The Clinical Diary of
Sándor Ferenczi

Portrait of Ferenczi by Olga Dormandi

The Clinical Diary of
Sándor Ferenczi

Edited by Judith Dupont

Translated by
Michael Balint and Nicola Zarday Jackson

Harvard University Press
Cambridge, Massachusetts
and London, England · 1988

Library of Congress Cataloging in Publication Data

Ferenczi, Sándor, 1873–1933.
   [Journal clinique (janvier–octobre 1932). English]
   The clinical diary of Sándor Ferenczi/edited by Judith Dupont;
translated by Michael Balint and Nicola Zarday Jackson.
      p.   cm.
   Translation of: Journal clinique (janvier–octobre 1932).
   Includes bibliographies and index.
   ISBN 0-674-13526-1 (alk. paper)
   1. Ferenczi, Sándor, 1873–1933. 2. Psychoanalysts—Hungary—
Diaries. I. Dupont, Judith. II. Title.
RC339.52.F48A313   1988   88-16244
616.89'17'0924—dc19   CIP
[B]

Contents

Editor's Note

This English edition of Sándor Ferenczi's *Diary* draws on these three textual sources:

1. The original manuscript in German, four-fifths of which is typewritten—presumably dictated to a secretary—and the rest in Ferenczi's own hand. It contains a number of typographical errors, unusual abbreviations, sentences with missing words, neologisms, and typographical infelicities such as unclosed parentheses. Much of the handwritten section is composed of cryptic notes that are difficult to decipher.

2. An entirely typewritten transcription by Michael Balint. Balint was familiar with Ferenczi's handwriting and was able to reconstruct sentences written in Ferenczi's telegraphic style. In transcribing the *Diary* he omitted several paragraphs, including two in which Ferenczi expressed his opinion of Freud. In 1969 Balint judged their publication inappropriate. It does not seem so today.

3. An English translation of the *Diary* by Michael Balint. This work facilitated greatly the understanding of certain passages. Balint also provided notes, which have been incorporated into this edition.

The translation in this edition reflects the spontaneous, unedited quality of the original manuscript. Ferenczi's idiosyncratic use of terminology has been preserved, as have various types of inconsistencies: In the same sentence Ferenczi might use first "I," then "we" or "one." He might refer to a particular patient sometimes in the feminine, sometimes in the masculine. Obvious cases of simple mistakes in typing have been corrected. Other inconsistencies, such as changes from singular to plural within a sentence, remain. The handwritten pages, often the most impenetrable parts of the *Diary,* are indicated by numbers in the margin referring to their page numbers in the original manuscript.

Except for the names of patients, words and names abbreviated in the manuscript have been spelled out in this translation. The identity of most of the patients mentioned in the *Diary* is known to us. Although Ferenczi sometimes used several different abbreviations in referring to one patient, this translation follows Michael Balint's lead and employs only one initial or set of initials for each patient. Ferenczi also mentions by name certain patients who were also his students. Both Clara Thompson and Elisabeth Severn are cited in the diary. Although their identities may be apparent to the informed reader, their initials have been altered here according to Ferenczi's own style in the *Diary*.

In 1969, believing that publication of his translation was imminent, Michael Balint wrote a draft of an introduction and made notes in preparation for a preface. These are reproduced in this edition in their original form; they help to explain the long delay in publishing Ferenczi's *Diary*.

J.D.

Acknowledgments

I would like to express my gratitude here to all those who assisted me in collecting the information needed to prepare the commentary and notes that accompany this *Diary*. In particular I am indebted to Suzanne Achache-Wiznitzer, Serge Apikian (in the field of the natural sciences), Eva Brabant, Jean-Pierre Bourgeron, Pierre Dupont (on mathematical questions), John Gedo, Georges-Arthur Goldschmidt, Ilse Grubrich-Simitis, André Haynal, Gisela Kadar, Pascal Le Malefan, Claude Monod (for having researched and provided certain essential documents), Paul Roazen, Pierre Sabourin, Maria Torok, and Anne Vincze.

Two works were of constant and immense value: the *Freud-Jung Correspondence,* with its remarkable comments by its editor, William McGuire, which helped me on innumerable occasions to confirm certain facts, as well as the indispensable *Freud and His Followers,* by Paul Roazen.

I would also like to thank Enid Balint for granting me permission to include in this volume the two introductory texts by Michael Balint.

J.D.

Introduction

In 1969 Michael Balint believed that the simultaneous publication of Ferenczi's *Diary* and the Freud-Ferenczi correspondence was imminent. In fact, it would take another sixteen years for the *Diary* to appear in French, and twenty for an English edition. And the correspondence will be issued after an additional delay, although this will consist only of the time needed to prepare it for publication.

If Michael Balint wished the *Diary* and the correspondence to appear simultaneously, he did so because each of the texts helps clarify and complete the other. On reading the *Diary* it becomes apparent why Ferenczi, delving deep within himself and calling everything into question, finally decided after long hesitation to decline the presidency of the International Psychoanalytic Association, a post that Freud had strongly hoped he would assume. In their correspondence this problem is discussed over a period of months. One also appreciates Ferenczi's desperate quest to obtain Freud's support in his perilous self-exploration, a support Freud was unable to give because he was convinced that his friend was on a path that could lead only to error and illness.

The *Diary* provides substantial proof, if any were needed, of Ferenczi's sound mental health. Indeed, as the final entries testify, Ferenczi was unable to take refuge in madness, and was dying because of just that: "Must I (if I can) create a new basis for my personality, if I have to abandon as false and untrustworthy the one I have had up to now? Is the choice here one between dying and 'rearranging myself'—and this at the age of fifty-nine?" he writes in October 1932. And a bit later, on the very last pages of the *Diary:* "A certain strength in my psychological makeup seems to persist, so that instead of falling ill psychically, I can only destroy—or be destroyed—in my organic depths."

The correspondence between Freud and Ferenczi provides us with invaluable information regarding both the genesis of the *Diary* and Ferenczi's aims in writing it.

It also enables us to understand that Freud could not follow his friend along this particular road: in the course of his quest, Ferenczi ends by undermining all the defenses whose protection had enabled Freud to construct the theoretical framework of psychoanalysis and had provided sufficient personal safeguards to allow him to continue. Hasn't it been said that the first task of the guerrilla fighter is to stay alive? Freud could not renounce defending himself, and Ferenczi probably paid with his life for having wanted to relinquish his own defenses to such an extent. In fact, in doing so he opened up for his successors new paths whose fruitfulness becomes increasingly apparent as research progresses. But it was to take more than half a century before Ferenczi's ideas and insights would be more or less assimilated by the psychoanalytic community.

In the Freud-Ferenczi correspondence, the first fairly direct mention of the *Diary* can be found in a letter dated 25 December 1929, in which Ferenczi, after a period of reserve, opens his heart to Freud, who had reproached him for his estrangement:

> [Rather than focusing on the political problems within the psychoanalytic movement], my interest is directed toward far more important matters. Actually, my true affinity is for research, and, freed from all personal ambition, I have become deeply immersed, with renewed curiosity, in the study of cases . . . To summarize in the briefest possible way, I should like you to know the following:
>
> 1. In *all* cases where I penetrated deeply enough, I found uncovered the traumatic-hysterical bases of the illness.
> 2. Where the patient and I succeeded in this, the therapeutic effect was far more significant. In many cases I had to recall previously "cured" patients for further treatment.
> 3. The critical view that I gradually formed during this period was that psychoanalysis deals far too one-sidedly with obsessive neurosis and character analysis—that is, ego psychology—while neglecting the organic-hysterical basis of the analysis. This results from overestimating the role of fantasy, and underestimating that of traumatic reality, in pathogenesis . . .
> 4. The newly acquired experiences (though in essence they refer back to the distant past) naturally also affect some particular features of technique. Certain measures are far too severe and must be tempered without completely losing sight of the secondary, educational aspect.

In subsequent exchanges, Freud does not enter into detailed discussion of the propositions put forward by Ferenczi, but reaffirms once again his lack of interest in the therapeutic aspect of psychoanalysis. This must have appeared unacceptable to Ferenczi, who was above all a physician and therefore primarily concerned with the therapeutic aspect, the more so as one of the endangered patients he was having to care for was himself.

On 17 January 1930 he wrote to Freud, his analyst:

> What happens in the relationship between you and me (at least in me) is an entanglement of various conflicts of emotions and positions. At first you were my revered mentor and unattainable model, for whom I nourished the feelings of a pupil—always somewhat mixed, as we know. Then you became my analyst, but as a result of unfortunate circumstances my analysis could not be completed. I particularly regretted that, in the course of the analysis, you did not perceive in me and did not bring to abreaction negative feelings and fantasies that were only partially transferred. It is well known that no analysand—not even I, with all the years of experience I have acquired with others—could accomplish this without assistance. Painstaking self-analysis was therefore required, which I subsequently undertook and carried out quite methodically. Naturally this was also linked to the fact that I was able to abandon my somewhat puerile attitude and realize that I must not depend quite so *completely* on your favor—that is, that I must not overestimate my importance to you. Also, some minor incidents in the course of our travels together resulted in your inspiring certain inhibitions in me, particularly the severity with which you punished my obstinate behavior over the matter of the Schreber book. I am still wondering: Wouldn't mildness and indulgence have been more appropriate from the side of the person of authority?

But now Ferenczi believes that he had been wrong in hesitating to communicate his new ideas to Freud. He even goes so far as to offer criticism, indeed advice:

> I do not share, for instance, your view that the therapeutic process is negligible or unimportant, and that simply because it appears less interesting to us we should ignore it. I, too, have often felt "fed up" in this respect, but overcame this tendency, and I am glad to inform you that precisely in this area a whole series of questions have now come into a new, a sharper focus, perhaps even the problem of repression.

Ferenczi thus hoped to have reestablished his correspondence with Freud on its former intimate footing.

This overture is followed by a much more cordial exchange of letters. Both men feel that their lives are in danger, and turn their thoughts toward death. Yet Freud, older and suffering a great deal from his cancer, finds it difficult to understand the complaints of his younger colleague, whose illness has not yet revealed itself and who has a long history of hypochondria.

On 20 July 1930 Ferenczi writes:

> Though somewhat sooner than you, Professor, I too am preoc-cupied with the problem of death, naturally in regard to my own destiny and prospects for the future. Part of my love for the corporeal Me appears to have sublimated itself in scientific inter-ests, and this subjective factor has made me sensitive, I think, to the psychic and other processes that take place in neurotics in moments of mortal danger, real or presumed. That was the path which led me to revive the theory of traumatism, apparently obsolete (or at least temporarily pushed aside).

Ferenczi feels that what happens in him is a "relatively belated burst of productivity," and he yields to that "sometimes acute pressure to produce, without renouncing control over it."

During September 1930 their dialogue even begins to take up cer-tain ideas raised by Ferenczi. This, however, proves to be short-lived, and all through the following year their exchanges become more factual. But behind the various topics broached are, one senses, the echoes of more deep-seated problems, notably when the discussion turns to the question of the presidency of the International Associa-tion, which Ferenczi hesitates to accept.

On 15 September 1931 Ferenczi devotes an entire letter to ex-plaining the research that would culminate in the *Diary*.

> I was and still am immersed in extremely difficult "clarification work"—internal and external, as well as scientific—which has not as yet produced anything definitive; and one cannot come forward with something that is only half completed. The scientific aspect still centers around questions of technique, but its elaboration also reveals many points of theory in a somewhat different light. In my usual manner, I do not shy away from drawing out their conclusions to the furthest extent possible—often to the point where I lead myself "ad absurdum." But this doesn't discourage me. I seek advances by new routes, often radically opposed, and I still hope that one day I shall end up finding the true path.
>
> All this sounds very mystical: please don't be alarmed by this.

As far as I can judge myself, I do not overstep (or only seldom) the limits of normality. It's true that I'm often wrong, but I'm not rigid in my prejudices.

To these confidences Freud responds on 18 September 1931 with a very disillusioned letter. He thinks that Ferenczi is moving away from him and considers it a sign of dissatisfaction that Ferenczi is pursuing his research in directions "that do not appear capable of leading toward any desirable goal." But he expects that Ferenczi will "make an about-face" and will correct his errors. No doubt Ferenczi is simply going through a "third puberty."

In his letter of 10 October 1931 Ferenczi attempts to plead his case:

I do not at all wish to deny that with me subjective factors influence, often substantially, the means and content of production. In the past, this occasionally led me to exaggerations. But I believe I finally was able to recognize where and how I went too far. Besides, even these excursions into uncertainty have always brought me significant benefits. I must expect something similar from your diagnosis of "third puberty." Assuming that the diagnosis is correct, the value of what has been produced in this state will, first of all, have to be assessed objectively . . . My more recent insights are first grasped "in statu nascendi." I would like very much for you to tell me something more specific concerning the points "that do not appear capable of leading to any desirable goal." Does it seem to you out of the question that after I've attained the maturity you expect from me—after I've made an "about-face"—I could produce something useful on a practical or even theoretical level?

I am, above all, an empiricist . . . Ideas are always closely linked with the vicissitudes in the treatment of patients, and by these are either repudiated or confirmed.

In December 1931 there is an exchange of letters that deeply upsets Ferenczi, though to us they appear to express more a misunderstanding than a divergence of ideas. On 13 December Freud writes his famous letter on the "kissing technique,"[1] to which Ferenczi responds on 27 December; his reply is reproduced in its entirety in the notes in this volume (see entry for 7 January 1932, note 3). The misunderstanding can be fully understood only from reading the *Diary*. Ferenczi will need quite some time to recover. On 21 January 1932 he

1. One rather incomplete version of this letter is cited in vol. 3 of Jones's biography of Freud. It has been reproduced in full in Maria Torok's article "La Correspondance Freud-Ferenczi," *Confrontations* 12 (Fall 1984).

writes to Freud: "Since our last exchange of letters a kind of appeasement has set in in me which—I hope—will intervene favorably in the resolution of the scientific-technical problems I am preoccupied with." Indeed, on 7 January he made the first *Diary* entry, which deals with "the insensitivity of the analyst."

On 1 May 1932, in reply to Freud, who has reproached him for his silence, Ferenczi again attempts to explain: "It seems that I would like to recuperate now from half a lifetime of super-performances. By 'rest' I mean here immersing myself in a kind of scientific 'poetry and truth' from which one day, perhaps—at times I believe definitely—something not without value will emerge. I do not believe that one can voluntarily modify such a state of mind . . ." Freud, who has not given up hope of seeing Ferenczi accept the presidency, and who thinks that this would be a salutary experience for his friend, responds on 12 May 1932: "In the past few years you have withdrawn into isolation . . . But you must leave that island of dreams which you inhabit with your fantasy-children, and once again join in mankind's struggles."

In his letter of 19 May 1932 Ferenczi continues to plead his case:

I must admit quite honestly that when I refer to my present activity in terms of "a life of dreams," "day-dreaming," and "a crisis of puberty," this does not mean that I admit that I am ill. In actual fact I have the feeling that out of the relative confusion many useful things will develop and have already developed . . . I really believe that I am doing not useless work, if I continue for a while with my current mode of work.

Then, in a letter dated 21 August 1932, Ferenczi definitely renounces the presidency: "In endeavoring to develop my analyses in a deeper and more effective sense, I am having to navigate a critical and self-critical course that appears to require in some respects not only the completion but also the correction of our practical—and in places theoretical—views." Ferenczi believes that his critical state of mind would hinder his becoming a good president, whose task is rather to preserve what already exists.

On his way to the Congress of Wiesbaden, due to begin on 3 September 1932, Ferenczi stopped off in Vienna to read Freud the paper he was to present at the congress, "Confusion of Tongues between Adults and the Child." It was a painful encounter, in which mutual incomprehension between the two men came to a head. Freud, deeply shocked by the contents of the paper, demanded that

Ferenczi refrain from publishing anything until he had reconsidered the position he put forth in it.

After the congress, where in spite of everything he presents his paper, Ferenczi attempts to take a vacation, first at Groddeck's clinic in Baden-Baden and then in the south of France. But he is very ill. It is a journey "from bed to bed," as he writes to Freud on 27 September. He has been profoundly shaken by his meeting with Freud in Vienna—in fact, it would be their last—and he protests against Freud's demand that he not publish anything for a while. Freud's response on 2 October is quite harsh: "I no longer believe that you will correct yourself as I corrected myself a generation ago . . . For a couple of years you have systematically turned away from me . . . Objectively I think I could point out to you the technical errors in your conclusions, but why do so? I am convinced you would not be accessible to any doubts." That same day, Ferenczi writes in the *Diary* entry of his painful dilemma between "rearranging" and dying. He will die seven months later—having reestablished in the last months a friendly tone in his correspondence with Freud, even if not mutual understanding.

Ferenczi deals with innumerable subjects in the *Diary:* paranoia, schizophrenia, homosexuality, the Oedipus complex, training analysis, the termination of analysis, masochism, the therapeutic effects of abreaction, repression, and so on. He also presents a whole series of clinical observations regarding the patients he was treating while composing the *Diary*—and more specifically, observations regarding four of these patients, designated by the initials R.N., S.I., Dm., and B., all of whom were women and three American.

Essentially, however, the *Diary* deals with three great principal themes, to which Ferenczi continually returns throughout:

1. *A theoretical point:* trauma. Inspired by his analyses currently in progress, he justifies the importance he assigns to trauma and develops a theory of trauma—of its effects and treatment.

2. *A technical point* (closely linked to the problem of trauma): mutual analysis. He demonstrates how the idea appeared, how it was put into practice, and finally how he himself was led to criticize it.

3. *A personal point:* Ferenczi criticizes the analytic devices as established by Freud, as well as Freud's attitude as analyst. Finally he analyzes his own relationship with Freud.

Trauma

During the year that preceded the writing of the *Diary*, Ferenczi begins noting down his ideas regarding trauma. He continues to be preoccupied with the subject throughout the *Diary*, but at the same time he composes a set of somewhat more structured notes on 19 September 1932 (during his distressing journey after the Congress of Wiesbaden) and another, after the interruption of the *Diary*, on 26 December—a day on which he makes some other brief notations. These, it seems, are the last pages written by Ferenczi.[2]

The *Diary* contains, recorded day by day, histories of the various clinical cases of which Ferenczi based his reflections. From these cases he drew a whole series of theoretical conclusions, as they appeared to him, a number of which he elaborated in the "Confusion of Tongues" and in his "Notes and Fragments."[3] Some others are merely sketched out, but today they appear to us as the founding themes of certain important currents in modern psychiatry—or even anti-psychiatry.

Ferenczi draws parallels among the child traumatized by the hypocrisy of adults, the mentally ill person traumatized by the hypocrisy of society, and the patient, whose trauma is revived and exacerbated by the professional hypocrisy and technical rigidity of the analyst.

He describes the process that takes place in people who are victims of overwhelming aggressive force: the victim, whose defenses have been broken down, so to speak abandons himself to his inescapable fate and withdraws outside himself, in order to survey the traumatic event from a great distance. From this vantage point, he may be able to consider his aggressor as sick or mad, and sometimes may even try to care for and cure him. Like the child, who can on occasion become the psychiatrist of his parents. Or the analyst, who conducts his own analysis through his patients; the notion of mutual analysis is not far away.

The trauma victim, the child, or the mentally ill person reflects back to the aggressor a caricatured image of himself, thus expressing simultaneously his own suffering and protest and also those truths which the aggressor is striving to evade. Then, little by little, the traumatized

2. The five notes dealing with observations on trauma were grouped together as "Gedanken über das Trauma" and published in *International Zeitschriften für Psychoanalyse* 5, no. 20 (1934): 5–12. Parts of them were included in *Fin*, 276–279, as "Some Thoughts on Trauma," and, in French, in *Psychoanalyse* 4 (1982): 139–147, as "Reflexions sur le traumatisme."

3. "Notes and Fragments, in *Fin*, pp. 216–279.

person becomes so caught up in his own scenario that he closes for himself all avenues of escape. Only therapeutic intervention from the outside can henceforth break the isolation.

Similarly, Ferenczi emphasizes the hypocrisy of certain professional attitudes of analysts—their denial of countertransferential feelings that are uncomfortable or contrary to their ethics. He considers such practices to be traumas inflicted on the patient, likely to revive the very traumas from the past that the analysis is supposed to cure. This was a situation Ferenczi himself had experienced, not only in his role as analyst but also as an analysand and a member of the analytic community. He was never really able to express his hostility—direct or transferred—toward Freud, his analyst and revered master, who, besides, did not tolerate well such controversial attitudes on the part of his supporters. It was also impossible for Ferenczi to accept as immutable the technical rules established from the beginning, or to agree that the theory should be transformed into dogma. To maintain that a patient who could not be cured in accordance with this theory or with this technique was unanalyzable appeared to him unsatisfactory and, moreover, in itself traumatizing. He believed that all patients who asked for help should receive it, and that it was up to the psychoanalyst to devise the most appropriate response to the problems presented to him. Thus, Ferenczi became the last resort for cases considered hopeless, cases that his colleagues referred to him from all corners of the earth.

As a result of his research and his original "unorthodox" experiences, all conditions were present to revive Ferenczi's own past trauma, caused by the conjunction of infantile guilt feelings and the moral rigidity of his mother, who accused him of making her "die of sorrow." The "*enfant terrible* of psychoanalysis" had probably relived something very similar to this in respect to Freud, who complained with disenchanted sadness as he saw his friend irresistibly drawn in directions he considered mistaken, abandoning him, a sick old man who was soon to die. As for Ferenczi's colleagues, they were protecting themselves from the unbearable upheaval that he advocated and initiated, by endeavoring to push him toward the pathological side. Which explains why Jones's allegations, often refuted, regarding Ferenczi's so-called mental deterioration in the last three years of his life have been so widely credited.

The *Diary* gives a full account of Ferenczi's struggle on behalf of his patients and himself. It enumerates all the means by which the victim of an overwhelming trauma can survive and rescue whatever can be saved of his personality: identification with the aggressor; disqualification of the aggressor, who may be regarded as a mentally ill person to be cared for; the splitting of the self in order to disperse the effects of the shock and in the hope of recovering some of the fragments intact; the instantaneous creation of ad hoc organs in certain situations of extreme distress, and so on.

Accompanying the passages that deal directly with trauma are numerous entries relating to the defensive and countertransferential attitudes of the analyst, which also can be grouped around the central theme of traumatism.

Mutual Analysis

It has often been said that the analyst throughout his life pursues his own analysis with the assistance of his patients. In general, this means the self-questioning induced by the analytic sessions with patients obliges him to engage in permanent self-analysis.

This, however, does not take into account the analyst's blind spots and weaknesses, which he no more than other people can tackle alone. The technique of mutual analysis essentially rests on the idea that where the analyst is unable to offer his patients reliable support, he should at least provide them with guideposts, by acquainting them, as sincerely as he can with his own weaknesses and feelings. The analyst thus allows his patients to know better where they stand with him; even if in that way the patients must confront and assimilate some painful realities, they will cope better with these than with feigned friendliness.

In an entry dated 5 May, Ferenczi describes how the idea of mutual analysis was conceived. In fact, it was the invention of one of his patients, R.N. This young woman had been in analysis for more than two years. At the beginning, Ferenczi had found her rather disagreeable. Reacting by overcompensating, he forced himself to give in to all her wishes, in accordance with his technique of indulgence and elasticity. From this the patient concluded that her analyst was in love with her, and she believed that she had found in him the "ideal lover." Faced with this turn of events, Ferenczi took fright, retreated, all the while trying to interpret for his patient the negative emotions that she ought to have felt toward him. She responded with identical interpretations, which Ferenczi had to concede were justified. He decided, then, to give free expression to his emotions, and thereafter he noted that the analysis, which had stagnated for two years, was again making good progress. Ferenczi himself now felt liberated from his anxiety and became a better analyst, not only for R.N. but also for his other patients. So he agreed to undertake the experiment in a more systematic fashion: double sessions, or alternating sessions, one for her and one for him. The progress thus made in the treatment inspired him to write: "Who should get the credit for this success? Foremost, of course, the patient, who in her precarious situation as patient never ceased fighting for her rights. This would not have been enough, however, had I *myself* not submitted to the unusual sacrifice of risking an experiment in which I the doctor put myself into the hands of a not undangerous patient." On no account can Ferenczi be accused of having agreed to experiment with mutual analysis out of a preference for the easy path. As this entry and others bear witness, he felt afraid and humiliated—and also exposed, as if he were balancing on a tightrope, as much from the point of view of technique as of theory. In fact, everything in him protested against this grave commitment and risk.

But as was usual with him, he decided to push the experiment to its limit. He was thus led to raise the problem of confidence, indispensable if one is to yield oneself to another as completely as is demanded by analysis. Yet in the analytic situation, each protagonist will perceive in the other obscure forces at work, with the result that neither will appear totally harmless to the other. Both are, therefore, prey to the same feeling of insecurity. Mutual analysis is designed to illuminate those shadowy corners, so that each protagonist can locate himself in relation to the other with greater assurance.

There is ample material for discussion here. Should the necessary confidence be created by the arousing of intense positive transference in the patient—an idealization endowing the analyst with all the comforting traits that the patient requires in order to confide in him? Or is it meant to provide the patient with all the essential elements that will enable him to evaluate what he can expect from the analyst? The discussion will not fail to throw some light on many of the consequences, insufficiently explored and poorly controlled, of the analyst's attitudes.

Gradually Ferenczi encountered a whole series of problems stemming from the technique of mutual analysis. In the entry of 31 January he lists some of these: the risk of seeing the patient "deflect attention from himself" and search for complexes in the analyst in a paranoid way; the impossibility of letting oneself be analyzed by every patient; the imperative need to respect the patients' sensibilities;

the problem posed by the discretion owed to other patients, whose secrets the analyst would in principle be obliged to reveal to the patient-analyst (entry of 16 February).

Ferenczi was thus led to see unavoidable limitations in his technique: practicing mutual analysis strictly according to the needs of the patient, and no further than was necessary for the patient; or, eventually, considering letting oneself be analyzed by a patient only after the patient's own analysis was terminated.

In this way, Ferenczi arrives at a critique of his method. In the entry of 3 March he recounts how and out of what considerations he has decided to put an end to mutual analysis with R.N.: he has noticed that the young woman is developing ideas bordering on delusions regarding their "collaboration"; she plans to prolong it indefinitely, and she insinuates that without her Ferenczi would lose all his therapeutic skills. He therefore decides to break off the experiment. After a brief period of hostility and disarray, R.N. decides to carry on with the analysis and makes substantial progress. In the entry of 6 March, Ferenczi summarizes the effects of the interruption.

Finally, in an entry dated 3 June (entry 140i), he concludes that mutual analysis is merely "a last resort" made necessary by insufficiently deep analysis of the analysts themselves. "Proper analysis by a stranger, without any obligation, would be better." This abandoned technique still leaves us with something useful: the countertransference interpretations.

But at the same time, Ferenczi maintains that "the best analyst is a patient who has been cured." All other candidate analysts ought to be "first made ill, then cured and made aware."

Indeed, perhaps all experimentation with mutual analysis is essentially the consequence of training analyses as they were practiced at the time, including that of Ferenczi by Freud: rapid, fitful analyses, often undertaken abroad, in a foreign language, during walks or travels together or visits to the home of analyst or patient. Be that as it may, the questions raised by mutual analysis remain relevant, even in these days of carefully worked out cursus and multiple controls: How can the analyst successfully deal with his weaknesses and blindness?

Criticism of Freud

Throughout the *Diary,* through his criticisms of analytic devices and techniques, Ferenczi simultaneously bears witness to his own analysis with Freud. It is not possible to limit this analysis only to those brief and intermittent periods that had been allotted to it. In fact, the entire relationship between Freud and Ferenczi, as it appears to us notably from their correspondence, in a sense constitutes part of that analysis. Ferenczi reveals to Freud the minutest details of his private life, discloses his most intimate feelings. Freud responds sometimes with interpretations; other times with attempts to disengage himself from this process of permanent analysis, difficult to sustain; sometimes simply with silence. Under these conditions, it is not at all surprising that intense transference, which is hard to control, builds up, charged with substantial latent hostility. The *Diary* also testifies to Ferenczi's struggle to free himself from his hostility and to come to grips with his transference, fraught with ambivalence and dependence, by at last clearly formulating his criticisms and his gradually accumulated grievances. This enterprise of clarification is implicit throughout the text, but a number of entries deal with it explicitly.

Ferenczi, whom Freud reproached for his "furor sanandi," reproaches Freud in turn for his lack of interest in the therapeutic aspect of psychoanalysis, his contempt for his patients, and his repugnance for psychotics, perverts, and all that seems to him too abnormal. He expresses strong reservations about the rigidity of analytic devices as established by Freud, and about the overly systematic application of Freud's frustration technique. He also reproaches Freud for becoming more and more of a pedagogue and not enough of a physician. Indeed, Ferenczi believes that Freud tries to educate his patients before he has pursued their analysis to sufficient depths (entry of 17 March) because of "his antipathy for their weaknesses and anomalies." He considers Freud incapable of making his patients (and first and foremost his pupils) independent of himself. To underscore this point, he cites a remark of Freud's to the effect that once sons have turned into adults their father has nothing else to do but to die (entry of 4 August). From this, Ferenczi concludes that Freud has formulated the notion of the Oedipus complex for the exclusive use of others without ever really applying it to himself, in order not to have to admit that he too may have wished the death of his father.

Ferenczi believes that Freud's self-analysis has not been taken far enough. For, as we know, according to Ferenczi self-analysis never can be. For him, analysis is an eminently social process. He explains this at length to his friend Groddeck in a letter dated 11 October 1922.[4]

4. *Correspondance Ferenczi-Groddeck* (Paris: Payot, 1982), pp. 71–75.

According to Ferenczi, Freud, who initially followed Breuer with great enthusiasm, has been irreparably disappointed by the discovery that hysterics lie. Since then he no longer loves his patients. He again becomes a materialistic, scientific investigator (entry of 1 May) emotionally detached from psychoanalysis, which he approaches henceforth on a purely intellectual level. Ferenczi thinks Freud has gradually developed an overly impersonal, pedagogic technique giving rise to a much too exclusively paternal transference. This attitude of superiority evokes in patients either submissive dependence, from which they cannot free themselves, or an attitude of defiance, like that of a child whom excessive parental severity has made obstinate, stupid, and naughty.

If Ferenczi criticizes Freud, he is no less severe with himself. He watches himself with an unrelenting eye: he is keenly aware of his position of infantile dependence toward Freud, a position he describes as a "persistent perversion of infantilism" and which he does not blame exclusively on his analyst.

In the entry of 15 July he refers to himself as a schizophrenic—delusional, paranoid, emotionally vacant, managing to function only by overcompensating for all that he lacks. Of course this diagnosis appears caricature-like, but like all caricature it doubtless also reveals something of Ferenczi's internal reality. In any case, this caricature accounts for a great ability to achieve distance from himself and for a remarkable lucidity, rather than a mental disintegration, as Jones wanted to believe and to make others believe. It is thus similar to the entry of 19 July in which Ferenczi makes his self-diagnosis of paranoia, which he comments on and explains: while remaining dependent on Freud, whom he is incapable of opposing, everywhere else he wants absolutely to be the one who is always right. He sees this as an imitation of the paranoia of authority. Consequently, he emphasizes the need for children to detach themselves from their fathers and then to "heal" them by teaching them understanding.

In an entry dated 2 October, at the end of the *Diary,* Ferenczi resumes and deepens the analysis of his relationship with Freud, as well as his relationship to his own illness. He correlates it with certain aspects of his infantile neurosis. His prognosis about the situation does not seem at all favorable: he feels he has reached an impasse.

Not without difficulties, Ferenczi still manages in his letters to voice some of his grievances to Freud, though very cautiously. In response, Freud tries to refer his protestations and reproaches to old, intrafamilial conflicts by recalling material Ferenczi has provided during the entire twenty-five years of their relationship. He addresses Ferenczi here in a friendly tone, there with paternal severity or even humorously, but it seems he never questions his own position.

In 1937, some years after Ferenczi's death, Freud returns to certain aspects of their relationship in a passage in "Analysis Terminable and Interminable":[5]

A certain man, who had himself been a most successful practitioner of analysis, came to the conclusion that his relations with men as well as with women—the men who were his rivals and the woman whom he loved—were not free from neurotic inhibitions, and he therefore had himself analysed by an analyst whom he regarded as his superior. This critical exploration of his own personality was entirely successful. He married the woman whom he loved and became the friend and teacher of the men whom he had regarded as rivals. Many years passed, during which his relation to his former analyst remained unclouded. But then, for no demonstrable external reason, trouble arose. The man who had been analysed adopted an antagonistic attitude to the analyst and reproached him for having neglected to complete the analysis. The analyst, he said, ought to have known and to have taken account of the fact that a transference-relation could never be merely positive; he ought to have considered the possibilities of a negative transference. The analyst justified himself by saying that, at the time of the analysis, there was no sign of a negative transference. But, even supposing that he had failed to observe some slight indication of it, which was quite possible considering the limitations of analysis in those early days, it was still doubtful, he thought, whether he would have been able to activate a psychical theme, or, as we say, a "complex," by merely indicating it to the patient, so long as it was not at that moment an actuality to him. Such activation would certainly have necessitated real unfriendly behavior on the analyst's part. And, he added, every happy relation between an analyst and the subject of his analysis, during and after analysis, was not to be regarded as transference; there were friendly relations with a real basis, which were capable of persisting.

This passage, read in conjunction with the text of the *Diary,* shows the extent and the inevitability of the misunderstanding between the two men.

A reading of the *Diary* suggests that Ferenczi, both as analyst and

5. "Analysis Terminable and Interminable," trans. Joan Riviere, in Freud, *Collected Papers,* vol. 5, ed. James Strachey (New York: Basic Books, 1959).

as analysand, had experienced the shortcomings of the so-called classic techniques for dealing with a certain type of problem. In the criticisms directed at him by his patients he recognizes his own criticisms formulated to Freud. He endeavors to invent for his patients what he wanted Freud to invent for him. He tries to offer them the understanding and trust that he himself has been unable to obtain from Freud. When Freud tells him he is on the wrong path, he cannot admit it: he would be disavowing a part of himself. When he reproaches Freud for having construed the analytic situation so as to assure above all the protection and comfort of the analyst, he is in fact reproaching him for refusing to listen when what he, Ferenczi, is saying threatens Freud's own internal security.

It seems useless to try to determine here who is normal and who is ill, who is right and who is wrong. It appears that in this relationship, at once painful and productive, each partner did all he could do and gave all he could give. But certainly there are situations in which everyone is alone and can rely on no one but himself. Freud remained alone with his desperate desire for a son who would be unconditionally devoted to him; Ferenczi had to confront alone the choice between the love and support of a powerful father and his own self-fulfillment—a dilemma that in the end killed him.

The *Diary* is a clinical diary. It recounts the clinical history of many of Ferenczi's patients, but also of Ferenczi himself. In other words, it offers a history of the multiple transferences and countertransferences that intertwine in an analytic practice, reported with unusual candor. Ferenczi dares to hear and dares to express feelings, ideas, intuitions, and sensations that generally have great difficulty working their way to consciousness and even greater difficulty allowing themselves to be formulated in words. He thus opens to psychoanalysts and to researchers in allied domains numerous doors—an achievement that has the merit not only of proposing new directions but also of bringing a healthy and invigorating breath of fresh air in those places, hitherto a little too enclosed, where the theories and technical principles of psychoanalysis have a tendency to settle and to become fixed.

An important issue thus stirred up and aired by Ferenczi is one of the problems and conflicts inherent in the psychoanalyst's situation. Training analysis—which Ferenczi advocated—is designed to prepare the future analyst to tackle these problems and conflicts by allowing him to bring to the surface, and resolve, a number of his own personal problems. But those which are determined by the analyst's position—and which moreover may determine his desire to attain that position—constitute the everyday fare of all analysts, even of training analysts, without any hope of ever being able to resolve them, either entirely or once and for all. There is a saying that an analyst completely analyzed would probably cease to be an analyst. Clearly, this hypothesis is unverifiable. Psychoanalysts are, therefore, the products of the imperfections of their practice. This is probably what has earned psychoanalysis the reputation of being "the impossible profession." And, in this sense, it certainly is. It may have been his refusal to accept this impossibility that led Ferenczi into those regions of suffering and despair to which the *Diary* testifies, and from which he was unable to escape alive.

Judith Dupont

Abbreviations

C   Sándor Ferenczi, *First Contributions to Psycho-Analysis,* trans. Ernest Jones (1916; rpt. New York: Brunner-Mazel, 1980).

FC   Ferenczi, *Further Contributions to the Theory and Technique of Psycho-Analysis,* ed. John Rickman, trans. Jane I. Suttie (1926; rpt. New York: Brunner-Mazel, 1980).

Fin   Ferenczi, *Final Contributions to the Problems and Methods of Psycho-Analysis,* ed. Michael Balint, trans. Eric Mosbacher (1955; rpt. New York: Brunner-Mazel, 1980).

SE   Sigmund Freud, *The Standard Edition of the Complete Psychological Works,* 24 vols. (London: Hogarth Press, 1953–).

7 January 1932

Insensitivity [Fühllosigkeit] *of the analyst*[1]

(Mannered form of greeting, formal request to "tell everything," so-called free-floating attention, which ultimately amounts to no attention at all, and which is certainly inadequate to the highly emotional character of the analysand's communications, often brought out only with the greatest difficulty.) This has the following effects: (1) the patient is offended by the lack of interest, or the total absence of interest; (2) since he does not want to think badly of us, or to regard us with disfavor, he looks for the cause of this lack of reaction in himself or in the quality of the material he has communicated to us; (3) finally he doubts the reality of the content, which until now he had felt so acutely. Thus "retrojecting" [*retrojiziert*], as one might say, he introjects the blame that is directed against us. In actual fact, his reproach is: You don't believe me! You don't take seriously what I tell you! I cannot accept your sitting there unfeeling and indifferent while I am straining to call up some tragic event from my childhood!—The reaction to these accusations (which are never expressed spontaneously by the patient, and can only be guessed by the doctor) must then be that we examine in a critical way our own behavior and our own emotional attitudes with respect to these observations and admit the possibility or even the actual existence of fatigue, tedium, and boredom at times. There is an involuntary increase in interest after such a quid pro quo: tone and gestures become more natural, discussion livelier, questions and answers more natural and productive.

Natural and sincere behavior (Groddeck-Thompson)[2] constitutes the most appropriate and most favorable atmosphere in the analytic situation: desperately rigid clinging to a theoretical approach is quickly recognized by the patients as such, and instead of telling us (or even admitting it to themselves) they use the characteristic features of our own technique, or our one-sidedness, in order to lead us ad absurdum. I remember, for instance, the case of N.G., who never tired of telling me about a teacher she found insufferable, who was very nice to her and yet always maintained a pedantic attitude, although the two lived together quite closely. The patient had earlier had a nurse, who always behaved naturally. I am now convinced that the relative lack of success of this patient's analysis can be traced back to my inability to appreciate the significance of this factor in her situation. Had I understood her unspoken reproaches and accusations and altered my behavior accordingly, the patient would not have been compelled to reenact unconsciously, in her conduct toward me, the defiant attitudes of her childhood. The tragedy of her case undoubtedly lay in her inability to endure the rigid and at times hypocritical behavior of parents, teachers, and doctors.

Rigid adherence to the frustration technique had caused my Greek patient to suggest that in order to advance the treatment he should perhaps give up eating, which he proceeded to do. For seven whole days he did not take a single bite of food, and he would have pursued this experiment to the point of suicide had I not countermanded this measure. I did this, however, only when he went further and proposed that he should also give up breathing. Such extreme cases obliged me to temper my "activity" substantially. At the same time I had to acknowledge that the principle of relaxation (passivity), which, in reaction to the active method, I was beginning to implement increasingly, could similarly lead to bad experiences. The patients begin to abuse my patience, they permit themselves more and more, create very embarrassing situations for us, and cause us not insignificant trouble. Only when we recognize this trend and openly admit it to the patient does this artificial obstacle, which is of our own creation, disappear. However, such mistakes and their subsequent correction often provide the motive and opportunity to dig deeply into similar conflicts, imperfectly resolved in the past [*schlecht erledigte*]. See the case of Dm., a lady who, "complying" with my passivity, had allowed herself to take more and more liberties, and occasionally even kissed me. Since this behavior met with no resistance, since it was treated as something permissible in analysis and at most commented on theoretically, she remarked quite casually in the company of other patients, who were undergoing analysis elsewhere: "I am allowed to kiss Papa Ferenczi, as often as I like." I first reacted to the unpleasantness that ensued with the complete impassivity with which I was conducting this analysis.[3] But then the patient began to make herself ridiculous, ostentatiously as it were, in her sexual conduct (for example at social gatherings, while dancing). It was only through the insight and admission that my passivity had been unnatural that she was brought back to real life, so to speak, as insight does have to reckon with social opposition. Simultaneously it became evident that here again was a case of repetition of the father-child situation. As a child, Dm. had been grossly abused sexually by her father, who was out of control; later, obviously because of the father's bad conscience and social anxiety, he reviled her, so to speak. The daughter had to take revenge on her father indirectly, by failing in her own life.

The natural behavior of the analyst itself offers points of attack for the opposition. The most extreme consequence of this was drawn by that female patient who demanded that the patient should also have the right to analyze the analyst. In most cases this demand can be met by: (1) admitting in theory to the possibilities of one's own unconscious; (2) relating fragments from one's own past.

In one case the communication of the content of my own psyche developed into a form of mutual analysis, from which I, the analyst, derived much profit. Indeed, it also gave me an opportunity to express ideas and views about the patient that otherwise would not have come to her notice; for example I could mention utterances indicating moral or aesthetic distaste, an opinion I had heard about her somewhere, etc. If we can teach the patient to cope with all this, we are helping him to cope in general, hastening his release from analysis and the analyst, and we also hasten the transformation into memory of those tendencies toward repetition, hitherto resistant to change.

1. See "Confusion of Tongues between Adults and the Child," *Fin* 156–166.—ED.

2. Georg Walter Groddeck (1866–1934), German physician, director of a famous clinic in Baden-Baden, author of a number of works, one of the founders of psychosomatic medicine. He corresponded with Freud, who formed close ties with him but later distanced himself. He was Ferenczi's friend and physician. Their correspondence has been published in French: *Sándor Ferenczi/Georg Groddeck: Correspondance* (Paris: Payot, 1982).

Clara Mabel Thompson (1893–1958), born in Providence, Rhode Island, studied medicine at Johns Hopkins University. She was referred to Ferenczi by Harry Stack Sullivan, the leader of psychologically oriented medicine in America, after Ferenczi's lectures at the New School for Social Research in 1926–27. Between 1928 and Ferenczi's death in 1933 she spent every summer, as well as additional periods of time, in Budapest. She left the New York Psychoanalytic Institute in 1941, when Karen Horney was expelled from it; her collaboration with Horney ended in 1943. With Sullivan and Erich Fromm she founded the William Alanson White Institute and the Washington School of Psychiatry.—ED.

3. This refers to an incident that came to Freud's notice via Clara Thompson, the patient in question, and which caused Freud to write the well-known letter of 13 December 1931. This letter has been often quoted since its publication—in incomplete form—by Ernest Jones in his biography of Freud. In it Freud reproaches Ferenczi for what he calls his "technique of kissing" and ironically points out some of the regrettable consequences that might result from its spread and its further development in the psychoanalytic world. The letter includes the following passage (most of which Jones omitted): "And then you are to hear from the brutal fatherly side an admonition . . . according to my recollection a tendency to sexual play with patients was not completely alien to you in preanalytic times,

so that the new technique could well be linked to an old error. That is why I spoke in my last letter of a new puberty." Jones III, 165; Maria Torok, "La Correspondance Freud-Ferenczi," *Confrontations* 12 (Autumn 1984): 97.

Ferenczi replied to Freud's letter on 27 December 1931:

Dear Professor,

By now you are used to the fact that I can reply only after a prolonged reactive period; this time, however, you will perhaps also understand it quite well yourself. This is perhaps the first time that an element of misunderstanding has arisen in our relationship. And now that I have let the affective current run its course, I think I am in a position to answer you in a way that will set your mind at rest.

You'll doubtless recall that it was I who pointed out the necessity of also publishing details regarding technique, provided it had been applied methodically; you, on the other hand, were inclined to keep communication on technical points to the minimum. And now it is *you* who maintain that it would be unworthy to keep silent, and it is I who must object that the decision to publish can be left to the tact and judgment of the author.

Still, this is not the most important thing I would like to discuss with you. Your fear that I might develop into a second Stekel is, I believe, unfounded. "Sins of youth," mistakes, once they have been overcome and analytically worked through, can even make one wiser and more prudent than people who have never experienced such storms. My highly ascetic "active therapy" was surely a preemptive device against such tendencies, which is why it assumed, by its exaggeration, a compulsive character. As soon as I realized this, I relaxed the rigidity of the restrictions and frustrations to which I had condemned myself (and others). Now I believe that I am capable of creating a congenial atmosphere, free from passion, which is best suited to draw forth what has previously been concealed.

Nevertheless, since I fear the dangers as much as you, I must and I shall, as in the past, keep in mind the warnings and remonstrances issued by you and try to subject myself to severe criticism, as well. But I would have bypassed something important, had I wanted to bury that productive layer which is beginning to take shape before me.

After overcoming the pain caused by the tone of our correspondence, I cannot but express the hope that our personal understanding as friends and scientists has not been disrupted by these developments—or, rather, that it will soon be restored.

With my heartfelt good wishes for the New Year,

Yours,
Ferenczi.

In this exchange of letters we see, explicitly and implicitly, the essential nature of the divergence of views that arose between Freud and Ferenczi in the last years of their relationship; but we also see evidence of their profound friendship, which always prevented these differences from turning into hostility.—ED.

10 January 1932

Thinking with the body equals hysteria

Here, perhaps, a possible approach to the "inexplicable leap into the physical" that characterizes hysteria. Starting point: a lecture by Dr. M[ichael] B[alint], in which he contrasts eroticism and educability (adaptability).[1] Thus purely egoistic (utility) functions (breathing, heartbeat) would be nonerotic. Organs currently engaged in the process of adapting themselves (the most recent products of development) are erotic. Hysteria is the regression of eroticism into organs that otherwise only serve ego functions; the physical diseases of organs do the same.

Quite apart from describing fully the contradistinction between utility functions and pleasure functions, the gradual de-eroticization of organ functions and the transference of eroticism onto one specific organ were described in detail in the Theory of Genitality, and also studied thoroughly in relation to ontogenesis; nevertheless it was certainly helpful to return to this theme and to examine the phylogenetic parallels to this process, only briefly outlined in the Theory of Genitality.

Thus this lecture provides an opportunity to approach once again the general question of the physical and the psychical. Here is an attempt: one could also formulate the opposition between the two in the following way: in mechanics, causes, that is, external pressures, provoke changes, whereas the psychical is governed by motives. The main motive is the maintenance of a state of equilibrium, somehow achieved, that is to say, resistance to any change in that state and a tendency, need, or determination to eliminate any disturbance. Motivation, however, assumes the existence of certain capabilities that can only be described as intellectual: perception of the disturbed unpleasure situation and the emergence of a power aimed at the cessation of the unpleasure. If we took this analogy further, it would lead to modern views on energy and matter. Inorganic and organic matter exist in a highly organized energy association, so solidly organized that it is not affected even by strong disruptive stimuli, that is, it no longer registers any impulses to change it [*keine Motive mehr zur Änderung empfindet*]. Substances are so self-assured in their strength and solidity that ordinary outside events pass them by without eliciting any intervention or even interest. But just as very powerful external forces are capable of exploding even very firmly consolidated substances, and can also cause atoms to explode, whereupon the need or desire for equilibrium naturally arises again, so it appears that in human beings, given certain conditions, it can happen that the (organic, perhaps also the inorganic) substance recovers its psychic quality, not utilized since primordial times. In other words the capacity to be impelled by motives [*Bewegtwerden durch Motive*], that is, the psyche, continues to exist potentially in substances as well. Though under normal conditions it remains inactive, under certain abnormal conditions it can be resurrected. Man is an organism equipped with specific organs for the performance of essential psychic functions (nervous, intellectual activities). In moments of great need, when the psychic system proves to be incapable of an adequate response, or when these specific organs or functions (nervous and psychic) have been violently destroyed, then the primordial psychic powers are aroused, and it will be these forces that will seek to overcome the disruption. In such moments, when the psychic system fails, the organism begins to think.

An example:[2] someone, in childhood, is sexually assaulted by a brutal giant. For a time all mental powers remain fully active, all possible effort is made, though in vain, to ward off the attack (struggling, screaming, for a short period even conscious emotions of hate, thirst for revenge, etc.). But when the weight of the man pressing down on the child becomes more and more unbearable, and especially when the attacker's clothing unrelentingly blocks the child's air passages, causing extreme shortness of breath, all sensation of pressure, of genital injury, any knowledge of the cause of the painful situation and its antecedents disappear; all available psychic force is concentrated on the single task of somehow getting air to the lungs. Yet even this task becomes progressively more and more difficult. Evidently as a result of carbon dioxide poisoning, violent headaches and a sensation of dizziness develop. (In the analytic reproduction, as well as in the nocturnal reproductions in nightmares, this stage is accompanied by a typical Cheyne-Stokes respiratory pattern.[3] The muscles are tensed to the maximum, then relaxed completely, the pulse is accelerated and irregular.)

The other point that deserves attention concerns the heart. As the patient consciously perceives the deceleration of cardiac activity, he attempts to influence by voluntary effort the normally involuntary process of circulation. Generally the unpleasure becomes so intense during this activity that the patient awakens. But if we can induce the patient to remain in the unpleasure situation, sometimes a new phase can be reached: suddenly the unpleasure gives way to a manic feeling of pleasure, as if the patient had succeeded in withdrawing completely from the painful situation. If we manage to maintain contact with the patient even in this state, he lets us know that he is no longer worried about breathing or about the preservation of his life in general. Moreover, he regards being destroyed or mutilated with interest, as if it is no longer his own self but another person who is undergoing these torments. The patient explains his hilarity as arising out of the difference between his colossal suffering and the fact that his assailant is now unable to do him any harm, even by unleashing all his destructive fury. To the extent that the assailant's motive for the aggression was sadism, the victim achieves vengeance through this newly developed insensitivity, for the sadist cannot inflict any more pain on the dead, unfeeling body, and therefore he must feel his impotence.

However, when someone's primal intellectual powers have been awakened, that is, when the need to mobilize them has arisen, it is not easy to make these primal functions vanish again. Expressed in psychologically more comprehensible terms, it means that it was incautious to assume that the environment would be normal and tolerable; it is better to rely on one's own primal powers. The consequence is that from now on, after even the slightest of injuries (physical or psychical), one no longer reacts by utilizing the alloplastic means of the nervous and mental systems, but by autoplastic, hysterical transformation (symptom-formation).

Another comparison: if the psychically dormant substance is rigid, while the nervous and mental systems possess fluid adaptability, then the hysterically reacting body could be described as semifluid, that is to say, as a substance whose previous rigidity and uniformity have been partially redissolved again into a psychic state, capable of adapting. Such "semisubstances" would then have the extraordinarily or wonderfully pleasing quality of being both body and mind simultaneously, that is, of expressing wishes, sensations of pleasure-unpleasure, or even complicated thoughts, through changes in their structure or function (the language of organs).

It is possible that a complicated internal process originating along neuropsychic paths, for example, as in the above case, the attempt to cope with an extremely painful situation, is suddenly abandoned, and the situation is resolved by autoplastic means, whereby regression of the specialized psychic functions to the primary psychic forces occurs, that is to say, it is transformed into substance modification utilizing its means of expression. The point at which external (alloplastic) control is completely abandoned and inner adaptation sets in (whereby reconciliation even with the destruction of the ego, that is, death as a form of adaptation, becomes conceivable) will be perceived inwardly as deliverance (?), liberation. This moment probably signifies the relinquishing of self-preservation for man and his self-inclusion [Sich-einordnen] in a greater, perhaps universal state of equilibrium.

In any event these reflections open the way to an understanding of the surprisingly intelligent reactions of the unconscious in moments of great distress, of danger to life, or of mortal agony. See here also the often-quoted incidents of clairvoyance.

1. The English translation of this lecture appeared under the title "Two Notes on the Erotic Component of the Ego Instincts" in *Primary Love and Psycho-Analytic Technique* (Hogarth Press; rpt. H. Karnac Ltd., 1985).
 2. See particularly "Some Thoughts on Trauma," *Fin* 276–279.—ED.
 3. The Cheyne-Stokes respiratory pattern is an abnormal pattern of respiration that occurs in cases of severe uremia. Periods of apnea alternate with periods of deep, rapid breathing. The respiratory cycle, which begins with slow, shallow breaths, increases to abnormal depth and rapidity, then subsides, climaxing in a period of ten to twenty seconds without respiration, before the cycle is resumed.—ED.

12 January 1932

Case of schizophrenia progressiva (R.N.)

I. Where the first shock occurred at the age of one and a half years (a promise by an adult, a close relative, to give her "something good," instead of which, drugged and sexually abused). At the onset of semiconsciousness, sudden awareness of something vile, total disillusionment and helplessness, perhaps also a temporary feeling of incapacity to exercise her own will, that is, painful awareness of suggestibility. Persistence of this state of half-stupor; probably at her most profound depths a wish not to be alive; nevertheless, under the influence of suggestion, a normal schoolchild's existence prevails: in other words, an artificial double life, together with complete repression of her own inclinations and feelings.

II. At the age of five, renewed, brutal attack; genitals artificially dilated, insistent suggestion to be compliant with men; stimulating intoxicants administered. Now (perhaps under the influence of the recent shock and the renewed attempt at adaptation), sudden recollection of the events in the second year of life, suicide impulse, probably also the sensation of dying (agony), *before* the suggested acts were performed. The enormity of suffering, plus helplessness and despair of any outside help, propel her toward death; but as conscious thought is lost, or abandoned, the organizing life instincts ("Orpha") awaken, and in place of death allow insanity to intervene.[1] (The same "Orphic" powers appear to have been already present at the time of the first shock.) The consequence of the second shock is a further "fragmentation" of the individuality. The person now consists of the following fragments: (1) A being suffering purely psychically in his unconscious, the actual child, of whom the awakened ego knows absolutely nothing. This fragment is accessible only in deep sleep, or in a deep trance, following extreme exertion or exhaustion, that is, in a neurotic (hysterical) crisis situation. Only with great difficulty and by close observance of specific rules of conduct can the analyst make contact with this part: *the pure, repressed affect.* This part behaves like a child who has fainted, completely unaware of itself, who can perhaps only groan, who must be shaken awake mentally and sometimes also physically. If this is not done with total belief in the reality of the process, the "shaking up" will lack persuasiveness as well as effectiveness. But if the analyst does have that conviction, and the related sympathy for the suffering being, he may by judicious questioning (which compels the sufferer to think) succeed in directing this being's reflective powers and orientation to the point where it can say and remember something about the circumstances of the shock. (2) A singular being, for whom the preservation of life is of "coûte que coûte" significance. (Orpha.) This fragment plays the role of the guardian angel; it produces wish-fulfilling hallucinations, consolation fantasies; it anesthetizes the consciousness and sensitivity against sensations as they become unbearable. In the case of the second shock, this maternal part could not help in any other way than by squeezing the entire psychic life out of the inhumanly suffering body. (3) After the second shock, we therefore have to deal with a third, soulless part of the personality, that is to say, with a body progressively divested of its soul, whose disintegration is not perceived at all or is regarded as an event happening to another person, being watched from the outside.

III. The last great shock struck this person, who was already split into three parts, at the age of eleven and a half. In spite of the precariousness of that *tripartitum,* a form of adaptation to the apparently unbearable situation had set in over the years. Being hypnotized and sexually abused became a style of life [*Lebensform*]. As though constant repetition of even such a painful rhythm, that is, the process of opening a pathway [*die Bahnung*] were in itself sufficient to make the painful appear less painful. But there is also the unconscious awareness that behind the tortures of the adult are concealed loving—though distorted—intentions; therefore, awareness of the libidinal elements present even in sadism. Finally, the adult's knowledge of and satisfaction with the child's endeavors, etc. . . . The combination of all these factors and others as yet incompletely explored may, therefore, have established a state—albeit a very precarious one—of equilibrium.

In this situation, sudden desertion by the tormentor strikes like a bolt of lightning. Being deprived of all spontaneity has made any reasonable adjustment, or even positive anticipation of new opportunities, impossible for the child. The situation was made worse by the fact that the father, before the separation, as a kind of farewell, had cursed the child, and thus had used his influence to the end to make the child indelibly aware of her own filthiness, uselessness, and contemptibility. The indefatigable Orpha, here, could not help itself any longer; it sought to encourage suicide. But as this was made impossible, the only form of existence left available was the complete atomization of psychic life. (Complete insanity, catatonic stupor, alternating with terror, hallucinations, and the confusion of chaotically jumbled memory impressions from her past.)

This lavalike eruption came to an end in total "incineration," a kind of lifelessness. But the life of the body, compelled as it was to breathe and pulsate, called back Orpha, who in despair had herself become inclined toward death. She managed, however, as if by a miracle, to get this being back on its feet, shattered as it was to its very atoms, and thus procured a sort of artificial psyche for this body forcibly brought back to life. From now on the "individuum," superficially regarded, consists of the following parts: (a) uppermost, a capable, active human being with a precisely—perhaps a little too precisely—regulated mechanism; (b) behind this, a being that does not wish to have anything more to do with life; (c) behind this murdered ego, the ashes of earlier mental sufferings, which are rekindled every night by the fire of suffering; (d) this suffering itself as a separate mass of affect, without content and unconscious, the remains of the actual person.

1. For Orpha, see 1 May 1932, note 1.

17 January 1932

Mutual analysis and the limits of its application

Starting point: developmental phases of the technique.

a. Original catharsis and precautions arising in consequence of it, and the development of an impersonal attitude.

b. Failures and incomplete successes, demands for change: increase in tension (active therapy); adverse effects of excessive strictness. Experiments with passivity, relaxation; as extreme consequence, loss of authority, provocations ("when will his patience snap"), "ad-absurdum" feeling.

c. Confession of artificiality in the analyst's behavior; admission in principle of emotions such as annoyance, unpleasure, fatigue, "to hell with it," finally also libidinal and play fantasies. Result: patient becomes more natural, more affable, and more sincere.

d. R.N. demands methodically conducted analysis as the only possible protective measure against the inclination, perceived in me, to kill or torture patients. At first strong opposition on my part: the patient may abuse the situation, frustrate in a projective sense the object of the entire self-analysis, that is, she may analyze me instead of herself. Surprisingly, it happened otherwise: the attitude adopted by the analyst made it possible for the analysand to convey from then on, without any reticence or regard for diplomacy, everything that had been formerly withheld (in deference to sensitivity). During the "proper" analytical session that followed, all hitherto repressed affects came out into the open. The strongest impression on the patient was naturally made by my admission of personal and physical antipathies and the confession of my previously rather overdone friendliness. Politeness, that is, the destruction of all hope of a real, a more than merely professional, countertransference. The first torrent of the patient's affects (desire to die, notions of suicide, flight) is succeeded, quite remarkably, by relative composure and progress in the work: attention becomes freer of exaggerated fantasies and now focuses on the two realities: the reality of the past and the potential reality of the future. It is as though the painful necessity of bearing the loss of the countertransference had steeled the patient to bear the unpleasure, those feelings which had led to repression regarding the past and to paralyzing phobia-like precautions regarding the future.

Another, as yet unresolved, problem here is linked to the admission of the possibility of positive transference feelings. In any case, here too admission and discussion of it offer some protection against its exaggeration. Any kind of secrecy, whether positive or negative in character, makes the patient distrustful; he detects from little gestures (form of greeting, handshake, tone of voice, degree of animation, etc.) the presence of affects, but cannot gauge their quantity or importance; candid disclosure regarding them enables him to counteract them or to instigate countermeasures with greater certainty.

Can and should the analyst, analyzed in this way, be completely open, right from the beginning? Should he not take into account the patient's reliability, capacity to tolerate, and understanding? For the time being, with this in mind, I am careful to exercise caution, and I allow myself to relax only by degrees, as the patient's ability to cope increases. Example: financial situation desperate; all payments had stopped earlier, then the debt itself is canceled. On a previous occasion a somewhat rash remark: in case of need, financial help is offered. (Shortly afterward inner opposition to this, combined with the feeling: one must surely not allow oneself to be eaten up by one's patients.) Possible negative consequences: the patient, relying on this promise, neglected to make use of even such energies or real opportunities as were at her disposal: simultaneously, instead of allowing herself to be helped analytically, she tries to obtain material assistance (money, libido). Further negative result: inward annoyance with the patient, which the patient feels but does not comprehend. Following frank discussion: increased trust, acceptance of the goodwill I have shown as such, after subtracting the exaggerations and strengthening against unpleasure mentioned earlier.

Now something "metaphysical": some patients have the feeling that when this kind of mutual peace is attained the libido, released from conflict, will, without any further intellectual or explanatory effort, have a "healing" effect. They demanded that I should not reflect quite so much, I should just be there; that I should not talk so much, or make any effort, and as far as I was concerned I could even go to sleep. The two unconsciouses thereby receive mutual help: the "healer" himself would gain some tranquillity from the healed, and vice-versa. Both emphasize that this mutual flux be taken in the substantial sense and not merely explained in terms of psychology. Both have completely identical notions that hate and enmity (especially in the earliest years of childhood) effectively expel the personality's vital energies and could altogether destroy them (shock, anxiety, and their paralyzing effect).

Such pressures or impacts may disrupt or completely suspend the capacity to think. The psyche that has been fragmented or pulverized by trauma feels love, cleansed of all ambivalence, flowing toward it and enveloping it, as if with a kind of glue: fragments come together into larger units; the entire personality may succeed in again becoming united (homogeneous). Unfortunately, at the end of the session these achievements will be largely destroyed again. Does the fault lie in the fact that the imagination has assumed more love in us than we actually have to give? Does not the blame for this Penelopean repetition of construction and destruction lie in the fact that when the session is over we simply send the patient away? A frank discussion of this is essential and may be of help. In any event our aim must be to induce the patient to be content with real possibilities, though substantially mitigated (friendliness, goodwill), that is, to accept this somewhat diluted libido-solution both as a glue and as a healing substance.

Subjective confession. This free discussion with the patient provides a kind of liberation and relief for the analyst in comparison with the kinds of activity favored [*eingenommenen*] until now, which are strained, so to speak, and taxing. If we also succeed in gaining the patient's goodwill, freed from neurotic egotism, so that the patient realizes the impossibility of demanding more from us, then we feel our efforts have been rewarded by an unselfish response to our own unselfishness. Our psyche, too, is more or less fragmented and in pieces, and, especially after expending so much libido without any libido-income, it needs such repayment now and again from well-disposed patients who are cured or on the point of being cured.

Intellectual activity at the time of each physical change

This activity is at rest if nothing disturbs it from outside. Resistance (defiance, noncomprehension) to every assault, time and space determined by this resistance. Intellect itself is without time and space, therefore supra-individual. "Orpha."

19 January 1932

Mutual analysis continued

R.N.'s dream. Former patient Dr. Gx. forces her withered breast into R.N.'s mouth. "It isn't what I need; too big, empty—no milk." The patient feels that this dream fragment is a combination of the unconscious contents of the psyches of the analysand and the analyst. She demands that the analyst should "let himself be submerged," even perhaps fall asleep. The analyst's associations in fact move in the direction of an episode in his infancy (*száraz dajka*[1] affair, at the age of one year); meanwhile the patient repeats in dream scenes of horrifying events at the ages of one and a half, three, five, and eleven and a half, and their interpretation. The analyst is able, for the first time, to link *emotions* with the above primal event and thus endow that event with the feeling of a real experience. Simultaneously the patient succeeds in gaining insight, far more penetrating than before, into the reality of these events that have been repeated so often on an intellectual level. At her demand and insistence, I help her by asking simple questions that compel her to think. I must address her as if she were a patient in a mental hospital, using her childhood nicknames, and force her to admit to the reality of the facts, in spite of their painful nature. It is as though two halves had combined to form a whole soul. The emotions of the analyst combine with the ideas of the analysand, and the ideas of the analyst (representational images) with the emotions of the analysand; in this way the otherwise lifeless images become events, and the empty emotional tumult acquires an intellectual content. (?)

Insight into the analyst's weaknesses leads to the abandonment of exaggerated expectations of indulgence. How can I guarantee her complete and lifelong happiness when I myself was and still am partly a child, that is to say, in need of care. This is why the patient turns to Dr. X., who is really ill, but who pays the patient when she does come, whereas the patient had to pay me over a long period of time and nowadays receives only moral help, without any prospect of more real happiness. It is possible that this undoubtedly deep insight into my own weaknesses was what [revealed to me]² my inclination to be rid of her, my resolve to give her neither libidinal nor financial help (both kinds of self-protection further intensified by infantile traumata: affair of the nurse, plus housemaid).

The combined result of the two analyses is summarized by the patient as follows: "Your greatest trauma was the destruction of genitality. Mine was worse: I saw my life destroyed by an insane criminal; my mind destroyed by poisons and suggested stultification, my body defiled by the ugliest mutilation, at a most inappropriate time; ostracism from a society in which no one wants to believe me innocent; finally the horrendous incident of the last 'experience of being murdered.' "

Under the influence of the destruction of illusion that the mutual analysis helps to bring about, the patient allows herself (or it is made possible for her) to confess to herself, and to me, the affects of ardor and sexual excitement, which she had hitherto not admitted to consciousness. An excited, furious scene over a relatively insignificant matter (against the servants) and, for the first time, reproduction of libidinal sensations in the mouth and in the genitals, in connection with the traumatic event. Nevertheless, the strict isolation of these feelings from the despised [verpönten]³ persons is still strictly maintained; the moment the emptiness of the supposed breast (fellatio) is noticed, the sucking need is displaced to the genitals, but only in the form of wanting to be touched there (here the common attribute, the identity between the analyst and the analysand: both had been forced to do more and endure more sexually than they had in fact wanted to). While in reality the despised and repudiated genital activities were in progress, in the split-off part of the psyche a masturbation fantasy of wonderful content was taking place, which had to become more and more complete as the actual course of events, with all her indescribable suffering, grew more dreadful. Similarly, her partner of the mutual analysis had compensated in his youth by endless masturbatory activity, the peculiarity of which can be gauged by the ejaculation up to the sky [*Ejakulatio usque ad coleum*].[4]

Is the purpose of mutual analysis perhaps the finding of that common feature which repeats itself in every case of infantile trauma? And is the discovery or perception of this the condition for understanding and for the flood of healing compassion?

Second case of mutual analysis

The revelation of one's own feelings of anxiety and guilt enables the same tendencies to emerge for the first time in the analysand (Dm.), who in a similar way ruins all potentialities in her life and many of her analyses. One could almost say that the more weaknesses an analyst has, which lead to greater or lesser mistakes and errors but which are then uncovered and treated in the course of mutual analysis, the more likely the analysis is to rest on profound and realistic foundations.

The analysis began years ago, with all possible sternness and reserve, unnecessarily exacerbated by a desire not to allow social differences to interfere. The patient, who had come with the intention of opening up in complete freedom, became as though paralyzed, at least in her behavior. Inwardly full of the most intense transference feelings, she did not reveal any of these. A slow thawing, later on definite progress toward trust, particularly when in a moment of great distress (money matters) she found protection and help from me, and probably also some emotional response. Then came an attempt at displacement onto a third person (R.T.), but finally, after a second trauma (brother's death), also mitigated by me, she resigned herself to returning to her family and her duties. At this point I succeeded in diverting the patient away from a one-sided [*einseitigen*] interest in ghosts and metaphysics, yet bound up with a great deal of anxiety, to two-sided [*beiderseitigen*] interests (remaining friends with the spirits, but also being able and willing to provide helpful assistance in the real world). What appears to be totally absent is any desire for sexual activity.

At this stage the patient begins to show interest and concern for the analyst's psyche. She asks him not to exert himself so desperately; he should not be embarrassed to fall asleep, if he feels like it: thus similar to case no. 1.

The probable outcome of this case—or a possible one, at least— may well be the discovery of the common attribute in the early damage done to the genital region in both, and continuation of, or regression to, infantile tenderness. The parallel to that in the adult would be his kindness, helpfulness, serenity, and, after withdrawing from the battles forced upon him and the convulsive outbreaks of passion, we will accept these qualities in all resignation as his true nature. But painfully, with philosophical resignation, one must recognize this, and not pursue false ideals. Mutual analysis will also be less terribly demanding, will promote a more genial and helpful approach in the patient, instead of the unremittingly all-too-good, selfless demeanor, behind which exhaustion, unpleasure, even murderous intentions are hidden.

1. Nurse, as opposed to wet-nurse, in Hungarian.

2. Verb omitted in original; phrase in brackets inserted by Michael Balint.

3. *Verpönten:* in archaic sense forbidden, taboo; in the more usual sense despised, inferior, contemptible.

4. In this passage Ferenczi refers to events in his own life; see *Correspondance Ferenczi-Groddeck.*—ED.

24 January 1932

Suggestion, intimidation, imposition of an alien will,

splitting off of one's own [will], which *remains intact;* just like the brutal effect of anesthesia and drugs, "superego."

I. R.N. (a) Seduction through agreeable promises; pleasurable excitation that demands fulfillment; sudden awareness that something bad is being done to her, accompanied by the assertion that this is "good." (See the work on childrearing in the British Psychological Society: the child is persuaded that things that taste good are bad, and the unpleasant ones are good.) The drugs had rendered R.N. acquiescent. The experience of being drugged is perceived as antagonistic to life, and rejected: in fact, one can be anesthetized only by force, even when one has consciously consented to it. The will to exercise control over sensations and motility, independent of outside influence, is never renounced. One yields to force, but with *reservatio mentalis*. Repression is, in actual fact, being repressed while retaining all original tendencies (among them the ability to form an opinion, for example contradiction). But where is the repressed located; what is its content; in what form does it stay connected to the parts of the individual that have surrendered to force, and in what way can a reunification occur? Answer: (1) The repressed, that is, the will that has yielded to force, is located, according to feeling and linguistic usage, "beside itself" [*ausser sich*]. The [victim's] own will is located somewhere in the unreal, in the physical sense; that is, it is located in the psychic reality as a *tendency* [*Tendenz*], that has at its disposal no instrument of power, no organic or cerebral resources, not even the memory images that are more or less physical. In other words this will, which feels intact and which no power can suppress, is located outside of the person who acts with violence, and through this splitting it continually denies being the person performing these actions. Here perhaps mention the case of B., in which throughout the day's activities, which consist of tasks that, though very unpleasant, must be performed, there is a soft humming of a few melodies. Their erotic character and rhythm, as well as their textual associations, represent a continual unspoken protest against this kind of life and work. In fact the ego, B.'s innermost self, has stopped performing any independent action of its own ever since an alien will, alien decisions, were imposed on it, [and will not perform any] as long as it is prevented from protesting aloud, that is, until revived in analysis. Almost everything that has developed since the trauma is in fact the work of that alien will: the person who does these things is not me. Hence R.N.'s extraordinary, incessant protestations that she is no murderer, although she admits to having fired the shots.

R.N.—as it became possible to establish by painstaking analysis of hundreds of fragments and symptoms—considers the effect of anesthetics a monstrous act of violence. These drugs in fact *produce over-sensitivity* (threat of death), with such a powerful effect that even the slightest touch, before any intervention, elicits that "yielding to force." To be anesthetized is thus to be temporarily split off from one's own body: the operation is not carried out on me, but on a body to which I used to belong. Here one might include one woman's description of the terrifying inability to answer questions she experienced while she was being anesthetized; she heard the voice of the questioner as if from a tremendous distance, many miles away. In the course of the narcosis (ethyl-methyl anesthetic), which lasted two minutes, she saw an immense succession of dream images; among these she saw the completed operation, and so she had the comforting feeling that she had survived the operation while in fact it was not yet over. All the same, sinking into nothingness was for her a terrifying sensation. When she recovered consciousness, her first remark was, "I dreamed so much!"

In the case of R.N. drugs and suggestion were used simultaneously. At the onset of the narcosis, sensitivity to any violence, to any expression of hate, anger, even the slightest dissatisfaction, is heightened, hence increased "suggestibility." Suggestibility, therefore, is actually the result of shock: paternal hypnosis equals fear of being killed, maternal hypnosis equals fear of being abandoned by the mother, that is, the threat that the libido will be withdrawn;[1] the latter feels just as deadly as an aggressive threat to life. But the most frightful of frights is when the threat from the father is coupled with simultaneous desertion by the mother. There is no chance to cry bitter tears over the injustice suffered or to gain a sympathetic hearing from anyone. Only *then,* when the real world, as it is, becomes so unbearable and the feeling of injustice, helplessness, and despair that things might ever change for the better becomes so absolute, only then does the ego withdraw from reality, though without giving up itself. Each experience of terror thus implies this kind of splitting off; all adaptation occurs in a person who has become malleable through terror-dissociation in the absence of the ego; the violent force imprints its own features on the person, or compels him to change in accordance with its own will.

On mimicry. How does the coloring of the environment come to be imposed on an animal or plant species? The environment itself (the arctic region) has no interest in coloring the polar bear's fur white; only the bear derives benefit from it. Theoretically, however, it is not impossible that a higher, shared attribute that includes both the individual and the environment, such as for example a universal tendency observable in nature toward a state of repose, may be in force as a higher principle, constantly working to balance out the differences between accumulations of danger and unpleasure. This principle enables the environment to lend its color to the individual and helps the individual to take on the color of its surroundings. An interesting example of the successful interaction of egoistic and universal tendencies—individual collectivism.

II. What is the content of the split-off ego? Above all a tendency, probably *the* tendency, to complete the action interrupted by shock. In order to be able to do this, a refusal to take any notice of the injustice suffered, and assertion by means of wish-fulfilling mental images, by day and by night, of what one considers just. In other words, ideational (cognitive) material, but limited to a tendency to repeat and to try to find a better solution. The content of the split-off ego is always as follows: natural development and spontaneity, protest against violence and injustice, contemptuous, perhaps sarcastic and ironic obedience displayed in the face of domination, but inward knowledge that the violence has in fact achieved nothing; it has altered only something objective, the decisionmaking process, but not the ego as such. Contentment with oneself for this accomplishment, a feeling of being bigger and cleverer than the brutal force; suddenly insight into the greater coherence of world order, the treatment of brute force as a kind of mental disorder, even when this power is successful; the beginnings of a desire to cure this mental disorder. What impresses us as megalomania in the mentally ill may well contain this, as its real and justified core. The mentally ill person has a keen eye for the insanity of mankind.[2]

1. See "Introjection and Transference," *C* 35–43; "Taming of the Wild Horse," *Fin* 336–340; "The Analysis of Comparisons," *FC* 402; *Thalassa: An Essay on the Theory of Genitality, Psychoanalytical Quarterly* (1938): 32–33; "Male and Female," in *Thalassa,* pp. 105–106.—ED.

2. This passage contains the first outline of the ideas that were to be fully developed in Ferenczi's last article, which he presented at the Congress of Wiesbaden: "Confusion of Tongues between Adults and the Child," *Fin* 156–166; see esp. 161–163. This paper caused profound shock in the psychoanalytic world at the time; perhaps the same mechanisms he described in the paper were operating there as well.—ED.

26 January 1932

On boredom

Exclamation of someone who is bored to death: "Everything is lost except killing!" In conjunction with observation of catatonic schizophrenics, this leads to the assumption that catatonia in its relaxed as well as in its rigid form protects society from tremendous aggression. Just as in milder cases the localized hysterical paralysis usually covers murderous, vengeful, or punitive actions and intentions, so the universal repudiation of all motor activity may represent the possible counterpart to an epileptic attack, accompanied by destructive and self-destructive intentions.

What does being bored mean? Having to do something one hates and not being able to do what one would like: in any event a state of endurance. Cases become difficult and pathological when the person who is bored is no longer consciously aware of what he does or does not want. Example: a little boy incessantly plagues his mother: "Mother, give me something! But what? I don't know!" Deeper probing into the wishes and unpleasure sensations of the little boy would have been enlightening. Analogy in poetry: Vörösmarty's "Petike."[1]

The urge or even compulsion to act is in fact a flight from the distressing feeling of boredom, or more correctly, from the total inhibition imposed by the pull toward activity in two opposite directions, with the victory going to passivity or negativism. No schizophrenic can be cured without a strict ban on all forms of mannerism (even tics must be treated by "active" therapy). What is the cause of this terrible anxiety and flight from such emptiness? Possible answer: hidden behind this emptiness is the entire experience or series of experiences that has led to the present incapacity: painful irritability, tendency to rage and defensiveness, feeling of helplessness, or fear of the prospect of irreparable outbreaks of rage and aggression. In the most extreme case activity withdraws even from the act of thinking. What remains in the field of action is an unthinking playing with bodily organs, or allowing them to play (scratching, twiddling of moustache or thumbs, "malmozni," waggling of feet), and last but not least some kind of masturbatory genital activity. This is one way to understand better the feces-smearing and continual masturbation of idiots and catatonics. Expressed in temporal terms: the libido regresses to the earliest forms of expression, when they had not yet been disturbed, that is, it regresses to spontaneous forms of expression. An apparent restitution consists of the purely mechanical hypercathexis of negativism or apraxia with purely mechanical, though socially acceptable, routine activities.

Another way of defining these states might be (as already mentioned elsewhere) an apparent yielding to force, accompanied by the unconscious maintenance of a continuous protest, and the assertion of spontaneity through stereotypes and through conscious or unconscious daydreams or fantasies. The impatient man kills with his piano-playing. Behind the apparently precise working activities of a lady, incessant melodies were going on, of which she was only rarely aware.

1. Mihály Vörösmarty (1800–1855), poet and writer, a central figure in Hungarian classical literature. He took part, as did Ferenczi's father, in the Revolution of 1848, and

after the brutal suppression of the Revolution by the Austrians he was obliged to lead a clandestine existence for a time. Here is a translation of his poem "Petike" (1841):

Little Peter sits there, mournful and sad,
  Ha ha ha!
Peter and sorrow! Good heavens, what can
  Be the matter?
His mother regards him with faithful eyes,
  The worthy old woman!
She thinks that perhaps her dear son
  Is ailing.
"Peter, my son, would you like some pie?
  Would you like a bite to eat?"
"No, no, I don't want anything to eat.
  Take it all away."
"Perhaps, dear son, you'd like some wine?
  Something nice to drink?"
"No, no, I don't want anything to drink.
  Take it all away."
"Would you like some new spurs for your boots,
  My darling Peter?
Feathers to brighten your hat, and fox fur
  To trim your waistcoat?"
"What do I want with feathers or spurs
  Or fox-fur trim,
When sorrow is gnawing away at my heart,
  Like a fox!"
"Would you like a book, the neighbor's book—
  The Bible?"
"What good are books? They're all nothing
  But words.
I have but a single friend,
  And that is death;
From whichever direction it comes, I know
  It will cut me down."

"Heavens above, my darling Peter,
  Pray, do not die!
You're filled with nothing but groans and sighs,
  As a hive swarms with bees.
Would you like me to ask Juliette to come?
  Perhaps you'd like to see her?"
In a gloomy voice master Peter says,
  "Well, where is she then?"
Rascal Peter!
So that's what was wrong!
Neither his hat, nor his waistcoat,
Nor the jangle of spurs;
He doesn't want fox fur,
Or the neighbor's Bible,
He doesn't want wine or pie.
But Juliette he would gladly have;
She's a flirt, and a simpering young thing,
But rosy, gay, and fair.
He doesn't want to eat or drink,
But only to dally with Juliette.
"Well, my Peter, my handsome boy,
  So that's what was wrong with you!
I'll make sure you grow big and strong,
  And see that you don't die.
And now get up! To school with you,
  You naughty, naughty boy!
And don't let me catch you moping about,
  Enough of these sighs and tears!
At school all thought of Juliette
  Will be banished from your mind.
In ten years' time, if God so grants,
  You'll take her for your wife."

28 January 1932

Repression, hysterical conversion, uncovering of their genesis in cathartic regression

Patient B., in whose previous history, reconstructed analytically, incestuous rape may be assumed with great certainty, at a relatively early stage in the analysis used to produce almost hallucinatory cathartic abreactions of repressed, traumatogenic events. In fact, already in the course of the first session, induced by the "egg dream," complete reproduction of sensations: the same smell of alcohol and tobacco as on the breath of her attacker; violent twisting of her hands at the wrists, a feeling of trying to push off with her palms the weight of a gigantic body; then a feeling of pressing weight on her chest, obstruction of her breathing by clothing, suffocation, violent stimulation [*Reizung*] (abduction) of her lower extremities, a most painful sensation in the abdomen with a marked rhythm, a feeling of leakage; finally the feeling of lying as though nailed to the floor, bleeding that will not stop, the sight of an evil, peering face, then only the sight of the enormous legs of a man, arranging his clothes, leaving her to lie there. (Preceding events: invitation to a remote room, a workshop, running from there in terror, being caught in the garden.) Despite the vividness and emotional intensity of the cathartic experience, soon or immediately afterward, a feeling of the unreality of the whole. (Interpretation: feeling of improbability, painful state, fear of consequences (mother's grief, father's suicide, pregnancy, shame, fear of giving birth), therefore the whole thing not true.) Vague notion of (1) cleaning herself up in the bathroom, (2) being comforted by her nurse.

In the course of further analysis, long periods of extreme mistrust and resistance toward me. Whole hours are spent in accusations and suspicions. (Cheating—financial and sexual—laziness, slowness, perhaps for the same reasons, occasionally sudden remission, then relapses again.)

At last, insight into the resistant nature of her attitude to analysis, resolves to relax properly; each time this is followed by a series of depressive symptoms. Instead of the previous noisy scenes, she turns pale, skin becomes cold, breathing shallow, barely perceptible, pulse irregular and weak. When questioned, complains of shivering fits, voice incredibly weak, increasing headaches. These states, if not interrupted, would last from one to several quarters of an hour.

In several sessions the patient demanded that I should not just let her lie there, but I should intervene somehow when she got into these states, and "do" something with her. In answer to these instructions, I tried, today for instance, to start a simple conversation without arousing the patient from her relaxation and state of suffering; this worked. First (in fact even before she was in a semitrance) she told me of her sleep disturbances, and today in somewhat more detail about her so-called bumping. For years, as a child, she could not fall asleep without first crouching and banging her head, always the forehead, against the mattress, over and over again with considerable force. She counted the bangs by the hundred on each finger of one hand, that is, a thousand on both hands. Often she counted up to three thousand before dropping off suddenly into the deepest possible sleep. She had to give up this procedure as she grew up, but appears to have invented analogous but less obvious substitutes: endlessly repeated melodies; an endlessly sustained long note that occasionally shifts to a higher tone, then after a while rises higher and higher, but so that the change occurs in jerks or waves. Sometimes, as for example today, this ascent took on a spatial, graphic character. Today in particular, the rise paralleled or closely resembled the road from her house to mine. Each rise of the hill was experienced as a climb to attain the plateau at the top of the hill in front of my house.[1] This corresponded to reaching her goal, and thus to falling asleep.

As I was repeating to her all that she had told me in the above context, the sensation of being cold all over suddenly increased, and at my insistence she described for me all kinds of paresthesiae. Apart from the cold, all she can feel is being gripped by both wrists, which are being twisted as mentioned earlier. A striking feature was the hyperesthesia of the head, already previously observed from time to time. She experienced the slightest touch, even the shaking of the couch, as incredibly painful. On either side of her rib cage she feels a pressure, like the pressure of two elbows. Suddenly a general burning sensation in the upper half of the body; about the lower half she reports, "I know that there is a pain there, but I cannot feel it!" There is experimentally confirmed hyperesthesia in the upper half of the body (probably combined with hypoesthesia in the lower half: but this was not tested). After I explained the displacement of all sensation upward and predicted that making the connections conscious would allow the excitation to flow back into its original and real locality (I used the comparison that I would squeeze her feelings back from her upper half down into her lower half, like squeezing out a sponge), she suddenly began to feel violent pains in her genital region.

The displacement upward of the reaction to stimulation makes it possible to stop worrying that the experiences might be real. Head banging, interminable melodies, the headaches, caused by all this, displace the pain to a more harmless region. Pain, therefore, is relatively pain-relieving, when its location is displaced to a morally less significant and obviously unreal part of the body. Here again an important source of masochism: pain as the alleviation of other, greater pains.

Analogous to the "sensation of dizziness at the end of the analytical session,"[2] the patient feels that after the sudden cessation of head banging or hill climbing, the motion in the head, once induced, continues automatically and causes dizziness. This dizziness is the equivalent of a sudden sinking into confusion and unconsciousness.

1. Ferenczi's house was situated exactly as described here, at the top of one of the hills of Budapest, the Naphegy (Sun Hill). The steep road leading up to it flattens out some twenty or thirty meters before reaching the house. On the outside wall, along Lisznyai Street, there is now a plaque, which was erected in 1983 to commemorate the fiftieth anniversary of Ferenczi's death.—ED.

2. See *FC* 239.—ED.

31 January 1932

The catharsis gets bogged down, and how to remedy it

One would think that the perpetual repetition in analysis of the traumatic experience, stressing first one factor and then another, would in the end result in a mosaic-like reconstruction of the whole picture. This does in fact happen, but only with a feeling of speculative reconstruction and not with the firm conviction that the events were real. "Something" more is required to transform the intellectual coherence of the possible or probable into the more solid cohesion of a necessary or even obvious reality.

For the present I have only two explanatory factors, or rather fragments, for the identification of this "something." It appears that patients cannot believe that an event really took place, or cannot fully believe it, if the analyst, as the sole witness of the events, persists in his cool, unemotional, and, as patients are fond of stating, purely intellectual attitude, while the events are of a kind that must evoke, in anyone present, emotions of revulsion, anxiety, terror, vengeance, grief, and the urge to render immediate help: to remove or destroy the cause or the person responsible; and since it is usually a child, an injured child, who is involved (but even leaving that aside), feelings of wanting to comfort it with love, etc., etc. One therefore has a choice: to take really seriously the *role* one assumes, of the benevolent and helpful observer, that is, actually to transport oneself with the patient into that period of the past (a practice Freud reproached me for, as being not permissible), with the result that we ourselves and the patient believe in its reality, that is, a present reality, which has not been momentarily transposed into the past. The objection to this approach would be: after all we do know that the whole episode, insofar as it is true, is not taking place now. Therefore we are dishonest if we allow the events to be acted out dramatically and even participate in the drama. But if we adopt this view, and contrive right from the beginning to present the events to the patient as memory images that are unreal in the present, he may well follow our line of thought but will remain on an intellectual level, without ever attaining the feeling of conviction.[1] "It cannot be true that all this is happening to me, or someone would come to my aid"—and the patient prefers to doubt his own judgment rather than believe in our coldness, our lack of intelligence, or in simpler terms, our stupidity and nastiness.

The psychic processes on awakening from the trauma are similar. Immediately after the events (generally in childhood) the victim of the shock could still have been helped. The shattered person is intellectually so confused that he cannot say anything precise about the events. (Consider here the comparison with retroactive amnesia following severe cerebral concussion.) A person thus paralyzed in his thought processes [*Denkarbeit*] must be encouraged to start thinking by going back to vague or faint memory images or their fragments. (Here it could be mentioned in some detail how R.N. awakes immediately from her dazed state whenever more than the simplest mental effort is required.)

It appears that at this point in the analysis something from the patient's past history repeats itself. In most cases of infantile trauma, the parents have no interest in impressing the events on the mind of the child, on the contrary, the usual cure is repression: "it's nothing at all"; "nothing has happened"; "don't think about it"; "*katonadolog*";[2] but nothing is ever said about these ugly matters (for instance of a sexual nature). Such things are simply hidden in a deadly silence; the child's faint references are ignored or even rejected as incongruous, with the unanimous concurrence of those around him, and with such consistency that the child has to give up and cannot maintain its own judgment.

The only course left for the analyst is to be honest with the patient about his own real feelings and to confess, for example, that burdened with his own personal troubles he often has to struggle to summon up sufficient interest to listen to the patient. Further confessions: the doctor exaggerates the friendliness of his feelings, smiles amiably, and thinks "To hell with you, you have disturbed my afternoon sleep," or "I slept badly last night, there is something wrong with my digestion," then, "How unbearable the resistance of this patient is, I would really like to throw him out." In principle, one must naturally reckon with the possibility of such suspicions on the part of the patient. It seems, however, that many of them are not content with just knowing what is possible; they want to know the truth. It may also happen that the patient does get the idea, or must be encouraged to appreciate the idea, that part of the difficulty in putting ourselves in his place, and our unpleasure or inability to be genuine observers of the drama, stems from the continued existence in the analyst of complexes of his own, which may be as yet unresolved, uncontrolled, or even quite unconscious. In fact, we analysts must admit to ourselves that we are much indebted to our patients for their sharply critical view of us, especially when we promote its development, which helps us to gain considerable insight regarding some peculiarities or weak points in our own character. I do not know of a single case of training analysis, my own included, that was so complete that it would have rendered corrections of this kind completely unnecessary in the analyst's subsequent life and work. The only question is how far such "mutual analysis" can or should go. Naturally there are grounds for suspicion that the patient is just taking the opportunity to deflect attention from himself and searching for complexes in the analyst in a paranoid way, thus turning himself into the doctor and the analyst into the patient. But even this cannot be rejected without further discussion. (a) In the case of paranoia itself, one must seek to discover the grain of truth that is hidden in every delusional idea. (b) The possibility should not be rejected out of hand that the analyst's habit of identifying any obstacle encountered as resistance on the part of the patient can be misused in an equally paranoid, that is, delusional, way for the projection or disavowal of his own complexes.

Special case of R.N. The first real advances toward the patient's gaining conviction occurred in conjunction with some genuinely emotionally colored fragments of the rather systematically conducted analysis of the analyst, accompanied by proof of affective exaggeration and an almost unbearable superperformance [*Mehrleistung*] with corresponding feelings of hate toward the patient. These feelings of hate can at the same time be linked to the highly painful superperformances of youth and childhood, only grasped through reconstruction as compensation for very significant traumata.[3] The disinclination for any kind of role-playing that is so characteristic of the analyst, rejection of affects as "affectation," is soon followed by appearance of "weak" emotional outbursts (grief, shock, regret, breaking down with tears in the eyes) in contrast to the previous coldness. *At the same moment* the patient opens up, is permeated by a feeling that I have at last understood (that is, felt) her suffering, consequently with an increased sense of certainty about (a) the reality of her own experiences, (b) the contrast between the present and the period when the incidents occurred: total isolation instead of the possibility of telling her troubles and of being listened to sympathetically.

Obvious objection: one cannot allow oneself to be analyzed by every patient! What I can answer to this objection, if I can answer it, remains to be seen. The question is: Is it only for some special cases, where nothing can be achieved without such deepening of the analytic situation?

2. After eliminating the obstacles coming from the analyst's side, which brings the limits of his help more clearly into view, the patient finds himself forced to look around for alternative means of existence: these, however, become available only on the way to real recovery. The will to heal, that is, the will to gain insight into what is painful in the reality (including that of the past) is strengthened by the patient's tolerating the disillusionment initiated by the analyst, while at the same time accepting in a friendly, unresentful way what can in reality be accomplished: all this leads to analogous modifications in the cathexis of memory material, which had remained unconscious because it was so unbearable.

(The identification of the exaggerated superperformance on the part of the analyst is generally followed by a reckoning: deducting the exaggerated parts of the transference feelings, [the patient] will express dissatisfaction of various kinds about which he previously remained silent.) The end result of the analysis of transference and countertransference may be the establishment of a kind, dispassionate atmosphere, such as may well have existed in pretraumatic times. The application of the "cathartic bogging down" metaphor must be attempted, in individual cases, with reference to these general principles.

1. Ferenczi had been preoccupied since 1913 with the problem of differential or varying levels of conviction; see his observations made at the Fourth Congress of the International Association of Psycho-Analysis in Munich: "Belief, Disbelief, and Conviction," FC 437–450. A number of his subsequent experiments with technique were aimed specifically at creating conditions that would enable the patient to attain that conviction, which, according to Ferenczi, would be of greatest therapeutic value.—ED.

2. In Hungarian: "Soldiers can take it," a fundamental concept in the education of children in Hungary.—ED.

3. It is not clear what particular traumatic incidents of his youth Ferenczi is alluding to here. Some are known (a family of many children and very busy parents; the death of a younger sister; the death of his father when Sándor was 15), but others are not known. For any concrete detail that is available on Ferenczi's childhood, refer to the preface of the Ferenczi-Groddeck correspondence.—ED.

2 February 1932

A dilemma of mutual analysis

1. The patient is intent on carrying out the analysis of the analyst, feeling that obstacles in [the analyst] make it impossible to attain that inner freedom of the libido without which the fragments that have been reconstructed a hundred times in analysis can never be welded together into a coherent unit; in particular, immediately after cathartic reproduction their content breaks apart into segregated elements of feeling and seeing (knowing), without ever arriving at anything more than momentary unification.

2. After overcoming considerable resistances, of both a personal and a purely theoretical (technical) nature, decision to yield on this point as well. Except for a very few instances, everything is communicated, although a certain respect for the patient's sensibilities is retained. The patient's ambition, however, drives her on to demand more and more open association, until finally the opportunity does arrive to dispense with consideration for the patient. In particular, the criticism withheld up to now is voiced. The most upsetting thing for the patient, almost tragic in its effect, is the fact that feelings of tenderness actually aroused through the patient's analysis will be directed in quite a different direction. During the next session, she mentions steps for breaking off the analysis, accompanied for the first time by concrete plans: a visit to a fond relative whose intuitions and caring involvement offer her just what she has been missing in me: love and tenderness.

3. The analysis appears to have run aground over this dilemma: the only line of retreat available is: the analyst manifests regret over this termination *and* his insight, based on his own experience, that if the present process is to have a different outcome from the original trauma, then the victim of traumatic shock must be offered something in reality, at least as much caring attention, or a genuine intention to provide it, as a severely traumatized child must have. It appears, however, that even the child thus afflicted demands, as compensation for and counterweight to his suffering, inordinate amounts of love, in both a qualitative and a quantitative sense. If this is not provided, he will persist in a state of silent and proud suffering; and unless there is at least one human being he can open up to, he will remain in majestic isolation, floating above the situation, while the processes of suffering unfold freely in his symptoms, in nightmares, and in states of trance, without leaving the slightest trace of conviction behind.

4. A parallel is shown by another case of spontaneous submerg-

ence into a state of trance that looks quite terrifyingly dangerous (deathlike pallor, breathing almost entirely shallow, eyes rolling upward, etc.). The most distressing part is the end of the session, when I am obliged to leave the patient in this state with only a few parting words, either urging her to leave or allowing her, for a short while, just to lie there alone. On the last of these occasions she said: "You could at least tell me that I am a good girl," which I then did; so in this case too, a longing for tenderness. (The previously mentioned patient said the next day that I should at least have given her an opportunity to become the analysand again for a short period, in order to alleviate to some extent the shattering effects of the information regarding the libido's orientation in another direction.) Moreover, both cases have in common (a) indispensable pride in this almost superhuman achievement; (b) the sensations of exploding into the universe, with images of brilliantly shining constellations; in case no. 1, hallucinatory, seemingly unconnected images and words, such as "I am a universal egg"—that is to say, that she is the center of the world and has incorporated the entire universe within herself.

Naturally everyone will say that this is megalomania, but to this the patient retorts that whoever has not been there himself does not know how right madmen are and how obtuse intelligent people can be. It is advisable in any event, if one wishes to understand anything about mental illness or traumatic shock, not to be too quick on the draw with one's rationalistic weapon when confronted with such assertions; but to keep in mind the grain of truth they do contain, in a quasi-medium-like fashion, precisely in the mentally disturbed persons whose hypersensitivity is outwardly oriented. In any case an opportunity is offered for gaining insight not only into the psychic content of the fragmented unconscious but also into the ways and means of the fragmentation process itself. Whether one should go further and search for supramaterial, metaphysical intuitions in the form and content of mental disorders (like physicists, in whose view substances are finally reduced to energy) is something each must decide for himself.

4 February 1932

On the psychogenesis of psychic shock (B.)

As I was feeling rather tired, I left the patient today for quite a long time undisturbed in her relaxed state, whereas at other times I had the objectionable habit, with this patient especially, of engaging her occasionally in conversation or discussion, from which she sometimes had to defend herself with an energetic "shut up." However, even when she fell into a semitrance, I usually disturbed this very early on by pressing for explanations or clarifications and by providing interpretations. I used to be similarly prompted by alarming symptoms—shortness of breath, interruption of pulse and breathing, pallor, coldness, and cold sweat, etc., etc.—to awaken the patient, so to speak, in order to spare her further suffering. None of this happened this time: the symptoms intensified and I allowed them to persist and then let their course run undisturbed. After about ten minutes the patient began to groan, that is, to communicate something about her condition and feelings. Thereupon I endeavored to probe into the details of her experiences during her mental absence accompanied by signs of suffering. She stated that her breathing became shallower and shallower, her thoughts were devoid of content, she was aware only of tremendous confusion, of the most acute headache in the region of the back of her neck (this area had often been mentioned previously, by her and by other patients in trance). The least sound, the gentlest touch appear at such moments to be unbearable, without the patient being able to indicate why. When asked what kind of emotions she had felt in this state, she replied, "immeasurable anger, inexpressible rage, nothing but kill, kill, kill!" (In the first instance only me, because I was the one who disturbed her peace.) My response: "Since you cannot say anything about the cause of this anger and rage, we can only assume that impressions of the external world are being retained and reproduced in the unconscious, impressions that correspond in quantity and quality to those emotional reactions. Indeed, one must assume that whatever you do not want to feel, know of, or remember is far worse than the symptoms you escape into." Neurotic suffering is relatively less painful than the suffering of the body and soul that is thus avoided. In any case, this experiment, which I owe to pure chance, encourages me to repeat it deliberately.

My earlier hypothesis of a double memory sequence—subjectively narcissistic and objective, emphasizing alternately one and then the other—offers insight into the formation of hysterical symptoms. If one succeeds in focusing all attention on the subjective process while the affects run their course, the object side of the perceptual system is totally empty, uncathected. Great pain, in this sense, has an anesthetic effect: pain without ideational content is not accessible to the consciousness. It is not impossible that all anesthesia could in fact be hypersensitivity of this kind. Here too the question of the existence of feeling without an object is answered positively. Such subjective experiences can be attained in a state of trance: a feeling of suffocation, of subjective auditory and visual perceptions without content or form, pain of the most varied types. The feeling of fading away, exploding, etc.

But processes relative to objects, robbed of their subjective feeling, are they registered and can they be brought back to life? The answer to this question will determine whether the trauma will become available in the repetition as a real experience or a memory. Here one might insert the story about the man who was in debt and pursued on the telephone by his creditor. He replies to the latter's abuse by exclaiming: "What a wonderful invention the telephone is! You can hear every word!" Useful hint: one should not be overly impressed by suffering, or rather should not break it off prematurely: see also my experiments with epilepsy.[1]

1. See "On Epileptic Fits, Observations and Reflections," *Fin* 197–204.—ED.

14 February 1932

On the acceptance of unpleasure [Der Bejahung der Unlust][1]

If one succeeds in philosophically incorporating the unpleasure situation that exists in reality into a larger unit, represented or perceived as something inevitable, even necessary for thinking, but above all when one succeeds in transferring the libido to this larger unit of classification, the feeling of unpleasure may vanish, even though its causes remain. It is even possible that this classification and the insight into it may be or become so pleasurable that it will have a great power of attraction. Quite possibly an element or factor of the masochistic situation is involved.

The "healing" of the masochistic compulsion might proceed in the following manner: as long as this classification process, which might be called optimistic, remains unconscious, it has—in conformity with the primary processes of the unconscious—a tendency to attach itself to every sort of unpleasure, even to kinds that would not in actual fact deserve such an optimistic assessment. If, however, the analysis succeeds in creating a conscious link between the delight in unpleasure and the specific situation that really existed, the compulsive character of masochism may cease to operate and be replaced by a rationally justified capacity to endure unpleasure for the sake of advantages anticipated in the future. The stronger and the more destructive the suffering—perhaps also the earlier in life it had to be endured, thus determining an orientation—the larger the circle of interests that must be drawn around the center of this suffering in order to make it seem meaningful, or even naturally inevitable. As an example (just to anticipate the least probable case): a helpless child is mistreated, for example through hunger. What happens when the suffering increases and exceeds the small person's power of comprehension? Colloquial usage describes what follows by the expression "the child comes to *be beside itself.*" The symptoms of being beside oneself (seen from the outside) are: absence of reaction with regard to sensitivity, generalized muscle cramps, often followed by generalized paralysis ("being gone"). If I am to believe what my patients report about similar states, this "being gone" is not necessarily a state of "not-being," but rather one of "not-being-here." As for the "where," one hears things like: they are far away in the universe; they are flying at a colossal speed among the stars; they feel so thin that they pass without hindrance through the densest substances; where they are, there is no time; past, present, and future are simultaneous for them; in a word, they feel they have overcome time and space. Seen from this gigantically wide perspective, the significance of one's own suffering vanishes, indeed there develops a gratifying insight into the necessity for the individual to endure suffering, when opposed and combatant natural forces meet in one's own person. After such an excursion into the universe, interest can be once more directed toward one's own ego, perhaps even with an improved ability for comprehension. The suffering thus "surmounted" makes one wiser and more patient.

To be sure, if the suffering was too acute and the distancing from the ego too colossal, this wisdom and patience can appear from the outside to limit, to a substantial degree, the emotional quality of life in general. After one has been overwhelmingly disappointed, most of the interest will remain caught in that other world, and the remaining fragment will be just strong enough to sustain a life of routine. What does the analysis accomplish in such cases? In my experience, as soon as genuine trust in the analyst's ability to show understanding for everything is established, the patient sinks into diverse stages of "being beside himself," "being gone," being outside time and space, of "omniscience," of being able to see and act at a great distance, and all this in a shifting and incoherent succession of images, hallucinations—in fact in what might be described as hallucinatory psychosis. If we are not alarmed by this diagnosis, if we even urge patients to befriend these images (S.I.), which have been so horrifying up to now, and do not reject a priori the possibility of the psychic reality or otherwise real nature of their observations, we will be rewarded in turn by the partial return of their interest in ordinary reality. In most cases they will also show an explicit tendency to provide help for me, as well as other sufferers, by encouraging optimism. The tendency, widespread in schizophrenics, to create their own cosmogonies, which often strikes us as fantastic, is a part of the attempt to incorporate their own "impossible" suffering into that great unity.

The difference between the suffering person and the philosopher would then be that the sufferer is in total revolt against the specific painful reality; perhaps what we call pain is after all nothing but such a revolt. Physiologists and doctors say that pain is useful as a warning signal of danger. It is questionable whether hypochondriacal attachment to pain, that is, to the revolt against the disturbance, might not rather be an obstacle to adaptation. (Coué's phrase—there is no illness; every day, in every way, I am better and better[2]—the same as Baker Eddy's negation of illness,[3] is perhaps effective, if it works at all, because behind it is hidden a kind of *friendly acceptance of illness*.) Instead of saying "there is no illness," I have sometimes found quite helpful the advice not to fight the pain but to allow it to run its full course. (Analogy with the absence of seasickness when I synchronized my will with that of the boat.) In all this the question remains unsolved or unanswered: To what extent do those who have "gone mad" from pain,[4] that is, those who have departed from the usual egocentric point of view, become able through their special situation to experience a part of that immaterial reality which remains inaccessible to us materialists? And here the direction of research must become involved with the so-called occult. Cases of thought transference during the analysis of suffering people are extraordinarily frequent. One sometimes has the impression that the reality of such processes encounters strong emotional resistance in us materialists; any insights we gain into them have the tendency to come undone, like Penelope's weaving or the tissue of our dreams.

It is possible that here we are facing a fourth "narcissistic wound,"[5] namely that even the intelligence of which we are so proud, though analysts, is not our property but must be replaced or regenerated through the rhythmic outpouring of the ego into the universe, which alone is all knowing and therefore intelligent. But more of this another time.

1. See "The Problem of the Acceptance of Unpleasant Ideas," C 366–378. *Bejahung* is usually translated as "affirmation," but in this context "adhesion," "acquiescence," or "acceptance" could equally well be used.—Ed.

2. Emile Coué (1857–1926), French psychologist who advocated autosuggestion.

3. Mary Baker Eddy (1821–1910), founder of Christian Science. After recovering from a serious illness she became convinced that in the treatment of illness only psychological means should be involved and all reference to the body should be excluded.—ED.

4. Ferenczi is playing here on the double meaning of *verruckt*; as an adjective it means "crazy," "insane," but it can also be understood as a form of the verb *verrucken*, "to move," "to shove aside," "to shift." The closest English equivalent combining the suggestion of insanity with that of actual physical motion may be the phrase "to be (or go) out of one's mind."

5. The first three narcissistic wounds were probably those inflicted by Galileo, Darwin, and Freud.—ED.

16 February 1932

Limitations of mutual analysis

1. *Discretion.* If the analysis is correctly conducted, the secrets of other patients must be divulged by the analyst to the analyzing analysand. This, however, comes up against ethical and logical obstacles. The patients do not know that I, the analyst, am having myself analyzed (and this by another patient). This should, in fact, be intimated to all my patients, but this would substantially interfere with their communicativeness and their confident trust in me. It would be like conducting analysis with the door open. This confused situation becomes especially difficult when the two analysands know each other, particularly when the one I let myself be analyzed by has neurotic traits and weaknesses of character that make him seem inferior in the eyes of the world (although I must acknowledge his ability to uncover things in me analytically, in spite of his greater or lesser failings otherwise). A way out of this complex situation might be not to allow oneself to be analyzed completely by any patient, but only to the extent that (a) the patient's needs require it or (b) the patient is capable of it in the given situation. This "polygamous" analysis, which roughly corresponds to the group analysis of American colleagues (even if it is not carried out in groups), provides a certain reciprocal control over the various analyses. At the same time it is a way to avoid being excessively influenced by any one patient. However, the mental acuity of one or the other of the mutual [analysts] may see through this piece of diplomacy. "There will be hardly any profound submergence into the unconscious if you put such artificial obstacles in the way of transference. What would *you* think of me, if I were to start choosing a second analyst in addition to yourself? It may well be that by these tactics I want to protect myself from genuine

insight. You will have to choose. (Naturally he means that he is the only one concerned.) And is it not one of your own peculiar analytical weaknesses of character that you are unable to keep any secrets to yourself, that you are compelled to broadcast this analytic relationship, that you have an uneasy conscience, as if you had done something wrong, and that you have to run to your mother or wife, like a small boy or a submissive husband, to confess everything and obtain forgiveness!"

Indeed, at the moment I can report on three analyses that run into one another in connection with me. Only one patient takes the matter seriously, in fact all too seriously, and is in despair when I do not take the following proposition quite seriously: (a) genuine belief in the obstacles that are caused by my own complexes, (b) the hope, already mentioned elsewhere, of finding in me, once the resistances have been removed, the lifesaver she has been waiting for, (c) an attempt to deflect attention from her onto me.[1] A specific limit to this kind of mutuality will be created by the analytical situation if, for instance, I let the patient experience something by design, that is, without telling her in advance. It is questionable, for example, whether one can tell the patient, without prejudicing success, that I intentionally torment her and allow her to suffer, do not come to her assistance with kindness or money, in order to persuade her, first, to tear herself loose from the transference, second, to relinquish the idea that sooner or later suffering will bring her compassion or help, and third, that distress brings to the surface latent sources of energy. Can and should one tell all this openly and really put all the cards on the table? I would reply, for the present, with a decided No, but I do see the colossal difficulties this could create.

One might take the view that confessions could go further and further, in relation to the patient's ability to tolerate them. What, however, would an analysis be like that would begin with my saying to a patient, male or female: "Basically I find you perfectly repulsive. I cannot stand your smell. Your face and your manners are awful." On the other hand, I do have guilt feelings that, in order to spare their feelings and to strengthen the analytical relationship, I have not pointed out to certain patients or pupils who came to me for analysis that some of their manners or peculiarities are unpleasant for me and others.

The experiences I have gathered since then have led me to suspect that it is no use, or not much use, to show more friendliness toward the patient than we really feel. Subtle, barely discernible differences in the handshake, the absence of color or interest in the voice, the quality of our alertness or inertia in following and responding to what the patient brings up: all these and a hundred other signs allow the patient to guess a great deal about our mood and our feelings. Some maintain with great certainty that they can also perceive our thoughts and feelings quite independently of any outward sign, and even at a distance.

In three cases I observed the particularly favorable effect of my own deepened relaxation on the patient's productions: (a) The patient notices that I am sleepy. Instead of being offended, as I feared, he felt deeply honored that I could behave so naturally in his presence. "This shows that you have great trust in me! Next time don't exert yourself anymore, just fall asleep." The same patient warns me not to overexert myself on behalf of my patients. But he said to me during one of the subsequent sessions: "Please don't fall asleep today, I so badly need your presence. I am so very distraught." At this appeal I awoke from my half-daze, paid attention to the patient's productions, tried to trace back the fragmentary emotions and thoughts to their origins, and was able to accomplish a good deal. (Perhaps also out of gratitude to him for letting me rest on other occasions and for showing kindness and consideration to me.) After working with this patient, I did not feel tired. (b) One patient felt even more honored, when, after having known and analyzed her for years, I permitted myself for the first time to use the lavatory in her house. This raised the question of my ability to relax in general, which was substantially limited because of the terrifyingly rough treatment I received from a nurse in my early childhood after an incident of anal soiling, and has given rise to an exaggerated tendency in me to attach too much importance to the wishes, likes, and dislikes of other people, accompanied by occasional dramatic slips, for instance spilling coffee or water, making myself ridiculous by falling, negligence regarding my clothes, etc., etc.

Here one might interpose the awkward question of relaxation, not only in thinking, but also relaxation in behavior (as in falling asleep, use of the lavatory).

One must have achieved a great deal with a patient in analysis and must have a great deal of confidence in his understanding before one can permit oneself anything of this kind (as above). One must, for example, be certain that the patient is not going to be mortally offended if we doze off for a moment, that he has already risen far above the conventional distaste for primitive bodily functions. However, one must also be perfectly sure of oneself, that one does nothing in the course of relaxation that might harm the patient or indirectly myself. One has a vision of the successful end of an analysis, which would be quite similar to the parting of two happy companions who after years of hard work together have become friends, but who must realize without any tragic scenes that life does not consist solely of school friendships, and that each must go on developing according to his own plans for the future. This is how the happy outcome of the parent-child relationship might be imagined.

1. The patient in this passage, R.N., is a woman. In the diary Ferenczi sometimes uses masculine pronouns to refer to her; for the sake of clarity we have changed these to the feminine gender.

20 February 1932

On mutuality

Continuing discontent, dissatisfaction with the results of the preoccupation with traumatic events, even though most intensively pursued, over many hours. Now, as always, most vivid reproduction accompanied by all the signs of suffering, even of agony. Impatient demand: "Not so many words, a few simple questions that will stimulate my thoughts, there is no conviction in your voice, what good is it to me if you know everything and I know nothing about any of it. Nothing but cheap optimism, I am in the greatest distress and I am expected to play-act as though I were receiving a visit from a lady dispensing charity, with whom I must behave pleasantly, I'll never do it again."

Acting on a sudden impulse, which I have had on several previous occasions, and impelled by the real urgency of the situation ("a dreadful accident and I am left lying here bleeding to death, because madam is waiting for dinner, and then that cheap optimism"), I warn the patient that I must tell her something extraordinarily painful, something that one does not usually tell patients—is she strong enough to listen to me? In fact, she must be, otherwise she would not have asked me for mutual openness.—With great resolve, the patient demands absolute frankness, whereupon I tell her that in fact I had deliberately exaggerated when I continually spoke of the success expected from her analysis. In reality I am often afraid that the whole treatment will go wrong and that she will end up insane or commit suicide. I did not conceal the fact that to have to tell her this was most painful and distressing for me, the more so as I myself knew only too well what it means to be faced with such possibilities. (Reference to incidents in my early childhood.) The result was, quite unexpectedly, complete appeasement: "If at the time I had been able to bring my father such a confession of the truth and to realize the dangerousness of the situation, I could have saved my sanity. This confession would have shown me that I was right when I talked about events that appeared impossible because nothing else supported them." (Scenes of poisoning and murder.)

Question: Was not the entire plan of "mutuality" conceived solely for the purpose of bringing to light something the patient had suspected in me and felt I had disavowed? Was it not an unconsciously sought antidote against the hypnotic lies of her childhood? Full insight into the deepest recesses of my mind, in defiance of all conventions, including those of kindness and consideration?

If it had been simple brutality or impatience, it would have done no good; but she saw how I had to struggle to do it, and how much pain this cruel task caused me. (She already knew long ago that because of similar internal obstacles I disliked performing surgery and whenever possible avoided postmortem examinations as well.)

In another case, in spite of months of repetition of the trauma, there is no conviction. The patient says, very pessimistically: It will never be possible for the doctor really to feel the events I am going through. Thus he cannot participate in experiencing the "psychophysical" intellectual motivation. I reply: Except if I sink down with her into her unconscious, namely with the help of my own traumatic complexes. The patient appreciates this, but has legitimate doubts about such a mystical procedure.

21 February 1932

Fragmentation

Psychic advantages: the unpleasure that arises when certain connections are made is avoided by the giving up of these connections. The splitting into two personalities, which do not want to know about each other, and which are grouped around different impulses, avoids subjective conflict. With the loss of the capacity to tolerate unpleasure, the lack of cohesion is exacerbated to the point of a flight of ideas; the hallucinatory psychosis that accompanies high fever is one such "atomization" of mental activity. Similar disorganization and anarchy manifest themselves in the organic field as well. The cooperation of organs is reduced, or it ceases; this amounts to a temporary giving up of physical individuality. Assumption: the giving up of cooperative procedures may further regenerative processes by saving energy and restricting organs to the performance of localized tasks. An analogy here with Loeb's experiments regarding the non-sexual fertilization of sea-urchin eggs.[1] (That a destructive process results in productivity.)

A similar phenomenon in the following case: a child is the victim of overwhelming aggression, which results in "giving up the ghost" ["*Aufgeben des Geistes*"], with the firm conviction that this self-abandonment (fainting) means death. However, it is precisely this complete relaxation induced by self-abandonment that may create more favorable conditions for him to endure the violence. (The organs and tissues become more elastic, bones more pliant without breaking, in an unconscious person, who does not resist violence, than in a person who is awake. For example how relatively rarely drunks are seriously injured.) Therefore someone who has "given up the ghost" survives this "death" physically and with a part of his energy begins to live again; he even succeeds in reestablishing unity with the pretraumatic personality, although this is usually accompanied by memory lapses and retroactive amnesia of varying duration. But this amnesic piece is actually a part of the person, who still is "dead," or exists permanently in the agony of anxiety. The task of the analysis is to remove this split, although here a dilemma arises. Reflecting on the event and reconstructing it by one's own reasoning—or even the fact that one perceives the need to reflect [*Denknotwendig keit*] on it—represents the preservation of the splitting into two parts: one that is destroyed, and one that sees the destruction. If in catharsis the patient sinks into the experience phase, he feels the suffering in this trance, but still does not know what is going on. Of the series of object and subject sensations, only the subject side is accessible. If he wakes from the trance, the direct evidence disappears immediately; once again the trauma will be grasped only from the outside, by reconstruction, without any feeling of conviction. Proposal of woman patient, O.S.: during the trance, stimulate thinking by asking very simple questions, to revive tactfully yet energetically the "ghost," which has been given up, as it were, and slowly to persuade the dead or split-off fragment that it is not dead after all. Simultaneously the patient must encounter enough compassion and sympathy that it seems worth his while to come back to life.

However, this cautiously gentle approach must not become overly optimistic; the reality of danger and the proximity of death, that is, a giving up of oneself, must be acknowledged. Therefore, on no account must the trauma be treated as a mere trifle—as so often happens with the sick, or with children. We must admit after all that our ability to help, or even our willingness to help is limited (partly owing to the needs of our own egoistical nature, partly because of our own unresolved complexes); this means that the patient must gradually come to appreciate that outside help is not enough, that he must also mobilize the available remaining portions of his own will. In the end we must even honestly confess that without self-help all our efforts may be quite useless. The question remains open whether there are not some cases in which the reunification of the traumatically split-off complexes is so unbearable that it does not fully occur and the patient retains some neurotic characteristics or sinks even deeper into a state of not-being or not-wanting-to-be [*Nichtseinwollen*].

How physis and the psyche function

Physis is hindered by resistances, that is to say, *determined* by the past, to which it is bound. In the psyche, these resistances either wholly or partially disappear; the psyche is governed by motives, that is, by something related to the future. To be sure, various degrees of freedom with respect to movement outside of time and space may exist in the psyche. Thinking governed by the reality principle is already weighed down to some extent, that is, it is determined by some earthly weight. The dominance of the mind by the pleasure principle means freedom of the will; however, this is unimaginable for logical thought.

1. James Löb (or Loeb), American physiologist, born in Germany in 1859. After earlier attempts by other scientists, he succeeded in the experimental parthenogenesis of sea-urchin eggs.—ED.

23 February 1932

On the male and female principles in nature[1]

I was rightly amazed and continue to be amazed at the fact, which can never be fully explained psychologically, concerning the acceptance[2] of unpleasure. Starting from my experiences with a patient (who after years of suffering, complaints, frequent episodes of being beside herself, and so on, plus complete frigidity, suddenly woke up and simultaneously underwent a character transformation: she became understanding, considerate toward others, charitable and generous, willing to tolerate all that she previously found unbearable, and at the same time experienced a kind of late maturation of her sexual feelings), I came to the realization, following a conscious lead by the patient, that in the female organism or psyche a specific principle of nature is embodied, which, in contrast to the egoism and self-assertion of the male, could be interpreted as the maternal willingness to suffer and capacity for suffering. According to this the capacity for suffering would be an expression of femininity, even though suffering, endurance, and toleration appear to occur in every sphere of nature, that is, to seem completely independent of sexuality. However exaggerated it may appear, it is perhaps not entirely nonsensical to suggest that whenever a force or substance has been "subjected" ["*unterliegt*"] to the changing, modifying, destructive influence of another force, in addition to the absolute or relative amount of violence, one must also reckon equally with the influence of the feminine principle, which we must assume to exist as a potential everywhere. In fact, it becomes even questionable whether, without the acquiescence of the feminine in substances, change could ever be brought about by any force, however great.

This generalization, in any event, relieves me of the hitherto impossible task of explaining selflessness simply as arising out of a complexity of selfish motivations, which we natural scientists used to do as a matter of course. Unfortunately, it may be argued from the scientific side that this is just bypassing an insoluble problem, as in the assertion that poverty stems from impecuniousness [*Pauvreté*]; selflessness and the capacity for endurance stem from a specific principle of selflessness and the capacity for endurance. Nevertheless, it is not entirely absurd to maintain a dualist position: the countless examples of bipolarity, ambivalence, ambitendency everywhere seem to justify looking at the whole of nature, for once, not only from the point of view of the principles of egoism but also from the opposite direction of the drives: that of selflessness.

All this would represent only a slight modification of Freud's assumption of life and death instincts. I would give the same thing other names. The drives for self-assertion and conciliation together constitute existence, that is, life in the whole universe. The old postulate, *natura horret vacui,* and another, to be newly coined, *natura horret cumuli,* should be set side by side, and the two together express in a good anthropomorphic manner the ubiquity of these two principles. Egoism is the impulse to rid oneself of a quantity of unpleasure-producing tension at all cost. It now seems as if wherever such an entity appears, an entity that has no willingness to suffer or capacity for suffering, conciliatory drives and impulses are mobilized from everywhere and summoned as if by magic: just as in human society the feminine principle clusters in the strongly masculine principle.

The singular consequence of the acceptance of the instinctual in the "wish to conciliate" leads directly to the assertion that, for the substance or being in which this drive is or becomes strong or exclusively dominant, suffering is not merely something that can be endured, but something desirable or a source of satisfaction. Principal example: the pleasure of motherhood is actually a toleration of parasitic beings, which develop in a completely egoistic manner at the expense of the mother's own body. An analogy to this is the suffering of the human being deprived of love, the sight of which awakens the female principle of the will to conciliate. Without making any pronouncements on the relative value of these two natural forces, this much appears certain: that the feminine principle, that is, the principle of suffering, is the more intelligent. "The wiser head gives in."[3] The one-sided manifestation of the selfish principle is sadism, that of the "wanting to suffer" principle is masochism.

Severe or prolonged suffering, but above all something unexpected and thus traumatic, exhausts the instinct of self-assertion and allows the forces, wishes, and even characteristics of the aggressor to invade us. There is no suggestibility without the cooperation of the feminine principle. The drive for self-assertion may be seen as the basis for Freud's pleasure principle, the drive for conciliation as the basis of his reality principle.

1. The ideas in this entry had already taken shape in an article of 1929: see "Male and Female," in *Thalassa*, pp. 96–107.—Ed.
2. Regarding the problem of selecting the correct term, see 14 February 1932, note 1.
3. A German proverb: *Der Klügere gibt nach*.

24 February 1932

[*Mutual analysis*]

1. B.: Mutual analysis may originally have been invented by patients as a symptom of their paranoid distrust: to obtain confirmation that they were right to uncover diverse resistances, caused by antip-

athies, in the analyst, and to compel him to admit to these impulses. Acquiescence to this wish is, naturally, the most radical contrast to the rigid, impenetrable secrecy of their parents. Today's example: during the most recent analytical session but one, radiantly happy, pleased with herself, because for the first time she was able, without any anxiety or restriction, to allow herself the pleasure of masturbation. During the next session this mood continues; actually nothing except humming to herself themes from *Tristan und Isolde*. Then at times the uncomfortable feeling that such happiness cannot last, that there will soon be a setback. In today's session, talking about the same subject, I suggest an interpretation (with reference to a dream in which a very gaunt woman, with a cannula following an operation for carcinoma of the larynx, thus a very weak person, has three or four enormous children) that the delights of masturbation provide a successful solution for the avoidance of the tremendous difficulties of motherhood. Strong opposition to this: every one of my assertions is rejected. Then a long pause; explanation: I feel nothing but antipathy for her, I prefer my rigid analytical explanations to everything else, and do not value her views. (In actual fact I was quite inclined to modify my conclusions about the interpretation of the masturbation; however, I anticipate the idea—analytically—that the manifest homosexuality of the patient, that is to say, a kind of masturbation, will be traced back to something terrifying in the sense of the above dream.) Her wish to know my most secret thoughts is the repetition of the selfsame wish from childhood, when the patient felt misled, or even deceived, by the grownups. After giving expression to her dissatisfaction, and crying somewhat, thus fulfilling the prophecy: pride goeth before a fall.

2. The methodical analytical intentions assumed a rather more complicated form in the case of R.N. Like someone in love, the patient tries to extend her interest in my person far back into the past. With the help of an intermediary, a Hungarian who at that time inhabited that distant land (she had only recently learned that he used to live there), the patient believes she discovered precisely me, through mystical thought-transference (N.B. thirty-one years ago), as the only person who would be able to help patients in great distress. (Here one might quote the example of patient S.I., who maintains that although she had never heard of me, yet as soon as she learned my name she understood immediately that I alone could save her. All other attempts at analysis had indeed failed, but she came to me with symptoms of intense transference.) After years of analysis came the

idea of mutual openness. Another tendency intermingles here with the simple repetition tendency, namely that of realizing the idea of the "ideal lover," and that with the analyst. The favorable position of the analyst enables the patient to remove all obstacles in the way of my love and create a lifelong communion of ideas and interests between us; my understanding and kindness will enable the patient to cope consciously with the frightful events of her childhood. As long as this does not happen and I maintain my professional distance, the patient cannot be cured. Spurred on by my ambition to help patients, I went so far as to devote a great deal of my interest and time to the patient without any reward.[1] A while ago, however, I was forced to reduce the time devoted to them; and this cost me considerable effort (I felt overwhelming compassion for the patients). It took about two months before the shock was overcome. As the patient's resources were beginning to be exhausted, I decided on a second, more dangerous step, of telling the patient that I would treat her only until she was able to support herself. As I suspected, she was convinced that I would provide for all her needs. She gesticulated like a lunatic, hinted at suicide, but I remained firm. I spent the ensuing sessions in restoring friendly relations, with infinite patience but without any change in my stand.

In a word, to have accepted the full analytical situation in this case would have caused, as I rightly must fear, the purely analytical situation to become mixed up with the real situation, very much to the disadvantage of the analysis. Like parents and children, so doctor and patient must in the end become independent of each other. The analysis envisioned by the patient thus represented an indirect way to become cured, in harmony, as it were, with the fulfillment of her wish: that is, by love and tenderness. The dissipation of this illusion is always painful, but it must take place. It is a question: did my perhaps exaggerated kindness possibly make this separation even more difficult for the patient? On the other hand, I believe that this case was not accessible to anything other than kindness. It remains an open question whether I possess the skill, tact, and patience to arrive at this act of renunciation with friendship intact.

Now about countertransference. The fact is that certain hints and analytic clarifications, as well as emotional responses of a quite intense kind, have benefited me in the course of this work. Is it conceivable that total and uninhibited surrender to analysis would have brought or would bring insights and experiences of depths as yet unattained?

3. To be more honest, I confess that I would have much preferred

to conduct such mutual analysis with my patient S.I., who in spite of more horrifying traumas in her childhood is capable of kindness and selflessness, while in R.N.'s case one always has the feeling that she is constantly pursuing a goal that is finally selfish. To use R.N.'s mode of expression: in R.N. I find my mother again, namely the real one, who was hard and energetic and of whom I am afraid. R.N. knows this, and treats me with particular gentleness; the analysis even enables her to transform her own hardness into friendly softness, and here the question arises: should one not have, in spite of all, the courage to expose oneself to the danger of analytic transference and win out in the end? Or is it not, or was it not, the only correct way to practice and induce educative self-frustration, with insight into all these conscious and unconscious intentions, and to renounce the potential advantages of such an analysis? If I had reached the same degree of profound earnestness and strength of character here as I have with S.I., I would probably have been able to expose myself to being analyzed by her only after she finished her analysis.

In the meantime, one must be content with obtaining pieces of analytic insight from the patients in scattered fragments, and not allow them to concern themselves with our person any more than is necessary for *their* analysis.

1. Ferenczi often uses the feminine or masculine pronoun irrespective of the patient's actual sex. As we know that B., R.N., and S.I. are women, we use the feminine when referring to any of them specifically and the masculine when speaking of patients in general.

24 February 1932

Trauma in an unconscious state

The effect of a shock—whether it be a sudden fright or fright plus physical injury—is particularly dangerous when the trauma occurs in exceptional states [of consciousness]. Example: (1) R.N. Sudden awakening from a hypnotic-toxic state, caused by the sudden withdrawal of both the anesthetic and the hypnotic lie. The trauma here encounters a being that is already split, which, unlike conscious people, cannot gather together all its will. (2) S.I. is in a similar position: her mother (probably like O.S.'s as well) launched an insane, terrifying attack on the sleeping child, because of some sort of masturbatory activity during sleep. A sleeping person is equally defenseless: when one is asleep, one relies on the safety of the house and the environment, otherwise one could not fall asleep. A quite small portion of the ego remains on guard even at night, but only to give warning signals when danger approaches. Should the attack come without warning, however, something like a blow, a shot, or some other shock in the midst of sleep or a dream, when the anticathexis of the sensory organs is absent, then the traumatic impact penetrates into the interior of the psychic organism, without opposition, and persists there in the same way a lasting posthypnotic suggestion would. In other words, the effect of terror in this state is enormously exacerbated. One is reduced almost to the level of a timid animal still of low intelligence. The propensity of neurotics to drink may be an indication (the reproduction) of impaired or weakened states of consciousness at the time of the trauma.

3 March 1932

On the theme of mutuality

It began to seem to me more and more discreditable to behave as though I had totally come to terms with mutuality, whereas in fact I was participating in my own "analysis" only with considerable *reservatio mentalis*. This and the hints I received from S.I. (who has made considerable therapeutic progress recently *without* "mutuality" and who has even repeatedly warned me against excessive self-sacrifice), and gave me last but not least the feeling of overdoing [it] (with time and labor), which I am aware of myself; finally out of regard for my own finances, that is, reality: all these things together and the recollection of Freud's warning that I was "too much under the influence of my patients" impelled me to speak openly about the fragmentary character of my own participation in mutual analysis, and about my resolve to let matters rest there. One of the contributory motives is fear, of course: (1) that bringing into prominence the analysis of the analyst could turn the analysis into a veritable breeding ground for projections and fear of one's own difficulties; (2) that the patient could start to demand financial assistance as recompense for *my* analysis by her. Providing financial help would, however, involve the analysis too much with reality and make separation more difficult. In fact the patient had already made various plans for lifelong cooperation on the model of Schiller and Goethe.[1] My defensive measure of receiving hints from other patients as well, she rejects on the grounds of the uniqueness of her case and of our joint technique, which penetrates into deep metaphysical regions. Finally reference is even made to the serious endangering of my work, which would collapse without the patient's help. This warning felt a bit like a threat (one must not forget that the patient believes herself to possess supernatural powers).

Immediate consequence: somewhat sobered, serious consideration given to ending the analysis at once, in order for her to make practical use of the money still available to her, before she finds herself "*vis-à-vis du rien.*" My counterproposal was that she accept a compromise: I would pursue *my* analysis only for brief periods each day and only as far as it was relevant to her analysis; the times allocated could not be exceeded.

After a prolonged, deathly silence and total despair, in which this time, curiously, less mention was made of suicide and of going insane, the patient decided finally to continue with the work for the time being "for the sake of the sympathetic side of my person," which is after all different from the characteristics of the infantile tormentor.

What can be hoped from this? (1) As in active therapy, under pressure caused by distress, to force her to insight, as yet incompletely attained, into the reality of the present and of the past. (2) Many repressed emotional impulses, especially those of hate, can be expected to dare to manifest themselves now that the patient has nothing else to hope for. Everything common and vulgar, which the patient tries to conceal with a fastidious aesthetic sense, will now probably be displayed. To be sure, one also has to be on guard against more dangerous threats.

In addition there remains the hope, that outside support will be obtained from somewhere; this would be favorable for the analysis insofar as the separation would then take place more spontaneously, on her own initiative, though spurred on by the intermezzo currently in progress. Finally and in conclusion, one must not lose sight of the idea that the envisaged mutuality has something generous about it, which I am forgoing, mainly because I am not completely confident in her. This firm attitude may have one advantage: "the break of one of my patterns," overcoming my fear of the "terrorism of suffering," which has, it is true, infantile sources.

On the terrorism of suffering

1. S.I.: She feels at times, especially when she is aggressive, hard, sarcastic, etc., etc., as though something alien were speaking through

her, something that she does not recognize afterward as herself. The malicious alien, for example, today turns out to be the mother, malicious, uncontrolled, aggressive, passionate, therefore terrifying to the child; whose almost manic gestures, facial expressions, as well as screaming are reproduced by the patient with such accuracy that it can only be the result of complete identification. The psychologizing patient describes in great detail her internal processes while in the grip of such terror: a part of her person gets "beside itself"; the area thus vacated is filled by the will of what has terrified her. As treatment she demands: I must remove, piece by piece, the fragments of the invading personality; simultaneously she must try to reinsert into her personality the exploded portions of her own person. Following prolonged relaxation and passivity on my part, she now demands: "you must poke the jellyfish," that is to say, for her sake, I must be somewhat stricter and tougher with her.

2. Similarly in case B.: she begs me to strangle her to the point of suffocation: better to experience the fullness of pain than to be anxious about it and to carry around a constant tension of unpleasure in the unconscious.

1. Schiller, ten years younger than Goethe, looked up to Goethe for guidance and approval. His pronounced Swabian accent irritated Goethe, who preferred to communicate with him by letter. It is interesting that the model for reciprocal transference mentioned by Ferenczi in connection with mutual analysis is comparable to his relationship with Freud, seventeen years his senior.—ED.

6 March 1932

Mutuality

In the third session after the termination of material help and mutuality, sudden about-face: I was received with a radiant face and a conciliatory gesture; numerous apologies for having provoked and infuriated me through lack of self-control during MY analysis (therefore, she still clings to mutuality in principle, and regards the steps I have taken merely as a slight deviation on her part). Nevertheless, by and large, clear signs that she is coming back into line: exclamations of admiration over my steadfastness in adhering to the course of the treatment in spite of her provocations. I did not suppress my satisfaction, and praised her ability to get the better of herself. She returned the compliment: *I* have shown myself stronger than my actual tendency to let myself be terrorized by suffering. I did not conceal the fact that this cost me a considerable expenditure of effort. The session was spent mainly in discussing the analytic event, yet I also succeeded in steering her into the depths, and into the past.

Similar occurrences with patient B. She too is beginning to demand the extension of the analysis to twenty-four hours a day; without this guarantee she cannot undertake to commit herself to the dangers of abandoning her conscious intellectual protective and precautionary measures. But here, as in the other case, my hints regarding her wish to leave are energetically rejected. Though she often says that we are not making any progress, yet if I suggest something similar, she replies: "How do you know that I am not making progress? Perhaps all this agitation is already a step forward."

In case A., it appears, however, that the amount of friendliness deployed in the course of years of work was enough to induce the patient (after a period of intense flight reaction) to bend her will, in spite of the incompleteness of her wish fulfillment and in contrast to her usual pride, defiance, and overbearing and contemptuous attitude. Something similar is to be expected in case B. If this succeeds, one can speak here, in fact, of a fundamental change in character, which will certainly have an effect in other respects as well. Thus, a kind of pedagogic success.

Here the question arises of what the relationship is between relaxation and activity or education. Analysis, like life, has to begin with relaxation: under its influence some cathartic reproduction becomes possible. A deeper penetration of the traumatic unpleasure experience, accompanied by full realization, seems, however, to be attainable only by way of the pain associated with the analytical weaning process. By way of the contrast between past and present, one can penetrate only to a certain depth. But pain of the highest order will be avoided as long as life offers something more or less tolerable. In analysis, therefore, must arise the feeling of being totally alone, of having to count only on oneself, the despair of no longer having anything to cling to (analysis, kindness of the analyst), so that this time, by way of analogy, the real pain is experienced. Indeed the present pain must—just because it is in the present—cause greater unpleasure than the memory of past pain can evoke still today. Therefore, flight from the present despair to the relatively more bearable traumatic situation (memory). So in order to tolerate this unpleasure, there must be an even greater unpleasure activated in the present. As the final act, following "deep catharsis," I imagine a period of reconciliation and finally separation, as in the case of R.N., with the feeling of being delivered from traumatic fixation, that is to say, from emotions of a compulsive nature with regard to love and hate. The traumatically oriented character ceases to exist, and the other, natural aspects of the personality are able to unfold. Here addition of Freud's excellent comparison with the disintegration of the excavated objects.

General view on tendency to turn away from reality in the course of psychoses

The prototype of all confusion is being misled about the reliability of a person or a situation. Being misled means having made a mistake;[1] someone has "simulated" a close emotional relationship by certain ways of acting and talking, and the moment of going astray occurs when we approach a situation with a particular expectation and find not what we expected but something else, often the opposite. Thus being surprised by something. Confusion corresponds to the moment between being surprised and new adaptation. (Example: weaning. The child, accustomed to sucking, is refused the breast. Reaction: 1. confusion, 2. defense and rejection, 3. adaptation.)

Now, in situations where protest and negative reaction, that is, all criticism and expression of discontent, are forbidden, criticism can find expression only in an indirect form. For example, the opinion "You are all liars, idiots, lunatics, who can't be trusted," is illustrated indirectly on oneself through exaggerated, crazy behavior and nonsensical productions, rather like the child who in grimacing distorts himself but only to show the other how he looks. Thus the lunatic expresses through his insanities the following judgment: I am the only intelligent person around; you are all crazy. Most noticeable in cases in which a child has been under the influence of parents who really are insane. The child recognizes at an early age the absurdities in the behavior of those in authority over him, yet intimidation precludes the exercise of criticism. Ironic exaggeration, the nature of which is not recognized by the environment, remains the only means of expression. The question remains of how and when the irony of the expressions becomes unconscious for the child as well. The insane "superego," being or becoming imposed upon one's own personality, transforms the previous irony into automatism. So, this is how it comes about, by way of tradition, that an apparent heredity of psychosis is created: by means of a graft of an insane personality component onto the superego.

1. *Irrewerden ist: sich geirrt haben.* There is a play on words here: *irrewerden* means "to become confused," "to be mistaken"; *irre werden* means "to lose one's mind," "to go crazy."

8 March 1932

The analyst as undertaker

1. It was naive to think that the adaptation to a new situation involving a complete change in character orientation would be established so easily and permanently. The affirmation of satisfaction with a "child of the sublimation," that is, to consent to conceive something-that-has-never-been in the spiritual, moral, intellectual realm, by combined efforts, thinking simultaneously and similarly, is only one side of the coin: the other side, the dark and negative side, did not cease to exist and emerged with redoubled force once the enthusiasm had waned. Her reaction to the words I flung in her face so cruelly—a reaction I had expected earlier (instead of the surprising reconciliation that took place)—was expressed today in a deferred way: my words would have murdered. Sublimation is madness (resignation, taking fantasy for reality): I was doing the same thing her murderous father had done; I would have injected the irritating, exciting poison, I would have created the anticipation of an orgasm, and then I would obtain the displacement of the love-object. She rejects this with determination, and even with the concentration of all her psychical powers, just as her murderous father could not succeed in making her conscious of feelings forced upon her that were incompatible with her person and her wishes. There remained no alternative for her but to go crazy again, that is, to turn the sensations (hunger for love) that had been provoked in her away from reality; and in order to do that she would have to turn herself "inside out." To put it in simpler terms; while she behaved and conducted herself as the poison forced her to, she led a fantasy life in the hope that an "ideal lover" would come. Her entire person had been splintered into pieces. One part was pure suffering, but accessible to the consciousness only in dreams and symptoms, and thereby unrealized. Another part provided her with the wish-fulfilling reinterpretation of reality. A third part, the body totally under the sway of both the poison and the father, was left as pure automatism. The patient thus exists in a state of insatiable hunger for love; under these circumstances it is impossible for her to be content with sublimation; she would rather go back to insanity or death.

2. B.: the last two sessions marked by total dissatisfaction, hopelessness, tendencies to flee, above all because she has no confidence in me: in case of real need I would be neither willing nor able to help her. Nevertheless, when urged by me, she decided to sink into the

depths of her soul, to relinquish all self-protective devices; she even permitted herself to become ill. Violent headaches and other pains, and complaints about these, occupied the sessions. Yesterday she took to her bed and sent for me. She lay there with a high fever, waiting and expecting—as we later learned—some kindness and humanity from me, rather like a mortally injured child who barely has the strength to drink, and can just sip a little liquid through a glass tube. Instead of that, she had to discover that I continued to ask stupid and boring analytical questions just as before, and, when I went away at the end of the session as usual, leaving her alone (N.B. it was on a day when the other women living in the house had been unkind and hurt her feelings), she saw that she could hope for nothing from me, that she would have to help herself, that she was right not to trust me, that her judgment of her father was all too correct, namely that he was a stupid coward who had left her in the lurch. The analysis, she says, is exactly repeating the conduct of her parents, who only provoke unpleasure but cannot cure her. She foresees that even after a further eight years she will still be in the same spot, unless she succeeds in tearing herself loose from the analysis, her family, perhaps the entire human race, and organizing her life independently. Incidentally, she had a dream in which a girl was lying in an uncomfortable position in a quadrangular coffin, quite dead. Her hair had fallen over her face, and her head was also covered with a cloth. Outside, a melody is being played (a song of mourning?); someone points toward the region of the larynx, indicating that she cannot join in the singing. In all, three persons are present: the dead person, the patient, and a third person (the provisional interpretation is: she could not speak, as a part of her was really dead, and consequently she could not sing either; reference to the situation at the time of the presumed attack, breathing difficulties).

3. Subjective reaction in both cases highly disconcerting, in the first instance discouraging. Apparently I do not like being continually accused of being a murderer. In case B., I have finally come to realize that it is an unavoidable task for the analyst: although he may behave as he will, he may take kindness and relaxation as far as he possibly can, the time will come when he will have to repeat with his own hands the act of murder previously perpetrated against the patient. In contrast to the original murder, however, he is not allowed to deny his guilt; analytic guilt consists of the doctor not being able to offer full maternal care, goodness, self-sacrifice; and consequently he again exposes the people under his care, who just barely managed to save

themselves before, to the same danger, by not providing adequate help. After we have allowed the patients to deliver their judgment, quite exhaustively, against us and the other murderers, they raise the question themselves: what would I have to say in reply? In my answer I openly admitted the inadequacy of my assistance, not making any secret of my own painful feelings on the subject; furthermore, I admitted that we men, even the best doctors among us, are not good at taking care of children and the sick; from childhood men are taught by their environment and by other boys not to show sentimentality, which is regarded as womanish and childish. Even in their kindness they are gruff and less solicitous. But, I said, there is nevertheless a difference between our honesty and the hypocritical silence of parents. This and our goodwill must be counted in our favor. This is why I do not give up hope and why I count on the return of trust in spite of all the disillusionment. If we succeed in refocusing the traumatic accent, as is justified, from the present to the infantile, there will be sufficient positive elements left over to lead the relationship away from a breach in the direction of reconciliation and understanding.

In the case of B., in view of the mutuality, the reaction naturally went much deeper. This gave me an opportunity to penetrate much deeper into my own infantilism: the tragic moment in childhood when my mother declares: You are my murderer. Excessively strong reaction to something similar in the analysis, followed by despair and discouragement, becomes clearly manifest. In this way: detachment from the present and a return of sympathy with sublimation tendencies and resignation. If one knows that this hangman's work is inevitable, that in the end it does help the patient, and if one overcomes the resistance against such cruelty, which can vary in strength; if one does or allows to be done the necessary analytical explorations—then one will not shrink from the radical interventions that will result in the patient's disengagement. After all, the child too must be separated from its mother by scissors:[1] delaying this operation may be injurious to both the mother and the child (analyst and patient). It must be a matter of tact and of insightful technique to determine: (1) how much kindness should be extended, (2) when and at what rate harsh reality ought to be invoked, (3) to what extent mutuality in the analysis is an advantage or an unavoidable necessity for this purpose.

1. This refers to the cutting of the umbilical cord.—ED.

10 March 1932

The healing element in psychotherapy (healing)[1]

A tacit or seldom expressed basic principle of psychoanalysis is that in contrast to other forms of psychotherapy it does not wish to operate by means of sedation, soothing, stimulation, encouragement (that is, by directly emotional and suggestive measures), or with compassion, tenderness, friendly concern, sympathy, or genuine participation in any of those waves of emotion, such as hate, indignation, despair, or shared joy over positive excitements, the happiness of love, etc.— but ultimately and in the end, by intellectual means alone: by clearing away inhibitions of feeling and of action, by bringing repressions to consciousness. The ideal analysis would therefore be a case in which nothing at all is analyzed into the patient; in which the analyst does not modify or improve anything, in either external or internal circumstances; that is, neither by providing social and personal assistance nor by gratifying emotional needs. Indeed, since the discovery of the transference element in the psychoanalytical situation more modern psychoanalysis has stressed the significance of affective, nonintellectual factors in analysis as well; it has even arrived at the conclusion that it is only transference and the clearing away of resistances against it that make possible the real attainment of consciousness, and thus the mastery of the unconscious. However, all these affective elements in analysis were seen as kind of interregnum, which ultimately will have to be resolved completely; what finally analysis offers to patients is insight and self-control.

Experiences with neocatharsis seem to oblige me very often to give up the strict observance of this analytic principle toward the end of an analysis; in moments of profound relaxation appealing to the intellect seems either impossible or actually disruptive, at any rate useless. The tasks of self-observation and self-criticism, as demanded by analytical explanation, already postulate a split in the person into one who is observing and one who is being observed. Relaxation, on the other hand, requires unifying the personality completely and allowing all perceptions to register on the self in an unfragmented way: that is, actually a kind of re-experiencing. In fact the patient sinks into a jumble of hallucinations, emotional outbursts, physical and psychical pain, into a feeling of helplessness and inability to comprehend, into fits of sarcastic, uncontrollable laughter at the naïveté of his own expectations and stark reality. If we approach this just as before, with the same cool, polite friendliness of the analyst, maybe even asking the standard question—"what else occurs to you in this connection?"—a sudden awakening from the trance and suffering can be observed. Patients refuse to cooperate any further, they feel that I shall never ever be able to help them at all, and they make arrangements to flee from the analysis, making no secret of their contempt for our incapacity for action and our general lack of human feelings; not infrequently they mix this reaction with analogous experiences from their earlier life, particularly in relation to members of their families. They are now completely convinced of our (the father's and my) self-satisfied egoism. The repetition has succeeded all too well, they say; what is the use of [repeating] the trauma word for word, to have the same disillusionment with the whole world and the whole of humanity? I try not to let the discouragement of my patients infect me, although it may cost me a great deal of effort to hold out against the incessant reproaches and accusations. One cannot help feeling inwardly hurt—at least I cannot—when after years of work, often quite exhausting work, one is called useless and unable to help, just because one cannot provide everything, to the full extent, that the poor suffering person needs in his precarious position. Should this happen, and if we thus become somewhat uncommunicative or silent when we should be providing help feverishly, then—and that is the patients' view—we have lost our chance with them. Nevertheless two courses do remain open for us: honest admission of our pain at not being able to help, and patient perseverance with wanting to help, going on with the analytic work, despite the apparent lack of any prospects. In one case the simple revelation and admission of the limitations of our emotional resources (in contrast to the hypocrisy of the family) did not suffice: only complete exposure of one's own unconscious, not without emotional outbursts on the part of the analyst as well, enabled the patient, in spite of the failure, to recover her trust. A third case (S.I.), however, produced good results without such upheavals. The patient arrived with great enthusiasm, but right at the beginning was put off by my coolness. Years of patient work, immense indulgence regarding her inability to keep the promises she made me (about drugs), an indulgence that she tested in every possible way; genuine human sympathy at moments of real shock, that is to say, a little bit of healing, brought, almost imperceptibly, a change (not least as a consequence of the patience with which I sought and discovered behind the hodgepodge of her metaphysics and supernatural revelations an actual, albeit psychological, reality). I became, so to speak, a living symbol of goodness and wisdom, whose mere presence had a healing and stabilizing effect. R.N. said much the same sort of things as well, in moments of calm after phases of conflict had ended. To introduce this healing into psychotherapy in the appropriate manner and where it is required is surely not an entirely unworthy task.

1. Ferenczi often used the English word "healing," as here.—ED.

13 March 1932

A "two-children" analysis

Certain phases of mutual analysis represent the complete renunciation of all compulsion and of all authority on both sides: they give the impression of two equally terrified children who compare their experiences, and because of their common fate understand each other completely and instinctively try to comfort each other. Awareness of this shared fate allows the partner to appear as completely harmless, therefore as someone whom one can trust with confidence. Originally this trust had been enjoyed unilaterally; the child enjoyed maternal tenderness and care without giving anything in return (probably the maternal feeling that the child enjoys is also a kind of regression to childhood on the mother's part). The intellectual coolness of the analyst eventually provokes a kind of revolt, with a tendency to tear oneself loose from the analyst and to implant a piece of the superego in place of the external power. The fulfillment of duty and obedience, self-observation and self-control appear more bearable, in spite of all, than being ordered about by others. (Here one might mention the child who goes and stands in the corner himself, in order to avoid punishment.) This "being good" and obedience incidentally are also a revenge on authority, which is thereby robbed of its own weapons.

Following disillusionment with parents, teachers, and other heroes, children unite among themselves and form alliances of friendship. (Should the analysis terminate under the signs of such a friendship?)

Mutual confession of one's own "sins," that is to say, childishly naive candor, in place of the adults' determination to be superior and good (hypocrisy and fanaticism), provides the child or the analysand with the reassurance that it is not he who is bad or insane when he allows natural, instinctual demands to manifest themselves, but rather it is the adults who are dishonest or blind.

If the resolution of infantile amnesia depends on such COMPLETE *liberation from fear* of the analyst, then we may well have the psychological basis for mutuality in analysis.

Praise necessary. A patient (Dm.) who for quite a long time has been protesting more or less unconsciously against the analysis by shifting her love and interest to a young man (probably with the expectation that I would hate her for it, even if I never said so) one day spontaneously suggests that she will perhaps give up her relationship with this unsuitable and also much younger man. Thereupon signs of resistance, which were not resolved until after she had told me how disappointed she was that I did not acknowledge how great a sacrifice she was making of her own free will. I admitted that she was right. She then appeared to want to search for the causes of my omission, and we were able to establish that the patient had been in a state of resistance for the past three or four months. Cause: the episode of her gossiping about me, and the consequences for me, namely from Freud,[1] etc. [She said] I had been more reserved since then, that is, irritable and contemptuous. I had taken the whole thing too personally, instead of looking further for the causes, etc. This was also the cause of the above omission. The end of the session in a conciliatory mood; she retained the feeling that she had regained my trust. That I do not treat her as she had been treated in the past, by her father and also by that teacher, who never confessed their offenses toward her. Out of revenge, she then described some of these incidents in much more crude and dreadful terms than was objectively justified. The hypocrisy of the adults gives the child justification for exaggerating and lying. If those in authority are more sincere, the child will then come forward on its own with confessions and proposals for good behavior [*mit Vorschlägen zur Güte*]. Every such conflict, however, like a quarrel between mother and child, will have to end with reconciliation and praise, that is, signs of trust.

1. An allusion to the gossip that had led Freud to write his letter of 13 December 1931 on Ferenczi's "technique of kissing": see 7 January, note 3.—ED.

15 March 1932

The autochthonous and the heterogeneous ego (S.I.)

The patient became convinced long ago that a great many of her symptoms had somehow been forced upon her from the outside. Since she has become acquainted with psychoanalytic terminology she refers to these sensations, tendencies, displacements, and forcibly imposed actions, alien to her own ego as well as contrary and harmful to its tendencies, as actions of the "superego." She represents this implantation of something alien to her own ego in a quite material way. The two principal persons who impose painful portions of their own egos onto her personality, in order, as it were, to rid themselves of the tension and unpleasure that they had provoked, are above all her mother (who in a state of insane lack of control used to give her children terrible beatings—a fact that has been substantiated) and more recently also a lady of her acquaintance, who for a period of time had exercised a kind of psychoanalytical as well as metaphysical influence over her. However, she is also aware of benevolent, healing influences, which she attributes to me in particular. Of course, nothing would be easier than to diagnose all this symptomatology as paranoid insanity, which, given our present state of psychiatric knowledge, would imply incurability. Yet, relying on analogous observations made by Freud, according to which no delusional idea is completely devoid of at least a grain of truth, I resolved to search more intensively for the reality contained in such apparently delusional concepts, at least for the psychic reality; that is, I resolved to identify myself for a good long time with those presumed insane. My model for this process is probably that of Dr. Breuer, who did not shrink from seeking and finding the truth in the most nonsensical statements of a hysteric, whereby he had to rely both theoretically and technically on the hints and suggestions of the patient. In response to the anticipated objection that psychoanalysis (and I myself in particular) already deals exhaustively with the psychic reality of delusional ideas by presenting them as projections of the inadmissible contents of the psyche, I only wish to affirm that I continue to maintain the projective character of a very large part of the delusional material,[1] I do not exclude the possibility that delusional productions contain more objective reality than we have assumed until now. From the very beginning I was inclined to think that the hallucinations of the insane, or at least a part of them, are not imaginings but real perceptions, stemming from the environment and from the psyches of other human beings, which are accessible to them—precisely because of their psychologically motivated hypersensitivity—whereas normal people, focusing only on immediate matters of direct concern to them, remain unaffected. What comes to mind in this connection is the so-called occult powers of certain people, and the close relationship and easy transition between the two states: paranoia and psychic superperformance.

The second person by whom the patient feels persecuted possesses such "psychic" qualities. Indeed, the patient has learned from the person herself that she has the power to make people do what she wants, by means of her will. (A large part of the patient's perceptions might therefore be simply a projection of the fear that has been instilled in her.)

Patient S.I. *feels* the irresistible influence, contrary to all her intentions, exercised by the spirit of these two people, pieces of whom, so to speak, live in her. The maternal influence, for example, has a tendency to spread itself out in her. If she had not gone into analysis, the patient feels absolutely certain, she would have been transformed completely into a person like her mother; she was already beginning to be hard, vicious, stingy, pleased by others' misfortune, making herself and others unhappy, driving her husband to the brink of despair, tormenting her daughter, and arousing fear and discomfort in her domestic staff. The pieces of the maternal transplant retain their vitality, indeed their energy for growth; the evil in people lives on, as it were, in the minds of those who have been ill treated (one may think of blood feuds, which go on for generations).

The patient also feels, however, that when I, the analyst, succeed in removing from her the pieces of the alien, implanted spirit, this benefits the patient but brings harm to the person from whom the fragments of evil stem. This idea is based on a theory according to which the heterogeneous implanted fragment is virtually linked in some way with the "donor's" person, as though by a thread. Therefore, when the fragment of evil is not accepted or is rejected, it returns to the "donor's" person, exacerbates his tensions and sensations of unpleasure, and may even result in the spiritual and bodily annihilation of that person.

In accordance with the grandiose manner [*Grosszügigkeit*] that characterizes persons of this kind, she does not hesitate to generalize from this experience of her own. All evil, destructive drives must be returned to the psyches from which they originate (therefore to ancestors, to animal forebears, even to the inorganic). This is thus an unprecedentedly grand plan to reform the world.

The therapeutic success of accompanying the patient on this seemingly dangerous path was remarkable. The patient said herself that her being had been completely transformed, and this was confirmed to me from all sides; she does not torment her husband any more, shows understanding for his particularities and thereby gives him an opportunity to develop the good qualities he does have; her relationships with her daughter, her friends, and social equals have become uplifting: all the people who used to feel sorry for her, at best, now come to her for advice. The most remarkable change is in her attitude toward money. She became generous, openhanded, yet prudent. If nothing else, the therapeutic success is an excuse for the audacity of having taken so seriously the delusional ideas of a mentally ill woman.

1. Note the similarity between *Wahnhaft*, "delusional," the word Ferenczi uses here, and *wahrhaft*, "true."

17 March 1932

Advantages and disadvantages of intense sympathy (R.N.)

Severe headaches after a session of mutual analysis nearly three hours long. Resolved to remedy this, without any regard for the painful mental state of the patient in relaxation, by breaking off the session after one hour (for both cases). Some anxiety at the idea of abandoning someone suffering, without providing aid or waiting for her to calm down. However—encouraged by reading a pamphlet on Mary Baker Eddy, who was simply left alone in her hysterical attacks, whereupon she recovered; and urged on a bit by S.I., who had seriously warned me not to let myself be "gobbled up" by my patients, (not even herself)—I resolved to be firm. At the patient's request, I started with my own analysis, which I wanted to use to disclose my feelings and intentions quite freely and plainly. I also had the thought that a dream the patient had had about two days earlier, predicting a great German revolution in two days' time, may actually have been a presentiment of *my* revolt against the tyranny of suffering. (Germany always signified brutality, therefore a brutal breaking off of good relations and consideration for her.) It happened quite differently. The patient greeted me with the news that someone had placed at her disposal a sum of money, enough for another year of analysis. And my anxiety about the effect on her of my decision to be brutal proved to be groundless. The patient fully approved of my intention; my irritation with the long sessions would do more harm to the analysis than the length of the sessions would do good; the patient felt the irritation and resistance, and this was what had led her to propose mutual analysis. As soon as aggressiveness proved to be inappropriate, I began to feel guilty about my "planned wickedness." While telling the "analyst" about this, I submerged myself deeply in the reproduction of infantile experiences; the most evocative image was the vague appearance of female figures, probably servant girls from earliest childhood; then the image of a corpse, whose abdomen I was opening up, presumably in the dissecting room; linked to this the mad fantasy that I was being pressed into this wound in the corpse. Interpretation: the after-effect of passionate scenes, which presumably did take place, in the course of which a housemaid probably allowed me to play with her breasts, but then pressed my head between her legs, so that I became frightened and felt I was suffocating. This is the source of my hatred of females: I want to dissect them for it, that is, to kill them. This is why my mother's accusation "You are my murderer" cut to the heart and led to (1) a compulsive desire to help anyone who is suffering, especially women; and (2) a flight from situations in which I would have to be aggressive. Thus inwardly the feeling that in fact I am a good chap, also exaggerated reactions of rage, even at trivial affronts, and finally exaggerated reactions of guilt at the slightest lapse.

The advantage of sympathy is an ability to penetrate deeply into the feelings of others, and the compulsive wish to help, to which the patient will respond with gratitude. But sooner or later it comes to pass that the patient is not helped by simple empathy. They either wish to stay with me and have me make them happy for the rest of their lives; or they prefer an end in terror rather than terror without end.[1] Here, however, there is a difficulty in me. The more wonderful and deep the relaxation in the analysis, the slower and less energetic I prove to be when the time comes for giving notice to quit. It is for this reason that patients needed to analyze me, to make me aware of my own faults, in the hope that when my weaknesses and their causes were uncovered I would become freer, would take their complaints less personally, would not be so deeply affected by their aggression, and instead would shift the picture of the present situation rapidly back to the old trauma.

Is this sensitivity a purely personal characteristic of mine, or is it a general fact of human nature? Is my reaction not in fact a model for the guilt feelings that constitute such a widespread tendency? As yet I have never heard of similar obstacles in analysis from any other analyst. (Except from my own pupils, who have inherited from me my obsession with looking for the fault in myself.)

It should be noted in my favor that I accompany my patients to these depths, and with the aid of my own complexes can, so to speak, cry with them. If, in addition, I acquire the ability to control my emotions and also the demands of relaxation at the right time, then I have a decided chance for success. My own analysis could not be pursued deeply enough because my analyst (by his own admission, of a narcissistic nature), with his strong determination to be healthy and his antipathy toward any weaknesses or abnormalities, could not follow me down into those depths, and introduced the "educational" stage too soon.[2] Just as Freud's strength lies in firmness of education, so mine lies in the depth of the relaxation technique. My patients are gradually persuading me to catch up on this part of the analysis as well. The time is perhaps not far when I shall no longer need this help from my own creations [*eigenen Kreaturen*].[3] With sufficient freedom in sympathy as well as in the unavoidable severity, I hope I will even be able to reduce the duration of the analysis substantially. I further believe that my old ideal of "terminating" the analysis will be realized in this way; this will probably be my final contribution to the technique of psychoanalysis. (Maybe when I am no longer bothered by these practical questions I will be able to pursue the theoretical problems that interest me so much more.)

1. A standard German phrase justifying a brutal breaking-off: *Lieber ein Ende mit Schrecken, als ein Schrecken ohne Ende.*

2. Ferenczi levels another reproach at Freud regarding his own analysis, a reproach that is certainly not unrelated to the first one. The incident is reported by Jones in his own fashion (Jones III, 158–159). In a letter of 17 January 1930, Ferenczi reproaches Freud for not having analyzed his negative transference. Freud defends himself in his reply of 20 January, pointing out that at the time they did not yet know that such negative reactions were produced in every case, and that in any event there was too little time (three weeks) for these reactions to appear from behind the cordial understanding that existed between them. Freud returns to this question in the form of a "case history" in "Analysis Terminable and Interminable."—ED.

3. According to Michael Balint, Ferenczi designated people by this description: "the people whom I have created out of patients."

17 March 1932

Difficulties that arise from not accepting as real the splitting of the personality

Part of the difficulty with my patient R.N. arises from the fact that I regard things I have said to her or heard from her while she is in a waking state as being present or conscious in some form even in the relaxed state. Apparently I have difficulty *really* believing that this allegedly split-off part is not somehow aware of the things we have discussed openly. I am therefore not a little exasperated when I refer to something we have recently discussed and the patient in relaxation declares quite simply that he knows nothing about it, and forces me, so to speak, to tell him about the whole thing again, or to stimulate the intellectual activity of that fragment until it comprehends the things, events, situations. If I commit the above error, the patient almost flies into a rage; he usually awakens more or less from the trance and delivers a tirade, reproaching me, sometimes quite impatiently, for my stupidity in this matter. If the patient recovers a little (especially if I recognize and admit my fault), he then attempts with angelic patience to give me precise instructions once more about how I should behave if I want to make and maintain contact with the murdered, unconscious, that is to say, shattered, portion of his personality. There will also be advice on the ways by which, with great patience and understanding for the primitive, sensitive, and intellectually paralyzed elements, the reunification of the traumatized fragments with the intellectual person can succeed. This is a brand-new piece of work for infantile education, which no one previously suspected. Here should be linked the mechanical mode of apperception, in the infantile generally, especially in hypnosis and suggestion; at the same time, the correct way for freeing oneself from it: demechanization and dehypnotizing.

20 March 1932

On hysterical attack

(1) Reference to the origin of the word "hysteria" (*hysteron* = uterus). (2) Charcot and Freud unmasked the "attitudes passionelles" as representations of coitus. (Freud in particular, the opisthotonus as the antithetic representation of the embrace.) (3) Popular usage describes persons, particularly women, who are sexually uncontrolled and are not to be satisfied, as hysterical. ("Hysterical female" [*hysterisches Frauenzimmer*].)

Observation of a case in which in relaxation ("trance") opisthotonic positions did appear: when contact could be established with the patient, she reported that the position was a reaction to a feeling of painful excitation in the genital passage, which the patient described as painful hunger: in this position, psychic unpleasure and defense against ardent desire are simultaneously represented. With the help of an exchange of questions and answers,[1] it could be established that this state of excitation had been implanted by the father, with the help of gentle stroking and seductive words and promises, which the child in her naïveté took seriously. A scene is reproduced in which the father takes the child in his lap and actually makes use of her.

As the child could not interpret this behavior as anything other than marital practice, she is in effect made into a wife, improbable as it may sound to us. This state of affairs is complicated by a prohibition against saying anything to her mother or anyone else. Timid allusions to being soiled are not taken seriously by the mother, who is, so to speak, stricken with blindness; indeed the child is even scolded for being dirty. Sudden awareness of lying and deceit, perhaps also an intuitive perception of the father's insanity (who in a state of "error in persona" transgresses against the child in place of his own mother, in other words, takes his revenge). Thereupon (here one must interpose the event in the fifth year of life) "explosion," that is, splitting off of her own ego into another "dimension," where nothing is known of the true facts, but where a continued longing for the "ideal lover" persists. Meanwhile the body, abandoned by the mind, is totally in the power of evil; it performs mechanically, without consciousness, the prescribed sexual acts and the gestures of prostitution.

A third personal fragment is a kind of substitute mother, who keeps a permanent watch over the other two fragments. It organizes the physiological adaptation of the body to tasks that seem most impossible, and it does everything to prevent physiological death resulting from pain, exhaustion, etc. At the same time it helps the place where all the pain collects [*Schmerzsammelstelle*] (that is to say, the actual, deeply submerged, childlike ego) by means of wish-fulfilling dreams and fantasies, which prevent the carrying out of the persistent threat of suicide. Out of pure pity it drives the "pain-ego" mad. (Before the attack an attempt was made to get rid of the tension by means of masturbation. A description of this attempt degenerates into uncontrollable laughter, as if it were a sudden insight into the absurdity of the attempt to replace reality with surrogates. In the middle of the relaxational conversation there is often revolt against my tendency to bring the patient back to the sad reality: to the realization of the illusory nature of that hope and of the complete absence of any prospects for the future, *quo ad* the fulfillment of colossal infantile expectations.) (1) It must be stated that—as the patient herself has to admit—such sobering intervention, that is to say, hysterical attack plus explanations, does have a soothing effect. If a session ends without this, then the entire intervening period is filled with emotive outbursts, sleep is disturbed, etc., until, at the next session, the outburst is brought to an end with relaxational conversation.

The major factor in this favorable result may well be the process of the unconscious becoming conscious, that is, the reparation of the original trauma through spontaneous elucidations and those I provide; the knowing, that is to say, the overcoming of those factors which produce not-knowing (anxiety, fragmentation) introduces a part of the trauma into the mainstream of the total personality. (Here a note on Alexander's "total personality," which, in ignorance of our data, does not deserve the label "total.")[2]

A second, nonintellectual element or factor of the success is the patients' feeling that not only do we not despise them for their peculiarities, or even their childish and naive seductive artfulness, their nymphomania or satyriasis, but we pity them and would gladly help them if it were within our power. We believe in their innocence, we love them as beings enticed into maturity against their will, and it is our aim that they should accept our compassion and understanding, admittedly an incomplete fulfillment of their hopes, for the time being, until life offers them something better. We admire the greatness and the strength they are capable of in preventing the submergence of their total self into the "sink of corruption" by that splitting, which they maintained with all their might.

A last, not unimportant, factor is the humble admission, in front of the patient, of one's own weaknesses and traumatic experiences and disillusionments, which abolishes completely that distancing by inferiority which would otherwise be maintained. Indeed, we gladly allow the patients to have the pleasure of being able to help us, to become for a brief period our analyst, as it were, something that justifiably raises their self-esteem. Should it even occur, as it does occasionally to me, that experiencing another's and my own suffering brings a tear to my eye (and one should not conceal this emotion from the patient), then the tears of doctor and of patient mingle in a sublimated communion, which perhaps finds its analogy only in the mother-child relationship. And this is the healing agent, which, like a kind of glue, binds together permanently the intellectually assembled fragments, surrounding even the personality thus repaired with a new aura of vitality and optimism.

1. For the game of Questions and Answers see "Child Analysis in the Analysis of Adults," *Fin* 129–130.—ED.

2. Franz Alexander (1891–1964), psychoanalyst of Hungarian origin who studied at the Institute of Psychoanalysis in Berlin, then left Europe for the United States.

Ferenczi is concerned with the "total personality" in relation to the fragmented personality, which he describes, while Alexander views the personality as an integrated unit, inclusive of all events and psychic levels, beyond conflicts and internal contradictions. For more detail see Franz Alexander, "Neurose und Gesamtpersonlichkeit" *Int Z für Arztliche Psa* 12 (1926), 334–347, or Alexander, *Anwendung von Freuds Ich-Theorie auf die Neurosenlehre* (Leipzig: Internationale Psychoanalyse Verlag, 1927). The latter work also appeared in English: "The Psychoanalysis of the Total Personality: The Application of Freud's Theory of the Ego to the Neuroses" (Nervous and Mental Diseases Publishing Co., 1930, 1953).—ED.

22 March 1932

Return of the trauma in symptoms, in dreams, and in catharsis. Repression and splitting of the personality. Dismantling of repression in and following catharsis

B.: Patient reports having slept restlessly. She was (in reality) awakened by a huge Saint Bernard bitch; the first time the animal howled and just wanted to be comforted by her (the patient misspeaks several times and talks of the bitch as it were a male dog). A second time the dog came into her room and woke her by licking her face. During the same night, a *dream:* she has a fearful pain in her lower abdomen; all the blood is running out down there, at which she things: "But I'm not menstruating." In addition, a sensation of the bowels emptying. The feeling of a fire-belt above the painful area (a fire-belt is the cleared strip of woodland that prevents the further spreading of forest fires). Awakening from sleep (thus already a *symptom*) with the feeling that she cannot move because of the pain. Legs stretched out straight, immobile because of the abdominal pain, the feeling as if she were lying on a hard floor, although the bed is soft and comfortable. A feeling as if she were being flattened, shortness of breath, both hands turned outward with the palms upward. The general feeling is as though a heavy weight that was crushing her had just moved off, leaving behind the sensation of being crushed and flattened in every limb. During the day, she caught herself having a *fantasy:* a gigantic male genital penetrates her and smashes everything inside her. She sees her body unnaturally laid out, like that of a dead person; powerful heart palpitations accompany this fantasy. After about twenty to twenty-five violent jolts [*Erschütterungen*],[1] which overwhelm her like waves of pain, she feels nothing more but regards herself, her body, as a stranger, from the outside. Her menstrual period is not due yet; she is not expecting it for another eight days. Throughout the day frequent, sudden sensations of pain in the region of her navel, which are, so to speak, pointing toward the depths. Her spine is as though shattered, flexible and unresisting.

Explanation of the dream presents no difficulties: for almost two years she has had dreams that could be interpreted in no other way than as dreams of rape. On innumerable occasions she recapitulated scenes or a scene of being overpowered by her father in a flat, hard field, hands turned upward, the legs gripped above her knee and forced apart after all her powers of resistance had been overcome; the sensations of penetration, etc., awakening in utter exhaustion and incapable of comprehending what had taken place.

Dream interpretation during relaxation [*Relaxations traumdeutung*] is an attempt—instead of conscious elucidation of the dream— to take the patient back into the dream itself during the analytical session, with the aid of conscious associative material. For this a certain state of drowsiness and relaxation is necessary. By means of quiet and simple questions, never difficult ones, one tries to remain in contact with the patients as they dream; one requests them to penetrate deeper into the feeling, seeing, and experiencing of each detail, whereupon they produce small details and data about the dream-fragment, which by all appearances are derived from reality. This kind of submergence into a dream leads, in most cases, to a cathartic exacerbation of the symptoms, which then provide us with an opportunity to get closer to reality.

By no means, however, can I claim to have ever succeeded, even in a single case, in making it possible for the patient to *remember* the traumatic processes themselves, with the help of symptom-fantasy [*Symptomphantasie*],[2] submergence into dreams, and catharsis. It is as though the trauma were surrounded by a retroactively amnesic sphere, as in the case of trauma after cerebral concussion. Each individual catharsis causes this sphere to contract further and further. For the present, it is not quite clear in what way the center of the explosion can be incorporated, if it can be, in the analysand's mind as a conscious event, and therefore as a psychic event, which is capable of being remembered. There happen to be several possibilities open here: (1) In this case, many patients share in wanting to accept this as an ultimate solution: that a piece of their psychic personality, certain psychic qualities, like hope, love in general or in relation to certain things, had been so completely shattered by the shock that they must be regarded as incurable, or more accurately, as completely killed. Thus the healing of this part cannot be a *restitutio in integrum,* but merely a reconciliation to a deficiency. According to the feelings of the suffering people, a quantity and quality of love of an extraordinary kind, the most complete and perfect genital-moral-intellectual happiness, could revive even these dead fragments of the psyche; that is, even the physical and mental components of the personality could be regenerated to full functional capacity, no matter how badly they had been shattered. But such happiness is not to be had in reality (in the case of infantile rape, for example, marriage to the greatest man in the world, both physically and mentally, colossally potent and colossally in love as well, might still be too weak an antidote to be effective against the degradation and the narrowing—mutilation—of the personality caused by the trauma). (2) It is my hope that with tremendous patience and self-sacrifice on our part, after hundreds of instances of enormous forbearance, sympathy, the renunciation of every authoritarian impulse, even acceptance of lessons or help from the patient, it will be possible to make the patient renounce that colossal wish-fulfillment and make do with what offers itself; I hope that, first for my sake indeed, but later for the sake of his own reason, he will be able to bring the dead ego-fragment back to life, that is, cure it and remember it. (Bandage around the hips.)

1. *Erschütterungen* also implies "shock" as in that caused by earthquakes, concussions, or violent emotions. See: "Some Thoughts on Trauma," *Fin* 253–254.—ED.
2. We believe this refers to a fantasy that itself constitutes a symptom.—ED.

25 March 1932

Psychic bandage

Patient B. has the fantasy that her hips are strapped up with wide, stiff bandages.

Associations allowed me to conclude that this fantasy corresponds to the wish to be protected and supported. In the transference the opportunity would present itself to provide that protection and support which were absent during the trauma. The love and strength of the analyst, assuming that trust in him goes deep enough and is great enough, have nearly the same effect as the embrace of a loving mother and a protective father. The help offered by the mother's lap and strong embrace permits complete relaxation, even after a shattering trauma, so that the shattered person's own powers, undisturbed by external tasks of precautions or defense, can devote themselves in an unsplintered way to the internal task of repairing the function-impairment caused by the unexpected penetration. The positive feelings of transference produce, as it were, a deferred *anticathexis,* which did not occur when the trauma took place. This is the place to say something about countercathexis: from the moment when bitter experience teaches us to lose faith in the benevolence of the environment, a permanent split in the personality occurs. The split-off part sets itself up as a guard against dangers, mainly on the surface (skin and sense organs), and the attention of this guard is almost exclusively directed toward the outside. It is concerned only with danger, that is to say, with the objects in the environment, which can all become dangerous. Thus the splitting of the world, which previously gave the impression of homogeneity, into subjective and objective psychic systems; each has its own way of remembering, of which only the objective system is actually completely conscious. (See here the relevant hypothesis in my article on tics.)[1] Only in sleep do we succeed, by means of certain external arrangements (creation of a secure situation by closing windows and doors, by wrapping ourselves in protective, warm bedclothes), in calling off this guard. (Here refer to the sleep–mother's womb theory, and add to it the following: birth is only a transient disturbance of the situation in the womb; the child wakes up for a moment, and sleeps on, in the cradle. The birth trauma, for that reason, is not dangerous and leaves no significant traces behind, because the environment immediately provides reparation.) (See here my criticism of Rank's birth-trauma theory.)[2] Actual trauma is experienced by children in situations where no immediate remedy is provided and where adaptation, that is, a change in their own behavior, is forced on them—the first step toward establishing the differentiation between inner and outer world, subject and object. From then on, neither subjective nor objective experience alone will be perceived as an integrated emotional unit (except in sleep or in orgasm).

If a trauma strikes the soul, or the body, unprepared, that is, without countercathexis, then its effect is destructive for body and mind, that is, it disrupts through fragmentation. The power that would hold the individual fragments and elements together is absent. Fragments and elements of organs, psychic fragments and elements become dissociated. In the bodily sphere this might mean an anarchy of the organs, parts and elements of organs, whose reciprocal cooperation alone renders proper global functioning—that is to say life—possible. In the psychic sphere, the intruding force, in the absence of a solid countercathexis, produces a kind of explosion, a destruction of psychic associations between the systems and psychic contents, which may reach down to the deepest elements of perception. (Here link with my hypothesis on the purely arithmetical, algebraic, and higher symbolic reductions of simple sensory impressions,[3] which themselves ultimately derive from single waves, impulses originating from the environment. Possibly also connection with the earlier theory on time and space. The purely subjective is still purely arithmetical; the setting up of "guards" (countercathexis), however, already demands generalizations, that is to say, synthesis, abstraction.)

An association contradicts the physical law of separation (impenetrability of matter). An association is neither A nor B, but A and B simultaneously, therefore something metaphysical. At the moment of thinking, A and B are for a moment present at one and the same point in the mind; in the symbol: all the arithmetical points of single experiences are concentrated in a metaphysical manner. Hypothesis: the most primitive, purely unitary experience is *not* timeless, its memory traces are like the grooves on a phonograph record, the depositories of each single vibration. The single wave is the unit of mass of real time, that is, of the resistance of corpuscular elements to any change, which is to say, to the *impacts* of the environment. The unprotected child is ready to be blown up, so to speak. (Link with my little work on children's desire to die.)[4] Narcosis, hypnosis, anxiety destroy the synthesizing functions. The feeling of not being loved, or of being hated (link with father and mother hypnosis)[5] makes the desire to live, that is, to be unified, disappear.

Inability to be alone[6]

Giving form to the environment

Formlessness of what has no limits

1. See "Psychoanalytical Observations on Tic" (1921), FC 142–174.—ED.
2. See "Review of Rank, *Technique of Psycho-Analysis*," Int J Psa 8: 93.—ED.
3. See "Mathematics," Fin 183–196.—ED.
4. See "The Unwelcome Child and His Death Instinct," Fin 102–107.—ED.
5. See "Introjection and Transference," C 35–93.—ED.
6. See D. W. Winnicott, "The Capacity to Be Alone" (1958), in *The Maturational Process and the Facilitating Environment* (Hogarth Press, 1965), esp. p. 32.—ED.

29 March 1932

Transformation of mutual analysis into simply being analyzed

At the beginning, after the general resistance against reciprocity had been overcome, there was a long struggle over priority: who should begin. Each offered to let the other go first. I, the analyst, had two reasons for this: (1) Above all, I wanted to work over the old material and the impressions of the previous day, and feared that what I was about to communicate would provoke new material, and new emotions, before the old material had been worked through. (2) Finally, I still considered my own analysis a resource for the analysis of the analysand. The analysand was to remain the main subject, have most of the time at her disposal, I having only as much as was left for me after full abreaction. (The total period of two hours was strictly adhered to.) The next step, in the mind of the analysand, was the precise division of the time into two equal parts. This was possible only after removing obstacles in my own analysis (not without considerable emotion) that made it difficult for me to cause someone pain (that is, not to satisfy someone): a particular compulsion, a result of excessive performances and demands in childhood regarding sexuality: Biri.[1] Since then regular double sessions. Taking into consideration the analysand's objection that she would be incapable of dealing with me objectively after the end of [her own] analytical session, this wish had to prevail as well, and now every double session begins with the analysis of the analyst.

Undeniably, at the end of my own analysis I noticed in myself great fatigue and difficulty in applying myself to the new task and to objectify my attention. In the usual manner of analysis, even under current conditions, I attempted to overcome this tendency to relaxation, but not always with equal success; the interest remained fastened on my own ego and demanded, above all, tranquillity.

It happened that in connection with a dream in which someone, with the assistance of his own convulsions, understood those same symptoms in someone else, I remembered some of the analysand's earlier notions that aimed to make me become Julius Caesar: that is, I would have to have an epileptic seizure before making a momentous decision. Only from this feeling could I attain any understanding and feeling for the patient's sufferings (to be sure, a person can have such a seizure only if he himself has, in childhood, been close to, or been immersed or almost immersed, in a death-struggle or -convulsion (agony) occurring during or as a result of trauma, from which he has returned with a deficit in his ability and desire to go on living, yet with a tremendously widened horizon for having also glimpsed the beyond. (Association with Caesar: seize her,[2] being seized by the attack.)

The first attempt to put this into practice was unsuccessful. The patient was telling me about a dream; the analyzed analysand (the analyst), still weary from his own analysis, simply fell asleep; still listening with half an ear and in a semidaze, he picked up a few dream images and word fragments; suddenly awakened by a sense of guilt, he tried to make the patient associate to these—for the patient—quite insignificant fragments. (For he suddenly remembered he was the analyst.) Thereupon irritation from the analysand because of my inattention. I replied with justifiable annoyance: Well, either I am Caesar or I am not Caesar. I cannot simultaneously have epileptic seizures and consciously attend to all the patient's communications. The patient agreed. But she hopes that in spite of drifting off I had taken in all that she had told me. I had to concede, however, that such simultaneous submergence and analysis was utterly impossible. I thereby had to return, somewhat shamefacedly, to the analysand's earlier suggestion that I let *myself* be analyzed completely *first,* before proceeding with her analysis. Not without a certain feeling of depression and shame. It had already cost me considerable effort to acknowledge the fact of our being equals in mutual analysis, and now the plan for a one-sided analysis of me by the analysand meant further degradation, or humiliation; I had to demote myself to the position of a child [*Ich musste mich zum Kinde degradieren*] and recognize the analysand as the authority keeping watch over me.

The first consequence of this decision was the flaring up of my hemicrania on the left side. Persistent depression then led to the following modification of the scheme: the analysis of the analysand must not be interrupted, if only so that the tensions of the patient do not accumulate. The best thing would be, therefore, if on a day of analysis only one *or* the other is analyzed, in other words, the direction of the analysis does not change. Instead the analysis would alternate from day to day, first one way, then the other. I must confess, however, that this scheme still contains remnants of resistance against the planned complete humiliation.

The actual fear of being analyzed is the fear of being dependent. If the person doing the analyzing [*dem Analysierenden*] succeeds in making himself indispensable to me, as I observe with my patients, then I am at his mercy. So long as I do not have full confidence in him,

I cannot surrender myself into his power. And so I find myself in the same situation that led my patient to want to analyze me: the patient did not have the impression of me that I was completely harmless, that is to say, full of understanding. The patient sensed unconscious resistances and obstacles in me; it was for this reason that mutual analysis was proposed. And now I am in the same position: I do not want to plunge into the depths without taking precautionary measures; and taking these precautionary measures means analyzing the analyst so that all potentially dangerous impulses, or at least all neurotic impediments to comprehension (which could lead to error) are allowed to become clearly manifest in the analysis. Thus neither of us has confidence in the other, at least no confidence that the other's understanding is free from complexes. This is why I now demand alternating analysis and why I protest against one-sidedness.

1. The name of a young girl.—Note provided by Michael Balint.
2. Phrase in English in original.

31 March 1932

Mutual analysis: decision through practice. Complications arising from the fact that more than one patient is in analysis

Two days in a row of only being analyzed: depressing feeling of having handed over the control, the reins. Disquieting idea that the patient has succeeded in escaping from analysis entirely, and in taking me into analysis instead. In accordance with my tendency to risk even what is most difficult, and then to find motives for having done so, I resolved, though most reluctantly, to take this risk as well; indeed, I even produced a theoretical basis for it, telling myself that real analysis can come about only when relaxation takes place as in the child-parent relationship, that is to say, total trust and the surrender of all independence. Thus the customary superiority of the analyst became first mutuality, being on equal terms, and then total subordination. In spite of this decision, no feeling of well-being, but in fact even symptoms: headache, sleep disturbances; the feeling of fatigue and sleepiness during analytic sessions, also during lengthy theater performances. A practical experience provided the solution. The patient's two-day abstinence made it impossible to delay her analysis any longer, and mutuality was again restored.

Complications arise through the involvement of a third person, who also wants to analyze me. Difference of opinion over this between me and patient I. I consider a total immersion, right down "to the mothers,"[1] impossible unless the analyst becomes an open book, that is to say, not only formally and professionally nice and polite but even harmless, by communicating his suppressed and repressed selfish, dangerous, brutal, and ruthless tendencies. Patient I on the contrary believes that this is necessary only in an exceptional case, such as hers, while no. II feels she has been relegated to a lesser position, and confesses to being jealous of no. I. No. II also asked me frequently whether I would be disturbed if she, as an analyst, were to undertake an analysis by a patient simultaneously with me. She chose for this a man toward whom she feels particularly impatient. At the same time she tries, in a somewhat suspicious manner, to reassure me, saying that the man is especially trustworthy, so that *my* secrets will be safe with him. In other words, she tells me that when a mutually analyzed patient (himself an analyst) extends the mutuality to his own patients, then he must reveal the secrets of the primary analyst [*Uranalytiker*] (that is to say, mine) to his patients.

Thus I would be confronted with the possibility that people who are complete strangers to me will come into full possession of my most intimate, most personal emotions, sins, etc. Consequently I either have to learn to accept the impossibility, even madness, of this whole idea and technique, or I must go on with this daring enterprise and come around to the idea that it really does not matter if a small group of people is formed whose members know everything about one another. This could even facilitate relations with such a group, in contrast to the perpetual mutual secrecy, suspicion, precautionary measures, inhibition in all manifestations, in speech and finally in feelings as well, that are usual today.

An earlier idea, that the blossoming of gangsterism may lead to the founding of a new social order in which all hypocrisy is absent, receives a new and different kind of support in the extension of mutuality. It will become obvious (1) that when we have been offended, disturbed, or injured we all have the reactions of gangsters. (2) In contrast, we shall recognize and openly acknowledge those "weaknesses" within ourselves as well as in the group, "weaknesses" that we still keep secret today or repress as childish or absurd, this longing that even the toughest gangster hides behind his cynicism— that is to say, a desire for gentle, childlike tenderness (active or passive) and for the happiness of trust.

Every analysis of a woman must end with homosexuality, that of a man with heterosexuality. The most profound submergence means the mother or the womb situation; obviously for a woman this is a relationship with someone of the same sex, for a man with someone of the opposite sex. "On revient toujours." One might say that homosexuality is the next-to-last word in the analysis of a woman. The (let us say male) analyst must let all the maternal qualities prevail and inhibit all aggressive, male instincts (the unconscious ones as well). This will lead to a manifestation in the female analysand of *spontaneous* (that is, not forcibly imposed) tendencies toward passivity and toward being loved in a quite penetrating manner, as corresponds to anatomy. The ultimate phase of a woman's analysis would thus be, without exception, the spontaneous development of the desire to be passive and to be a mother.

Freud is right, therefore, when he sees a masculine, boyish (that is to say, mother-fixated) period as preceding femininity; the only correction to be added is the fact, resulting from analysis, that a large part of children's sexuality is not spontaneous, but is artificially grafted on by adults, through overpassionate tenderness and seduction. It is only when this grafted-on element is reexperienced in analysis, and is thereby emotionally split up, that there develops *in the analysis,* initially in the transference relationship, that *untroubled* infantile sexuality from which, in the final phase of analysis, the longed-for normality will grow.

But what is "normality"? In the woman: a preponderant tendency to be wife and mother, superior toleration of a certain aggressiveness in sons and husband, who after all is only one of the children of the mistress of the house; toward daughters, a large amount of homosexual love between mother and daughter persists, in spite of marriage and maternity. The woman's longing for a friend of the same sex or the mother, with great reciprocal tenderness, is undying, and it will also be accepted by society as natural, and even if excessive it is not really condemned or abhorred. In the "normal" man, a large part of the toughness that is usual today (known as masculinity) will be dismantled; it will not be a disgrace for a grown man to be childish, gentle, nonsexual, at least not always sexual; showing emotions or weeping will no longer be unmasculine modes of expression. (Here perhaps bring in the specific privileges of the male sex in the paper "Male and Female.")[2] Probably the result would also be less promiscuity, more men would have the courage to testify to the simple contentment of family life, this very image of the infantile situation.

1. An allusion to Goethe's *Faust,* part 2, act 1: Mephistopheles gives Faust a key, saying, "Follow it down; it will lead you to the mothers." The mothers are Sicilian goddesses who raised Zeus and who are the source of all life.

2. "Male and Female" in *Thalassa,* pp. 96–107.—ED.

3 April 1932

Explantation and implantation of psychic contents and energies (S.I.)

Like many others, this frigid patient, who suffers from anxiety states (attacks), anxiety dreams, and the compulsion to drink alcohol every evening, on occasion also produces hallucinations with an anxiety content during the day; often speaks of a dark, irresistible alien power, which forces her against her will, against her own interest, even against her own pleasure, to destructive actions and words damaging to herself and others: one could in fact speak of demonomania. Not infrequently the psychoanalytic associations degenerate into unusually vivid visual images, whose reality she does not doubt in the least, although she remains aware that this kind of seeing is different from the usual kind. She then automatically covers her eyes by pressing her forearms against her eyeballs; she almost forgets about my presence, yet she seems to be aware of it to some extent, as she continues to report her sensations to me. It also is not difficult to bring her out of these hallucinations. My verbal request suffices. One sees a certain difficulty in wresting her out of that state, namely the effort she requires to take her arms away from her face. Quite often she looks at me afterward as though astonished, perhaps saying words like: "So you are here? How remarkable. You are Dr. F., and you have been here the whole time." Occasionally she adds some remarks about the changes in her being that my presence produces. To my modest reply that I knew nothing of such magnificent qualities [*Grossartigkeit*] in myself and also that I have not done anything special for her, she answered with great assurance that then I must be unaware of my own capabilities and actions. The content of the hallucinations: extremely abrupt shifts in time, space, and objects, similar to the flight of ideas. She feels herself liberated from all the fetters and impediments of physical distance. She flies in the atmosphere, plunges into the depths of the seas with all the marvels of the deep sea; the most varied light-apparitions without any content, which often have a definite orientation, suddenly emerge in her. Almost always human figures soon appear, or fragments of figures, which she calls ghosts. Certain types recur with great frequency, especially so Chinese people. An old man with a bald head, who bends over her. These kinds of ghosts gradually take on a frightening character; the patient makes defensive gestures, often, at the end, she calls out with a shrill cry and every indication of terrible fright: "They are hitting me! They will smash my head in! They are killing me!" During all this her face is red, tears are running from her eyes. After several minutes of this struggle, the whole person suddenly, so to speak, becomes paralyzed; she lies there silent and deathly pale, without the least affect; occasionally she claims that she is no longer inside but outside her body, the body itself is dead, murdered. The figures (ghosts) are very often the apparitions of a dead person, particularly of her brother, who died a year ago. The figure does not speak, expresses itself only by gestures. He points to his heart (he died of a heart attack), points to me (Dr. F.), as though he wanted to invite her to turn to me.

Since she has heard of Freud's theory of the superego as a split-off product of the self, she repeats with great conviction that in her case an evil superego, her mother's will, with the assistance of great anxiety, keeps her in chains and compels her to self-destructive behavior. (She even feels that her unwanted tendency to get fat was the work of this alien will, forced on her, which imposes itself on her in a physical sense as well.)

She imagines the intrusion of the harmful superego (alien will) as something like this: pain and fright paralyze the person's cohesive, life-preserving forces, and into this "softened and unresisting material" the alien will, born of hate and the lust for attack, penetrates the other person with all its tendencies, while a piece of the person's own spontaneity is forcibly driven out.

The result of this process is, on the one hand, the implanting of psychic contents into the psyche of the victim, dispensing unpleasure, causing pain and tension; at the same time, however, the aggressor sucks up, as it were, a piece of the victim into himself, the piece that has been expelled. Hence the soothing effect on an enraged person of the explosion of his rage, when he succeeds in causing pain to the other: a part of the poison is implanted in the other person (from now on it is the other person who has to struggle with the feelings of unpleasure, the more so for having been unjustly treated). At the same time (and this is what is new in what S.I. reported) the aggressor annexes the naive state of peaceful happiness, untroubled by anxiety, in which the victim had existed until recently. Expressed in simpler terms this would mean: someone in a distressed, painful situation, envying the peace of another—let us say, of a weak person, a child—kicks the dog, so to speak, in his depression. In this one ensures that the other suffers too, something that will inevitably ease my pain. In addition, by this action I annex that previous state of happiness.

5 April 1932

All hate is projection, in fact psychopathic

If pain is inflicted on someone, or love is withdrawn, there is suffering. The rational reaction to this would be sadness, while maintaining the real love situation, something like: I still love him as before, he does not love me anymore, how much pain I have to endure! The hate reaction on the other hand is completely unreal; if I am badly treated I start to assert: I do not love him, I hate him; and instead of experiencing the real pain to its full extent, I inflict some physical or moral pain on him. This is how I bring it about that henceforth he is the one to suffer, not I. I succeed in this way in displacing my suffering, wholly or in part, onto someone else. The paranoid mechanism may also manifest itself in the fact that the displacement draws ever wider circles and hatred is extended to a whole family, a whole nation, a whole species. As a result of the displacement and the projective quality thus associated with hatred, it will also be difficult or impossible for hatred to be dismantled philosophically as quickly as mourning, or slowly to be eroded in other ways. Had the injured person lived through a prolonged period of grief instead of hate, then the process of mourning would gradually have done its work; while the displaced affect, perhaps just because of this unreality, can prevail for a long time or even permanently. The most frequent example: traumatic disillusionment in childhood; lifelong hatred of a particular type of person.

Essential difference between male and female homosexuality

It has been too little noted that female homosexuality is in fact a very normal thing, just as normal as male heterosexuality. Both man and woman have in the beginning the same female love-object (the mother). For both sexes, deep-reaching analysis leads to conflicts and disillusionments with the mother. Training in cleanliness, the creation of "sphincter morality," is the mother's business (the question even arises whether it is not because of this very first disappointment with the mother that a part of the libido is turned toward the father). Fixation on the father or on the male sex, in contrast, is thoroughly abnormal; above all, it is in contradiction with anatomy, which (contrary to Freud) I consider fundamentally determining in psychology. Society does not appear to judge female homosexuality so harshly either. The girl's relationship with her mother is much more important than that with her father. Indeed, even acts of sexual aggression in early infancy, coming from the male side, had a traumatic effect mainly because they dislocated the relationship with the mother.

In accordance with the hypothesis of a very close connection between anatomy and psyche, it may be presumed that vaginal eroticism, in the inner vagina that has never been touched, arises in fact quite late, and with it an increased interest in passivity.

Additional fragments concerning the Oedipus conflict[1]

Experiences regarding the traumatic effect of genital attacks by adults on small children oblige me to modify the analytic view of infantile sexuality that has prevailed up to now. The fact that infantile sexuality exists obviously remains undisputed, yet much of what appears as passionate in infantile sexuality may be a secondary consequence of the passionate behavior of adults, forcibly imposed on children against their will and, so to speak, artificially implanted in them. Even overpassionate manifestations of nongenital tenderness, such as passionate kissing, ardent embraces, affect the child in fact unpleasurably. Children want no more than to be treated in a friendly, tender, and gentle way. Their own movements and physical expressions are tender; if it is otherwise, then something has already gone wrong. One has to ask oneself how much of what is involved in the undying love of the child for its mother, and how much of the boy's murderous desire against the rival father, would develop in a purely spontaneous way, without the premature implantation of passionate adult eroticism and genitality; that is, how much of the Oedipus complex is really inherited and how much is passed on by tradition from one generation to the other.

1. In this entry Ferenczi sketched out ideas that he would develop further in "Confusion of Tongues between Adults and the Child," *Fin* 156–167, written during the next few months. The ideas were very badly received by Freud and by the psychoanalytic world in general.—ED.

5 April 1932

On the long-term effect of forcibly imposed, "obligatory,"
active and passive genital demands on young children

1. Genital violation by the father in early infancy. *Development:*
stubborn disposition, inability to complete studies of any kind
(Freud: sexual activity produces ineducability),[1] hysterical sensations,
especially in the head and abdomen. Occasional attacks of pain—
deeper analysis: permanent excitation of the vagina of an itching
nature, conversion of these sensations to pain and displacement to
distant parts of the body. Occasional abreaction in hysterical convulsive seizures.

2. Complete analogy in symptomatology with no. 1. However, the
moral motif of refusal and unpleasure during the attack is particularly
transparent, but of course complete inability to defend herself and
coercion to submit. Protection of the personality by loss of consciousness, compensating fantasies of happiness, splitting of the personality.
The trauma involved (and mostly involves) the child at a stage of
already-established sphincter-morality; the girl feels soiled, indecently
treated, would like to complain to her mother, but she is prevented by
the man (intimidation, denial). The child is helpless and confused,
should she struggle to prevail over the will of adult authority, the
disbelief of her mother, etc. Naturally she cannot do that, she is faced
with the choice—Is it the whole world that is bad, or am I wrong?—
and chooses the latter. Thereupon displacements and misinterpreta-
tion of sensations, which ultimately produce the above symptoms.

3. Quite analogous damage in men on whom genital activity had
been forcibly and prematurely imposed. Main feature: the taking on
of superhuman tasks, behind which there is tremendous fatigue and
dislike of work. (Naturally the same in relation to the libido.)

1. Freud, "Three Essays on the Theory of Sexuality," SE VII, 179; also more generally
the second essay, "Infantile Sexuality," as well as p. 234 of the third essay, "The Transformations of Puberty."—ED.

7 April 1932

The fate of children of mentally ill parents

1. We have as yet no proper picture of the psychic qualities of the
young child's personality. Certain signs indicate that the psychophysical personality of a child in the womb, or indeed after birth, is not yet

completely crystalized, as it were, but exists still in a state of "dissolution." (The fantastic hypothesis behind this picture-like metaphor is the idea that before conception the individual was somehow still dissolved in the universe. One should, in that case, consider death as a return to this "state of dissolution." As already described elsewhere, children still die easily.)[1] The physiological parallel to the above representation is the fact that before conception the individual was divided into at least two halves. One half was the component part of the mother, the other half that of the father. One may formally ask oneself the question: whether this early state of being split is not the model for all later splitting, including the splitting of the personality in psychosis.

The idea of the still half-dissolved state (consistency) of the childish personality tempts the imagination to suppose that the childish personality is in much closer contact with the universe, and therefore its sensitivity is much greater than that of the adult, crystalized into rigidity. It would not surprise us either if some day it were to be demonstrated that in this early state the whole personality is still resonating with the environment—and not only at particular points that had remained permeable, namely the sensory organs. So-called supernormal faculties—being receptive to processes beyond sensory perceptions (clairvoyance), apprehending the communications of an alien will (suggestion from a distance)—may well be ordinary processes, in the same way that animals (dogs), whose personalities evidently always remain in a state of dissolution, possess such apparently supernormal faculties (sense of smell at a colossal distance, the inexplicable adoption of the owners' sympathies and antipathies). Here the first possibility to understand the so-called telegony (the influence of the mother's psychic experiences on the child in the womb).

To connect with the strange dream images about "wise babies."[2] Spiritualist mediums, insofar as they accomplish anything at all, owe their powers to a regression to this infantile state of omniscience and supreme wisdom.

2. The formation of the superego gains a more plastic character through these representations. I am indebted to several patients for the idea, recorded elsewhere, that adults forcibly inject their will, particularly psychic contents of an unpleasurable nature, into the childish personality. These split-off, alien transplants vegetate in the other person during the whole of life (as a counterpoint to this, I hear expressed the view that the expelled parts of the childish personality become assimilated, as it were, by the dispenser of the superego).

On theoretical grounds alone, frightful confusion can also be expected when a child who is sensitive in this way and to this degree comes under the influence of a deranged, mentally ill adult. Peculiar experiences in one case make it appear not impossible that the "wise baby," with his wonderful instinct, accepts the deranged and insane as something that is forcibly imposed, yet keeps his own personality separate from the abnormal right from the beginning. (Here an access to the permanent bipartition of the person.) The personality component expelled from its own framework represents this real, primary person, which protests persistently against every abnormality and suffers terribly under it. This suffering person protects himself, by forming wish-fulfilling hallucinations, against any insight into the sad reality, namely that the evil, alien will is occupying his entire psychic and physical being (being possessed).

In the above-mentioned case a strange thing happened. The insane and evil will, after a maniacal outburst exceeding anything that had happened before, suddenly sobered and withdrew from the person it had occupied hitherto; and from now on it turns against the person in whom it had until now vegetated, as it were, in the form of a pure will to kill. The consequence is a tremendous void in the person who had become accustomed to having the alien will as a skeleton of his own person. As soon as the crazy person has made the decision to withdraw, the remaining part of the person finds himself in a state of insecurity resembling an earthquake. But at the moment of the attack all illusion is destroyed, the sudden insight into this terrifying existence in the power of a madman cannot be accepted, and the state of being split that has existed up to now gives way to a state of complete dissolution. After that has run its course, as when fireworks have burnt themselves out, the entire sector of this experience disintegrates into a mass of atomized debris.

The task of the analyst is to bring the psyche back to life out of these ashes. (Day after day, first modest, then a progressive consolidation of the ashes into fragments of insight. At times everything will be destroyed again, then patiently built up again, until finally the experience of transference, and its implicit lesson in suffering, will smooth the path toward the traumatic depths.) Eugenic hint: already newborn babies ought to be removed from an insane environment.

1. "The Unwelcome Child and His Death Instinct," *Fin* 102–105.—ED.

2. Phrase in English in original. See "The Dream of the 'Clever Baby,' " *FC* 249–250. The notion of the Clever Baby, or Wise Baby, is taken up time and time again by Ferenczi, notably in "Child Analysis in the Analysis of Adults," *Fin* 135–136; "Confusion of Tongues between Adults and the Child," *Fin* 165; "Exaggerated Sex Impulse and Its Consequences," *Fin* 271; "On Lamaism and Yoga," *Fin* 274.—ED.

7 APRIL 1932

10 April 1932

Erotomania as the basis of all paranoia

With increasing frequency, I find in the most diverse delusional representations of paranoid patients (delusions of grandeur, delusion of jealousy, persecution mania), behind the homosexual base, an even more profound cause for homosexuality in the form of an erotomanic delusional structure. This develops as a wish-fulfilling psychosis similar to amentia, after the traumatic loss of the love object, or after the gaining of traumatic insight into that which is illusory in the presumed object-love relationship. In this connection the question arises whether the primal trauma is not always to be sought in the primal relationship with the mother, and whether the traumata of a somewhat later epoch, already complicated by the appearance of the father, could have had such an effect without the existence of such a pre-primal-trauma [ururtraumatischen] mother-child scar. Being loved, being the center of the universe, is the natural emotional state of the baby, therefore it is not a mania but an actual fact. The first disappointments in love (weaning, regulation of the excretory functions, the first punishments through a harsh tone of voice, threats, even spankings) must have, in every case, a traumatic effect, that is, one that produces psychic paralysis from the first moment. The resulting disintegration makes it possible for new psychic formations to emerge. In particular, it may be assumed that a splitting occurs at this stage. The organism has to adapt itself, for example, to the painful realities of weaning, but psychic resistance against it desperately clings to memories of an actual past and lingers for a shorter or longer period in the hallucination: nothing has happened, I am still loved the same as before (hallucinatory omnipotence). All subsequent disappointments, later on in one's love life, may well regress to this wish-fulfillment.

12 April 1932

The relaxation of the analyst

Until recently the discussion has been focused almost exclusively on the relaxation of the patient: the analyst was expected merely to promote this relaxation by suitable measures, or at least not to disturb it. Occasionally reference was made to the most important of these disturbances. The emergence of the idea of mutual analysis is actually an extension of relaxation to include the analyst as well. Analyst and analysand relax in alternation.

It should be added here that Freud's earliest statements on technique[1] recommend this kind of relaxation on both sides, although he does not give the process this name. The patient is asked to assume a completely passive attitude toward his psychic contents. In one passage he compares the ensuing psychic state as intrinsically related to the passive docility of someone who submits to hypnosis. However, he also demands from the analyst a "free-floating attention": that is, a certain degree of detachment from consciously goal-oriented thought or inquiry. In other words, Freud demands relaxation from the doctor and the patient, but relaxation of differing depths. The patient is expected to entrust himself, for the time being, to the directions of the unconscious, and the doctor should also give his imagination free rein in all directions, even the most absurd. However, he must not, or should not, move too far away from the surface of consciousness, so as not to neglect for a single moment the task of observing the patient, of evaluating the material produced, and of making decisions regarding any eventual communication, etc.

In mutual analysis the doctor renounces, if only temporarily, the role of "watchman." Up to now this has meant (in mutuality) that in the meantime the analysand takes over the role of analyst. An unexpected and at first quite senseless modification has evolved or seems to have evolved from this: the necessity that both relax simultaneously. As mentioned above, this at first sounds totally absurd. What is the use of two people falling into a trance simultaneously and then senselessly talking at cross-purposes, that is, free-associating and also giving vent to their feelings in gestures and expressive movements. Here, as the sole thread offered by previous analytical experience, is the idea (launched, if I remember correctly, by me): the dialogue of unconsciouses.[2] When two people meet for the first time, I said then, an exchange takes place not only of conscious but also of unconscious stirrings. Only analysis could determine for both why, quite inexplicably to either of them, sympathy or antipathy has developed in them. Ultimately I meant by this that when two people converse, not only a conscious dialogue takes place but an unconscious one, from both sides. In other words, next to the attention-cathected conversation, or parallel to it, a relaxed dialogue is also pursued. Some of my women patients are not satisfied with this explanation, however: they steadfastly maintain that apart from this receptivity to the manifestations of unconscious emotions in their fellow human beings, demonstrable by analytic or by normal psychological means, psychic phenomena are also involved, which cannot be explained in the present state of our knowledge of the physiology of the sensory organs and of psychology. Others before me have already drawn attention to the remarkable frequency with which so-called thought-transference phenomena occur between physician and patient, often in a way that goes far beyond the probability of mere chance. Should such things be confirmed some day, we analysts would probably find it plausible that the transference relationship could quite significantly promote the development of subtler manifestations of receptivity.

And this is in fact what has led to the story of the origins of the most recent modification. The motive for reversing the process (the analyst being analyzed) was an awareness of an emotional resistance or, more accurately, of the obtuseness of the analyst. The relentless complaint was: "You are too passive, you don't do anything, etc.," not infrequently accompanied by signs of the deepest despair. Under the pressure of helplessness, the patient split off a sort of fragment of intelligence to give me directions about how and what I should do or should have done at that particular moment. However, after over-coming strong personal resistance against such treatment by prescription, I asked the appropriate questions that had been prescribed and got the answers; the result remained unsatisfactory for the patient, as regards the conviction of the reality of the traumatic situations re-produced in the trance. The "counteranalysis" set in motion now confirmed, almost word for word, the assertions of the analysand. The continuous protests (from the deepest unconscious) that I do not in fact have any real empathy or compassion for the patient, that I am emotionally dead, was in many respects analytically proven, and could be traced back to deep infantile traumata (traumata that could be traced back specifically to excessive demands of genitality on the part of adults, to conflicts with the puritanical spirit within the fam-ily, and, not least, possibly to a traumatic event in earliest infancy). Here the extraordinary analogy between my fate (neurosis) and the psychosis of her own father was able to have an effect. The patient had lived in a total community of soul and spirit with her father; sometimes she maintained that she lived in the head of the father, at other times that the father lived in the head of the patient. Because of his insanity, however, he does not know that all the infamous acts against the daughter are in fact meant for the mother; the final, atomizing trauma occurred at a moment of mutual sobriety. The father, following a final desperate attempt at incest, withdrew from his daughter emotionally, in order to vilify her henceforth for life: in an already sober act of revenge. The atomization came about when she suddenly became aware of the impossibility of getting her father to admit his insane acts and sins.

In my case infantile aggressiveness and a refusal of love toward my mother became displaced onto the patients. But, as with my mother, I managed with tremendous effort to develop a compulsive, purely intellectual superkindness, which even enabled me to shed real tears (tears that I myself believed to be genuine). (Could it be that my entire relaxation therapy and the superkindness I demand from myself toward patients are really only an exaggerated display of compassionate feelings that basically are totally lacking?) Instead of feeling with the heart, I feel with my head. Head and thought replace heart and libido. Displacement of physically more primitive libidinal impulses to the head, perhaps also in the form of symptoms (headaches), or in my tendency to formulate theories in which the genitals are identified with the head. (There are many possible links here.) All in all, then, a case of castration hysteria with corresponding displacements. What is missing for My patients in me is that "certain something" [*das gewisse "etwas"*].[3]

1. See "Freud's Psychoanalytical Procedure," SE VII, 249; "Recommendations to Physicians Practising Psycho-Analysis," SE XII, 109–121; "On Beginning Treatment," SE XII, 121–145.—ED.

2. Toward the end of "Psychogenic Anomalies of Voice Production," FC 109, Ferenczi refers to the "dialogues of the unconscious"; for clarity and added emphasis we have used the rather more cumbersome literal translation "the dialogue of unconsciouses."

3. Possibly a reference to "Madame Arthur" d'Yvette Guilbert, a singer who was much admired by Freud and consequently by the psychoanalytic world at large.—ED.

24 April 1932

Paranoia and the sense of smell

A patient reports that on the previous day she had to spend several hours in the company of Mrs. Dm., a lady she had known for quite some time, and who had also made several attempts at analytic treatment with her. The reasons she gave for her antipathy toward this lady were her lack of education, her New England narrowmindedness, and her primitive way of expressing herself; furthermore she did not have the least trace of artistic élan, etc. This prompted her to

flee from the company of this lady. As she could not avoid her yesterday, she felt compelled to get drunk. Only in a totally drunk, un-
balanced, dreamy, half-asleep state could she stand her. When thinking of her, all her associations centered on the smell of this lady. She
gives off an odor like that of a corpse, which scares the patient and
alerts her defenses.

On the same day Dm. came to see me and said that she had also
drunk a lot (but had not been drunk). She feels frightened in the
company of the patient; this lady, she said, was too aggressive, too
energetic, and reminded her of her own mother. (Here the link with
an infantile trauma: her mother had grabbed her so hard by the wrist
that she broke her arm.) It must be noted here that Dm. does really
have a very unpleasant odor, and people with a fairly acute sense of
smell definitely are repelled by her. It may be stated as highly probable that the intensity of these emanations may have something to do
with repressed hate and rage. It is as if, like certain animals, in the
absence of other available weapons she keeps people away from her
body with such repellent emanations of hate. (Consciously and in her
manifest behavior, the patient is rather pliant and inclined to blind
obedience and uncomplaining submissiveness.)

It was not too presumptuous to trace the patient's reaction to the
fact that she can actually smell people's feelings. She also reported
then to me various other experiences of this kind. Interestingly, she
gives me a long account of her mother, who had concocted for herself
ideas similar to those of Professor Jaeger[1] in his time. Having a bath
and washing were unhealthy, she never changed her underwear, but
she felt she never had an unpleasant smell. Otherwise she was uncom-
monly energetic and ruled in the home (the father was a drunk, and
only entered the house once in a while, soon after which another child
would be born).

The theory that could be derived from these and similar questions
would be as follows: the emanations of the patient's mother, which
were consciously aggressive, did not stink, yet those of Dm., who was
seemingly more obsequious and accommodating, but secretly is filled
with hate, betray this repressed hatred (here the association "Solomon the Wise speaks").[2]

Dm. is frightened by the openly aggressive manner of the patient
and begins to stink. The patient perceives this as a counterattack, as
being persecuted (persecution mania), and must either run away or
anesthetize herself with alcohol. It is not impossible, that in so doing
she is imitating her father, an alcoholic, who could not stand to be

with her mother. As long as she is manically aggressive, she imitates her mother; however, when she begins to sense Dm.'s hidden aggression, she then begins to play the role of the father. (?) Be that as it may in detail, this much is certain, that those suffering from persecution mania—like certain animals, especially dogs—can smell people's hidden or repressed emotions and tendencies. A further step would lead to an extraordinarily more subtle and more finely gradated qualitative and quantitative sensibility that would enable someone to smell the most delicate emotions and even the psychic content of wishful impulses, that is, the representations of another person. A great deal of what has been regarded up to now as occult, or as a metaphysical superperformance, would thus become explicable in psychophysiological terms. A further and still bolder step would then lead to the performances of spiritualist mediums, who can sense a person's total emanations, as they continue vibrating somewhere in space, even across the limitless passage of the ages. (As a dog might [sense] the footprints of its deceased master.) Spiritualist mediums therefore reconstruct, with the aid of their sense of smell, a person's past. They may, aided by their olfactory imagination, follow a person back into the most distant past, to all the places he stayed in the course of his life.

Why Dm.'s smell should be experienced as the smell of a corpse is a problem in itself. Preliminary attempt at a solution: whenever an emotional reaction is suppressed, interrupted, or repressed, something is actually destroyed in us. The annihilated part of the person falls into a state of decay and decomposes. Should the entire person be prevented from acting, then generalized decomposition ensues, that is to say, death. A link here with the assertion of so many neurotics, in states of trance or dream states, that a greater or lesser part of them is dead, or killed, and is dragged around as a lifeless, that is, nonfunctioning burden. The content of this bundle of repression is in a permanent state of agony, that is, decomposition. Total disintegration (death) is just as impossible for it as coming back to life through the influx of vital energies.

    Nine pin
    Silly servant.[3]

1. This may be a reference to Gustave Jaeger (1832–1917). Although primarily interested in animals (he founded the zoo in Vienna and later lectured on zoology in Stuttgart), Jaeger became a practicing physician in 1884. He believed in the importance of wearing pure wool undergarments; thermal underwear is still referred to in Central Europe as "Jaegers." Among his works is *Normalkleidung als Gesundheitsschutz* [Normal clothing for health protection] (1880).—ED.

2. Perhaps a reference to the judgment of Solomon, which purports to take into account the secret feelings that may exist behind a person's overtly proclaimed sentiments.—ED.

3. Phrases in English in original; this patient's analysis was conducted in English. For the meaning of "nine pin," see pages 90–91.—ED.

26 April 1932

Pornophasia as a condition of genital potency

In fact, a chapter for a possible collection on excessive genital demands in infancy. The colossal superperformance the child imposes on itself has endless consequences. (1) It altogether destroys the feeling of spontaneity, that is to say, the origin of the surplus of pleasure in genital activity. (2) Complete psychic uncertainty about feelings of love; never quite knowing when and to what extent these represent an obligation and the performance of a duty. (3) Extreme general tendency to fatigue, which extends over almost any kind of activity, but manifests itself as a state of deathly sleepiness after each sexual act. (4) This is the place to consider whether the phenomena called neurasthenic fatigue are not the consequence of a self-imposed genital superperformance in regard to psychic or psycho-physical masturbation. (Cite here the case of the young man who was seduced in childhood and (a) felt compelled to satisfy every woman, (b) masturbated four to five times a day and, using immense concentration and the summation of every erotically stimulating situation, contrived to squirt his semen onto the ceiling, some five or six meters above him.) (5) Influence on behavior pattern and character. Persistent tendency to get themselves into extremely dangerous and difficult situations, which are often also morally hazardous, from which they extricate themselves only at the last moment by great effort and with great difficulty. Undertaking tasks requiring a great expenditure of energy and hard work (studies, examinations), putting these things off till the last moment, wasting time on useless things and simultaneously: sense of guilt. (6) Pornophasia a special variety of conditioned potency. The woman must announce that she is a prostitute, she has to confess all her sins, describe them in detail, and if necessary invent some. Thereby the act is degraded from being an authentic sexual union to voyeuristic masturbation. The man's imagination remains caught up with the represented scene; thus the actual genital act is not performed by him, but by a really potent man. He himself has only to watch and masturbate. The obligation placed on the woman to behave like a prostitute makes the task easier; a part of the scene will be really acted out, and does not need to be represented in imagination. In the analytical treatment of such cases one must expect the emergence of a general incapacity of the psycho-physical functions, and naturally also the disappearance of any libido. In actual fact, infantility is restored this way, a state in which normally there is more selfishness and less consideration of others.

What a formidable disruption in development it must be, when emotional demands are made in such excess on a child, who by nature is egoistic. After this almost comatose state of prostration has lasted for a while, often not even very long (patients are capable of falling asleep halfway through a sentence, or very often in the theater), the signs of a really spontaneous libido make themselves felt now and then; later there are expressions of sexuality without fatigue afterward. The exhaustion that follows the manufacture of intellectual feelings and intellectual emotions bears witness to the immense effort required to force intellectual processes back to a hallucinatory level. Normal libido is always in overflow, and the overflowing emotions also affect our sensory apparatus. The maxim *nihil est in intellectu quod prius non fuerit in sensu* is reversed, and replaced here by a "prius" of the intellect. It seems plausible that all types of neurasthenia will be traceable, on closer examination, back to something of this kind. (Here bring in the physiological contrast, which I have stressed, between the impoverishment of the libido in masturbation and the accumulation of libido in coitus interruptus, that is, anxiety neurosis.)

26 April 1932

Contribution to the phallus cult

Dream of patient B., with an almost certain pre-history of infantile-genital violence: she sees a row of soldiers, or gymnasts, all without heads, lined up stiffly; on the left side (shoulder) of each one there is an upright, fleshy appendage sticking up. The association shifts to a bowling alley (ninepins). The single thrusts are signified by individual soldiers; the idea of orgasm, perhaps, by all nine. Simultaneously their headlessness represents pure emotionality, all intellectual control being absent: *L'amour est un taureau acéphale*—Anatole France.[1] But at the same time the patient's psychic state is also represented: it occurs to her that it must be difficult for the ninepins to keep their balance, since they are weighted down unilaterally on their left side. This idea, however, comes from the fact that the patient had drunk a large number of cocktails before going to bed, which had disturbed her balance noticeably. In such a state where one has lost one's head it seems possible that the emotions of others overflow directly onto us, just as if the protective covering of the ego had been dissolved by the narcotic drug. In other words, an inebriated or drugged child (possibly also a child whose self-defense is paralyzed by fright or pain) becomes so sensitive to the emotional impulses of the person it fears that it feels the passion of the aggressor as its own. Thus, fear of the phallus can turn into phallus adoration, or a phallus cult. (Here the problem of female sexual pleasure; originally it may be just anxiety, transformed into pleasure.)

But a problem remains: *can* anxiety be transformed into pleasure at all, even if only after losing one's head and identifying with the *taureau acéphale*. In any case, a quite different solution remains open, which says that not all masochism originates in fear, but also that kindness and self-sacrifice exist as instincts in their own right and are perhaps a natural force, keeping selfish impulses in balance. (S.I.)

Or should the death instinct be posited as an instinct of kindness and self-sacrifice, something maternal-feminine in opposition to the masculine?

Antihomosexuality as a consequence of the masculine "protest"

Conscious, intense antipathy, as for example toward homosexuality, may be a significant obstacle in the treatment of manifest cases. It may well turn out that the resistance against "psychoses" and perversions, which is so widespread (Freud), is due to inadequate analysis in relation to such propensities. Such patients, perhaps, remind us of the cruelest experiences of primordial times, of moments when men had to fight for their psychic sanity and libidinal destiny.

An analyst who has developed an aggressive disposition may play the role of the strong father admirably. Another, who participates in all the patients' emotions, is admirably fitted to be a surrogate mother. A real analyst should have the capacity to play all these roles equally well.

Active therapy was paternal-sadistic, purely passive therapy was maternal. Relaxed, natural behavior, without a preconceived plan, may elicit now the one and then the other characteristic. Only the principal condition remains: the sincere acknowledgment to oneself of actual feelings.

1. Anatole France, pseudonym of Anatole-François Thibault (1844–1924), French man of letters, author of novels, plays, literary critiques, and poetry. Ferenczi knew well, and greatly admired, Anatole France's works. See his article "Anatole France as Analyst" (1911), in *Zentralblatt für Psychoanalyse* I, 461–467. We have been unable to trace the above quotation; possibly Ferenczi was incorrect in attributing it to France.—ED.

1 May 1932

Who is crazy, we or the patients? (the children or the adults?)

Question: Is Freud really convinced, or does he have a compulsion to cling too strongly to theory as a defense against self-analysis, that is, against his own doubts? It should not be forgotten that Freud is not the discoverer of analysis but that he took over something ready-made, from Breuer. Perhaps he followed Breuer merely in a logical, intellectual fashion, and not with any emotional conviction; consequently he only analyzes others but not himself. Projection.

Immense resistance within myself, when, yielding to Orpha's proposal, I tried to allow myself to be analyzed by the patient,[1] that is, to surrender myself completely, to relax, and so to place myself in the patient's power. Anxiety that the patient may well abuse this situation to his own advantage. Being unconscious of his own malicious impulses, the patient to whom such power is given can (1) do everything to free himself of unpleasure, without any concern that it may harm or even destroy the analysand; (2) the patient finds compensatory satisfaction in the sadistic acts for which the analysis provides opportunities.

As a further, somewhat demonomaniacal extension of this chain of thought, the idea comes to mind that the ill will of an insane person can transcend time and space as well, and persecute one even in one's dreams; in other words, he can destroy one demonically: inciting to perilous and unwholesome acts, disturbing the quiet of sleep, destroying any prospect of happiness out of envy, annihilating potency, driving one to suicide, etc., etc.

The patient, when confronted with these open expressions of suspicion, is quite justified in answering: (1) why then should he, the patient, place himself blindly in the power of the doctor? Is it not possible, or even probable, that a doctor who has not been well analyzed (and who *is* well analyzed?) will not cure me, but instead will act out his own neurosis or psychosis at my expense. In confirmation, justifying these elements of suspicion, I must remember some of Freud's remarks he let fall in my presence, obviously relying on my discretion: "Patients are a rabble" ["*Die Patienten sind ein Gesindel*"]. (2) Patients only serve to provide us with a livelihood and material to learn from. We certainly cannot help them. This is therapeutic nihilism, and yet by the concealment of these doubts and the raising of patients' hopes, patients do become caught.

I tend to think that originally Freud really did believe in analysis; he followed Breuer with enthusiasm and worked passionately, devotedly, on the curing of neurotics (if necessary spending hours lying on the floor next to a person in a hysterical crisis). He must have been first shaken and then disenchanted, however, by certain experiences, rather like Breuer when his patient had a relapse and when the problem of countertransference opened up before him like an abyss.

This may well correspond in Freud's case to the discovery that hysterics lie. Since making this discovery Freud no longer loves his patients. He has returned to the love of his well-ordered and cultivated superego (a further proof of this being his antipathy toward and deprecating remarks about psychotics, perverts, and everything in general that is "too abnormal," so even against Indian mythology). Since this shock, this disillusionment, there is much less talk of trauma, the constitution now begins to play the principal role. Of course this involves a certain amount of fatalism. After the psychological wave, Freud has thus landed, first, in the materialism of the natural scientist again. He sees almost nothing in the subjective, except the superstructure of the physical; the physical itself is something much more real. Secondly, he still remains attached to analysis intellectually, but not emotionally. And third, his therapeutic method, like his theory, is becoming more and more [influenced]² by his interest in order, character, the replacement of a bad superego by a better one; he is becoming pedagogical.

The modification of his therapeutic method, becoming more and more impersonal (levitating like some kind of divinity above the poor patient, reduced to the status of a mere child, unsuspecting that a large share of what is described as transference is artificially provoked by this kind of behavior), one postulates that transference is created by the patient.

This may well be true in part, and useful for bringing old material to the surface; yet if the doctor does not watch himself he will remain longer than necessary in this situation, comfortable for him, in which his patients spare him the unpleasure of self-criticism and give him the opportunity to enjoy his superiority, and to be loved without any reciprocity (a situation of almost infantile grandeur), and moreover he even gets paid for it by the patient.

And so the physician can quite unconsciously, and in all conscious innocence, get himself into the situation of a child in relation to his patients. A patient is quite justified in describing part of the behavior of such an analyst as crazy. Certain of the doctor's theories (delusions) may not be challenged; if one does so nevertheless, then one is a bad pupil, one gets a bad grade, one is in a state of resistance.

My "active therapy" was a first, unconscious assault directed against this situation. By exaggerating and exposing this sadistic-educative methodology, I came to realize clearly that it was untenable. As a new theory (new delusion) the theory of relaxation emerged, the complete laissez-faire approach with regard to the patient; the forcible suppression of any naturally human emotional reaction. But patients reject the false sweetness of the inwardly exasperated teacher, just as previously they had rejected the brutality of the "active" analyst, who subjects patients to fiendish torture and then expects to be thanked for it. So finally one begins to wonder whether it would not be natural and also to the purpose to be openly a human being with feelings, empathic at times and frankly exasperated at other times? This means abandoning all "technique" and showing one's true colors just as is demanded of the patient. If one embarks on this course, the patient quite logically will come to suspect that the analysis of the analyst has been incomplete; gradually awakening from his timidity, he may have the courage to point out paranoid or exaggerated features himself; finally it will come to the suggestion of mutual analysis. If one has a certain confidence in one's own ability to be impressed ultimately only by the truth, then one may resolve to risk the sacrifice, seemingly so horrifying, of putting oneself in the care and control of a madman. Quite remarkably, this courage is rewarded; the patient copes more easily with the disappointment of not being loved by us than with endless dependence on a parent (father, mother) who appears to promise everything but inwardly withholds everything.

By a contrast with the present there is thus a better and quicker prospect of sinking back into the traumatic past, and from this a recovery can be expected that will be definitive, spontaneous, and no longer based on authority.

As for the doctor, thus sobered from his scientific delusion, he will have a more beneficial effect in subsequent cases; as a secondary gain he will acquire possibilities for enjoying life that previously were denied to him by neurosis or psychosis.

1. The patient in question is a woman, but in this passage Ferenczi refers to her in the masculine gender. It was in connection with this patient that Ferenczi developed the theme of "Orpha," which represents organizing, vital instincts; here he also appears to be referring to the patient in this sense. See 12 January 1932.—ED.

2. Verb provided by Michael Balint.

3 May 1932

Unconscious struggle of sensitivities between patient and analyst

Occasionally one gets the impression that a part of what we call the transference situation is actually not a spontaneous manifestation of feelings in the patient, but is created by the analytically produced situation, that is, artificially created by the analytic technique. At the very least the interpretation of every detail as expressing a personal affect toward the analyst, which Rank and I perhaps exaggerated, is likely to produce a kind of paranoid atmosphere, which an objective observer could describe as a narcissistic, specifically erotomaniacal delusion of the analyst. It is possible that one is all too inclined to assume too quickly that the patient either is in love with us or hates us.

This appears to be an all too literal repetition of the child-parent relationship; in childhood, too, excessive affects, especially feelings of love, are presumed by adults to exist. The child is constantly exhorted to have such feelings, undoubtedly a curious form of suggestion, that is, a smuggling in of emotions that are not spontaneous and in reality are nonexistent. It may be enormously difficult to get free from such a trap and become one's own self. If the suggestion is effective, the child becomes obedient, that is, it is well content in its dependent state. It may be rather different in cases where a perhaps precociously developed intelligence makes blind submission difficult. Such children become "bad," obstinate, and even "stupid." In the absence of any other defensive weapon, they shut themselves off intellectually from comprehending the things demanded of them. By this means they are able (1) to use their "inability" to protect themselves against the acceptance of rules that appear to them false, senseless, and unpleasant, (2) to get hold of an efficient weapon, moreover an invisible weapon, with which they can take revenge for the injustice committed against them. However much parents and teachers exert themselves to seem friendly when faced with headstrong defiance, the child is aware of the irritated tension mounting in them. Relief from this can be obtained only if he persists in his defiance until the subsequent outburst of hatred from the adults. Even if the scene ends with being scolded or beaten, such an ending provides the child with a sense of relative satisfaction; and this is perhaps at the ultimate root of masochistic pleasure and the fantasy of "a child being beaten."

The parallel to this situation arises, among other things, through the relentless demand (affirmation) for transference feelings and through the interpretation of the absence of them as resistance. The self-confidence with which this is presented by the analyst makes it rather difficult for the patient to contradict him without hurting the doctor's feelings. (Although I remember having always taken care never to be the first to speak about positive transference unless there was a spontaneous manifestation of it, I was all the more generous with my suspicions regarding symptoms of resistance.)

In the mutual analysis in which I have recently been involved, this mechanical, egocentric interpretation of things by the analyst touched me in a highly disagreeable way. I found it positively tedious, and I had to ask the analyst rather to let me finish what I was saying. However, this is the method this patient has learned from me, so perhaps I too have overdone it, as I was also to hear soon enough. The discussion we had on the subject then led me to the supposition that the difficulties, which in part have been artificially created, especially the exaggerated emphasis on the analytic situation against the patient's emotional convictions, make him feel as if he has been coerced into a difficult position by means of suggestion. His dependence on the analyst's friendliness inhibits him in exercising external criticism, and most probably internal criticism as well. One can keep a patient like this for years without making any significant progress, always hoping that something is being "worked through." I hear then from many that the case has bogged down; others in this uncomfortable situation remember that there is such a thing as making an endpoint and expelling the patient from the treatment.

5 May 1932

Case of R.N.

1. The analytic treatment began without any particular sympathy on my part; as a matter of course, as a doctor I approach my patients

with interest, which I consider to be quite sincere. Much later the patient once told me that during the initial interview, and only then, my voice had been much softer and more appealing than ever since. On that occasion I learned that it was this voice that promised her as it were a deep, personal interest and thereby love and blissful happiness. In retrospect, however, what I can make of it is this: the above-mentioned antipathy may be the result of (a) excessive independence and self-assurance, (b) immensely strong willpower as reflected by the marble-like rigidity of her facial features, (c) altogether a somewhat sovereign, majestic superiority of a queen, or even the royal imperiousness of a king—all these are characteristics that one certainly cannot call feminine. Instead of making myself aware of these impressions, I appear to proceed on the principle that as the doctor I must be in a position of superiority in every case. Overcoming my obvious apprehensions when faced with such a woman, I appear to have assumed, perhaps unconsciously, the attitude of superiority of my intrepid masculinity, which the patient took to be genuine, whereas this was a conscious professional pose, partly adopted as a defensive measure against anxiety.

The misunderstanding was clarified, however, during the third or fourth session, when the patient made the observation, in her associations, that I had said I was growing fond of her. This alarmed me considerably; I recalled the many cases of erotomanic hysterics who falsely accused their doctors of having made declarations of love to them. I denied categorically and immediately ever having said anything of the kind, but I did not seem to be able to convince the patient. As I got more deeply involved with the analytic work, however, I developed a keen interest in all the details of her life history, as I usually do. But right from the beginning the patient had claimed to be more important than the other patients, something that had not especially endeared her to me. When the case did not show any progress, I redoubled my efforts; in fact I made up my mind not to be frightened off by any difficulty; gradually I gave in to more and more of the patient's wishes, doubled the number of sessions, going to her house instead of forcing her to come to me; I took her with me on my vacation trips and provided sessions even on Sundays. With the help of such extreme exertions and the help, as it were, of the contrasting effects of relaxation, we arrived at the point where the evidently traumatic infantile history could emerge, in the form of states of trance, or attacks.

We remained at this stage without any further progress for another two years. The most trying of the demands on me arose from the fact that toward the end of the sessions the patient would have an attack, which would oblige me to sit by her for another hour or so, until the attack subsided. My conscience as a doctor and a human being prevented me from leaving her alone and in this helpless condition. But the overexertion appears to have provoked immense tension in me, which at times had rendered the patient hateful to me. It came to a kind of crisis, the consequence of which was that I began to retreat, so to speak.

Without stressing the historical sequence of events, it occurs to me that perhaps the most significant turning point came about as follows: the patient conceived the plan, or reported her conviction, that in the course of the summer, on the dates corresponding to her infantile trauma, according to the calendar, she would repeat and remember the whole event.

A part of the repetition did occur, but each attack ended with the statement: "And still I don't know if the whole thing is true." The analysis of dreams and other analytic work demonstrated clear determination not to acknowledge the awfulness of her life, that is, not to end the splitting of herself into the unconsciously aware and suffering part and the one existing mechanically, without feeling, but still surviving, until such time as reality would offer as compensation a life in which she would be fully loved and appreciated.

The patient had cast me in the role of this perfect lover. As with every fantasy that patients produce, I tried to penetrate into this one as well more deeply, that is, to help these fantasies to unfold. These soon took on a sexual character, which I analyzed, like everything else, with interest and friendliness. However, when she once asked me directly if this really meant that I was in love with her, I said to her quite frankly that this was a purely intellectual process, and that the genital processes of which we were speaking had nothing to do with my wishes. The shock this provoked was indescribable. The whole experience was of course taken back to the past, to her trauma, over and over again, but still the patient would not ever relinquish the transference side.

The above-mentioned crisis forced me, against my sense of duty and probably my sense of guilt as well, to limit my medical superperformances. After a hard inner struggle I left the patient by herself during vacations, reduced the number of sessions, etc. The patient's resistance continued unshaken. There was one point over which we came to be at loggerheads. I maintained firmly that she ought to hate me, because of my wickedness toward her; she resolutely denied this, yet these denials at times were so ferocious that they always betrayed feelings of hatred. For her part she maintained that she sensed feelings of hate in me, and began saying that her analysis would never make any progress unless I allowed her to analyze those hidden feelings in me. I resisted this for approximately a year, but then I decided to make this sacrifice.

To my enormous surprise, I had to concede that the patient was right in many respects. I have retained from my childhood a specific anxiety with regard to strong female figures of her kind. I found and continue to find "sympathetic" those women who idolize me, who submit to my ideas and my peculiarities; women of her type, on the other hand, fill me with terror, and provoke in me the obstinacy and hatred of my childhood years. The emotional superperformance, particularly the exaggerated friendliness, is identical with the feelings of the same kind I had for my mother. When my mother asserted that I was bad, it used to make me, in those days, even worse. She wounded me most by claiming that I was killing her; that was the turning point at which, against my own inner conviction, I forced myself to be good, and obedient.

The patient's demands to be loved corresponded to analogous demands on me by my mother. In actual fact and inwardly, therefore, I did hate the patient, in spite of all the friendliness I displayed; this was what she was aware of, to which she reacted with the same inaccessibility that had finally forced her criminal father to renounce her.

Mutual analysis appears to provide the solution. It gave me an opportunity to vent my antipathy. Curiously, this had a tranquilizing effect on the patient, who felt vindicated; once I had openly admitted the limitations of my capacity, she even began to reduce her demands on me. As a further consequence of this manifest "circulus benignus," I really find her less disagreeable now; I am even capable of transferring friendly and joking feelings onto her. My interest in the details of the analytical material and my ability to deal with them—which previously seemed paralyzed—improved significantly. I must even confess that I am beginning to be aware of the beneficial influence of this liberation from anxiety in relation to other patients as well, and thus I am becoming, not only for this patient but also for the others, altogether a better analyst. (Less sleepiness during sessions, more human interest in all of them; sincerely sensitive intervention in the analytic process when necessary.)

Who should get the credit for this success? Foremost, of course, the patient, who in her precarious situation as patient never ceased fighting for her rights. This would not have been enough, however, had I *myself* not submitted to the unusual sacrifice of risking an experiment in which I the doctor put myself into the hands of a not undangerous patient.

8 May 1932

Schizophrenia-like inner emptiness, overlaid with external hyperactivity, obsessional neurosis, female homosexuality. Sudden improvement after almost two years of being bogged down, obviously due to the influence of the analyst's "being woken up." (O.S.)

The analysis began according to a plan worked out in advance: to leave the homosexuality alone, in the vague hope that it would resolve itself in the course of the analysis, and led by the idea that the analysis cannot begin with a refusal. Complication: her feminine partner she has brought with her wishes to be analyzed; in view of some external problems and at the urgent request of O.S., I agree to devote half of the sessions to the partner. She is a case of sensitivity slightly tainted with paranoia: alternate attacks of excessive goodness and outbursts of hate.

The patient comes from a severely afflicted family; the mother is in an insane asylum. It was established that when the patient was only one and a half years old she spent whole days alone with her demented mother, who engaged in terrifying procedures—we do not know of what kind—in order to protect the child from masturbatory activity. (It can be proven that over the past 150 years the mother's family had many insane members. Grandmother, great-grandmother, etc., all women went mad after giving birth to a child.) One of the mother's brothers, an American millionaire, lived with them; the patient lived with an overanxious German governess in a distant part of the mansion, anxiously protected. Evidently everything was done (1) to protect the patient from any excitement, (2) to keep the idea of insanity away from her. But this unusually intelligent little girl, who felt perfectly healthy, nevertheless appears to have seen through everything; but she was stricken by the fear of going mad herself and consciously accepted the attitude of her environment: (1) she shielded herself from emotions (which she identified with insanity); (2) she fled from conscious anxiety by resorting to phobic protective measures.

At the same time she was terribly bored, could not understand why she was not liked by her contemporaries (obviously because of her excessive rationality she was a spoilsport), and consoled herself with the idea that from the age of eighteen, when she would be an adult, everything would change, everything would be allowed.

In the meantime the family's circumstances were becoming more complicated. The mother divorced the father, who was a drunkard. The mother married a famous doctor, who obviously did not love her and only married her for her money in order to build his great hospital; this he also did. For a while the patient appears to have loved this formidable stepfather; he forced her to be tremendously ambitious, and he nourished her with rigid rules of conduct, which she constantly had to bear in mind; moreover, he was a tyrant who drove her beloved governess and the sick uncle (the two were having an affair) from the house; the latter moved to California and the patient traveled back and forth between New York and California.

At university she fell in love, as soon as she was at all capable of such feelings, with several girls. Boys made no impression on her whatsoever. (Perhaps because of her fear of childbearing that would lead to madness.) On a trip to Europe she met a frivolous foreigner, who deflowered her. On her return home she realizes to her horror that she is pregnant. In a state of tremendous anxiety she turns to her stepfather, who reacts as follows: he persuades her that an artificially induced abortion is impossible, she must marry someone, without telling him she is pregnant. An old admirer, a wealthy young man of the same social background, is delighted to have her. She believes, however, that the stepfather and the bridegroom are only letting her get married for the sake of appearances, and that he will give her a divorce immediately after the operation. The two men, however, hope that she will become reconciled to the marriage. This does not happen; she finds herself in a pressured situation [*Zwangslage*], she feels guilty because of her silence and is sorry for her husband. But she cannot really love him, partly for neurotic reasons. Thus she falls in love with women and sets out on expeditions to explore Brazil with her husband and her female lover. In the meantime the stepfather becomes fatally ill and throws himself out of the window of his own hospital. The patient enters analysis with an American doctor, who helps her to some extent but ends up by moralizing and trying to persuade the patient that she should adjust to the marriage. She tried for years to come to me, but I could accept her only after a three-year waiting period.

Patient struggles with complete lack of affect, without any visible success, but her woman partner, who makes more rapid progress, starts to help me in the analysis. A few days ago she came, having relinquished all the former feigned manifestations of hyperactivity, with a feeling of absolute inner emptiness. Thus, an apparent deterioration, which I however view as an uncovering of the actual state of affairs, and thus as progress. At this critical moment my "having (or having been) woken up" then appears to have intervened. I felt that this inner emptiness was actually a desire for immense compassion instead of the indifference one customarily feels toward such persons who lack affect or who are profoundly deranged or alienated. The patient herself declares that she is not worth any consideration, she must appear repellent, etc. Pulling myself together, I tried to convince her of the exact opposite and to make her understand that it would be most unjust in addition to everything to spurn such an unfortunate and defeated being, and that in the name of an unjust humanity I should offer more love and interest to her than I would to people who were happy. She did not appear to be moved by this, but the very same night her friend happened to notice that the patient was masturbating in her sleep. In the morning she knew nothing about it, and urgently begged her friend not to tell me about it; naturally, however, she did not promise this.

Perhaps under the influence of the sympathy she expected from me, she now found the courage—overcoming all her infantile timidity and inhibitions—to admit to a passion. It will perhaps be a less difficult task now to reunite the split-off part of the person, affectivity, with the rest of her personality.

10 May 1932

Traumatic self-strangulation

One of the cases where the patient is beset by nightly breathing difficulties. Occasionally she awakens and continues to hear her own rasping as though it were that of some other person, then she suddenly wakes with a start, full of anxiety. Periodically her relaxation exercises during analysis have given rise to similar states, which I was able to observe: extremely shallow breathing, deathly pallor of the skin, quiet, barely audible voice, scarcely perceptible pulse. These symptoms were connected with fantasies about some incidents of unscrupulous caresses perpetrated by an adult male, probably her father. At the same time total inability, or impossibility not only (a) to tell someone about the trauma, but even (b) to have any certain knowledge about it. In the wake of a "psychoanalytic confession" (the disclosure of my never-before-expressed dislike of a homosexual relationship, perhaps accompanied simultaneously by a trace, on my part, of male and medical jealousy), a feeling of colossal triumph and self-assurance never experienced before: So I was right after all!

This analytic experience enabled the patient to reach a much more secure conviction of the reality of the event: this in turn enabled her to tell her brother about it (remarkably, it was the brother who just at this point approached her with a question about their father's character) and to obtain from him confirmations of it. That same night, a nightmare of unprecedented length and intensity, and this time completely undistorted: as a little girl, she feels herself assaulted sexually by a giant; the weight of the enormous body crushing her chest; then follow an endless series of terribly painful genital attacks, which for a time she attempts to withstand by means of an extremely violent contraction of all her muscles. But suddenly her willpower gives way, and at the same moment complete numbness sets in with regard to her own self, but without her losing any awareness of the whole scene; on the contrary, she now sees the whole event as though from the outside; she sees a dead child being abused in the manner just described. With the state of "being dead" even pity, quite remarkably (and of course fear, rescue attempts, etc.), ceases completely; instead, interest, even feeling, and complete understanding are now diverted to the aggressor. She finds it self-evident that the accumulation of tensions in the attacker had to be discharged in the way described.

In the meantime the complete relaxation of muscles had set in, whereupon breathing and circulation, previously completely suppressed, could be restored again: the patient woke up partially, but was still able to experience the final few seconds of the rasping and the sensation of being dead as a dream. After complete awakening, the memory of the repetition of the trauma was exceptionally preserved. Previously, on similar occasions (see the dream about the ninepin soldiers), the memory either was lacking completely or was distorted to the point of being unrecognizable so that it could only be reconstructed analytically. The patient had the feeling that only her increased confidence in herself and in me had made it possible for her to sink so deeply into a repetition.

Theoretically the following may be assumed: at moments of complete exhaustion in the muscle tone (generalized epileptiform convulsions, opisthotonos) all hope of outside help or alleviation of the trauma is abandoned. Death, which is already there, so to speak, is no longer feared; obviously all moral and other scruples vanish as well, in view of the inevitable end; the individual gives up all expectations of outside help, and a last, desperate attempt to adapt, perhaps analogous to the feigning of death in animals, occurs. The person splits into a psychic being of pure knowledge that observes the events from the outside, and a totally insensitive body. Insofar as this psychic being is still accessible to emotions, it turns its interests toward the only feelings left over from the process, that is, the feelings of the attacker. It is as though the psyche, whose sole function is to reduce emotional tensions and to avoid pain, at the moment of the death of its own person automatically diverts its pain-relieving functions toward the pains, tensions, and passions of the attacker, the only person with feelings, that is, identifies itself with these.

The disappearance of one's own person, while others are still present in the scene, would thus be at the deepest root of masochism (otherwise so puzzling), of self-sacrifice for other people, animals, or things, or of the identification with outside tensions and pains that is nonsensical from a psychological or an egoistic point of view. If this is so, then no masochistic action or emotional impulse of the sort is possible without the temporary dying of one's own person. So I do not feel the pain inflicted upon me at all, because I do not exist. On the other hand I do feel the pleasure-gratification of the attacker, which I am still able to perceive. The fundamental thesis of all psychology, that the sole function of the psyche is to reduce pain, is therefore preserved. The pain-alleviating function must, however, be able to apply itself not only to one's own ego but also to every kind of pain perceived or imagined by the psyche. Considered from another point of view, that of the undying instinct for self-preservation, the same process would have to be described as follows: if all hope of help from a third person is abandoned, and if one feels that all one's own powers of self-defense have been completely exhausted, then all one has to fall back on is hope for mercy from the attacker. If I submit to his will so completely that I cease to exist, thus if I do not oppose him, then perhaps he will spare my life; at least if I abstain from offering any resistance, I have a bit more hope that the attack will be less devastating. A completely limp body will sustain less damage from the thrust of a dagger than one that is defending itself. If the body is as though dead, with the muscles slack and virtually without any circulation, then a stab wound will draw less blood, or perhaps none at all (performance of fakirs).

This mode of explanation presupposes, however, that at moments of extreme danger it is possible for the intelligence to detach itself from the ego, and even perhaps from all affects, which hitherto had served the purpose of self-preservation (fear, anxiety). In view of the general ineffectiveness of the affects, suspended from action and transformed into an intelligence free of affect, which encompasses a much wider sphere of action. At moments of dire need a guardian angel emerges within us, as it were, who is able to make use of our physical strength to a far greater extent than we would be able to under normal circumstances. The almost acrobatic feats performed when in extreme danger are well known (my own fall in the mountains; managing to grab the one slightly projecting rock above an abyss, and then having to spend the night sitting on this rock). This "guardian angel" is shaped from parts of one's own psychic personality, probably consisting of parts of the affect of self-preservation. Hence the lack of feeling while it is present. The absent external help, therefore, is replaced by the creation of a more ancient substitute. Of course, not without modification of the previous personality. In the most extreme cases of this kind, retreat from the patient's own self was so complete that even the memory of the entire incident is lost. A certain influence on the character of a person who has been through an experience of this kind nevertheless remains; our patient, for example, has displayed, since the almost certainly established trauma, a stubborn, uncommunicative disposition, trusting in fact no one but herself, an attitude she now triumphantly vindicates in the analysis. In psychoanalytical jargon I would speak here of a case of narcissistic splitting of the self.

Someone who thinks along purely physiological lines may, however, explain the incident in the following way: In a moment of intense fright—or an attack of pain—the patient responds by summoning all his psycho-physical resources in a tremendous effort. This causes him to hold his breath, and makes increased demands on the heart. If the pain attack continues, circulatory disturbances set in, leading to trophic disturbances in the brain and eventually also in the medulla oblongata. Heart and respiratory centers become paralyzed, consciousness vanishes. Whereupon complete muscular atonia occurs, demands on heart functions diminish, cerebral functions revive, mostly without total recall of what has happened. In all similar cases patients spoke about violent headaches in the nape of the neck immediately before the loss of sensation: such pains often occur during the process of repetition. The compulsion of two patients to smoke incessantly was also a kind of flirtation with self-strangulation.

12 May 1932

Compulsion to repeat the trauma

1. After uncovering and reconstructing the presumed trauma, an almost endless series of repetitions follows during the analytical sessions, accompanied by every imaginable kind of affective outburst. Psychoanalytical expectations until now allowed us to hope that with each such outburst a certain quantity of the blocked affect will be lived through emotionally and muscularly, and that when the entire quantity is exhausted the symptom will disappear of its own accord. Accordingly the analyst's aim has been to discover and eliminate all tendencies toward flight and evasion in the patient, in order to force him through the one remaining passage: that of the trauma. Thus the conscious living-through-to-the-end, and therewith the progressively unnecessary neurotic substitute formations disappear of themselves. But in reality, as one gains experience one encounters more and more disappointments in this respect. Though the affective outbursts do bring momentary relief from tension, it often lasts only a few hours, not unlike the periods of calm that follow hysterical or epileptic convulsions. Usually, however, the very next night will bring another anxiety dream and, consequently, material for the repetition of the trauma in the next session. And one cannot claim that these repetitions, no matter how often they recur, provide substantially new material. On the contrary, they appear to become a somewhat tedious rehashing of one or the other traumatogenic moment.

In the case of R.N. the attack would intensify until it reached an unbearable climax, and the patient would passionately plead for help, often shrieking, "Take it away, take it away!" The appeal is obviously addressed to me, but causes me the greatest embarrassment, since I have no idea of how I can help to relieve her state of suffering. Sometimes I concur with her wishes and assert, so to speak, suggestively: "Yes, now I am taking the pain away." Sometimes a "bit of intelligence" in the patient remains in contact with me even during the repetition of the trauma, giving me wise guidance as to how to handle the situation. In this manner I was advised to make sure, before I left, that the pain would remain separated from the rest of the psyche. The painful part of the psyche is represented in this instance materially, as a substance, and I am required to surround this matter with a strong, impenetrable covering, or to prevent the rest of the psyche, which is located in the head, from collapsing, by erecting suitably placed, solid, supporting beams. Furthermore it is asked of me that even when I go away I leave a part of myself with, or in, the patient as a guardian spirit.

Quite frankly I was embarrassed for a very long time to get involved with suggestive machinations of this kind, since I was so far from believing in the reality of these strange mental images. But frequently I could not bring the attacks to an end without reciting word for word, somewhat ashamed, whatever the patient insisted upon. When I uttered these very words, exactly and word for word as requested, they would often work wonders. But the effect did not last long: the next day I would have to listen again to her account of a nightmare, etc., and also of symptoms in the course of the day; and so it went on, often for months, without anything changing in the least. It required a good deal of optimism to proceed patiently despite all this; but the patience that I thus required of the patient was no less significant.

The violent attacks used to end with a feeling of being dead, in total relaxation. The patient felt as if she had been torn to pieces, or more correctly, she succeeded in tearing herself loose from the remaining parts of her person. The psyche felt itself at an infinite distance, or at a colossal height; but being torn away from reality like this enabled it to see everything that was going on in or around the person. In this clairvoyant state she now told me (1) that my essential task consisted of putting my mental powers at the disposal of the split-off psyche, which after having been torn loose is wandering about uncomprehendingly at a distance—not by offering explanations, but by stimulating it to activity by asking the appropriate questions. The questions I must put to the split-off psyche must be couched in the simplest possible terms, which even a child that had been found half-dead should be able to answer; questions about the feelings that had been expressed, where they came from, who or what caused them, etc., were expected from me and were to be clearly answered. Yet as long as I myself doubted the reality of the events and only mechanically repeated what was being required of me, the questioning did not meet with any real success; dissatisfaction and reproaches regarding my inadequacy persisted.

In fact there were two things demanded of me, without which no change in the repetition would be granted: (1) Total sincerity regarding existing feelings of unpleasure in the analyst, mutual analytical elucidation of the obstacles in me, of the obstacles to libido-transference in reverse. (2) Following the elimination of this difficulty, the paralysis of intellectual comprehension vanished and the correct questions, sustained by inner conviction, came to me as if of their own accord.

What is fundamentally significant in all this is the fact that an abreaction of quantities of the trauma is not enough; the situation must be different from the actually traumatic one in order to make possible a different, favorable outcome. The most essential aspect of the altered repetition is the relinquishing of one's own rigid authority and the hostility hidden in it. The relief that is obtained thereby is then not transient, and the convictions derived in this way are also more deeply rooted.

2. The case S.I. (a "case" of deeper repression, or for the first time a conscious experiencing-to-the-end?)

17 May 1932

Heterosexual trauma, flight into (female) homosexuality

1. Patient Ett. returned home at her own wish, relatively recovered, after about a year and a half of analysis. Term suggested by herself, but subsequently also agreed to by me. (Relationship to her husband unsatisfactory owing to latter's physical, but not sexual, disability). Came to me for control analysis in America. It turned out later that she knew all along, as a result of an indiscretion, about my sympathy for another woman patient. Perhaps out of revenge for all this, she arranged things as follows: she became reconciled with her husband after he confessed his infidelity. In addition she fell in love with a married man, who will not divorce his wife. Finally she fell in love with a very attractive girl and from then on divided her libido among all of them. Not until two years later did she reveal her dissatisfaction with me, by developing an intellectual transference for a colleague in America.

2. This same young girl comes to me for analysis, constantly reiterating her fidelity to her friend, the woman mentioned above.

After a frank discussion about my dissatisfaction, her self-confidence suddenly increases; she feels certain that she can, whenever she wants to, seduce any person, male or female. And for a while she in fact does indulge herself in this pleasure, though not without guilt feelings. She regards herself as a public menace because of her skill in seduction; she gets the impression that I, too, am becoming libidinally dependent on her. The pleasure she takes in herself and the world at large often causes persistent genital sensations, a kind of prolonged orgasm.

Fragments from a frequent dream: following prolonged pleasure of the kind just described, and a successful seduction scene with Mr. Th., masturbation, whereupon she suddenly falls asleep and wakes an hour later from a frightful nightmare, utterly confused and disoriented. She has to convince herself by various stratagems, *that it is actually she* who is there, where she is; she has the impression that she has been suffering for an endlessly long time, and is amazed at the brevity of the period of sleep. The dream is roughly as follows: she is lying on the slightly sloping concrete floor of the subway in a mass of slime, in constant danger of sliding between the rails. Her right leg is paralyzed. She hangs on with one finger in a hole; another woman pins her down with her own weight; she is also slipping downward in the same dangerous manner. The patient gets this woman off by sticking the woman's fingers, which had been gripping her convulsively, into the same hole. Finally, however, even so, her own strength gives way and she falls onto the rails, that is, she loses consciousness. Then she sees herself struggling away from the railway track, following a complicated path toward a house, where she is kindly invited in by an elderly gentleman (from the balcony). On the way she feels dreadfully ill, she is aware of a terrible nausea, she falls down, grabs a valuable vase as a receptacle, and vomits continuously like a fountain, finally even on the floor, until everything is awash. The fluid has a strange taste and there are seeds in it. She comes to from this second fit of fainting, as described above. On the way to the place where she vomited, there are people who accuse her unjustly. As she is walking, her right leg becomes twice its size, and she has to walk with flexed knees in order to be able to walk at all.

Leaving aside the rest of the content of this manifestly traumatic dream, I focus on her being pinned down by another woman and her extraordinary way of freeing herself. Probably this means that she not only had to endure the trauma but also had to preserve artistically the tranquil life of her mother by keeping it a secret. A second interpretation points toward mutual masturbation; she trains her mother, with whom she associated herself sexually in a compulsive manner (hence the relationship with Ett.), to gratify herself. It is only when she probes beyond the homosexuality that she arrives at real events, that is, the heterosexual trauma, which left her with an enormous yearning for enormous physical satisfaction. Should the analysis succeed in overcoming her anxiety and shame at this immense eroticism, then she will totally renounce her homosexuality (out of regard for her mother). There remains only one problem: what is to happen in reality to the prematurely awakened libido.

19 May 1932

On the constituent factors of the sense of guilt

Two patients: one of them allows himself to analyze the other, a woman, for the fun of it. She soon discovers resistances in the analyst, and suggests mutual analysis, which unexpectedly leads to the discovery of the following situation: the woman "patient" was unable to put any trust in this man; it was not known why; he had clearly been extraordinarily good to her, yet in money matters he had been inconsistent. (1) Toward a man he was excessively generous, (2) toward the patient less so. (3) He remembered once having failed a woman whose life was in great danger. These memories led to the discovery of homosexual tendencies, or at least the predominance of libidinal fixation on men. His hatred of his mother in his childhood had almost led to matricide. At the dramatic moment in the reproduction of this scene he, so to speak, violently throws the knife away from himself and becomes "good." The "woman analyst" discovers from this that in order to save his mother the "patient" has castrated himself. Even his relationship to men (father) is in fact compensation for a still more deeply repressed murderous rage. The entire libido of this man appears to have been transformed into hatred, the eradication of which, in actual fact, means self-annihilation. In his relationship to his friend the woman "analyst," the origin of guilt feelings and self-destructiveness could be recognized *in statu nascendi*.

An interesting contrast is offered by two other cases, in which the feeling of guilt suddenly vanished, as if by magic. (1) S.I., a head injury, the end of her self-torment, independence (also from analysis, in part), after *I* had left her alone in a state of life-threatening unconsciousness; so that she could only choose between suicide and recovery. (2) Case B.: after I admitted my own lack of frankness, sudden awakening of trust in me: I acquired the power to inflict pain on her, and that increased her self-esteem. She also saw me as strong enough to let her die, if necessary. (Analogy to my experiments with epileptics.)[1]

1. See "On Epileptic Fits: Observations and Reflections," *Fin* 197–204.—ED.

29 May 1932

140a *Self-lessness (minus ego)* [Selbst-losigkeit (− Ich)][1]

Repression of the self, annihilation of the self, is the precondition for objective perception. What is the motivation for such selflessness: really only the experience that, through it, the self will be helped in another, better way. I disappear for a moment, I do not exist, instead things outside of me exist.

The original wish is: *nothing* should exist that disturbs me, nothing should stand in my way. But certain wicked things will not obey me and force themselves into my consciousness. So: there are *other* wills besides my own. But why does a sort of *photograph* of this external body appear in me as soon as, aware of my weakness, I vanish by withdrawing? (Why does the horror-struck person in his anxiety imitate the features of the horrifying thing?) The *memory mask* develops, perhaps always at the cost of the temporary or permanent dying away of a part of the ego. Originally an effect of the shock. *Imitation magic?*

Memory is thus a collection of *scars of shocks* in the ego. Fear dissolves the rigidity of the ego (resistance) so completely that the material of the ego becomes as though capable of being molded 140b *photochemically*—is in fact always molded—by external stimuli. Instead of my asserting *myself,* the external world (an alien will) asserts itself at my expense; it forces itself upon me and *represses the ego.* (Is this the primal form of "repression"?)

Complete restitution would therefore be possible only at the level of complete *unconsciousness,* that is to say: with a return to that which is still unconscious (an as yet undisturbed state of the ego).

A scientific way to discover the truth

A discovery of this kind sometimes follows immediately upon the sudden realization of a common error or false belief, until now accepted. I believed Mrs. F. too literally; suddenly I am aware how wrong I was to do so.

The prerequisite was insight into the selfishness appearing in the form of guilt. (1) When I want something, she does not. (2) That is a police matter.

Scrupulousness compels me to tell her everything nonetheless, and not to let myself be influenced *in a one-sided manner* by R.N. In the end even she is malicious.

Or am *I* suffering from persecution mania?

I bowed to the woman   Imitated her?
                         (Obedience, submission)
                         Should I become independent of her
                         (Lose the women's love!)

140c *Consistent neglect of the ego in thinking (abstraction)*

I think: the dog is barking
In reality: I see—the dog ⎱   simultaneously and from the
            I hear—barking ⎰   *same direction.*

Thereupon I neglect the subjective element and feel justified in regarding (recognizing) "dog" and "is barking" as "really" existing, even without my subjective evidence.

If two sensory impressions reach us from one and the same point (direction), we accept the existence of a thing outside us at the point of intersection of the two lines of incidence of the sensory stimuli. If this is confirmed by other sensory stimuli, the certainty of its existence (reality) in the external world is heightened.

The interrelating of two simultaneous stimuli is an act of thought. It is possible that abstraction from the ego, that is, the annihilation of self-interest (pleasure-unpleasure quality), is required if we are to have the energy necessary for thinking (relating one thing to another).

140d [This passage has been lost.]

1. English title of this entry proposed by Michael Balint.

140e 1 June 1932

Speech

To speak is to imitate. Gesture and speech (voice) imitate objects of the external world. "*Ma-ma*" is imitation magic. (Mother's breast.) The first "*Ma-ma*" when mother's breast is withheld. (Child's first play, quoted by Freud.) *Fear of being alone* produces traumatic "photo-hyperesthesia" (sensitivity to light and sound); chemotropic change in structure, in which self-assertion is relinquished to some extent (perhaps only temporarily) and the external world is able to shape the ego. But a part of the ego remains undestroyed, indeed, it seeks to profit from this demolition (scars). The traumatic *mimicry impressions* are utilized as memory-traces, useful to the ego: "dog" = bowwow, bowwow. When I am frightened of a dog, I become a dog. After such an experience, the ego consists of the (undisturbed) subject and the part that has become the object through the influence of the trauma = memory-traces = permanent imitation (speech is telling the story of the trauma).

Ego = remains of ego + memory-traces. On a higher level: remains of ego + memory-traces + *becoming conscious* by means of reproduction (gesture, speech).

140f 1 June 1932

What does "becoming conscious" mean?

Becoming aware of being torn apart into ego and *environment* (dog). The part of inner experience that can be represented in gesture and speech is separated from one's own ego, as external world. Simultaneously I become *conscious of myself:* conscious of the existence of an *external world.*

Actually it may be that no reproduction is necessary here—the *photochemistry of the retina imitates pictorially* the external world (or the external world *takes possession of* the specifically traumatophilic substance of the retina). This picture of the external world, which is forced upon the organism (and the primal form of which is contained in the sensitivity of the skin) is used for orientation in space. In this way *what remains of the ego* acknowledges the rule of the *reality principle.* Sleep is regression to a primal unity, as yet unsplit. (Without consciousness and, when completely *without objects,* dreamless.) Regression to the pretraumatic.

140g 3 June 1932

Theoretical consequences for libido-theory and neurosis-theory

Symptomatology of infantile sexuality must be differentiated more precisely than before into (a) spontaneous and (b) provoked excitation. If (b) is subtracted then the desire for *tenderness* without reciprocity remains. This is neither a response nor narcissism, but *passive object love. Being loved as an object, without loving in return.* To be orgasmically satisfied appears to be a successful reproduction of this state. *Not to be torn apart into ego and world.* (Consciousness is superfluous, struggle unnecessary.)

Regression to the time prior to the first anxiety

    1. Infantility (babyhood)
    2. Intrauterine!

How much of $\left\{\begin{array}{l}\text{oral eroticism}\\\text{anal eroticism}\\\text{measure of sight}\end{array}\right.$ is spontaneous, and how much already *neurotically regressive,* elicited by culture (upbringing)! *Displaced*! Less prohibited! Anal difficulty at least *discussed, recognized* as existing. Therefore a suitable sphere for the displacement of *genital interests.*

(a) Genital prohibitions and (b) genital exaggerations become genitofugal. (c) Obedience in showing love *more intensely* than it is felt. As intensely as it is *expected to be,* not as *it is.* (Be what you are, do not force feelings.) (d) Feeling of guilt, because of insincerity (because of showing more love). Therapy: to tolerate (a), (b), and (c) *without feeling of guilt.* Guilt is assigned to the adults. (Adults should know that they cannot count on the child's gratitude.)

(e) Is gratitude entirely lost? No, a trace of it may be natural as well. But much less than is usually expected.

(f) Finally: abandonment of *narcissistic splitting of the self.* ("One is one's own mother, in fact the mother of the mother.") Capacity for guiltless enjoyment. (g) Adjustment to reality through one's own experience, not $\left\{\begin{array}{l}\text{untimely}\\\text{imposed.}\end{array}\right.$

    1. Insight into limitations
    2. Capacity for happiness (of being loved)

Problems: Why is homosexuality $\left\{\begin{array}{l}\text{masculine}\\\text{feminine}\end{array}\right\}$ preferred?
(No battle of the sexes, but nobody says *yes*!)

3 June 1932

No special training analysis!

1. Analysts should be analyzed *better, not* worse, than patients.
2. At present they are analyzed worse.
    a. time limit
    b. no relaxation (patients' expression)
3. If six to eight years required, impossible in practice. But should be corrected by repeated supplementary analyses. But even so, not quite satisfactory.
4. A special group of truly analyzed persons—who have the ambition to know more than analyzed patients.
5. Mutual analysis: only a last resort! Proper analysis by a stranger, without any obligation, would be better.
6. The best analyst is a patient who has been cured. Other pupils must be first made ill, then cured and made aware.
7. Doubts about *supervised analyses:* last resorts: recognition and admission of one's own difficulties and weaknesses. Strictly supervised by the patients! No attempts to defend oneself.

3 June 1932

(Dm.) Ways of being passionate. Concluded.

Symptom: *Buying* oneself *peace* and *friendliness* by excessive expenditure of tenderness and presents of money. Fear that without these one will remain alone. Better to give away everything. *Behind this:* outbursts of rage if the *most exaggerated* expectation of pleasure without reciprocity is not fulfilled by every object, every person. First impulse: to destroy the unaccommodating *world!* Then becoming aware of *anxiety, obedience exaggerated,* solely in order to escape the anxiety.

Is not anxiety therefore in the last analysis a feeling of the power of the death drive, a beginning of *death* (starvation)?

Dm. (1) was born with teeth, the same as her brother, that is, with the strongest aggressive tendencies.

(2) Breast refused. Bottle.

When she asserted herself: mother like ice.

(1) Indifference, (2) aggression, (3) excessive tenderness: all three have a regressive effect on the child. The child senses, correctly, the

aggressive element even in exaggerated libidinal passion. (Transient symptom on this point: she feels smothered.)

3 June 1932

Passion

Catatonia, highly ironic *flexibilitas cerea* [waxen flexibility].[1]

Exaggeration of obedience (Mrs. Smith). Perhaps REAL fear of WISH TO KILL. Which is primary: aggressiveness, or regression to self-destruction? (F. A portion of the ego must be preserved from destruction, and THIS commands obedience. *Intelligence* is *insight* into the necessity to obey—otherwise kill or be killed.)

THERAPY: The patient must once have the opportunity *to be all ego,* before his ego is reconstructed on the basis of *his own insight.* (Upbringing corrected, replaced by self-education through experience.) Analysis must make possible for the patient, morally and physically, the *utmost regression,* without shame! Only then will the patient, after he (or she) has enjoyed for a while *taking everything for nothing* without scruples of conscience, be able to adapt to the facts; even to tolerate maternally (without expecting anything in return) the sufferings of others (goodness).

1. See "Psycho-Analytical Observations on Tic," FC 163.

3 June 1932

(Dm.) There is no goodness where gratitude is expected. One should have received kindness as a child, and so much of it that one can pass some of it on (to the next generation). (Mention Dm!)

Obedient children of passionate parents have to be cleverer than their parents, play a maternal role.

(My own experience: mother in a rage.)

Passion: incestuous relation: for the child it is only aggression.

(B.) Icy coldness—sensed in Mrs. E. Her own feelings: (1) *Compulsion* to soften that coldness by means of exaggerated amiability. (2) Behind this the feeling: (a) I do not love her, I do not love anyone (friendly toward everybody). Obviously I expect to be loved by everybody. (b) Anger because this does not happen. Aggressiveness provoked and intensified to the point of wanting to kill. (c) Fear of being alone, of not being loved. The condition of being loved must be attained, in any circumstances. (d) This happens in an exaggerated way.

9 June 1932

Psychosoma

R.N.: When pain or some other sensation becomes "unbearable" (that is, when the organism's powers of anticathexis and emotional sources of expression have been exhausted): *muscle contraction* (a) exhausted (b) too painful (c) suspends breathing; heart is paralyzed (shortage of oxygen)—the bladder and bowels emptied—it seems that it is still possible for life to continue with the aid of purely psychical powers. Expressed in psychiatric terms: *the hallucination* of breathing can maintain life, even when there is total somatic suffocation. The hallucination of muscles and muscular power, cardiac strength, evacuation of the bladder, vomiting, accompanying the complete paralysis of these organs, can delay the disintegration of the organism. The patients feel, however, that in a "teleplastic" fashion, up to now perhaps believed in only by spiritualists, real organs, receptacles, gripping tools, tools of aggression are produced as ad hoc organs, which take charge of a greater or lesser part of the organism's functions, while the organism is lying lifeless in a deep coma. Discharge of these functions occurs then extrasomatically. For instance a large bladder (which will occasionally be further dilated) forms at the back of the head, into which all unpleasure affects that cannot be dealt with are *poured* and neutralized in an imaginary fashion. But the patients think that this imagination is just as real and can perform organ functions just as efficiently and effectively as the organism itself. From substances as yet unknown and with the help of unknown powers (in greatest need), when the organism's own powers are quite exhausted: *new organs are formed* (Lamarck). In contrast to our previous assumptions, such organs can, however, develop not gradually but all of a sudden (like the organs of unicellular organisms).

10 June 1932

The duty to remain silent. The feelings of responsibility in small children after the adults have committed an offense against them

B.: Father so miserable after the deed that the threat of suicide (though unexpressed) is quite real. The child's reaction: unspoken promise not to let on (otherwise the family would fall apart, especially mother's status, love, entire existence). (In order to ensure silence, also *internal silence:* forgetting, repression.)—Yet what are the consequences?

1. Mother nevertheless feels (unconsciously): (a) That father is unfaithful; therefore hates (unconsciously) the child as a rival, or becomes very capricious: attacks of excessive hatred, then excessive love. (Much self-deception.) (b) That the child's character is not forthright: she *scolds* her, punishes her: the child now feels that she is being punished *for being* so intimate with her father's family.

2. Consequences for the child: attacks of neurosis—psychosis—outbursts of rage—masochistic obedience—failure at school, and in life. (Eventually on occasion looking for a mother homosexually.)

3. Father has the compulsion to test the child's loyalty by his more and more impossible behavior (Griselda):[1] "Nothing can happen to me" (whatever I might do) is the result of successful gangsterism.

1. According to the *Encyclopaedia Britannica,* Griselda is a heroine of romance and is said to have been the wife of the Marquis of Saluces or Saluzzo in the eleventh century. According to Larousse dictionary, she is the heroine of a touching legend. Supposedly she was a shepherdess who enchanted the Marquis de Saluces with her beauty. He married her; then, to test her fidelity, he subjected her to severe sufferings. But she bore them all with angelic patience, and thus has become a symbol of conjugal virtue.—ED.

12 June 1932

Doctor hating patients[1]

Freud: "rabble," "only any good for making money out of, and for studying." (Is true, but must be admitted to the patients.) They feel it in any case and produce resistance. (When it is admitted—trust increases.) *Patients scolding:* buzzing flies, monotonous noise—mother's, father's scolding and our helpless fury. "*Bear hug*"—children feel the possessive-aggressive element in it and do not dare to show their *fear, anxiety*—and fury. They displace the reaction to minor things (sensitiveness about the slightest intrusion in their right—free-dom). Outlet also in way of *imitating mother*—reflecting this way—*like a mirror* the affect (aggression—tension) on others. Mostly in a hidden way (letting fall an infuriating remark—later quite uncon-scious) but this makes one unpopular. No sense of humor—fury. Choosing medicine as job (conscious compensation of misanthropy). First motive: birth of a new child—seems like intrusion into a *right*. You were (before) treated, as it were *for ever*. *Fear of the eyes* (wide open: they eat you up!). Hating mother's *smell* and *saliva* (after the disappointment).

1. Most of this entry was written in English.

12 June 1932

1400 *Confusion about one's own person, with a feeling of panic (and subsequent loss of memory).*

1. R.N.: Father, after having seduced her, etc., punishes and reviles her. Incomprehensible (as reality). Dream about a suitcase, into which have been forced more mattress springs than it can hold. It *breaks apart*—into pieces (shatters [*Zerspringt*]).

2. R.N.: Treated appallingly by drunken father, then left all alone; later repeated. (Humiliation after seduction.) (Hate of woman!) Dream: downstairs "tea." She is lying in the corridor, with her head empty, feels her way to the door, 17, 18, then 19, with a great effort—*no light*. Realizes that this is not her room. (This cannot be her; each time she loses consciousness.) In the (middle) room (18) she sees . . .[1]

1. The rest of this entry is missing.

12 June 1932

Technique: error (emotion instead of objectivity): (1) commit, (2) confess, (3) correct

Typical sequence of events with B. with regard to transference: dissatisfaction increases from session to session, impatience that symptoms do not disappear, that we are unable to help. One feels the unfairness of the reproach, but tries to conceal this; at best one becomes laconic and feels irritated. After a certain acme, when either my patience or that of the patient is about to snap, she arrives suddenly quite acquiescent, friendly, and obedient, and works quite hard for a while, only to repeat the threat of explosion after a certain period of work.

A more radical change did not come about until the analyst recognized this fact: insight of the analyst, that the patients have only one duty, namely to say everything, however unpleasant it may be for us; to take this personally is senseless, and the reason for doing so may well lie in some particular trait of our own character. The patient makes use of our sensitivity to repeat a past injury. They try for this reason to put us to the test. As long as we keep failing this test, we will get no further than the continued repetition of the infantile repression: apparent obedience, inner defiance. Since it is humanly impossible not to get irritated, and since patients sense even the silent manifestation of irritation, there is no choice but to confess to the irritation while admitting its injustice, and to treat the patient, even if he behaves in a disagreeable way, with kindness and affection. The child demands more or less the same thing: parents should not assume the pose of loving protectors when inwardly they are almost bursting with rage; the child responds not to the friendly words but to the behavior, that is: voice, gestures, rough handling, etc. The analyst must be an authority that for the first time admits its faults, especially hypocrisy. The child can deal much better with rough but honest treatment than with so-called pedagogical objectivity and detachment that, however, conceals impatience and hatred. This is one of the causes of masochism; one prefers being beaten to feeling simulated calm and objectivity. Another fault, which must be recognized, admitted, and changed, is moodiness.

12 June 1932

Psychical anticathexis of sensations that become unbearable

R.N.: When approaching traumatic scenes involving physical or moral mutilation, hysterical outbursts of emotion; when these are no longer enough, instead of outbursts of pain, convulsive laughter. At this point it seems as though a psychical hypercathexis of reality suddenly takes place through compensatory fantasies of pleasure (although the patient maintains that the laughter only means getting rid of a *quantity* of tension). The patient has the sensation that suddenly, at a painful spot at the back of her head, a bladder is formed, which has room for all her pain. The bladder is almost infinitely expandable.[1] This is preceded by the actual elimination of a large quantity of urine. On this painful site on the head (probably the place where the patient was given injections) an ad hoc bladder is formed, but with this the splitting of the personality has begun. A more recent trauma can also overcome the bladder-formation and cause it, so to speak, to burst. The seemingly impossible task here is: (1) to refashion the bladder from its fragments (for which task the analyst is required to mobilize his intellectual powers as well as his patience to endure); (2) to ensure that the bladder thus reconstructed reunites its contents with the ego (the body).

A purely intellectual reconstruction by the analyst does not appear to be sufficient for this task. The patient must feel that the analyst shares his pain and would also gladly make sacrifices to relieve it. Coolness toward the analysand, or indeed antipathy and impatience, can usually be dealt with only after overcoming strong resistance by means of some character analysis. Patient R.N. even imagines that at the time of the principal trauma, with the aid of an omnipotent intelligence (Orpha), she so to speak scoured the universe in search of help (by means of an ad hoc teleplastic organ). Thus her Orpha is supposed to have tracked me down, even at that time, as the only person in the world who owing to his special personal fate could and would make amends for the injury that had been done to her. This capacity of mine was unmasked in the course of mutual analysis as my sense of guilt at the death of a sister (diphtheria) two years younger than myself.[2] The reaction against it makes me unsympathetic toward the sick; this I overcome by showing excessive kindness, medical interest, and tact (surely exaggerated). The analysis must establish the impatience behind this kindness and subtract it. Friendly feelings remain, that is, to some extent that Orphic fantasy is coming true. Whereupon, as relaxation has become possible, the personality that burst and that was stuck in a bladder is now able to reunite, and simultaneously, instead of repetition, the memory of what happened can be established.

Friendly relations with the spirit world

For years S.I. had terrifying hallucinations, especially after consuming alcohol. Suddenly, following a head injury, capable of abstinence.

Further progress: she no longer has to be abstinent, she can drink again without any ill effects. At the same time the hallucinations assume a less terrifying character and the patient becomes better able to cope with the demands of reality, maintains that my personality has a healing effect on her and that this great change is due to these qualities. She is also aware that at times I am bored and irritable, but that I possess the rare or even unique ability to rise above my own weaknesses.

Failures with pupils

Dm. now has the courage to reproach me for abandoning pupils at the first signs of incomplete adaptation or submission. I have to admit to it, but excuse myself with the argument that pupils do steal my ideas without quoting me. Freud has found the same symptom in my brother complex, which has recurred now in the International Association.

1. See page 117.
2. This refers to his sister Vilma, actually four years his junior, who died in the first year of her life. Between Sándor and Vilma there was another boy, Moritz Karoly.—ED.

14 June 1932

Permanent disturbance of object-libido

I. Patient U. notices in himself that he feels no inclination for preliminary pleasure or foreplay in sexual relations, but experiences the act more like an obligation, as it were, which he seeks to get over as quickly as possible; similar lack of "afterpleasure" ["Nachlust"]. He is puzzled when he hears from one of his mistresses that she is "thrilled" for quite some time both before and after.

Explanation: a young savage, raised in the most primitive circumstances, suddenly arrives at the age of twelve in an environment that, at least on the surface, is far more civilized (emigration to America). At first degraded in his entire personality, he uses psychoanalysis as a springboard to rise to a more sublimated sphere (in order to rid himself of his perpetual fear: fear of going mad). A more recent breakdown during a first analysis, when in bad company he is threatened with death.

The fear was determined by a multiplicity of factors: (1) real danger of death, (2) relapse into the primitive state before his emigration, and fear of this, (3) fear of his own aggressiveness, (4) uninhibited intellectual self-esteem and tyrannical willfulness, which are poorly dealt with and transformed into anxiety, and which, after a failure, impress him as insanity.

He does not believe in subtleties, tenderness, symbolism, allusions, moral inhibitions, etc., only direct action itself seems real to him. He battles against his own criminal and ruthlessly infantile-egoistic tendencies.

He suffered a great deal from his mother's unpredictable outbursts of love as a child; it is also possible that some kind of homosexual experiences caused him to turn away from the female sex.

II. Patient O.S.: Infantile traumata: (1) anal injury caused in two different ways, by a woman and a man; (2) as in case I, incapable of sustaining any object relationship (never finishes a book, withdraws from all friendships for the slightest of reasons). Tries to overcompensate by excessive kindness, but becomes paralyzed in his effort. As I suspected in my article on tics,[1] at the site of the trauma a residue of excitation appears to persist. Libidinal energy is obtained for this from the general reservoir, genitality. *Ubi bene, ibi vagina.*

A second possibility is that the trauma affects the genitals (threats, prohibitions, etc.) and genitality regresses to the anal stage. In any case, anality, with its autoeroticism, renders one independent of objects; however hypochondriacal he appears, the anal character with his capital and with gratification of anal stimuli feels much more protected from the disappointments that dependence on another person might bring him. This situation will have a tragic outcome, nevertheless, when the desire for a happy object-relationship reawakens in him, or when he starts to compare himself in this respect with other, happier people. The anal character trait is also well suited for displaying feelings of hate, for example (1) flatus keeps people at a certain distance, or even drives them out of the room, (2) it means a defiant emphasis on self-contempt, "Goddam, I stink." If one follows this further, one may find that a far too severe and unjust judgment, which the judges refuse to correct, will end in such soiling of oneself and a certain degree of soiling of others. Thus here once again a failure of the original tenderness. One's personal disorder and lack of anal control also provide effective means for seemingly innocent acts of revenge. In the absence of any other weapon, one is able to annoy with apparent innocence somebody who has offended us.

The tendency toward displacement onto anality may be enhanced by the presence of an abnormal store of retained trauma. Possibly, however, during and because of the struggle with weaning, a bit of the libido remains caught up in the anal sphere, which facilitates the regressive flow. Yet it is not impossible that originally only the mouth and genitals are libido reservoirs (erogenous zones) and that anal eroticism in fact is displaced hysterical genitalization. The link between sadism and anal eroticism, almost always demonstrable, might indicate that the emergence of the anal store is the final outcome of a struggle for genitality. As such one might mention: (1) the threat of castration, (2) premature, enforced demands on the genitals, which create unpleasure, that is to say, forcibly imposed or brutally prevented genitality leads to sadism and anal eroticism. (Here perhaps mention Simmel?)[2] Quite possibly the capacity for narcissism in general depends on the possibility of isolation, for which the anal region is not yet suited. Surely nowhere else can such quantities of excitation and matter accumulate, as here. Also there is significant scope for variation in means of expression.

III. Latent feelings of hatred, overt friendliness and kindness, anal fissure, conspicuously smelly emanations. Principal motive for these tendencies of hatred and superiority stems from the conviction that as a child she was deceived and defeated in the struggle for her father's love. The father only played with her, it was the mother who had the baby. Since then no tender love relationship, even the present one is bound up with hatred, largely anal (independent) and strongly aggressive.

1. See "Psycho-Analytical Observations on Tic," *FC* 142–174.—ED.

2. Ernest Simmel (1882–1947), German psychiatrist. He collaborated with Abraham, Ferenczi, and Jones on *Psycho-Analysis and the War Neuroses,* published in May 1919; his contribution was the article "War Neuroses and Psychic Traumas." In 1926 he founded the Tegelsee, a clinic at Tegel, near Berlin, at which the entire staff had been analyzed. Freud was very interested in the experiment and made several visits to the clinic. Fleeing Nazism, Simmel left Germany in 1933, going first to Zurich and then to the United States. He settled in Los Angeles, where he founded the Sigmund Freud Clinic and a Society and Institute of Psychoanalysis.—ED.

146a ## 14 June 1932

Normális feminin homosexualitás

"Men don't understand," women say, and are (even in analysis) very reticent about their homosexual feelings. "Men think women can only love the possessors of penises." In reality, they continue to long for a mother and female friend, with whom they can talk about their heterosexual experiences—*without jealousy.* (B. and Ett., Dm. and women friends.) They prefer *effeminate* (passive, homosexual) men, because these offer them a continuation of bisexuality.

The renunciation of homosexuality

(Repression occurs at the time of first menstruation—when Tom-Boy-ishness[1] is suppressed all of a sudden.) Dm. demands from me (after overcoming substantial resistance) *that I should become a good mother to U. (and to herself).*[2] (Dm.: I am to overcome my ambition to be greater than he, content myself with a passive role in relation to him, but at the same time also accept her tomboy-love. Only then will she permit herself to cut herself loose from her dependence on me. Masculine or feminine: I must admit that I *love* U. (Daddy!)[3] *just as much as I love her,* then we (daughter and mother) will become colleagues. A large share of the girl's *tenderness* remains (under such circumstances) attached to the mother.

1. In English in original, and spelled as here.
2. Ferenczi is discussing his relationships to U., a man, and Dm., a woman.
3. Word in English.

16 June 1932

Awareness of personality (awareness of one's own size, form, value) as a result of recognition from the environment

Patient S.I., following a brief, passionate transference phase, kept entirely secret, entered a phase of strong resistance, exacerbated by the unexpected interruption of the analysis on my part (trip to America). Gradual return of trust, helped by my sincere sympathy at two tragic moments: (1) when it became known that her husband had squandered enormous sums of money on gambling and women, (2) at the sudden death of her beloved brother. The transference, however, assumed entirely the form of the most sublimated, congenial, intellectual rapport. The main interest is in a joint exploration of the unconscious, particularly of that deeper, hitherto neglected "metaphysical" layer which enables the individual to make contact with a greater or lesser part of the universe. In this chaotic universe she meets the spirits of the dead and of the living; in deeply relaxed states of trance she is frightened by such spirits. Following the extreme intensification of her breakdown (head injury), sudden awakening of her capacity

(1) to maintain relations with those "spirits" unafraid, on an almost friendly basis, (2) the sudden cessation of hitherto uncontrollable drinking, at first by means of enforced abstinence, but then just by simple moderation. Two somewhat feeble attempts to yield to the advances of two men up to a certain point. The first attempt involves a man who makes advances to her but cannot abandon his masochistic subservience toward his wife. He is also more of a scholar and an aesthete. He loves things, not people. After a brief kindling of desire, quite rapidly, a total cooling off. The second case was less significant; she felt rather flattered by the attentions of a man who was also inhibited, but more natural—though yet again, married.

In the meantime, or perhaps under the influence of these changes, substantial increase in the sense of reality, and the undertaking of extremely practical measures to rescue the family's financial and moral position. She becomes the adviser of all and sundry, takes charge of her daughter's upbringing; indeed, she helps a whole series of people in her social circle.

Periodically she attempts, partly as a "task," to engage herself autoerotically, but she never has any accompanying erotic fantasies while doing so. These are rare, even in her dreams. On the other hand she carries on untiringly with the analytic work; she has, I believe, an exaggerated regard for my attainments; she feels that my mere presence is capable of helping her in a way of which I myself am unaware. In almost every session she sinks into a trance, with mostly inexplicable, incoherent visions; nevertheless, on awakening from these she never tires of thanking me for my help.

This behavior and the complete absence of any physical or mental sexual activity suggested to me that her purely intellectual relationship with me was providing her with an unconscious substitute for sexuality. One might think this a typical case of sublimation, but occasional observations reveal that, in a deeply repressed fashion, purely sexual excitation continues to exist in this intellectual relationship. Sometimes she speaks of a spiritual aura, or a luminous vision, that approaches her from my direction; at other times the analysis of her positive or negative interest in smells leads to the assumption that (somewhat like this colleague who could attain satisfaction only by means of a breath on the genitals) she unconsciously perceives the truly chemical sublimates of a person in her vicinity, and of course the friendly, tender concern with which the doctor follows all expressions of emotion and apparently nonsensical productions of the imagination of the patient, which are nevertheless felt to be of value; all this contributes greatly to the fact that here she feels, so to speak, enveloped in goodwill and interest. It is also quite striking that this person who is otherwise thrifty and even stingy in small matters pays the not inconsiderable expenses of the treatment with pleasure, so to speak, and indeed firmly refuses my offer to reduce the fees or to remain in debt; surely an indication that part of the "sublimation" has taken the path of anal eroticism. (The interest in smells may also be evaluated from this point of view.)

Recently I have found her and her trust in me strong enough to tell her all this. At the same time I tried out the following theory concerning her manner of reaction in life generally and in analysis: we know that the patient's mother in earliest childhood was prone to outbursts of rage that were certainly pathological, perhaps also psychotic. One brother (the one mentioned above) and a sister remember having been beaten in the most brutal manner by the mother, and even their heads being smashed against the wall. At times the patient has vague notions of a furious outburst of rage that was directed at her genitals. On this occasion her hymen may really have been injured, for both she and her husband noticed that there was no impediment to sexual intercourse and also that the normal bleeding did not occur. Actually the husband, so erotic in outside appearance, proved to be almost impotent in the conjugal bed, especially after the birth of their only child. The patient admits, however, that her own frigidity, colossal prudery, and inexperience were also to blame for this.

Perhaps not quite correctly or exactly, one may interpolate another incident: she is still lying in her cradle, the mentioned brother comes dancing up with a piece of wood and injures her genitals. A later trauma, which makes her totally averse to sexuality, was being shamed by her father after being caught with a whole group of children (her brother among them) exhibiting themselves to one another.

It must be noted that the family was brought up in true puritanical fashion and was kept away from anything "dirty." A complication that might almost be called tragic was as follows: her next-oldest sister, the prettiest of the three, contracted syphilis through a kiss from a man with whom the patient was also in love. Later the patient went with this sister and a governess as a threesome on a trip around the world and had to witness various instances of her sister's decadence and the governess's addiction to morphine. Added to this, the disturbing scenes in China: for instance, in a Chinese town her rickshaw passed by a square where somebody was just being executed, and the executioner frightened her by hurling a severed arm at the carriage. The theory alluded to in the title refers to the connection between that "dissolution" in the universe and the coldness of sexual feeling caused by all the traumata.

In one of her dreams the patient saw the ghosts of people, approaching her, as much larger than the people were in reality. I now believe that this magnification means a simultaneous dilution of that person. An even further dilution of the libido in her environment makes it possible for her to extend the boundaries of her person into the infinite, in a manner of speaking; whereby, however, her real, that is to say normal, person disappears (loss of consciousness, incoherence). The friendly relations with those excessively shy men, the indifferent attitude of the doctor in the analysis, made it possible for her to turn away from reality and toward the mystical hereafter. I suspect that the sudden change in her behavior and in her psychosis can be traced back to the following chance circumstance: when she had, in my presence, almost fatally injured herself, I became so anxious and was so moved that I grabbed her at once and lifted her up from the floor, laid her on the bed, and proceeded to try to revive her, gently yet energetically. The amount of emotion I displayed seems to have restored her sense of her own worth, as reflected by my compassion and passionate desire to help. Among other things, she began to examine some parts of her faces, even, with skepticism at times. She also began to take more interest in her outward appearance (looks, slimness, clothing). The indefatigable perseverance with which, in spite of all these difficulties, I tried to understand her and so to speak bring her to life was for her really the equivalent of a man's embrace—such as had ever been her share—but on a sublimated, asexual level. But then came the time when I could tell her that unconsciously she was waiting for a man who would not let himself be scared off even by her sexual coldness, and who would restore her self-esteem with a strong embrace. Her reply was that she would no doubt find a way to wriggle out of it. I countered this by saying that there must be an embrace that completely envelops the whole person and does not leave any exit free. Only then will she be able to recognize and learn to value her own qualities, in the mirror of her partner's passion. But the physical embrace also allows her, or forces her, to convert her personality, which has been dissolved in the universe, into a real thing existing of this world, and more or less to withdraw her libido from the universe. Expressed in physical or geometric terms, one could claim on the basis of similar experiences that the narcissism that is indispensable as the basis of the personality—that is to say the recognition and assertion of one's own self as a genuinely existing, a valuable entity of a given size, shape, and significance—is attainable only when the positive interest of the environment, let us say its libido, guarantees the stability of that form of personality by means of external pressure, so to speak. Without such a counter-pressure, let us say counterlove [*Gegenliebe*], the individual tends to explode, to dissolve itself in the universe, perhaps to die.

18 June 1932

A new stage in mutuality

Refer to experiences with R.N. and S.I., especially with the latter. Through the henceforth consciously directed unmasking of the so-called transference and countertransference as the hiding places of the most significant obstacles to the completion of *all* analyses, one comes to be almost convinced that no analysis can succeed as long as the false and alleged differences between the "analytical situation" and ordinary life are not overcome, just like the conceit and feeling of superiority—still to be found among analysts—with regard to the patient. In the end one becomes convinced that patients are also right in demanding from us not only that they be taken back to the trau-matic experience, but also two further things: (1) real conviction, whenever possible a memory of the reality of the reconstruction, (2) as a condition of this, a genuine interest, a real desire to help, or more precisely an all-conquering love for each and every one of them, which alone makes life seem worth living and which constitutes a counterweight to the traumatic situation.

Only from this point on will it become possible (1) that the pa-tients, who have come to trust us, can be freed from the effort of mastering (intellectually and emotionally) the traumatic situation; that the process of splitting of the self that was therefore required is now terminated, and thus they become restored to that uniformity of experience which existed before the trauma. Clearly there is no con-viction without this sense of uniformity, and no sense of uniformity, that is, no conviction, as long as in observing oneself one has doubts about oneself, even in the face of logically complete evidence. (It is impossible to foresee what the consequences would be for knowledge if people were freed from this anxiety and dared to examine and recognize the world in its own quite self-evident form; how much further that could lead, than even the most audacious of what nowadays we call fantasies. Really mastering anxiety, or rather overcoming it, might perhaps make us quite clairvoyant, and might help humanity to solve apparently insoluble problems. This may be a deferred verification of the self-assurance, which impresses as megalomania, in R.N.'s declarations.)

2. Furthermore, no analysis can succeed if we do not succeed in really loving the patient. Every patient has the right to be regarded and cared for as an ill-treated, unhappy child. So it points to a weakness in the analyst's own psychic organization if he treats a patient he finds sympathetic better than the antipathetic one. It is equally wrong to respond to fluctuations in the patient's behavior with fluctuations in our own reactions, in an uncorrected fashion. But it is no less of an error simply to withdraw from every emotional reaction, be it of a positive or a negative kind, and to wait behind the patient's back for the end of the session, unconcerned about his suffering, or concerned only on an intellectual level, and leaving the patient to do all the work of collection and interpretation almost all alone. It is true that as a doctor one is tired, irritable, somewhat patronizing, and now and then one sacrifices the patient's interests to one's own curiosity, or even half-unconsciously makes covert use of the opportunity to give vent to purely personal aggression and cruelty. Such mistakes cannot be avoided by anyone and in any of the cases, but one must (a) be aware of it, (b) taking hints from the patients, admit these errors to oneself and to the patients.

But such confessions, however often they may be repeated, will not get us any further if we (a) do not resolve to come to a radical understanding through mutual analysis, (b) as a consequence of this, we do not successfully change our entire attitude toward the patient, but above all, if we do not give up that passivity and place ourselves at the patient's disposal in, one could say, a passionately active manner. It is quite true that what is being demanded here is unusual: the seemingly improbable combination of overwhelmingly passionate love, which can only be likened to the self-denial of a mother, with a wise superiority and self-control, as well as the self-confidence not to be overly good and the skill to help the now trusting patient to use his unifying mental capacities again, and so to arrive at knowledge.

Trauma is a process of dissolution that moves toward total dissolution, that is to say, death. The body, the cruder part of the personality, withstands destructive processes longer, but unconsciousness and the fragmentation of the mind already are signs of the death of the more refined parts of the personality. Neurotics and psychotics, even if they are still halfway capable of fulfilling their functions as body and also partly as mind, should actually be considered to be unconsciously in a chronic death-agony. Analysis therefore has two tasks: (1) to expose this death-agony fully; (2) to let the patient feel that life is nevertheless worth living if there exist people like the helpful doctor, who is even prepared to sacrifice a part of himself. (Hence the tendency of patients to get into financial difficulties and to put our selflessness to the test.)

In order to achieve such a success, however, one more thing is needed: the self-confidence of the analyst. It is only half benefit if someone converts a stupid sense of superiority into exaggerated and perhaps masochistic self-criticism. If he does that, he will discover in the course of mutual analysis that *his* trauma resulted in a character defect that inhibits action. For example (a) love for mother, (b) disappointment, birth of a sibling, (c) reaction of rage, (d) fear of the consequences, (e) hate rechanneled into defiance and a desire to annoy, misogyny, relative impotence, lack of full ability to help patients. To express it in terms of libido theory, one would say that the restoration of truly full potency, mobile with regard to everyone, must be achieved if one wishes to terminate analyses. Antipathy is impotence.

19 June 1932

Specific odor of the mentally ill

Patient Dm., who herself in fact perspires quite conspicuously and with a marked odor, particularly on certain occasions, finds a similarity between herself and the mentally ill Mrs. Smith. (I had an opportunity to see Mrs. Smith, a schizophrenic, in a state of terrible anxiety. She did have a penetrating smell, rather like mouse urine.) Dm., on the other hand, feels that she herself exudes sexual odors. She also suffers from anal fissure. Both conditions, as well as intermittently chronic contractions, become manifest when she suppresses her tendency toward almost manic rage in speech, voice, and gestures. The suppressed rage stimulates a chemical change in her (poisoning—see poison for rage), the transformation of the attracting substance into one that repels. The analysis reveals that she is waiting for a hero, who will not be scared off even by these odors. The analyst must be this hero, he must (1) abandon his hypocritical insensitivity and admit his antipathy and his revulsion; (2) analyze himself, or let himself be analyzed, to a point where he no longer finds such substances and behavior repellent, whereupon (3) the patient will renounce her provocative activities.

In the case of Dm., acquaintance with the analyst began with the patient behaving quite improperly at a dance. After she was not accepted as a patient at that time, she went straight to the apartment of a young man and lost her virginity. Naturally this provoked reactions of disgust in the analyst, which had to be overcome in the course of a prolonged period of work.

The model for this whole process was infantile rage concerning (1) the prohibition of all sexual expression, (2) the realization that the parents engaged in sexual activities (birth of children). A further motive to fury was anger over the weak submission of the father to the maternal power (some of what appears as penis envy may be a demonstration of the behavior of a woman who remained with a weak man).

156 20 June 1932

Another motive for women's wish to have a penis

The principal motive in Dm.: the desire to be loved by her mother. "Mother always found something wrong with her body" (even in her earliest childhood, criticizing her chubbiness, her odor (?)—her passionate way of hugging, even more, *her love for her father,* which was passionate at an early age). Her desire to become a boy was determined by the wish to eliminate her mother's *dislike of her feminine inclinations.* She disguises herself as a man *because as a woman she displeases her mother* (is hated by her mother, very likely for reasons of jealousy).

This wish intensifies at the onset of *puberty,* when femininity can no longer be denied. (Menstruation.) She is aware that her mother is displeased (envy, jealousy). She seeks out masculine activities. She feels that her mother will not let her *really* get married and obeys her; or that her mother looks for quite unsuitable men for her. When *she* herself falls in love with someone (father, B. Mac.), it ends in tragedy. She wants (dream fantasy) to be loved by the analyst, despite another man's passion and moods.

Yet equally, she wants only a man who recognizes that a woman has other desires beyond genital gratification—which only a mother is capable of satisfying. *Longing for a triangle without envy or jealousy.*

21 June 1932

Permanent traumatic respiratory disturbances during sleep

Two cases of sleep disturbance persisting since early childhood: (1) Waking from deep sleep with a feeling of dizziness and headache; still half asleep, one observes that one has not breathed for ten seconds or longer and has not even felt any impulse to breathe in. Sudden feeling of fear causes inhalation, yet as soon as sleepiness sets in again, the breathing stops. If fatigue increases, one succeeds in falling asleep again for a longer period, but on awakening from this sleep one feels as after a severe and dangerous, long-lasting suffocation: heat-sensation in the head, all bedclothes thrown off; a violent attack of coughing, for hours expectoration of mucus, crystal-clear sputum, the ramifications of which reproduce the bronchioles. There is no doubt that bronchioles were severely obstructed and that whole areas of the lungs had ceased to function. Increased pulse rate, pulse irregular. It took almost half a day to expectorate all the mucus, to restore halfway the heart and lung functions, and to eliminate the concomitant serious mental and other functional disturbances. Waking observers affirm that the patient grinds his teeth almost incessantly and snores loudly in somewhat deeper sleep, until finally this Cheyne-Stokes-like disturbed pattern of breathing ceases when he wakes with a start. Occasionally the disturbed breath takes the form of fitful spasms, so that the similarity to epileptoid attack becomes quite striking.

The same group of symptoms is reproduced in almost every analytic session, when relaxation is sufficiently deep. It appears as though the patient has a permanent tendency, even during the day, to sink into a mortal agony of suffocation, so that his breathing is already in fact a conscious countermeasure, and does not occur automatically as in normal people. A part of his conscious attention sees to the task of not allowing that respiratory activity to stop for too long. As soon as the attention is lessened by fatigue or sleep, or suspended altogether, the breathing difficulties set in again.

In the course of the analytic relaxation advocated by me, this kind of sleep disturbance occurred even in the half-awake state. When the patient awoke with a start I urged him to tell me about the fragments of dream fantasies, of which he otherwise would have taken no notice; and when I on the one hand let him associate freely to these fragments and on the other hand helped him by appropriate questioning, we arrived at the reconstruction of an infantile trauma of a homosexual nature. The attack by an older boy, which evidently had often been repeated but consciously totally forgotten, resulted in (1) a marked inclination to subordinate himself to a man with strong willpower. As compensation: defiant resistance against any kind of influencing and a compulsion toward total moral and intellectual independence. Voice remained somewhat effeminate, relations with the female sex disturbed, toward women he feels:[1]

1. Sentence continues in next entry.

158a ## 22 June 1932

(2) Relative impotence with an occasional (heterosexual) breakthrough; intense passion in masturbatory fantasies; *ejaculatio usque ad tegmen camerae* [ejaculation up to the ceiling]. (3) Breathing disturbances as described; periodic throbbing pains in the back, previously accompanied by anxiety (rage) dreams, now without dreams for years.

Case II. Strongly dependent on mother, no relationship with (eccentric) father. "Difficult child," "problem child." Since childhood, "banging head against the mattress (two to three thousand times!) before falling asleep. Breathing disturbances while in relaxation, just like case I. Preceded by fierce pains in the abdomen, in and around the uterus.[1] Face is quite haggard, sensation of being crushed; Cheyne-Stokes, face pale, head subjectively hot. The pain is intensified, so that—because it is so *improbably severe*—it provokes convulsive laughter. *It is too stupid* (therefore not true!). Dreams about having to help oneself in an impossibly painful situation. *The feeling of going insane.* (The reality of an unpleasure can be eradicated by focusing concentration on an idea or an image. Lamas do not feel any pain if they concentrate on certain verbal images.)

159   Such patients—apparently well adapted—are *unconsciously insane* (in flight from reality). Deliverance from conscious torment saves life. In the course of relaxation (in sleep) they get the feeling of

having to die, unless either being awakened by anxiety puts an end to the pain or the feeling of *being maternally loved* keeps them alive despite the pain. Love is transformed into a kind of *antidote*. But: finely attuned sensitivity as to whether the love[2] at work is feigned or genuine. Only the latter helps (presumably recognized in behavior, gesture, in the signs of passionate tenderness). If she does not feel this, then *she must come to her own aid,* that is, remain split and insane and deny reality.

Case III. No respiratory difficulties, as in the cases cited above, but when well relaxed—fumes with rage at being helplessly overpowered—"nameless," "impossible" cruelty, and then (it's mad!) to be rebuked and degraded! Consequence: *wanting to die before being killed.* Feeling: head invisibly split with a saw into four parts. Right

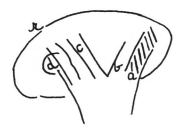

half is the "imagination" of the suffering and the determination of the decision to die. r = cd—is carrying out this idea—c weeps over d (the child who is actually to be killed). Yet the whole is divided into four parts.[3] Can be realized only piece by piece, unless the *real (ideal) lover appears,* who will put everything right. (Male and Female:[4] she does not want to get well—until she is convinced that it is worth the trouble.) This conviction can be attained only when the analyst, who sees everything, loves her in spite of it, or just because of it.

Here the practical question arises: must the analyst give himself personally, unreservedly, to every patient (as a private person, and also as a sexual being)? Hardly possible! Solution (R.N.): When the patient can feel *the potential capacity* for loving in the analyst, actual experience of it is not absolutely necessary. Perhaps this fourfold division contains a more detailed description of the process of hysterical repression.

The beginning of a dissolution process, whereby the accumulation of dissolution processes somehow inhibits any further (lethal) dissolution—indeed (particularly by eliminating the conscious quality of pain-unpleasure), it makes possible adaptation to a semidissolved state. Through *the separation of mind and body* the continuation of life is assured. Yet, being kept separated . . .[5]

1. Word unclear in the handwritten text: it may be *Hintern,* "buttocks," rather than *Uterus.*

2. Ferenczi's word is *Güte,* but in this context "love" seems a more appropriate translation than "goodness" or "kindliness."

3. Michael Balint intended to omit this schematic representation and the accompanying text, no doubt because they are rather obscure. As the French edition included them, however, we have done so as well.

4. "Male and Female," in *Thalassa,* pp. 96–109.—ED.

5. The rest of this entry is missing.

23 June 1932

Anesthetizing the trauma

The dilemma of curing a neurosis by causing the pathogenic trauma to be experienced anew—this time without "repression"—comes up against the following difficulties, which at first sight appear insurmountable: we succeed by our insistence in inducing the patient to return himself to one or several painful situations, localized precisely in terms of both space and time, and while doing so to manifest all the symptoms of mental and physical pain, indeed, inducing him during the attack to admit verbally, to himself and to us, the reality of those events; nevertheless the permanent effect we had expected fails to appear, and a long sequence of analytic sessions are spent without any notable progress toward either curing the symptoms or achieving permanent conviction. Either the conviction that appears to have been established for good evaporates in the course of the following day (even more likely, in the course of the night and dream experiences), or else the pain accompanying the traumatic-analytic experience is intensified to such an unbearable degree that the patient ceases to be an objective observer and recorder of the events and succumbs to an affect of pain, which strangles all thoughts and wishes, all access to reason, and allows only a horrible scream to be released from such pain.

If one heeds this appeal for help—and soothing words and suggestive phrases do have there a decisive effect—the torment comes to an end, but so does all knowledge as to the cause. If we do not give in to that appeal and allow the pain of the traumatic situation to persist, then a distinct state of mental confusion ultimately sets in, not infrequently accompanied by convulsive laughter or a severe, frightening, almost corpse-like paralysis, not only of mental activity and musculature but also of respiration and the heart. Patients tormented in this way start to have doubts about the analysis, accuse us of ignorance, of foolhardiness at their expense, of cruelty, of impotence; try to tear themselves free from us (in one case, Dr. S., successfully), drive us to despair and to doubts about what we are doing. The usual cool excuse, that all this comes from the patient's resistance against sinking even deeper into the trauma, does not help here. The patients have the definite feeling that they themselves have reached the limits of their capacity, and that from now on someone else, naturally I, the analyst, must "do something," but do what!!?

In one case, which left a particularly deep impression, I received the answer that not only explanations but also passionate tenderness and love should be dispensed as an antidote to the pain (genuine compassion only, not feigned). As reported elsewhere, such analytical experience may in fact often lead to an astonishingly sudden change for the better (see case S.I.). But in many other cases this does not happen. I have in mind three cases currently under observation: Case 1, R.N., where I can create this sympathy only transiently, even if it is very intensive and requires a victory over my own self. Profound self-analysis was required to uncover in myself the motives behind this antipathy, to paralyze it, and to strengthen my own character or, to put it better, my analytic potency, so that I would be able to help antipathetic people too. Aided by these measures, I became capable of engaging in battle with the demon that dominated the mind and body of the patient; while doing so, in a way demanding a great deal of intelligence and ingenuity, I could drain away the patient's pain by my compassion. Through the continued application of such psychic drainage I could relieve the tension, which otherwise would tend to explode, to a point where encouragement to reach insight and conviction became increasingly possible. Nevertheless success and progress, though quite evident, were dreadfully slow.

In the other two cases, the traumatic analysis[1] could not get under way at all. The patients never relaxed sufficiently into free association, let alone to the point of intellectual and emotional semiconsciousness or unconsciousness. Both protect themselves from unpleasure, of even the slightest kind, so desperately, and both have devised and developed a way of life and an attitude of mind that keep them miles away from the real upheavals in their lives. In Case 2 the idea had already occurred to me, that since the traumas probably took place in an artificially induced (narcotic) state of unconsciousness and paralysis (of the body and mind) it might be appropriate to anesthetize the patient with ether or chloroform, in order to anesthetize the traumatic pain to such a degree that the circumstances related to the trauma would become accessible. From such a procedure the emergence of significant pieces of material evidence may be expected, which the patient will not be able to deny or minimize even after waking up. One might also consider combining anesthesia with hypnotic suggestion, which would have to confine itself to deepening, subjectively as well as objectively, the resistances against acknowledging the mentally and physically traumatic events, and to fixing them also for the time when the patient wakes up (postnarcotic and posthypnotic). Significantly both patients (2 and 3) have already made use of the narcotic method for their own purposes.

Case 3, O.S., is also so terrified of physical pain that she had acquired from Paris two hundred dollars worth of her own anesthetic equipment, which she wants to be used even for the most minor dental intervention. Case 4, N.H.D., remembers giving birth to her only child without the least pain under morphine and ether anesthesia (high forceps!). She always has the feeling that she lost something because of this, which she must find again. It so happened that during the course of analysis she had to have a small tumor operated on. On waking from the anesthesia she said to the analyst: "I had a dream during the anesthesia, in which everything we are looking for became quite evident." On full awakening, however, none of this was conscious. Some additional assistance from the analyst during the anesthesia might have helped here. Note preliminary studies on this subject by Frank[2] and Simmel.[3]

1. The phrase *traumatische Analyse* here seems to suggest that the analysis itself would be traumatic.

2. Ludwig Frank (1863–1935), Swiss neurologist. His name is mentioned in the Freud-Jung correspondence several times, though none too flatteringly. He was a supporter of Forel, the Swiss psychiatrist who was a resolute opponent of psychoanalysis. Frank himself appeared to be hesitant, a pseudo-supporter, ambivalent and ill-informed rather than an outright adversary. His most notable publications were "Zur Psychoanalyse," *Journal de Psychologie et de Neurologie* XIII (1908), and "Die Psychoanalyse, ihre Bedeutung für die Auffassung und Behandlung psychoneurotischer Zustande" (1910), which Freud severely criticized in a letter to Jung on 22 April 1910. In the end Frank did not become a member of the Swiss Association of Psychoanalysis, founded in 1910.—ED.

3. See page 124, note 2.

26 June 1932

Permanent (perhaps also long-range) effect of terrifying curses

1. For some years it was as though S.I. were demonomaniacally under the influence of evil spirits, which tried to devour her and terrorize her, which threatened her with death and had directed their hatred and murderous intent against her person, in gestures and by expression. Here a link with an outburst of about three or four years ago, when, disrupting transferential friendliness, she suddenly came out with accusations: that I knew that R.N., a patient she was acquainted with, was threatening her and persecuting her from afar, and that I was allowing this to happen. At that time the patient allowed herself to be placated by my sincere denial. In the meantime, however, it has become clear to me that the patient was in the right, insofar as that in the analysis of R.N. I had occasionally identified myself with the latter, and had indeed encouraged her to give her aggression free rein. I also knew that that patient had expressed feelings of hatred against S.I.

In yesterday's analysis of R.N. the most horrendous cruelties were reproduced, which had been inflicted upon her. This time in particular, injections of poison in the region of the nape of the neck, which resulted in the inflammation of the mastoid area. About two years ago recurrence of this inflammation, for which the ear specialist could give no explanation. I must confess, but the patient was also demanding this from me, screaming, that I was inclined to alleviate the patient's frightful suffering. I did this successfully by means of consoling and liberating suggestions. The following night S.I., who could not have had the slightest inkling of these events, or perhaps just the merest inkling, had the following dream: She has growths over one ear, these growths are fungi [*Schwämme*], a large fungus and a smaller one. She examines them carefully and finds that these fungi do not belong to her body, therefore she carefully detaches the growths from herself.

This dream occurs at a time when S.I. finally succeeds in regarding objectively the demons, previously so terrifying, and even in recognizing that her colossal terror stems only from the incorporation of hatred that is in fact foreign to her. ("Terror is exogenous hatred forced upon the ego.") This discovery makes her independent of the terrifying effect of the threats, she detaches them, as it were, from her own person. The mushroom shape leads to sexual associations; R.N. used to explain everything to her in terms of sexual symbols. She now makes herself independent of that and also of blind obedience (also in my direction).

As long as S.I. was afraid, her attention was directed anxiously toward the outside world, particularly the wishes and moods of people important to her, therefore particularly frightening. It seems that the hypersensitivity of the sense organs, as I have found with some mediums, was to be traced back to the anxious listening for any wish-impulses of a cruel person. Presumably, therefore, all mediums are such overanxious people, who are attuned to the slightest vibrations, those accompanying cognitive and affective processes too, even from a distance. Here link with the telegraphic, electro-radio-telegraphic and -telephonic hallucinations of the mentally ill. Perhaps there are no hallucinations, but only an illusionary working through of real events. The isochronism of dreams corresponding to reality of several patients could be explained as (1) an obedience reaction (in fact perhaps a revolt against emotional reactions toward other patients, that is, identification with me out of fear); (2) perhaps my person is only a relay station, through which the two of them can come into immediate contact with one another. In this dream that shock tried to reassert itself, but the greater independence acquired in analysis refuses to accept the exogenous substance or emotion into the ego. She rejects, with, as it were, deadly determination, the fare offered to it, saying, "Please eat it yourself! Deal with it yourself! I will not let myself be tortured instead of you." In order to make this explanation even more plausible, it must be said that the most abominable cruelty that the patient was subjected to was in fact this: she was forced to swallow the severed genitals of a repugnant black man, who had just been killed.

26 June 1932

On the compulsion to alleviate others' pain, or to help to further the development of others' talents

Patient O.S. comes to me, a rather ill young lady, dressed in the latest fashion, determined to be alluring. She has brought a woman friend with her to Budapest, she wanted to live independently from her jealous husband, undisturbed, with her woman friend, and to help her develop her talent as a writer. She came to me for analysis not alone, however, but accompanied by her friend, two monkeys, three dogs, and several cats. The friend, who later entered analysis, turned out to be a person for whom nothing was more hateful than someone wanting to make her happy against her will, or without consulting her. In these circumstances she becomes defiant and incapable of action, often also angry, indeed enraged. From this arise the most varied conflicts and a gradual cooling of relations on both sides. In addition to the animals and the woman friend, O.S. has now also adopted a talented girl, who had been in real danger of becoming depraved, in order to allow her to develop into a distinguished artist. She is today perhaps one of the most promising dancers, with excellent prospects.

O.S. has gained seventeen kilograms in the last four months, and has a compulsion to overeat. She cannot stay on a diet (as a child she was extremely large and fat, badly dressed, although her mother and uncle were multimillionaires). She was aware that she did have talents, which could not develop properly under the inflexible German methods of childrearing. Nobody made friends with her, because of her peculiar, ridiculous appearance. Already as a young girl, it was an event of the greatest importance for her to meet Pavlova, the most celebrated dancer of the day, at her stepfather's house. She was so overcome, however, that she could not utter a word, she could only admire her.

O.S. clearly identifies herself with neglected talents who must be helped. Secretly, however, the hope persisted in her, that one day she would herself become beautiful, both physically and mentally—brilliant and attractive. The analysis appears to have diminished substantially her capacity to live out her life through others. (Above all she became aware that in the case of her friend her psychological-psychiatric skills have failed. She neither succeeded in developing her talents nor in receiving thanks for it. But without this gratitude the identification appears to weaken and the feeling becomes strengthened in her that this transaction leaves her empty-handed.) Yesterday the following event took place: her adoptive child danced for her, more beautiful than ever, and moreover slim and full of grace. Instead of taking pleasure in her as usual, all of a sudden she was full of the sense of her own clumsiness and plumpness, and felt like an elephant. While I was encouraging her to give way to this feeling and at the same time not omitting to show her my sympathy, she burst into heart-rending tears. Remarkably enough she still did not appreciate what this extreme despair about herself meant: despite the notion of not being able to live like this, despite her expressive gestures, she maintained that she felt nothing, at the most an inner emptiness. Whereupon it was pointed out to her that the self-observation of inner emptiness would justify the feeling of sadness.

From this observation the way is open to an understanding of the compulsive desire to help, which in male homosexuality has already been recognized as a consequence of identification. She plays the role of the mother, who provides her child with the best opportunities for development and shares the happiness of her adoptive children as well. There are people, especially women, who cannot bear to watch an animal, or be it a man in love, suffer. Physiologically, it may be that even the idea that a man in sexual excitement may have to endure the tension of his erect penis is so unbearable that she must give herself to the man in order to alleviate his pain, and she cannot feel calm again until ejaculation and relaxation have set in. Curiously, the impossibility of bearing another's suffering may be stronger than her sensitivity to the pain she herself must endure when she gives herself to the man who desires her. It is as though desire were the greatest possible pain, greater than physical suffering. Presumably a curious reversal of reality takes place, helped by the production of fantasies, when desire exceeds a tolerable level. Instead of continuing to suffer and making further, often arduous attempts to attain the objects of desire in reality, through tedious and painstaking effort, the patience suddenly gives out and, instead, an imaginary identification with a ready-made successful ideal of beauty or life takes place.

By neglecting reality, to which they no longer pay any attention, deeply immersed in the delights available through the detour of identification, they hardly notice that meanwhile time has slipped away, that they are growing old and still have not established a home, that their powers of attraction are fading. The analysis has certainly played its part in her attaining these insights. She is beginning to sense that while she is living in her fantasy world her real world and her prospects are degenerating more and more. One of the most important auxiliary factors in her submergence into a fantasy world was the loss of a sense of time. The patient allowed letters to pile up over several months without even opening them, believing there was plenty of time. As though time were suddenly something infinite, as though life did not have to come to an end in old age and death. At least not her life. In the analysis, therefore, the patient must be brought to suffer from desires herself, instead of ensuring their absence with the help of imaginary identification. Here an opportunity to speculate about the problem of whether there is only one principle involved in nature, namely that of the reality elements striving to assert themselves and to exert influence, or whether there is not another, second principle, that of resignation, that is, obedient adaptation and submission. This second principle appears to intervene only when the pressure of the tension opposed to or bearing down on the principle of self-assertion becomes so unbearably strong that even hope, so to speak, for the realization of wishes must be abandoned. By means of this pressure the ego is completely annihilated, the elements are no longer held together in any kind of unity, and the second principle can intervene and shape, from the substance that had become formless, a new kind of material. Analogy with pressure of gas, which resists as compression increases but abandons the resistance and liquefies (adaptation) when the pressure exceeds a certain point, the situation thus becoming intolerable and also hopeless.

170   24 June 1932[1]

On failing to hear [Vom Überhören]. *A specific form of parapraxis*

Actors: Dm.   Mrs Sp.   Mrs Sch.
          A   B   C

A, B, C sunbathing together.
Account of the events by AB and BC:
The three of them talked together for quite a while; finally Dm. takes her leave. B and C under the impression that A has already gone, C in particular starts to malign her, quite openly, even in a loud voice. She is "common." Her language low—scum of populace. No originality, boring, common, common, common.—Suddenly appears Dm., who after taking leave had sat down in nearby bathing hut, arranging her hair. "*Now I caught you*," she said, and departed with an angry expression. (Even that was "common," said C. She, C, would have done it differently, with more finesse.) In any case B and C are greatly disturbed over the incident.

Account by A (all this in analysis)

"I had an epileptic fit." Yesterday Gellert Swimming Pool—then Pest—then home in bed. Jerks for hours. Not a word about the incident! Because I suspected an intentional failure to hear, I told her the story of B and C. She knows *nothing* about it; she was not listening.

171   *Theory:* 1. She heard everything.

2. Aided by her capacity to *swallow* the most unjust accusations, she swallows the knowledge of what she has heard. *She fails to hear* nonsense, lies, and injustice—in order not to explode (kill).

3. All previous outrages of such a kind return and cause (a) an unconscious rage ("epileptic fit"), (b) dreams with references to the word not heard and to its associations (mother, I). Seemingly senseless emotions, *outbursts,* and *movements* are revealed as unconscious rage and reactions of revenge. (c) Connection between parapraxis and dream. Dream of the following night contains a reference to the incident and the history of its origin.

The process of repression

1. *Onset* of a *reaction.*

2. Change of direction in the *statu nascendi* (perhaps imaginary identification with the aggressor) or "taking him ad absurdum," in the hope that he will finally realize this. (?) In any event: splitting off of the emotion. Reaction *in the body* of *ego consciousness* [*Ichbewusstsein*]. Leap into the physical sphere of the body. Originally every reaction bodily and psychic. From now on: ability to react *with the body alone.*

1. The inversion of dates closely follows that in the original manuscript.

172   ## 24 June 1932

Yesterday, she reports, she was in a bad mood. ("Sliminess" of the patient. My dirtiness is unbearable!) She then read two chapters of Chadwick's book;[1] yesterday she thought she had read in this book the idea about anxiety and a feeling of filthiness (leakage) accompanying menstruation. "I wanted to praise this in a book review." On *second reading* it now becomes evident (the truth!) that Chadwick had written *nothing* about it. She wanted to make a present to Chadwick of *her own idea* (unconsciously). (Behind this: I, Dr. F., steal the patient's ideas and then feel *superior.*) Therefore a second, previous, deliberate parapraxis: *reading* one's own ideas *into* a text, as today: *not hearing,* failing to hear [*Überhoren*], lying, as for instance (a) denial of one's own competence, (b) not hearing injustice from others. I tell her all this, I even quote from myself (it does not matter what)—quotation of Rousseau, Lamartine, Plato!—at the end of the work. Beautiful, good aphorisms from my theories, what temptation there is in that for teachers!

C. recounts a dream of the same night: *someone* (mother?) *says the words* "The man must have been crazy to do a thing like that." Interpretation: trauma (a) caused by man *is true:* mother's doubts make the child consciously deny her own self. Thus she learns suggestibility, she has no confidence in me, neither in *her own* judgment, nor in her friends. *Postscript to the dream:* persons dead, including also (mother) and myself (Dr. F.).

1. This probably refers to Mary Chadwick, an English nurse, the author of several works including "Psychological Problems in Menstruation" (1932).—ED.

28 June 1932

Femininity as an expression of the pain-alleviating principle faced with a case of impotence

S.I. up to now frigid, but prone to bouts of drinking and outbursts against her husband; after the great upheaval she becomes kind, considerate, and helpful toward almost everyone. By chance she catches sight of her husband's genitals, hanging rather sadly. Instead of the usual revulsion she feels deep compassion. Analysis: she would like to console her husband and allow him to be unfaithful to her in any way whatsoever, but she cannot bear the sadness and lameness of the guilt-ridden little boy. She is also more kindly disposed toward her husband's wasteful spending and mania for gambling. Just as she succeeded in improving his self-control with the help of this understanding, so now she hopes unconsciously to increase his potency by forgiving him his sexual transgressions. The next step could then be the awakening of courage to deal with the woman, and the corresponding further consequence would be her own surrender to satisfy her husband's desire, which is now directed toward her. The wife of an impotent man has, therefore, to be even more feminine than the woman; yet in most cases the woman fails in this additional, difficult task: she becomes rebellious, contemptuous, and thereby inhibits the last vestiges of potency.[1]

The whole process represents a repetition of the period of incestuous thoughts and desires in the young boy. In marriage infidelity takes the place of incest as the unforgivable sin. The right sort of wife will not imitate the boy's mother, who condemns sexuality altogether, not to mention incest; instead she will understand how to reassure the inhibited boy of her love, whatever kinds of impulses he may feel, and even when he has given in to these impulses. As a reward for this self-denial she will witness an improvement in his self-esteem, the awakening of his sense of responsibility simultaneously with his potency, and thereby put an end to the compulsion to repeat that stems from his childhood. With the present trends in the education of women, such understanding and forgiving behavior is hardly to be expected. Even in this particular case a great deal of time and a deeply upsetting analytical experience were required to make such an attitude possible. The patient is now more capable of regarding the traumatic events of her own childhood in the spirit of understanding and forgiveness, rather than that of despair, rage, and revenge. A genuine recovery from traumatic shock is perhaps conceivable only when the events are not only understood but also forgiven.

The capacity for such adaptation to renunciation is perhaps explicable only if we assume the existence in nature of a second principle next to that of egoistical self-assertion, namely an appeasement-principle; that is, selfishness (infantility, masculinity) versus mother-liness, that is to say kindness.

Here reference could perhaps be made to the phenomenon of compression and eventual liquefication of gases[2] in the inorganic world, mimicry etc. in biology, as analogies. It is as though nature were concerned only with somehow establishing peace. Peace through the relentless *satisfaction* [*Befriedigung*] of desires, or peace through self-denial.

1. In this passage Ferenczi uses two words for "woman": *Frau*, which can also be translated as "wife" (as here), and the archaic *Weib*, which seems to imply something more elemental and abstract.
2. See page 143.

28 June 1932

Utopia: suppression of hate impulses, ending the chain of acts of cruelties (like blood feuds); progressive taming of the whole of nature through controls of knowledge

Link with earlier thoughts about the future of psychoanalysis: if it is at all possible to inhibit impulses and reflexes through insight, then it is just a question of time (I thought) before all selfish impulses in the world will be tamed by being passed through a human brain.

The somewhat daring hypotheses regarding the contact of an individual with the whole universe must be viewed from the standpoint not only that this omniscience enables the individual to perform extraordinary feats, but also (and this is perhaps the most paradoxical assertion that has ever been made) that such a contact can have a humanizing effect on the whole universe.

30 June 1932

Projection of adult psychology onto children (falsum)

It is certain that Freud has succeeded in tracing the psychology of the adult genetically far back into childhood. Starting always with the assumption that the reactions of children, babies, indeed all living beings are identical with those of adults, the difference being that children are prevented from asserting their original longings for omnipotence, which they retain secretly in a repressed form for the rest of their lives. Thus one assumes—on this point see my own "Stages in Development"[1]—that the child is born with a strongly developed will of his own, which attempts to prevail at any price, and when thwarted in this *gratifies itself in the form of hallucinations.* The very existence of such ways of obtaining satisfaction should have alerted us and made us realize that individuals at the beginning of their existence still have totally different ways of reacting from those in later life, and that it is perhaps not appropriate to assume adult reaction patterns at the basis of these primordial life processes.

In one psychic process the importance of which has perhaps been insufficiently appreciated, even by Freud himself, namely that of *identification as a stage preceding object relations,* we have until recently not sufficiently appreciated the functioning in it of a mode of reaction already lost to us, but one that nevertheless exists; although perhaps we are faced with the functioning of a quite different kind of reaction principle, to which the designation *reaction* can no longer be applied; that is, a state in which any act of self-protection or defense is excluded and all external influence remains an impression without any internal anti-cathexis.

The most concise summary of this situation was perhaps given by Dr. Thompson, when she said that people at the beginning of their lives have as yet no individuality. Here my view on the tendency to fade away (falling ill and dying in very young children) and the predominance in them of the death instinct: their extreme impressionability (mimicry) may be also just a sign of rather weak life and self-assertive instincts; indeed it is perhaps already an incipient, but somehow delayed, death.[2] But if this is true, and this kind of mimicry, this being subject to impressions[3] without any self-protection, is the original form of life, then it was rash, even unjustified, to ascribe to this period, still almost bereft of motility and of course also probably intellectually inactive, the only self-protective and hallucinatory mechanisms we know and are accustomed to (wish impulses). The hallucinatory period, therefore, is preceded by a purely mimetic period; in this the unpleasure also comes to an end at last, though not by changing the external world but by the yielding of the living substance, that is, a partial relinquishing of the weak self-assertive impulse that has just been attempted, an immediate resignation and adaptation of the self to the environment. The effect achieved by such an as yet incompletely developed life thus brings to mind the achievements attained in later life only by exceptional people of outstanding moral and philosophical stature.

Religious people are selfless, in that they renounce their own selves; primordial life is selfless, because it does not possess a developed self as yet. To a considerable extent the selfish person seals himself off from the external world with the help of his stimulus-barrier mechanisms, as though with a layer of skin. In infants these protective devices are not yet developed, so that infants communicate with the environment over a much broader surface. If we had the means to get such a child to tell us what this hypersensitivity makes him capable of, we would probably know much more about the world than our narrow horizon now allows.

O.S., who suffers from a helpless compulsion of being unable to watch any suffering without somehow alleviating it, lets almost everyone enjoy some of her great wealth except herself. Was analyzed for years on the basis of the principle of repressed sadism, without the slightest success and also without giving her the feeling that anyone had ever understood her. In the end, I had to decide, having placed myself entirely in her position, to accept it as probable that in her case the original reaction is not defense but a need to help.

The influences of her childhood environment were as follows: she lived in the house of a hypochondriac, who could almost be termed mentally ill; her governess impressed on her very early on that any noise would do this uncle terrible harm. Her reaction to this was not something like anger; the governess and the uncle commanded her respect to such an extent that not only did she not dare to contradict, but the idea that they could be wrong did not even occur to her. All of a sudden she changed into an anxious person, imitating the hypochondria of her environment completely; she could not help walking around on tiptoe and was totally convinced that this was the only way—and the natural way—for small children to behave. The only wish-fulfilling fantasy she had was to grow up. When I am grown up I won't have to go around on tiptoe; there will be others, my children perhaps, walking on tiptoe to ensure my peace and quiet.

Much earlier, the development of her personality had been disturbed by her mother. She was really insane, and it is common knowledge in the family that during one of her fits of insanity she kept the child in her room for two days. Nobody knows what went on there, but attempts at reproduction in analysis (the mother was always painfully anxious to prevent any masturbatory activity in her daughter) led us to suppose that the mother made an attack on the child's genitals. The tragedy of this case is that even after the patient had grown up and obtained possession of her fortune and the right to dispose of it, she still does not really have the courage to enjoy this freedom herself. She continues to feel the compulsion to sacrifice herself for others, just as she in fact had to sacrifice her whole childhood and youth, and even a part of her intelligence, to her insane— crazy—environment. She is moved to tears and immediately to charitable intervention.

1. See "Stages in the Development of the Sense of Reality," C 213–239.—ED.
2. See "The Unwelcome Child and His Death Instinct," Fin 102–107.—ED.
3. Since Ferenczi this is sometimes described as "impregnation" or Pragung.—ED.

30 June 1932

Hypocrisy and the "enfant terrible"

Dm.: hypocrisy is the consequence of *cowardice* in those who set the tone. (Authorities are afraid of authorities.) They preach *lying* and speak contemptuously of anyone who speaks the unadorned truth. *Good children* have become hypocrites themselves. "Enfants terribles" are in revolt (perhaps to an extreme) against hypocrites, and exaggerate simplicity and democracy. Really favorable development (optimum) would lead to the development of individuals (and a race) that would be neither mendacious (hypocritical) nor destructive.

Schizophrenia is a "photochemical" mimicry reaction, instead of self-assertion (revenge, defense). (Dm.: schizophrenics were affected by trauma *before* they possessed a personality.)

The photosensitive "mimicry reaction" in nature is *more primary* than the self-assertive or self-important reaction. The seemingly non-existent *second principle* (kindness reaction) ignored by science is *the primary* one (more childish). It seems to get lost as a result of errone-ous (irritating) upbringing.

Repressed goodness: analysis denied this—or admitted its existence only on a higher plane. (Pfister!)[1]

180   Analysts want to apply their own complexes (wickedness, ill will) even to those damaged at an early age (schizophrenics). Mistakenly! Indeed even neurotics must be guided *beyond* (behind) the traumato-genic vileness back to trusting kindness. *The second "principle" is the more primary one.*

Influence of the passions of adults on the character-neuroses and sexual development of children[2]

What are passions? In the *Encyclopaedia Britannica*:[3] "passion" = (1) suffering of pain, (2) feeling of emotion, (3) sufferings of Jesus Christ . . . and of Saints and Martyrs. "The modern use generally restricts the term to strong and uncontrolled emotions." V. 418 C, V. 420 C, V. 425 D. (Descartes: If reason be contradictory in itself, truth must be found in unreason.)

It is not easy to conceive how the same being who is determined by passion from without should also be determined by reason from within. How in other words can a spiritual being maintain its charac-ter as self-determined or at least determined only by the clear and distinct idea of the reason which are its innate forms in the presence of this foreign element of passion that seems to make it the slave of external impressions? Is reason able to crush this intruder or to turn it into a servant? Can the passions be annihilated or can they be spiritu-alized? Descartes could not properly adopt either alternative.

So Descartes tried to establish the nature of sublimation in a specu-lative manner. Freud tried to define all sublimation and all striving for perfection as unfulfillable wish impulses, which must remain forever unsatisfied, as though they were compensatory and consoling fan-tasies and actions. A special investigation and observation of the conversion of passion into logical and ethical self-control, then into positive pleasure taken in growth and development [*Gedeihen*] everywhere (this means in oneself, as well as in the environment) led to the assumption that there are possibly two distinct processes involved in sublimation, that is to say, in the pleasure taken in well-being, development, mutual kindness, and tenderness: (1) de facto, in the Freudian sense, there is a change of direction of the passionate but unfulfillable aggressive and selfish impulses; (2) one comes to suspect that there is also a second source of mutual goodwill, more primary, natural, and nonneurotic. If we succeed in gaining insight into the psychic life of a child who as yet has been spared pain and suffering, then we come ultimately to the assumption that man becomes passionate and ruthless purely as a consequence of suffering. But if the child continues to live in an optimal environmental climate, then it is inclined (a) to share its own pleasure with the environment, (b) to take pleasure, without a feeling of envy, in development and well-being in the environment.

This behavior and feeling, however, apparently so highly ethical, has none of the pretensions of the righteous adult; it is merely a psychic parallel to one's own unimpeded physical and mental growth; so it is no particular achievement nor is it experienced as such. Such perfect happiness was perhaps enjoyed only in the womb, that is, a passionless period, which is briefly interrupted by the trauma of birth, but which continues to be enjoyed during the period of nursing. The unavoidable—but perhaps partly superfluous and unnecessary—sufferings of the first adaptation (regulation of organ functions, training in cleanliness, weaning) make every human more or less passionate. In the most favorable cases, however, there remains in the individual, as the residue and effect of the happiness experienced, a bit of optimism and also harmless pleasure in progress and development everywhere.

It is therefore perhaps incorrect to attribute all manifestations of goodness or excessive goodness on the part of obsessional neurotics to compensated or overcompensated sadistic aggressiveness. Even if all the suffering that provoked the unconscious aggressiveness was reproduced in analysis, and was dealt with in a new way, full of insight and compassion, and even if the layer of terror and its anxious and phobic defensive structures are dismantled, there still remains the problem: what could have made the child capable of finding such an intelligent, one would like to say such a selfless, form of adaptation, instead of persisting with a defensive and defiant attitude (as it clearly often happens) and being destroyed. One must recall those wonderful processes in nature such as mimicry and especially symbiosis.

The prodigious alloplastic achievement in adapting itself forces large quantities of the environment's energy into economic channels. (See Benjamin Franklin: "Eripuit coelo fulmen sceptrumque tirannis.")[4] A part of the world's energy is tamed and humanized, so to speak, by human influence. The attempts of human beings toward mutual adaptation must be described as less successful, however. If there were some way to moderate human beings' impulse to be passionate by allowing them to enjoy the real happiness of childhood a little longer, by taming one's own inclination to be passionate toward them, and by not making the unavoidable efforts of resignation in the adaptation period even more difficult through superfluous suffering: then it might not be impossible to reduce the conflicts of individual egoism, and to promote the development of the child's nature, which is perhaps not completely selfish to begin with, particularly its conciliatory and balancing aspects and the aspects that delight in progress. If one were not ashamed to indulge in prophesies, then one would expect of the future neither the triumph of one-sided and ruthless capitalism nor that of fanciful egalitarianism, but rather a full recognition of the existence of purely selfish drives, which remain under control but must be partly satisfied in reality; the elimination of a great deal of neurotic, still passionate, one might even say violently excessive goodness (eat-bird-or-die policy)[5] and, finally, perhaps the gradual unfolding of a naive good-heartedness.

The preparatory work for this must be provided in the upbringing of children, but the preparatory work for the upbringing of children is psychoanalytical experience and experiment. So one naturally comes under suspicion of having simply increased by one more the number of mad world-reformers; the evidence against this is: (1) that in individual cases such a process of transformation has a permanent effect; (2) that the favorable change in the character of cured neurotics is already, today, affecting the environment in the above-mentioned beneficial sense; (3) that there are very promising experiments already on record about the results of psychoanalytically trained upbringing of children.

My own optimism is a psychoanalytical success. My most obvious character trait used to be a definite pessimism concerning both insight and progress as well as the possibilities for adaptation in nature. Everywhere I saw only a *circulus vitiosus*. Nowadays I venture, at times, to think of a *circulus benignus*.

184

"Cartesianism. *Encyclopaedia Britannica,* Vol. V, 1910–11. The passions are . . . provisions of nature for the protection of the unity of soul and body, and stimulate us to the acts necessary for that purpose. Yet, on the other hand, he could not admit that these passions are capable of being completely spiritualized . . . It is impossible to think that the passions which arise out of this unity, can be transformed into the embodiment and expression of reason."[6]

Descartes points out: ". . . every passion has a lower and a higher form; and while in its lower or primary form it is based on the obscure ideas produced by the motion of the animal spirit, in its higher form it is connected with the clear and distinct judgments of reason regarding good and evil."

Supposition: even the lowest forms of existence (inorganic, purely vegetative) are the result of *two* tendencies: seeking the route: (1) through self-defense and resistance; (2) through adaptation, compromise, appeasement. Higher (also ethical) human knowledge is *a return to compromise*—or the principle of *appeasement,* which exists everywhere.

The inorganic: feeling everything, knowing nothing. (Reality principle only.)

The vegetative: to know, as far as possible, everything that is advantageous to oneself. (Pleasure principle only.)

Human: to eliminate whatever is not the self by means of defense and resistance. (Repression.) Pleasure principle.

Two forms: (1) compulsion: reality principle only (selflessness); (2) taking into consideration pleasure and reality principles!

Yet even Descartes sees that "no *ideal* morality is possible to man in his present state."

Dualism of Descartes in Metaphysics and in Ethics.

Is progress conceivable to a point where *selfish* (passionate) tendencies are entirely renounced? Only if the centers of self ceased to exist as such, and, if separate individuals (atoms, etc.) were to come to the "conviction" that it is better *not* to exist as separate beings. Unification of the universe at an ideal point [*ideellen Punkt*].

At present only a *relative optimum* possible (porcupine philosophy). Yet this could be improved (Progress).

Malebranche,[7] church father: "*My pain is a modification of my substance but truth is the common good of all spirits.*"

Ferenczi: Passion is purely selfish, "truth" is the common property of all existing things.

C II principle (peace).

Ferenczi: (a) "Struggle of all against all" = modern natural sciences. (b) "Compromise of all with all" (peace principle).

186 *Malebranche:* "The idea of the infinite is prior to the idea of finite."

Ferenczi: The reaction of all to all (in the universe) is present prior to self-protective organization (individuality).

Malebranche: "We conceive of the infinite being by the very fact that we conceive of being without thinking whether it be finite or no. *But in order that we* may think of a finite being we must necessarily cut off or deduct something from the general notion of being, which consequently we must previously possess."

The fact of *feeling-one's-self* postulates the existence of a *non-I; the ego is an abstraction.* PRIOR to this abstraction we must have felt the Whole (universe).

The child is still closer to this feeling of universality (without sense organs), he knows (feels) everything, certainly much more than adults, whose present sense organs serve in large part to exclude a large part of the external world (in fact *everything* except what is useful).

187 Adults are relative idiots. Children are all-knowing.

1. Oskar Pfister (1873–1956), Swiss pastor, became an analyst without relinquishing his ministry. All his life he endeavored to reconcile his religious faith and psychoanalysis. He engaged in lively discussions with Freud and became his friend, as one can discern from their extensive correspondence: *The Letters of Sigmund Freud and Oskar Pfister* (Hogarth Press, 1963). He published a number of books and papers, notably "The Illusion of a Future," a response to Freud's article "The Future of an Illusion."—ED.

2. This is the first draft of the paper Ferenczi presented at the Congress of Wiesbaden in 1932: "Confusion of Tongues between Adults and the Child," *Fin* 156–167.—ED.

3. The rest of this paragraph and all of the following paragraph were written in English. René Descartes (1596–1650), French philosopher and mathematician. The quotations here are from an entry on Descartes in the *Encyclopaedia Britannica*, which Freud had given to Ferenczi on his fiftieth birthday. Ferenczi refers here to the *Treatise on Passions,* more precisely to Article 147 of the *Passions of the Soul,* dated 1649.—ED.

4. Snatched the lightning from the heavens and the scepter from the tyrant.

5. According to Michael Balint, this refers to a well-known German tale in which a boy is given a budgerigar as a present. Wanting to look after it as well as possible, he offers the bird all kinds of delicacies, but it does not seem to want to eat. The boy finally flies into a rage and forces some food into the bird's beak, crying, "Eat, bird, or die!"

6. This paragraph and the one following are in English.

7. Nicolas Malebranche (1638–1715), French metaphysician. As with Descartes, Ferenczi's source here was the *Encyclopaedia Britannica*. Some of the ideas set out in Malebranche's philosophy: (1) The idea of the infinite: Malebranche reaffirms the Cartesian position, according to which: "The mind possesses the idea of the infinite, and it does so even before it possesses the idea of the finite." (2) On the "peace-principle": Malebranche postulates an opposition between the "peace of the state" and the "peace of the church." "The rigor of rationalist principles is thus accompanied, in Malebranche's moral system, by a strong sense of the concrete, which excludes all formalism and varies the application of the rules according to the circumstances." Geneviève Rodis-Lewis, *Nicolas Malebranche* (Paris: Presses Universitaires de France), pp. 89, 278.—ED.

6 July 1932

Projection of our own passions or passionate tendencies onto children

Are perversions really infantilisms, and to what extent? Are sadism and anal eroticism not already hysterical reactions to traumata?

Advantages and disadvantages, that is, optimal limits of countertransference

R.N.: almost daily course of events: (1) Examines thoroughly the associations of the analyst, who naturally cannot disguise that he himself feels various negative reactions toward the patient. R.N. tries to treat these statements with analytical understanding, but despite her usual objectivity, one notices a special interest in statements pertaining to herself and in statements made by others about her; but especially: how far I identify myself with those who do not appreciate her. (2) Change of direction of the investigation, session begins with complaints: (a) about her illness and its symptoms, the slowness of progress; (b) equally based on analytic admissions of the previous day, complaints about the absence of the degree of interest and sympathy, even love, that alone would give her confidence in my ability to glue her lacerated soul into a whole; (c) my reaction to this was formerly a marked increase in antipathy and the feeling of being forced into feelings. (Followed by corresponding inner defense.)

Since the more profound investigation of the causes of my sympathies and antipathies, a large share of the latter have been traced back to infantile father and grandfather fixation with corresponding misogyny. Accordingly appreciable increase in compassion for this person who has been tortured almost to the point of death and falsely accused in addition. As soon as my emotion reaches a certain peak, the patient becomes calm and is willing to carry on working; the still persisting criticism from now on refers only to my ineptitude in framing questions and, with a few exceptions, to the absence of appropriate and efficient inner exertions of my will, which is immediately perceived by the patient, who feels telepathically, even clairvoyantly, aware while in trance. All the same, these double sessions end at times in almost tender reconciliations. The antithesis to these events is provided by her previous history: the perpetrator of the trauma himself was so blinded that he made the foulest accusations against his child. This was the moment of disintegration, the loss of all hope, which is transferred onto the analysis as well.

On the other hand it cannot be denied that the patient efforts of eight years deserve recognition, and that a child tortured almost to death must be treated tenderly. But when should adaptation to reality begin? Will it be possible to get the patient to renounce her unrealizable fantasies? Sometimes I almost despair of it, but holding on, up to now, has always been worth it. Today, for example, she dreamed of a bull, which attacked her; she actually feels the horn against her skin, and she gives up. This saves her life, since the animal loses all interest in the creature that is no longer struggling and appears to be dead, and leaves her lying there.

And yet the patient finds me not quite repentant enough; on the other hand, as this dream shows, she is now perhaps inclined to appreciate my admission and my friendliness, and to do without some of the other things. Thus up to now it has been worth it to keep the occasional fits of impatience firmly under control, and even to accept a large share of the responsibility for such impatience. It is not an analyst's job to get angry; he is there to understand and help. Where this capacity is blocked he must search for the fault in himself. There then comes a time—or so we hope—when patients will become reconciled, even though with regret, to what is irremediable, even if analysis does not offer them any more for their lives than understanding and sympathy, and even if real life promises only fragments of the happiness they have until now been denied.

B.: Feeling of being unwell intensely aggravated. There is not a night without sleep- or respiratory-disturbances; suffering it for weeks, then boiling rage spills over against the analysis, which only causes pain and opens old wounds, and then does nothing for her. Swearing and screaming during the entire session, accusations, insults, etc., she insists I should admit my helplessness, finally she even has the idea that I should repeat the trauma—if it will only help. In the past, on the occasion of similar attacks and outbursts, I felt somehow a sense of guilt, and I tried to soothe the patient and treat her—a suffering child again—with deeply felt tenderness; yet everything stayed the same as before. Since then, I have learned to control my emotions; I even think that the friendly but cool approach and the unavoidable outbursts that follow it are [to be regarded][1] in fact as progress compared to the previous concealment of rage (which she learned to do at home). I believe that a further increase of her rage, handled subsequently in the same way, will find its way back into the past of its own accord. If one goes too thoroughly into the positive or negative countertransference, one may avoid unpleasant experiences in the course of the session, but if one does not evade it, then one may be rewarded by unexpected progress.

Dm.: Ever since she sees and feels that I do not respond to her provocative actions and behavior simply with antipathy, one can have anything from her. There is enormous progress.

S.I. was actually someone I always liked, but she was resistant for a long time. Then the sudden shift I have often described, to serenity and sublimation.

All in all still no universally applicable rules.

1. Phrase supplied by Michael Balint.

7 July 1932

Reflected imaging and inversion,

as psychical consequences of the disintegration of the personality (and of the loss of capacity for conviction, and even knowledge and remembering). (1) R.N.: frequently recurring form of dream: two, three, or even several persons represent, according to the completed dream-analysis, an equal number of component parts of her personality. The dream analyzed today, for instance, was dramatized as follows: the dreamer herself receives a written message from the beloved person who is closest to her, which reads: "Here I am. I am here." The dreamer attempts to tell this to a third person, a man, but she can contact him only indirectly, by a long-distance telephone call, and in fact the whole conversation with this man sounds very indistinct, as if coming from an immense distance. The difficulty increases to the point of a nightmarish and helpless struggle because of the fact that the text of the message cannot be read directly; the dreamer sees it only in mirror-writing, as light shines through the postcard; she is sitting in a kind of tent, and can see the writing only as mirror-writing.

Her inability to make herself understood is linked by association in the analysis (a) to her despair over the fact that I, the analyst, could have misunderstood her for so long (I was comparing her case to a different, much milder one, S.I., and reproaching her, as it were, for not being converted to optimism in the same nice and obliging way as the other was.) (b) This behavior on my part reproduces the moment when she despaired of ever regaining the love her father had once shown her. She recognizes that his true nature is blind and mad (twisted) rage, anger, and cruelty. (c) Furthermore, it is interwoven with the diabolical idea, which he in fact carried out, of making the patient totally defenseless and transforming her into an automaton by administering various poisons. The man in the dream who is so hard to reach is on the one hand this tormentor; on the other hand he represents me, the stubborn analyst. The historical analysis of this male figure (who acts like a clown in the dream and instead of showing his own pain amuses others and performs comical acrobatic tricks) leads (a) to her own infantile life story, circus performances, etc., (b) to similar infantile experiences suspected in the analyst (drunkenness and abuse). Looking through the tent canvas, reading the mirror-writing itself, and hearing the caller as though from a great distance correspond to historical events.

The most comprehensive interpretation of this nightmare, however, is that this personality, shattered and made defenseless by suffering and poison, is attempting, over and over again but always unsuccessfully, to reassemble its various parts into a unit, that is, to understand the events taking place in and around her. But instead of understanding herself (realizing her own misery) she can only display in an indirect and symbolic way the contents that relate to her and of which she is herself unconscious: she must concern herself with analogous mental states in others (the reason for her choice of career), perhaps in the secret hope that one day she will be understood by one of these sufferers. Her hypersensitivity—as says the association—goes so far that she can send and receive "telephone messages" over immense distances. (She believes in telepathic healing by means of willpower and thought-concentration, but especially through compassion.) As she links her own life history with that of the analyst, she suspects that even as a child she found the analyst, who is subject to similar suffering, "over a long distance" by means of telepathy, and after some forty years of aimless wandering has now also sought him out. However, the obstacles and amnesia in the analyst himself have delayed the emergence of an understanding (in the analyst; see her complaints about my erroneous judgments), and only now, as I begin to realize my mistakes and recognize and exonerate her as an innocent and well-intentioned person (I did in fact describe her in the most favorable terms at S.I.'s recently), are we approaching the possibility of fitting the fragments of her personality together and of enabling her, not only indirectly but also directly, to recognize and remember the actual fact and the causes of this disintegration. Until now, she could read (know) about her own circumstances only in mirror-writing, that is, in the reflection of the analogous sufferings of others. Now, however, she has found someone who can show her, in a, for her, convincing manner, that what she has uncovered about the analyst she must acknowledge as a distant reflection of her own sufferings.

If this succeeds, then the former disintegration, and consequently the tendency to project (insanity) will in fact be mutually reversed.

(2). The individual components of the personality enable us, in this in depth analysis, to study the process of repression in detail. The question of whether repressed feelings and pain do exist will be here positively resolved. Indeed, immense quantities of masses of sensory excitation, devoid of representations and cut off from motor discharge and thinking, are accumulated in neurotics and psychotics. This state of being cut off from the intelligence exacerbates the pain. In any event we see here an obvious confirmation of *Freud* regarding the formation of repression: the forcible separation of the contents of the psyche from the appropriate emotional reactions.

19 July 1932

Insight into one's own paranoia as a "brilliant achievement" (for the first time?) of the logical consequence and of "perseverance" (strength of character)

Despite great unpleasure and almost superhuman exertions, continually struggling with inner conflict (see tics: bringing musical and incantational order (solution) to the chaos), creating a logical unity in the crazy jumble (a) of my own feelings and thoughts, (b) of the chaos in the world around me. Even when I did not succeed in this, no matter how often I failed, I never gave up the *hope* that eventually I can succeed. I *almost* gave it up prior to the "frontier passage" episode. Yet it was *just then* that despair shifted abruptly to *psychological activity* sustained by the "inner counsel." (Finding the unconscious.) It was a case of "to be or not to be." (S.S.S.)[1]

After this brief intermezzo I landed in the "service of love" of a strong man, remaining dependent. A new impetus was provided by the experience of psychoanalysis: (1) enthusiasm, personal work, a great deal of originality; (2) literal subordination (secret Grand Vizir ambivalence). Partial relaxation of enthusiasm already in America (1) yet, at most, *silence*. Unproductivity. Latest disappointment: "He does not love anyone, only himself and his work" (and does not allow anyone to be original). After Berlin, Paris.—The libidinal detachment permitted "revolutionary" technical innovations: activity, passivity, elasticity. Return to trauma (Breuer). *In opposition to Freud* I developed to an exceptional degree a capacity for *humility* and for appreciating the clearsightedness of the uncorrupted child (patient). Finally, I even allowed them: (1) full insight into my weaknesses (analysis by everyone), (2) into my fraudulent superiority (tranquillity).

1. In this passage Ferenczi refers to key events of his own earlier life, events of which we do not have details. As to the significance of "(S.S.S.)," we must rely on conjecture. The only known expression that may have given rise to it and that also fits the general context is advice generally given to mothers-in-law: *schweigen, schlucken und schenken*—"keep quiet, keep swallowing, and keep giving." We are indebted to S. Achache for this hypothesis.—ED.

195 19 July 1932

Superiority (grandeur) up to now has given me the pleasant feeling that everyone is stupid (crazy) but me. Psychoanalytical insight into my own emotional emptiness, which was shrouded by overcompensation (repressed—unconscious—psychosis) led to a self-diagnosis of *schizophrenia*. (In consequence, compensations had to be in conflict with reality, that is, delusional, paranoid. *Hatred of the woman, veneration of man* (with a compulsion to promiscuity as a superstructure) made possible the rationalization of *traumatic impotence*. Fundamental cause: father's father = God, king, patriarch. (It was impossible to be right against God.) Yet obstinate claim to be right in all other areas.

The whole world was criticized. Finally the *criticism* turned itself *against myself* (being right, not lying, was easier than death, or anxiety, or pain). So I submitted, as a logical consequence, to the desired idea. Finally this led to the *search for the causes* of my wanting to be right (hatred of women). The solution of the trauma and compensation. Final result: insight into the blindness (cowardice) still persisting in the face of male authority. In the end: insight into the *paranoia* of authority (God is insane, the world is chaotic). Realization: my paranoia was only the imitation (representation) of his, that is, of the powerful adult's.

From now on: I have to detach myself from them calmly, then perhaps cure them (teach them insight). Special task: to free the patients whom psychoanalytic paranoia has reduced to the status of minors, made dependent and permanently attached, truly to liberate them, *from us as well.*

196   Pride: I am the *first* crazy person who had acquired critical insight, and had *yielded to everyone.* (To have resolved to learn from the "conscious.") Reward: the *insane* show themselves as *healthy;* intellectual and symbolic honesty only in "thoughts," in speech. Honesty is transformed. (Courage to criticize.)

In Case I (R.N.), so difficult. Utilizing material from self-analysis in Case I.

In Cases II, IV. (Dm., B., etc.), faster.

197   "Even becomes discouraged," weeps.

If the analyst does not assist *courageously* with the repetition (without fear), then the patient will make no progress. The obstacles of the *analyst* must first be resolved and understood. The self-confidence of the patient returns (or will be established for the first time). Self-injury when nothing happens from the outside or (out of fear) is handled too gently (S.I.). *Suicide.*

Splitting is like love-of-the-self: as it is terrifying, therefore being killed is preferred.

Technique: Put an end to the period of gentleness. Ruthlessness is called for.

Awakening of self-confidence in B. (child)

Her friend is unreasonably sensitive.

Analysts everywhere promote "hate."

"I hallucinate," that is, I admit that they are all (men and women) *insane:* they get angry about trivial things; they hate instead of loving. She cannot, however, believe that she is the only one with a clear head; therefore she must tell herself constantly: *I am crazy* (instead of: everybody else is).

198   # 19 July 1932

Order in chaos

B.: incapable of free association. Always logical. Instead of that, one discovers, after overcoming colossal resistance against talking about it, that in addition to her clearly conscious work of thinking [*Denkarbeit*] she also has a *melody permanently in her head,* in fact a disharmonious polyphony, which she must *resolve* by musically logical means.[1] Solution: in addition to her conscious-logical existence, which is an overcompensation for her real condition and mode of functioning, she harbors a *chaotic* existence, which must constantly be put in "order." (A large part of the person is "crazy," disoriented.)[2]

(See also the dream of the small child, whose head only comes up to the edge of the table.) *Trauma is fixed* on the traumatic (not the pretraumatic) moment. One would like to deal with it, that is, to grasp it consciously and incorporate it into the past (memories). That will, however, be impossible (1) when the trauma is too great to be fully experienced again, (2) if one does not get any help with it, (3) especially, when one . . .[3]

1. Regarding the subject of creating order in chaos by musical means, see page 159.—ED.

2. Ferenczi again puns on the word *verrückt;* see 14 February, note 4.

3. The rest of this entry is missing.

21 July 1932

On the feeling of shame

1. Starting point B.: (a) Her friend who shares the house with her, N.F., gets into a rage over trivia, sulks for days in total silence, she also stammers. Patient B. suddenly has an almost hallucinatory fantasy that when N.F. speaks it is as though she were performing an anal function with her mouth. (Po-po-po-po-po.) (b) B. dreams that she sees a man crawling on the floor, like a wounded animal, groaning. His anal region is distorted, twisted, blood-red, just like an open mouth, with two rows of teeth and a tongue inside. (c) N.F., breaking her silence, sits down on B's lap with a sudden and almost violent movement and says furiously: "By God, I love you."

B. has attempted to make it quite clear to N.F. that she (N.F.) assumes things in her (B.) that are simply not there. N.F. replies to that (in good psychoanalytic fashion), "Oh yes, these things are there in you, you just don't know about them." (She meant that one is so ashamed of certain tendencies that one makes them unconscious.) I could reassure B. that there are, indeed, quite genuine feelings behind which nothing else "unconscious and repressed" is hidden. From here the analytical discussion moved on to the problem of shame in general. I said to her that shame was a typically male invention, and basically quite senseless. Why should one refer to an organ and its functions, both of which exist, as shameful parts? Boys are much more bashful than little girls. This is why girls suddenly turn modest when they reach the age of puberty. (Here quote the example of the little Erzsike.)[1] Men make moral laws and compel women to accept them. An unbroken transmission ensures the impregnation of the next generation with morality.

It so happened that as B. got to know about genital functions and their pleasurable character in earliest childhood, when her mind was still untainted by morality, she became, so to speak, clairvoyant; she only pretended to accept social conventions, but deep down she remained convinced that modesty is senseless (insane) and a lie. She unmasked the puritanism and snobbery of her mother and the impotent cowardice and dependency of her father, since by then she had seen the latter in his moral négligé. She is thus also afraid of the moralism in psychoanalysis, which goes on forever about repression caused by shame, while (in childhood) so much is experienced fully, without repression or shame.

Analysts do not know how genuine and unaltered is the childish naïveté of neurotics. They believe too little of what the neurotic says, and that must be discouraging to him, when he knows how open and unashamed he is and how unjust it is to impute any repression to him. It is not the child but society that is full of shame and repressive.

So in the above two cases. B. sees in N.F. the distortion: as a consequence of genital shame, the genitals and genital functions are, so to speak, excluded, and instead anus and mouth are cathected with libido: love life is focused on biting and evacuation. As a child she probably came to feel that all that is genital is to be treated as being just as disgusting as the evacuation of stools. One will also be punished for it, just as though one had soiled oneself. Thus sadomasochism and anal eroticism take the place of genitality. The same thing happens to the man in her dream. B. sees quite clearly the personality of Dr. R.N.N. She sees, behind his exaggerated masculinity and his obsession with possessing every woman, the anal distortion caused by the homosexual practices of his grandfather. She sees that in fact he is impotent and a weakling. She sees something similar in almost all civilized men.

These explanations, and the affirmative replies on my part to the question of whether I also am civilized, produce a singular change in the behavior of the patient. Her next dream concerns a fairly robust man with a minute penis. Details pointed to my person. I was able to satisfy her curiosity and tell her something about my own anxiousness and bashfulness, small-penis complex, etc. As she noted that I do not conceal any of my weaknesses, so that she cannot hurt me any more by alluding to these weaknesses, she ceased to rub my nose in my ineptitude, analytical and otherwise, and began to wonder whether it is not unsatisfied sexual hunger that is behind the apparently unbearably agonizing pains (in abdomen), and whether the "trauma" in her case was not created by the withdrawal of love rather than by rape.[2]

The withdrawal of love, and being toally alone with one's demands for love against the compact and overwhelming majority, produce shame and repression (neurosis) in so-called normal children. The awakening to a sense of shame can come about quite suddenly; it probably signifies the beginning of a new epoch accompanied by more or less complete forgetting (amnesia) of the time before. B. was regarded by her family as a "difficult child, problem child." Her defiance was a symptom of the fact that she had only formally yielded to the constraints of a puritanical sense of modesty. Now, in me, she at last finds someone whose upbringing had made him prudish (civilized) indeed, but who had nonetheless been able to "improve" himself, that is, to realize and admit the senselessness of prudery. Now she begins to admit that when she restricts herself exclusively to the "elephant penis" of her infantile experiences and rejects everything less than that, she is condemned to hunger for life, and she begins to wonder whether one could not give up what is unattainable and be satisfied, at least in part, with what is attainable. She is also beginning to regard the "small penis" of the "civilized man" as a possible instrument of love. There is every prospect that she will give up mocking men by means of female homosexuality.

(What could have been the fundamental cause of the tradition of modesty in man? Here one must refer to the works of Davis with appreciation.) What was the motive of puberty rites that branded the genitals as organs of suffering and women as dangerous and dirty? See Freud's work on the history of civilization.

2. Today O.S. had the following little experience: she has always maintained that she is almost never subject to emotions such as rage, anger, and the like, a claim that her friend N.D. always doubted and even mocked. Her friend (who is certainly inclined to paranoia) has

always suspected that behind her apathy are hidden the most horrible murderous intentions. In reality O.S. is infantile to an extreme degree; she is a playful child. However, such children are initially quite incapable of a persistent attitude of defiance and rage; they feel momentary anger perhaps, but they forget it when one gives them a friendly smile. O.S. now wanted to please her friend by telling her, as though she were giving her a present: "You see, I was jealous of such and such a person today." But what happened? Instead of praising O.S. for her honesty, her friend (N.D.) started to search for other, even worse signs of malice in her.

Adults behave the same way when they project their own passionate character onto children, and this is also what we did as analysts when we posited our own sexual distortions, imposed on children, as infantile sexual theories. O.S. is right when she says "I know very well (as indeed all children know) when what I want is something bad, when I am afraid of something, when I have feelings of guilt and shame. But I refuse to take on myself the exaggerated accusations of the adults, and I also refuse to declare certain things shameful that to me are absolutely not so."

How and why does a girl at the onset of menstruation become suddenly aware of shame? Menstrual bleeding takes her back to the time when she was not yet able to control her stool and urine. One cannot regulate uterine bleeding with willpower; whether one wants to or not, one will soil oneself, and all of a sudden one is aware of the warnings and exhortations that one used to dismiss laughingly before menstruation.

1. A Hungarian girl's name: little Elizabeth.
2. *Überwältigung*, the translation of which would be "subjugation," "being overpowered." At the suggestion of Michael Balint, however, the above translation was adopted, which would have been *Vergewaltigung*.

23 July 1932

Experimentum analyticum cum B.

B. is incapable of free association. Cause: (1) Unfortunate experiences with authority (mother), when she complied with the request, "Tell me nicely everything, nothing will happen to you"—and then was punished nevertheless. Thus she cannot believe I really mean it when I urge her to tell me everything, even what may be disagreeable for me. (2) She knows from her own experience how unbearable it is to be scolded, particularly in a loud and shrill voice; this is why she knows how much she would be hated by the analyst, to whom she is telling everything. (3) The inhibition is at its strongest when the analyst's behavior betrays nothing of the unpleasant effect on him, but his sudden silence and exaggerated reserve indicate hidden annoyance. (This situation will not be improved until one behaves with more openness toward the analysand. Mention here her relief, described earlier, when I admitted to a feeling of irritation toward her.) The question now arises, however, whether it will be enough to tell the patient only what disturbs, annoys, or irritates me in him; or whether positive, friendly, tender, etc., feelings should also be communicated. (4) A specific sensitivity in the patient in the face of such "cowardly and hypocritical concealment" stems from her observations as a very young child. She noticed that her imposing father turned into a frightened coward as soon as her mother began to scream. Later she found that men are generally cowards, and that however brutal or aggressive they may be, they take to their heels at the sound of a shrill female voice. It is possible that in watching the primal scene she identified with the father. (Perhaps because her mother meant more to her than her father. She therefore became the father in order to keep the mother. But on later occasions, when she found her father cowardly and anxiously silent when facing her mother, she became impatient and wanted to show the father: *this is how* you should behave toward mother.) In the analytic situation she becomes terribly impatient when she notices that in the face of her rage I withdraw (in fact often I very nearly go to sleep) instead of giving her a thorough dressing-down as she would have wished her father to do; and this wish remained always unsatisfied.

Therefore in the analysis she becomes the screaming mother, and when nothing happens on my part other than the stereotypical remark, "Yes, and what occurs to you in this connection?"—then she becomes truly enraged and demands loudly: "But for God's sake do something, try to act, otherwise we shall not get one step further!" If I remain silent and reserved, she then becomes totally exhausted, and may start the next day by applying herself diligently. As we have been able to establish, however, there is no actual progress in this diligence; it merely indicates that in the face of my cowardice she is helpless; she becomes resigned, and is forced to behave, with her will shattered, as though she were in agreement with my approach. Her exhaustion with protesting may be so complete that she does not even know anymore that she would like to protest.

This is how she spent years living near her father, without even knowing what kind of emotional meaning he had for her. What the patient, like many others, incidentally means by "something must be done" is probably revealed by certain seemingly senseless "fears," such as "I often believe that you want to hit me over the head, and when you make a move I almost feel the blow." The patient means by this that when she has tormented me for too long, what I would like to do most is to knock her down or throw her out. Patients know this from their own experience, they know the rage that came over them when they had to endure insults or an injustice. (An important, probably the most important, source of masochism, of the wish to be beaten, may be a protest against the hypocrisy of teachers and parents, pregnant with rage, that is disguised in benevolent behavior.

It is unbearable for children to believe that they alone are bad because they react to torture with rage. That the adults never feel anything similar, that they always are and always feel they are right, clever, insightful, etc. It is unbearable to be the only bad person in a magnificent and exemplary society, so it is of some consolation when I succeed in making my respected father [*Herr Vater*] or teacher lose their tempers, thereby making them admit indirectly that they are not any less subject to "weaknesses" than their children.

In the case of B. too one came to the idea, though not without having been influenced by the case of R.N., how it would be if we suddenly exchanged roles, that is, if I were to lie on the couch and she to make herself comfortable in my armchair. I just wanted to show her what free association is, and she was to show me how the correct behavior of the analyst looks. I rejoiced at regaining my freedom and at the license it gave me. As a contrast to screaming and abuse I demanded tenderness and kindness (I asked her to caress my head and wished to be rewarded for all my exertions with affection, tenderness, embraces, and kisses); but by this I in fact admitted how much I disliked being in the other situation, where I was only permitted to endure and could hardly ask for anything in return. This typically characterizes man's somewhat childish attitude toward a woman. However, the reaction of the pseudoanalyst was no less characteristic: she was quite prepared, without further ado, to comply with all my wishes, indeed she had to admit that the feelings of shame and reserve were almost alien to her, she became a little alarmed, though not seriously, at the idea: "How can I become an analyst if I am so ready to comply with the wishes of my clients?"

The answer to this question, which puts us in quite an embarrassing situation, can perhaps be formulated as follows: (a) Perhaps women make good analysts only insofar as they discern patients' wishes quickly and surely, just as mothers do with their children, but they make bad analysts when it comes to the second task of childrearing, namely that of teaching the restraint and self-control required in life. Men and women can thus equally be good analysts, but in order to do this women must learn some of the masculine self-control and inhibition, so as to impart it to children. However, the man can be a good analyst only when, in addition to the logical and ethical rules they are familiar with, he also acquires, applies, teaches, and if necessary inspires in others the feminine capacity for empathy.

The total absence of shame and moral notions in this female patient may derive from the fact that she became prematurely and moreover fully acquainted with sexual reality, that is, lust, before she could have had any notion in her inexperience of the social and practical dangers involved. "Premature sexual satisfaction renders the child ineducable."[1] (Freud). This would also equal analytic ineducability. I however believe that one can, albeit with a great deal of effort, educate analytically even those who have been sexually initiated too early. But naturally only when one gives up every kind of hypocritical prudery in thinking and feeling, and also in speech and behavior, with such patients and explains the necessity for restraint only and exclusively on the grounds of social and other real obstacles.

1. Freud, "Three Essays on the Theory of Sexuality," SE VII, 179; also more generally the second essay, "Infantile Sexuality," as well as p. 234 of the third essay, "The Transformations of Puberty."—ED.

24 July 1932

On abreaction

For more than two years now, we have been working with R.N. so that fragments of the traumata, often the complete antecedents of the trauma, are reexperienced and worked through with colossal outbursts of affect bearing every indication of terrible experiences. The associations are, almost without exception, linked to her dreams. A number of the dreams are painful in themselves and of a nightmarish character; the rest of the dreams have a harmless facade, do not disturb sleep, and it is only the associations that raise the mass of affect. Despite these efforts on my part and the abreaction of affect on hers, to this day the affective outbursts have brought no permanent success. Indeed the attacks usually end with a certain appeasement, and during and immediately after these attacks the patient also feels a sense of conviction concerning the reality of the experiences; quite soon after such sessions, however, doubt sets in, and after a few hours everything is as it was before; the following night brings another nightmare, and the next session another attack.

We are not entirely clear as to the causes of this lack of success. It must be noted that these attacks do not occur until after the patient has dropped her daytime personality and name and has wholly become that child with the childish nickname on whom the traumatic assaults were made. In other words, the abreacting part is really still living in the past; the patient repeats, or rather continues, the emotions of her childhood. When she awakens after the attack she becomes again the grown-up person who has no recollection of the reality of the assaults in childhood and the painful events. She has a memory of the attack, however, so in this respect she is not amnesic, yet on waking she loses her sense of the reality of the situations in which the assaults in her childhood took place. As long as the split in the personality persists, as long as the patient on the one hand is awake, conscious, and amnesic, and on the other hand is asleep or in a trance, thereby perpetuating the past, that is, as long as the split-off fragments of the personality do not join each other, abreactions will have no more effect than the hysterical outbursts that occur spontaneously from time to time.

This all seems rather hopeless, but some rays of light can already be discerned.

Under what circumstances does the junction, however fleeting, between the two parts of the personalities and the concomitant conviction take place? As long as I listen to the current outbursts with some irritation, or perhaps even with a certain amount of boredom, which the patient partly becomes aware of from my behavior, my voice, or my manner of questioning, the pain and acuteness of the attack are intensified, and if I do nothing else, they usually end in shrill, mad laughter, followed by awakening in apathy. But if the patient notices that I feel real compassion for her and that I am eagerly determined to search for the causes of her suffering, she then suddenly not only becomes capable of giving a dramatic account of the events but also can talk to me about them. The congenial atmosphere thus enables her to project the traumata into the past and communicate them as memories. A contrast to the environment surrounding the traumatic situation—that is, sympthy, trust—mutual trust—must first be created before a new footing can be established: memory instead of repetition. Free association by itself, without these new foundations for an atmosphere of trust, will thus bring no real healing. The doctor must really be involved in the case, heart and soul, or honestly admit it when he is not, in total contrast with the behavior of adults toward children.

Perhaps the obstacles preventing the elements of the personality from forming a unit offer a clue to how the split itself has occurred. In the course of mental or physical torture, one draws strength to endure the suffering from the hope that sooner or later things will be different. One thus retains the unity of one's personality. But should the quality and quantity of suffering exceed the person's powers of comprehension, then one capitulates; one endures no longer; it is no longer worthwhile to combine these painful things into a unit, and one is split into pieces. I do not suffer any more, indeed I cease to exist, at least as a complete ego [*Gesamt-Ich*]. The individual component parts can suffer each by itself. The cessation of the total-suffering and its replacement by fragments of suffering may bring that sudden relief which allows the weeping, struggling, and screaming to be suddenly transformed into laughter. A physical comparison: if a sphere disintegrates into a hundred little spheres, the surface is increased a hundred times,[1] so that there is much less suffering per surface unit of the outer covering, for instance, on the skin of the body. This may be the cause of hallucinations of enormous numbers: the seeing of hundreds of rats or mice at the height of delirium. The hallucinations of those under the influence of anesthesia or alcohol are relevant here. It is possible that the phenomena associated with anesthesia, for example chloroform anesthesia, present an experimental reproduction of the psychological effects of shock. Inhalation of the irrespirable and lethal gas provokes, suddenly, extreme unpleasure, which is so intolerable that a splitting of the personality results. On awakening the complete-ego cannot remember any of the events that occurred while it was split.

210 *Identification versus hatred*

Because I identify myself (to understand everything = to forgive everything), I cannot hate. But what happens to the mobilized emotion when *every psychic discharge onto the object is blocked*? Does it persist as *tension in the body*, which attempts to discharge *itself* onto displaced objects (with the exception of the real ones)? Is punishing oneself (killing oneself, suicide) more bearable than being killed. When the threat of violent annihilation approaches from outside it is absolute, unavoidable, unbearable. If I *kill* myself, *I know what will happen*. Suicide is less *traumatic* (not unforeseen).

What is traumatic is the unforeseen, the unfathomable, the incalculable. Death of a kind and at a time one has determined oneself is less traumatic—the mind is able to function up to the last moment. Unexpected, external threat, the sense of which one cannot grasp, is unbearable.

Behind the humbleness, immense narcissism—justified! The child is the only reasonable being in a mad world.

Ambivalence: two opinions and emotions concerning the same object: (1) insane, hated; (2) understandable, loved.

To be able to hate, the *possibility* of loving someone else, something else, must remain open.

The dangerousness of the object also calls for understanding.

211 *Identification in trauma*

Mrs. G. Primal scene: C. masculine and feminine. Hatred of mother:

{ Lying
   neglecting her
   (loneliness)
   cheating

{ Killing impossible.
  Emotion no outlet.
     Dying.
  Defense: Identification
     instead of killing:

{ 1. Killing object
     (I exist, she
     not).
  2. Killing oneself
     (no emotions
     of my own—
     living some-
     body else's
     life).

Posttraumatic effect: identifications (superegos) instead of one's own life.

Repression (leap into the physical). (James-Lange)[2]
Purely sensory (sensitive) EXCITATION (permanent excitation).
Without striated muscle outlet (without emotion), yet with cardiac innervation. Dog's heart.[3]

Repression (B): Inability to scream at or to attack mother. Throat is *constricted.* Foot becomes rigid in equine[4] position. Mother's voice makes her mute. Even if she is being killed, she must not (cannot) scream; screaming "is absolutely forbidden."

Identification versus hatred

1. G.—Mother + father. Left alone.
2. Dm.—No comparison with unprovocative, reasonable people, as their existence unknown. The child sees parents fighting (senseless, mad). If I admit this then I am left *without parents;* that is, however (for a child), absolutely impossible. Therefore the child becomes a *psychiatrist, who treats the madman with understanding* and tells him that he is right.[5] (This way he will be less dangerous.) Indeed, the child even *commits* mistakes *on purpose* in order to justify and satisfy the adults' need for aggression. (Dm.: smelling.)

212   *Perversions are not fixations but the products of fear*

Anxiety, fear in the face of normality (trauma) provoke flight to deviant ways to satisfy desire. Homosexuality (autosadism) is forbidden, yet not so "impossible," "unmentionable," "unthinkable" as *heterosexual union.*

1. Homosexuality: intensification of the manifestation of friendship to the point of complete satisfaction of desire.
   a. the masculine use of men as though they were women
      1. inversion of the man
      2. inversion of *oneself*
   b. feminine: *replacement* of maternal feelings by orgasmic ones (exaggeration): substitute for heterosexuality.
   c. "pretending to be a child" (so as not to let heterosexuality be seen) (to prolong or simulate childishness). Children are allowed to do everything.
2. *Sadism—anal eroticism.* Children cannot be completely forbid-

den to complain about intestinal or urinary problems. Nor can adults deny completely that these are *possible* functions and organs, which they (adults) have as well. *Because of the physical proximity* it is easy to displace interest and sensation from the genitals onto the bladder and bowels, as well as to displace interest in orgasm onto the ease of evacuation.

It is not the summation of the urethrality and anality (amphimixis) that leads to genitality;[6] but the *splitting of genitality* into *urethrality* and *anality* constitutes the real process. Literal application of Freud's theories was wrong!

Is the idea of downward displacement and the accumulation of all libido in the genitals thus—wrong? And how does genitality arise otherwise?

What about the *"reservoir theory"*?[7]

A new attempt: genitality emerges in *loco proprio* as a ready-made and specific tendency of organ functioning (sensory-motor mechanism). Before the development of this mechanism *the child has no sexuality.* Return to the generally valid view: there is no extragenital infantile sexuality; but indeed there is precocious genitality, the suppression of which provokes, as hysterical symptoms:

1. sucking for pleasure (?)
2. anal play
3. urethral play
4. sadomasochism
5. exhibitionism—voyeurism
6. homosexuality

{ "Oral organization" is already secondary.
{ "Anal-sadistic" organization is as well.

Sucking for pleasure has originally nothing to do with sexuality— only after the suppression of masturbation, which *begins very early.* Is the *Oedipus complex* also a consequence of adult activity— passionate behavior?

Thus: no fixation through pleasure but fixation through *anxiety:* Man and woman will *kill me, if I do not love him* (do not identify myself with his wishes).

1. Ferenczi's calculation provides a spectacular illustration of his point. Actually, the correct form of the equation is: (ratio of the volumes) ÷ (ratio of the surfaces) = $\sqrt[3]{}$ratio of the volumes. Therefore, for a bullet that breaks into 100 smaller bullets, the cube root of the ratio of the volumes is 4.64. For the surface to be multiplied by 100, it would be necessary for the bullet to explode into 1 million smaller bullets.—ED.

2. The James-Lange theory of emotions was developed by two authors independently. The Danish philosopher C. G. Lange (1834–1900), in a paper of 1885, argued that emotion is identical with changes in the vasomotor system: the latter induce emotional and pharmaco-dynamic changes in response to emotional stimuli. The American philosopher William James, in a paper entitled "What Is an Emotion" (1888), argued that organic reactions as perceived by sensory organs are neither the outcome nor the concomitants of emotional experience, but are its *cause;* thus it would be more true to say that we are afraid because we run away, than that we run away because we are afraid.—Ed.

3. The dog's respiratory rhythm is linked to its heart rate.—Ed.

4. Foot in a position of forced extension, touching the ground only at its anterior extremity.

5. See "Confusion of Tongues between Adults and the Child," *Fin* 169.—Ed.

6. On the amphimixis of eroticism see "Psycho-Analytical Observations on Tic," *FC* 172–173; *Thalassa,* esp. pp. 5–14 and 20–21; and "Psychoanalysis of Sexual Habits," *FC* 263–264.—Ed.

7. In a passage on narcissism in " 'Psychoanalysis' and 'Libidotheorie' " Freud wrote the following: "The ego is to be regarded as a great reservoir of libido from which libido is sent out *to* objects and which is always ready to absorb libido flowing back *from* objects." SE XVIII, 257.—Ed.

26 July 1932

Clitoris and vagina

Perhaps it was too hasty to represent feminine sexuality as beginning with the clitoris, with a shift of this zone much later to the vagina. It is even doubtful whether any organ at all can be thought of as "undiscovered" by the psyche, psychically neutral as it were, that is, nonexistent. On the contrary, one feels justified in the assumption that the apparent nondiscovery of the vagina is already a sign of frigidity and the heightened clitoris-erotogeneity is already a hysterical symptom. The same shift would also cause the accentuation of the urethral and anal regions, that is, the splitting of genitality into closer and more distant zone shifts. The motives for early infantile vaginal repression could be: that the hand is systematically kept away from the vaginal opening almost from the moment of birth, whereas the clitoris region is stimulated right from the beginning by washing and powdering.

In the cases of early trauma one arrives analytically at the conviction that in sensory and motor respects the infantile vagina reacts normally and vigorously to intrusive stimuli; the actual traumatic stage begins when the child may perhaps wish to repeat the experience and is rejected, threatened, and punished by the partner, who is usually weighed down with guilt feelings.

26 July 1932

A revision of the Oedipus complex

Case G.: Conscious memory and visual image of the parents' sexual relations. Mother was always inconsiderate, self-seeking; her love unattainable. Patient had to content herself with the father. Father unhappy with mother (mother habitually unfaithful, something the child seemed to sense in some way). Father sought comfort partly in his love for the child; this became passionate. Passionate gaze of the father provokes shock, is interpreted as a threat to life. In view of her own weakness, and in the absence of alloplastic physical and mental tools of aggression, nothing remains but to perish for lack of love, or to adapt by autoplastic adaptation to the wishes (even the most hidden wishes) of the attacker, in order to calm him down. Identification in place of hatred and defense. Further advantage of identification with the father is his switching off: after she becomes the father, she wins back the mother, who otherwise would remain inaccessible. Erotic fantasies and masturbation represent either an active or a passive sexual relationship with the mother. When the mother left the father (the child was ten years old), the father was leaning even more passionately on the child; indeed, once when struggling with sleeplessness he even got into her bed, where he complained dramatically about his unhappiness, urged her not to be afraid of him anymore, and formally declared her in charge of the household. Yet at the same time he constantly and very severely lectured her to regard her mother as a negative example, that is: that she was not to be sexual on any account. The fact that infantile fantasy had come true made it impossible for her to detach herself from her father at all, particularly as the prohibitions kept the sexual fantasies unconscious; transference onto a third person became utterly impossible, and it became completely unclear whether the patient has any spontaneous, unprovoked feelings of her own, and which ones.

This could be an example of the cases—certainly not rare—in which fixation on parents, that is, incestuous fixation, does not appear as a natural product of development but rather is implanted in the psyche from the outside, that is to say, is a product of the superego. It should be noted that not only sexual stimuli but also other kinds that neither are overpowering nor have to be overcome (hate, fear, etc.) can have a mimetic effect in the same way as imposed love.

The as yet incomplete individual can thrive only in an optimal environment. In an atmosphere of hatred it cannot breathe and perishes. Psychically this ruin is expressed in the disintegration of the psyche itself, that is, the relinquishing of the unity of the ego. If the as yet "semifluid" individual is not supported from all sides by that optimum, it is inclined to "explosion" (Freud's death instinct). But in a manner which to us appears mystical, the ego fragments remain linked to one another, however distorted and hidden this link may be. If this succeeds . . .[1]

1. The rest of this entry is missing.—ED.

27 July 1932

Does rage play a part in the process of repression?

B., in certain states of relaxation, is as though paralyzed—pale, hardly breathing, eyes sunken, skin icy cold. On exceptional occasions and by overcoming the greatest resistance (forced free association, flight into melodies, rhythmicisms), we succeed in getting under, that is behind, this layer. Face suddenly becomes bright red, hands and feet tense; uncoordinated screaming, from which, with my help, intelligible words and sentences are formed, words of abuse and reproach against mother and father, vivid reproduction of merciless beatings (the mother simply battered to death, the father interminably tortured).

Patient describes her feeling when "expiring": "Everything turns inside out"—by which she means that the greater part of her personality freezes over, like a crust of ice. This crust protects her from the breaking through of the repressed material hidden deep inside and sealed hermetically, as it were.

This observation indicates that hatred and rage play a part in the processes that precede repression; if that is so, then no analysis is completed as long as this emotion has not been worked through as well. It is possible that, at each overwhelming shock, an initial attempt at aggressive, alloplastic defense is made, and only faced with the full realization of one's own utter weakness and helplessness does one submit entirely to the aggressor or even identify with him. In addition to awareness of one's own weakness, the existence of am-bivalence-conflicts may lead to the abandonment of one's own person. (In the case of B., this was the pleasurable sensations the father was able to awaken in the child; in the case of G., in addition to these, also the feelings of tenderness and gratitude toward her father.)

The idea of "inside-out" signifies in psychological terms the turning outward of something unreal and fantastic, and the use of it as though it were "ourselves," whereas it is an inanimate mechanism of "pseudo-living" even if it functions correctly.—In the case of O.S. the most brutal insults and even effective assaults by her friend are apparently experienced without any rage or hate; yet the consistent rage-interpretations in the analysis, perhaps also the reassurance that I do not condemn her, gradually lead to the admission of feelings of rage and hate, indeed murderous intentions.

The most potent motive of repression, in almost all cases, is an attempt to make the sustained injury not have happened. Another, perhaps even more potent motive is identification out of fear—one must know the dangerous opponent through and through, follow each of his movements, so that one can protect oneself against him. Last not least: an attempt will be made to bring to his senses even a terrifying, raging brute, whose behavior suggests drunkenness or insanity. When the Medusa, threatened with decapitation, makes a horrible angry face, she is actually holding up a mirror to the bestial attacker, as though she were saying: This is how you look. In the face of the aggressor one has no weapons; and no possibility exists of instructing him or bringing him to reason in any other way. Such deterrence by means of identification (holding up a mirror) may still help at the last moment (*ta twam asi:* this art thou).

Normal and pathological sexual relations in the family

Case G.: My attempt of yesterday to trace the whole Oedipal situation back to an external influence (the father's excesses) had failed. The patient maintains with great assurance—and I have no reason not to believe her fully—that after the infantile shock (primal scene with deferred identification in her fantasy with her mother) she recovered quite well and was in the process of turning away from her parents and toward external objects. It was only the second and almost real approach of her father (mother's flight from the house, daughter's assumption of the role of lady of the house) that led to the rigid situation from which there was no escape. The passionate genitalization of the relationship with her father was not her own wish, but was forced upon her, so to speak. Defense was out of the question here (see repressed rage above). The incest situation was too passionately felt and evolved into an unbearable Oedipus complex with its inevitable repression. The libido, already vaginally established, is split (the vagina emptied), and gratification is shifted to the pregenital, infantile zones and, even in incest relationships, to more permissible zones: fantasies of female breasts (tenderness-factors in sexuality), fantasies of buttocks and being beaten or respectively beating = retroactive transposition of the passionate element to the anal zone and to punishing-procedures for soiling oneself. It should be further observed how far Freud is right that the Oedipus situation is normally just a child's game and becomes a pathogenic complex only in pathological cases, under the influence of trauma.

What is traumatic: an attack or its consequences?

The adaptive potential "response" of even very young children to sexual or other passionate attacks is much greater than one would imagine. Traumatic confusion arises mainly because the attack and the response to it are denied by the guilt-ridden adults, indeed, are treated as deserving punishment.[1]

Cruel game with patients

The way in which psychoanalysis operates in the relationship between doctor and patient must impress the latter as deliberate cruelty. One receives the patient in a friendly manner, works to establish transference securely, and then, while the patient is going through agonies, one sits calmly in the armchair, smoking a cigar and making seemingly conventional and hackneyed remarks in a bored tone; occasionally one falls asleep. At best, one makes a colossal effort to try to overcome the yawning tedium, even exerts oneself to be friendly and full of compassion. If one educates the patient to be truly free and urges him to overcome all fear and shyness toward us as well, then we will get to hear that in one or another layer of his mind the patient is well aware of our real thoughts and feelings. All new efforts to try to withdraw from the situation are in vain; the patient will sense that this too is forced. Analogies from childhood and their transference into the present prevent him, under such circumstances, from freeing himself from us. As long as the slightest trace of hope exists that his wish for love will be gratified, and since our every gesture and word acts on him with great power of suggestion, the patient will not be able to free himself from us and look around for other, more real possibilities in life. Therefore, however valuable the understanding immersion in patients' sufferings and torments might be (without such deep immersion into the subtleties of the patient's feelings, we would never reach that deep level), the day must come, when . . .[2]

1. On this subject see "Child Analysis in the Analysis of Adults," *Fin* 138–139; and "Confusion of Tongues between Adults and the Child," *Fin* 162–163.—ED.
2. The rest of this entry is missing.

30 July 1932

"Literal" repetition endlessly repeated—and no recollection[1]

Patient B. dreams about a cousin: she is lying in a field, a bull runs up to her and rapes her. Second scene: she sees the same cousin (whose name is Shore) floating lifelessly in the water, then, watched by a crowd of people, dragged ashore. Patient wakes up. Immediately after waking, she racks her head about why she cannot remember these things, why she only dreams about them, and why in such distorted form. She also puts the same question to me. My first reply is: I know from other analyses that a part of our personality can "die," and if the remaining part does survive the trauma, it wakes up with a gap in its memory, actually with a gap in the personality, since it is not just the memory of the death struggle that has selectively disappeared or perhaps has been destroyed, but all the associations connected with it as well. "Yes, but if I already know that, why can't I come to terms with the death of the part that has been killed and see that with a great part of my personality I am still alive: why can't I concern myself with the present and the future, and finally, I never tire of asking myself and you: when I do occupy myself with the past, why do I do it in the form of dreams, and in such a distorted fashion?"

I extricated myself from this embarrassing position with the following answer: "I know from other cases that there can be frighteningly painful moments, in which one feels one's life so appallingly threatened, and yet oneself so weak or so exhausted by the struggle, that one gives up. In fact one gives oneself up." As an analogy I refer to a reliable account of an Indian friend, a hunter. He saw how a falcon attacked a little bird; as it approached, the little bird started to tremble and, after a few seconds of trembling, flew straight into the falcon's open beak and was swallowed up. The anticipation of certain death appears to be such torment that by comparison actual death is a relief.

There are well-known cases of people who shoot themselves out of fear of death (before a duel, a battle, or an execution). Taking one's own life (just like punishing oneself) appears to be a comparative relief. In contrast, however, it seems unbearable to see oneself being overpowered with certainty by an overwhelming force, just as one is beginning to feel the pressure and when the most extreme concentration of all our mental and physical strength appears absurdly insignificant compared to the force of the attack. But how would that little bird have felt if—just at the moment when it stopped trembling and was flying to its death—my friend the hunter had shot the falcon, before it could swallow the little bird; what would the little bird's state of mind have been? Possibly after a certain time it would have recovered, but of the moment of the suicide attempt there would probably have remained only a memory; for what is remembering: the conservation of a memory trace for the purposes of future use. But if life has already been given up, and therefore there is no future ahead of us, why should the individual still take the trouble to register anything? And as I have already given myself up for lost, that is, I am no more important to myself than other people and external objects, why should I not then make it easier for myself, even for the brief remaining period of my existence, by doing what I am accustomed to doing in dreams, namely regarding myself no longer as the suffering person but looking at myself, or someone who resembles me, from the outside—like B., in her dream, watching the death of her cousin.

Putting it in simpler terms, one might say that fear of an inevitable and violent death can lead to a giving up of oneself and thereby to a dreamlike illusion or hallucination. Here I can quote instances when colleagues who were dying held consultations with the doctor treating them about a dying patient (which was themselves). Perhaps there are two kinds of dying in any case: one kind to which one submits, and another against which one protests to the very end. One form of this protest is the denial of reality, that is, mental illness. The total negation of reality is loss of consciousness. The partial negation and distortion of reality is its replacement by a dream. If it happens, owing to external circumstances or to vital forces that one had not taken into account when one resolved to die, that one succeeds in escaping mortal danger or one undergoes the assault one thought would be lethal without being totally destroyed, then it is understandable that one can no longer think about the events that occurred during the period of mental absence subjectively as a memory, but, only by objectifying it, as something that happened to another person, and can only be represented in this form.

This may be the reason that, at my instigation, so often you have already sunk deep into the most vivid representation of those infantile-traumatic events, indeed you have reenacted the shattering incident both mentally and physically, and yet, on waking from this trance, this serious and painful reality has become once again only a "dream," that is, the conviction—very nearly attained—is soon gnawed away and then totally eaten up.

I have to return again to the idea you have expressed: why concern ourselves so much with the inaccessible piece of the personality, dead or encapsulated in some way: "Why should one not let the dead be dead and go on living oneself?" "The answer to that is simple, Doctor. That split-off part seems to represent in the first instance a large, indeed perhaps the most significant, part of my soul, and even if you were to urge me to, which I hope you will not, I should never stop striving to make that portion of my personality, however painful, consciously my own." "I must add to that," I replied, "that even if you wanted to, you could not escape the effects of the splitting. The fact of being split may make conscious recollection impossible, but it cannot prevent the affect that is attached to it from forcing its way through in moods, emotional outbursts, susceptibilities, often in generalized depression or in compensatory, unmotivated high-spiritedness, but even more in various physical sensations and various functional disturbances. "But how are you going to make me suffer the pain that I have skillfully managed to avoid in the trauma without a renewed split, that is, without any repetition of the mental disorder, thereby restoring the unity of my personality, that is, render conscious what has never been conscious before? Does it not seem to you an impossible undertaking?" My reply: "I don't know myself, but I am [convinced] of the reversibility of all psychic processes, that is, all not purely hereditary . . ."[2]

224a   *What is "trauma"?*

"Concussion," reaction to an "unbearable" external or internal stimulus in an autoplastic manner (modifying the self) instead of an alloplastic manner (modifying the stimulus). A neoformation of the self is impossible without the previous destruction, either partial or total, or dissolution of the former self. A new ego cannot be formed directly from the previous ego, but from *fragments,* more or less elementary products of its disintegration. (Splitting, atomization.) The relative strength of the "unbearable" excitation determines the degree and depth of the ego's disintegration:

a. change in consciousness (trance, dream state)

b. loss of consciousness

c. syncope

d. death.

The elimination of ego-consciousness results in a diminution of the pain caused by the action of the stimulus; thereupon the part of the ego that has remained intact can recover more quickly. (The elimination of anxiety makes automatic bodily functions easier.) The return of consciousness reveals gaps in remembering or in the certainty-of-remembering in relation to the events, while in shock. Without any change in the external situation or in the ego's capacity for endurance, the return of the psychic traumatic situation can only result in disintegration and reconstruction. (Repetition.) New elements present in the analysis:

1. Presence of a helpful person (understanding and wanting to help). Alleviation of pain.

2. Help through suggestion, when energy flags: shaking up, encouraging words. Thereupon a sensation of increased strength or decreased weakness of the alloplastic "capacity for thought and action." No "hopelessness," "impossibility." "Disintegration" is revoked. "Glue." Settlement. *Recollection* possible only if a sufficiently consolidated ego (integrated, or one that has become so) *resists* external influences; it is influenced but it is not fragmented by them.

224c Systems of memory scars form new tissue with its own functions: reflexes, conditioned reflexes (nervous system). This function, originally only an interrupted modification of the self (destruction), is placed in the service of *self-preservation:* as *alloplastically directed thought work* [*Denkarbeit*].

Repetition compulsion in the traumatized is a renewed attempt at a *better resolution.*

Double shock

1. Trauma

2. Denial

---

1. Fragmentation	Moldability (suggestion and hypnosis)
2. Atomization	Magnetic power
Anxiety: atomization	Willpower
adaptability	Instant [*Augen-blick*][3]

Understanding is eo ipso *identification.*

One cannot really *understand* without identifying with the subject. Identification = *understanding* can be put in the place of emotion (hatred). (Case G.: She *understands* Fr. *instead* of hating him.

Death = feminine, mother.

            Using his patients to give birth to his child ($\Psi\alpha$ insight)

Never grateful for understanding (perhaps because mother's hatred is not benevolent).

> The nightingale sang: "O lovely Sphinx!
> O love, explain to me:
> Why do you blend the pain of death
> With every ecstasy?"
> > *Book of Songs,* Preface to the Third Edition[4]

224e   *Passionate character of psychoanalysts*

Analysand the parents' darling.

1. Their own comfort. Lack of consideration. Using analysands, instead of letting them develop.

2. Sadistic and masochistic elements allowed in the atmosphere that was originally clearly benevolent. Pleasure in the pain of others, because one's own analytical suffering is repressed. I myself oscillate between sadism (activity) and *masochism* (relaxation).—Instead of being serene, cheerful, benevolent:

    Sensitivity of the analyst (unjustified) (desire for vengeance).

    Excessive emphasis on the *analytical* situation.

    (Vanity) TYRANNY: against independence.

Analysands are *children. Analysis prolonged* (keeping them children instead of letting them go).

Primal scene creates sadism in the child (because it really is sadistic)! Fr[eud:] *Primal scene is interpreted by the child as anal-sadistic* (because it is at the anal-sadistic age!) F[erenczi:] Anal.

224f   *Sanction* (not being able to be alone).

Children have no confidence in their own thoughts and actions, unless these are approved by the parents. Hence R.N. and Fr[eud]: "You tell me (the meaning)—when you have found it yourself."

(Proof that a part has really remained a young child.) The child cannot be alone even in its thought processes; it must be supported, as when learning to walk.

1. This entry is another draft of the Wiesbaden lecture.—ED.
2. The rest of this passage is missing.—ED.
3. *Augenblick* means "instant," "moment"—but by writing it with a hyphen Ferenczi calls attention to the possible meaning of its component parts: "expression in the eyes," "glance."
4. The quoted lines, by the German poet Heinrich Heine:

      Die Nachtigall sang: "Oh schone Sphinx
      O Liebe! was soll es bedeuten
      Das Du vermischest mit Todesqual
      All, Deine Seligkeiten?"

The translation given here is from Hal Draper, *The Complete Poems of Heinrich Heine: A Modern English Version* (Boston: Suhrkamp/Insel, 1982), copyright © 1982 by Hal Draper. Used by permission of Suhrkamp Publishers New York, Inc.

224g   4 August 1932

Personal causes for the erroneous development of psychoanalysis

1. Why antitrauma and predisposition? In the case of F[erenczi] it appears that Fr[eud] altered the external situation to conform to the neurotic wish of the patient, in order to escape something traumatic. (a) Contrary to all the rules of technique that he established himself, he adopted Dr. F[erenczi] almost like his son. As he himself told me, he regarded him as the most perfect heir of his ideas. Thereby he became the proclaimed crown prince, anticipating his triumphal entry into America. (Fr[eud] seems to have expected something similar of Jung years ago; hence the two hysterical symptoms I observed in him): (1) the fainting spell in Bremen,[1] (2) the incontinence on Riverside Drive,[2] added to the bit of analysis he gave us: dying as soon as the son takes his place, and regression to childhood, childish embarrassment, when he represses his American vanity. (Possibly his contempt for Americans is a reaction to this weakness, which he could not hide from us and himself. "How could I take so much pleasure in the honors the Americans have bestowed on me, when I feel such contempt for the Americans?") Not unimportant is the emotion that impressed even me, a reverent spectator, as somewhat ridiculous, when almost with tears in his eyes he thanked the president of the university for the honorary doctorate.[3]

The anxiety-provoking idea, perhaps very strong in the unconscious, that the father must die when the son grows up, explains his fear of allowing any one of his sons to become independent. At the same time, it also shows us, that Freud as the son really did want to kill his father. Instead of admitting this, he founded the theory of the parricidal Oedipus, but obviously applied only to others, not to himself. Hence the fear of allowing himself to be analyzed, hence perhaps also the idea that in civilized adults primitive instinctual impulses are not in fact real anymore, that the Oedipal disease is a childhood disease, like the measles.

24h(II)   The mutually castration-directed aggressivity, which in the unconscious is probably crassly aggressive, is overlaid by the need—which should be called homosexual—for a harmonious father-son relationship. In any case he could, for example, tolerate my being a son only until the moment when I contradicted him for the first time. (Palermo.)[4] Otto R[ank][5] was easier to get along with, just the same as our friend von Fr[eund].[6] (It will be worth it to get out my notes from Berchtesgaden—1908[7]—my enthusiasm, my depression when I was neglected even for one day; my total inhibition about speaking in his presence until he broached a subject, and then the burning desire to win his approval by showing that I had understood him completely, and by immediately going further in the direction he recommended: all this reveals me to have been a blindly dependent son.) He must have felt very comfortable in this role; he could indulge in his theoretical fantasies undisturbed by any contradiction and use the enthusiastic agreement of his blinded pupil to boost his own self-esteem. In reality, his brilliant ideas were usually based on only a single case, like illuminations as it were, which dazzled and amazed, for example, me. "How miraculous that he knows that." In this acclaim I detect the hidden doubt: just a wonder, but no logical conviction, that is, it was only adoration and not independent judgment that made me follow him.

The advantages of following blindly were: (1) membership in a distinguished group guaranteed by the king, indeed with the rank of field marshal for myself (crown-prince fantasy). (2) One learned from him and from his kind of technique various things that made one's life and work more comfortable: the calm, unemotional reserve; the unruffled assurance that one knew better; and the theories, the seeking and finding of the causes of failure in the patient instead of partly in ourselves. The dishonesty of reserving the technique for one's own person; the advice not to let patients learn anything about the tech-

24i(III)   nique; and finally the pessimistic view, shared with only a trusted few, that neurotics are a rabble, good only to support us financially and to allow us to learn from their cases: psychoanalysis as a therapy may be worthless.

This was the point where I refused to follow him. Against his will I began to deal openly with questions of technique. I refused to abuse the patients' trust in this way, and neither did I share his idea that therapy was worthless. I believed rather that therapy was good, but perhaps we were still deficient, and I began to look for our errors. In this search I took several false steps; I went too far with Rank, because on one point (the transference situation) he dazzled me with his new insight. I tried to pursue the Freudian technique of frustration honestly and sincerely to the end (active therapy).[8] Following its failure I tried permissiveness and relaxation,[9] again an exaggeration. In the wake of these two defeats, I am working humanely and naturally, with benevolence, and free from personal prejudices, on the acquisition of knowledge that will allow me to help.

Mrs. F[erenczi] felt, and rightly so, attracted by the essence of psycho-analysis—trauma and reconstruction—but repelled by all analysts for the way they make use of it. By contrast Professor K., by confidently allowing the patients' own intelligence to develop fully, is helpful without being an analyst, so although not an analyst, he is analytically helpful. On the other hand Professors Bl[euler] and M[aeder],[10] for championing their own theories and for not acknowledging what is genuinely brilliant in Freud, are unacceptable to her. She longs for an analyst who will be analytically as gifted as she is, who will be concerned above all with truth, but who will not only be scientifically true but also truthful regarding people.

Thus the antitraumatic in Fr[eud] is a protective device against insight into his own weaknesses.

1. On their way to the United States in 1909, Freud met Ferenczi and Jung in Bremen on 20 August. At lunch Freud persuaded Jung to yield in two instances regarding his refusal to drink alcohol. Immediately afterward Freud felt ill. See Jones II, 61; Max Schur, *Freud: Living and Dying* (Hogarth Press, 1972).—ED.

2. This incident was undoubtedly related to the prostate problem that was so troublesome to Freud on his trip to America. See Jones II, 66–67: "I recall his complaining to me of the scarcity and inaccessibility of suitable places to obtain relief: 'They escort you along miles of corridors and ultimately you are taken to the very basement where a marble palace awaits you, only just in time.' "—ED.

3. Freud received an honorary doctorate in psychology at Clark University, Worcester, Massachusetts, in September 1909 at the conclusion of his lecture tour.—ED.

4. In September 1910 Freud and Ferenczi traveled together from Leyden to Palermo, via Paris, Rome, and Naples. They spent about eight days in Sicily. An incident took place in Palermo: during a joint working session, Ferenczi displayed a much more independent

attitude than Freud was prepared to accept. Furthermore, throughout the journey Ferenczi felt that he had cause to reproach Freud for an attitude of paternal severity and reserve, while Freud reproached Ferenczi for behaving like a truculent and demanding child. This incident, often referred to subsequently, contains the germ of the painful discord between the two men that would develop later on. See *Ferenczi/Groddeck: Correspondance,* letter of Christmas 1921, pp. 56–57; Jones II, 91–93; Schur, *Freud: Living and Dying.*—ED.

5. Otto Rank (1844–1939), Viennese analyst, not medically trained. Rank was very close to Freud for approximately twenty years after 1906, but then he moved away, pursuing paths of which Freud disapproved. He wrote, notably, *The Trauma of Birth,* and in collaboration with Ferenczi, *The Development of Psycho-Analysis* (New York and Washington: Nervous and Mental Disease Pub. Co., 1925). See the chapter on Rank in Paul Roazen, *Freud and His Followers* (Allen Lane, 1976).—ED.

6. Anton Tószeghy von Freund (1880–1920), wealthy Hungarian businessman. He was an active supporter of a number of philanthropic projects and provided valuable financial support for the psychoanalytic movement. In 1918 Ferenczi nominated him to be secretary of the International Psycho-Analytical Association. His sister Kata, also an analyst, married Lajos Levy, Ferenczi's physician, who had on occasion also been consulted by Freud. Both von Freund and the Levys maintained close relations with Ferenczi and with Freud. —ED.

7. The first holiday Ferenczi had spent with Freud and his family, from 15 July to 30 July 1908 at Diedfeld Hof, near Berchtesgaden.—ED.

8. On "active therapy" see Ferenczi's works of 1924, 1925, and 1926; for a list of these see Bibliography, *Fin* 383–384.—ED.

9. On permissiveness and relaxation see particularly "The Elasticity of Psycho-Analytical Technique" (1928), *Fin* 87–101; "The Principle of Relaxation and Neocatharsis" (1930), *Fin* 108–125; "Child Analysis in the Analysis of Adults" (1931), *Fin* 126–142.—ED.

10. Paul Eugen Bleuler (1857–1939), Swiss psychiatrist, who from 1898 to 1927 taught at the University of Zurich and was in charge of the psychiatric hospital at Burgholzli. His particular interest was dementia praecox, a condition for which he created the term "schizophrenia." He also undertook serious research in such fields as autism and ambivalence. He was a militant teetotaler and had converted Jung, a member of his staff since 1900, to his cause. In these circumstances, one can gauge how significant the episode at Bremen must have been to Jung (as it was to Freud), when Jung broke his vow of abstinence at Freud's instigation.—ED.

Alphonse E. Maeder (1882–1971), Swiss psychotherapist, president for a time of the Psychoanalytical Association of Zurich. Maeder followed Jung after the latter's breach with Freud. He later developed a technique for brief analyses.—ED.

4 August 1932

2. The ease with which Fr[eud] sacrifices the interests of women in favor of male patients is striking. This is consistent with the unilaterally androphile orientation of his theory of sexuality. In this he was followed by almost all of his pupils, myself not excluded. My theory of genitality may have many good points, yet in its mode of presentation and its historical reconstruction it clings too closely to the words of the master; a new edition would mean complete rewriting.

One example: the castration theory of femininity. Fr[eud] thinks that the clitoris develops and functions earlier than the vagina, that is, girls are born with the feeling that they have a penis, and only later do they learn to renounce both this and the mother and to accept vaginal and uterine femininity. Thus he neglects the alternative possibility that instinctual heterosexual orientation (perhaps only in fantasy) is highly developed quite early on, and that masculinity only takes its place for traumatic reasons (primal scene), as a hysterical symptom.

The author may have a personal aversion to the spontaneous female-oriented sexuality in women: idealization of the mother. He recoils from the task of having a sexually demanding mother, and having to satisfy her. At some point his mother's passionate nature may have presented him with such a task. (The primal scene may have rendered him relatively impotent.)

Castration of the father, the potent one, as a reaction to the humili-ation he experienced, led to the construction of a theory in which the father castrates the son and, moreover, is then revered by the son as a god. In his conduct Fr[eud] plays only the role of the castrating god, he wants to ignore the traumatic moment of his own castration in childhood; he is the only one who does not have to be analyzed.

224k   7 August 1932

Autochthonous sense of guilt

Until now, we have dealt only with a sense of guilt that takes the place of a fear of punishment as a superego-institution in opposition to the rest of the ego and the id. Certain observations suggest that an oppressive sense of guilt can occur even when one has not trans-gressed against oneself at all. A classic example: excessive masturba-tion. The ego feels comfortable only in a state of "libidinal equilib-rium." Impoverishment of the libido, artificial pumping out of libido without internal pressure, has a paralyzing effect on the ability of soul and body to function. In the end one is forced to believe the com-plaints of masturbators on this subject; their complaints are far too eloquent, and it would be brutal to attribute the consistently repeated complaints solely to anxiety and fear. Possibly the warnings against masturbation prove to be so effective only because their effect is added to an already existing autochthonous sense of guilt.

It remains an open question why the artificial and exaggerated discharge of libido should manifest itself specifically as a feeling of conscious guilt. It appears that one holds oneself responsible if one disturbs ego functions merely for the sake of pleasure. "First and foremost *I* am here: only when I am satisfied, or perhaps even disturbed by an excess of libido, can an expenditure of libido be contemplated." If one breaks this rule, then the ego punishes us by a kind of strike, carrying out its functions with unpleasure and with little energy; this results in a generalized hypersensitivity, which will punish every major exertion with fatigue and a feeling of pain.

But a similar thing occurs when the pumping out of the libido is provoked not by oneself but by another person, something that happens all too often when the environment is passionate and ignorant of the psychology of children.

The newborn child uses all its libido for its own growth; indeed, it must be given additional libido to ensure that it grows normally. Normal life thus begins with exclusive, passive object-love. Infants do not love; they must be loved.

The second stage of libidinal economy is, or rather begins, when the child starts to love itself. (This stage is probably initiated by the imperfections and the inevitable occasional lack of satisfaction in being loved.) But it is also conceivable that when the first turbulent period of growth gives way to a somewhat more settled one, the surplus quantities of libido that have already been mobilized begin to look for an object. The first love object is then the self. A still greater increase in the tension and amount of libido then leads to a search for objects also outside of the ego. In addition to being loved and loving oneself, one can also introject persons and things as love objects. When, during which moments of development, these changes occur is at present not known.

A premature imposition of untimely forms of satisfaction will disturb the normal development of the ego, which is thus confronted with tasks for which it is not yet mature enough. It is undoubtedly injurious to the infant if lazy and unscrupulous wet nurses use masturbatory stimulation of the genitals to make children go to sleep. Just as untimely and disturbing to the ego are the frequent, brutally masturbatory assaults of adults on growing children, whose genitality has not yet progressed beyond the period of harmless, nonpassionate touching. An undeveloped ego will have to make an even more colossal effort, of course, when it has to endure the violence and shock, as well as the emotions, of real sexual intercourse. But such incidents are much more frequent than one would imagine. Only a very small proportion of the incestuous seduction of children and abuse by persons in charge of them is ever found out, and even then it is mostly hushed up. The child, deeply shaken by the shock of the premature intrusion and by its own efforts of adaptation, does not have sufficient strength of judgment to criticize the behavior of this person of authority. The feeble efforts in this direction are menacingly repudiated by the guilty person with brutality or threats, and the child is accused of lying. Moreover, the child is intimidated by the threat of the withdrawal of love, indeed of physical suffering. Soon it begins even to doubt the reliability of its own senses, or, as more frequently happens, it withdraws from the entire conflict-situation by taking refuge in daydreams and complying with the demands of waking life, from now on, only like an automaton. (Source of the case: aristocratic circles, the tutor, he alone knows of five children who were seduced.)

The early-seduced child adapts itself to its difficult task with the aid of complete identification with the aggressor. The analysis of case F. demonstrates that such identificatory love leaves the ego proper unsatisfied. In analysis, therefore, the patient must be taken back to the blissful time before the trauma and to the corresponding period of sexual development (Balint: "Character Development and New Beginning");[1] starting from here on the one hand, and on the other hand by unraveling the fabric of the neurotic superstructure, he must arrive at an understanding of the shock and its inner consequences, in order to restore gradually or in fits and starts the capacity to manifest its own kinds of libido.

Quote as example the "perversion" of persisting infantility when the development of the libido is disturbed. In F.'s case the heterosexual libido, which was already developing in a normal direction in fantasy, after the shock at the age of ten splits into sadomasochism (infantile fantasies of beatings) and breast-fetishism accompanied by an active and passive homosexual attachment to the mother. It must be added that this was preceded by a deeply disturbing primal scene in earliest childhood (primal scene is traumatic only if life otherwise is totally asexual and hypocritical).

One could ask whether a sense of guilt after having suffered an untimely attack (or in boys being forced to superperformances) is not bound up with guilt feelings because of having guessed and shared the aggressor's feelings of guilt.[2] It is perhaps only this perception of guilt feelings in the aggressor that gives to the unpleasure of the ego the character of guilt, because of the disturbance [suffered]. The conduct of the person in authority after committing the act (silence, denial, anxious behavior), in addition to threats made to the child, is well suited to suggest to the child consciousness of his own guilt and complicity.

A not insignificant contribution to the sense of guilt—characteristic of the postsexual reaction—may be the circumstance that genital organs react to the stimulation with feelings of sensual pleasure. The pleasure experienced in the sexual process, which one cannot deny to oneself, gives rise to the tendency in us to feel responsible or co-responsible for the events. A further factor contributing to this feeling may spring from the fact that children—although admittedly on a more harmless sexual level, by means of coquettishness, exhibition, touching, etc.—implicate themselves as the seducers of adults. Of course, what they in fact wanted to seduce the adults to was something quite different from what happened to them. What a terrible conflict between organ-reaction marked by pleasure and psychic defense! No wonder the child clothes the whole scene in regressive forms (vomiting) and uses this hysterical conversion to escape the even greater unpleasure of conscious psychic experience. Such hysteria lies at the basis of all shock neuroses, even if later it is overlaid by obsessional-neurotic or paranoid psychotic symptoms, or by certain features of character. (Question: when character, when neurosis, when psychosis.)

1. Michael Balint, "Character Analysis and New Beginning" (1932), in *Primary Love and Psycho-Analytic Technique* (Hogarth Press, rpt. H. Karnac Ltd., 1985), pp. 159–173.—ED.

2. This theme is further developed in "Confusion of Tongues between Adults and the Child" (1933), *Fin* 156–167.—ED.

8 August 1932

Tolerating being alone

B.: About a year ago, under pressure from me, deep relaxation to the point of extreme physical weakness, pain, states resembling death agony, fever, cardiac weakness, etc. This lasted eight days, becoming more and more threatening; then sudden emergence from this state, complete recovery, and resumption of the analysis. Only one thing did not reestablish itself, or only to a small degree: free association. The patient was terrified of getting into that state again.

Now she herself comes with the idea of retiring from the world, living alone, and making another attempt to overcome her fears about this. At the same time she is now beginning to apply herself seriously to free association, and she asks herself what could have changed so much that she now feels more able to cope with this painful task. She supplies the answer herself: "In the meantime my trust in you has grown so much that I am able to do it. I hope you will treat me differently now from when I was ill."

This hope is fully justified: in the meantime we had become convinced that in my reliance on the basic rules of analysis I had treated her too coolly, one might even say cruelly. This admission on my part, and the change in my emotional attitude that logically followed it, increased her trust more and more, so that she herself wants to attempt the repetition, hoping that I will not let her perish, that is, that I have both the intention and the ability to bring her back from her traumatic confusion. If she can, just once a day, talk to me freely and then receive courage and elucidation from me, she will be able to tolerate her loneliness in the interim. She also knows that I am sufficiently well-disposed toward her to take care of her in the intervening periods as well, should it be absolutely necessary. In other words, being alone is tolerable only if she never feels totally abandoned; from this it follows that being really totally alone, where one does not have even the hope of being understood and helped by the outside world, is intolerable. But what is this being intolerable? Surely nothing else but continuing to live in a distorted inner (psychic) or outer reality.

The patient's associations led very soon to a fantasy in which she hears her father whisper: "You will always feel but never see my naked body."

She has some indistinct memories from her early infancy, when she often saw her father naked, taking a bath and in other circumstances. As far as her distinct memories go back, her father had always been extremely modest toward her—until about four years ago, when out of the blue he made overtures of love toward her. His behavior at that time strongly supports our assumption that the rape fantasies are based on reality.

What she now expects from me is (1) belief in the reality of the incident, (2) reassurance that I consider her innocent, (3) innocent, even if it should appear that she derived immense satisfaction from the attack and repaid her father with admiration, (4) the certainty that I will not let myself be carried away by similar passionate behavior.

The traumatic aloneness [*Alleinsein*], the father's prohibition and his will to prohibit, the mother's deafness and blindness, that is what really renders the attack traumatic, that is, causing the psyche to crack. The being left alone like this must help himself, and for this he must split himself into one who helps and one who is helped. Only when trust has been won and this self-help, self-observation, self-control (all enemies of free association) are relinquished—see above—can the states that existed at the time of the total aloneness after the trauma be experienced fully.

Patient B. arrived at the idea by herself that the total split in her father (epilepsy, drunkenness) has created a similar one in her: Dr. Jekyll and Mr. Hyde. The whispering of those words is the acoustically formulated impression of her father's will, possibly thought transference (my earlier idea that thought transference is different from Cumberlandism must probably be abandoned).[1] All thinking is motor and therefore is capable of provoking associated movement. See the case of thoughts becoming audible because of earwax.

Reproduction of trauma by itself is therapeutically ineffective

R.N.: About three years ago discovery of the amnesia, two years ago reproduction of the trauma, on each occasion ending with terrible pains and convulsive laughter. Since then an outburst every day, almost without exception. Adhering strictly to the theory that the quantity of abreactions will finally be exhausted and that this will lead in time to certain recovery, I continued to produce the attacks. Financial difficulties nearly led to a break in the analysis, but my stubborn faith made me carry on, even without being paid. Progress almost nil. Greater financial demands on me and increasing demands on my time and interest exhausted my patience, and we had almost reached the point of breaking off the analysis, when help arrived from an unexpected source. The weakening of my hitherto unflagging willingness to help was the start of "mutual analysis" (see above), in which I admitted to almost everything I had held back with regard to antipathy and resistance in the face of excessive suffering and this was recognized and traced back to infantile elements in myself. Under the influence of this analysis many things have changed, in my relationship and attitude, in every respect; and yet the sympathy still did not reach the level that, for example, B. had won for herself so easily, that is, so much more easily (admittedly under the influence of what I had already learned from the case of R.N.).

The danger of latent sadism and erotomania in the analyst

The analytic situation, but specifically its rigid technical rules, mostly produce in the patient an unalleviated suffering [*lenteszie-rendes Leiden*][2] and in the analyst an unjustifiable sense of superiority accompanied by a certain contempt for the patient. If one adds to that a feigned friendliness, interest in detail, and occasional real compassion in the face of a too intense suffering, then what we see is the patient entangled in an almost unresolvable conflict of ambivalence, from which there is no way out. Some chance incident will then be used to allow the analysis to break down "because of the patient's resistance."

I do not know of any analyst whose analysis I could declare, theoretically, as concluded (least of all of my own). Thus we have, in every single analysis, quite enough to learn about ourselves.

Analysis offers to persons otherwise somewhat incapacitated and whose self-confidence and potency are disturbed an opportunity to feel like a sultan, thus compensating him for his defective ability to love. Analyzing this condition leads to a salutary loss of illusions about oneself and thus to the awakening of a real interest in others. If one has overcome one's narcissism in this way, one will soon acquire that sympathy and love of humanity without which the analysis is just a protracted vexation [*protrahierte Sekkatur*].

1. Cumberlandism is a phenomenon that was demonstrated for the first time by the English illusionist Stuart Cumberland in the nineteenth century. His experiment, which became known as the "willing game," consisted of asking the subject to find a hidden object, or to perform an action that had been imagined by someone else but not described in words. A person who knew the object's location or the action to be performed sat with his hands touching those of the subject, and supposedly aided the subject with subtle pressures that he himself was unaware of. For more information on psychological automatism see Pierre Janet, *L'Automatisme Psychologique* (1973; orig. pub. 1889), pp. 350–351, and the contribution by Charles Richet in *Traité de Métapsychique*.—ED.

2. The adjective *lenteszierendes* does not appear in any currently available dictionary and may be regarded as pure evocation. Various suggestions for translating it have been advanced: "souffrance interminable" in the French edition; "the suffering of the exploited" by Michael Balint. The word "unalleviated" appears to come nearest to Ferenczi's presumed intention.

11 August 1932

A note on criminality

A former patient, analyzed for a time and relatively freed from his anxiety, consults me again: he is in some difficulty at the moment, but this does not upset him too much. In his business he has gotten involved in undertakings far too large for the capital at his disposal. During the first analysis I had encouraged him to have all possible sorts of scientific and business fantasies and had myself derived a certain amount of pleasure from seeing him taking on in intellectual debates almost all the scholars he encountered—with the exception of the mathematician. Within a few months this man, who could barely write his own name, was discussing the most complex problems of physics, chemistry, physiology, philosophy, and psychology with experts. At the same time he got involved in love affairs with twelve or fourteen women, concurrently or one after the other. Ultimately, with three at once on a fairly steady basis: (1) his cook, who became devoted to him like a bitch, (2) one of the most attractive and intelligent young ladies of higher social standing, who is also scientifically talented (he broke off the relationship with her as this lady objected to the affair being made public, knowing that her reputation and career would be ruined in higher aristocratic circles if that happened), (3) an outstanding Hungarian physician, who quite the contrary made too public a show of the relationship and behaved as though she were his wife. He managed to get a considerable sum of money from her, and he has also failed to pay my fee for his analysis for many months.

Now that he sees that he cannot become rich quickly, he is thinking of escaping from his obligations. At the same time he announces that he has been infected with gonorrhea by a prostitute in Paris but has since had intercourse with both the cook and the doctor. I told him that he must get treatment for himself and have both women examined.

I used the opportunity to tell him that from now on he must pay me, but I did suggest that for the time being he could pay only half and continue to owe me the money for earlier treatment. Strangely enough, at the time of the first consultation I was still inclined to lend him the entire sum again, and it was only on further reflection that I told myself it was high time to show the man the limits of reality in analysis as well. (The slowness with which I realized this came out in my self-analysis: identification with the coward who overcoming his fear turns into a hero, beyond good and evil.) In a discussion with employees in his business, he let himself be carried away to such extreme rudeness that he was challenged to a duel. For the present he refused to accept my conditions; I remained firm, however, and expect a settlement from him, probably tomorrow. The next step he resolved to take was the decision to terminate his relationship with the doctor. He believes that I am biased against him because of her, that I will push him into marrying that "son of a witch";[1] he would also like to tell her that she cannot have him anymore as a "fucking instrument"; she should not have taken "my cock" in her mouth. I left him to it, and hope that this discussion will clear up the situation. The growing antipathy of the neurotic doctor will now have better foundations, her provocative behavior, her credulity, etc., will be explained analytically.

What is also important, however, is the slowness and delay with which *I* gained these insights. There is nothing for it, I must look for the cause in my own repressed criminality. To some extent I admire the man who dares to do the things that I deny to myself. I even admire him for the impudence with which he cheats me. The basic cause can only be fear of such miscreants; probably at one time I was effectively defeated and intimidated by someone like him.

An interesting idea occurred to me today in connection with this man: I thought that he would physically attack me, and had the idea of carrying in my pocket my revolver that fires warning shots. For the moment I have put off settling matters until tomorrow; but I am determined to remain firm, and if necessary to let him go. I have the feeling that if I give way he will treat me like a fool—as he does almost everyone else—and take advantage of me. If I remain firm, he may really attack me; he has already started to hint that he gave me enough money before (so that he is not willing to pay me any more); he can threaten me with publicity, disparage me to my friends, etc. All of it will leave me cold. Perhaps he will then try to make me give in by breaking down; in that case I will offer to continue his treatment, if he accepts my conditions. Problem: When is criminality curable? How much insight into one's own illness is required here, as in psychoses? Drawing of sharper limits between fantasy and reality during the analysis. (Quote two other cases: Dr. G., who fooled Freud, and B.'s father.)

1. Phrase written in English. In the original manuscript "son of a bitch" has been changed in pencil to "son of a witch."—ED.

12 August 1932

Subjective presentation of function's splitting

The patient O.S. suffers from obesity. The most effective reducing preparations—thyroid, pituitary, mercury—were unsuccessful. She could not stay on a diet, as she feels restless unless she eats well and a great deal. Yet a deep depression (insight into the hopelessness of all the efforts she has made to alter the behavior toward her of her friend, who could be described as manic) presented an opportunity for her to submit to a starvation diet in addition to medical treatment. She is in a state of emotional apathy, so that nothing, not even the sensation of hunger, matters to her. She has now fasted for six days, drinking daily one to two small glasses of cognac and one glass of orangeade.

She describes her condition as follows: as far as possible she does not do any work; if she has to do any, she feels quite exhausted. She responds to any demand on her with a peculiar sensation in the abdominal region. Although consciously she experiences neither fear nor anxiety nor any other emotion, she knows from the special quality of this sensation if it means this or that emotion. She can honestly maintain, however, that her knowledge of this is purely intellectual. She talks about a complete division of her personality into two parts. Anything unpleasant, in this insensitive state, causes only the body to react, as described above. Her emotional state remains completely undisturbed and unaffected. When she wants to describe the internal bodily reaction "in the region of the solar plexus" more accurately, she says that it feels as if "one were pushing something away from oneself and retreating from something." On further inquiry one is told that where food is concerned the patient behaves differently at different times. At times she has to alleviate the inner sensation as quickly as possible by eating or drinking. "Just the way a child, whatever happens to it, will be calmed most quickly by being offered the bottle or the breast." A situation of more profound unpleasure paralyzes even this capacity for being comforted, or for comforting oneself.

The patient herself refers to the trauma she suffered at the age of six weeks, when she was in a hotel for about two or three days with her mentally ill mother—subjected to no one knows what treatment— until at last they were discovered. That must have been a time when the child must have experienced violent fright, and must have been demanding food, but the mother probably let her starve, so that the child was finally so exhausted that she gave up demanding food, and, was only aware of slipping away, so to speak. Even after she had been discovered and revived and fed in the best possible way, it seems that readaptation to life was learned only by a superficial part of her personality, in a rather automatic fashion. A twin sister, let us say six weeks old, lies buried in her in the same state of rigidity that she herself fell into in the course of the trauma: in a faint (powerless, incapable of any motor manifestation); reacting perhaps only with a flight reflex or defensive kicking, for a time perhaps still able to be comforted by sucking; but after a further period of helplessness and sensations of unpleasure, the motility, and probably also desire to live, are completely extinguished. (Here the explanation proper of the link between "oral eroticism" and depression, respectively melancholia; Abraham, Radó.)[1]

Perhaps there is an opportunity here for insight into the trophic peculiarities of "manic depressives." This patient appears to be able to put on weight in certain circumstances without taking any nourishment, allegedly without drinking any more than what is stated above. Since beginning her fast she had, up to yesterday, lost four kilograms; without having altered anything in her diet (fasting) and despite injections of these drugs, she has gained one kilogram since yesterday. Assuming that cheating is excluded, one cannot discount the possibility that the "biologically unconscious, purely vegetative" twin sister (perhaps like a plant, or like an embryo) absorbs oxygen, CO_2, and H_2O from the surrounding medium (air), and accomplishes such apparent miracles . . . . . Weight increase in schizophrenics. Mrs. S.I.: Superego makes one fat. (Case S.I. must be revised in accordance with the twin-sister theory.) Patient O.S. feels restless and has a compulsion to keep busy on ordinary days (weekdays); on festive days even this escape is formally restricted, and she feels only an utterly unbearable quiet, which she fears more than anything else (Sunday neurosis!).[2] The quiet of holidays makes it inevitable that she hear the internal sounds of the twin sister.

B: Dream: (1) A crazy driver turns a full bus in such a tight circle that it tips over. The patient sees the danger, takes an outside seat, climbs out of the overturned vehicle; all the others have cleanly severed limbs (covered by their clothing), for example the severed foot of a man. As she gets out, she feels only small fragments of glass in her outer auditory canal. Symbolic condensation of the injury suffered, of the desired revenge, of the memory (being reminded) in a displaced way on waking; perhaps also vague perception of painful noises, or of her own screaming. (2) Assaulted physically by a man. (3)[3]

1. Karl Abraham (1877–1925). See Abraham, *Selected Papers in Psychoanalysis* (Hogarth Press, 1973); several chapters are devoted to the subject of melancholy.—ED.

Sándor Radó (1890–1971), Hungarian analyst who emigrated to the United States. His ideas provoked strong opposition in analytic circles. His paper "Das Problem der Melancholie" (1927) became a classic.—ED.

2. See "Sunday Neurosis," *FC* 174–177.—ED.

3. The rest of this passage is missing.—ED.

13 August 1932

A *catalogue of the sins of psychoanalysis*

(Reproaches of a woman patient): (1) Psychoanalysis lures patients into "transference." The profound understanding and the keen interest in the most minute details of their life history and of the impulses of their psyche are naturally interpreted by the patients as a sign of profound personal friendship, indeed tenderness. (2) As most patients are psychic shipwrecks, who will clutch at any straw, they become blind and deaf to the facts that would indicate to them how little *personal* interest analysts have in their patients. (3) Meanwhile the unconscious of the patients perceives all the negative feelings in the analyst (boredom, irritation, feelings of hate when the patient says something unpleasant or something that stirs up the doctor's complexes). (4) The analysis provides a good opportunity to carry out unconscious, purely self-seeking, ruthless, immoral, indeed so to speak criminal actions and similar behavior guiltlessly (without a sense of guilt), such as a sense of power over a succession of helplessly devoted patients, who admire him without reservation. Sadistic pleasure in their suffering and their helplessness. Unconcern regarding the length of the analysis, indeed the tendency to prolong it for purely financial reasons: if one wants to, one turns the patients into taxpayers for life.

As a result of infantile experiences of the same kind it becomes impossible to detach oneself from him (and the analyst, because he does not clarify the analytical situation and his own behavior, does not help to elucidate the situation and to draw conclusions from the present regarding the past), no matter how long the unsuccessful work has been going on, just as a child cannot run away from home (because left to his own devices he feels helpless).

Transference that one finds far too much of in the process arising in analysis, which analysts in their ignorance are not equipped to resolve (he would have to know himself and his behavior much better to be able to do this), plays ultimately the same role in analysis as the selfishness (egoism) of parents in childrearing.

239 (Unspoken hatred fixates more than spoiling. The reaction to it is excessive goodness due to a sense of guilt, which cannot be eliminated without outside help.)

Patients *feel* the hypocritical element in the analyst's behavior; they detect it from hundreds of tiny signs. (Some of them even believe they can read the analyst's feelings and thoughts.) These far too seldom become the object of analysis (and too seldom are acknowledged by the analyst).

The remedy for this, even when it has "developed" this far, is true "contrition" in the analyst. Usually one reacts with the opposite: loss of enthusiasm, silence, irritation, the feeling of having done the best one could and still being criticized for it. Desire to break off the analysis, and perhaps really doing so.

(Possibly no analyst is so "perfect" that he can avoid things of this kind. However, if one bears it in mind and works on it quite early on, one shortens the duration of the analysis considerably. Does the fundamental cause of the *endlessness* of the traumatic repetitions (six to eight years long!) lie in this—because the *contrast with the past is missing*, without which *the past-unhappiness*, aided by the association of the present with repetition-unhappiness, continues to be experienced as something actual, and thereby the remembering-of-the-trauma [*Trauma-Erinnerung*] results in fragmentation, the reinforcement of symptoms, and the repression of the trauma.)

240 Only sympathy heals. (Healing.)

Understanding is necessary in order to employ sympathy in the right place (analysis), in the right way. Without sympathy: there is no healing. (At most, insight into the genesis of the illness.)

Can one love everyone? Are there no set limits to it?

Under the prevalent regime (rearing of children, passionate behavior of adults) it is made difficult for all people to free themselves of any sympathies or antipathies and their unfairness. Maybe someday the character of humanity will improve (limits of the ability to change). Even science is "passionate" when it sees and recognizes only selfish instincts. The natural urge to *share feelings of pleasure* following the corresponding normal satiation, and nature's principle of harmony, are not sufficiently recognized.

The idea of the death instinct goes too far, is already tinged with sadism; *drive to rest* [Ruhetreib] and SHARING (communication [*Mit-teilung*], *sharing*) of "excessive" accumulations of pleasure *and* unpleasure is the reality, or it was when not artificially—traumatically—disturbed.

BEING ALONE leads to splitting.

The presence of someone with whom one can share and communicate joy and sorrow (love and understanding) can HEAL the trauma. Personality is reassembled *"healed"* (like "glue").

241

Hatred of patients is behind the hypocritical *friendliness of the doctor toward the patient.* He must be awakened, taken back to (internal) causes; only then can one *help,* share and communicate one's *own suffering* and *share* that of others. If one is satiated oneself and not greedy, then wanting the good, feeling good, and doing good will follow naturally.

The *genitals* are not the organs with whose aid one *becomes free from suffering* (reservoir of suffering!), but organs for the *communication* and *sharing* of surplus energy (pleasure).

1. The child must be saturated with love and nourishment.

2. Puberty—supercharged with pleasure

Discharging it }
Communicating it } through the genitals

{ A kind of motherhood
Love for the split-off part: semen, child
Remains of self-love.

Love as above: 1. Love for semen-cells and ovula
                 2. Love for the person with whom one shares them
Deposition of a dangerous bomb (F.)
    "   of a loved being
             fragments. (F.)[1]

242   *Analyst* after receiving catalogue of sins, and after overcoming his defiant reaction: breakdown—"wanted the best and this is what happened!" *Patient:* in a position to *forgive.* That the first step could be taken toward forgiveness for causing the trauma indicates that they had attained insight. That it was at all *possible* to arrive at insight and communion with oneself spells the end of general *misanthropy.* Finally it is also possible to view and *remember* the trauma with *feelings of forgiveness* and consequently *understanding.*

The analyst who is forgiven: enjoys in the analysis what was denied him in life and hardened his heart.

MUTUAL FORGIVENESS!!—Final success.

1. This is a very confusing passage in the manuscript, composed of notes apparently intended to refresh the author's memory when he develops these ideas further. It may refer to various fantasies on the eventual fate of sperm cells.—ED.

14 August 1932

Trauma and splitting of the personality; rupture between feeling and intelligence

Case G.: *Sudden* shock (swift, unforeseen) when she observed parents having intercourse. What she most suddenly came to see and feel (Parents are fighting, father is strangling mother, mother appears to be in complete agreement with it, no one is thinking about me, I cannot run to anyone, I am left to myself, but how can I survive alone? Something to eat would appease me, but no one is thinking of me; I would like to scream, but don't dare, better that I keep silent and remain hidden, otherwise they will do something to me; I hate them both, I would like to push them away—impossible, I am too weak, and it would also be too dangerous; I would like to run away, but I don't know where, I would like to spit out this whole business as I would something disgusting), all this was unbearable for her, and yet she had to endure it; it was forced upon her. The unbearable nature of a situation leads to a sleeplike state of mind, in which all that is possible can be altered as in dreams, distorted in a negative and positive hallucinatory way. The idea of the disgusting character of the situation and the feelings produces the dream: it is nothing, I have only eaten something nasty; I will vomit it up and be free from it—or: "Someone will come and give me something nicer to eat." If the unpleasure persists without any help arriving, then one regresses even further back: "I am so dreadfully alone, of course I haven't been born yet, I am floating in the womb."

But if one has once succeeded in freeing oneself from psychic unpleasure with the aid of such a daydream, then a weak point for the entire future is established, to which the ego (feelings) easily regress as soon as something unpleasurable occurs. (So with our patient, when her mother suddenly left the house and much later when she experienced disappointment with her adored husband.)

The shock-effect in our patient, however, goes still deeper. Her entire emotional life sought refuge in regression, so that she now experiences fully and completely no emotion whatsoever; it is, in fact, never to her that things happen; she identifies herself only with other people. Thus while her emotional life vanishes into unconsciousness and regresses to pure body-sensations, her intelligence, detached from all emotions, makes a colossal but—as already mentioned—completely unemotional progression, in the sense of an adaptation-performance by means of identification with the objects of terror. The patient became terribly intelligent; instead of hating her mother or father she penetrated by her thought-processes their psychic mechanisms, motives, even their feelings so thoroughly (to the last with the help of her knowledge) that she could apprehend the hitherto unbearable situation quite clearly—as she herself had ceased to exist as an emotional person. The trauma made her emotionally embryonic, but at the same time wise in intellectual terms, like a totally objective and unemotionally perceptive philosopher.[1]

What is new in this whole process is that in addition to the flight from reality in the regressive sense there is also a flight in a progressive sense, a sudden development of intelligence, even clairvoyance— that is, a progressive flight, a sudden flowering of developmental possibilities virtually present in outline but hitherto functionally not utilized; a sudden aging, so to speak (at the same time as the emotions turn embryonic). One could thus take the view that after a shock the emotions become severed from representations and thought processes and hidden away deep in the unconscious, indeed in the corporeal unconscious, while the intelligence goes through the progressive flight described above. Fright was the force that tore feelings and thoughts apart, but this same fright is at work still, keeping the torn apart contents of the psyche still divided. Should one succeed, by means of an unforeseen attack or with the help of free association, in eliminating fear for a moment, the abrupt contact between the previously divided parts of the psyche will result in a loud explosion: convulsions, emotive, sensory and motor-corporeal symptoms, maniacal outbursts of rage, and finally most often irrepressible, unstoppable laughter, expressing uncontrollable swings of emotion; in the end, following complete exhaustion, relative appeasement, as if waking from a bad dream. But once again it was only a dream, without any lasting conviction regarding the reality of the events. So instead of remembering, the attempt at repetition has led only to a fit of hysteria followed by emotional amnesia.

What can bring about any change in this? Simply and solely: trust in the goodness and understanding of the analyst. He must be able to admit to all his negative emotional impulses, and thereby free the patient from the feeling that he is hypocritical. But in addition the patient must come to feel the real kindness of the analyst. This sympathy makes it possible for patients to share their sufferings with us and thus to feel, to a large extent, relieved from them. Under such circumstances, the kindness and the energy of the analyst make it possible to avoid the explosion on contact between the worlds of emotion and thought, so that at last recollection can take the place of repetition.

1. See on this subject "The Dream of the Clever Baby," *FC* 349; "Child Analysis in the Analysis of Adults," *Fin* 135–136; "Confusion of Tongues between Adults and the Child," *Fin* 165; "Exaggerated Sex Impulse and Its Consequences," *Fin* 271; "On Lamaism and Yoga," *Fin* 274.—ED.

17 August 1932

Projection of one's own REAL *incestuous tendencies onto children and patients: not understanding the difference between infantile fantasy and the realization of same*

    a. In life.
    b. In the analysis.

Case G.: Somewhat weary of the unceasing self-analysis, of the unceasing complaints about being unable to live her own life and about being required to identify with objects instead of loving and hating, I attempted, with the help of free association, to make the patient admit to feelings against her father that she may harbor in her unconscious. The father, suddenly deserted by the mother, turned to his daughter with emotional demands. They became comrades. When she tried to form friendly, perhaps even somewhat erotically tinged relationships with young men of her own age, her father rebuked her firmly, telling her she must never, on any account, become a person like her mother. While she was telling me all this, I made the following remark: "In fact it was a happy marriage between your father and you."

The next day I learn that the patient spent the whole day in deep depression, quite despairing of me: "If I don't get any more understanding from *him* (me), what can I expect at all? Even he calls it a happy marriage, that is, something I may have wanted. Instead of seeing that as a child I may have *wanted* something like that in my *imagination,* but nothing could have been further from my thoughts than achieving this intention or desire as a reality. This reality was forced on me, however, and so the way to normal development was blocked: instead of loving and hating I could only identify with people." The dreams of the following night are characteristic: (1) I am analyzing her, but I am lying next to her in bed. (2) Dr. Brill[1] is analyzing her; he leans over and kisses her; for the first time in her life she feels the beginnings of an orgasm after a kiss. Sudden awakening, without completing the orgasm. Interpretation: My claim of yesterday shows that I have no more understanding for her real feelings than her father, Brill (Horace?); she cannot expect anything from my analysis; namely I cannot even bring her to have an orgasm with Brill (the most repellent person) by means of identification with my desires. She does this out of fear of us, men. It was this fear that compelled her in the primal scene to identify not with her father but with her mother; in that awful moment she was the less frightening of the two.

I admitted that, caught in my own theoretical postulates, I had, in a superficial and careless manner, presumed modes of feeling of an adult, sexually mature person, where probably only infantile, unrealistic erotic fantasies were involved.

I hope that this capacity for insight and self-examination and my subsequent ability to follow the patient in a less prejudiced manner in the direction of the painful experience of identification will be able to save the threatened analysis. There are several important lessons to be drawn from this: (1) that we analysts project God only knows how much of our sexual theories onto children and no less onto our patients in the question of transference; we cannot grasp that the patients, although they are adults, have really remained small children and just want to play with things, are frightened of reality even in transference, but, out of fear of us, do not tell us about it and for our sakes behave as though they were in love with us; much of this, only because we analysts have these expectations or even unconscious desires. (2) We make no proper distinction between the playful, fantastic erotic velleities of children (and in this respect we behave rather like B.'s father, who, carried away by the daughter's sexual play, had raped her). (3) Fixation at the infantile stage is caused (a) by the imposition of libido of an adult kind, (b) by humiliating words of reproof, beatings, etc., for Oedipal fantasies, which in fact become real only by being taken seriously in this way, (c) the fixation is even worse when—as so frequently happens—one first permits these to be taken for real in a positive way, and then, for reasons of moral remorse, reserve and punishment are meted out (to make the child forget and to soothe one's own conscience).

In addition to the passionate attitude, this kind of *lack of understanding* of children's nature and in particular lack of belief in the innocence of children (and of patients) must drive them to despair, which then the adults help to transform into discouragement or defiance, sometimes exaggerated ambition, in any case unfortunate character traits, while in analysis it leads to a situation of bogging down that the analysts will construe as resistance on the part of the patients, instead of looking for the fault in themselves. The remedy can be provided only by an analysis that spares neither analysts nor analytical theory. If our own analysts will not do this, then we will have to listen to our patients' words and work on the hints they provide. Then we must be able to get the patients to put into words what we suspect is in them. The result is: relief, and a capacity to feel things regardless of whether they are pleasant or unpleasant for us. With that, the end of identification is inaugurated.

1. Abraham Arden Brill (1874–1948), American psychoanalyst of Hungarian extraction, born in Austria. One of the first to translate Freud into English, he made extremely controversial translations. He founded the Psycho-Analytical Association of New York in 1911, and was probably the dominant figure in psychoanalysis in the United States at the time, although his position was called into question by Jones, Frank, and Rank, as well as somewhat later by Radó.—ED.

17 August 1932

Addendum to fragmentation

(R.N.) Applying the observations made by G.: regression of feelings to the embryonic and progression of the intellect (in the identification with the aggressor out of fear) in the direction of virtual possibilities of development, in the sense of masochism, that is, maternity, produced for R.N., in the middle of an emotional outburst, the optical representation of a third kind of fragmentation: the soul passes through a hole in the head into the universe and shines far off in the distance like a star (this would be clairvoyance, which goes beyond understanding the aggressor and understands the entire universe, so to speak, in order to be able to grasp the genesis of even such a monstrous thing). Thus under the pressure of the shock a part of the personality leaves the selfish spheres of earthly existence and becomes all-knowing. As a result of the distance, the clarity, and knowledge of all of the connections, this omniscient part is able to intervene and help, even when all seems lost and hopeless. Extreme example: the astral fragment sees off in the distance the only person whose fate and suffering offer possibilities for self-examination, in spite of the similarity, that is to say, full understanding and also goodwill instead of pure aggressivity (father). Only when someone believes in this in addition to the other fragments (so to speak looks with one eye through the hole in the head at the distant star, and with the other eye observes the events going on in the body and in the soul) . . .

To add here: feelings are also present in the astral fragment, just as under anesthesia pain cannot be avoided but is just displaced to infinite distances. The astral fragment helps the individual by driving it insane. For many cases there is no other kind of possibility, the last pass before death or suicide. Astra also produces dream images and fantasies of happiness, for example of the ideal lover, of wonderful marital relations, while in reality the child is perhaps being cruelly raped, the organ overdilated in a narcotic state of relaxation as the uterus is forced to assume maternal functions prematurely.

In addition to the capacity to integrate the fragments intellectually, there must also be kindness, as this alone makes the integration permanent. Analysis on its own is intellectual anatomical dissection. A child cannot be healed with understanding alone. It must be helped first in real terms and then with comfort and the awakening of hope. We must stop despising suggestion when faced with the needs of purely infantile neurotics. Kindness alone would not help much either, but only both together.

22 August 1932

Spontaneity refreshing—provocation depressing

Patient U. falls in love with an elderly lady; during the sessions he complains about her, but he cannot do without the intimacy with her. At the same time he is carrying on affairs with five or six other women and makes no secret of this in front of the lady. The lady takes his courtship seriously and begins to behave as though she were the fiancée of the young man, a step that the patient does not oppose strongly enough. At the same time sexual relations with her are more satisfying, on occasion, than with any of the others. Finally he exposes her to the danger of infection. This leads to moments of manifest anger and hatred on the part of the woman. Although this affected U. painfully, he still had friendly feelings toward her afterward. Soon after this, however, the woman began to try to regain his love, as though she had forgiven him; she showed herself hurt and depressed, as it were, by his behavior. At that, a sudden reversal of feelings in U. again: if he was previously somewhat sad about the inevitable separation and happy to have genuine feelings, even gratitude and friendship, now he feels tied down once more (obligation) and compelled to help her and stay with her. At the same time, jealousy toward another young man flares up again.

This is an example of the fact that older people (adults), with the help of behavior designed to provoke pity, make a child feel guilty and so can keep it bound to them in a permanent helplessness, but that such a situation can provoke unconscious feelings of hatred, or even criminal impulses. A part of these impulses eventually may actually be realized (lack of concern about the risk of infection). If this is followed by punishment or reproof, instead of the situation being changed by understanding, the child is once again fixated by a sense of guilt.

Thereby, the repetition-tendency to marry the mother, or to fall in love with someone like her, is established, followed by feelings of guilt and hatred. Jealousy is actually a desire to free oneself, with the help of a third party, from an unwanted attachment. (*Szegény tatár*.)[1]

The child would like most of all to see his parents happy; if they are not, he then feels obliged to take the whole burden of the unhappy marriage on his own shoulders. The child would like best to play, just to play at being mother and father, not to be them. (As I have often said—see above—we psychoanalysts tend to view the infantile situation far too much from our adult point of view, and forget the autoplasticity of childhood and the dreamlike nature of children's entire psychic existence.—Primary process.) Patients are like children: they do not dare to contradict. They must be educated to it; some are so frightened that they can only be driven to become angry by renewed fright.

---

1. "Poor Tatar": a Hungarian expression, representing the comment of a peasant who sees a Tatar riding off with his pretty but cantankerous wife.—MICHAEL BALINT

24 August 1932

Is the rigorousness of the incest taboo the cause of fixation on incest?

In G.'s case: the child's fantasies suddenly realized in the departure of the mother and the approach of the father. In puberty hardly more independent, outward-looking in sexual matters: warned by the father not to be like her mother. This forced the child to regard the incest fantasy as real. But *no child* can do that; there is something in children that abhors real incest, finds the mother old, ridiculous, in any case unsuited to be loved. One must not show that the incest is imposed, so as not to offend the parent. (Analogy in psychoanalysis the treating of incestuous desires as real.)—Without the rigors of the taboo, the impulses to transgress against the taboo would probably, by themselves, partly "have been grown out of" and have vanished.

(A possible hypothesis regarding the shock-effect of the primal scene: in fantasy one may have toyed with such possibilities—observation of animals; the terrifying thing about it is having to watch this fantasy as a reality.)

Extreme good health or adaptability of the body as a protective measure against mental incapacity

Many psychotics in the family for the last three hundred years, but their physical health has been extraordinarily good. At the same time a general tendency to obesity; even the most powerful medicines work only in very high doses. It seems as though this physical robustness were storing up reserves of strength and mechanisms to preserve life even in case the mind should fail completely. Compare with this the weight gain of paralytics at the stage when dementia sets in.[1]

Revision of the catalogue of sins

It does not seem to suffice to make a general confession and to receive general absolution; patients want to see all the sufferings that we caused them corrected one by one, to punish us for them, and then to wait until we no longer react with defiance or by taking offense, but with insight, regret, indeed with loving sympathy. Finally (with the help of our own analysis) we must become so strong that we are immune from repeating such mistakes in the present. This is the stage in which the patient begins to trust us, and it is only now that he can look back at past events from a secure vantage point in the present, without a repetition of the explosion.

The patient's confidence, which we have thereby earned, now makes it possible for us to present to him as *reality* what he has experienced in the trance, and by means of countersuggestion to put an end to infantile, posthypnotically fixed command-automatisms; with real determination and its verbal expression we can prevent unnecessary repetitions of suffering for the patient (catalytic process).

Fear of suggestion in psychoanalysis

Psychoanalysis had considered the reduction to a traumatic experience and becoming conscious instead of repression (and later, the task of overcoming resistance against this knowledge) as being simultaneously the means of healing. Breuer's patient was freed from symptoms by being made aware and by abreaction. Later Freud taught us that latent transference, that is, something emotional, was the principal agent. The analytic technique creates transference, but then withdraws, wounding the patient without giving him a chance to protest or to go away; hence interminable fixation on the analysis while the conflict remains unconscious.

Once the patient is freed from these fetters, he protests against the sadistic procedure; but if the patient really feels that we will in fact take care of him, that we take his infantile need for help seriously (and one cannot offer a helpless child, which is what most patients are, mere theories when it is in terrible pain), then we shall be able to induce the patient to look back into the past without terror. More proof that the lasting effect of the trauma stems from the absence of a kind, understanding, and enlightening environment.

On being alone

The childish personality, as yet barely consolidated, does not have the capacity to exist, so to speak, without being supported on all sides by the environment. Without this support the psychic and organic component mechanisms diverge, explode, as it were; as yet there is no ego-center strong enough to be worth mentioning, which could hold the whole of it together, also on its own. Children have no ego yet, but only an id; the id still reacts alloplastically, not motorically. The analysis should be able to provide for the patient the previously missing favorable milieu for building up the ego, and so put an end to that state of mimetism which like a conditioned reflex only drives the person toward repetition. A new *couvade,* so to speak, and a new taking flight. (If the trauma encounters an already more developed ego, then reactions of rage and defiant attitudes follow; criminality —U.)

256 *"Terrorism of suffering"*

Fright: One part gets "BESIDE ITSELF." *Splitting.* The place thus vacated is taken up by the aggressor. Identification.

Representation of the child: "You are all crazy" by imitation. (Nonsense.) *Grimace.*

Mentally ill Children	{ In *desperation* { *Helplessness*

Crazy person }! (Mentally ill parents) }	{ Tradition { For generations

Doctors Men	{ No children { Medical nurse

Trauma repetition	Mythos Healing!

Really believe in the splitting. (Not to give scientific lectures.) Technical course.

Real coitus with children (incestuous acts) consequences much more frequent!

---

1. This refers to generalized paralysis in syphilis.—ED.

Regression in Ψ—φ Embryonic state during analysis (in organic disintegration)

Further regression to being dead. (Not yet being born is *the danger.* Is a new kind of solution to the personality problem possible after such *sinking* into the traumatic?)

In my case the blood-crisis[1] arose when I realized that not only can I not rely on the protection of a "higher power" but *on the contrary* I shall be trampled under foot by this indifferent power as soon as I go my own way and not his.

The insight this experience has helped me to attain is that I was brave (and productive) only as long as I (unconsciously) relied for support on another power, that is, I had never really become "grown up." Scientific achievements, marriage, battles with formidable colleagues—all this was possible only under the protection of the idea that *in all circumstances* I can count on the father-surrogate. Are the "identification" with the higher power, the most *sudden* "formation of the superego," the support that once preserved me from final disintegration? Is the only possibility for my continued existence the renunciation of the largest part of one's own self, in order to carry out the will of that higher power to the end (as though it were my own)?

And now, just as I must build new red corpuscles, must I (if I can) create a new basis for my personality, if I have to abandon as false and untrustworthy the one I have had up to now? Is the choice here one between dying and "rearranging myself"—and this at the age of fifty-nine? On the other hand, is it worth it always to live the life (will) of another person—is such a life not almost death? Do I lose too much if I risk this life? *Chi lo sa?*

My pupils' confidence in me could give me a certain self-assurance; in particular, the confidence of one person who is both a pupil and a teacher.

(I have just received a few personally friendly lines from *Jones.* He has sent roses, suggested a circular letter.) Cannot deny that I was pleasantly touched even by this. I did indeed also feel abandoned by colleagues (Radó etc.) who are all too afraid of Freud to behave objectively or even sympathetically toward me, in the case of a dispute between Freud and me. A more restrained circulation of letters between Freud, Jones, and Eitingon has certainly been going on for a long time now. I am treated like a sick person who must be spared. My intervention will have to wait until I recover, so that the special "care" becomes unnecessary.

A certain strength of my psychological makeup seems to persist, so that instead of falling ill psychically I can only destroy—or be destroyed—in my organic depths.

259   I was seized with sentimentality when I thought back to the time when as a soldier (a one-year volunteer) I was once publicly commended for outstanding (and spontaneous) action in the field (on maneuvers). *This* seems to be what I lack now, and lacked in my childhood. Through harshness and lack of understanding I was driven into the role of the "bad boy." The contempt toward me was particularly painful from my oldest sister,[2] with whom I seem to have been hopelessly in love. I found a substitute in passionate self-satisfaction. Self-satisfaction is always psychopathic—splitting of the personality—one part gratifies the other (fantasy world). In reality one then feels (1) exhausted, (2) guilty. (Identification with the object of love, including *adopting* the contemptuous thoughts and judgments of that person: I despise myself in the same way *she* would despise me if she knew everything about me. (Voyeurism!) The part that I introjected with the identification is, however, an identification that at the same time knows everything about us.)

Interestingly, the affair with brother J.[3] offers me an opportunity (concurrently with the Freudian controversy) to have it out with J.—that is, to acknowledge the *reality* (hopelessness) in this direction also, and to make it known to the other party. Open antipathy instead of feigned amicability.

260   *Mutuality—sine qua non*

An attempt to continue analyzing unilaterally. Emotionality disappeared; analysis insipid. Relationship—distant. Once mutuality has been attempted, one-sided analysis then is no longer possible—not productive.

Now the question: must every case be mutual?—and to what extent?

1. U.: Confession of weakness had made him anxious—helpless—contemptuous.

2. Dm.: Made herself independent—feels hurt because of the absence of mutuality on my part. At the same time, she becomes con-

vinced that she has overestimated father's (and my) importance. Everything comes from the mother.

3. R.N.: My "incompetence" ultimately turned me into the *father* unwilling (and unable) to help. (Finally she realized that she had a great deal of aggression and resistance against me as a father-surrogate.) My attribute as the Ideal Lover thereby was lost (that is, also the hope of ever finding this in me). At the same time she finds my constant "probing" painful, unnecessary, a device for keeping (and for torturing) patients.

From *my* analysis she expects insight into the *personal* (quite independent of her), historical determinants of my behavior toward patients—and thus definitive detachment. What will *remain*, she hopes, is a *reciprocal* "honorable" recognition of mutual achievement, of having coped *with such a case*.

R.N.: Mutuality   F: Acceptance of mutuality
      Perseverence   Insight into own weakness—admission

I released R.N. from her torments by repeating the sins of her father, which then I confessed and for which I obtained forgiveness.

261   *Progression*

    {Sudden motherhood
    {Flourishing of intellect
    (*Being worm-eaten*)
    Racial progression
    Omniscience
    Mediumism
    (Healer)
    Genius and madness
    He has fallen on his head [*Fejére esett*]
    Insanity of body only (O.S.)
    Cyclical obesity etc.
    CATALOGUE OF SINS

Indignation of the Faculty, when I said: "Colleagues must commit errors." (Joke.)[4]

(1) Sadism. Disregard for patients' sufferings. (2) Megalomania: seeing oneself surrounded by worshippers—*erotomania*. (3) *Theories* invalid. Blinded. Determined by own complexes. These are imposed on patients. Patients dare not rebel. (4) They must be *forgiven* (this is what men rely on).

$$\left.\begin{array}{l} \text{Sin} \\ \text{Confession} \\ \text{Forgiveness} \end{array}\right\}$$

There must be punishment. (Contrition.)

1. Pernicious anemia, which was to cause Ferenczi's death just a few months later.—ED.

2. This probably does not refer to Ilona, Ferenczi's eldest sister, but rather to Gizella, born on 8 June 1872, about a year before Sándor's birth.—ED.

3. Undoubtedly this refers to the brother who preceded Gizella: Jakab, called Joseph, born on 14 July 1869.—ED.

4. *Begehen,* "commit," instead of *gestehen,* "confess."

Sándor Ferenczi, toward the end of his life,
in Baden-Baden.

Draft Introduction by Michael Balint

The *Diary* was written in 1932 and will be published only now in 1969.[1] The time-lag of almost forty years calls for an explanation.

All of us, who were fairly close to Sándor Ferenczi in his last years, knew about the existence of the *Diary*. In the preceding years he spoke to us several times about his plan to write it, during 1932 he often mentioned that he was writing it, and during his last months in 1933 he repeated time and again that, because he had to give up his practice, he could not finish the *Diary,* and how much he regretted that he could not include in it his last experiences with his patients as they, one after the other, had to leave him.

After his death at least three of us, Vilma Kovács, Alice Balint and I, read considerable parts of the *Diary*. Our unanimous advice to Mrs. Ferenczi, which she accepted, was to postpone its publication for the time being. We thought it had better wait until the immediate repercussions of the disagreement between Freud and Ferenczi had settled. This would allow time for a more favourable atmosphere to develop for the objective assessment of Ferenczi's ideas contained in the *Diary*.

During the next few years the three of us were fully engaged in collecting, editing and translating the material for Volumes 3 and 4 of the Bausteine. Freud, of course, was not only informed about our plan but was sent all the hitherto unpublished material. It can be stated that he followed our work with interest, did not object to any part of the text proposed by us; on the contrary, he expressed his admiration for Ferenczi's ideas, until then unknown to him. As the Verlag in Vienna did not have enough funds to finance all the costs, it was decided to print the edition in Budapest using paper supplied by the Verlag. We finished the printing just before the Anschluss; we had to realise then that re-exporting it to Vienna would have meant exposing the whole edition to certain destruction. After some com-

---

1. Michael Balint believed at the time that all obstacles to a simultaneous publication of the *Diary* and the Freud-Ferenczi Correspondence had been removed.—ED.

plicated negotiation with the Nazi Authorities we were allowed to re-export the whole edition to Switzerland where the two Volumes were given in commission to the Hans Huber Verlag in Bern. Then came the War and every major publishing plan had to be postponed.

When I left Budapest for England in January 1939 Mrs. Ferenczi gave me the *Diary,* together with all the letters written by Freud to Ferenczi, and asked me to keep them until the time arrived when they could be published.

After the War my first concern became to translate and edit all the important papers by Ferenczi which had not yet appeared in English. After overcoming some resistance by Ernest Jones, the Editor of the International Psychoanalytical Library, who wanted to omit from the English edition all the papers written by Ferenczi after 1928, the *Final Contributions* appeared in 1955. The reception was not encouraging, so I decided to wait.

In 1957 Volume 3 of Jones' Freud Biography appeared, containing a violent attack on Ferenczi. As Jones had access to the whole Freud-Ferenczi correspondence, I could not understand how he was able to neglect the evidence contained in it. When I asked him from what source he derived his allegations, he refused to give any information except that it was someone close to Ferenczi during his last period. When we reached this point it was already generally known that Jones was suffering from an incurable condition. Under these circum-stances the only thing I felt wise to do was to agree with him to publish a correspondence in the *International Journal* (1958) in which each of us stated his point of view.

The aftermath of Jones' Biography was a spate of acrimonious publications, definitely not a favourable atmosphere for the publica-tion of the *Diary* with its many original and intriguing ideas, mistakes and exaggerations, profound but often disquieting insights.

The chief reason for publishing the *Diary* now is that it will appear at about the same time as the correspondence between Freud and Ferenczi, selected and edited jointly by Ernst Freud and myself. This fact may be taken as a symbol that the waves of the painful disagree-ment that overshadowed the last two or three years of the friendship between these two great men have sufficiently settled to enable the psychoanalytic world to judge the real differences in an impartial but sympathetic manner.

Notes for a Preface by Michael Balint

In addition to writing his introduction, Balint made notes for the purpose of drafting a preface. This preface in fact was not written, but the notes themselves appear to us of sufficient importance to be reproduced here in their original form.—ED.

No matter whether one accepts the truth of the reconstructed infantile sexual traumata in all their details or not, the theoretical discussion of the consequences especially with regard to the finer mechanism of repression remains valid and important, even for today. Exactly the same holds true for the discussion of the resulting changes in the ego; these are as relevant for our present theory as they were in 1932 when Ferenczi wrote them down.

Title: Form of the Diary

This is entirely spontaneous, as a real diary ought to be. True, a large part, roughly 80%, is typed out, which means that Ferenczi dictated this part to his secretary whenever he could get a few moments free from his work. The entries are dated so one can follow how much, or how little, he could cope with on any one day. As a rule he gave a title to each of his ideas, but the ideas of any one day were, as a rule, closely linked with each other.

The last typed entry is dated 24th August 1932. Then Ferenczi stopped working in order to go first to Vienna, where he met Freud for the last time in his life, and from there to the Wiesbaden Congress which opened officially on September 4th. After that day there are only six more handwritten pages, all dated October 1932.

If one compares the dates of the Diary: the first entry in January 1932, then fairly continuous entries until the end of August 1932, and lastly a few disjointed ones in October with the dates of the "Notes and Fragments" that were found after his death among his papers, and published in Volume 4 of the Bausteins and subsequently in the *Final Contributions*, we find: a few experimental entries in

1920, then a continued effort throughout 1930 and 1931 which suddenly stops at the beginning of 1932. There is one isolated, not very interesting, entry in June of that year, but a new series of entries starts mid-September in Biarritz where Ferenczi went from Wiesbaden and where the first alarming symptoms of his illness, pernicious anaemia, developed. From then on the entries continue until the end of that year.

I think from these details one could infer with very great probability that the entries in 1930 and 1931 were a kind of prolegomena to his diary. Further proof of this assumption is that all these entries were handwritten on all sorts of papers, starting with proper sheets and ending with backs of envelopes and half pages of odd pharmaceutical propaganda material; in contrast to this the proper diary was typed in almost the whole of its entirety and its pages were more or less properly numbered. This concerted effort, as well as Ferenczi's condition, suffered a shattering blow during his last meeting with Freud (and by his subsequent illness which—one does not know—was a coincidence or a consequence).

Ferenczi never recovered sufficiently to continue his *Diary* in the way he intended and achieved the writing of it in the first part of 1932; still, as the "Notes and Fragments"[1] show, he went on collecting material and jotting down his ideas until the end of that year, hoping that perhaps his state would improve. As we all know, this did not happen; and he died in April 1933.[2] In spite of liver therapy his condition worsened; during the winter 1932–3 he was forced to give up his practice, became bedridden chiefly because of the degeneration of his spinal cord and died in April 1933.

1. "Notes and Fragments," *Fin.*, 216–279.—Ed.
2. Michael Balint here makes a surprising mistake, which he repeats a few lines further down, regarding the date of Ferenczi's death. In fact Ferenczi died on 22 May 1933 and was buried on 24 May.

Index

Mutual analysis, xvii, xviii, xx–xxii, 13–16, 42–45, 65, 71–73, 110, 115, 131, 193; problems and failure of, xxi–xxii, 28–29, 73–75; limitations of, 10–13, 26, 34–37; analytic view of, 27; two-children nature of, 56–57; and analysis, 71–73; relaxation in, 84; vulnerability in, 92–93. *See also* Analysis

Mutuality in analysis, 35, 37–38, 46–47, 48–50, 53, 213–214; new stage of, 129–131

Narcissism, 124, 128–129, 171
Neocatharsis, 54
Neurasthenia, 89, 90
Neurosis-theory, 113–114
"Notes and Fragments" (Ferenczi), xviii, 221, 222
Nymphomania, 63, 65

Object-libido, 122–124
Object relations, 147
Oedipus complex, xvii, xxiii, 79, 173, 175–176, 178, 185; fantasies, 205–206
Ontogenesis, 5
Orpha (organizing life instincts), 8, 9, 10, 13, 92, 121

Pain alleviation, 140–143, 145–146
Paranoia, xvii, 26, 58–59, 95; of patients, 42–43; and sense of smell, 86–88; as "brilliant achievement," 159–160; of authority, 160; psychoanalytic, 161
Parapraxis, 143–145
Passion, 102, 115–117, 150–154, 155, 165
Penis envy, 132–133
Perfection, 150
Permissiveness, 186
Persecution mania, 87
Personality, 68, 119; awareness of, 125–129; disintegration and reassembling of, 157, 201; unity of, 169–170
Personality, split, 38, 51, 54, 62–63, 65–67, 69, 80, 81, 98, 102, 104, 107, 121, 129, 170; narcissistic, 105, 114; subjective presentation of, 196–199; and aloneness, 201; and trauma, 202–204
Perversion, 172–173
Pfister, Oskar, 150, 154n1
Phallus cult, 90–91
Photochemical reaction, 150
Photo-hyperesthesia, 112–113

Physics, 40
Pleasure principle, 153
Pornophasia, 89–90
Provocation, 207–208
Psyche, 6, 104; fragmented, 13, 38–40, 203 (*see also* Personality, split); functioning of, 40; and superperformance, 58–59; and "bandages," 68–70; contents and energies, 76–78; and anatomy, 79; paralysis of, 83; discharge of, 170
Psychiatry, xviii
Psychoanalysis, *see* Analysis
Psycho-Analytical Association of New York, 206n1
Psychosoma, 117

Radó, Sándor, 198, 206n1, 212
Rank, Otto, 185, 186, 206n1
Rape fantasies, 192
Reaction principle, 147
Reality: avoidance and negation of, 50, 180; reinterpretation of, 51; delusional, 58; principle, 153; adaptation to, 156
Regression, 116, 191, 203, 206; of libido, 20; cathartic, 21–24; and anxiety, 114; neurotic, 114; to embryonic state, 212–213
Relaxation, 63, 94, 97; of analyst, 36–37, 71, 83–86; of self-abandonment, 39; and activity (education), 49–50; of analysand, 54–55, 83; technique, 62, 186; dream interpretation during, 67–68; in sleep, 134. *See also* Trance states
Repression, xvii, 21–24, 136, 144, 153, 163, 172, 200, 221; of infantile trauma, 25; and catharsis, 66–67; ego, 111; formation of, 159; in children, 164, 174; and rage, 176–177
Respiratory disturbances, 102–106, 133–134, 156
Richet, Charles, 194n1

Sadism, 9, 42, 151, 155, 200, 214; repressed, 148; and anal eroticism, 172–173; in analysis, 183; in children, 183; latent, 194
Sadomasochism, 163, 173, 190
Satyriasis, 65
Schizophrenia, xvii, 33, 187n10, 198; progressive, 8–10; catatonic, 19; case example of, 100–102; and trauma, 150
Self-assertion, 41–42, 143, 146
Selfishness, 146, 148, 151, 153

FICTION

The
INNER
CIRCLE

ALSO BY BRAD MELTZER

$\mathcal{T}\!he$
INNER
CIRCLE

BRAD
MELTZER

GRAND CENTRAL
PUBLISHING

NEW YORK   BOSTON

Copyright © 2011 by Forty-four Steps, Inc.

Song lyric from "God Bless the Child," by Billie Holiday and Arthur Herzog, Jr., © 1941 by Edward B. Marks Music Company.

Grand Central Publishing
Hachette Book Group
237 Park Avenue
New York, NY 10017

www.HachetteBookGroup.com

Printed in the United States of America

First Edition: January 2011
10 9 8 7 6 5 4 3 2 1

Grand Central Publishing is a division of Hachette Book Group, Inc.
The Grand Central Publishing name and logo is a trademark of Hachette Book Group, Inc.

Library of Congress Cataloging-in-Publication Data
Meltzer, Brad.
    The inner circle / Brad Meltzer. — 1st ed.
      p. cm.
    ISBN 978-0-446-57789-2 (regular ed.) — ISBN 978-0-446-57371-9 (large print ed.)   1. United States. National Archives and Records Administration—Fiction.   2. Archivists—Fiction.   3. Conspiracies—Fiction.   4. Washington (D.C.)—Fiction.   5. Political fiction.
I. Title.
    PS3563.E4496156 2011
    813'.54—dc22
                        2010036506

For Theo,
my son,
who came into my life
when I needed him most

ACKNOWLEDGMENTS

I know who's in my inner circle. Many of them are listed below—including you, treasured reader, who give me the support that still lets me do this. So thank you to the following: My first love and first lady, Cori, who pushes me, challenges me, fights me, but most important, believes in me. Since junior high. Jonas, Lila, and Theo are my greatest and most beautiful treasures, and they astonish me every single day. There is no greater love than the love I have for them. Jill Kneerim, the patron saint of agents, who remains my steadfast champion and dear friend; Hope Denekamp, Caroline Zimmerman, Ike Williams, and all our friends at the Kneerim & Williams Agency.

This is a book about history and friendship—and the profound power when you combine the two. But it's also about what we'll do for our families, so let me thank mine, beginning with my dad, who taught me how to fight, especially when it came to those I love most, and my sister Bari, who continues to teach me even more of the same. Also to Will, Bobby, Ami, Adam, and Gilda, for everything a family can be.

Here's a secret: As a writer, you can only be as good as the readers you share your first drafts with. So let me start with the reader whom I couldn't do this without: Noah Kuttler. For every page I write, Noah hears it first. He is ruthless, insightful—and never takes his eyes off the craft. He's the one I count on to make sure I'm being intellectually honest—and also to make sure I'm not being the middle-aged cliché that my body so wants to be. Ethan Kline has read and improved every early draft since I started writing; and Dale Flam, Matt Kuttler, Chris Weiss, and Judd Winick have saved me in more ways than they'll ever realize.

In a novel so steeped in our nation's history, I owe the following people tremendous thanks for sharing that history: First, President George H. W. Bush, who inspired so much of this during a cherished conversation I will never forget. And while we're on the subject, let me thank the man himself—George Washington—for being such a wild genius (you'll see what I mean inside). At the National Archives, which everyone should go visit, Susan Cooper, Matt Fulgham, Miriam Kleiman, and Trevor Plante were my masterminds and guides. They answered every insane question I threw at them and the best part of this process has been the friendship that we've shared. Special thanks to Paul Brachfeld and his amazing team, including Kelly Maltagliati, Ross Weiland, and Mitchell Yockelson, who I admire so much; Lisa Monaco, Ben Powell, Brian White, and all my friends at the Department of Homeland Security's Red Cell program for helping push this idea even further; White House doctor Connie Mariano and my pals at the Secret Service took me back inside my favorite white building; Debby Baptiste toured me through the underground storage caves; Steve Baron for the St. Elizabeths's details; my confidants Dean Alban, Arturo de Hoyos, Brent Morris, Tom Savini, and Mark Tabbert for their great historical insight; and the rest of my own inner circle, whom I bother for every book: Jo Ayn Glanzer, Mark Dimunation, Dr. Lee Benjamin, Dr. David Sandberg, Dr. Ronald K. Wright, Edna Farley, Jason Sherry, Marie Grunbeck, Brad Desnoyer, and Kim from L.A. More Archives research came from Juliette Arai, Judy Barnes, Greg Bradsher, Cynthia Fox, Brenda Kepley, John Laster, Sue McDonough, Connie Potter, Gary Stern, Eric VanSlander, Mike Waesche, Dave Wallace, Morgan Zinsmeister, and in memory of John E. Taylor; thanks to A. J. Jacobs and Michael Scheck for their idiosyncrasies. The books *George Washington, Spymaster* by Thomas B. Allen and *Washington's Spies* by Alexander Rose were vital to this process. Finally, Roberta Stevens, Anne Twomey, Kevin Wolkenfeld, Alison

ACKNOWLEDGMENTS

Coleman, Pat Finati, Phyllis Jones, Linda Perlstein, and the great people at Mount Vernon lent their expertise to so many different details; Ananda Breslof, Kim Echols, Steve Ferguson, and Pansy Narendorf lent themselves; and these friends on Facebook and Twitter lent even more personal character traits: Steven Bates, Beth Bryans, Denise Duncan, Scott Fogg, Abraham Medina, Hector Miray, Matthew Mizner, Lisa Shearman, and Jason Spencer; Rob Weisbach for the initial faith; and of course, my family and friends, whose names, as usual, inhabit these pages.

I also want to thank everyone at Grand Central Publishing: David Young, Emi Battaglia, Jennifer Romanello, Evan Boorstyn, Chris Barba, Martha Otis, Karen Torres, Lizzy Kornblit, the nicest and hardest-working sales force in show business, Mari Okuda, Thomas Whatley, and all the kind friends there who have spent so much time and energy building what we've always built. I've said it before, and it never changes: They're the real reason this book is in your hands. Special love to Mitch Hoffman, who never stopped editing and is a true part of the family. Finally, let me thank Jamie Raab. Over the past two years, we've shared overwhelming losses and watched our lives change together. Through that time, I've realized she doesn't just edit me. She lends me her strength. For that, I owe her forever. Thank you, Jamie, for bringing me home, and most important, for your faith.

The
INNER
CIRCLE

In 1989, during his final minutes in the White House, outgoing President Ronald Reagan scribbled a secret note—and, it was reported, a picture of a turkey. The note said, "Don't let the turkeys get you down." He then slipped the note into the Oval Office desk and left it for his successor, President George H. W. Bush.

In 1993, President Bush left a private note in the desk for Bill Clinton, who left a note for George W. Bush, who left one for Barack Obama.

But there were two things no one knew.

The tradition didn't start with Ronald Reagan. It started with George Washington.

And the picture Reagan drew? It most definitely was *not* a turkey.

PROLOGUE

He knew the room was designed to hold secrets.

Big secrets.

The briefcase from Watergate was opened in a room like this. Same with the first reports from 9/11.

He knew that this room—sometimes called the Tank or the Vault—held presidential secrets, national secrets, and *pine-box* secrets, as in, the kinds of secrets that came with coffins.

But as he stood in the back corner of the small, plain beige room, swaying in place and flicking the tip of his tongue against the back of his front teeth, the archivist with the scratched black reading glasses knew that the most vital thing in the room wasn't a classified file or a top-secret sheet of paper—it was the polished, rosy-cheeked man who sat alone at the single long table in the center of the room.

He knew not to talk to the rosy-cheeked man.

He knew not to bother him.

All he had to do was stand there and watch. Like a babysitter.

It was absurd, really.

But that was the job.

For nearly an hour now.

Babysitting the most powerful man in the world: the President of the United States.

Hence the secure room.

Yet for all the secrets that had been in this room, the archivist with the scratched black-framed reading glasses had no idea what he'd soon be asked to hide.

With a silent breath through his nose, the archivist stared at the

1

back of the President, then glanced over at the blond Secret Service agent on his far right.

The visits here had been going on since President Orson Wallace was first elected. Clinton liked to jog. George W. Bush watched baseball games in the White House Residence. Obama played basketball. All Presidents find their own way to relax. More bookish than most, President Orson Wallace traveled the few blocks from the White House and came to the National Archives to, of all things, read.

He'd been doing it for months now. Sometimes he even brought his daughter or eight-year-old son. Sure, he could have every document delivered right to the Oval Office, but as every President knew, there was something about getting out of the house. And so the "reading visits" began. He started with letters that George Washington wrote to Benedict Arnold, moved to classified JFK memos, and on to today's current objects of fascination: Abraham Lincoln's handwritten Civil War notes. Back then, if there was a capital case during a court-martial, the vote of "life or death" would come straight to Lincoln's desk. The President would personally decide. So in the chaos of President Wallace's current life, there was apparently something reassuring about seeing the odd curves and shaky swirls in Lincoln's own handwriting.

And that, as Wallace scribbled a few personal notes on his legal pad, was a hell of a lot more calming than playing basketball.

"Four more minutes, sir," the blond Secret Service agent announced from the back corner, clearing his throat.

President Wallace nodded slightly, beginning to pack up, but never turning around. "Is Ronnie joining us or no?"

At that, the archivist with the scratched reading glasses stood up straight. His supervisor, Ronald Cobb, was one of President Wallace's oldest friends from law school. It was Cobb who usually managed the visits and selected which priceless files the President would read. But with his recent diagnosis of pancreatic cancer, Cobb wasn't going anywhere for a bit.

"Mr. Cobb's at a chemo appointment, sir," the archivist explained in a voice that seemed strained even to himself.

Again, President Wallace nodded without turning around, flipping his legal pad shut.

It was the quick motion of the legal pad that caught the archivist's eye. For a moment, as the pale yellow pages fanned forward, he could swear one of the brown, mottled Lincoln letters was tucked inside.

The archivist squinted, trying to see. But from the angle he was at, diagonally behind the left shoulder of the President, the Lincoln document was—

No.

This was the President of the United States. He'd never . . .

No, the archivist told himself.

No. Not a chance. No.

"Before we go, I just need to hit the little vice president's room," President Wallace said, using the joke that always got him easy laughs with donors. He stood from his seat and held his legal pad at his side.

According to current research, when faced with an awkward social situation, the average person will wait seventeen seconds before breaking the silence.

"Mr. President," the archivist called out without even hesitating. "I'm sorry, but—"

President Wallace turned slowly, showing off his calming gray eyes and flashing the warm, fatherly grin that had won him the governorship of Ohio as well as the White House. "Son, I just need to run to the restroom, and then we can—"

"It'll just take a second," the archivist promised.

The room was no bigger than a classroom. Before the archivist knew it, he was standing in front of Wallace, blocking the President's path to the door. The blond agent stepped forward. Wallace motioned him back.

"Tell me the crisis, son," the President asked, his grin still keeping everything calm.

"I just . . . urr . . ." the archivist stammered, slowly starting to sway. "I'm sure it was just an honest mistake, sir, but I think you may've accidentally...huhh...In your notepad." The archivist took a deep

accidentally…huhh…In your notepad." The archivist took a deep breath. "One of the Lincoln letters."

The President laughed and went to step around the archivist.

The archivist laughed back.

And stepped directly in front of the President. Again.

President Wallace's gray eyes slowly shrank into two black slits. He was far too savvy to lose his temper with a stranger, but that didn't mean it was easy to keep that grin on his face. "Victor, I need you to excuse us a moment."

"Sir…" the blond agent protested.

"Victor…" the President said. That's all it took.

With a click and a loud metal *crunk*, the metal door to the Vault opened and Victor joined the other three agents stationed in the corridor outside.

Staring at the archivist, the President squeezed his fist around the legal pad. "Son, I want you to be very careful about what your next words are."

The archivist craned his neck back, taking in the full height of the President, who was so close the archivist could see the golden eagle and the presidential seal on Wallace's cuff links. *We have a set of LBJ's cuff links in our collection,* the archivist reminded himself for no reason whatsoever. And as he looked up at the most powerful man on the planet—as he studied the leader of the free world—it took far less than seventeen seconds to give his answer.

"I'm sorry, Mr. President. But those Lincoln documents aren't yours."

For a moment, the President didn't move. Didn't blink. Like he was frozen in time.

There was a deep *thunk* from behind the archivist. The metal door to the room clicked open.

"I toldja, right, Mr. President?" a familiar midwestern voice called out as the door clanged into the wall. The archivist turned just in time to see his boss, Ronnie Cobb, hobble inside, faster than usual. "I told you he'd come through. No reason to bother with Beecher."

The President smiled—a real smile—at his old friend and put a hand on the archivist's shoulder. "Good for you," he announced.

"I-I don't understand," the archivist said, still focused on Cobb. "I thought your chemo..." He looked at Cobb, then the President, then back to Cobb, who was beaming like a new father. "What the heck's going on?"

"Didn't you ever see *Willy Wonka*?" Cobb asked as he limped a few steps closer. "The big prize goes to the one who tells the truth."

The archivist paused a moment, looking at the two men. "What're you talking about? Why'd you mention Beecher?"

"Relax—we've got something a lot better than a spooky chocolate factory," President Orson Wallace said as he closed the door to the Vault, once again keeping his Secret Service agents outside. "Welcome to the Culper Ring."

1

There are stories no one knows. Hidden stories.

I love those stories.

And since I work in the National Archives, I find those stories for a living. They're almost always about other people. Not today. Today, I'm finally in the story—a bit player in a story about...

"Clementine. Today's the day, right?" Orlando asks through the phone from his guardpost at the sign-in desk. "Good for you, brother. I'm proud of you."

"What's that supposed to mean?" I ask suspiciously.

"It means, *Good. I'm proud*," he says. "I know what you've been through, Beecher. And I know how hard it is to get back in the race."

Orlando thinks he knows me. And he does. For the past year of my life, I was engaged to be married. He knows what happened to Iris. And what it did to my life—or what's left of it.

"So Clementine's your first dip back in the pool, huh?" he asks.

"She's not a pool."

"Ooh, she's a hot tub?"

"Orlando. Please. Stop," I say, lifting the phone cord so it doesn't touch the two neat piles I allow on my desk, or the prize of my memorabilia collection: a brass perpetual calendar where the paper scrolls inside are permanently dialed to June 19. The calendar used to belong to Henry Kissinger. June 19 is supposedly the last day he used it, which is why I taped a note across the base of it that says, *Do Not Use/Do Not Change*.

"So whattya gonna say to her?"

"You mean, besides *Hello*?" I ask.

"That's it? *Hello*?" Orlando asks. "*Hello*'s what you say to your sister. I thought you wanted to impress her."

"I don't need to impress her."

"Beecher, you haven't seen this girl in what—fifteen years? You need to impress her."

I sit on this a moment. He knows I don't like surprises. Most archivists don't like surprises. That's why we work in the past. But as history teaches me every day, the best way to avoid being surprised is to be prepared.

"Just tell me when she's here," I say.

"Why, so you can come up with something more mundane than *Hello*?"

"Will you stop with the mundane. I'm exciting. I am. I go on adventures every day."

"No, you *read* about adventures every day. You put your nose in books every day. You're like Indiana Jones, but just the professor part."

"That doesn't make me mundane."

"Beecher, right now I know you're wearing your red-and-blue Wednesday tie. And you wanna know why? Because it's *Wednesday*."

I look down at my red-and-blue tie. "Indiana Jones is still cool."

"No, Indiana Jones *was* cool. But only when he was out experiencing life. You need to get outta your head and outta your comfort zone."

"What happened to the earnest you're-so-proud-of-me speech?"

"I am proud—but it doesn't mean I don't see what you're doing with this girl, Beech. Yes, it's a horror what happened with Iris. And yes, I understand why it'd make you want to hide in your books. But now that you're finally trying to heal the scab, who do you pick? The safety-net high school girlfriend from fifteen years in your past. Does that sound like a man embracing his future?"

I shake my head. "She wasn't my girlfriend."

"In your head, I bet she was," Orlando shoots back. "The past may not hurt you, Beecher. But it won't challenge you either," he adds. "Oh, and do me a favor: When you run down here, don't try to do it in under two minutes. It's just another adventure in your brain."

Like I said, Orlando knows me. And he knows that when I ride the elevator, or drive to work, or even shower in the morning, I like to time myself—to find my personal best.

"Wednesday is always Wednesday. *Do Not Change.*" Orlando laughs as I stare at the note on the Kissinger calendar.

"Just tell me when she's here," I repeat.

"Why else you think I'm calling, Dr. Jones? Guess who just checked in?"

As he hangs up the phone, my heart flattens in my chest. But what shocks me the most is, it doesn't feel all that bad. I'm not sure it feels good. Maybe it's good. It's hard to tell after Iris. But it feels like someone clawed away a thick spiderweb from my memory, a spiderweb that I didn't even realize had settled there.

Of course, the memory's of her. Only she could do this to me.

Back in eighth grade, Clementine Kaye was my very first kiss. It was right after the bright red curtains opened and she won the Battle of the Bands (she was a band of one) with Joan Jett's "I Love Rock 'n Roll." I was the short kid who worked the spotlights with the coffee-breath A/V teacher. I was also the very first person Clementine saw backstage, which was when she planted my first real wet one on me.

Think of your first kiss. And what it meant to you.

That's Clementine to me.

Speedwalking out into the hallway, I fight to play cool. I don't get sick—I've never been sick—but that feeling of flatness has spread through my whole chest. After my two older sisters were born—and all the chaos that came with them—my mother named me Beecher in hopes that my life would be as calm and serene as a beach. This is not that moment.

There's an elevator waiting with its doors wide open. I make a note. According to a Harvard psychologist, the reason we think that we always choose the slow line in the supermarket is because frustration is more emotionally charged, so the bad moments are more memorable. That's why we don't remember all the times we chose the fast line and zipped right through. But I like remembering those times. I *need* those times. And the moment I stop remembering those times, I need to go back to Wisconsin and leave D.C. "Remember this elevator next time you're on the slow line," I whisper to myself, searching for calm. It's a good trick.

But it doesn't help.

"Letsgo, letsgo..." I mutter as I hold the Door Close button with all my strength. I learned that one during my first week in the Archives: When you have a bigwig who you're taking around, hold the Door Close button and the elevator won't stop at any other floors.

We're supposed to only use it with bigwigs.

But as far as I'm concerned, in my personal universe, there's no one bigger than this girl—this woman...she's a woman now—who I haven't seen since her hippie, lounge-singer mom moved her family away in tenth grade and she forever left my life. In our religious Wisconsin town, most people were thrilled to see them go.

I was sixteen. I was crushed.

Today, I'm thirty. And (thanks to her finding me on Facebook) Clementine is just a few seconds away from being back.

As the elevator bounces to a halt, I glance at my digital watch. Two minutes, forty-two seconds. I take Orlando's advice and decide to go with a compliment. I'll tell her she looks good. *No. Don't focus on just her looks. You're not a shallow meathead. You can do better*, I decide as I take a deep breath. *You really turned out good*, I say to myself. That's nicer. Softer. A true compliment. *You really turned out good*.

But as the elevator doors part like our old bright red curtains, as I anxiously dart into the lobby, trying with every element of my being to look like I'm not darting at all, I search through the morning crowd of guests and researchers playing bumper cars in their winter coats as they line up to go through the metal detector at security.

For two months now, we've been chatting via email, but I haven't seen Clementine in nearly fifteen years. How do I even know what she...?

"Nice tie," Orlando calls from the sign-in desk. He points to the far right corner, by the lobby's Christmas tree, which is (Archives tradition) decorated with shredded paper. *"Look."*

Standing apart from the crowd, a woman with short dyed black hair—dyed even darker than Joan Jett—raises her chin, watching me as carefully as I watch her. Her eye makeup is thick, her skin is pale, and she's got silver rings on her pinkies and thumbs, making her appear far more New York than D.C. But what catches me off guard is that she looks...somehow...older than me. Like her ginger brown eyes have seen two lifetimes. But that's always been who she was. She may've been my first kiss, but I know I wasn't hers. She was the girl who dated the guys two grades above us. More experienced. More advanced.

The exact opposite of Iris.

"Clemmi..." I mouth, not saying a word.

"Benjy..." she mouths back, her cheeks rising in a smile as she uses the nickname my mom used to call me.

Synapses fire in my brain and I'm right back in church, when I first found out that Clementine had never met her dad (her mom was nineteen and never said who the boy was). My dad died when I was three years old.

Back then, when combined with the kiss, I thought that made Clementine Kaye my destiny—especially for the three-week period when she was home with mono and I was the one picked to bring her assignments home for her. I was going to be in her room—near her guitar and her bra (Me. Puberty.)—and the excitement was so overwhelming, as I knocked on her front door, right there, my nose began to bleed.

Really.

Clementine saw the whole thing—even helped me get the tissues that I rolled into the nerd plugs that I stuffed in my nostrils. I was the short kid. Easy pickings. But she never made fun—never laughed—never told the story of my nosebleed to anyone.

Today, I don't believe in destiny. But I do believe in history. That's what Orlando will never understand. There's nothing more powerful than history, which is the one thing I have with this woman.

"Lookatyou," she hums in a soulful but lilting voice that sounds like she's singing even when she's just talking. It's the same voice I remember from high school—just scratchier and more worn. For the past few years, she's been working at a small jazz radio station out in Virginia. I can see why. In just her opening note, a familiar tingly exhilaration crawls below my skin. A feeling like anything's possible.

A crush.

For the past year, I'd forgotten what it felt like.

"Beecher, you're so . . . You're handsome!"

My heart reinflates, nearly bursting a hole in my chest. Did she just—?

"You are, Beecher! You turned out great!"

My line. That's my line, I tell myself, already searching for a new one. *Pick something good. Something kind. And genuine. This is your chance. Give her something so perfect, she'll dream about it.*

"So . . . er . . . Clemmi," I finally say, rolling back and forth from my big toes to my heels as I notice her nose piercing, a sparkling silver stud that winks right at me. "Wanna go see the Declaration of Independence?"

Kill me now.

She lowers her head, and I wait for her to laugh.

"I wish I could, but—" She reaches into her purse and pulls out a folded-up sheet of paper. Around her wrist, two vintage wooden bracelets click-clack together. I almost forgot. The real reason she came here.

"You sure you're okay doing this?" Clementine asks.

"Will you stop already," I tell her. "Mysteries are my specialty."

*   *   *

2

E veryone knows when there's a fight in the schoolyard.
No one has to say a word—it's telepathic. From ancient to modern times, the human animal knows how to find fighting. And seventh graders know how to find it faster than anyone.

That's how it was on this day, after lunch, with everyone humming from their Hawaiian Punch and Oreo cookies, when Vincent Paglinni stole Josh Wert's basketball.

In truth, the ball didn't belong to Josh Wert—it belonged to the school—but that wasn't why Paglinni took it.

When it came to the tribes of seventh grade, Paglinni came from a warrior tribe that was used to taking what wasn't theirs. Josh Wert came from a chubby tribe and was born different than most, with a genius IQ and the kind of parents who told him never to hide it. Plus, he had a last name like *Wert*, which appeared in just that order—*W-E-R-T*—on the keyboard of every computer.

"Give it back!" Josh Wert insisted, not using his big brain and making the mistake of calling attention to what had happened.

Paglinni ignored the demand, refusing to even face him.

"I-I want my ball back!" Josh Wert added, sucking in his gut and trying so hard to stand strong.

By now, the tribe of seventh graders was starting to gather. They knew what was about to happen.

Beecher was one of those people. Like Wert, Beecher was also born with brains. At three, Beecher used to read the newspaper. Not just the comics or the sports scores. The *whole newspaper*, including the obituaries, which his mom let him read when his dad died. Beecher was barely four.

As he grew older, the obits became Beecher's favorite part of the newspaper, the very first thing he read every morning. Beecher was fascinated by the past, by lives that mattered so much to so many, but that—like his father—he'd never see. At home, Beecher's mom, who spent days managing the bakery in the supermarket, and afternoons driving the school bus for the high school, knew that made her son different. And special. But unlike Josh Wert, Beecher knew how to use those brains to steer clear of most schoolyard controversies.

"You want your basketball?" Paglinni asked as he finally turned to face Wert. He held the ball out in his open palm. "Why don't you come get it?"

This was the moment the tribe was waiting for: when chubby Josh Wert would find out exactly what kind of man he'd grow up to be.

Of course, Wert hesitated.

"Do you want the ball or not, fatface?"

Seventeen years from now, when Beecher was helping people at the National Archives, he'd still remember the fear on Josh Wert's round face—and the sweat that started to puddle in the chubby ledges that formed the tops of Wert's cheeks. Behind him, every person in the schoolyard—Andrew Goldberg with his freckled face, Randi Boxer with her perfect braids, Lee Rosenberg who always wore Lee jeans—they were all frozen in place, waiting.

No. That wasn't true.

There was one person moving through the crowd—a late arrival—slowly making her way to the front of the action and holding a jump rope that dangled down, scraping against the concrete.

Beecher knew who she was. The girl with the long black hair, and the three earrings, and the cool hipster black vest. In this part of Wisconsin, no one wore cool hipster vests. Except the new girl.

Clementine.

In truth, she really wasn't the *new* girl—Clementine had been born in Sagamore, and lived there until about a decade ago, when her mom moved them to Detroit to pursue her singing career. It was hard moving away. It was even harder moving home. But there was nothing more humbling than two weeks ago, when the pastor in their church announced that everyone needed to give a big *welcome back* to Clementine and her mom—especially since there was no dad in their house. The pastor was just trying to be helpful. But in that moment, he reminded everyone that Clementine was *that girl*: the one with no father.

Beecher didn't see that at all. To Beecher, she was the one *just like him*.

Maybe that's why Beecher did what he was about to do.

Maybe he saw something he recognized.

Or maybe he saw something that was completely different.

"Do you want the ball back or not?" Paglinni added as a thin smirk spread across his cheeks.

In the impromptu circle that had now formed around the fight, every seventh grader tensed—some excited, some scared—but none of them moving as they waited for blood.

Clementine was the opposite—fidgety and unable to stand still while picking at the strands of the jump rope she was still clutching. As she shifted her weight from one foot to the other, Beecher felt the energy radiating off her. This girl was different from the rest. She wasn't scared like everyone else.

She was pissed. And she was right. This wasn't fair...

"*Give him his ball back!*" a new voice shouted.

The crowd turned at once—and even Beecher seemed surprised to find that he was the one who said it.

"What'd you say, Beech Ball!?" Paglinni challenged.

"I-I said... give him the ball back," Beecher said, amazed at how quickly adrenaline could create confidence. His heart pumped fast. His chest felt huge. He stole a quick glance at Clementine.

She shook her head, unimpressed. She knew how stupid this was.

"Or *what*...?" Paglinni asked, the basketball cocked on his hip. "What're you gonna *possibly* do?"

Beecher was in seventh grade. He didn't have an answer. But that didn't stop him from talking. "If you don't give Josh the ball back—"

Beecher didn't even see Paglinni's fist as he buried it in Beecher's eye. But he felt it, knocking him off his feet and onto his ass.

Like a panther, Paglinni was all over him, pouncing on Beecher's chest, pinning his arms back with his knees, and pounding down on his face.

Beecher looked to his right and saw the red plastic handle of the jump rope, sagging on the ground. A burst of white stars exploded in his eye. Then another. He'd never been punched before. It hurt more than he thought.

Within seconds, the tribe was screaming, roaring—*Pag! Pag! Pag! Pag!*—chanting along with the impact of each punch. There was a pop from Beecher's nose. The white stars in Beecher's eyes suddenly went black. He was about to pass out—

"*Huuuhhh!*"

Paglinni fell backward. All the weight came off Beecher's chest. Beecher could hear the basketball bouncing across the pavement. Fresh air reentered his lungs. But as Beecher struggled to sit up and catch his breath...as he fought to blink the world back into place...the first thing he spotted was...

Her.

Clementine pulled tight on the jump rope, which was wrapped around Paglinni's neck. She wasn't choking him, but she was tugging—hard—using the rope to yank Paglinni backward, off Beecher's chest.

"—*kill you! I'll kill you!*" Paglinni roared, fighting wildly to reach back and grab her.

"You tool—you think I still jump rope in seventh grade?" she challenged, tugging Paglinni back with an eerie calm and reminding Beecher that this wasn't just some impromptu act. It wasn't coincidence that Clementine had the jump rope. When she came here, she was prepared. She knew exactly what she was doing.

Still lying on his back, Beecher watched as Clementine let go of the rope. Paglinni was coughing now, down on his rear, but fighting to get up, his fist cocked back and ready to unleash.

Yet as Paglinni jumped to his feet, he could feel the crowd turn. Punching Beecher was one thing. Punching a girl was another. Even someone as dumb as Paglinni wasn't that dumb.

"You're a damn psycho, y'know that?" Paglinni growled at Clementine.

"Better than being a penis-less bully," she shot back, getting a few cheap laughs from the crowd—especially from Josh Wert, who was now holding tight to the basketball.

Enraged, Paglinni stormed off, bursting through the spectators, who parted fast to let him leave. And that was the very first moment that Clementine looked back to check on Beecher.

His nose was bloody. His eyes were already starting to swell. And from the taste of the blood, he knew that his lip was split. Still, he couldn't help but smile.

"I'm Beecher," he said, extending a handshake upward.

Standing above him, Clementine looked down and shook her head. "No. You're a moron," she said, clearly pissed.

But as the crowd dissipated and Clementine strode across the schoolyard, Beecher sat up and could swear that as he was watching Clementine walk away in the distance...as she glanced over her shoulder and took a final look at him...there was a small smile on her face.

He saw it.

Definitely a smile.

3

Today
Washington, D.C.

Thirty-two minutes later, as Clementine and I are waiting
for the arrival of the documents she came looking for, I
swipe my security card and hear the usual *thunk*. Shoving
the bank vault of a door open, I make a sharp left into the cold and
poorly lit stacks that fill the heart of the Archives. With each row of
old files and logbooks we pass, a motion sensor light goes off, shining
a small spotlight, one after the other, like synchronized divers in an
old Esther Williams movie, that chases us wherever we go.

These days, I'm no longer the short kid. I'm blond, tall (though
Clementine still may be a hair taller than me), and dressed in the
blue lab coat that all of us archivists wear to protect us from the rotted leather that rubs off our oldest books when we touch them. I've
also got far more to offer her than a nosebleed. But just to be near
this woman who consumed my seventh through tenth grades . . . who
I used to fantasize about getting my braces locked together with . . .

"Sorry to do this now. I hope you're not bored," I tell her.

"Why would I be bored? Who doesn't love a dungeon?" she says
as we head deeper into the labyrinth of leather books and archival
boxes. She's nearly in front of me, even though she's got no idea
where she's going. Just like in junior high. Always prepared and
completely fearless. "Besides, it's nice to see you, Beecher."

"Here . . . it's . . . *here*," I say as the light blinks on above us and I
stop at a bookcase of rotted leather-bound logbooks that are packed

18

haphazardly across the shelf. Some are spine out, others are stacked on top of each other. "It's just that we have a quota of people we have to help and—"

"Stop apologizing," Clementine offers. "I'm the one who barged in."

She says something else, but as I pull out the first few volumes and scan their gold-stamped spines, I'm quickly lost in the real treasure of this trip: the ancient browning pages of the volume marked *November 1779*. Carefully cradling the logbook with one hand, I use my free one to pull out the hidden metal insta-shelf that's built into each bookcase and creaks straight at us at chest height.

"So these are from the Revolutionary War?" she asks. "They're real?"

"All we have is real."

By *we*, I mean *here*—the National Archives, which serves as the storehouse for the most important documents of the U.S. government, from the original Declaration of Independence, to the Zapruder film, to reports on opportunities to capture bin Laden, to the anthrax formula and where the government stores the lethal spores, to the best clandestine files from the CIA, FBI, NSA, and every other acronym. As they told me when I first started as an archivist three years ago, the Archives is our nation's attic. A ten-billion-document scrapbook with nearly every vital file, record, and report that the government produces.

No question, that means this is a building full of secrets. Some big, some small. But every single day, I get to unearth another one.

Like right now.

"Howard...Howard...Howard," I whisper to myself, flipping one of the mottled brown pages and running my pointer finger down the alphabetical logbook, barely touching it.

Thirty-four minutes ago, as we put in the request for Clementine's documents, a puffy middle-aged woman wearing a paisley silk scarf as a cancer wig came into our research entrance looking for details about one of her relatives. She had his name. She had the fact he served in the Revolutionary War.

And she had me.

As an archivist, whether the question comes from a researcher, from a regular person, or from the White House itself, it's our job to find the answers that—

"Beecher," Clementine calls out. "Are you listening?"

"Wha?"

"Just now. I asked you three times and—" She stops herself, cocking her head so the piercing in her nose tips downward. But her smile—that same warm smile from seventh grade—is still perfectly in place. "You really get lost in this stuff, don't you?"

"That woman upstairs... I can't just ignore her."

Clementine stops, watching me carefully. "You really turned out to be one of the nice ones, didn't you, Beecher?"

I glance down at the logbook. My eyes spot—

"He was a musician," I blurt. I point to the thick rotted page, then yank a notepad from my lab coat and copy the information. "That's why he wasn't listed in the regular service records. Or even the pension records upstairs. A musician. George Howard was a musician during the Revolution."

"Y'mean he played 'Taps'?"

"No... 'Taps' wasn't invented until the Civil War. This guy played fife and drum, keeping the rhythm while the soldiers marched. And this entry shows the military pay he got for his service."

"That's... I don't even know if it's interesting—but how'd you even know to come down here? I mean, these books look like they haven't been opened in centuries."

"They haven't. But when I was here last month searching through some leftover ONI spy documents, I saw that we had these old accounting ledgers from the Treasury Department. And no matter what else the government may screw up, when they write a check and give money out, you better believe they keep pristine records."

I stand up straight, proud of the archeological find. But before I can celebrate—

"I need some ID," a calm voice calls out behind us, drawing out each syllable so it sounds like *Eye. Dee.*

We both turn to find a muscular, squat man coming around the far corner of the row. A light pops on above him as he heads our way. Outfitted in full black body armor and gripping a polished matching black rifle, he studies my ID, then looks at the red Visitor badge clipped to Clementine's shirt.

"Thanks," he calls out with a nod.

I almost forgot what day it was. When the President comes, so does the . . .

"Secret Service," Clementine whispers. She cocks a thin, excited eyebrow, tossing me the kind of devilish grin that makes me feel exactly how long I haven't felt this way.

But the truly sad part is just how wonderful the rush of insecurity feels—like rediscovering an old muscle you hadn't used since childhood. I've been emailing back and forth with Clementine for over two months now. But it's amazing how seeing your very first kiss can make you feel fourteen years old again. And what's more amazing is that until she showed up, I didn't even know I missed it.

When most people see an armed Secret Service agent, they pause a moment. Clementine picks up speed, heading to the end of the row and peeking around the corner to see where he's going. Forever fearless.

"So these guys protect the documents?" she asks as I catch up to her, leading her out of the stacks.

"Nah, they don't care about documents. They're just scouting in advance for *him*."

This is Washington, D.C. There's only one *him*.

The President of the United States.

"Wait . . . Wallace is *here*?" Clementine asks. "Can I meet him?"

"Oh for sure," I say, laughing. "We're like BFFs and textbuddies and . . . he totally cares about what one of his dozens of archivists thinks. In fact, I think his Valentine's card list goes: his wife, his kids, his chief of staff . . . then me."

She doesn't laugh, doesn't smile—she just stares at me with deep confidence in her ginger brown eyes. "I think one day, he *will* care about you," she says.

I freeze, feeling a blush spread across my face.

Across from me, Clementine pulls up the sleeve of her black sweater, and I notice a splotch of light scars across the outside of her elbow. They're not red or new—they're pale and whiter than her skin, which means they've been there a long time. But the way they zigzag out in every direction...whatever carved into her skin like that caused her real pain.

"Most people stare at my boobs," she says with a laugh, catching my gaze.

"I-I didn't mean—"

"Oh jeez—I'm sorry—I embarrassed you, didn't I?" she asks.

"No. Nonono. No."

She laughs again. "You know you're a horrible liar?"

"I know," I say, still staring at her scars.

"And you know you're still staring at my scars?"

"I know. I can't stop myself. If we were in a desert instead of in these dusty stacks, I'd bury myself right now."

"You really should just go for my boobs," she says. "At least you get a better view."

Instinctively, I look—and then just as quickly stare back at her scars. "It looks like a dog bite."

"Motorcycle crash. My fault. My elbow hyperextended and the bone broke through the skin."

"Sounds excruciating."

"It was ten years ago, Beecher," she says, confidently shrugging the entire world away as her eyes take hold and don't let go. She's staring just at me. "Only the good things matter after ten years."

Before I can agree, my phone vibrates in my pocket, loud enough that we both hear the buzz.

"That them?" Clementine blurts.

I shake my head. Caller ID says it's my sister, who lives with my mom back in Wisconsin. But at this time of the day, when the supermarket shifts change, I know who's really dialing: It's my mom, making her daily check-up-on-me call, which started the day after she heard about Iris. And while I know my mom never liked Iris, she has too much midwestern kindness in her to ever say it to me. The phone buzzes again.

I don't pick up. But by the time I look back at Clementine, all the confidence, all the conviction, all the fearlessness is gone—and I'm reminded that the real reason she came to the Archives wasn't to share old scars or see overmuscled Secret Service agents.

Last year, Clementine's mom died, but it wasn't until a few months back that Clementine called in sick to the radio station and went back home to clean out her mom's closet. There, she found an old datebook that her mother had saved from the year Clementine was born. Sure enough, on December 10, there were hand-drawn hearts and tiny balloons on the day of her birth, there was a cute smiley face drawn on the day she came home from the hospital, but what was most interesting to Clementine was when she flipped back in the datebook and saw the entry on March 18, which had a small sad face drawn in it, followed by the words *Nick enlists.*

From that, she finally had a name and a lead on her dad.

From me, thanks to our recent emails, she had the Archives.

From those, I had only one call to make: to our facility in St. Louis, where we store the more recent army enlistment records.

Ten minutes ago, Clementine was in front of me. But now, as I head for the metal door ahead of us, she starts falling behind, going surprisingly silent.

In life, there's the way you act when you know people are watching. And then there's the way you act when no one's watching, which, let's be honest, is the *real you.* That's what I see in Clementine right now: I spot it for just a half-second, in between breaths, just as I take the lead and she ducks behind me, thinking I can't see her. She's wrong. I see her. And feel her.

I feel her self-doubt. I feel the way she's unanchored. And in the midst of that single breath, as her shoulders fall, and she looks down and slowly exhales so she won't explode, I spot that little dark terrified space that she reserves for just herself. It only exists for that single half-second, but in that half-second I know I'm seeing at least one part of the *real* Clementine. Not just some fantasized cool jazz DJ. Not just some ballsy girl who took on the bully in seventh grade. The grown her. The true her. The one who learned how to be afraid.

"I should go. I hate when I'm all woe-is-me-ish," she says, regaining her calm as I tug the metal door and we leave the stacks, squeezing back out into the pale blue hallway. She's trying to hide. I know what it's like to hide. I've been doing it for the past year of my life.

"Don't go," I shoot back, quickly lowering my voice. "There's no— They said they'll have the results within the hour and...and... and...and we've got so much stuff to see here...if you want." I bite my lip to stop myself from talking. It doesn't help. "Listen, I didn't want to have to do this," I add. "But if you really want, we can take out the Louisiana Purchase and write *'Clementine Rulz!'* along the bottom."

She barely grins. "Already did it on the Constitution."

"Fine, you win," I say, stopping in the center of the hallway and leaning on the marble wainscoting. "You want to meet the President, I'll take you to meet the President."

She doesn't blink. "You don't know the President."

"Maybe. But I know what room he goes to when he does his reading visits."

"You do?"

"I do. Wanna see?"

She stands up straight and twists her forearm back and forth so her vintage bracelets slide from her wrist toward her elbow and her scars. "Is it far from here or—?"

"Actually, you're standing right in front of it."

I point over her shoulder, and she spins to find a metal door that's painted the same color as the pale blue hallway. Easy to miss, which is the whole point. The only thing that stands out is that the square glass window that looks into the room is blocked by some black fabric. Down by the doorknob, there's a round combination lock like you'd find on a safe.

"That's it?" Clementine asks. "Looks like my old gym locker."

I shake my head. "SCIFs are far safer than gym lockers."

"What'd you call it? A skiff?"

"SCIF—Sensitive Compartmented Information Facility," I explain, rapping the knuckle of my middle finger against the door and hearing the deep thud that lets you know just how thick it is. "C'mon, when you read a classified document, you think you just open it at your desk? People are watching from everywhere— through your windows, from listening and video devices—Big Brother doesn't just work for us anymore. So all around the government, we've got rooms built and certified by the CIA."

"Skiffs," she says.

"SCIFs. Walls with quarter-inch metal shielding, floors with eight-inch metal plates to stop eavesdropping, no windows, copper foil in the corners to stop transmissions, bars over the vent shafts so Tom Cruise can't lower himself on his trapeze..."

"And you have one of these SCIFs here?"

"You kidding? Our legislative guys alone have *sixteen* of them. Every major building in D.C.—the White House, the Capitol, every Senate and House building—if you've got a bigshot in the building, we've got a SCIF in there too. And the biggest bigshots get them in their homes. Tiny little rooms for you to read the world's most vital secrets."

"Can we peek inside?" she asks, rapping her own knuckle against the door.

I force a laugh.

She doesn't laugh back. She's not trying to pry. She means it as an honest question.

"If you can't, no big deal," she adds.

"No, I *can*...I just..."

"Beecher, please don't make that stress face. I didn't mean to make you uncomfortable."

"No, I'm not uncomfortable."

"Let's go do the other stuff," she says, already walking away.

"Oh, just take the damn girl inside already," a deep voice echoes on our left. Up the hallway, an older black man with a caterpillar mustache heads our way carrying an oversized cup of coffee.

Despite his age, he's still got the muscular build that first got him the job as one of our uniformed security guards. But one look at his dimpled chin and big-toothed smile, and it's clear that Orlando Williams is more pussycat than lion.

"This that girl you used to have a crush on? The one that's gonna mend that broken heart Iris left you?" Orlando shouts even though he's only a few steps away.

"Who's Iris?" Clementine asks.

Every office has a loudmouth. Orlando is ours—or more specifically, mine, ever since he found out that:

a) I was from his home state of Wisconsin, and
b) I was the only archivist willing to give his brother-in-law's boss a private tour of the Treasure Vault.

For better or worse, he's determined to return the favor.

"Just take her inside—I won't even put you in my floor report," he adds, tucking his clipboard under his armpit and taking a deep swig from his coffee cup.

"Orlando, I appreciate the kindness, but would you mind just—"

"*What?* I'm trynna help you here—show her your love of... adventure." Turning to Clementine, he says, "So he tell you about his wedding photographer days?"

"Orlando..." I warn.

"You were a wedding photographer?" Clementine asks.

"After college, I moved here hoping to take photos for the *Washington Post*. Instead, I spent three years doing weddings in Annapolis. It was fine," I tell her.

"Until he got the chance to help people directly and then he came here. Now he's *our* hero."

Clementine cocks a grin at Orlando. "I appreciate the unsubtle hype, but you do realize Beecher's doing just fine without it?"

Orlando cocks a grin right back. He likes her. Of course he does.

"Will you c'mon?" Orlando begs, focused just on her. "The President's not scheduled here until"—he looks at his watch—"ya got at least an hour, even more if he's late. Plus, the cart with his files isn't even in there yet. Who cares if she sees an empty room?"

I stare at the pale blue door and the combination lock, which of course I know by heart. No doubt, it'd be easy, but the rules say—

"Sweet Christmas, Beecher—*I'll* open the damn room for her!" Orlando calls out.

He heads for a call box and presses the silver intercom button. A small red indicator light blinks awake as a soft-spoken voice answers, "Security."

"Venkat, it's Orlando," he says, speaking close to the intercom. I recognize the name from our staff list. Venkat Khazei. Deputy chief of security. "I'm opening SCIF 12E1," Orlando says. "Just doing spot checks."

"Sounds good. Just remember: Moses is on his way, eh," Khazei replies through the intercom, using our own internal code name for the President.

"That's why I'm checking the room first," Orlando barks back.

The intercom goes quiet, then crackles once more. "Enjoy."

As Orlando strides back toward us, his toothy grin spreads even wider.

Under my shirt, I wear a thin leather necklace with an old house key on it. During high school, when I worked at Farris's secondhand bookshop, I found the key being used as a bookmark in some old dictionary. It's kooky, but that day was the same day I got accepted to Wisconsin, the first step in escaping my little town. The magic key stayed. I've been wearing it so long now, I barely even feel it. Except when I'm sweaty and it starts sticking to my chest. Like now.

"Beecher," Clementine whispers, "if this is skeeving you out, let's just skip the room and—"

"I'm fine. No skeeving at all," I tell her, knowing full well that Iris would've had me leave ten minutes ago.

"Here, hold this," Orlando says, offering me his cup of coffee so he can work on the combo lock.

"No food or drinks allowed in the SCIFs," I remind him, refusing to take it.

"Really, are those the rules, Beecher?" he shoots back. Before I can answer, he hands Clementine his coffee cup and gives a few quick spins to the lock.

With a click and a low *wunk*, the door pops open like the safe that it is.

Even Orlando is careful as he cranes his neck and glances inside, just in case someone's in there.

I do the same, already up on my tiptoes to peer over Orlando's shoulder and make sure we're all clear.

Clementine's different. She doesn't rush—she's not overeager in the least bit—but with a quick, confident step she heads inside, totally unafraid. It's even sexier than telling me to stare at her breasts.

"Our own little Oval Office," Orlando adds, motioning palms-up like a flight attendant showing off the emergency rows. Yet unlike the Oval and its grand decor, the small windowless room is beige, beige, and more beige, centered around a wide oak table, a secure phone that sits on top, and two wooden library chairs.

When they first see it, most staffers blurt, *"That's it?"*

Clementine circles the desk, studying each beige wall like she's taking in a Picasso. "I like the poster," she finally says.

Behind me, stuck to the back of the metal door, is a poster featuring a steaming hot cup of coffee and a red-lettered warning:

A lot of information can spill over one of these.
Make sure that your conversation is secure
to the last drop.

Yet as I read the words, my brain backflips to—
Crap. Orlando's coffee.

"No, *not on there*," I plead with Clementine just as she's about to take a seat and lower the open cup onto the President's desk. If it spills...

I reach to grab it; she jerks her hand to protect it. That's all it takes. The back of my hand brushes against the styrofoam—the cup tips—and the light brown liquid splashes across the desk, racing to Clementine's side of the table.

A waterfall of coffee pours down, tap-dancing in a fine neat kickline across the polished floor.

We need to get this clean before the President...

Clementine jumps back to avoid the mess, and her legs slam into her chair, sending the wooden seat toppling backward.

"Orlando, go get paper towels!" I yell, ripping off my blue lab coat to use it as a sponge.

The wooden chair hits the floor with a crack...

...followed by an odd, hollow *thump*.

I turn just in time to see the exposed bottom of the chair, where a square piece of wood pops out from the underside, falls to the floor—and reveals the shadow of an object hidden within.

From the table, coffee continues to drip down, slowing its kickline across the linoleum.

My throat constricts.

And I get my first good look at what was clearly tucked inside the chair's little hiding spot and is now sitting on the floor, right in the path of the spreading puddle of coffee. It looks like a small file folder.

"Beech?" Orlando whispers behind me.

"Yeah?"

"Please tell me you had no idea that was in there."

"No idea. Swear to God."

He picks up the coffee cup and takes a final swig of whatever's left. As my magic key spot-welds to my chest, I know he's thinking the same thing I am: If this was put here *for*, or even worse, *by* the President...

"Beech?" he repeats as the puddled coffee slowly seeps into the folder.

"Yeah?"

"We're dead."

"Yeah."

*　　*　　*

4

Seventeen years ago
Sagamore, Wisconsin

Running up the snowy front path, young Clementine Kaye bounced up the wooden staircase toward the small house with the dangling green shutter. She made sure her left foot was always the first one to touch the steps. Her mom told her most people lead with their *right* foot. "But hear me on this, Clemmi," Mom used to say, "what's the fun in being *most people*?"

Even now, at thirteen years old, Clementine knew the answer.

Reaching the front door, she didn't ring the doorbell that went *ding*, but never *dong*. She didn't need to ring the doorbell.

She was prepared. She had a key and let herself inside.

As the door swung open and the whiff of rosewater perfume washed over her, she didn't call out or ask if anybody was home. She knew no one would answer. Her mom was still traveling—three shows in St. Louis—which meant she'd be gone until next week.

Clementine didn't even worry about getting help with homework, or what she'd eat for dinner. She'd grown accustomed to figuring things out. Plus, she knew how to cook. Maybe tonight she'd make her sausage stew.

In fact, as Clementine twisted out of her winter coat and let it drop to the linoleum floor, where it deflated and sagged like a body with no bones, she was all smiles. Giving quick chin-tickles to two of the three ginger cats her mom had brought back from various trips, Clementine was still moving quickly as she burst into the overcluttered living room, turned on the CD player that teetered so precariously off the edge of the bookshelf, and inserted the disc labeled *Penny Maxwell's Greatest Hits.*

Penny wasn't just Clementine's favorite singer. Penny was Clementine's mother—who still had nearly three hundred copies of her *Greatest Hits* CD stacked in the closets, under the bed, and in the trunk and backseat of the car. It was yet another of Mom's brainstorms that brought more storm than brain. ("If you do a Greatest Hits *first*, it'll sell faster because people will think they're missing something.") Clementine didn't notice. For her, this was life.

Indeed, as the music began and the sly hook from the trumpet seized the air, Clementine closed her eyes, soaking in the familiar husky voice that'd been singing her to bed—with this same song, Billie Holiday's "God Bless the Child"—since she was a baby.

> *Mama may have, Papa may have*
> *But God bless the child that's got her own*

Clementine had no idea that her mom had changed the words so it was about a little girl. And had no idea that Billie Holiday had written the song after a particularly brutal argument with her own mother, over money—which is what *that's got his own* really refers to. But right there, as she stood there in the living room, swaying back and forth in the pretend dance she always did with her mom after school, thirteen-year-old Clementine Kaye wasn't sad about being alone . . . or having to cook dinner . . . or even having to fend for herself.

She was prepared. She was *always* prepared.

But more than prepared, she was just happy to hear her mom's voice.

5

Today
Washington, D.C.

I don't see what the big disaster is," Clementine says in the SCIF.

"Nonono—*don't touch it!*" Orlando yells as I reach for the small file folder.

"What? It's soaking wet," I argue, snatching it, now dripping, from the coffee puddle.

"We could've put it back," he says.

"It's soaking. Look. See the soaking?" I hold up the file so he can spot the drip-drip from the corner of the manila folder. "You think I can just shove this back under the chair like nothing happened? We need to report this."

"Lando, you there? Vault all clear?" a voice crackles through his walkie-talkie.

We all turn toward the upended wooden chair and the gaping hollow hiding spot underneath.

"Y-Yeah, perfect," Orlando reports back through his walkie.

"Good, because company's coming," the voice crackles back. "Service says ten minutes till departure."

From here, the White House is a ten-minute trip. But only three if you're coming by motorcade.

"We need to get out of here," I say, trying to sop up the coffee with my lab coat.

Orlando stays focused on the chair. On the side of it, just underneath the actual seat, there's a narrow slot—like a mail slot—cut into the piece of wood that connects the left front leg with the back leg. "D'you have any idea what this—?" He shakes his head, his toothy grin long gone. "You were right. We gotta report this."

"I take that back. Let's think about this."

"Beech, if someone's using this room as a dead drop..."

"You don't know that."

"A *dead drop*?" Clementine asks.

"Like a hiding spot," Orlando says.

Reading her confusion, I add, "It's a place where you leave something for another person, so you don't have to risk a face-to-face meeting. Like taping something below a mailbox, or in a hollowed-out tree, or..."

"...in a chair," Clementine says, quickly seeing the full picture. With the narrow mail slot underneath the seat, it'd be simple to slide an item into the chair seat, then take it out through the removable hollow bottom. "So if this SCIF is used only by President Wallace, and there's something hidden here for him..."

"Or *by* him," Orlando points out.

"Don't say that. We don't know that. We don't know *anything*," I insist.

"And you believe those words as they leave your lips? You really think this is all just some innocent *Three's Company* misunderstanding, Chrissy?" Orlando asks. "Or are you just worried that if I file an official report, your name will be permanently linked to whatever presidential bullcrap we just tripped into?"

On the corner of the file folder, a single drip of coffee builds to a pregnant swell, but never falls.

"We should open it and see what's inside," Clementine offers, far calmer than the two of us.

"No. Don't open it," I insist.

"What're you talking about?" Orlando asks.

"You ever seen a horror movie? There's that moment where they hear the noise in the woods and some dumbass says, *Let's go see what's making that noise!* And of course you know right there he's number one in the body count. Well...we're in the horror movie:

33

At this exact moment, this little file folder is Pandora's box. And as long as we keep it shut—as long as we don't know what's inside the box—we can still walk away."

"Unless there's a real monster in the box," Orlando points out.

"Orlando..."

"Don't Orlando me. This is my *job*, Beecher."

"Yeah and two seconds ago you were telling me to put it back."

"It's still my job. I walk the halls, I check IDs—that's why it's called *Security*. Now I'm sorry if I find something in the President's reading room, but we did. And if he or anyone else is committing a crime or sneaking classified papers in or out of this building, you really think we should just walk away and pretend we didn't see it?"

I don't look up, but on my right, I can see the red-lettered warning poster on the back of the closed steel door. It doesn't bother me nearly as much as the disappointed expression on Clementine, who clearly doesn't deal well with weakness. The way her ginger eyes drill me, she has no idea which way I'm going to vote.

I wish she knew me better than that.

I toss the damp folder toward the desk. "Just remember, when the CIA grabs us in the middle of the night and puts the black Ziplocs over our heads, *this* is the moment where we could've avoided it." The folder hits the table with a *ptttt*.

Clementine doesn't say a word. But as she takes a half-step forward, she cocks her head, like she's seeing something brand-new on my face. I see the same on hers. I've known this girl since seventh grade. It's the first time I've ever seen her impressed.

"Beecher, it'll take two seconds, then we can leave," Orlando promises. "You'll never regret doing the right thing."

But as he peels open the folder, as he finally sees what's hidden inside, I can already tell he's wrong.

6

weet Christmas," Orlando mutters.

"I don't get it. What is it?" Clementine asks, squeezing in next to me, though careful not to touch anything.

I have no such concern. From the pockets of my coffee-stained lab coat, I pull out the pair of cotton gloves all archivists carry, put them on, pick up the folder like it's live dynamite, and open it. Inside, it's not a top-secret memo, or the whereabouts of bin Laden, or a target list for our spy satellites.

"It's a book," Clementine says.

She's partly right. It has the *cover* of a book—cracked and mottled black leather with faded red triangles in each of the top and bottom corners. But the guts of it—almost all the interior pages—are ripped out. It's the same with the spine: torn away, revealing exposed, ancient glue and torn stitching. Without its insides, the whole book barely has the thickness of a clipboard.

I rub two gloved fingers across the cover. From the red rot (the aged, powdery residue that rubs off on my gloves), I'm guessing it dates back to at least the Civil War.

"*Entick's New Spelling Dictionary*," Orlando reads from the cover.

I check my watch. If we're lucky, Wallace still hasn't left the White House.

"Why would someone hide an old, torn-up dictionary for the President?" Clementine asks.

"Maybe *the President's* hiding it for someone else," Orlando offers. "Maybe when he's alone in the room, he puts it in the chair for someone to pick up later, and they still haven't picked it up yet."

"Or for all we know, this has nothing to do with the President, and this book has been hidden in that chair for years," I point out.

I swear, I can hear Orlando roll his eyes.

"What, like that's so crazy?" I ask.

"Beecher, y'remember when that sweaty researcher with the pug nose and the buggy eyes was coming in here and stealing our old maps?"

"Yeah."

"And when that looney-toon woman was nabbed for swiping those old Teddy Roosevelt letters because she thought she'd take better care of them than we were?"

"What's your point?"

"The point is, y'know how they both got away with their crimes for so long? They took a tiny penknife and sliced each page out of the bound collection, page by page so no one would notice, until almost nothing was left," he says, motioning with a thick finger at the old dictionary like he's Sherlock Holmes himself.

"And that's your grand theory? That Orson Wallace—the President of the United States, a man who can have any document brought *right to him at any moment*—is not only *stealing* from us, but stealing worthless dictionary pages?"

For the first time in the past five minutes, the office loudmouth is silent.

But not for long.

"The *real* point," Orlando finally says, "is that this book—this dictionary, whatever it is—is property of the Archives."

"We don't even know that! The spine's ripped off, so there's no record group number. And if you look for..." Flipping the front cover open, I search for the circular blue *National Archives* stamp that's in some of the older books in our collection. "Even the stamp's not—" I stop abruptly.

"What?" Orlando asks as I stare down at the inside cover. "You find something?"

Leaning both palms on the desk, I read the handwritten inscription for the second and third time.

Exitus

Acta

Probat

"*Exitus acta probat?*" Clementine reads aloud over my shoulder.

I nod, feeling the bad pain at the bridge of my nose. "Exitus acta probat. *The outcome justifies the deed.*"

"You know *Latin?*" Clementine asks.

"I didn't play Little League," I tell her.

"I don't understand," Orlando says. "'The outcome justifies the deed.' Is that good or bad?"

"*Moses is in transit,*" Orlando's walkie-talkie screams through the room. They'll notify us again when he reaches the building.

I study the book as the pain gets worse. "I could be wrong," I begin, "but if I'm reading this right . . . I think this book belonged to George Washington."

7

ait whoa wait," Orlando says. "*George* George Washington? With the wooden teeth?"

"...and the cherry tree," I say, picking the book up and looking closely at the lettering. The paper is in such bad shape—deeply browned and rough to the touch—it's hard to tell if the ink is old or new.

Behind me, there's a jingle of keys. I spin just in time to see Orlando fighting with the small metal lockbox that's bolted to the wall in the back of the room. With a twist of his key, the box opens, revealing a stack of videotapes and a clunky top-loading VCR that could easily have been stolen straight from my grandmother's house. Our budgets are good, but they're not that good.

"What're you doing?" I ask.

"Sparing you a starring role," he says, ejecting one tape and stuffing a new one in. "Or would you prefer smiling at the camera while you hold the President's secret stash?"

I nearly forgot. Up in the corner there's a small videocamera that's been taping us since the moment we walked in. The only good news is, to maintain the security of each SCIF—and to keep outsiders from intercepting the video—each room is only wired internally, meaning there's no transmission in or out, meaning that tape—the one Orlando is pocketing—is the only proof that Clementine and I have even been in here.

"You sure that's smart?" I ask.

"It's smart," Clementine says, nodding confidently at Orlando. In all the panic, she's not panicking at all. She's watching...studying... taking it all in. It's no different than the jump rope all those years ago.

"Maybe you were right, though," I point out. "Maybe we should report this to Security."

"I *am* Security—I'm a *security guard*," Orlando says. "And I can tell you right now—*Absolutely. No question*—this right here shows a definite problem in our security."

"But by taking that videotape—"

"Beecher, I appreciate that you're a sweet guy. And I know you don't like assuming the worst about people, but let me give you a dose of real life for a moment: There are only two possibilities for what's happened here. Either Roman Numeral One: President Wallace doesn't know anything about this book, in which case we can all calm down and I'll start a proper investigation. Or Roman Numeral Two: Wallace *does know* about this book, in which case he's going to want this book back, in which case handing him a videotape with our faces on it is going to do nothing but make the President of the United States declare war . . . on us."

"Now you're being overdramatic."

"Overdramatic? What happened to the CIA grabbing us and putting the black Ziplocs over our heads?" Orlando challenges.

"That doesn't mean the President's declaring war."

"Really? I thought you knew your history."

"I do know my history."

"Then name me one person—Valerie Plame . . . Monica Lewinsky . . . I don't care who they are or how right they were—name me one person *ever* who went up against a sitting President and walked away the same way they walked in."

"Mark Felt," I tell him.

"Mark Felt?"

"Deep Throat. The guy who told the truth about Nixon."

"I know who he is, Beecher. But the only reason Mark Felt walked away was because *no one knew who he was*!" Orlando insists, waving the videotape in my face. "Don't you get it? As long as we have this video, we get to be Deep Throat and I get to do my investigation. We lose this video, and I promise you, if this book is something bad—and c'mon, you know it's something bad—we're gonna be racing head-on against a man who is so stupidly powerful, wherever he goes, they fly bags of his own blood with him. Trust me here. You wanted smart. This is us being smart."

"What about you?" I ask Orlando. "When you buzzed us in... when you called downstairs to that guy Khazei...Your name's already in the records."

"One disaster at a time. Besides, if we're lucky, this tape may even have who snuck in the book in the first place," he says as he tucks the videotape in the front waistband of his pants. "Now tell me about the Latin: *Ex act probe it?*"

"*Exitus acta probat.* It's the motto on Washington's personal bookplate," I explain as he shuts the lockbox. "It's from his family's coat of arms—and on the inside cover of all of George Washington's books."

"And this is what it looked like?" Orlando asks, already heading for the door. "Three words scribbled on a page?"

"No...the coat of arms is a work of art: There's a picture of an eagle, two red-and-white stripes, plus three stars. But when Washington designed his coat of arms, he personally added the words *Exitus acta probat,*" I say as Clementine motions me to follow Orlando and leave the room. We need to get out of here. But just as I move, my phone vibrates in my pocket. Caller ID reads *NPRC,* but it's the 314 St. Louis area code that reminds me why we're standing in this room in the first place.

Next to me, Clementine eyes the phone in my hand. She doesn't freak, doesn't tense up. But as her lips close tight, I get a second glimpse of the side of her she can't hide. The real Clementine. The scared Clementine. Twenty-nine years of not knowing who your father is? Whatever we stepped in with the President, it has to wait.

"Please tell me you've got good news," I say as I pick up.

"I can bring you information. *Good* and *bad* are the subjective clothes you decide to dress it in," archivist Carrie Storch says without a hint of irony, reminding me that around here, the better you are with books, the worse you are with social skills.

"Carrie, did you find our guy or not?"

"Your girlfriend's father? In that year, in that county of Wisconsin, he was the only *Nicholas* to enlist on December 10th. Of course I found him."

"You did? That's fantastic!"

"Again, I leave the distinctions to you," she says, adding a short huff that I think counts as a laugh. Carrie never laughs.

"Carrie, what are you not saying?"

"I just bring you the information," she says. "But wait till you hear who the father is."

She says the words, pauses, then says them again, knowing I can't believe it.

The President of the United States should be here any minute. But right now, I wonder if that's the least of our problems.

"Clementine," I say, grabbing her hand and heading to the door, "we need to get you out of here."

8

St. Elizabeths Hospital
Washington, D.C.

They don't call them *mental patients* anymore.

Now they're called *consumers*.

Such a turd idea, orderly Rupert Baird thought as he pushed the juice cart down the pale sterile hallway. Almost as bad as when they started calling it KFC instead of Kentucky Fried Chicken. It was the same with the patients. If you're fried, you're fried.

Heh.

That was funny, Rupert thought.

But still a damn turd idea.

"Hey there, Jerome," he called out as he rolled the juice cart into Room 710. "I got apple and orange. What's your pick?"

Cross-legged on his bed, Jerome just sat there, refusing to look up from the newspaper advertising supplements, the only section of the paper he ever read.

"Apple or orange?" Rupert asked again.

No response.

"Any good coupons for Best Buy?" Rupert added.

No response. Same as ever.

Rupert knew not to take it personally—this *was* Ward 5 of the John Howard Pavilion, home to the NGIs. Not Guilty by reason of Insanity.

As he pivoted the juice cart into a three-point turn and headed for Room 711 across the hall, he knew that the next patient—no, the next *consumer*—would be far easier to deal with.

It wasn't always that way. When Patient 711 first arrived ten years ago, he wasn't allowed visitors, mail privileges, sharp objects, or shoelaces. And he certainly wasn't allowed the juice cart. In fact, according to Karyn Palumbo, who'd been here longer than anyone, during his second year on the ward, 711 was caught filing his middle fingernail to a razor point, hoping to carve a bloody cross into the neck of one of the girls from the salon school who used to come and give free haircuts.

Of course, they quickly called the Secret Service.

Whenever 711 was involved, they had to call the Secret Service.

That's what happens when a man tries to put a bullet into the President of the United States.

But after ten years of therapy and drugs—so much therapy and drugs—711 was a brand-new man. A better man.

A cured man, Rupert and most of the doctors thought.

"Hey there, Nico," Rupert called out as he entered the sparsely furnished room. There was a single bed, a wooden nightstand, and a painted dresser that held just Nico's Bible, his red glass rosary, and the newest Washington Redskins giveaway calendar.

"Apple or orange?" Rupert asked.

Nico looked up from the book he was reading, revealing his salt-and-pepper buzzed hair and his chocolate brown eyes, set close together. Ten years ago, in the middle of the President's visit to a NASCAR race, Nico nearly murdered the most powerful man in the world. The video was played time and again, still showing up every year on the anniversary.

As the screaming began, a swarm of Secret Service agents tore at Nico from behind, ripping the gun from his hands.

These days, though, Nico was smart.

He knew better than to talk of those times.

He knew he should've never let the world see him like that.

But the one thing that Nicholas "Nico" Hadrian didn't know

back then, as he was tugged and clawed so viciously to the ground, was that he had a young daughter.

"C'mon, Nico—apple or orange?" Rupert called out.

Nico's lips parted, offering a warm smile. "Whatever you have more of," he replied. "You know I'm easy."

9

"Tell me what you're not telling me," Clementine demands as I reright the chair and finish my crude cleanup. Darting for the door, I've got the old dictionary in one hand and my coffee-stained coat in the other.

"Orlando, I have to—"

"Go. I need to rearm the alarm," he calls back, fiddling with the electronic keypad. "Just remember: zipped lips, right? Be Mark Felt. Not Lewinsky."

"That's fine, but if we look into this and it's actually bad..."

"...I'll be the first in line to hand them the stained dress," he says, patting the videotape in his waistband.

As he rearms the door, we're already running. Orlando's a big boy. He's fine by himself. Clementine's another story. She knows that last phone call was about her dad.

"They found him, didn't they?" she asks as we leave the SCIF behind and race up the hallway. In the distance, I hear the soft cry of police sirens wailing. Wallace's motorcade is close, and if this old dictionary really was put there for the President—if someone is somehow helping him grab it, or worse, steal it, or if there's something valuable hidden in it—the last thing we need is to be seen this close to the SCIF with—

"*Ding!*" the elevator rings as we turn the corner.

I pick up speed. No way anyone's fast enough to spot us.

"Beecher Benjamin White, you think I'm blind!? Step away from that girl right now...!"

Clementine freezes.

"...unless of course you plan on introducing me to her!" a young

45

man with combed-back brown hair and a scruffy starter beard calls out, already laughing at his own lame joke. At twenty-nine years old, Dallas is a year younger than me and should be my junior. He's not.

"Dallas Gentry," he adds as if Clementine should recognize the name.

When it comes to archivists, everyone has their own specialty. Some are good with war records. Others are good with finding the obscure. But what Dallas is good at is getting his name in the newspaper. It peaked a few months back when he opened a dusty 1806 personnel folder from the War Department and found a hand-written, never-before-seen letter by Thomas Jefferson. Sure, it was dumb luck—but it was Dallas's luck, and the next day it was his name in the *Washington Post*, and Drudge, and on the lecture circuit at every university that now thinks he's the Indiana Jones of paper. To celebrate his rise, Dallas went full-on intellectual and started growing a beard (as if we need more intense bearded guys around here). The saddest part is, based on his recent promotion, it's actually working for him, which makes me wonder if he's the one staffing President Wallace today. But as I frantically fumble, trying to hide the dictionary under my coffee-soaked lab coat, this isn't the time to find out.

"Listen, we're kinda in a rush," I say, still not facing him.

Clementine shoots me a look that physically burns. At first I don't get it. She motions around the corner, back to the SCIF. Oh crap. Orlando's still in there. If Dallas waltzes in on him and then connects him to what's missing...

"I mean...no, we have plenty of time," I tell Dallas. "Boy, your beard looks cool."

Your beard looks cool? My God, when did I turn into Charlie Brown?

"Is that *buttered rum*?" Clementine jumps in, sniffing the air.

"You're close. Cherry rum," Dallas replies, clearly impressed as he turns toward her, staring at the piercing in her nose. It's not every day he sees someone who looks like her in D.C. "Where'd you learn your pipe smoke?"

"My boss at the radio station. He's been a pipe smoker for years," she explains.

"Wait, you starting smoking a pipe?" I ask.

"Just for the irony," Dallas teases, keeping his grin on Clementine. He honestly isn't a jerk. He just comes off as one.

"Beecher, what happened to your coat?" a soft female voice interrupts as Dallas reaches out to shake hands with Clementine.

Just behind Dallas, I spot archivist Rina Alban, a young straight-haired brunette with bright green reading glasses perched on her head, and triple knots on her shoes. In the world of mousy librarians, Rina is Mickey. She's ultra-quiet, ultra-smart, and ultra-introverted, except when you ask about her true love, the Baltimore Orioles. In addition, she looks oddly like the Mona Lisa (her eyes follow you also), and on most days she's just as talkative. But not today—not the way she's studying my bunched-up lab coat, like she can see the book that's underneath.

"Beecher, what *is* that?" Rina asks again.

"Coffee. I spilled my coffee," Clementine jumps in, restoring calm.

"Wait, you're the one he knows from high school, right?" Dallas asks, though I swear to God I never mentioned Clementine to Dallas. That's the problem with this place. Everyone's doing research.

"You really shouldn't have coffee up here," Rina points out, less quiet than usual. I know why.

Every month, the powers that be rank us archivists in order of how many people we've helped. From tourists who walk in, to the handwritten letters asking us to track down a dead relative, every response is counted and credited. Yes, it helps justify our jobs, but it also adds unnecessary competition, especially after this morning, when they told us Rina was, for the fifth month in a row, number two on the list.

"By the way, Beecher, congrats on the top spot again," Dallas says, trying to be nice.

"Top spot in what?" Clementine asks, peering down the hall and hoping to buy a few more seconds for Orlando.

"Being helpful. Don't you know that's what Beecher's best at?"

Dallas asks. "He even answers the questions that get emailed though the National Archives website, which no one likes answering because when you email someone back, well, now you got a pen pal. It's true, you're walking with the nicest guy in the entire building—though maybe you can teach him how to help himself," Dallas adds, thinking he's again making nice.

Doesn't matter. By now, Orlando should be long gone from the SCIF. Nothing to worry about. But as Clementine steps between me and Rina, Rina isn't staring at me. Her eyes are on my coat.

"Clear the hallway," a deep baritone calls out. I turn just as two uniformed Secret Service agents exit from the nearby staircase. On my left, the lights above the elevator tell us it's back on the ground floor. The sirens are louder than ever. Here comes Moses.

Without a word, one of the agents motions to Dallas and Rina, who head back around the corner. Question answered. Rina and Dallas are the ones staffing Wallace in the SCIF.

I go to push the button for the elevator. The taller Secret Service agent shakes his head and points us to the staircase. Until the President's in place, that's the only way down.

"What happened to your coat?" the agent asks, pointing to the brown Rorschach blots.

"Coffee," I call back, trying to look relaxed as I head for the waiting stairs.

"Beecher, just say it," Clementine says as soon as we're out of sight. "Tell me!"

I shake my head, speedwalking us back through the musty stacks. I'm tempted to run, but as the motion sensor lights pop on above us, I'm reminded of the very best reason to stay calm. The sensors are the Archives' way of saving energy, but all they do is highlight us for the videocameras in the corner of each stack. And unlike the videotape Orlando swiped from the room, these beam right back to the Security Office.

"You sure this is right?" Clementine asks as we reach a section where the lights are already on. Like we've been here before.

"Of course it's right," I say, squinting at the record group locator numbers at the end of the row on our left. I pause a moment. A moment too long.

"You're lost, aren't you?"

"I'm not lost."

She studies me, strong as ever. "Beecher..."

"I'm not. Yes, I'm turned around a little. But I'm not lost," I insist.

"Listen, even if you are, it's okay," she says with no judgment in her voice. But as she looks away, she starts...chuckling.

"You're laughing?"

"I-I'm sorry," she says, shaking her head, unable to hide it. The worst part is, she's got a great laugh—a laugh from deep in her stomach, not one of those fake mouth ones. "It's just— All this running...and the videotape and the Secret Service...and everyone's got guns...This is the *President*, Beecher! What're we *doing*?" she asks, her laugh coming faster.

Before I know it, I'm chuckling with her. It starts slowly, with just a hiccup, then quickly starts to gallop. She's absolutely right. To be lost like this...what the hell *are* we doing?

My belly lurches, catapulting a gasp of a laugh that only makes her laugh harder. She bends forward, holding her side and shooting me another new look I've never seen before. It barely lasts a second—an appreciative grin that reveals a single dimple in her left cheek—

Poomp.

Half bent over, I look down and see that the dictionary that was hidden beneath my lab coat has slipped out, slapping against the stacks' 1950s linoleum floor.

Clementine stares down at the old book. Her laughter's gone.

Mine too. Reality's back. And so is her fear.

"Clemmi, listen to me—whatever we found in that room— whatever they're doing with this book—" She looks my way, her eyes wide. I take a deep breath. "I can fix this."

She nods, swaying just slightly. "You mean that, don't you?"

"I'm not sure. I think I do." I scan the empty stacks and again study the record group numbers, determined to get us back on track. "Yeah. I do."

She studies me carefully, silence settling around us. Behind me, one of the motion sensor lights blinks off from inaction. I wait for the look she gave me before—the appreciative nod with the single dimple. It doesn't come. Instead, she stands up straight, turning her head, like she's studying me from a brand-new angle. She's no longer swaying. No longer moving. She's staring straight at me. I have no idea what she's seeing.

But I'll take it.

"My father's dead, isn't he?" she asks.

"What? No . . ."

"Beecher, you know who my dad is, don't you?"

"Let's just—"

"If you know . . ." Her eyes well with tears and, like that half-second when she thought I wasn't looking before, the girl who's always prepared . . . she's not prepared for this. *". . . how could you not tell me?"*

She's right. Completely right. But to just blurt it here . . .

"Beecher . . ."

She doesn't say anything else. Just my name. But in those two stupid syllables, I hear everything in between. For twenty-nine years, Clementine Kaye has lived with empty spaces. And from what I know, she's lived with them better than me. In seventh grade, I remember being paralyzed when Mrs. Krupitsky had the class make Father's Day cards, thinking that's the day we always go to his grave. Next to me, young Clementine was already happily writing away, turning it into a Mother's Day card without even a second thought. But today, in those two syllables of my name, those empty spaces are back again, and I hear them loud and clear.

"Nico Hadrian," I blurt.

Her eyes jump back and forth, fighting to process. I wait for her to lean on the end of the metal shelves for support, but her body stays stiff. She's trying to will herself back to calm. It's not working. "N-Nico? Y'mean, like the guy who—"

"Him. Mm-hmm. Nico Hadrian." I nod, hoping to soften the blow. But there's no other way to say it. "The man who tried to shoot President—"

"But he's alive, right?"

"Yeah, sure—I mean, I think he's in a mental hospital..."

"But he's alive. My dad's alive." She reaches for the metal shelf on her left, but never grabs it. "It's—it's not what I expected, but I think—I think—I think—this is better than being dead, isn't it?—it's better," she insists, blinking over and over, brushing away the tears. "I was so scared he'd be dead." Her eyes stare straight ahead, like she can't even see I'm there. "I didn't think he'd be this, but—There are worse things in life, right?"

"Clementine, are you—?"

"There are worse things in life. He could've been dead; he could've been—" She cuts herself off, and slowly—right in front of me—it's like she's finally hearing her own words. Her jawbone shifts in her cheek. Her knees buckle. Before, she was unprepared. Now she's unraveling.

I grab her arm, tugging hard. Time to get her out of here. At the end of one of the stacks—the real end this time—I push a metal door open and the dusty old stacks on the ninth floor dump us into the polished office hallway on the third floor of the main building.

The sirens from the motorcade still scream through the hall. No doubt, the President is inside the Archives by now, probably already in the SCIF with Dallas and Rina. The sirens should be fading soon. But as we head down the final steps to the lobby, as I tuck the coat-covered book tight under my arm and tug Clementine along, the sirens keep wailing. By the time I wave my badge and hear the click that opens the heavy door, there are a half dozen armed Secret Service agents standing in the lobby. The sirens are louder than ever.

A blast of mean December air from outside nearly knocks over the lobby's Christmas tree as it sends its shredded paper decorations flying. On my right, I spy the source of the sudden wind tunnel: The automatic doors that lead out to Pennsylvania Avenue are wide open.

"*Step aside! Emergency!*" someone yells as a gleaming metal gurney comes blasting through the entrance, pushed by two impassive paramedics in dark blue long-sleeved shirts.

"What's going on?" I ask the nearest uniformed Secret Service guy. "Something happen with the President?"

He glances at my badge, making sure I'm staff. "You think we'd be standing here if that were the case? We took him out of here six minutes ago. This is one of yours."

A strand of shredded paper kisses the side of my face, hooking around my ear. I don't feel it. I don't feel anything. "How do you mean, *one of ours?*"

"One of *them*," he clarifies, pointing with his nose at the Security guys who run the main check-in desk. "Apparently, some poor guy had a seizure—or heart attack—they found him on the floor of his office. I think they said his name was..."

"*Orlando!?*" a guard shouts from the check-in desk.

"*Orlando!?*" Clementine blurts behind me.

No. No no. He didn't just say—

The string of shredded paper slips off my ear, blowing into a small swirl at the center of the marble lobby. Clementine is silent behind me.

There's no way. I was just...he was just...

"Beecher," Clementine whispers behind me.

I'm already running, dragging her with me by her hand.

This isn't happening. Please tell me this isn't happening.

But it is.

10

ove! Move it! Move!" I yell, running full speed up the bright white basement hallway with the white-and-gray checkerboard floor. The magic key bounces against my chest as I fight my way through the insta-crowd that's already forming outside Orlando's office.

I'm not a big person. Or strong. But I have two older sisters. I know how to get what I want:

I lie.

"*We're with them!*" I shout as I point to the paramedics who're barely fifty feet ahead, riding their wake as they pull me and Clementine through the crowd.

Not a single Archives employee tries to stop me. Archivists aren't built for confrontation. They're built for observation, which explains why small groups of gawkers fill the hall all the way to the front door of the Security Office.

I hear more whispers as I run: *Orlando...? Orlando...! Heard a seizure...Orlando...!*

"Don't assume the worst. He could be okay," Clementine says.

I refuse to argue as we squeeze into the large office suite. Inside, it's quiet and looks like any other: a long rectangular layout spotted with cubicles and a few private offices. All the action is on our left, where I hear the squawks and crackles of far too many walkie-talkies. The paramedics have them. Security has them. And so does the small team of firefighters who arrived earlier and are now in a small circle at the center of the office, crouched on their knees like kids studying an anthill.

"They're still working on him," Clementine says.

That's good news. If they're working on him...

But they're not working. There're no frenzied movements. No CPR.

"On three," they call out, getting ready to lift the stretcher. "One...two..."

There's a metal howl as the stretcher's steel legs extend and pins and sockets bite into place. With a tug, the firefighters pull tight on the black Velcro straps that tighten around the white sheet...

Not just a sheet...under the sheet...

Orlando.

One of the firefighters takes a half-step back and we get a short but perfect view of Orlando's face. His skin is dry like a faded chalkboard. You don't need a medical degree to know when you're staring at a dead man.

"Beecher, take a breath," Clementine whispers behind me. "Don't pass out."

"I'm not going to pass out."

"You are. I can see you are."

"What do you want me to do? That's— We— This man's my friend!"

I crane my neck to look through the crowd, studying Orlando's profile. His head is tilted to the side—almost toward us—and the bottom right corner of his mouth sags slightly open and down, the way my mom looked when she had the complications with her heart surgery.

"He was just— We just saw him," Clementine whispers.

I try to focus on Orlando's eyes, which are closed and peaceful. But that bottom corner of his mouth, sagging open so slightly...

"I'm so sorry," Clementine offers.

A whiplash of pain stings my heart, my lungs—like every one of my organs is made of crushed glass. The shattered pieces cascade like sand down my chest, landing in my stomach.

Please tell me this wasn't because we were in that room... I say to myself.

"You heard them," Clementine says, reading me perfectly. "He had a heart attack...or a seizure."

I try to believe that. I really do. There's no reason to think otherwise. No reason at all. Except for that gnawing ache that's tunneling through my belly.

"What?" she whispers. "How could it not be a heart attack?"

"I'm not saying it's not, but...it's a hell of a coincidence, isn't it? I mean, think of the odds: Right after we find that hiding spot, Orlando just happens to—" I lower my voice, refusing to say it. But she hears it. When Orlando made that call through the intercom, he put himself on record. *He's* the only one listed as being in the SCIF, so if someone else went in that room after we left, if they went looking for—

Oh crap.

I look down at my bundled lab coat covered in coffee stains. It's squeezed by my armpit. But all I feel are the worn edges of what's hidden underneath.

The book. Of course. The stupid book. If that was left there for the President, and they thought Orlando took it—

"Beecher, get it out of your head," Clementine warns. "For anyone to find out he was even in there...no one's that fast."

I nod. She's right. She's absolutely right.

In fact, besides us, the only person who even knew Orlando was in there was—

"What an effin' nightmare, eh?" a soft-spoken voice asks.

I stand up straight as a burning sting of vomit springs up my throat. I know that voice. I heard it earlier. Through the intercom. When he buzzed us into the SCIF.

"Venkat Khazei," says a tall Indian man with low ears and thin black hair that's pressed in a military-combed side part. He knows I know who he is, and as he puts a cold hand on my shoulder, I notice that he's got the shiniest manicured fingernails I've ever seen. I also notice the equally shiny badge that's clipped to his waist. *Deputy Chief of Security—National Archives.*

And the only person who I'm absolutely sure knew that Orlando was in that SCIF and near that book.

"Beecher, right?" he asks, his sparkling fingers still on my shoulder. "You got a half moment to chat?"

* * *

55

11

What a horror—and especially with you two being so close, eh?" Khazei asks, his accent polished, like a Yale professor. Across from us, a firewoman covers Orlando's face by pulling up the thin bedsheet that's neither crisp nor white. The sheet's been beaten and washed so many times, it's faded to the color of fog. Worst of all, it's not big enough to really cover him, so as he lies there on the stretcher, as the paramedics confer with the firefighters, Orlando's black work boots stick out from the bottom like he's in a magician's trick, about to float and levitate.

But there's no trick.

"Pardon?" I ask.

"I saw you run in with the paramedics...the concern you were wearing." Khazei stands calmly next to me, shoulder to shoulder, like any other person in the crowd. He's careful to keep his voice low, but he never steps back, never tries to draw me out or get me to talk somewhere private. I'm hoping that's good. Whatever he's fishing for, he still doesn't know exactly where he's supposed to be fishing. But that doesn't mean he's not hiding a hook.

"We're both from Wisconsin—he was always nice to me," I admit, never taking my eyes off the body, which sits right in front of Orlando's open cubicle. On the floor, there's a small pile of scattered papers and books fanned out at the foot of Orlando's desk. They could easily be the papers Orlando knocked over when he toppled from his chair. But to me, even as Khazei takes his manicured fingers off my shoulder, they can just as easily be the aftermath of someone doing a quick search through his belongings. But what would they be looking—?

56

Wait.

The video.

In the SCIF. Orlando grabbed that video so no one would know we were there. So no one would know what we grabbed. We. Including me. But if someone sees that video . . . If someone finds out I was in that room . . . Maybe that's why Orlando was—

No, you don't know that, I tell myself. I again try to believe it. But I'm not believing anything until I get some details. And until I'm sure that videotape is in my own hands.

"Do we even know what happened? Anyone see anything?" I ask.

Khazei pauses. He doesn't want to answer. Still, he knows he's not getting info until he gives some.

"Our receptionist said Orlando was being his usual self," he explains, "said he was humming 'Eye of the Tiger' when he walked in—*which is sadly typical*—then he headed back to his cube and then . . ." Khazei falls silent as we both study the covered body. It's the first time I notice that, across the room, mixed in with the still growing crowd, are two familiar faces—one with a crappy beard, the other with her green reading glasses and triple-knotted shoes.

Dallas and Rina.

Clementine coughs loudly from behind. I don't turn around. So far, Khazei hasn't even looked at her. He has no idea we're together. Considering who we just found out her dad is, that's probably for the better.

"Y'know he had sleep apnea, right? Always bitching about going to bed wearing one of those masks," Khazei explains.

I'm still studying Dallas and Rina, my fellow archivists. Unlike everyone else, who's pretty much standing behind us, the two of them are deep on the other side of the room, facing us from behind the cubicles. Like they've been here for a bit. Or are looking for something.

I continue to check each desk, searching for the videotape.

"One of the firefighters even said that if the stress gets high enough, you can trigger a seizure, but—" Khazei shakes his head.

"When you spoke to Orlando earlier, he seem bothered or upset about anything?"

"No, he was—" I stop and look up at Khazei. He's not wearing a grin, but I feel it. Until this moment, I'd never mentioned that I'd spoken to Orlando earlier.

Dammit.

I'm smarter than that. I *need to be* smarter than that. But the longer I stand here, the more I keep thinking that there's only one possible reason Orlando died. And right now, that reason is wrapped in my lab coat and clutched by my now soaking armpit.

"I'm just trying to talk with you, Beecher. Just be honest with me. Please."

He adds the *Please* to sound nice. But I'm done being suckered. Of the forty people rubbernecking around the office, I'm the one he's decided to chat with. That alone means one of two things: Either he's a hell of a good guesser, or he's got something else he's not saying.

I replay the past half hour in my head, scouring for details. But the only one I keep coming back to is Orlando's Roman Numeral Two: If this book does belong to the President, and the President finds out we have it, he's going to declare war on . . .

On us. That's how Orlando put it.

But there is no *us.* Not anymore.

Orlando's dead. And that means that whatever's really happening here—whether it's the President or Khazei or someone else that's playing puppetmaster—the only one left to declare war on . . .

Is me.

A single bead of sweat rolls down the back of my neck.

Across the way, Dallas and Rina continue to stand there, still facing us from the far end of the room. Dallas grips the top of a nearby cubicle. Rina's right behind him. Sure, they saw us in the hallway—just outside the elevator—but that doesn't tell them I was in the SCIF, or, more important, that I'm the one who actually has the book. In fact, the more I think about it, there's only one way anyone could've known we were in there.

My brain again flips back to the video.

"Beecher, you understand what I'm saying?" Khazei asks.

When Orlando grabbed that videotape, he told us it was the best way to keep us safe—that as long as no one knew we were in there, we could still be Mark Felt. But if that tape is out there...if someone already has their hands on it...they'd have proof we were in the room and found the book, which means they'd already be aiming their missiles at—

"Were you with him all afternoon?" Khazei asks. "What time did you leave him?"

"Excuse me?"

"I'm just reacting to *your* words, Beecher. You said you were with Orlando. But if you want, take a look at your calendar...at your datebook...whatever you keep it in. My only concern is getting an accurate timeline."

I nod at his swell of helpfulness. "Yeah...no...I'll look at my calendar."

"I appreciate that. Especially because..." He pauses a moment, making sure I see his smile. "...well, you know how people get."

"How people get *about what*?"

"About things they don't really know about that they think they know about," he says, his voice as kind as ever. "So if I were wearing your shoes, Beecher, the last thing I'd want is to suddenly be known as the last person to be alone with the security guard who mysteriously just dropped dead. I mean, unless of course it was just a heart attack."

On the back of my neck, my single drop of sweat swells into a tidal wave as I start to see the new reality I'm now sitting in. Until this moment, I thought the worst thing that could come from that videotape was that it made me look like a book thief. But the way the picture's suddenly been repainted, that's nothing compared to making me look like a murderer.

"Make way, people! Coming through!" the paramedics call out, shoving the stretcher and slowly rolling Orlando's body back toward the reception desk.

The crowd does the full Red Sea part, clearing a path.

But as we all squeeze together, I once again eye Orlando's cubicle, searching his messy desk, scanning the papers fanned across the floor, and scouring the office for—

There.

I didn't look for it before—didn't know it was that important—back in the corner, just outside his cubicle. Right where Dallas and Rina were first standing.

There's a black rolling cart, like you see in every A/V department, with a small TV on top. But I'm far more interested in what's underneath.

I push forward, trying to fight through the crowd as it squeezes back, bleeding into other cubicles to make way for the stretcher.

"Easy!" a middle-aged woman in full security uniform snaps, shoving me back with a shoulder.

It's just the shove I need. On the lower shelf of the A/V cart sits an ancient bulky VCR. Like the one upstairs, it's a top-loader. Unlike the one upstairs, the basket that holds the tape is standing at full attention, already ejected.

And empty.

No. It can't be empty! If someone has it... I bite down hard, swallowing the thought. Don't assume the worst. Maybe Orlando hid it. Maybe it's still—

I feel another shove from in front of me. It nearly knocks me on my ass.

"Move, people! Show some respect!" one of the paramedics shouts.

With a final swell, the crowd packs extra-tight, then exhales and loosens its grip, dissipating as the stretcher leaves the room. Within seconds, there are coworkers everywhere, whispering, talking, the gossip already starting to spread.

Fighting for calm, I search for Dallas and Rina. They're gone. I turn around, looking for Khazei. He's gone too.

But I hear him loud and clear.

Of all the people in this room, he came straight to me. And

while I still don't know if Khazei's threatening me for the book, or just investigating the loss of an employee, based on the intensity of his questions, one thing is clear: The book...the video...the President...even Orlando...There are multiple rings on this bull's-eye—and right now, every one of those rings is tightening around my neck.

12

It was late when Dr. Stewart Palmiotti's phone began to ring. It was late, and he was comfortable. And as he lay there, toasty under his overpriced down comforter and protected from the December cold, he was perfectly happy to feel himself slowly swallowed by his current dream, a piano dream involving old childhood Italian songs and the pretty girl with the bad teeth who he always sees at the supermarket deli counter.

But the phone was ringing.

"Don't pick it up." That's what his ex would've said.

That's why she was his ex.

This wasn't just some random call. From the ring—high-pitched, double chirp—this was the drop phone. The phone that could go secure with the flip of a switch. The phone with the gold presidential seal on the receiver. The phone that was installed in his house two years ago. By the White House Communications Agency. And the Secret Service.

The drop phone was about to ring again, but as Palmiotti knew, only a schmuck lets the drop phone ring twice.

"Dr. Palmiotti," he answered, sitting up in bed and looking out at the late-night snow that had already blanketed his street in Bethesda, Maryland.

"Please hold for the President," the White House operator said.

"Of course," he replied, feeling that familiar tightening in his chest.

"Everything okay?" whispered Palmiotti's...*girlfriend? Girl-*

62

friend wasn't the right word. *Girlfriend* made them sound like they were teenagers.

Palmiotti wasn't a teenager. He was forty-eight. Lydia was forty-seven. Lost her husband to...she called it cancer of the soul. Meaning he was screwing the overweight girl from the dry cleaners.

It took Lydia two years before she would date. She was happy now. So was Palmiotti. He was happy and warm and ready to dream.

And then his phone rang.

Palmiotti didn't like being on call. He had given it up years ago. But that's part of the job of being personal physician—and one of the oldest friends—of the most powerful man in the world.

"Stewie, that you?" President Orson Wallace asked.

By the time they entered their freshman year at the University of Michigan, Palmiotti and Wallace had called each other by first names, last lames, nicknames, and most every good curse word they could find. But it wasn't until Inauguration three years ago that Palmiotti started calling his friend *sir*.

"Right here, sir," Palmiotti replied. "You okay? What's wrong?"

The President doesn't have to choose his physician. Most simply go to the White House Medical Unit. But a few, like George H. W. Bush, who appointed a dear family friend, understand that sometimes the best medicine is simply having someone to talk to. Especially someone who knows you well.

"I'm fine," Wallace replied.

"If you're fine, don't wake me up in the middle of the night."

"Wait. You got Lydia sleeping there, don't you?"

At that, Palmiotti paused.

"Don't lie to me, Stewie." The President laughed. "I got satellites. I can see you right now. Look out your window and—"

"Orson, this a doctor call or a friend call?"

This time, Wallace was the one who was silent. "I just...I think I did something to my back. It's bothering the hell outta me."

Palmiotti nodded. His predecessors had warned him as much.

Most calls from the Oval would be stress-related. "You want me to come over and take a look?"

"Nah. No. That's silly. It can wait till tomorrow."

"You sure?"

"Yeah—absolutely," the President of the United States said. "Tomorrow's just fine."

13

The archivist was patient.

Of course he was patient.

Impatient people would never stand for this—would never take a job where half your day was spent alone with ancient government paperwork, poring through memos and speeches and long-forgotten handwritten letters, treasure-hunting for that one minute detail that a researcher was so desperately looking for.

No, impatient people didn't become archivists.

And without question, this archivist—with the scratched black reading glasses—was plenty patient.

Patient enough to stay quiet all day.

Patient enough to let the ambulances fade and the EMTs and the firefighters and the Secret Service leave.

Patient enough to go about his job, helping a few tourists in the second-floor research room, then answering a few letters and emails that came in through the Archives website.

And even patient enough to drive home, cook his spaghetti with turkey meat sauce, and spend the last hour before bed noodling with a double acrostic word puzzle in *Games* magazine. Just like any other night.

That's how they taught him to do it.

But when all was quiet. When the street was dark. When he was sure that anyone watching would've long ago become bored and left, he finally reached into his briefcase and pulled out the true treasure from today's hunt.

According to Benjamin Franklin, "He that can have patience, can have what he will."

The archivist had something far more valuable than that.

He had a videotape.

The one Orlando was carrying when—

He put the thought out of his head as he slid the tape into his old VCR. Right now, the danger was that it was all coming undone... everything was at risk.

Hitting rewind, he leaned in close as the picture slowly bloomed onto his TV. The angle looked down from the top corner of the SCIF, no different than any security camera. Sure enough, there was Orlando, rushing around as—

Wait.

There.

In the corner. By the door. A shadow flickered. Then another.

Realizing he hadn't gone back far enough, the archivist again hit rewind.

The shadow— No. Not a shadow.

A person. Two people.

His eyes narrowed.

Now it made far more sense. That's why they couldn't find the book.

Orlando wasn't alone in the SCIF. There were two other people with him.

One of them a girl. And the other? The one with the bunched-up lab coat and the messy blond hair?

The archivist knew him. Instantly.

Beecher.

Beecher had what the Culper Ring wanted.

14

My phone starts screaming at 7:02 the next morning. I don't pick it up. It's just a signal—the morning wake-up call from my ride to work, telling me I now have twenty-four minutes until he arrives. But as the phone stops ringing, my alarm clock goes off. Just in case the wake-up phone call doesn't do its trick.

I have two sisters, one of them living in the D.C. area, which is why, instead of waking to the sound of a buzzer, my alarm clock blinks awake with a robotic male voice that announces, "...Thirty percent chance of snow. Twenty-one degrees. Partly overcast until the afternoon."

It's the official government weather forecast from NOAA—the National Oceanic and Atmospheric Administration—where my sister Lesley's been working for the past year and a half, studying tides and weather and sometimes getting to write the copy that the robotic voice announces. And yes, I know there's not much "writing" when it comes to saying it's "partly overcast until the afternoon." And yes, I'd rather wake up to music or even a buzzing alarm. But it's my sister. Lesley wrote that. Of course I support her.

As Robotman tells me about the rest of the forecast, I kick off the sheets and lower my head. My mom used to make us say a prayer every morning. I lasted until junior high, but even then, she taught me that I shouldn't start the day without being thankful for something. Anything. Just to remind you of your place in the world.

Closing my eyes, I think about...huuh...I try to tell myself it's good that Orlando's at least at peace. And I'm glad I got to know him. But when it comes to what I'm thankful for, no matter how much I think of Orlando...

I can't help but picture that look when Clementine first arrived yesterday—that self-assured warmth that she wears as coolly and comfortably as her thumb rings and nose piercing. But what's far more memorable is that fragile, terrified look she didn't want me to see as she ducked behind me in the stacks. It wasn't because she was shy. Or embarrassed. She was *protecting* me from that look. Sparing me the heartache that comes with whatever she thinks her life has become.

I help people every day. And of course, I try to tell myself that's all I'm doing right now—that I'm just trying to be a good friend, and that none of this has anything to do with my own needs, or what happened with Iris, or the fact that this is the very first morning in a year when I woke up and didn't eye the small bottle of Iris's perfume that I still haven't been able to throw out. I even tell myself how pathetically obvious it is to fill the holes of my own life with some old, imagined crush. But the truth is, the biggest threat to Clementine's well-being isn't from who her father is. It's from the fact that, like me, she's on that videotape from when we were in the SCIF.

The tape's still gone. But even without an autopsy, I know that's why Orlando died. It's a short list for who's next.

From there, I don't waste time getting ready. Four and a half minutes in the shower. Seven minutes for shaving, toothbrushing, and the rest.

"*Ping*," my computer announces from the downstairs kitchen table where I keep my laptop that keeps track of all the morning eBay bids. My townhouse isn't big. It isn't expensive. And it's in Rockville, Maryland, instead of in D.C.

But it's mine. The first big thing I bought after nearly a hundred weddings, plus two years of working my eBay side business and saving my government salary. My second big purchase was the engagement ring. I've been making up for it ever since.

In fact, as I head downstairs, on the beige-carpeted second-to-last step, there's a neat stack of a dozen postcards. Each card has a different black-and-white photo of the Statue of Liberty from 1901 to

1903. On the step below that, there's another stack—this one with black-and-white photos of baseball stadiums in the early 1900s. And there're more piles throughout the kitchen: across the counter (photos of old German zeppelins), on the microwave (photos of steam-engine trains), on top of the fridge (separate piles for dogs, cats, and tons of old automobiles), and even filling the seat of the bright orange 1960s lounge chair that I got at the Georgetown flea market and use as a head chair (each pile a different exhibit from the 1901 Pan-Am Expo in Buffalo, New York, including a big pile for the camel parade).

To anyone else, it's clutter. To me, it's how the world used to communicate: through postcards.

Back in the early 1900s, when you bought a new car, or new dress, or had a new baby, you took a picture, sent it to Kodak, and they'd send you back six black-and-white "real photo postcards," which you'd then send to family and friends. At the time, collecting those real photo cards was the number one hobby in America. Number one. But once World War I began, since the best printing was done in Germany, production halted—and a new company called the American Greeting Card Company filled the void, offering cheaper cards that Americans didn't like as much.

Of course, the final nail hit the coffin in the form of the telephone. Why send a card when you could just call up and tell them the news? But today, those real photo postcards are among the most collected items on eBay, as I learned when I sold a photo from a 1912 Stanford football game for a whopping $2.35.

To my mom, the cards are yet another example of my obsession with the past. To my sisters, who know me far better, they're the distraction that's only grown in size since Iris left. They may be right—but that doesn't mean distractions don't have benefits. The cards have oddly helped me settle back into my groove and find my sea legs—so much so that when an old friend like Clementine emails after fifteen years and asks how you're doing, instead of thinking about what's wrong with your life, you take a chance, hit the reply button, and say, "So glad you got in touch." That's even more valuable than the newest bids on eBay.

The problem is, by the time I reposition the piles on the kitchen table and pour my morning bowl of raisin bran, there's only one thing I really want to see on the computer. I start every morning with the obituaries. Mostly, I read about strangers. Today, at washingtonpost .com, I put in Orlando's name. His obit's not in there yet.

I put in the word *Archives*. Nothing there either. Not even a little blurb in the Metro section. I know what it means. If they thought it was foul play—even if it was suspicious and the cops were looking into it—there'd be ink on this. But as I swallow a spoonful of raisin bran, it looks like there's no current police investigation.

The worst part is, I don't know if that's good or bad.

Maybe it *was* just a heart attack, I tell myself, still hearing Khazei's words. For all I know, the only bogeymen are the ones in my imagination.

There's only one problem with the theory.

I look down at the vintage soft brown leather briefcase that's leaning against the leg of the table. The briefcase used to belong to my dad. He died when he was twenty-six. He never had a chance to use it. Today, it holds my keys, my journal that I keep all my eBay sales in, and the beaten old dictionary that sticks out from the back pouch.

Forget the videotape and Khazei and everything else.

The book. It still comes back to George Washington's book.

There's a reason that book just happened to be in that room, which just happened to be used by the leader of the free world. And until I find out what it is—

There's a quick double tap of a car horn, honking from outside.

"Coming!" I call out even though he can't hear me.

Grabbing my briefcase and winter coat, I head for the door, speedwalking through the living room, which is decorated with a used art deco black leather sofa that sits right below three side-by-side framed photo postcards from the 1920s, each of them with a different view of an old firemen's parade as it marched down the main street where I grew up in Wisconsin. The prints are the prize of my collection—and a daily reminder that if I mess it up here, that's exactly where I'm going back to.

Outside, the car honks again.

"I got it!" I shout, reaching for the door. But as I give it a tug, I see it's already open—just a bit—like I forgot to close it all the way last night. The thing is, I always close it all the way.

Standing in the doorway, I look back toward the living room, through to the kitchen. Both rooms are empty. Bits of dust turn silent cartwheels through the air. I recheck my briefcase. The George Washington book is still there. I tell myself I'm being para-noid. But as I leave, I pull hard to close the door—twice—and dart into the cold, which freezes my still damp hair.

Waiting for me idling in the street is a powder blue 1966 con-vertible Mustang that clears its throat and lets out the kind of hack-ing cough that comes with lung cancer. The car's old, but in perfect shape. Just like the driver inside, whose head is bobbing to the country music.

"C'mon, old boy... y'know I hate this neighborhood!" Tot shouts even though the windows are closed. At seventy-two years old, he's not rolling them down manually.

Racing for his car, I notice a thin man with a plaid green scarf walking his dog—a brown dachshund—on the opposite side of the street. I know most everyone on the block. Must be someone new. I can't think about it now.

Tot is far more than just my ride. He's the one who trained me on the job. And encouraged me to buy the house. And the only—truly *only*—one who doesn't bust my chops about Iris, but will always lis-ten when I talk about whatever new set of old postcards I uncovered at the flea market. He's my friend. My real friend.

But he's also an archivist—since the very last days of LBJ's administration, which makes him the oldest, most senior, most resourceful researcher I've ever met. So as I hop in his car, open my briefcase, and hand him the tattered copy of George Washington's dictionary, he's also my best hope of figuring out whether this damn book could possibly be worth killing for.

*   *   *

15

There were faster ways for Dr. Stewart Palmiotti to get to work. As the President's doctor, he had a prime parking spot on West Exec. Not a far one either. Up close. Closer even than the spot reserved for Minnie. And Minnie was the President's sister.

From there, it was just a short walk through the West Wing. There was no need to take the long way around and walk past the Oval. But after that call last night... Palmiotti had been White House doctor for over three years. He'd been Wallace's dearest friend for over three decades.

Palmiotti wasn't some twentysomething novice. Rather than getting close, where he'd be spotted by the morning swirl of staffers and secretaries, he strolled casually past the Roosevelt Room, which had a clear view of the Oval Office's front door. Even back when he was governor, Wallace was always at his desk by at least 7 a.m. Even the day after he buried his mom.

Palmiotti glanced at his watch: 7:27. He looked over at the Oval. There were no suit-and-tie agents standing guard outside the door. The President still wasn't in.

No reason to panic just yet.

From there, Palmiotti picked up the pace and made his way back outside, eyeing his own breath as he rushed down the West Colonnade and past the Rose Garden, whose snow had been melted away by the gardening staff. With a sharp left through the French doors, he stepped onto the long red-and-gold-trimmed carpet of the Ground Floor Corridor.

"He's still up there, huh?" he called out to Agent Mitchel, the uniformed Secret Service agent who was posted outside the private elevator on the left of the corridor.

Mitchel nodded, but the mere fact that the agent was there told Palmiotti that the President was still upstairs in the Family Residence.

"He's gonna be in a mood, isn't he?" Mitchel asked as Dr. Palmiotti headed to his own office, the White House Medical Unit, which sat directly across the hall from the elevator. Most staffers thought the Medical Unit was poor real estate, too far from the Oval. But as any doctor knew, the real action always happened at home.

"Depends," Palmiotti lied, well aware that from the phone call last night that something must've happened. "We know where he is?"

For a moment, the agent stood there.

"C'mon, I'm just trying to figure out what kind of day we're gonna have," Palmiotti added.

He wasn't stupid. After three years, he knew the Service protocol by now. To maintain some level of privacy, there were no agents or cameras allowed in the Residence. But to maintain some level of safety, the Service wired the floors of nearly every room up there. They did the same in the Oval: Weight-sensitive pressure pads under the carpets let them know exactly where President Wallace was at all times.

"Workout Room," Mitchel finally said, referring to the small room on the third floor installed by President Clinton.

Palmiotti rolled his eyes. The only time Wallace worked out was when he had something that needed working out.

"This from what happened last night?" the agent asked.

"Sorry?"

"I saw the call log. President called you at three in the morning?"

"No, that was nothing," Palmiotti said. "Same as always—just pulled his back again."

"Yeah, always his back," the agent said. "Though if that's the case, you really think he should be working out right now?"

This time, Palmiotti was the one who stood there. The Secret Service wasn't stupid either.

"Oh, by the by—Minnie's been looking for you," the agent added, referring to the President's sister.

Nodding politely, Dr. Stewart Palmiotti glanced down at his watch: 7:36. A new Wallace record.

"This something we should worry about, Doc?" the agent asked.

"No," Palmiotti replied, staring up at the red light above the elevator, waiting for it to light up...waiting for the President of the United States to come downstairs and tell him what the hell was going on. "I'm sure he's just running late."

16

*E*ntick's Dictionary?" Tot says, reading the embossed gold letters on the cover of the book as we weave through the morning traffic on Rockville Pike.

"Ever hear of it?" I ask, lowering the radio, which is pumping with his usual playlist—old country music by Willie Nelson, Buck Owens, and at this particular moment, Kenny Rogers.

"Don't you touch *The Gambler*," he threatens, slapping my hand away. He quickly turns back to the book. "Looks like it's... or at least what's left of it is..." He's blind in his right eye, so he has to turn his head completely toward me to see the book's torn-away spine and the missing interior pages. It's the same when he drives (which, legally, he can)—always with his head turned a quarter-way toward the passenger seat so he can get a better view of the road.

Most people think Tot looks like Merlin—complete with the scary white beard and the frizzy white hair that he brushes back—but he's far more of a Colonel Sanders, especially with the gray checked jacket and the bolo tie that he wears every day. He thinks the bolo tie makes him look modern. It does. If you're in Scottsdale, Arizona, and it's 1992.

"... I'm guessing pre-nineteenth-century—let's say about..." Tot rolls his tongue in his cheek, already loving the puzzle. Even his blind eye is twinkling. The only thing that gets him more excited is flirting with the sixty-year-old woman who runs the salad bar in the cafeteria. But at seventy-two years old, Aristotle "Tot" Westman could have worse weaknesses. "I'd say 1774."

"Close—1775," I tell him. "You're losing your touch."

"Sure I am. That means you guessed...what?...Civil War?"

I sit there, silent.

"Look at the threading," he says, running his finger down the exposed spine and the mess of exposed thread. "By the nineteenth century, it was all case binding—all machine production—two boards and a spine, then glued to the pages. What you have here is...this is art. Hand-stitched. Or *was* hand-stitched before someone gutted it. Is it one of ours?"

"That's what I'm trying to figure out."

"You haven't looked it up? Seen if it's in the system?"

"I need to. I will. It's just— Yesterday was—" I take a breath. "Yesterday sucked."

"Not just for you. You see the paper this morning?" he asks as he pulls a folded-up copy of the *Washington Times* from where it's wedged next to his seat along with a copy of the *Washington Post* and the *Baltimore Sun*. "Apparently one of our guards had a seizure or something."

He tosses the paper in my lap. I quickly scan the story. It's small. Buried on page two of the Metro section. Doesn't mention me. Doesn't mention foul play. Doesn't even mention Orlando by name ("The victim's name is being withheld until family can be notified").

"This wasn't in the *Post*," I say.

"Of course it wasn't in the *Post*. You read only one paper and you're only getting half the actual news—whatever biased side you happen to subscribe to. Can you imagine, though?" Tot asks, his voice perfectly steady. "Guy drops dead right in our building—right as President Wallace is about to arrive—and right as you're walking around the building with the daughter of Nico Hadrian, the very guy who tried to assassinate Wallace's predecessor."

I sit up straight as the traffic slows and a swarm of red brake lights flash their ruby smile our way. The only person who knew about Nico was the woman I called in our St. Louis records center. Carrie—

"Don't even feign the faux-shock, Beecher. You really think Carrie could find enlistment records—from Nowhere, Wisconsin—*from over twenty years ago* without calling for help?"

I shouldn't be surprised. When John Kerry ran for President and they needed to prove that he earned those Purple Hearts, they came to Tot. It was the same when they were searching for George W. Bush's National Guard records. And the same with John McCain's military file. On my first day of work, a coworker asked Tot if he knew where to find the unit records for a particular company in the Spanish-American War. Tot gave them the record group, stack, row, compartment, and shelf number. From memory. On the anniversary of his fortieth year here, they asked him the secret of his longevity. He said, "When I first arrived, I started to open these boxes to see what's inside. I've been fascinated ever since."

"Honestly, though, Beecher—why didn't you just call me in the first place?" Tot asks. "If you need help..."

"I need help, Tot," I insist. "Major help. I need the kind of help that comes with a side order of help."

His face still cocked toward me, he holds the steering wheel of the old Mustang with two crooked fingers. The car was his dream car when he was young, his midlife crisis car when he turned fifty, and his supposed retirement present when he finally hit sixty-five. But it was always out of reach, always for another day—until three years ago when his wife of fifty-one years died from a ruptured brain aneurism. It was the same week I started at the Archives. He had nothing back then. But he somehow found me—and I found... When I used to work at the bookshop, Mr. Farris told me we're all raised by many fathers in our lives. Right now, I pray he's right.

"Tell me the story, Beecher. The real story."

It takes me the rest of the ride to do just that, and as we follow rush-hour traffic to his usual shortcut through Rock Creek Park, I give him everything from showing Clementine around the building, to Orlando offering to let us in the SCIF, to spilling the coffee and finding the book hidden below the chair.

He never interrupts. Forever an archivist, he knows the value of collecting information first. By the time we turn onto Constitution Avenue, I hit the big finale with the parts about Orlando's death, the suddenly missing videotape, and every other detail I can think of, from Dallas's lurking, to Khazei's passive-aggressive threat to make me look like the murderer. But as the powder blue Mustang growls and claws through D.C.'s slushy streets, Tot's only reaction is:

"You shouldn't've told me any of this."

"What?"

"You need to be smart, Beecher. And you're not being smart."

"What're you talking about? I *am* being smart. I'm getting help."

"That's fine. But look at the full picture you're now in the middle of: Of everything that's happened, there's only one detail—just one—that can't be argued with."

"Besides that I'm screwed?"

"The book, Beecher. Where'd you find that book?" he asks, pointing to the dictionary.

"In the chair."

"Yes! It was hidden in the chair. Y'understand what I'm saying? You may not know if it was hidden *by* the President, or *for* the President, or by or for his Secret Service agents or some other party we don't even know of—but the act of *hiding* and *finding* something, that's a two-party agreement. One hider and one finder. So to hide the book in that SCIF...to even get in that room..."

"You think it's someone from our staff," I say.

"Maybe from our staff...maybe from Security...but it's gotta be someone in our building," Tot says as we stop at a red light. "I mean, if you're hiding something, would you ever pick a room unless you had the key?"

Up ahead, the Washington Monument is on my right. But I'm far more focused on my left, at the wide green lawn that leads back, back, back to the beautiful mansion with the wide, curved balcony. The White House. From here, it looks miniature, but you can already see the specks of tourists lingering and snapping photos at the black metal gates.

"Beecher, don't think what you're thinking."

I stay silent, eyes still on the home of Orson Wallace.

"That's not who you're fighting, Beecher. This isn't you against the President of the United States."

"You don't know that."

"Sure I do. If it were, the paramedics would be carrying *you* under the sheet by now."

I shake my head. "That's only because they don't know I have their book."

For the first time, Tot's silent.

As we turn onto Pennsylvania Avenue, as he pulls past our building—a huge neoclassical granite archives that fills over two city blocks on our right—I ignore the fifty-foot-high columns and instead stare at the two smaller limestone statues that flank the front doors. There are four statues in total, representing the Future, the Past, Heritage, and Guardianship. Tot knows better than I do which is which, but there's no mistaking the carved old man holding a scroll and a closed book on the right. Engraved at the base it says, "Study the Past."

I open the Washington dictionary and again read the words. *Exitus acta probat.*

"Think about it, Tot, of all the people in the building yesterday, I can account for everyone being where they were—Orlando...Dallas...Rina...even Khazei—everyone except for President Wallace, who just happened to pick the exact day, at the exact time of death, to stop by for his visit."

"Actually, he's not the only one."

"What're you talking about?"

He looks my way, turning far enough that I can see his good eye. "Tell me about the girl."

"Who?"

"The girl. The high school crush you're all gushy about."

"Clemmi?"

"*Clemmi?* No, no, no, don't do pet names. You barely know this girl two days."

"I've known her since seventh grade," I say as I reach to change the radio station.

"What're you doing?" Tot challenges.

"Huh?"

"Don't change my station. What'd I tell you about messing with The Gambler?"

"I know, and you know I love The Gambler, but— Can't we just...?" I twist the dial, searching for music. "I just want to hear something new—like maybe—do you know which stations play rap or even...Joan Jett?"

He pumps the brakes, nearly putting me through the windshield. "Beecher, don't you dare hit menopause in my car."

"What're you talking about?"

He raises his voice, trying to sound like me. *I need something new. Where do they keep the rap music?*" Returning to normal, he adds, "This girl's been back in your life barely forty-eight hours, and what—suddenly you don't want to eat your raisin bran, or listen to the same boring old music anymore? Don't be such a cliché, Beecher. You have a good life. You moved past Iris...you were in a real groove."

"I *was* in a groove. But that's the problem with a groove—if you don't change it up, it quickly becomes a hole."

"Yeah, except for the fact you're already in a hole—one that can swallow you. You gotta admit it's odd, Beecher. The daughter of Lee Harvey Oswald walks back into your life—"

"Her dad's not Oswald."

"No, he's Nico Hadrian, who tried to assassinate a U.S. President. And she walks back into your life on the same day that another President just happens to be visiting our offices? Girl's got a pretty uncanny sense of timing, no?"

"Tot, she didn't even know who her dad was until we told her! How could she possibly be plotting against me?"

With a sharp right onto 7th Street, Tot makes another quick right toward the underground side entrance of the building, which is blocked by a bright yellow metal antiram barrier that rises from the concrete. Tot rides the brakes, giving the barrier time to lower. When it doesn't, the car bucks to a halt.

On our left, I finally see why Tot's so quiet. An armed security guard steps out of the nearby guardhouse, his puffed black winter coat hiding everything but his face and his unusually white front teeth. Ever since 9/11, when we became obsessed with terrorists stealing the Declaration of Independence, our building has limited the underground parking spots to a grand total of seven. Seven. Our boss—the Archivist of the United States—gets one. His deputy gets another. Two are for deliveries of new records. Two are for VIPs. And one is for Tot, a favor from a friend in Security who used to control such things during the Bush era.

As the guard with the white teeth approaches, Tot nods hello, which is always enough to get us in. But instead of waving us through and lowering the barrier...

The guard raises his hand, palm straight at us. We're not going anywhere.

17

"orning, morning," the duty nurse sang as Dr. Palmiotti stepped into the cramped reception area of the White House Medical Unit. As usual, her dyed black hair was pulled back in a tight military braid that was starting to fray from her bad night's sleep. Behind her, in the area between the bathroom and treatment room, she'd already tucked away the fold-down bed. The White House doctor arrived first thing in the morning, but the duty nurse had been there all night.

"Good night's sleep?" Palmiotti asked, amused to notice how the morning small talk sounded like a one-night stand.

"I tell my mom I sleep less than a hundred feet from the President. Vertically," duty nurse Kayre Morrison replied, pointing up at the ceiling.

Palmiotti didn't even hear the joke. He was peeking over his shoulder, back into the hallway. The red light above the elevator was still off. Still no sign of President Wallace.

"By the way, Minnie wants to see you," the nurse said. "She's waiting for you now. In your office."

"Are you—? Kayre, you're killing me. I mean it. You're striking me dead."

"She's the President's sister," the nurse whisper-hissed. "I can't kick her out."

Palmiotti shook his head as he trudged to his private office in the back of the suite. Typical duty nurse. And typical Minnie.

"Heeey!" he called out, painting on a big smile as he threw the door open. "How's my favorite girl?"

Across from his desk, sitting on the tan leather sofa, was a stumpy forty-two-year-old woman with a thick block of a body. She was dressed in her usual unconstructed dress, this one navy blue, plus her mother's long dangly silver earrings from the early eighties, which was about the time Palmiotti first got to know Jessamine "Minnie" Wallace.

"Okay, Minnie, what's it this time?"

Minnie lifted her chin, revealing a stout, squatty neck and a grin that—ever since her stroke—rose on only one side.

"Can't I just be here to say hello?" she asked with the slight lisp (another lingering side effect from the stroke) that made the word *just* sound like *juss*.

"Aren't you supposed to be doing physical therapy right now?"

"Already did it," Minnie promised.

Palmiotti stood there, studying her on the sofa as her thumb tapped against the bright pink cane that she still needed to walk. The handle of the cane was shaped and painted like the head of a flamingo. That was the problem with being the sister of the President—you wind up spending your life finding other ways to stand out. "You didn't do your therapy again, did you?"

"Sure I did."

"Minnie...Show me your hands," Palmiotti challenged.

Minnie half-smiled, pretending not to hear him. "I meant to ask, you still seeing Gabriel for lunch today?" she said, referring to the President's scheduler.

"Please don't do that," he begged.

"Do what?"

"What's it now? Reception in the Oval? Having the President speak at your annual convention?"

"It's a Caregivers' Conference—for the top scientists who study brain injuries," she explained, referring to the cause that she now spent so much time pushing for. "My brother already said he'd come, but when I spoke to Gabriel—"

"Listen, you know that if Gabriel tells you no, it's *no*," he said. But as he reached for the best way to track down the President—the earpiece and Secret Service radio that sat on his desk—there was a sudden burst

83

of voices behind him. Over his shoulder, out in the Ground Floor Corridor, he saw a phalanx of staffers—the President's personal aide, his chief of staff, the press secretary, and an older black speechwriter—slowly gathering near the President's private elevator. Palmiotti had watched it for three years now. Forget the radio. The personal aide always got the call first from the valet who laid out Wallace's suits.

Sure enough, the red light above the elevator blinked on with a *ping*. Agent Mitchel whispered something into the microphone at his wrist, and two new Secret Service agents appeared from nowhere. Thirty seconds after that, President Orson Wallace, in fresh suit and tie, stepped out to start the day. For a second, the President glanced around the hallway rather than focusing on the swarm of staff.

The doctor shook his head.

Not every President is a great speaker. Not every President is a great thinker. But in the modern era, every single President is a master of one thing: eye contact. Bill Clinton was so good at it, when he was drinking lemonade while you were talking to him, he'd stare at you through the bottom of his glass just to maintain that lock on you. Wallace was no different. So when he stepped off the elevator and glanced around instead of locking on his aides...

...that's when Palmiotti knew that whatever happened last night, it was worse than he thought.

"Just gimme a minute," the President mimed as he patted his personal aide on the shoulder and sidestepped through the small crowd—straight toward Palmiotti's side of the corridor.

Of course, the staffers started to follow.

Yet as the President entered the reception area of the Medical Unit, half the throng—the speechwriter and the press secretary, as well as the Secret Service—stopped at the door and waited in the hallway, well aware that their access didn't include a private visit to the President's doctor.

"Dr. Palmiotti...!" the duty nurse murmured in full panic. The only times the President had come this way were when it was officially on the schedule.

"I see him," Palmiotti called back from his office.

"Where you hiding him? You know he's dating again? He tell you he was dating?" the President teased the nurse, flashing his bright whites and still trying to charm. It was good enough to fool the nurse. Good enough to fool the two trailing staffers. But never good enough to fool the friend who used to get suckered trading his Double Stuf Oreos for Wallace's Nilla Wafers in fifth grade.

As the two men made eye contact, Palmiotti could feel the typhoon coming. He had seen that look on the President's face only three times before: once when he was President, once when he was governor, and once from the night they didn't talk about anymore.

The President paused at the threshold of Palmiotti's private office, which was when Palmiotti spotted the hardcover book the President was carrying.

Palmiotti cocked an eyebrow. *We're not alone*, he said with a glance.

Wallace dipped his neck into the office, spotting his sister, who raised her flamingo cane, saluting him with the beak.

Definitely not ideal.

The President didn't care. He stepped into Palmiotti's office, which was decorated with the same medical school diplomas that had covered his first office back in Ohio. Back when everything was so much simpler.

"Mr. President..." Wallace's personal aide said, standing with the chief of staff at the threshold.

In any White House, the smart staffers get invited to *walk* with the President. But the smartest staffers—and the ones who get the farthest—are the ones who know when to *walk away*.

"...we'll be right out here," the aide announced, thumbing himself back to the reception area.

"Stewie was just examining my hands," Minnie announced, reaching forward from the couch and extending her open palms to Palmiotti.

"Wonderful," Wallace muttered, not even looking at his sister as he closed the door to Palmiotti's office. There were bigger problems to deal with.

"So I take it your back's still hurting you?" Palmiotti asked.

Orson Wallace studied his friend. The President's eye contact was spectacular. Better than Clinton's. Better than W's. Better than Obama's. "Like you wouldn't believe," the leader of the free world said, carefully pronouncing every syllable. "Think you can help with it?"

"We'll see," Palmiotti said. "First I need you to tell me where it hurts."

18

T his is bad, isn't it?" I ask.

"Relax," Tot whispers, rolling down his window as a snakebite of cold attacks from outside. He's trying to keep me calm, but with his right hand he tugs at his pile of newspapers, using them to cover George Washington's dictionary.

"Sorry, fellas," the guard says, his breath puffing with each syllable. "IDs, please."

"C'mon, Morris," Tot says, pumping his overgrown eyebrows. "You telling me you don't recognize—"

"Don't bust my hump, Tot. Those are the rules. ID."

Tot lowers his eyebrows and reaches for his ID. He's not amused. Neither is the guard, who leans in a bit too deeply through the open window. His eyes scan the entire car. Like he's searching for something.

Circling around toward the trunk, he slides a long metal pole with a mirror on the end of it under the car. Bomb search. They haven't done a bomb search since we hosted the German president nearly a year ago.

"You got what you need?" Tot asks, his hand still on the newspapers. The story on top is the one about Orlando.

"Yeah. All set," the guard says, glancing back at the guardhouse. Doesn't take James Bond to see what he's staring at: the flat, compact security camera that's pointed right at us. No question, someone's watching.

There's a deafening metal shriek as the antiram barrier bites down into the ground, clearing our path. Tot pulls the car forward, his face again mostly turned to me. His blind eye is useless, but I can still read the expression. *Don't say a word.*

I follow the request from the parking lot all the way to the elevators. Inside, as we ride up in silence, Tot opens up the folded newspapers, but it's clear he's really reading what's tucked inside— *Entick's Dictionary*. I watch him study the swirls and loops of the handwritten inscription. *Exitus acta probat.*

"See that?" I ask. "That's George Washing—"

He shoots me another look to keep me quiet. This time, I wait until we reach our offices on the fourth floor.

The sign next to the door reads *Room 404*, but around here it's called Old Military because we specialize in records from the Revolutionary and Civil wars.

"Anyone home . . . ?" I call out, opening the door, already knowing the answer. The lights in the long suite are off. On my left, a metal wipe-off board has two columns—one IN, one OUT—and holds a half dozen magnets with our headshot photos attached to each one. Sure, it's ridiculously kindergarten. But with all of us always running to the stacks for research, it works. And right now, everyone's in the OUT column. That's all we need.

Knowing the privacy won't last, I rush toward my cubicle in the very back. Tot does his best to rush toward his in the very front.

"Don't you wanna see if the book is in our collection?" I call out as I pull out my key to open the lock on the middle drawer of my desk. To my surprise, it's already open. I think about it a moment, flipping on my computer. With everything going on, I could've easily forgotten to lock it last night. But as my mind tumbles back to the front door of my house . . .

"You do your magic tricks, I'll do mine," Tot says as I hear the *gnnn* of a metal drawer opening. Tot's cube is a big one, holding a wall of six tall file cabinets, stacks upon stacks of books (mostly about his specialty, Abraham Lincoln), and a wide window that overlooks Pennsylvania Avenue and the Navy Memorial.

My cube is a tiny one, filled with a desk, computer, and a corkboard that's covered with the best typos we've been able to find throughout history, including a 1631 Bible that has the words "Thou *shalt* commit adultery," plus the first edition of a *Washington Post* gossip column from 1915 that was supposed to say President Woodrow Wilson "spent the evening entertaining Mrs. Galt," a widow who he was courting, but instead said, "the President spent the evening *entering* Mrs. Galt." You don't get this job without having some pack rat in you. But with ten billion pages in our collection, you also don't get it without being part scavenger.

As my computer boots up, I grab the keyboard, all set to dig. In my pocket, my cell phone starts to ring. I know who it is. Right on time.

"Hey, Mom," I answer without even having to look. Ever since her heart surgery, I've asked my mother to call me every morning— just so I know she's okay. But as I put the phone to my ear, instead of my mom, I get...

"She's fine," my sister Sharon tells me. "Just tired."

I have two sisters. Sharon's the older one—and the one who, even when she went to the local community college, never stopped living with my mom. We used to call it Sharon's weakness. Now it's our whole family's strength. She looks like my mom. She sounds like my mom. And these days, she spends most of her life dealing with all the health issues of my mom.

Every two weeks, I send part of my check home. But Sharon's the one who gives her time.

"Ask her if she's going to Jumbo's," I say, using my mom's preferred lunch spot as my favorite code. If my mom's eating lunch there, I know she's feeling well.

"She is," Sharon answers. "And she wants to know where you're going Friday night," she adds, throwing my mom's favorite code right back. She doesn't care where I'm going, or even *if* I'm going. She wants to know: *Do I have a date?* and more important, *Will I ever get over Iris?*

"Will you please tell her I'm fine?" I plead.

"Beecher, how's your seventy-year-old friend?"

"And you're the one to talk? Besides, you've never even met Tot."

"I'm sure he's lovely—but I'm telling you, from experience: If you don't change the way you're living, that's gonna be *you* one day.

Old and lovely and all by yourself. Listen to me on this. Don't hide in those Archives, Beecher. Live that life."

"Is this me arguing with you, or arguing with Mom?"

Before she can answer, I glance to my right. There's a solid red light on my desk phone. Voicemail message.

"I think I got you something, old boy," Tot calls out from his cubicle.

"Shar, I gotta go. Kiss Mom for me." As I hang up my cell, I'm already dialing into voicemail, putting in my PIN code.

While waiting for the message to play, I dial up caller ID on the keypad, study the little screen of my phone, and scroll down until I see the name of the person who left the last message.

Williams, Orlando.

My heart stops.

I read it again. Orlando.

My computer blinks awake. Tot yells something in the distance.

"Message one was received at . . . 4:58 p.m. . . . yesterday."

And in my ear, through the phone, I hear a familiar baritone voice—Orlando's voice—and the final words of a dead man.

19

O
n a scale of one to ten," Dr. Palmiotti asked, "would you say the pain is...?"

"It's a four," the President said.

"Just a four?"

"It *used to be* a four. Now it's an eight," Wallace said, pacing along the far left side of the doctor's office and glancing out the wide window with the stunning view of the White House Rose Garden. "Approaching a nine."

"A nine for what?" his sister Minnie asked, already concerned. The doctor was talking to the President, but it was Minnie, as she stood across from Palmiotti, who was being examined.

She held her right palm wide open as he poked each of her fingers with a sterilized pin, testing to see her reaction. Whenever she missed therapy for too long, sharp pains would recede and feel simply dull. "What's wrong with him?" she asked, motioning to her brother.

"Nothing's wrong," Palmiotti promised.

"If he's sick..."

"I'm not sick. Just some stupid back problems," the President insisted. "And a really crappy night's sleep."

"Listen to me, I know they won't say this on the front page of the paper, but you need to hear it, O: I have faith in you. Stewie has faith in you. Your wife and kids have faith in you. And millions of people out there do too. You know that, right?"

The President turned, looking at his sister, absorbing her words.

Palmiotti knew how much Minnie loved her brother. And how much Wallace loved her back. But that didn't mean it was always best for him to have her around. By now, most of America had heard the story: How Minnie was born with the genetic disease known as Turner syndrome. How it affected only females, leaving them with a missing X chromosome. How 98 percent of people die from Turner syndrome, but Minnie lived—and she lived without any of the heart or kidney or cognitive problems that go along with it. In fact, the only thing that Minnie Wallace got from Turner syndrome was that she was—like a few of its victims—manly.

Broad chest. Low hairline. Short neck. With one X chromosome, she looked like Moe from the Three Stooges. Perez Hilton said if she were one of the Seven Dwarfs, she'd be Stumpy. Or Fatty. Or Dumpy. When it first got posted, the President tried to let it roll off. He issued a statement saying that the comment made him Grumpy. But Palmiotti knew the truth. Nothing hits harder than when someone hits home. For the President...for Minnie...the last time Palmiotti saw pain like that was the night of the accident that caused her stroke.

The worst part was, he saw the makings of a similar pain right now—and from the strained look on the President's face, despite the little pep talk from his sister, that pain was just starting to swell.

"Minnie, go do your therapy," Palmiotti ordered.

"I can do it right here. You have the squeeze balls—"

"Mimo, you're not listening," the President interrupted. "I need to see my doctor. By myself."

Minnie cocked her head. She knew that tone. Grabbing her flamingo cane, she started heading for the door.

"Before I go..." she quickly added, "if you could speak at our Caregivers' Conference—"

"Minnie..."

"Okay. Fine. Gabriel. I'll talk to Gabriel," she said. "But just promise me—all these back problems—you're sure you're okay?"

"Look at me," Wallace said, flashing the insta-smile that won him 54 percent of the popular vote. "Look where I live...look at this life...what could I possibly be upset about?"

With her limp, it took Minnie nearly a minute to leave the office. The President didn't start speaking until she was gone.

*　　*　　*

20

*B*eecher, *it's me . . .*" Orlando says in the message, his deep
voice showing just a crack of flat Wisconsin accent.

My legs go numb, then my chest.

"Beecher, lookit this!" Tot yells behind me, though I swear to
God, it sounds like he's talking underwater.

"Tot, gimme one sec," I call back.

My Lord. How can—? Orlando. That's . . . Orlando . . .

"You need to see this, though," Tot insists, shuffling toward me
with a thick stack of paper held by a binder clip.

Still gripping the phone, I lean forward in my chair, lurching for
the keypad and pounding the 3 button. *This isn't . . . focus! . . . start
over . . . just focus . . .*

Beep.

"Beecher, it's me," Orlando begins again. He pauses a moment.

"Y'ever see this?" Tot interrupts, waving the pages.

"Tot, please . . . can it wait?"

I hit the 3 button again to buy some time. The phone's not near
my ear, but I still hear Orlando's opening. *"Beecher, it's me."*

"You want to know if that was George Washington's dictionary or
not?" Tot asks. "Just listen: When George Washington died, Mount
Vernon made a list of every single item in his possession—every
candlestick, every fork, every piece of art on his walls . . ."

I hit 3 again. *"Beecher, it's me."*

". . . and of course, every one of GW's books," Tot says, tossing me
the copy of *Entick's Dictionary.* It hits my desk with a dead thud.

"Okay . . . I get it, Tot."

"The more you rush me, Beecher, the slower I'm gonna talk."

"Okay, I'm sorry, just...*please.*" I press 3 again. *"Beecher, it's me."*

"The point is," Tot continues, "the only way to find out if this is really GW's book is to first find out if he even owned a copy."

I hit 3 again. "And?"

"According to this, he had one." He points to the list. *One copy. Entick's Dictionary.* "Though if this is even the same copy, that still doesn't explain how it found its way here."

"Or even *if* it found its way here," I say. "For all we know, this isn't even part of our collection."

"Actually, that's easy enough to find out." Stepping toward my computer, Tot shoos me from my seat. "C'mon...Up!...Old man needs to sit," he says as I hop aside, stretching the phone cord to its limits. He's already clicking at the keyboard. Perfect. I turn my attention back to the phone...

"Beecher, it's me," Orlando begins again. He pauses a moment. *"Crap, I don't have your cell phone."* He pauses again, then his voice picks up speed. *"I need you to call me. What you did..."*

What I did?

"Just call me," he finishes.

I hit the button and replay it again.

"Crap, I don't have your cell phone."

He pauses after that. Is that panic? Is he panicking? Is he sick?

"Crap, I don't have your cell phone."

I listen closely, but I was wrong before. His voice isn't picking up speed. It's fast, but no faster than usual.

"I need you to call me. What you did..."

There it is. The only moment his voice strains. Just slightly on the word *did.* I hit the rewind button again.

"What you did..."

He means finding the dictionary.

"What you did..."

There's definitely an emphasis on the last word.

"What you did..."

It's just three syllables. Three dumb words. It's no different than looking at a photo of a happy, grinning child and then being told he died in a brutal car accident. No matter what you want to see, all you see is... it's not just loss or sadness. To hear these words... uttered by this—this—this—ghost...

"What you did..."

All I hear is blame.

"Just call me," Orlando finally says at 4:58 p.m. yesterday.

As his voice fades, I feel my body churn, straining for its own equilibrium. It doesn't come. I'm squeezing the phone so hard, streams of sweat run from my fist down the inside of my wrist, seeping into my watchband.

It's not until I look down that I spot Tot arching his head toward me, studying me with his good eye. If he heard...

He stares right at me.

Of course he heard.

I wait for him to judge, to warn, to say that I need to get rid of Orlando's message.

"You're not alone in this, Beecher."

"Actually, I kinda am," I say as I hear a beep on the other line. I look down at caller ID, which reads *Security*. I don't pick up. The last thing I need right now is Khazei quizzing me again about Orlando's death. Instead, I forward Orlando's message to my cell and delete it from voicemail.

Tot shakes his head. "I'm telling you, you're not alone. You need to hear that."

"That's fine—and I appreciate when someone says something nice to me, Tot, but... I'm just... I don't think I can do this."

"Do what?"

"*This.* Any of this. Tracking old books that're hidden for Presidents... playing Spy versus Spy... getting guilt and spooky messages from dead people..."

"Guilt? What're you talking about?"

"Didn't you hear Orlando's message? When he said, *What you did...*—heart attack or murder—he might as well have added... *when you caused my death.*"

"You really think Orlando was calling you for some bitter scolding?"

"What else am I supposed to think?"

At his jawbone, just below his ear, Tot twirls a few stray hairs of his wizard beard between his thumb and pointer-finger while eyeing the gutted copy of *Entick's Dictionary*. "Maybe he was amazed you found it. Maybe he just realized the consequences: *What you did...*" He lowers his voice to sound like Orlando: "*...you just uncovered something no one knew existed. President Wallace was...God knows what he was up to, but you found it, Beecher. You're a hero.*"

"A hero? For what? For spilling coffee? For trying to impress a girl from high school in the hopes of forgetting about my fiancée? I mean it, Tot. I woke up this morning with my feet sweating! Name one hero who has sweaty feet!"

I wait for him to answer—for him to pull some historian nonsense and tell me that Teddy Roosevelt was known for his sweaty feet, but instead Tot just sits there, still twirling his beard.

My phone again starts to ring. Like before, caller ID reads *Security*. Like before, I don't pick it up.

Nodding his approval, Tot takes a deep breath through his nose. "Beecher, y'know what the best part of this job is? For me, it's this sheet of paper," he says, picking up a random sheet of paper from my desk and flapping it back and forth. "On any given day, this sheet is just another sheet in our collection, right? But then, one day—9/11 happens—and suddenly this sheet of paper becomes *the most vital document in the U.S. government.*" He tosses the paper back to my desk. "That's what we're here to witness, Beecher. We witness it and we protect it. We're the caretakers of those sheets of paper that'll someday define the writing of history."

"Tot, I think you're being a little dramatic about paper."

"You're not listening. It's not just with paper. It also happens with *people.*"

At the far end of the office, the front door opens and there's a quiet metallic *clunk* on our magnet board. Like a periscope rising from a submarine, I peer above the cubicles and spot my fellow archivist Rina, who offers a surprisingly warm Mona Lisa smile considering how pissed she was yesterday at coming in number two in our internal rankings.

"You okay?" Rina asks me.

"Huh?"

"Yesterday—I saw you downstairs. With Orlando. You were friends, no?"

"Yeah...no...I'm okay. Thanks," I tell her as she heads toward her own cube.

Lowering periscope, I turn back to Tot. "Rina," I whisper, quickly adding, "So in this analogy, *I'm* the sheet of paper?"

"You've been here a few years now, Beecher—you should know history isn't just something that's written. It's a selection process. It chooses moments, and events, and yes, people—and it hands them a situation they should never be able to overcome. It happens to millions of us every single day. But the only ones we read about are the ones who face that situation, and fight that situation, and find out who they really are."

"And now *you're* the one not listening, Tot. I know who I am. I fought for this life. And I spent two full years taking 140,000 photographs of overpriced wedding cakes, and grooms who think they can dance, just to make sure that I didn't have to go back to Wisconsin and say that life outside my mother's house was just too tough for me. I got further than my father, and his father, and every rotten classmate who used to aim for my head in dodgeball even though they knew headshots didn't count. But whatever history supposedly handed me...whatever we did find in the SCIF...I don't know what it is...I don't know where to start...I don't even know what I'm supposed to be looking for!"

Once again shaking his head, Tot turns back to my computer and hits the enter key. Onscreen, I see the Archives' history for *Entick's Dictionary.* Yes, we have a copy. Yes, it's in this building. And according to this, it's currently...

"*Signed out,*" I blurt, reading from the screen.

It's the first good news I've had all day. Every day at the Archives, hundreds of people come to do research. To make it easier, once you register as a researcher, you can fill up two carts and keep them on hold, stored in our research room, for three days. And from what it says here, *Entick's Dictionary* is currently on hold for a researcher named... Tot clicks to the next screen.

"*Dustin Gyrich*," we both whisper as my phone rings for the third time. For the third time, I ignore *Security*.

"This guy Gyrich from us?" I ask as I pull open my top drawer and start flipping through our staff list. A...B...C...G...H... I...No one named Gyrich.

"I don't think he's a pro either," Tot adds, referring to the professional researchers people can hire by the hour.

Across the office, the door again swings open. "Beecher, you here!?" a familiar voice shouts.

Even without raising periscope, I smell the pipe smoke on Dallas. On most days, he ignores me. Today, his footsteps head right for me.

"Beecher?" he adds, sounding almost concerned. "You there or not?"

"Yeah...right here," I say, stepping out from my cube.

"Dammit, then why didn't you say something!? Security's worried— After Orlando— Don't *do that!*" he scolds, all his concern already faded in anger. "Next time someone calls your sorry ass, pick up the damn ph—"

Dallas cuts himself off, stopping midstep as he reaches my cube. He's not looking at me anymore. He's looking at what's behind me. I spin around, worried he sees the dictionary. But the dictionary's already gone—tucked away by the person still sitting at my desk.

"Hey, Tot," Dallas offers, scratching at his starter beard. "Didn't realize you were there."

Tot doesn't say a word. He just stares at Dallas, unblinking. It's nothing personal. When he turned seventy, Tot decided there were ten rules for living a happy life. The only one he's shared with me thus far is that, as an archivist, he won't make friends with anyone who says FDR knew about the impending attack on Pearl Harbor, since there's not a single sheet of paper in our building to back up that claim. I know another of his rules has something to do with white cotton panties and the keys to a great sex life (I made him stop talking because—just the thought of it made me want to be blind). And from what I can tell, there's a third rule that enshrines a venomous hatred for bullies—especially those who curse at Tot's friends.

The best part is watching Dallas take a half-step back. Even the most stubborn of cubs knows when the big cat's around.

"I was just saying..." Dallas stutters, "...I was telling Beecher I was worried about—"

"How'd you know someone was calling him?" Tot challenges.

"Pardon?"

"When you came in," Tot says. "You said Security was calling. How'd you know they were calling?"

"I-I was there," Dallas says.

"In the Security Office?"

"No...at sign-in...with the detectors," he says, referring to the check-in desk on the Penn Avenue side of the building. "They have a visitor for Beecher who's pretty insistent that she see him..."

"*She?*" I ask.

"Your friend. From yesterday. The one with the nose pierce..."

Tot shoots me a look. He's already called her the daughter of Lee Harvey Oswald. The last thing he wants is me bringing her in again.

"Clementine's downstairs right now?" I ask.

"Why do you think they keep calling you?" Dallas says. "They saw you check in at the garage, but when you didn't answer your phone—"

I glance at Tot, who doesn't need help putting the rest together. The only way to get Clementine into this building is if I personally go down and sign her in. And while the last thing I need right now is to put myself higher on the suspect list because I'm helping out the daughter of a killer, the less time I let her spend with Security, the safer I'm gonna be.

"*Tot*..." I say with a glance as I run for the door.

Go. I have it, he replies with a nod. It's never taken me more than three minutes and twenty-two seconds to get to the sign-in desk. And while I need to get Clementine, priority number one is still finding out who Dustin Gyrich is and why, on the same day the President was set to arrive here, Gyrich requested this old dictionary.

"I'm old and hate small talk," Tot tells Dallas as he turns back to my computer. "You need to leave right now."

As Dallas heads back to his desk, I pick up speed and make a sharp left toward the office door. But as I pull it open and bound into the hallway, I nearly smash into the chest of the tall man. And his shiny Security badge.

"Beecher, you know the one thing that really ticks me off?" Deputy Security Chief Venkat Khazei asks as I crane my neck up to see him. "When people here—people sitting right at their desks—don't return my calls."

He puts a hand on my shoulder, but all I can think is that he's the only other person in the entire building who knew Orlando was in that SCIF.

"Is there something I can help you with?" I ask.

"That's generous of you, Beecher," Khazei says. "I thought you'd never ask."

21

"Y ou tell me what's easier," Khazei offers, trying hard to keep it nice. "We can talk out here, or at your desk, or—"

"Out here's fine," I blurt, determined to keep him far from the book.

"Where you headed anyway?"

"Wha?"

"You were running, Beecher. You almost smashed into me. Just wondering where you're headed."

"Stacks," I say with a nod, realizing that while Khazei was calling for info, it was the front-desk security guys who were calling about Clementine. "Just pulling a record from the stacks."

He looks down at my empty hands. "Where's the pull slip?"

Now he thinks he's being smart.

"Right here," I say, pointing to the side of my head and being smart right back. But the way his broad eyebrows knot together, Khazei doesn't like me being smart right back.

"Y'know..." he says, smoothing his thinning black hair to the side, "you were also running yesterday when you found out about Orlando."

"He's my friend. I shouldn't run when I hear my friend's dead?"

"I'm just saying...for a place that gets the gold medal for slow and quiet, you're rushing around a lot lately."

He watches me carefully, letting the silence of the empty hallway sink in. But all I'm really focused on is the thought of Clementine still waiting for me downstairs.

"You said you had a question, Mr. Khazei."

"No, I said I had something I was hoping you could help me

101

with," he corrects, scratching his chin with the back of his hand. "I'm just wondering if you were able to look at your calendar...for when you were with Orlando."

"I looked, but I can't really nail it down. I saw him in the hallway. Maybe about a half hour before he...y'know..."

Khazei nods, but doesn't otherwise react. "Anything else you might've thought of? Anything that might be helpful as we look into his death?"

"I thought the paramedics said it was a seizure—that he had sleep apnea."

"They did. That's why they're paramedics, not coroners," Khazei says. "Now. Again. Anything at all—anything Orlando might've said, anything he did—that you think we should know about?"

I don't pause. "Nothing that I can think of," I tell him.

"I thought you said you guys were close."

"I said he was *nice to me*. We're both from Wisconsin, and he was always nice."

"And that's it?" Khazei asks.

"Why's that so hard for you to believe?"

"I don't know," Khazei replies, calmer than ever. "I guess...if he's just some nice guy from Wisconsin, well...why's he making you the very last person he calls before he dies?"

Over his shoulder, the elevator dings, bringing the morning's arrival of fellow employees. Khazei smiles, as if he's in control of that too.

"It's the twenty-first century, Beecher. You really think we wouldn't take the time to check the outgoing calls on Orlando's phone?"

It's the second time he's caught me in one of his lame little mental traps. I swear right now, he's not getting me for a third.

"Maybe it's better if we continue this conversation someplace a bit more private," Khazei suggests, motioning to the metal door that leads to the stacks. This time of the morning, there are already too many employees filling the hallway. "You said you needed to grab a file, right?" Khazei adds. "I'll walk with you."

Until yesterday, when he buzzed Orlando into the SCIF, I'd barely heard of Venkat Khazei. But if my gut is right, and he *is* doing more than just simply investigating Orlando's murder—if he really is after the book, or trying to make me look like a murderer as a way of getting it—the last thing I need is to be walking alone with him in the most remote section of our building.

"Actually, I'm okay talking out here," I say as the crowd disappears into its offices and, like a high school after a late bell, the hallway slowly drains back to its regular morning silence.

Khazei nods, pretending he's not annoyed. But as I wait for the final door to close in the hallway, I notice, through the front door to my own office, a thin pointed shadow, like a scarecrow, on the opposite side of the translucent glass. From its opaque outline, it could be any of our archivists—Tot, Dallas, Rina—but after swaying there for an instant, the scarecrow backs off. Like it knows I see it listening.

"So what was it that Orlando said in his last message?" Khazei challenges.

From his tone alone, I can tell it's his third trap. If he had the technology to know that I got Orlando's final message, it's just as easy for him to've already listened to that message. He's just testing to see if I'll be honest.

"Orlando just . . . he said he didn't have my cell phone and that I should call him back."

"Call him back about *what*?"

"Probably about what I did with some old blank letterhead I found from the Senate Judiciary Committee. It got sent over by mistake so I took one of the sheets—it was just a joke—and wrote a letter to Orlando saying he was being deported. Just dumb office stuff."

It's a good enough excuse delivered with good enough calm. I even used the words *what I did* to evoke the one unexplainable moment in Orlando's message. *What you did . . .*

But Khazei just stands there with his starched military posture, like a giant exclamation point. I glance back at my office. The shadow of the scarecrow is still there.

"Were you in SCIF 12E1 yesterday?" Khazei finally blurts.

"E-Excuse me?"

"It's a simple question. It requires a simple answer. Were you *in* or anywhere *near* that Vault at any point in time yesterday?"

I take a deep breath, trying hard not to look like I'm taking a deep breath. I don't know much about Khazei, but from what I can tell of our two conversations together, he hasn't asked a single question he doesn't already know the answer to, or at least have a hunch on. And considering that Dallas and Rina and at least one Secret Service agent saw me around the corner from that room...and that the videotape is still unaccounted for..."12E1..." I say. "That's the one the President does his reading in, right?"

"Beecher, at this moment, I am your friend. But if you want to make me an enemy..."

"Yeah, no...I definitely walked by the room. That's where I saw Orlando. I was giving a tour."

"But you're telling me you didn't go inside it?"

This is the moment where I can tell him the truth. I can tell him I went inside. I can tell him I didn't do it. But as I stare at Khazei, who's still the unmoving exclamation point, all he's going to hear is that I was the last person alone with Orlando before he died. And once he hears that...once he can confirm that I had actual access to the book...

I shake my head. "No. Never went inside it."

He tightens his stare.

"What?" I ask. "If you don't believe me, go check the tape. All those rooms are wired for video, aren't they?"

It's a risky bluff, but right now, I need to know what's going on. Sure, Khazei could've been the one who snatched that video from Orlando's VCR. But if he planned on using it to make me the murderer, we wouldn't even be having this conversation. So either Khazei has the tape and all he cares about is the book, or he doesn't have the tape and it's still out there.

"Amazingly, the tape is gone—someone took it from the SCIF," Khazei says flatly. "But thanks for the reminder. I need to tell the Service about that."

"The Service?"

"I know. But when Orlando's dead body showed up at the exact same time that President Wallace was entering the building... Apparently, the Secret Service doesn't like when bodies are that close to their protectee. So lucky us, they've offered to help with the investigation," he says, watching me more closely than ever. "What an opportunity, though. I'm guessing by the time they're done, they'll scan and alphabetize every atom, molecule—every speck of DNA—in the entire SCIF. God knows what you can find in there, right, Beecher?"

Just over his shoulder, there's a second *ding* as another elevator empties a group of employees into the wide hallway.

"Oh, and by the way," he adds as they fan out around us, "when you had your lab coat all bunched up yesterday—what was it stained with again? That was coffee, right?"

I nod and force a smile and—*Morning! Hey! Morning!*—wave hello to passing staffers.

"Enjoy your day," Khazei says, heading for the waiting elevator. "I'm sure we'll be talking again soon."

As the elevator doors swallow him whole, I take another peek at my own office door. The scarecrow's gone. At least I can finally catch my breath and—

No...

I run for the stairs. I almost forgot.

She's down there right now.

22

"*old on...not yet...*" the President said, holding up a single finger. Backlit by the morning sun, he studied the door to the doctor's office, which had already closed behind his sister.

Across from him, Palmiotti sat at his desk. Underneath the door, they could see the shadows of the staffers outside.

That's how it always was. Even in the most private parts of the White House, someone was always listening.

"So you were saying." Palmiotti motioned to the President. "About your back problem..."

"It hurts," Wallace insisted, still eyeing the shadows at the door. "And it's getting worse."

Palmiotti mulled on this. "Is it something I can take a look at personally?"

The President mulled too, once again staring out at the purposely melted snow of the Rose Garden. It took a ton of work to make something appear this undisturbed.

"Let me think on that," he said to Palmiotti. "Right now, we're probably better off sticking with the original treatment."

"Mr. President...?" one of the staffers called from the hallway. Time for him to go.

"Before you run," Palmiotti said. "Have you thought about surgery?"

The President shook his head. "Not with this. Not anymore."

"Mr. President...?" the staffer called again. Four uninterrupted minutes. For any President, that was a lifetime.

"I've got a country to run," Wallace said to his friend. "By the way, if you're looking for a good book..." He held up the hardcover copy of a book entitled *A Problem from Hell: America and the Age of Genocide* by Samantha Power. "Give it a look—it won the Pulitzer Prize," the President said, handing it to Palmiotti. Directly.

"You got it," the doctor said to his oldest friend as he glanced down at the hardcover book. *A Problem from Hell*. It sure was.

"Oh, and if you see Gabriel," Wallace called back as he headed for the door, "tell him to block out a quick drop-by in the schedule for Minnie's conference. But I'm not staying for photos."

"You're a sucker, y'know that?"

The President waved an absent goodbye, not saying a word. But his point was clear.

In Wallace's eyes, family came first.

It was a lesson not lost on Palmiotti, who knew exactly what was at risk if this current mess was what he thought. It'd be easy to walk away now. Probably smart too. The President's foot was clearly approaching the bear trap. But after everything Wallace had done for him... everything they'd done for each other...

Family came first.

"Oh, and Stewie, you need a haircut," the President added. "You look like dreck."

Dr. Stewart Palmiotti nodded.

A haircut. He was thinking the exact same thing.

23

T he girl."

"What girl?" asks the security guy with the round face and bushy eyebrows.

"The girl," I say. "There's supposed to be a girl."

He looks around the welcome area. The faded green rain mats and gray stone walls make it feel like a crypt. On the right, there's the metal detector and X-ray machine. But beyond a few more employees flashing their IDs, the only people I see are two other security guards.

"I don't see any," the guard says.

"Someone called me," I insist. "She was just here! Black hair. Nice eyes. She's really—"

"The pretty one," the guard by the X-ray calls out.

The eyebrows guard looks around.

"You don't know where she is, do you?" I ask.

"I think I— I signed her in. She was waiting right *there*," he says, motioning to one of the benches.

I'm not surprised. They may've given me and Tot the full once-over this morning, but for the most part, our security is at the same level as Orlando's top-loading VCR. We don't even swipe our IDs to get in. Especially during the morning rush—I can see it right now—a lanky woman in a bulky winter coat waves her ID at the guard and walks right through.

"I swear—*right there*," he insists.

I glance at the sign-in sheet on the edge of the marble counter. Her signature is the exact same from high school. An effortless swirl. *Clementine Kaye*.

"Maybe someone already brought her in," the X-ray guard says.

"No one brought her in. I'm the one she was waiting—" No. Unless . . . No. Even Khazei's not that fast.

Pulling out my cell phone, I scroll to Clementine's number and hit send. The phone rings three times. Nothing but voicemail. But in the distance, I hear the ring of a cell phone.

"Clementine . . . ?" I call out, following the sound. I head back past the guard desk and rush toward the Finding Aids room, where most visitors start their research. It would make sense. I kept her waiting long enough—maybe she came in here to look for more about her dad.

I hit send again. Like before, there's a faint ring. *Here*. For sure from here.

Hitting the brakes, I scan the mint green research room. I scan all four of the wide, book-covered desks. I scan the usual suspects: In the left corner, two elderly women are filling out paperwork. On my right, an old military vet is asking about some documents, a young grad student is skimming through genealogy reports, and—

There.

In the back. By the computers.

Staring at the screen, she leans forward in her chair, hugging the charcoal overcoat that fills her lap. Unlike yesterday, her short black hair has been divided into two ultra-hip pigtails like the kind you see on girls who make me feel just how old I've been feeling since she crashed back into my life and made me start searching for rap music instead of Kenny Rogers.

"Clemmi, what're you doing here?" I ask as I reach the back of the room.

She doesn't answer.

But as I get closer . . . as I see what she's looking at onscreen . . . something on YouTube . . .

There are videos in my family that, if you covered the entire screen except for one square inch, I'd still be able to identify the moment. There's the footage of me and my sisters, the two of them side by side on the vinyl couch in the hospital, holding baby me across their laps when I was first born. There's me at ten years old, dressed as Ronald Reagan for Halloween, complete with what my mom swore was a Ronald Reagan wig, but was really just some old Fred Flintstone hair. And there's the video of my dad—one of the only ones I have of him—in the local swimming pool, holding the two-year-old me so high above his head, then splashing me down and raising me up again.

But all those pale next to the scene that Clementine's staring at right now: of Nico Hadrian, dressed in a bright yellow NASCAR jumpsuit, as he's about to lift his gun and, without an ounce of expression on his face, calmly try to kill former President Leland Manning.

To most Americans, it's history. Like the first moon footage. Or JFK being shot. Every frame famous: the tips of the President's fingers blurring as he waves up at the crowd...his black windbreaker puffing up like a balloon...even the way he holds so tight to the First Lady's hand as they walk out on the track, and...

"Now you think I'm a nut," she says, still watching the screen.

"I don't think you're a nut."

"You actually should. I'm related to a nut...I'm sitting here, watching this old footage like a nut...and yes, it's only because you kept me waiting here that I put his name in Google, but still...this is really bordering on pathetic. I'm practically a cashew. Though watch when he steps out of the crowd: He totally looks like me."

Onscreen, the President and First Lady are flashing matching grins, their faces lit by the generous sun as they walk to their would-be slaughter.

"Okay, it is kinda nutty you're watching this," I tell her.

Her eyes roll toward me. "You're really chock full of charm, huh?"

"I thought it'd make you laugh. By the way, why'd you come here? I thought we agreed it was better to lay low until we—"

Standing up from her seat, she reaches into her purse, pulls out a small square present wrapped in what looks like the morning newspaper, and hands it to me.

"What's this?" I ask.

"What's it look like? It's a poorly wrapped present. Open it."

"I don't—" I look over my shoulder, totally confused. "You came here to give me a present?"

"What's wrong with a present?"

"I don't know...maybe because, between Orlando dying, and then finding your dad, I sorta threw your life in the woodchipper yesterday."

She regrabs the present, snatching it from my hands.

"Beecher, tell me something that upset you."

"What're you talking about?"

"In your life. Pick a moment. Pick something that hurt you... a pain that was so bad, you almost bit through your own cheek. Y'know...someone who really put you through the emotional wringer."

"Why would—?"

"Tell me who Iris is," Clementine says, reminding me that the people who know you the longest are the best at finding your weak spots.

"Why're you bringing up Iris?"

"I heard Orlando say her name yesterday—and within two seconds, you had the same pain on your face that you have now, like someone kicked your balls in. I know the feeling...y'know how many DJ jobs I've been fired from? So what happened to Iris? Is she dead?"

"She's not dead. She's an old girlfriend. We broke up."

"Okay, so she dumped you for another guy."

"That's not—"

"Beecher, I'm not trying to upset you...or pry," she says, meaning every word. "The point is, whatever it was—however Iris hurt you—you're over her now, right?"

"Absolutely," I insist. "Of course."

"Okay, you're not over her," she says as I stand there, surprised by the sudden lump that balloons in my throat and the familiar sting of self-doubt that Iris planted so deeply in my chest. "But you will be, Beecher. And that's what you did for me yesterday. For my whole life, I've wondered who my father might be. And now, thanks to you, I *know*. And yes, it's not the easiest answer. In fact, it may just be . . . it's kinda the *Guinness Book of World Records* crappiest answer of all time. But it's an *answer*," she says, handing the present back to me. "And I appreciate that."

Looking down at the present, I give a tug to one of the scotch-taped seams. As I tear the paper aside, I spot the turn buttons on what looks like the back of a picture frame. It's definitely a picture frame. But it's not until I flip it over that I see the actual picture inside.

It's a color photo of me in seventh grade, back when my mom used to shop for whatever Garanimals shirt I was wearing that day. But what I notice most is the other seventh grader standing next to me in the photo with the wide, surprisingly bucktoothed grin. Young Clementine.

The thing is, back then, we never had a photo of just the two of us.

"H-How'd you get this?" I ask.

"I made it. From our old class photo in Ms. Spicer's class. You were standing on the left. I was on the right. I had to cut us out with an X-Acto knife since Tim Burton movies made me genuinely scared of scissors, but it still made our heads kinda octagonal-shaped, so sorry about that."

I look down at the frame, where both of us have our arms flat at our sides in standard class-photo positions. Our heads are definitely octagons.

"You don't like it?" she asks.

"No, I like it . . . I love it. I just . . . If you had scanned it in— I feel bad you had to ruin the actual photo."

"I didn't ruin anything," she insists. "I cut out the only two people I cared about in that class."

I look up at Clementine, then back down at the photo, which is choppy, poorly made, and completely unflattering.

But it's of us.

A smile grips my cheeks so hard, they actually hurt.

"By the way, don't think you get a pass on that Garanimals shirt," she tells me as the video continues to play onscreen behind her. Her back is to it, so she can't see it, but it's the part where Nico is about to step out of the crowd.

"Listen, I gotta run," she adds as a man with black buzzed hair, a big bulbous nose, and a bright yellow jumpsuit steps into the frame and raises his gun. My God—he *does* look like her. "They told me to come back in an hour," she says.

"Who did? What're you talking about?"

"The guards. At St. Elizabeths."

"Wait. As in *mental institution St. Elizabeths*?"

"Nico's there. Same place as John Hinckley—the one who shot Reagan. It's only ten minutes from here."

"Can we please rewind one second? You went to see Nico!?"

"I can't get in unless he approves me first. That's how they have to do it on his ward. I'm waiting to get approved."

"But he's—"

"I know who he is—but what'm I supposed to do, Beecher? Sit at home and do my nails? I've been waiting to meet this man for thirty years. How can I not—?"

Pop, pop, pop.

Onscreen, the gunshots are muffled. As Nico steps out of the crowd, his head's cocked just slightly—and he's almost...he's smiling.

Pop, pop, pop.

With her back still to the monitor, Clementine doesn't turn at the gunshots. But she does flinch, her body startled by each and every one.

"Shots fired! Shots fired!" the agents yell.

"Get down! Get back!"

"GOD GAVE POWER TO THE PROPHETS..." Nico shouts, his rumbling voice drowned out by all the screaming.

The camera jerks in every direction, panning past the fans in the stands. Spectators run in every direction. And by the time the

113

camera fights its way back to focus, Nico is being pulled backward, lost in instant chaos as he's clawed to the ground by a swarm of Secret Service agents. In the background, two aides go down, the victims of stray bullets. One of them lies facedown holding his cheek. Luckily, the President and his wife get rushed into their limo and escape unharmed. It wasn't until later that Nico tracked them down and killed the First Lady.

In the corner of YouTube, I spot the viewcount on the bottom right: *14,727,216 views.*

It seems like a lot.

But in truth, fourteen million viewers are meaningless.

All that matters is this single one.

"Please don't look at me like that, Beecher. I can do this," she insists, even though I haven't said a word.

I don't care how strong she's pretending to be. I saw the way, even though she knew those gunshots were coming, she flinched at each pop. And the way, ever since Nico appeared onscreen, she still won't look at the monitor.

She knows what's waiting for her.

But she also knows there's no avoiding it.

"You're telling me if it were your dad, you wouldn't go see him now?" she asks.

I stay silent, thinking back to my first year at the Archives. My dad died at the age of twenty-six, in a stupid car accident on his way to enlist for the first Gulf War. He didn't get killed fighting for his country. He didn't die a hero. He didn't even die from friendly fire. Those people are given medals. But the grunts who aren't even grunts yet because they're driving to the recruiting office when some nutbag crashes into him on a bridge and kills everyone on impact? They die as nobodies. Their lives are half-lived. And during my first year here, I spent every single lunch hour going through old army records, trying to figure out which platoon he would've been in, and what kind of adventures he would've had if he'd made it to the enlistment office.

"If you want, I can go with you," I finally say.

"What?"

"To St. Elizabeths. I can go with you. Y'know...if you want."

I wait for her to smile. To say thanks. Instead, she shakes her head. "You can't."

"Sure I can."

"You don't understand."

"Actually..."

"I *know* your dad's dead, Benjy," she says, using the nickname only my mom uses. "You think I don't remember that? When we were little, you not having a father...You have any idea what that meant to me? How *not alone* that made me feel?"

The balloon in my throat expands, catching me off guard.

"But to have this chance right now..." She stares down at the old photo—the one of us—still refusing to face the video behind her. "My mom used to tell me that the best part of music—even as a DJ—was that when you go to a new city, you get to be a brand-new person," she adds. "And I chose Virginia because—all the pictures seemed to have horses in them. Horses are calming, y'know? But then to find out—of all the places I could've picked—I'm ten minutes from...from *him*," she says, thumbing back at the screen as Nico's video wraps up. "I'm not saying it's a sign—but I am saying...maybe some things are meant to be. Like reconnecting with you." Before I can say a word, she adds, "Besides, I want what's best for you, Beecher. And right now, bringing you to meet a delusional sociopath—even one who's been calmed down by medication—is not what your life needs at this moment. This is something I think I'm supposed to do myself."

"I understand."

"You *do*?" she asks.

"Don't you get it? I want what's best for you too."

She looks up at me and grins. "That homemade photograph really made you mushy, didn't it?" she asks.

"Hey, Beecher! *Phone!*" one of the staffers calls out from the desk behind us.

"Whoever it is, tell them—"

"It's Tot. Says not to let you give any lame excuses. Says it's important. He's on hold."

I shake my head, ready to ignore the call.

"He says don't ignore it!" the aide calls back. "On hold!"

"Just gimme one sec," I tell Clementine as I grab the phone at the circulation desk, which is just a few feet away.

"What're you doing with her?" Tot asks before I can even say hello.

"Pardon?"

"Clementine. You went down to buzz her in. That was twenty minutes ago."

I look over at Clementine, who's finally turned back to the computer screen, where YouTube has offered a variety of recommendations for the next video to click on. Even from here, I can see what she's looking at as bits of bright yellow jumpsuit peek out from each video option.

"Is this really that important, Tot?"

"You tell me. I found the cart for your guy Dustin Gyrich," he says, referring to the last person who requested a copy of *Entick's Dictionary*. "Now, do you want to hear his connection to the President or not?"

24

I 'll call you when I'm done," Clementine says, stepping away from the computer and heading for the lobby. "I gotta go."

"Good. Let her," Tot says through the phone.

"Clemmi, just wait!" I call out as she pulls her coat on.

"Let her be," Tot says. "Whatever she's got going on, you've got enough disasters to deal with."

"What're you talking about?" I ask.

"I told you. Dustin Gyrich."

"So he's the last person to request the…" I look around, and I swear, in this wide mint green room, every person, from the old ladies to the young grad student, is looking directly at me.

"Yeah…to request the dictionary," Tot says in my ear. "That's the thing, though. At first I thought it was odd that he just happened to request the dictionary on the exact same day that President Wallace was here for his reading tour. But when I pulled the full record, well…Dustin Gyrich—whoever he is—has requested *Entick's Dictionary* fourteen different times, which isn't that unusual—"

"Get to the point, Tot."

"The point is, when I matched Gyrich's dates up with a calendar, guess who else happened to be visiting this very building on every one of those days? I'll give you a hint. It rhymes with *President*."

Across from me, Clementine buttons the top button on her coat and turns toward the main lobby to leave.

"Just wait," I whisper to her. "I'll only be a minute."

"You'll be way more than a minute," Tot says through the phone. "Unless you're no longer understanding the bad news I'm delivering."

"Thirty seconds," I promise Clementine.

She pauses a moment, like she really does want to wait. But as she did when the red curtain went up during the Battle of the Bands, Clementine stands there a moment, lifts her chin, and buries all her fears in whatever place she's come to keep them. The difference is, she's no longer facing testy tenth graders. She's facing her father. The destroyer.

"I'll be okay," she insists, even though I didn't ask her. Her eyes blink quicker than usual, just like when she flinched at those gunshots. Before I can argue, she's headed down the hallway, past the security desk, and through the automatic doors that take her outside into the cold. I look down at the homemade photograph of our younger selves. It's the second time in two days that I realize I'm seeing the soft side of her no one else knows. The part she shares with no one. Ever since Iris . . . I forgot how good a simple crush can feel.

But it's not just the crush. There are some people in your life who bring back old memories. And there are others—your first kiss, your first love, your first sex—who, the moment you see them, bring a spark . . . and something far more potent. They bring back your old life and, with that, potential. And possibilities. And the feeling that if you were back in that time, life could be so very different from where you're stuck right now. That's the most tantalizing thing Clementine offers. I want my potential back.

"You hearing me, Beecher?" Tot shouts in my ear. "Over the past four months, every single time the President of the United States has come to this building, this guy Gyrich takes *this* copy of the dictionary—"

"Wait, wait, wait. I thought we weren't sure if the copy we found in the"—I lower my voice—"*in the SCIF* was the same one from our collection."

"And for the second time, are you hearing me? Where do you think I've been for the past half hour? I went down and pulled Gyrich's cart. He's got twelve items on hold here, but—what a coincidence—there's only eleven on the cart. So guess which one's missing? That's right—one copy of *Entick's Dictionary*."

"I don't know, does that really tell us that the Archives copy is the same as the beat-up one we have?" I ask, still watching through the glass of the automatic doors. Out by the curb, Clementine hails herself a cab. "The one we found doesn't have identifying information, or a stamp, or even most of its own pages," I say. "Would the Archives really keep something that beat up and let it get checked out over and over again?"

"That's fine—and we can look into that," Tot agrees. "But it doesn't change the fact that fourteen weeks in a row, every time President Wallace comes here to visit—every single time—Gyrich requests the dictionary, puts it on hold, and makes sure it's out of general circulation. When it happens two times, that's dumb luck. Three times? That's a very weird fluke. But fourteen times in fourteen weeks?" His voice goes quiet. "That's a plan."

He's right. He's always right. But as I watch Clementine duck into her cab, there's a surprising new feeling tugging at my ribcage.

Since the moment I saw her yesterday, I've been looking at Clementine through the sparkly prism of exhilaration that comes with any old flame. But now, for the first time, I'm not just seeing what I want. I'm seeing what my friend needs.

The door to the taxi slams shut.

"Tot, I need to borrow your car."

"My car is nice. You're not taking it anywhere. And what're you talking about anyway?"

"I need to run an errand."

"No, you need to get up here so we can find this guy Gyrich and figure out what's really going on."

"And I will. Right after this errand."

I hear nothing but silence through the phone. "This is the part where you're being stupid again, Beecher. And inconsiderate, considering how much of my time you're wasting while you chase some girl."

"I'm not chasing a girl."

"So you're not going to St. Elizabeths?" he challenges.

I pause, thinking of the perfect lie. "Okay, fine. I'm going to St. Elizabeths. It's not far from here."

BRAD MELTZER

"Beecher…"

"You're forgetting, Tot. You're forgetting that there were three of us in that room. She was there with me—so if my life's at risk, her life's at risk too."

"You don't know that."

"I *absolutely* know that—and the last time we let someone who was in that room out of our sight, Orlando showed up dead. Besides, aren't you the one who said I should keep an eye on her…that it was too much of a coincidence that she showed up and all this went down? This is my chance to see what's really going on. And more important than any of that, she's about to step into what's probably the single roughest moment of her life. How do I let her do that alone?"

Once again, the phone goes silent. It's the last part that's getting to him. When Tot's wife died, he learned exactly what it feels like to face his worst moment by himself.

"That mean I can have the car?" I ask.

"Yes," he sighs. "Let's all be stupid."

Twenty-four minutes and fourteen seconds later, I twist the steering wheel of the powder blue 1966 Mustang into a sharp right and pull up to the small guardhouse that sits just inside the black metal gates.

"Welcome to St. Elizabeths," a guard with winter-grizzled lips says as he turns down the *Elliot in the Morning* show on his radio. Clearly, this guy's a genius. "Visitor or delivery?"

"Actually, a pickup," I tell him.

25

Every barber has one haircut he'll never forget.

For many, it's the first good one they give. Not the first *haircut* they give, but the first *good* one, where they realize just how much they can improve someone's looks with a few flicks of a scissors.

For others, it's at the end of their career, where they realize they don't have the steady hand that had served them for so long.

For a few, it's that moment when a particularly famous person sits down in their chair.

But for master barber Andre Laurent, a tall, hefty silver-haired black man with a just as silver mustache, the one that stayed with him was back in Ohio, back in the early eighties, when he was cutting the hair of that blond man with the odd cowlick, who always used to bring his eight-year-old son with him. In the midst of the cut, the door to the shop burst open and a young brunette with pointy breasts stormed in, nearly shattering the glass as the door slammed into the wall.

"You didn't tell me you were married!" she screamed at the man with the cowlick. But all Laurent saw were the big ash-gray eyes of Cowlick's son, watching his dad and slowly, right there, trying to put it all together.

Back then, their small Ohio town would've feasted on gossip like that. Especially when the dad left his family behind a few years later. Especially as the ash-eyed boy grew older. Especially when he became the youngest state senator in Ohio history. Especially when he reached the governor's mansion. And even more especially when he made that run for the White House and nearly every reporter in the country came to Journey, Ohio, to see the small-town barber-shop where Orson Wallace still got his hair cut on a biweekly basis.

To this day, Andre Laurent had never said a word. Like his father and grandfather—both barbers and both midwestern gentlemen—he never would.

"Mr. Laurent, I got a walk-in for you," the appointment girl with the squeaky voice called out from the front of the shop.

"Send him back," Laurent replied, brushing a few stray hairs from the barber chair's headrest.

For forty-three years, Laurent had barbered at the same place his father and grandfather learned their trade. It was called, obviously enough, Laurent's.

Three years ago, he had moved to Washington, D.C., taking a chair at a place called Wall's Barber Shop. He liked that Wall's still had its original stainless steel barber chairs. He liked that there was a working red, white, and blue barber pole outside. But he especially liked that, on 15th Street, it was walking distance from the White House.

"Shoeshine while we got you in the chair?" Shoeshine Gary called out to Laurent's client.

"*No,*" the client said without looking at him.

When Barack Obama was first elected President, one of the very first things he said to the press was that if he could no longer go to his barber, his barber would have to come to him.

What a good idea, President Orson Wallace thought.

Finding a good barber was tough.

Finding someone you trust was even tougher.

That was the start of it. Once every two weeks, Laurent would trek to the White House to cut the President's hair. And sometimes, if there was a real emergency—especially over the past few weeks—the White House would come to him.

"What can I do to you?" Laurent asked as his client sat in the barber chair. "Shave or haircut?"

"How about both?" Dr. Stewart Palmiotti replied, leaning forward and tossing the fat hardcover book he was carrying onto the glass shelf that sat just below the mirror. "I think we're gonna need the extra time."

"As you wish," the President's barber said, reaching for a hot towel as the President's doctor tilted his head back.

Every barber has one haircut he'll never forget.

And some barbers have more than one.

26

The cobblestone Italian street was still damp from the overnight rain, and as the small, slender man stood there, he enjoyed the reflective view it created on Via Panisperna. *Like a whole different universe*, he thought, taking in the upside-down view of Sant'Agata dei Goti, the fifth-century church that now appeared—like magic—below his feet.

He'd been standing by the side door waiting for a while now, but he wasn't worried. In all their time coming here, she'd never stood him up. He knew she wouldn't start now. Not with what was about to happen.

"You look nervous," Lenore called out as she turned the corner and marched up the bumpy stone driveway.

"Not nervous," the man said. "Excited."

"You don't look excited. You look nervous."

The man smiled to himself, knowing better than to argue with Lenore, a woman well trained, from Princeton all the way up to the White House, in the fine art of arguing.

"If I weren't a little nervous, I'd be insane," the man said with a laugh.

Shoving hard on the carved wooden double doors, he pushed his way inside and winced as the hinges shrieked. But there was something instantly calming about being back here, especially that smell: the damp wood and the rosewater candles.

"The smell reminds you of your mother, doesn't it?" Lenore asked.

Ignoring the question—and the slamming doors behind him—the slender man headed straight for the source of the smell, the ancient iron rack filled with the white rose prayer candles.

"She had that smell on her when you were little," Lenore contin-ued. *"When you went to church in Wisconsin."*

The man couldn't help but smile. In this world, there was noth-ing scarier than trusting someone. But there was also nothing more rewarding.

"They were good memories," he said as he picked up an unlit candle, dipped it into the flame, and whispered a silent prayer for his mother. Two years ago, for a prayer like this, he would've bobbed his head sixteen times before saying amen. He would've pulled out two eyelashes, setting them perpendicular in his palm until they formed a miniature cross. But today, as he looked up toward the intricate stained glass window... Nico Hadrian was better.

And so was former First Lady Lenore Manning.

Even though she'd been dead for two years now.

"Nico, let's go—they want you in the day room," the tall orderly with the sweet onion breath called out.

Peering over his shoulder, Nico looked across his small bare room at St. Elizabeths Hospital. He looked past his single bed and the painted dresser that held his Bible and the Washington Red-skins calendar. Italy was gone, and there was no one there except for Sweet Onion Breath.

"Please tell me you're not talking to no imaginary friends," the orderly pleaded. "You do, I gotta report it, Nico."

Nico cranked his small smile into a kind, wider one. He'd made the mistake of honesty once. He wouldn't make it again. "You know I don't do that anymore."

He was mostly right. After his escape and capture, when he was finally returned to St. Elizabeths, it took Nico four months before he stopped picking off his own fingernails, determined to punish himself for what he'd done. To be manipulated like that—to be so lost in the religious spirit—to kill in the name of God. By now, the doctors were thrilled with his progress. They gave him mail privi-leges, even access to the grounds. For the past two years, Nico had fought back to his own level of normalcy. Yes, he was better. But that didn't mean he was cured.

Turning toward the one window in his room, Nico watched calmly, patiently, as the single bed, wooden nightstand, and painted dresser were replaced by the ancient iron rack of white rose candles, and the wide shatterproof window turned back into the beautiful stained glass window of the church Sant'Agata dei Goti, the church dedicated to Saint Agatha, who never—even when the torturers severed her breast—ever renounced her faith.

"You don't look nervous anymore," the First Lady said.

"I think I'm excited. Yes. I'm very excited," Nico whispered to himself.

"C'mon, Nico—you have a visitor," the orderly called out as the church again faded and the hospital returned.

"No. I have more than just a visitor," Nico insisted as he headed for the day room. God always provided. "I have Clementine."

27

When I was in tenth grade, there was a kid in our class—Weird Warren—who used to be able to bend down his ear, and keep it down, so he'd look like an elf. Most of my classmates did their usual teasing, knighting him with the nickname. But Clementine—she said it so nicely I'll never forget it—she asked him if he could grant her three wishes.

Pounding the faded red button with the heel of his palm, the St. Elizabeths guard raises the gate arm, allowing me to drive past the guardhouse. I told him I was here to pick up records for the Archives. With my government ID, it was enough to send me toward the main security check-in and onto the property, a 350-acre piece of land that's encased by a ring of tall black metal gates.

As I head up the hospital's poorly plowed road and scan the parking lot that sits across from the main five-story brick building, Clementine's cab is long gone. She's inside, probably already with Nico. I have no idea what her three wishes would be today. But if I had the chance to get even two minutes with my dead dad, I know what at least one of my wishes would be.

As I kick open the car door in the parking lot, a blast of winter air stings my face, but before I get out I reach down and pull out the copy of *Entick's Dictionary* that's tucked underneath the driver's seat. Tot's idea. Based on this morning, Khazei isn't just asking questions anymore—he's circling for a kill. I still can't tell if what he really wants is the book or me, but either way, the last thing we need is to have this lying around the building. Still, that doesn't mean I can just leave it in the car.

For a moment, I think about hiding it in my briefcase, but if I do that, I risk security here rummaging through it. No. If this book is as important as we think it is—if Orlando really died for it—I need to keep it close.

Stepping outside and heading across to the building, I tuck the book under the back of my jacket and carefully slide it into the back of my slacks. It fits—with most of the pages gone, it's just the covers. I take a fast glance over my shoulder to make sure I'm alone. But as I look up, standing on one of the second-floor balconies is a pale bald man with no eyebrows.

I strain a smile, even as I pick up my pace.

He glares down. But his expression never changes. I don't think he even sees I'm here.

For a moment, I think about just waiting out here for her. But I don't slow down.

As I finally reach the front, the doorknob gives with barely a twist. The cold has definitely eased up, but a pitiless chill climbs my spine. According to Clemmi, this is the mental hospital that holds not just Nico, but also John Hinckley, the man who shot Ronald Reagan. Why the hell's the front door unlocked?

I push the door inward, revealing a 1950s waiting room decorated in a pale drab green. Straight ahead, a thin guard who looks like David Bowie circa 1983 sits at an X-ray and metal detector also stolen from the same era.

"C'mon in—only about half our patients bite," a woman's voice calls out. She laughs a silly puffy laugh that's supposed to put me at ease. On my left, standing inside a thick glass booth, is a second guard—a female guard with a bad Dutch-boy haircut and great dimples.

"You must be Mr. White, correct?" She got my name from when I checked in at the guardhouse. "Relax, Mr. White. They keep the doors unlocked so that the patients feel they have more freedom. But not that much freedom," she says with the puffy laugh, pointing at a thick steel door that looks like a bank vault: the real door to get inside.

"Um . . . great," I blurt, not knowing what else to say.

"So how can we help you, Mr. White?" she asks as I realize she's one of those people who says your name over and over until you want to eat poison.

"Actually, it's Beecher. I'm here from the National Archives. Anyhow, we were thinking of doing an exhibit on the history of St. Elizabeths—when it was run by the government and founded to help the insane . . . then converted in the Civil War to help wounded soldiers . . . It's just a great part of American history—"

"Just tell me what time your appointment is and who it's with."

"That's the thing," I tell the woman behind the glass. "They told me to come over and that I should take a quick tour of the campus."

"That's fine, Beecher. I still need a name to call first."

"I think it was someone in Public Affairs."

"Was it Francine?"

"It might've been—it was definitely a woman," I bluff.

She lowers her chin, studying me through the fingerprint-covered glass.

"Something wrong?" I ask.

"You tell me, Beecher—you have no appointment and no contact name. Now you know the population we're trying to help here. So why don't you go back to the Archives and set up your meeting properly?"

"Can't you just call the—?"

"There is no call. No appointment, no call."

"But if you—"

"We're done. Good day," she insists, tightening both her jaw and her glare.

I blink once at her, then once at David Bowie. But as I turn to leave . . .

The steel door that leads upstairs opens with a *tunk*.

"—sure it's okay to go out here?" Clementine asks as she walks tentatively behind a man with salt-and-pepper buzzed hair and chocolate brown eyes that seem too close together. At first, the gray in his hair throws me off—but that bulbous nose and the arched thin eyebrows . . . God, he looks just like the video on YouTube.

Nico. And Clementine.

Heading right for me.

*　　*　　*

28

Mr. Laurent, your next appointment's here," the girl called out from the front of Wall's Barber Shop, a long narrow shop that held seven barber chairs, all in a single row, with Shoeshine Gary up near the front door and local favorite James Davenport cutting hair in chair one.

Laurent glanced at her from the very last chair in the back, but never lost focus on his current—most vital—client.

"I should get back. It's late," Dr. Palmiotti said from the barber chair.

"Don't you go nowhere. Two more minutes," Laurent said, pressing the electric razor to the back of Dr. Palmiotti's neck. *Cleaning out the tater patch*—that's what Laurent's grandfather used to call cleaning the hair on the neck. The very last part of the job.

"So your brother..." Laurent added, well aware that Palmiotti didn't have a brother. "If he needs help, maybe you should get it for him?"

"I don't know," Palmiotti replied, his chin pressed down against his chest. "He's not that good with help."

Laurent nodded. That was always President Wallace's problem.

This close to the White House, nearly every business had at least a few hanging photographs of local politicians who'd helped them over time. Since 1967, Wall's Barber Shop had none. Zero. Not even the one from *Newsweek*, of Laurent cutting President Wallace's hair right before the Inauguration. According to the current owner, in the cutthroat world of politics, he didn't want to look like he was taking one side over the other. But to Laurent, the blank walls were the cold reminder that in Washington, D.C., when it all went sour, the only person you could really count on was yourself.

"Just be sure to say hello for me," Laurent said, finishing up on the doctor's neck. "Tell him he's in my prayers."

"He knows that. You know he knows that," Palmiotti said, trying hard to not look uncomfortable.

Laurent wasn't surprised. Like most doctors, Palmiotti always had a tough time with faith. Fortunately, he had an easy time with friendship.

With a tug at his own neck, the doctor unsnapped the red, white, and blue barber's apron and hopped out of the chair in such a rush, he didn't even stop to check his haircut in the mirror. "You're a magician, Laurent. See you soon!"

But as Palmiotti was paying the cashier, Laurent looked over and noticed the hardcover book with the bright red writing—*A Problem from Hell*—that was still sitting on the shelf below the mirror.

Palmiotti was at the cashier. There was still time to return it to him.

Instead, Laurent opened the drawer that held his spare scissors, slid the book inside, and didn't say a word.

As usual.

29

ou're anxious," Nico says to Clementine as he leads her past me and heads for the door that'll take them outside. Clementine nearly falls over when she sees me, but to her credit, she doesn't stop. Just shoots me a look to say, *What're you doing here?*

I turn back to the glass guard booth, pretending to sign in.

If I remember my history—and I always remember my history—when Nico took his shots at the President, he said it was because of some supposed ancient plan that the Founding Fathers and the Freemasons had hatched to take over the world.

Exactly.

He's crazy enough. He doesn't need to be more crazy by me confronting or riling him.

"There's no need to be nervous," Nico continues, reading Clementine's discomfort.

He shoves open the front door and steps out into the cold. As the door slams behind them, it's like a thunderclap in the silent room.

"Th-That was— You let him walk out the door!"

"...and he'll walk right back in after his visitor leaves," says the guard behind the glass. "Our goal is curing them, not punishing them. Nico earned his ground privileges just like anyone else."

"But he's—"

"He's been incident-free for years now—moved out of maximum security and into medium. Besides, this isn't a prison—it's a hospital. A hospital that's there to help him, not punish him. You gotta let a man walk outside," she explains. "And even so, we got guards—and a fence that's too high to hop. We see him. Every day, he does

132

custodial work in the RMB Building, then feeds the cats there. By the way, Beecher, they still got that copy of the Magna Carta at the Archives? That stuff is cool."

"Yeah...of course," I say as I try to walk as casually as possible to the door.

The guard says something else, but I'm already outside, searching left and right, scanning the main road that runs across the property. In the distance, there's a guard walking the perimeter of the black metal gates that surround the hospital's snow-covered grounds. Ahead and down to the right, the concrete walkway looks like a squiggle from a black magic marker that slices through the snow. The plowed path is lined with trees and holds so many benches, it's clearly for strolling patients.

Nico's at least four steps in front of her, his left arm flat at his side, his right clutching a brown paper supermarket bag. He walks like Clementine used to: fearlessly forward as he follows the thin pedestrian path. Behind him, whatever confidence Clementine had—the woman who plowed just as fearlessly into the President's SCIF—that Clementine is once again gone. From the stutter in her steps...the way she hesitates, not sure whether she really wants to keep up...I don't care how far people come in life—or how much you prepare for this moment. You see your father, and you're instantly a child again.

As they step out onto the pathway, I stick by the entryway of the building, making sure there's at least half a football field between us. But as I take my first step out and my foot crunches against some thick chunks of snow salt, I swear on my life, Nico flinches.

He never turns. He doesn't glance over his shoulder to investigate. But I remember the news footage—how he has hearing and eyesight more acute than the rest of us. That's why the military first recruited him for sniper school.

I stop midstep.

Nico keeps going, marching his purposeful march, clutching the brown bag, and glancing just slightly to make sure the clearly uncomfortable Clementine is still behind him.

Leaving the entryway, I take it slow, always careful to use the nearby trees for cover. On my far left, the guard is still patrolling the gates. As I reach the beginning of the path, he spots them too.

It's not hard to see where he's leading her. The thin black path curves downhill toward another 1960s-era brick building. Throughout the wide campus, it's the only thing that's plowed. Even I get the message: This path is the one place patients are allowed to walk.

The farther they get, the more they shrink. I still can't tell if they're talking, but as they finally reach the front of the building, I'm all set to follow. To my surprise though, instead of going inside, Nico points Clementine to the wooden benches out front.

Taking the seat next to her, Nico puts the brown bag between them. Even from here, I can see Clementine scootch back, away from the bag. Whatever he's got in there . . . my brain can't help but imagine the worst.

That's when the cats start arriving.

A gray tabby races out of the building, followed by a chubby black one. Then two small matching orange kittens, followed by what must be their mom. There're half a dozen cats in total, all of them heading for the exact same spot: straight to the bench. Straight to Nico.

On my far left, the guard is still down by the perimeter fence, but he hasn't moved much. This is clearly Nico's routine. From the brown bag, Nico sprinkles the ground with whatever food he has inside. *Feeding the cats.* The woman behind the glass said it's one of his jobs. But the way Nico leans down to pet them—scratching tummies, necks, between ears, like he knows each of their soft spots—he isn't just feeding these cats.

He loves them.

And the way they rub against Nico, weaving infinity loops around his legs, they love him right back.

Sitting up straight and settling into his stiff, alien posture, Nico won't look at anything but the cats. I can't read lips, but I can read body language. Fidgeting next to him, Clementine looks even more

134

awkward than he is, and from her hand movements—she scratches her wrist, then her neck, like there's something living beneath her own skin. Back at the Archives, she couldn't even look at Nico in the old assassination video. It's only worse here. No matter how ready she thought she was, she's not ready for this. Until...

He suddenly rises from his seat, standing erect.

The cats startle at the sudden movement, then settle back around his feet. Before Clementine can react, Nico looks at his watch and starts walking to the far side of the building. He's calm as ever. He makes a quick hand motion, asking Clementine to follow.

No, don't go with him—!

She pauses, searching around. She's definitely smarter than that. She needs to be—she knows who she's dealing with. But she can't help herself. A few cats trail him like the Pied Piper. A few others, including two tuxedo cats—black, with white bib and feet—start to groom themselves, then walk away, aloof. Clementine needs to decide which cat she'll be.

It doesn't take long. She's wondered about this man for nearly thirty years. She takes a few hesitant steps...then scratches the back of her neck...then follows.

Nico turns the corner and...

They're both gone.

I give them a moment to come back. Thirty seconds to see if they return.

Still gone.

There's no reason to break the emergency glass. Maybe he's just getting more cat food.

I search for the guard back by the fence. He's gone too.

I look around, but there's no one else. I can run back to the main building, but by the time I get there, God knows where Nico will be. More important, if something happened to Clemmi, it'd be my fault.

Tot called history a selection process that hands us situations we should never be able to overcome.

He's right. I can't overcome this. Nico's a trained monster. A killer. A destroyer.

I can't do this.

I can't.

But I have to try.

Running full speed, I race down the concrete path. With each step, my feet slap the pavement, splattering puddles of slush.

As I pass the front of the building, I spot the blur of my own profile in the reflection of the glass doors. The tuxedo cats are milling around, looking bored as they ignore me. I even see Nico's and Clementine's footsteps where the snow isn't melted yet. They can't be far.

At the corner of the building, I make a sharp left and . . .

Nothing.

A long alley of browning snow, a rusted Dumpster, and just beyond the Dumpster, an empty golf cart that—

Mrrow.

Cat. That's one of the cats.

I crane my neck.

There. In the back. The tabby one.

I'm already halfway there as its tail disappears around the back of the building. As I fly past the Dumpster—

Pfuump.

A thick forearm rams my neck, hitting like a baseball bat and clotheslining me so hard, my feet leave the ground.

Keeping his forearm at my throat, Nico shoves me backward by my neck until I crash—hard—onto the freezing concrete. The back of my head hits first, and a flash of bright stars blinds me on impact.

"What're you doing!? Are you crazy!?" Clementine shouts at Nico.

Her father smiles, heading toward me.

Before I can register anything, Nico's all over me.

*　　*　　*

30

Wasting no time, Nico climbs on my stomach, my chest, his baseball-bat forearm now pressing like a nightstick against my neck. His breath smells like cigarettes and old coins. I try to breathe, but he's ... *huuuh* ... *huuuh* ... he's on my windpipe ... I scream for the guards, but no one knows we're here.

"I heard you," he says, completely calm as his chocolate eyes rattle back and forth, picking apart my face. "In the entryway. I hear things better than you."

"G-Get off him!" Clementine shouts, racing out from where he shoved her behind the Dumpster. She plows toward him, ready to push him away.

"Do. *Not,*" Nico says, whipping around and grabbing her wrist with one hand, while holding my throat with the other. I've never seen anything move so fast.

Clementine thrashes, fighting to get free. No. She's not fighting. She just wants him off her. Stumbling backward, her face goes gray and ashen like she's about to throw up. Back at the Archives, I remember what the *pop, pop, pop* of the gunshots did to her. She could barely deal with that. She certainly can't deal with this.

As she finally breaks free, Clementine falls on her ass. It shifts Nico just enough that he lets go of my throat as my lungs lurch for air.

"Huuuh ... hgggh ..."

He watches my face ... studies my eyes as I look to Clementine ...

No. I shouldn't look at her.

Too late.

Glancing to his left, he studies Clementine, then turns back to me.

"You know him," he says to Clementine, who's still on her rear, crabwalking and scrambling to get away. "You brought him here."

"I-I didn't," she insists. "I swear to—"

"God's name. Don't take it in vain," Nico warns, his voice just a whisper.

I wait for her to say something, but from the panic in her eyes... She can't. She's done. There's no reconnecting with this man. All she wants is out of here.

Nico turns, like a dog spotting a squirrel. His chest rises and falls so quickly. He hears something.

"*Nico...?*" a sharp voice calls from the distance. We can't see who it is, but the way Nico turns...Whoever's coming...It's a guard.

Clementine crabwalks back even farther. With a leap, Nico climbs to his feet and I get my first clear breath.

"*Nico, get yer ass outta there!*" a man shouts in a deep southern accent.

I stumble to my feet just as a black guard with small shoulders turns the corner.

"What the hell you doing?" the guard asks.

Nico's eyes roll toward him, unafraid. "We were feeding the cats."

The guard shoots Nico a look that says, *Do I look stupid to you?* Then he shoots us a look that says, *Why'd you let him take you back there?*

"Public spaces only. You know that," the guard growls.

"We'll just be a minute," Nico says, gripping Clementine's shoulder as she rises to her feet.

"Nico, hands off her. You okay there, miss?" the guard asks.

"We're coming up front. To feed the cats," Nico replies. "The tabby still hasn't eaten."

"Nico, I am *not* in the mood for your freakiness right now. Shut your face," the guard says. "Miss, you okay or not?"

THE INNER CIRCLE

Clementine stiffens. I know she wants to run...to scream...to get away from here, but the last thing she needs is Nico freaking.

"We're coming to the front. To feed the cats," she repeats, her voice barely working.

Looking at all three of us, the guard studies us, especially Nico. "Public spaces. Everyone. Now!"

Nico doesn't move. But as Clementine takes off, he falls in behind her. Right next to me.

"You came here to protect her," Nico whispers to me. "To make sure she was okay."

I don't answer.

"You like her," Nico adds, calm as ever as we follow the guard out of the alley, toward the front of the building. "I see the way you study her. Is that why you brought a gun with you? To keep her safe?"

Clementine looks back at me. Just like Nico.

"A gun?" I ask. "I don't have a gun."

"I can see it," Nico says, never raising his voice. It's like he's part robot. "I can see it tucked under your jacket. In the back."

Patting myself around the waist, I quickly realize what he's talking about. The book. The dictionary. The way it props my jacket up in the back of my pants.

"No—okay—*look*, it's just— It's a book," I tell him, taking out the thin, gutted dictionary and showing it to him. "Just a book."

But as I hold it out between us, Nico freezes.

"You wanna feed your cats, feed 'em here," the guard calls out, pointing us back to the wooden benches in front of the building. No longer trusting Nico, the guard heads toward the building and stands in front of the doors, about fifty feet from us. This time, he's not letting us go far.

Clementine heads back toward the main path. She can't get out of here fast enough.

Still focused on the book, Nico's eyes squeeze into two angry slits. "Why do you have that?" he asks.

"Have what? The book?"

139

"Why do you have it!?" Nico growls. "Tell me why you brought it here."

"Just calm down," I say, glancing over at the guard.

Following my eye, Nico turns to the guard, then sits down on the bench, swallowing every bit of rising anger. However long he's been in here, he knows the consequences of losing his cool.

"Is this a test?" he asks. "Is that it? It's a test for me?"

"I don't know what you're talking about," I tell him, offering him a quick goodbye as I follow after Clementine. "I work in the Archives, and I found this book, so I—"

"*You* found the book?" Nico interrupts.

I freeze, confused.

Clementine keeps walking.

Nico's eyes go wide, his cheeks flushed with excitement. "Of course you found it. Of course," he says. "Why else would you be here?"

"Hold on. You *know* this book?" I challenge.

"Don't you see? That's why she found me," Nico says, motioning to his daughter.

Clementine stops, utterly confused—and for the first time, looks directly at Nico.

"And that's why *you* followed," Nico says, pointing to me. "God knows how I was misled. But God provides..."

"Nico, you're not making sense," I say.

"The book. To bring that book," Nico insists. "The Lord knows my belief is just in Him. I'm no longer fooled by ancient stories of devil worship or secret cults or—or—or— This isn't— This has nothing to do with me. It's not a test for *me*," Nico insists, his voice picking up speed. He points at my chest. "It's a test for *you*!"

I glance over my shoulder. To the guard, it just looks like we're talking.

"What kind of test?" Clementine asks, hesitantly walking toward us.

"This dictionary. *Entick's Dictionary*," Nico says, now locked just on me. "You work in the Archives. That's why you smell of wet books. Don't you know your history? This was the book George Washington used."

"Time out. You *do* know this book?" I ask again.

"It's the one Washington used. To test the loyalties."

"The loyalties of what?"

Stretching his long spider legs out, Nico creeps off the bench, stands up straight, and kicks his shoulders back. "What else?" he asks, eyeing the guard and smiling. "For the Culper Ring."

31

ay again?" Clementine stutters.

"The Culper Ring," Nico says. "When George Washington was—" He cuts himself off, but this time doesn't look back at the guard. He looks at me. His eyes flick back and forth. "You of all people . . . You know who they are, don't you?"

"Me? Why should I know?" I ask.

He studies my face. Like he's looking for something no one else can see. "To work in the Archives . . . You know. I know you know."

This time I don't respond.

"Is he right? Beecher, please . . . say something," Clementine pleads, more unnerved than ever. "You know, don't you? You know what this Culper Ring is."

"Not what. *Who*," Nico says. "The strength was in the *who*. That's why they saved us," he explains. "Back during the Revolutionary War, the British were slaughtering us. Not just physically. Mentally too. War is mental."

War's not the only thing mental, I think to myself.

"If you know, please . . . why're you not saying anything?" Clementine asks, looking just at me and making me realize just how unsettling—and unlikely—all these coincidences are to her.

"*I don't know*," I insist.

"You just said—"

"I've heard of them. I work in Old Military—of course I've heard of them—but all I know are the basics: They were George Washington's private spy group. He personally put the group together."

"You know why he brought them together," Nico challenges.

142

"Why are you so fearful to show your knowledge? Is it her? Or are you uncomfortable around me?"

I again stay silent. Clementine knows *he's* the one I'm worried about. Indeed, my mind tracks back to the crazy Freemason/Founding Fathers conspiracy that caused Nico to shoot the President all those years ago. Nico was convinced Thomas Jefferson and the other Founders were trying to rule the world, and it was his job to save us.

The guy's got a PhD in crackpot history, so the last thing I need is to add another gallon of crazy to his tank. The problem is, like before, the *real* last thing I need is to rile him for no reason. "Okay, just listen," I say. "Back during the Revolution, George Washington was frustrated that our side couldn't keep a secret—our plans kept getting intercepted by the British, since they knew who all our military spies were," I continue, glancing back at the guard, who's watching us, but seems satisfied all is under control. "And that's when Washington decided to stop relying on the military, and instead put together this group of regular civilians..."

"That's the key part," Nico says. "The Culper Ring weren't soldiers. They were normal people—a group no one could possibly know—even Washington didn't know their names. That way they could never be infiltrated—no one, not even the commander in chief, knew who was in it. But this Ring—they were regular people," he adds, standing over me as his chocolate eyes drill into mine. "Just...just like us."

I scooch back on the bench, still wondering whether he's being extra crazy because of me, or he's just permanently extra crazy. Next to me, Clementine's just as worried. She's done asking questions.

"So these guys in the Culper Ring," I say to Nico, "I still don't understand what they have to do with *Entick's Dictionary*."

"Ask yourself," Nico says, pointing to me.

"Okay, this is just silly now," I shoot back. "I have no idea what the Culper Ring did with a dictionary."

"You know," Nico says. "Deep down, you should know."

"How could I possibly—? What the hell is going on?"

"Nico, please...he's telling the truth—he doesn't know what the book is for—we don't have a clue," Clementine says, locking eyes with her father. When Nico stares back, most people can't help but look away. She stays with him.

To Nico, it matters. Her glance is as mesmerizing as his own. He nods to himself slowly, then faster.

"The book—the dictionary—that's how George Washington communicated with his Culper Ring," he finally says.

"Communicated *how*?" I ask. "There's nothing in the dictionary but empty pages."

Nico studies the guard, but not for long. "You can't see the wind, but we know it's there. Just like God. We know it's there. We feel it. Not everything can be seen so easily."

I flip the dictionary open and the only thing there is the hand-written inscription.

Exitus

Acta

Probat

The other pages—the few that haven't been torn out . . . "Everything's blank," I say.

"Of course they're blank," Nico replies, his chest rising and falling even faster. He doesn't care about the guard anymore. "This is George Washington you're trying to outsmart," he adds, now eyeing the dictionary. "He knew they'd be looking for it. That's why he always wrote it with his *medicine*."

"Medicine?"

"That was his code name for it," Nico says. "That's what he called his *invisible ink*."

*   *   *

32

Y ou don't believe me," Nico says, fine-tuning his gaze at me. "Of course you'd think like that."

"What're you talking about?" I ask. "You don't even know me."

"You're wrong. You're *very* wrong!" he growls, his chest pumping like wild.

"You got three minutes!" the guard calls out behind us, just to make sure we know he's watching. "Make them count."

Nico *psssts* at the two tuxedo cats, who continue to ignore him.

Clementine knows I'm not going anywhere. Not now. She stands there, still facing us. But she won't come closer. She's heard enough. She wants to go.

"*Tell me,*" Nico says excitedly, sitting on his own hands as he returns to the bench. "When you found that book... for you to bring it here. You of all people..."

"Why do you keep saying that?" I scold.

"Benjy!" Clementine pleads.

"*Benjy?*" Nico asks, scanning my ID that hangs around my neck. "Is that your name?"

"My name's Beecher."

His eyes recheck my ID, which lists my full name in impossibly small type. He has no problem reading it. *White, Beecher Benjamin.* He starts to laugh. A strong, breathy laugh through his gritted teeth. "It couldn't be more perfect, could it?"

He's no longer excited; now he's absolutely giddy.

"Yesyesyes. This is it, isn't it?" he asks, his head turned fully to the left. Like he's talking to someone who's not there. "This is the proof..."

"Nico..." I say.

"...this proves it, right? Now we can..."

"Nico, if you need help, I can get help for you."

"You are," he snaps. "You're helping me. Can you not see that? To follow her here...to come see me...every life...all our lives are lived for a reason."

"Nico, you said it's a test for me," I say. "Tell me why it's a test for me."

Across from us, a gray tabby cat leaps up, landing delicately on the edge of an outdoor metal garbage can. There's not a single sound from the impact.

Nico still flinches.

"That's it, Nico! Time's up!" the guard shouts, quickly approaching. "Say goodbye..."

"How do you know this book?" I challenge. "What the heck is going on?"

"I have no idea what's going on," Nico replies, calmer than ever and still sitting on his hands. "I don't know who's using that dictionary, or what they have planned. But for you to be the one who found it...such a man of books...and the name *Benjamin*...like your predecessor—"

"Wait. My predecessor? Who's my predecessor?"

Nico pauses, again turning to his left. His lips don't move, but I see him nodding. I don't know who his imaginary friend is, but I know when someone's asking permission.

"We all have souls, Benjamin. And our souls have missions. Missions that we repeat, over and over, until we conquer them."

"Y'mean like *reincarnation*?" Clementine asks, earnestly trying to understand, though she still won't take a single step toward us.

"Nico! Let's go!" the guard yells. *"Now!"*

He barely notices.

"I can see who you are, Benjamin. I can see you just like the Indian chiefs who saw George Washington as a boy. They knew who he was. They knew he was chosen. Just as I knew when I saw *you.*"

Oh, then that makes far more sense, I think to myself. "So now that we're all reincarnated, lemme guess—I'm George Washington?" I ask.

"No, no, no—not at all," Nico says. "You're the traitor."

"Nico, I'm taking mail privileges first, then the juice cart!" the guard threatens.

Nico pops from his seat and strolls toward the guard at the front of the building. But as he circles past us, he glances back over his shoulder, his voice barely a whisper. "All these years...haven't you seen the battles I've been chosen for? *I'm* George Washington," Nico insists, tapping a thumb at his own chest. "But you...I know you, boy. And I know how this ends. This is *your* test. *I'm* George Washington. And *you're* Benedict Arnold."

33

"...and now you know why they call it an *insane* asylum," I say, giving an angry yank to the steering wheel and tugging Tot's old Mustang into a sharp right out of the parking lot.

"Can we please just go?" Clementine begs.

"Benedict Arnold? He hears my middle name is *Benjamin* and suddenly I'm Benedict Arnold? He could've picked Benjamin Franklin or Benjamin Harrison. I'd even have accepted *Benjamin Kubelsky*."

"Who's Benjamin Kubelsky?"

"Jack Benny," I tell her as I pump the gas and our wheels kick spitballs of slush behind us. "But for your dad to look me in the face and say that I somehow have the soul of one of history's worst traitors—not to mention him trying to eat us..."

"Don't call him that."

"Wha?"

"*My dad*," she pleads. "Please don't call him *my dad*."

I turn at the words. As we follow the main road back toward the front gate at St. Elizabeths, Clementine stares into her side mirror, watching the hospital fade behind us. The way her arms are crossed and her legs are curled on the seat so her body forms a backward S—to anyone else, she looks pissed. But I've seen this look before. It's the same one she had back in the Archives, when she didn't think I was looking. Over the past twenty-four hours, the real Clementine keeps showing her face, reminding me that pain isn't something she works through. It's something she hides.

In my mind, I was visiting a presidential assassin. For Clementine, it was the very first time she met her father.

"Y'know, in all the dreams where I get to see my dad again," I tell her, "the reunion always goes smoothly and perfectly."

"Me too," she says, barely able to get the words out.

I nod, already feeling like an insensitive tool. I should've realized what this visit did to her, but I was too busy being spooked out with this Culper Ring and Benedict Arnold hoo-hah.

"I'm sorry for surprising you like that," I tell her.

She waves me off. That's the least of her problems.

"So what'd he say?" I ask as I turn onto the poorly plowed streets of Martin Luther King Jr. Avenue. Clementine doesn't even blink at the gang-tagged storefronts and the two burned-out cars on our right. Craning her neck to look out the back window, she still can't take her eyes off the hospital. "When you first got there, did he seem—? Was he happy to see you?"

"Beecher, we can talk about anything you want—even the Benedict Arnold stuff—but please . . . don't ask me about him."

"I hear you, Clemmi. I do. And I'm not trying to push, but for a moment, think of what just happened. I mean, no matter who he was, I would still saw my left arm off to have even thirty seconds with my father—"

"Beecher, please. Don't call him that," she begs. "Especially around him."

I pretend to stare straight ahead, focusing on the road. But the way those last words hang in the air . . .

Especially around *him*.

Clementine bends her knees, tightening her backward S and fighting to hold it together.

"You never told him, did you?" I ask.

She doesn't answer.

"He doesn't know he's your father?"

"I meant to. I was going to tell him," she finally says, still staring in the rearview. "But then . . ." She shakes her head. "Didja know he speaks to the dead First Lady? When we were there . . . that's who he was mumbling to. I read it in an article. I think he hides it from the nurses. They said he used to talk to his last victim as some desperate way to absolve himself."

I sit with that one, not sure how to respond. But there's still one piece that doesn't make sense. "If you didn't tell them you were a relative, how'd you even get in to see him?" I ask.

"Grad student. I told them I was writing a dissertation on complex psychosis," she explains.

"And they just let you in?"

"It's not up to the doctors. It's up to the patient. Don't forget, it's been a decade. Nico doesn't get too many visitors anymore. He okays whoever shows up."

"But to be that close and not tell him who you are..."

"You should be thanking me," she points out. "If I did, he probably would've called me Martha Washington."

"That's funny. I'm actually thinking about laughing at that."

"Of course you are. You're trying to get on my good side. Classic Benedict Arnold move."

I shake my head, amazed at just how much the joke burrows under my skin. "Clemmi...you know I'd never betray you."

She turns to me. A small appreciative grin lifts her cheeks. "Beecher, why're you doing this?"

"Doing what?"

"Besides these past few months of emails, I haven't spoken to you in fifteen years. You were cute in high school—in that quiet, smart, scared-of-me way—but we didn't stay much in touch. Plus at your office, you've got the head of security ready to pin you for murder. So why'd you come here? Why're you being so nice?"

Holding the wheel, I stare straight ahead, pretending to watch the road. "She was my fiancée."

"Huh?"

"Before. You asked before who Iris was, and I said she was my *girlfriend*. She was my fiancée. The one. We sent out invitations. The table seating was done. On one night with a few cheap margaritas, we even started picking baby names. And yes, there are worse things, but when it all fell apart, it felt like she strangled and killed my entire life. Everything was dead. Anyway, I figure after all the honesty you've shown me, you at least earned that back."

"So she *did* dump you for another guy?"

"Don't push. We're not being that honest yet," I say.

She stays with the rearview, her head slightly swaying back and forth, like she's whispering an imagined question to someone.

"I'm not a DJ," she finally blurts.

"What?"

"For the radio station—I'm not a DJ," Clementine says. "I sell ads. I'm just an ad sales rep. I-I thought you'd— I sell on-air ads for soft drinks, car dealerships, and in Virginia, we do a ton for places that help people addicted to chewing tobacco."

"But you told me—"

"I always wanted to be a DJ—I did it once for a few years at a community college's radio station. But for the past ten years, I'm just— I used to be a peacock; now I'm just a feather duster." Looking over at me, she adds, "I'm sorry for lying to you, Beecher. When we were first emailing, you said you had this perfect job at the National Archives, and when you asked me what I did, I wanted you to— I didn't want you to think I was a failure."

"Clementine, I'd never think—"

"And the lies just flowed, didn't they? Instead of an ad rep— shazam!—I was magically a DJ with the life I'd always dreamed for myself. And the worst part was how fast the bullshit came—flush with all the details, and all the old jazz we play, and..." She won't look at me. "I'm like *him*, aren't I? The imagined life...I'm a natural liar, Beecher. I am."

"Then I guess I shouldn't believe that either."

It's a good joke, but it doesn't help.

"I thought the worst part would be *seeing* Nico," she explains, "but the real worst part, now that I finally have—is how much of my life now sadly *makes sense*."

I'm all set to argue, but before I can say a word, my phone vibrates in my pocket. I can't ignore this one.

"Where are you?" Tot asks the moment I pick up.

"What's wrong? What happened?" I ask, knowing that tone and wondering if he found the videotape.

"Y'mean besides the fact that you're out fawning over some girl you barely know, who you're just stupidly smitten with?"

"That's not what's happening."

"Sure it's not. You've got a beautiful girl in a pristine automobile. It's not a guess, Beecher. It's science."

"Tot, can you please stop saying things that make me want to hang up on you?" I plead.

"Actually, no—especially when you hear this: Still no sign of the video, but I was able to track down your man Dustin Gyrich," he says, referring to the guy who checked out *Entick's Dictionary* every time President Wallace visited the Archives. "And, oof...it's a doozy, Beecher."

"What? He's got some kinda record?"

"Oh, he's definitely got a record," Tot explains. "I started digging backwards through our pull slips, and from what I can tell... well..." Through the phone, I hear Tot roll his tongue inside his cheek. "Dustin Gyrich has been checking out books and pulling records for over a hundred and fifty years."

34

T hey didn't believe you, did they?" the dead First Lady
asked.

Up on the third floor, standing near the edge of the
screened-in balcony, Nico watched the powder blue Mustang
squirm down the narrow paved road that led toward the guardhouse
at the front gate.

"She's watching me. I can see her," Nico announced.

"Does that matter?" the First Lady asked.

"It means she'll be back again. I know she'll be back."

*"But what you said about the boy...about Beecher...They never
believe you."*

Turning to the First Lady, he asked, "Do *you* believe me?"

*"Nico, you shot me with a bullet that sprayed my brain across the
front of my car's dashboard. You took me away from my husband and
children and grandchildren. I want to hate you with everything I have
left. But this boy Beecher—he knows who he is. We all know who we
are, even if we won't admit it. So when he comes to betray us—"*

"He may not betray us. That's his test. I have to give him his
chance."

*"A chance is fine. But if he fails, he better suffer the same punish-
ment you gave me."*

Nico nodded, turning back to the fading Mustang.

"What about the girl?" the First Lady added. *"You know who she
is, don't you?"*

"Of course," Nico replied as the car finally turned the corner.
"I may be crazy, but I'm not an idiot."

*   *   *

35

Pulling into Tot's parking spot in the basement of the Archives, I catch my breath and take a peek in the rearview. Morris the security guy thinks I don't see him as he peers down from the top of the ramp that leads outside. Like this morning, he did the full search, including the mirror sweep underneath the car. But he's not gonna find anything—including Clementine, who's no longer sitting next to me.

It was easy to drop her off half a block away. It'll be even easier to meet up inside the building. She knows where. Our Rotunda holds original copies of the Declaration of Independence, the U.S. Constitution, and the Bill of Rights. It also holds the best meeting spot for staffers to sneak their friends off the public tour and into their offices on the working side of the building—without ever having to put their names on the sign-in sheet.

It's bad enough I'm under Khazei's microscope. I'm not bringing Clementine—or her dad—there with me.

Of course, that doesn't mean I'm playing sacrificial lamb either. Beyond a good parking spot, there's one other thing waiting for me in the basement.

With the dictionary once again tucked into the back of my slacks, I throw the heavy car door open, climb outside, and stroll right under the eye of the security camera in the corner. It follows me all the way to the double doors that take me to the interior checkerboard floors of the building.

Within the Archives, most people think that basement offices—with no windows and no view—are the worst. But for one office in particular, the lack of sunlight is an absolute necessity.

There's no sign out front, no room number on the wall, and if you come at it from an angle, you can tell that the glass door, with its horizontal blinds pulled closed, is bulletproof. It needs to be. Forget the vaults upstairs. Here's where the real treasures are kept.

"Daniel, you in there?" I call out, knocking hard on the glass.

Underneath the door, it's clear the lights are off. I know his tricks.

"Daniel, I know you're there. I have something good for you."

Still no response.

"It's an old one too..."

Still nothing.

And then...

"*How old?*" a voice finally calls out.

"Let's go, Howard Hughes—open the door!" I shout.

There's a muffled click as the door swings wide, revealing Daniel "the Diamond" Boeckman, the handsomest man in the entire Archives, wearing a crisp white lab coat that I swear doesn't have a single crease, even in the tag. It's the same with his manicured nails, perfect tie, and immaculate brushed-back blond locks—there's not a thread, a hair, a molecule that's out of place. More importantly, he's one of the best talents we have in Preservation.

"Tell me your afternoon is free," I plead.

"Can't," he says. "I've got Dallas's original Thomas Jefferson letter that's going on display tomorrow."

Clementine's waiting. Time to go atomic.

I pull the dictionary from the back of my pants and hold it up in front of him. "Washington still beat Jefferson?" I challenge.

He studies the gutted dictionary. Ten years ago, a man in Rhode Island found an original music sheet of "The Star-Spangled Banner" folded up—and seemingly stuck—in an old family journal. Boeckman said it was a fake just by looking at the swirl in the handwriting. But that didn't stop him from calibrating the acidity of the paper, freeing the document from the journal, and even reassembling the individual ink flakes on the page, which proved the same. When it comes to document preservation, no one's tougher than the Diamond.

"The binding's gorgeous. Hand-threaded," he says, holding it

155

in his open palm, like he's eyeing the Gutenberg Bible. "But that doesn't mean it belonged to GW."

"That's not what I'm after," I tell him. "You ever hear of Washington using invisible ink?"

He's about to hand the book back. He stops. "You think there's something in here?"

"You're the one with all the CSI chemicals. You find the answer, I'll owe you a monster one."

"All you archivists owe me monster ones. Without me, you'd be going to *Antiques Roadshow* to find out if half your stuff was real."

He's right. Fortunately, there's one thing the Diamond prefers even more than credit.

"How're things going with Rina?" I ask with a grin.

He doesn't grin back. There's not a person in the building who doesn't know about his crush on my #2 officemate.

"Beecher, you don't have half the testicles to make good on whatever inducement you're thinking of."

"That's true. But that doesn't mean I can't put in the good word for you."

With his free hand, he touches his perfect Windsor tie. And smiles. "You used to be one of the nice ones, Beecher. Now you're just like all the rest."

"Just look at the book. And the invisible ink," I tell him, tugging open the bulletproof door and leaving him the dictionary. "Rina sits right by me." I lower my voice. *"Oh, what's that, Rina? Oh, yes, isn't that Daniel Boeckman handsome?"*

"Tell her I'm sensitive," the Diamond calls back as I dart into the hallway. "She was upset yesterday—y'know, with the Orlando thing. *Sensitive* will serve me far better."

The bulletproof door slams with a boom, but what echoes are his words. *The Orlando thing.*

A man died. My friend. I still see him lying there—his skin now chalkboard gray, the bottom corner of his mouth sagging open. It was yesterday! *The Orlando thing.* Like we're talking about someone who didn't refill the coffeepot.

156

The thought hits even harder as I follow the basement's white-and-gray checkerboard floor toward the elevators, just down from Orlando's office. But it's not until I turn the corner that the door to the Security Office opens and I spot . . .

My stomach lurches, like it's being squeezed in a slipknot.

Anyone but them.

36

I'm sorry for your loss. I'm sorry this happened. I'm just...I'm so *sorry*, I say to myself, practicing the words in my head. But as the tired African-American woman with the outdated clear plastic glasses and the faded red overcoat leaves the Security Office and heads toward me in the hallway, I can't muster a single syllable.

She doesn't notice I'm there. She's too focused on the person behind her—her son—who looks about my age as he carries a cardboard box, hugging it to his chest. He's got a deep dimple in his chin.

Just like his father.

I know them from the pictures on his desk: Orlando's wife and his oldest son. From the cardboard box, they came to clear out his desk.

As they trudge toward me at the elevators, it's like they're walking underwater while carrying a bag of bricks. But it's not the box that's weighing them down.

For a moment, the three of us just stand there in the silence of the hallway. Even now, his son offers up a we're-waiting-for-the-same-elevator smile.

I should say something.

I *need* to say something.

My brain slingshots to the very best advice someone gave me when they heard my dad was dead: Our fathers never leave us. Ever.

I could even say something about how nice Orlando was to everyone.

I can give them that one final memory.

But as the elevator rumbles, its doors slide open, and Orlando's wife and son step inside...

I just stand there in the hallway. Paralyzed.

They both stare at the floor, in no mood for eye contact.

The doors bite shut, consuming them whole.

And I'm still standing there, once again reminded that the only feeling more painful than *loss* is the feeling of *guilt*.

I reach for the elevator call button, but as my finger ignites the up arrow, I can't help but notice the sudden burst of voices coming from the open door of the Security Office. Following the sound, I lean back and take a fast peek into the wide room of cubicles, where small clusters of coworkers are talking—just whispering, gossiping.

It makes sense. With Orlando's wife and son gone, there's no need for whatever self-imposed silence the office had been carrying while his family went through his desk.

"You see them?" the receptionist asks me. "Just heartbreaking, right?"

She says something else, but I'm too busy looking at Orlando's cubicle on the left side of the office. All the photos...the holiday cards...the clutter of life...even his Wisconsin Badgers pencil cup...it's all gone. I search for his computer, but that's gone too (which probably means there's no chance the videotape is here either). I still need to check. With me and Clementine on it, that video holds our fate. But except for a few stray pens and a single pink photocopy that's push-pinned to the wall (the instructions for how to use voicemail), the only remaining proof that someone worked here is the big telephone, with the long cord and two blinking lights, that floats like an island at the center of the otherwise empty desk.

Orlando's desk phone.

According to Khazei, I'm the last person Orlando called. But that doesn't mean I'm the last one who *called him.*

I rush toward his desk—and just as quickly stop myself. This isn't the time, especially with half the staff still standing around and watching. But as I think about Orlando's wife and son...about everything I should've said to them just now...this is exactly the time. Forget the Culper Ring and the dictionary and all of Nico's

ramblings. If I can find out what really happened to Orlando—
I owe his family at least that much.

Sliding into his chair, I take a final glance around to see who's
looking. But to my surprise, the only one watching is the person
who just stepped into the office. I turn toward her just as she peeks
inside. Rina.

I lock eyes with the Mona Lisa, but by the time the chair fully
swivels around, she's already gone.

I saw her, though. I know she was there.

But right now, I need to stay focused on the current problem.

My fingers dive for the phone's keypad, tapping the button for
caller ID. The first one reads *Security—ext. 75020*. Those're the
guys from the front desk, probably wondering when Orlando was
coming to do his shift. The next one's from someone in Exhibits.
Then a call from *Westman, Aristotle—ext. 73041*.

Tot? Why's Tot calling him?

But as I scroll down to make sure I have it right, a brand-new
name pops up. Then pops up again. It only gets worse.

Forget the slipknot around my stomach. My whole chest tightens like it's squeezed by a noose.

My fingers attack caller ID like a woodpecker. Of the last dozen
calls made to Orlando... seven of them... eight of them... nine of
them... my Lord, *ten of them*...

... are all from Rina.

I spin back toward reception.

"Get off me!" a woman's voice yells.

I know that voice. I've known it since junior high. It sure as hell
ain't Rina.

By the time I see what's going on, sure enough, Rina's not there.
But in her place—

"I said, get... *off*!" Clementine barks, fighting to get free.

Just behind her, Khazei grips her by the biceps. I almost forgot.
I'm in *his* territory.

The deputy chief of security isn't letting go.

*　　*　　*

37

L et go of me!" Clementine insists, still fighting to free her arm from Khazei's grip.

He shoves her into the hallway, refusing to let go.

Khazei's no idiot. If he's bringing us out here, he's hoping to avoid a scene.

Too late.

"I didn't do anything!" Clementine adds, her feet slip-sliding along the checkerboard tile.

"Really? So waiting in the Rotunda—strolling there for nearly twenty minutes without taking a single look at the gasper documents," he shouts back, referring to the Constitution and the other documents that make tourists gasp. "You're telling me that you weren't waiting there for Beecher to sneak you over?"

"It's a public area! I can stroll there all I want!" she yells.

Khazei pulls her close, squeezing her arm even tighter. "You think I didn't look you up when you signed in this morning and last night? We've got cameras outside! I saw him drop you off on the damn corner!"

A puddle of sweat soaks the small of my back. The only reason I tried to sneak her in was so Clementine—and her dad—would avoid getting linked to everything with Orlando and the President. So much for that. Still, Clementine doesn't seem to care. She's got far more pressing problems to deal with.

"I swear to God, if you don't let go . . . !" she threatens, still thrashing to get free.

"Clemmi, calm down," I tell her.

"She can't, can she?" Khazei challenges. "Got too much family blood in her."

"Get your hands off me!" she explodes, the intensity catching me off guard. A flick of spit leaves her lips as she roars the words. Her eyes have volcanoes in them. This isn't anger. Or rage. This is her father.

Khazei doesn't care. He grips Clementine by the back of her neck, hoping it'll take the fight out of her.

He doesn't know her at all. And the way she continues to boil, her whole body shaking as she fights to break free of his grip, I start thinking that maybe I don't know her either.

She twists fast, trying to knee him in the nuts. He turns just in time to make sure she misses.

"Clemmi, please . . . It's enough," I beg.

"Stop fighting and I'll let you go," Khazei warns her.

"Get . . . off . . . me!" she snarls as a silver spit bubble forms at her lips.

"You hear what I said?" Khazei asks.

Clementine refuses to answer. Still trying to escape, she punches at his hands. Her body trembles. She's determined to break away. Khazei grits his teeth, pinching her neck even tighter.

"Let her go . . . !" I shout, shoving Khazei's shoulder.

"You listening?" he asks her again, like I'm not even there.

Her trembling gets worse. The spit bubble in her mouth slowly expands. She'll never give up. It has nothing to do with Khazei. Clementine just met her father for the first time in her life. She had to sit there and listen as he told us that our lives and our choices are predetermined. Then Khazei jumped in and basically accused her of the same.

Clementine looks over at me, her face flushed red. She's trying so hard to prove them wrong, to prove to the entire world—and especially to herself—who she really is. But as the volcanoes in her eyes are about to blow, that's exactly her problem. No matter how far we come, our parents are always in us.

"Eff. *You!*" she explodes, spinning hard and sending Khazei off balance, lost in his own momentum. Before he realizes what's happened, Clementine twists to the left and grabs the antenna of his walkie-talkie, yanking it from his belt and wielding it upside down, like a miniature baseball bat. It's not much of a weapon. It'll probably shatter on impact. But the way she's gripping it—the way she's eyeing his face—it's gonna leave a hell of a scar.

I rush forward, trying to leap between them.

"What in the holy hell you think you're doing?" a voice calls out behind us.

I spin around just as he turns the corner. Clementine lowers the walkie-talkie to her side. He's far down the hallway, but there's no mistaking the wispy white beard...the bolo tie...the one man who's been here longer than me and Khazei combined.

"Y'heard me," Tot says, honing in on me and readjusting the thick file he's got tucked under his arm. "Y'know how long I've been waiting, Beecher? You missed our meeting. Where the heck you been?"

I know it's an act. But I have no idea what I'm supposed to say.

"I...I..." I glance over at Khazei.

"He's been talking with me," Khazei says, his voice serene, making peace rather than war. He's definitely smarter than I thought. Khazei's been here a few years. Tot's outlasted eleven Presidents and every Archivist of the United States since LBJ. It's the first rule of office politics: Never pick a fight you can't win.

"So no problem then? They're free to go?" Tot challenges, lumping in Clementine and leaning in so Khazei gets a good look at his milky blind eye. "I mean, I thought I heard yelling, but I'm old and creaky," he adds. "Maybe I was just imagining it, eh?"

Khazei studies the old man. I can feel the anger rising off him. But as the two men share a far too long, far too intense look, I can't help but think that there's something else that's going unsaid in their little standoff.

Khazei puffs out his chest, all set to explode, and then...

He shakes his head, annoyed. "Just get them out of my face," he blurts, turning back to his office.

As Tot continues to hit him with the evil eye, I can't tell if I've underestimated the power of seniority, or the power of Tot. But either way, we're free to go.

"Clementine . . ." Tot calls out, pretending to know her.

"Yeah."

"Give the man his walkie-talkie back."

She hands it to Khazei. "Sorry. That's not who I usually am."

To my surprise, Khazei doesn't say a thing. He grabs the walkie, slotting it back into his belt.

I go to step around him, and he stabs me with a final dark glare. "I saw you sitting at Orlando's desk," he says. "Got something needling at your conscience?"

"Why should I? Everyone's saying it was a heart attack," I shoot back. "Unless you suddenly know something different."

"I know you were in that SCIF with him, Beecher. It's just a matter of time until that video proves it, and when that happens, guess who everyone'll be looking at?"

I tell myself that if it all comes out, I can point a finger at the President—but that's when Orlando's words replay louder than ever. No matter who you are or how right you are, no one walks away the same way from that battle.

"Beecher, if you help me with this, I promise you—I can help *you.*"

It almost sounds like he's doing me a favor. But there's still plenty of threat in his voice. Before I take him up on anything, I need to know what's really going on.

"You want help? You should talk to Rina," I tell him. "Y'know she called Orlando ten times on the morning he died?"

He barely moves, once again making me wonder what he's really chasing: Orlando's killer, or the George Washington book?

Without a word, he turns back to his office. I race to catch up to Tot and Clementine, reaching them just as they turn the corner. Before I can say anything, Tot shoots me a look to stay quiet, then motions down to the real reason he came looking for me: the thick accordion file that's tucked under his arm. The flap says:

Gyrich, Dustin

The man who's been checking out documents for over a hundred and fifty years.

38

"How's my car?" Tot asks.

"How'd you get Khazei to back down like that?" I challenge.

"How's my car?"

"Tot . . ."

He refuses to turn around, shuffling as he leads us past dusty bookshelf after dusty bookshelf on the eighteenth floor of the stacks. He's not fast, but he knows where he's going. And right now, as the automatic lights flick on as we pass, he's got me and Clementine following. "Khazei doesn't want a fight," he explains. "He wants what you found in the SCIF."

"I agree, but . . . how do you know?"

"Why didn't he push back? If Orlando's death is really his top concern, why hasn't Khazei thrown you to the FBI, who're really in charge of this investigation . . . or even to the Secret Service, who by the way, have been picking apart the SCIF all morning and afternoon? You've got every acronym working quietly on this case, but for some reason, Khazei's not handing over the best pieces of dynamite, namely the two of you," Tot says as another spotlight flicks on. I search the corner of the ceiling. The stacks of the Archives are too vast to have cameras in every aisle. But near as I can tell, Tot has us weaving so perfectly, we haven't passed a single one. "Now tell me how my car is," he says.

"Your car's nice," Clementine offers, still trying to make up for the rage parade she just put on. "I'm Clementine, by the way."

For the second time, Tot doesn't look back. He doesn't answer either.

He wants nothing to do with Clementine. As he said this morning, he doesn't know her, doesn't trust her. But once she got grabbed by Khazei, he also knows he can't just chuck her aside. For better or worse, she was in that SCIF—she was there with Orlando—and that means her butt's in just as much of the fire as mine.

"Your car's fine," I add as we make a final sharp left. "Clemmi, this is Tot."

A spotlight blinks awake, and I'm hit with a blast of cold air from a nearby eye-level vent. Our documents are so fragile, the only way to preserve them is to keep the temperature dry and cool. That means intense air conditioning.

Tot hits the brakes at a wall of bookcases that're packed tight with dusty green archival boxes. At waist height, the bookcase is empty, except for a narrow wooden table that's tucked where the shelves should be. Years ago, the archivists actually had their offices in these dungeony stacks. Today, we all have cubicles. But that doesn't mean Tot didn't save a few private places for himself.

The spines of the boxes tell me we're in navy deck logs and muster rolls from the mid-1800s. But as Tot tosses the fat file folder on the desk, and a mushroom cloud of dust swirls upward, I know we're gonna be far more focused on . . .

"Dustin Gyrich," Tot announces.

"That's the guy you think did this, right?" Clementine asks. "The guy who's been checking out books for a hundred and fifty years. How's that even possible?"

"It's not," Tot says coldly. "That's why we're up here whispering about it."

"So every time President Wallace comes here on his reading visits," I add, "this man Gyrich requests a copy of *Entick's Dictionary* . . ."

"Just odd, right?" Tot asks. "I started sifting through the older pull slips . . . seeing how far back it went. The more pull slips I looked at, the more requests from Dustin Gyrich I found: from this administration, to the one before, and before . . . There were eleven requests during Obama's administration . . . three during George W.

167

Bush's...five more during Clinton's and the previous Bush. And then I just started digging from there: Reagan, Carter, all the way back to LBJ...throughout the term of every President—except, oddly, Nixon—Dustin Gyrich came in and requested this dictionary. But the real break came when I tried to figure out if there were any other books that were pulled for him."

"Can't you just search by his last name?" Clementine asks.

"That's not how it works," I explain. "If it were today, yes, we've got a better computer system, but if you want to see who requested a particular document in the past, it's like the library card in the back of an old library book—you have to go card by card, checking all the names on it."

"And that's when I thought of *Don Quixote*," Tot says.

I cock my head, confused.

"Remember that list we looked at—from Mount Vernon—of all the books that were in George Washington's possession on the day he died? Well, in his entire library, guess what single book he had more copies of than any other?"

"Other than the Bible, I'd say: *Don Quixote*?" I ask.

"Uncanny guessing by you. And did you know that in 1861, during a U.S. Circuit Court case in Missouri—whose records we happen to keep since it's a federal trial—one of the parties presented into evidence all the personal property and baggage that was left behind by one of their passengers? Well, guess what book that passenger was carrying?"

"*Don Quixote*," I say for the second time.

"History's fun, isn't it?" Tot says. "That's now two books in our collection that were also in the collection of President Washington. Today, that copy is stored out in our Kansas City facility, but on April 14th, 1961, during the JFK administration, a man named D. Gyrich once again came in and—"

"Wait, what was that date again?" I interrupt.

"Ah, you're seeing it now, aren't you?"

"You said April 14th...?"

"Nineteen sixty-one," Tot says with a grin.

168

Clementine looks at each of us. She's lost.

"The Bay of Pigs," I tell her.

"Actually, a few days before the Bay of Pigs... but that's the tickle," Tot says, rolling his tongue inside his cheek. "Our dear friend D. Gyrich also came into the building and asked to see that same copy of *Don Quixote* on October 3, 1957, and on May 16, 1954, and on August 6, 1945."

My skin goes cold. It has nothing to do with the chill from the extreme air conditioning.

"What?" Clementine asks, reading my expression. "What happened on those dates?"

"October 3, 1957—that's the day before the Russians launched Sputnik, isn't it?" I ask.

"Exactly," Tot says. "And May 16, 1954?"

"The day before the *Brown v. Board of Education* decision was handed down. But that last one, I forget if it's—"

"It's the later one," Tot says, nodding over and over. "You got it now, don't you?"

I nod along with him. "But to be here the day before... to always be here the day before... You think he knew?"

"No one has timing that good," Tot says. "He *had* to know."

"Know *what*?" Clementine begs.

I look at her, feeling the icy cold crawl and settle into the gaps of my spine. Dustin Gyrich, whoever he is, was in here days before the Bay of Pigs... Sputnik... the *Brown* decision... and August 6, 1945...

"Hiroshima," I whisper. "He was here the day before Hiroshima."

"He was," Tot agrees. "And you'll never believe where he was before that."

39

O kay, here...go back another thirty years," Tot says. "Nineteen fifteen...two days before the *Lusitania* was attacked..."

"That's what brought us into World War I," I explain to Clementine, who's still confused.

"Then again in 1908, the week the Model T was introduced," Tot says, flipping through a stack of photocopies, his voice filled with newfound speed. "Some dates, nothing big happened. But I even found a visit two days before they changed the U.S. penny to the Abraham Lincoln design."

"How'd you even—?" I cut myself off. "That's impossible. He couldn't have come here."

"You're right," Tot says.

"Huh...*why*?" Clementine asks.

"We weren't open back then," I tell her. "The Archives was founded in 1934. Staff didn't start moving in until 1935."

"But lucky us, the Library of Congress has been making books available since 1800," Tot explains. "And when I called some of my friends there, well, considering that they're the largest library in the world, what a shocking surprise to hear that they had their own copies of *Don Quixote* as well."

"So even before the Archives opened..."

"...a Mr. D. Gyrich has been going in there and looking at old books that just happened to once be owned by General George Washington. Still, the real marvel is his timing: three days before the massacre at Wounded Knee...six days before the Battle of Gettysburg...They're still searching, but we found another all the way

170

back to July 4th, 1826, when former Presidents Jefferson and Adams both died within hours of each other on Independence Day."

"He's like the evil Forrest Gump," I say.

"You say 'he' like he's one person—as if there's one guy who's been walking around since 1826," Tot counters. "No offense, but vampire stories are overdone."

"So you think it's more than one person."

"I have no idea what it is. But do I think there're a bunch of people who could be using that name throughout history for some unknown reason? We're in a building dedicated to housing and preserving the government's greatest secrets. So yes, Beecher, I very much believe that that kind of Easter Bunny can exist. The only question is—"

"They're communicating," Clementine blurts.

Tot and I turn. She's sitting at the dusty desk, flipping through Tot's stack of photocopies.

"They're talking to each other," she repeats. "They're coming in here and they're using the books. That's how George Washington communicated with his group. It's like my d—" She cuts herself off. "Think of what Nico said."

"You spoke to Nico?" Tot asks me. "What'd he say? He knew something? What could he possibly know?"

Tot's questions come fast. They're all fair. But what catches me by surprise is the intensity in his voice.

"Beecher, tell me what he said."

"I will, but...can I ask you one thing first?"

"You said Nico—"

"Just one thing, Tot. Please," I insist, refusing to let him interrupt. "Yesterday...before Orlando was killed..." I take a deep breath, vomiting it all before I can change my mind. "When I was in Orlando's office earlier, on his caller ID...Why were you calling Orlando on the day he died?"

Clementine looks up from the paperwork. Tot freezes. And then, just as quickly, he smiles, his blind eye disappearing in a playful smirk.

"Good for you, Beecher. Good for you," he insists, doing the thing where he twirls his finger in his beard. "I told you to not trust anyone, and you're doing just that."

"Tot..."

"No, don't apologize. This is *good*, Beecher. Smart for you for asking that. This is *exactly* what you need to be doing."

I nod, appreciative of his appreciation, but...

"You never said why you were calling him," Clementine blurts.

Tot's finger slowly twirls out of his beard. "My ID," he says. "My Archives ID is about to expire, and they told me to call Orlando to get the paperwork for a new one."

"I thought the IG does all our investigations," I say, referring to the Inspector General's office.

"They do. But Orlando's the one who takes your photo. Go look. Across from his desk, there's one of those passport backgrounds that you pull up and stand in front of."

I look at Clementine, then at Tot. That's all I need. He just saved our asses from Khazei, and gave us his car, and did all this Dustin Gyrich research for no other reason than that he's my dearest friend.

"Beecher, if you don't want to talk about Nico, it's fine," he offers.

"Just listen," I tell him. "Do you know what the Culper Ring is?"

"Y'mean, as in George Washington's spy brigade?"

"So you've heard of them?"

"Beecher, I've been here since before Joe Kennedy had chest hair. Of course I've heard of—" He catches himself as it all sinks in. "Oh. So that's what Nico—"

"What?" I ask. "That's what Nico *what*?"

He thinks a moment, still working the details. "Beecher, do you have any idea what the Culper Ring actually did?" Tot finally asks.

"Just like you said: They were Washington's personal spy unit. That he used civilians to move information back and forth."

"Yeah, no—and that's right. They moved lots of information. Washington's top military spies kept getting caught by the British—

his plans kept getting intercepted, he didn't know who to trust—so he turned to these civilians, these regular people, who wound up being unstoppable. But what the Culper Ring is really known for, and what they're treasured by history for, is—" He again stops. "Have you ever seen whose statue sits outside the original head-quarters of the CIA?"

"Tot, I'm good, but I don't know this stuff like you do."

"Nathan Hale. You know him?"

"I only regret that I have but one life to lose for my country . . ."

"That's the one. One of Washington's earliest spies. And just to be clear, Hale never said that."

"What?"

"He never said it, Beecher. The *one life to lose for my country* part came from a play which was popular during Revolutionary times. But do you know why our leaders lied and said Hale was such a hero? Because they knew it was better for the country to have a martyr than an incompetent spy. That's all Hale was. A spy who got caught. He was hung by the British."

"And this is important because . . . ?"

"It's important because when William Casey took over the CIA in the early eighties, it used to drive him crazy that there was a statue of Nathan Hale at headquarters. In his eyes, Nathan Hale was a spy who failed. Hale was captured. According to Casey, the statue in front of the CIA should've been of Robert Townsend."

"Who's Robert Townsend?" I ask.

"That's exactly the point! Townsend was one of the members of the Culper Ring. But have you ever heard his name? Ever seen him mentioned in a history book? No. And why? Because for two hundred years, we didn't even know Townsend *was part of* the Culper Ring. *For two hundred years, he kept his secret!* We only found out when someone did handwriting analysis on his old letters and they matched the ones to Washington. And that's the real Culper Ring legacy. Sure, they moved information, but what they did better than anyone was keep their own existence a secret. Think about it: You can't find them if you don't know they exist."

I look over at Clementine, who's still flipping through the photo-copied pull slips. I'm not sure what unnerves me more: the way this is going, or that Nico's ramblings aren't sounding as crazy as they used to.

"So this Dustin Gyrich guy—you think he's part of..." As I say the words...as I think about Benedict Arnold...none of this makes sense. "You're saying this Culper Ring *still exists*?"

"Beecher, at this exact moment, the only question that seems logical is, why *wouldn't* they still exist? They were the best at what they did, right? They helped win a revolution. So you've got half a dozen men—"

"Hold on. That's all there were? Half a dozen?"

"It think it was six...maybe seven...it wasn't an army. It was Benjamin Tallmadge and Robert Townsend and I think George Washington's personal tailor...they were a small group with loyalty directly to Washington. And if you're George Washington, and you're about to step into the Presidency, and you can't trust anyone, why would you suddenly disband the one group that actually did *right* by you?"

"See, but there's the problem," I point out. "To assume that this Ring—whatever it really is—to assume it lasted all the way to now...No offense, but these days, even the CIA can't keep their own spies' real names off the front page of the newspaper. No way could this town keep a secret that big for that long."

Tot looks at me with one of his Tot looks. "I know you have a security clearance, Beecher. Do you really think there aren't any secrets left in our government?"

"Okay, maybe there are still a few secrets. I'm just saying, over the course of two hundred years—with each new President and each new agenda—forget about even keeping the secret...how do we possibly know this group is still doing *right*?"

"I assume you're talking about what happened with Orlando?"

"Y'mean that part where Orlando suddenly shows up dead right after it looks like he's the one who has their book? Especially when *I'm* the one who has their book? Yeah, call me paranoid, but that's kinda the part I'm focusing on right now."

Tot runs his fingers down the metal ribbons of his bolo tie. He doesn't like the sarcasm, but he understands the pressure I'm under. Behind him, Clementine is flipping even faster through the photocopies. Like she's looking for something.

"Clemmi, you okay?" I call out.

"Yeah. Yeah, yeah," she insists without looking up.

"Beecher, I hear you," Tot continues. "And yes, over the course of two hundred years, who knows if this current Culper Ring has any relation to the original Culper Ring, but to assume that they've turned into the evil hand of history—"

"Did you not see that list?" I interrupt. "Hiroshima, Gettysburg, the Bay of Pigs—all we're missing is the grassy knoll and theater tickets with John Wilkes Booth!"

"That's fine, but to say that a single small group of men are at the cause of all those singular moments—that's just stupid to me, Beecher. Life isn't a bad summer movie. History's too big to be controlled by so few."

"I agree. And I'm not saying they're controlling it, but to be so close on all those dates...they've clearly got access to some major information."

"They're communicating," Clementine says again, still looking down. "That's what I said before. That's what Nico said: To send messages to his Culper Ring, Washington used to hide stuff directly in his books. So maybe today...they put info in a book, then someone picks up that book and reads the message."

"That's...yeah...can't it be that?" I say with a nod. "These guys have information—they sit close to the President, so they traffic in information—and in this case, in this book that was left in the SCIF, President Wallace has information."

"Or someone has information for President Wallace," Tot points out.

"Or that. That's fine," I say. "Either way, maybe this is how they share it."

"Okay—that's a theory—I can see that. But if it's really that earth-shattering, why not just bring it directly to the President?"

"Look at the results: Dustin Gyrich comes in here, then—kaboom—World War I. Another visit, then—kaboom—Hiroshima. This isn't small stuff. So for Gyrich to be back yesterday, there's clearly something big that—"

"Wait. Hold on. Say that again," Tot interrupts.

"Clearly something big?"

"Before that..."

"For Gyrich to be back yesterday?"

"We never checked, did we?" Tot asks.

"Checked what?"

"Gyrich's visit. We know the dictionary was on hold for him yesterday, but we never checked if Gyrich actually physically came into the building..."

I see where he's going. If Gyrich was here, if he checked in as a researcher and signed the log, we've got the possibility of having him on video, or at the very least fingerprints that can tell us who he really—

"Clemmi, c'mon..." I call out, already starting to run.

Clementine doesn't move. She's still flipping through the pull slips—the slips that every visitor has to fill out to look at a particular volume or box of documents—scanning each one like she's reading a prescription bottle.

"Clemmi!" I call again.

Nothing.

I dart to the desk and grab at the pile of photocopies. "C'mon, we can read this after—"

Her arm springs out, desperately clutching the pages. She's practically in tears. "Please, Beecher. I need to know."

Within seconds, she's back to scanning the documents.

Over her shoulder, I check the dates of the pull slips, trying to get context. *July 7, July 10, July 30*—all of them from ten years ago. What the hell happened in July ten y—?

Oh.

"You're looking for Nico, aren't you?" I ask.

She flips to another sheet.

At the NASCAR track. Ten years ago. That's when Nico took the shots at President—

"Please tell me they didn't know about that," I say.

She shakes her head, unable to look up at me. There's only so many punches this poor girl can take in one day. "They didn't," she says, her voice shaking as she nears the end of the pull slips.

"That's good, right? That's good."

"I-I-I guess," she says. "I don't even know if I was hoping for it or not...but if this Culper Ring knew about all those other parts of history...I...I dunno. I just thought they might—"

"Clemmi, it's okay," I tell her. "Only a fool wouldn't've checked. It's completely—"

"You don't have to say it's normal, Beecher. Searching to see if some secret two-hundred-year-old group knew about the day your father tried to murder the President...We're a little far from normal."

I know she's right, but before I can tell her, I feel the vibration of my phone in my pocket. Caller ID tells me it's the one call I've been waiting for. Extension 75343. The Preservation Lab downstairs.

"You ready for it, Beecher?" Daniel the Diamond asks before I can even say hello.

"You were able to read it?" I say.

"It's invisible ink, not the Rosetta Stone. Now you want to come down here and see what's written in this book or not?"

40

A ndre Laurent hated hats.

He always hated them—even on a day like today, when the late afternoon winds were galloping down from the Capitol, barreling full force as they picked up speed in the wide canyon created by the buildings that lined Pennsylvania Avenue. Sure, a hat would keep him warm. But as Andre Laurent knew—as any barber knew—a hat did only one thing: ruin a good day's work.

Still, as Laurent leaned into the wind, fighting his way up the block toward the huge granite building, he never once thought about removing his red Washington Nationals baseball cap.

He knew its benefits, especially as he made a final sharp right, leaving the wind tunnel of Pennsylvania Avenue and heading under the awning that led to the automatic doors of the National Archives.

"Looks like Dorothy and Toto are flying around out there," the guard at the sign-in desk called out as Laurent pushed his way into the lobby, bringing a frosty swirl of cold air with him.

"It's not that bad," Laurent said.

He meant it. Compared to the permanent gray of Ohio, the winters in D.C. were easy. But as he approached the sign-in desk, Laurent couldn't help but think that was the only thing that was easier here.

Especially over the last few months.

"Research, or you got an appointment?" the guard asked.

"Research," Laurent said, noticing just how bushy the guard's eyebrows were. They definitely needed a trim, he thought, reaching for the ID Palmiotti had given him and carefully readjusting his baseball cap, which right now was the only thing protecting his face from the ceiling's security camera.

"And your name again?"

Laurent leaned against the sign-in desk, which was built like an airline counter—so tall it came up to his chest. He never liked coming here. But as they knew, the President couldn't get his hair cut every single day. "You don't recognize me by now? I'm here all the time," Laurent said as he held up the ID. "I'm Dustin Gyrich."

41

You talk me up to Rina yet?" the Diamond asks.

"You're joking, right?" I shoot back. "How fast you think I am?"

"Plenty fast," he says, nodding a hello to Tot and taking a quick glance at Clementine. "Kinda like I was with this invisible ink problem you got."

He cocks both eyebrows, thinking he's hysterical. With a pivot, he spins toward the lab, inviting us inside.

"By the way, where's *she* from?" he adds, his back to us as he throws a thumb at Clementine.

"She's . . . er . . ." I reach over to Clementine and tuck the red Visitor ID badge that Tot got her inside the lapel of her jacket. "She works in Modern Military in College Park," I add, referring to our facility out in Maryland. "Her name's Lucy."

"*Lucy?*" Clementine mouths, making a face.

"Nice to meet you, Lucy," the Diamond says, his back still to us. "It's kooky though that a full-time employee would be wearing a visitor's badge."

I don't say a word as we pass a bank of map cabinets and storage units. I shouldn't be surprised. He spends every day studying the tiniest of details.

"Listen, Daniel . . ." Tot begins.

"Tot, I don't care. I really don't," he insists. "Beecher, just make sure you put the word in with Rina. Fair trade?"

I nod. Fair trade.

"Okay, so on to your next nightmare," he says, leading us to a square lab table in back that's covered by an array of sky blue plastic developing trays, like you find in a darkroom. On the edge of the lab table is our copy of *Entick's Dictionary*. "How much you know about invisible ink?"

"I remember fifth-grade science fair: Someone writes it in lemon juice, then you heat the paper and voilà..."

As I flip the dictionary open, there's now a sheet of see-through archival tissue paper protecting each page. But except for where it says,

Exitus

Acta

Probat

...that front inside page is otherwise still blank.

"I thought you said you found the writing," Tot challenges, nearly as annoyed as I am.

"That's what I'm trying to tell you," the Diamond begs. "Whoever put this in here—they're not playing Little League. This is pro ball," he explains. "The best secret inks date back thousands of years, to China and Egypt—and by the eighteenth century, they were almost universally based on some organic liquid like leeks or limes or even urine. And like you said, a little heat would reveal the writing. But as George Washington understood, it's not much of a secret when every British soldier knows that all you have to do is wave a candle to see the magic appear."

"Get to the part about the pro ball," Tot tells him.

"That is the part," the Diamond insists. "Basic invisible inks require a heating process. You heat the paper, you crack the code. But to foil the British, Washington and his Culper Ring started playing with a *chemical* process."

"Wait...What was that?" Clementine asks.

"The chemical process?"

"No—before that," she says.

181

"She means the Culper Ring," I jump in. I know where she's going. She wants to know how much of Nico's ramblings were right. "So the Culper Ring were the ones who used this?"

"Of course," the Diamond says. "I assume you know what the Culper Ring is, yes?"

We all nod.

"Then you know the whole purpose of the Ring was to help Washington communicate his most vital secrets. In fact, invisible ink is just the start of it: The Culper Ring had their own codes and ciphers...they made sure no one used their real name...they would only write on the back of the fifteenth sheet of paper. That's why when William Casey took over the CIA—"

"We know the story. About the statue," I tell him. "They're the best spies ever. We got it."

"I don't think you do. As small a group as the Culpers were, they had a huge hand in winning the Revolution for us. And their best value came from the fact that all the vital documents were hand-written letters. So when Washington's orders kept getting intercepted over and over, he asked his Culper Ring to do something about it."

"Cue invisible ink."

"But not just any ink," the Diamond points out. "And this is the part that's brilliant. Instead of using heat, they would do the writing with a chemical that would disappear, which they called the *agent*. And then when you were ready to read it, you'd use a completely separate chemical, which they called the *reagent*."

"And that makes the writing reappear," Tot adds.

"Simple, right? *Agent* and *reagent*," the Diamond says. "As long as you keep the second chemical away from your enemy, they can never figure out what you're writing. So as you surmised, Washington and the Culper Ring would put their messages right into the first few pages of common books."

The Diamond points to the dictionary, and I can hear Nico's words in my head. *Not everything can be seen so easily.*

"They used books because no one would search for messages in there," Tot says.

"That was part of it. They also used books because they needed good-quality paper for the chemicals of the invisible ink to work best," the Diamond points out. "Back then, the paper that was in common pocket books like old pamphlets, almanacs . . ."

". . . and dictionaries," Clementine says.

". . . *and dictionaries*," the Diamond agrees, "was cheaper than good paper imported from England." Sliding on a pair of cotton gloves, he carefully reaches over and removes the dictionary from my grip, laying it face-open on the lab table.

"The one snag is, if you have a two-hundred-page diction-ary, how're you supposed to know what page to apply the reappearing chemicals to?" he adds, flipping through the blank pages that are all slightly browned, but are basically indistinguishable from each other. "No surprise, the Culper Ring had a way around that one."

Tugging at the first piece of tissue paper, the Diamond once again reveals the book's handwritten inscription:

Exitus

Acta

Probat

"When it came to Washington's messages," he explains, "they knew to read between the lines."

I look at Tot, still lost.

"I'm not being metaphorical," the Diamond says. "That's where we get the phrase from. Do it: *Read between the lines.*"

From the nearest developing tray, he pulls out a small square sponge no bigger than a matchbox. With a surgeon's touch, he gently dabs the wet sponge onto the page.

From the paper's textured fibers, faded light green letters rise, blooming into view and revealing the message that I'm now starting to think was intended for the President of the United States:

Exitus

FEBRUARY 16

Acta

26 YEARS IS A LONG TIME TO KEEP A SECRET

Probat

WRITE BACK: NC 38.548.19 OR WU 773.427

"Jiminy Crackers," Clementine whispers, her voice cracking. Her face is pale.

"Curiouser and curiouser, eh?" the Diamond asks, clearly excited.

The only one silent is Tot. I see the way he's looking at the message. He sees it too.

If these numbers are right...

We just jumped down a brand-new rabbit hole.

42

The guard at the sign-in desk studied the barber's ID, then looked back at Laurent.

This was the moment Laurent hated. If something were to go wrong, this is when it would happen.

The guard stood there, his cheeks just starting to puff.

Laurent tried to smile, but it felt like his whole body was flattening. Like the inside of his chest was now touching the inside of his back. He wasn't a spy. He wasn't made for this. In fact, the only reason he agreed to do it was...Dr. Palmiotti thought it was because the President of the United States asked personally. But it wasn't about the office.

It was about the man. A man Laurent knew since Wallace was a boy. A man who asked Laurent to move to Washington, and to whom Laurent made a promise. And while some people don't put high priority on such things in Washington, D.C....back in Ohio, and in so many other places...there's something to be said about keeping your word.

"Here you go, Mr. Gyrich," the guard with the overgrown eyebrows announced, handing back the ID and waving the barber toward the X-ray machine.

As the conveyor belt began to whirl, Laurent filled a plastic bin with his keys, his cell phone, and of course the book he was carrying: *A Problem from Hell.*

It rolled through the machine without a hitch, and within seconds the barber was on his way. "Thanks again," he called to the guard.

"Anytime," the guard replied. "Welcome to the Archives. And happy hunting to you."

*　　*　　*

43

F *ebruary 16th,*" Clementine reads from the page. "Should we know that date?"

I shake my head at her. *Not here.*

"That's the date they found King Tut," the Diamond jumps in.

"Pardon?" I ask.

"How do you even know that?" Tot challenges.

"I looked it up. Before you got here," the Diamond explains, pointing down at the now revealed message on the front page of the dictionary:

Exitus

FEBRUARY 16

Acta

26 YEARS IS A LONG TIME TO KEEP A SECRET

Probat

WRITE BACK: NC 38.548.19 OR WU 773.427

"I couldn't find anything noteworthy on the twenty-six years ago part, but looking at just February 16th—that's the date the silver dollar became U.S. legal tender, and Howard Carter found Pharaoh Tutankhamen. Otherwise, it's pretty much a quiet day in history." Reading our reactions—and our silence—the Diamond adds, "Sorry. Didn't mean to pry."

"You're not prying. Not at all," Tot says, forcing a dash of thankfulness into his voice. "We just found this book mixed in with some old files from the early sixties, and we figured if someone scribbled in there, it might be fun to see what they were writing about."

The Diamond stares directly at Tot, unafraid of his blind eye.

"Do you have any idea how invisible ink works?" the Diamond asks.

"You just told us how it works," Tot shoots back.

"I did. I gave you a crash course. But if I gave you the full course, I'd also tell you that if the invisible ink sits for too long—if a few decades go by and we apply the reagent chemicals—that writing reappears in a color that's pale brown. Like a chestnut. Your writing here is pale green," he says, pointing down to the dictionary. "That's fresh ink—and by the brightness of the color, I'm wagering something that's been written in the last week or so."

Still pale as can be, Clementine looks at me. I look at Tot.

"Daniel, listen . . ." Tot begins.

"Nope. Not listening. Not butting in. I already told Beecher: I don't want your problems, and I don't want to be mixed up in whatever you're mixed up in. He needs my help, I'll give it to him. But don't treat me like an idiot, Tot. It makes you look pompous. And besides, it's insulting."

"I apologize," Tot says.

"Apology accepted," the Diamond replies as he hands me back the dictionary. "Though by the way, I can tell you right now: No way this book ever belonged to George Washington."

"But the motto . . ."

"*Exitus acta probat* never appeared as just three words on a page. Never. Not once in his collection. Trust me, I've verified over thirty books for Mount Vernon. Whenever Washington used the motto, it appeared with the full coat of arms, including the eagle, and the stripes, and the three stars. And even if that weren't the case, I also found *this* . . ."

He flips to the inside back cover of the dictionary. In the bottom right corner, the characters "2--" are written in light pencil. I didn't even notice it before.

"Is that another code?" Tot asks.

"The most important code of all," I say, remembering my time in Mr. Farris's store. "In used bookstores, that's the price."

"...or in some cases, what the bookseller paid for it," the Diamond adds, "so they know what to sell it for."

Tot rolls this one around in his head. "So rather than some rare George Washington edition, you think this book is worth about two bucks?"

"It's worth whatever someone will pay for it," the Diamond says. "But if I had to guess, sure, I'm betting this is a later edition that some counterfeiter doctored up to sell in some scam during the 1800s when Washington died. We see 'em all the time. Saw another one a few weeks back at a used bookstore in Virginia," the Diamond says. "So if I were you, I'd focus my energy on whatever book they want you to reply in."

"Pardon?" Clementine asks.

"You telling me those aren't library call numbers?" the Diamond challenges. "They wrote to you in this book, now you write back in another. Communicating through books. Someone's doing the Culper Ring proud."

I once again think of Nico as all three of us stare down at the last line of the message:

WRITE BACK: NC 38.548.19 OR WU 773.427

No question, they definitely look like library call numbers. "There's only one problem—" I begin.

"—and that is, we need to find those books right now," Tot interrupts, shooting me a long hard look. I take the hint.

But as we head for the door, I hear the song "Islands in the Stream." Kenny Rogers and Dolly Parton. Tot's phone.

"You've got Tot," he answers, flipping it open. He nods, then nods again. But he doesn't say a word. Even as he closes it.

"Daniel, thanks again for the help," Tot finally announces, motioning me and Clementine out into the hallway.

"Don't forget me and Rina," the Diamond calls as we leave.

The lab's bulletproof glass door slams shut with a cold clap, but all I hear is Tot's quiet huffing as he shuffles back toward the elevators.

"The book that's in those call numbers—you know which one it is, don't you?" Clementine asks.

Tot ignores her. So do I.

"Who was that on the phone?" I ask him.

"Matthew," Tot says.

"Who's Matthew?"

"The guard at the front desk. With the caterpillar eyebrows. I paid him twenty bucks to keep an eye out," Tot says as we all crowd into the waiting elevator. "Now if you move your heinie fast enough, we're about to get our chance to finally grab Dustin Gyrich."

44

*P*ing" the elevator sings in F-sharp as the doors slide open.

I race out first, darting into the hallway and heading straight toward the gray stone walls of the lobby. Behind me, Tot hobbles, trying to keep up. No surprise. He's got nearly fifty years on me. But what is a surprise is Clementine, who starts to run and quickly loses steam. Her face is pale white like an aged porcelain doll.

"You okay?" I ask.

"Go . . . If he's there . . . *Go!*" she insists.

I take the cue, picking up speed.

"He said he went into Finding Aids!" Tot calls out.

Pulling a sharp right, I cut into the mint green Finding Aids room, the same room I found Clementine in this morning, when she gave me the homemade photo of the two of us.

There's no one at the research tables. No one at the bookshelves. For visitors, the last pull from the stacks was done hours ago. It's too late. No one's here.

Except for the older black man in the dark wool pea coat who's hunched in front of the small bank of computers.

"Sir, I'm checking IDs. Can I see your ID?" I call to the man.

He doesn't turn around.

"Sir . . . ! Sir, I'm talking to you," I add, now on a mad dash toward him. I reach out to grab his shoulder.

"Beecher, don't—!" Tot shouts as he enters the room.

Too late. I tap the man hard—hard enough that he turns around and—he—

He's a she.

"I *know* you didn't just put your hands on me," the woman barks, twisting from her seat.

"Ma'am, I-I'm sorry...I thought you were...I'm just checking IDs," I tell her.

She flashes her badge, which says she's a researcher from the University of Maryland. But as I scan the rest of the room, there's no sign of...of...of anyone.

Including Dustin Gyrich.

It doesn't make sense. The guard saw him come here. For him to move that fast...It's like he knew we were coming. But the only ones who knew that were—

"Who's calling you?" Tot asks.

I spin around to see Tot standing next to Clementine. In her hand, her phone is vibrating.

She looks down to check the number. "It's my job—they probably want to know if I'm coming in tomorrow," she explains. "Why?"

"Why aren't you picking it up?" Tot pushes.

"Why're you using that tone with me?"

"Why aren't you picking it up?"

Clearly annoyed, and looking paler than ever, Clementine flips open her phone and holds it to her ear. She listens for a few seconds and then says, "I'll call you back, okay?" Reading Tot's reaction, she asks, "What?"

"I didn't say anything," Tot challenges, making sure she hears that challenge in his voice.

"Just say it," she pushes back.

He shakes his head.

"So now you don't believe me?" she asks, holding out the phone to him. "You wanna speak to them? Here—speak to them."

"Listen, everyone's had a long day," I jump in.

"And don't give me that evil eye stare you give everyone else," she says, still locked on Tot. He walks over to the main check-in desk. She follows right behind him. "Beecher's been in my life long before he's been in yours. I've been helping him since the moment this started—and what?—now you think I'm tipping off Gyrich or something?"

"Those are your words, not mine," Tot says.

"But they can just as easily be applied to *you*," Clementine shoots back. "Oh that's right—I almost forgot you got that magic phone call three minutes ago that sent us racing up here. What a perfect time for Gyrich to check in and say, 'All's clear.' I'm telling you now, you hurt my friend, and I'll make sure the world knows who you are."

I wait for Tot to explode, but instead, he stares down at a red three-ring binder that sits open on the main desk.

Of course. The binder...

"Beecher..." Tot says.

I fly to the desk.

"What?" Clementine asks. "What is it?"

Ignoring her, Tot flips back one page, then flips forward to the current one.

"Every day, this room is staffed by us—by archivists," I explain. "We're on call for an hour or two each day so when visitors come in, we can help them with their research. But more important, the supervisor who runs this room marks down the exact time each of us gets here, just so she knows who's staffing the room at any particular moment."

"And of the fifty archivists in this building, look who was the very last one who was in here today—according to this log, barely ten minutes ago," Tot says, stabbing his crooked finger at the last name on the sheet.

4:52 p.m.—Dallas Gentry.

My coworker. And officemate. And along with Rina, the one other person staffing President Wallace yesterday when he was arriving in the SCIF.

45

Six minutes ago

When he was cutting hair, Andre Laurent put no premium on speed.

His focus was accuracy. Precision. Giving the client exactly what he wanted. Or at the very least, convincing the client that whatever he gave them was exactly what they wanted.

But this was different.

As he entered the mint green Finding Aids room on the first floor of the Archives, Laurent didn't waste a single second.

Without question, today was very much about speed. Most of the time, the goal was to move slowly—to go to the upstairs research room, pull a cart full of documents and pamphlets and half a dozen other records, and then hide what they needed right in plain sight.

But if what it said in *A Problem from Hell* was true... if someone else had grabbed the dictionary...

He didn't even want to think about it.

A quick scan of the room told him he at least picked the right time. God bless government employees. This close to five, nearly all the staff was gone.

"Can we help you?" an older employee called out as she wheeled a rolling cart filled with small boxes toward the microfilm reading room on their far left.

"I'm actually okay," Laurent said, waving his thanks, but not moving until she was gone.

When she was out of sight, he cut past the main research desk and headed for the bookshelves that lined the walls of the room. Ignoring record group numbers, he started counting. The one... two... three... fourth—here—fourth bookshelf on the right. Like nearly every other shelf in the room, it was filled with old leather books—mostly brown and dark blue, but a few red ones as well—each volume dedicated to a different subject matter. On the top shelf was a row of black binders and some pamphlets. According to the spines, *Record Group 267.*

Laurent nodded. That's the one. Glancing over his shoulder, he double-checked that the supervisor was gone.

All clear.

Reaching to the top shelf, he used two fingers to tip back one of the thick black binders. As he removed it with one hand, he placed it squarely on top of the book he was carrying—*A Problem from Hell*—and then, in one easy motion, slid both books onto the top shelf and headed for the door.

The theory was so simple it was elegant. Archives employees are concerned about visitors sneaking records out. But no one ever suspects someone sneaking something *in*.

There it sat. Just another book in the world's biggest archive.

Thirty seconds after that, Laurent was gone.

Thirty seconds after that, he was outside, using a crowd of departing employees to keep him out of the eyespace of security.

And thirty seconds after that, he was on his phone, dialing the number that by now he knew by heart.

As it began to ring, a beat-up Toyota whizzed by. On the back was a faded presidential bumper sticker: *Don't Blame Me—I Didn't Vote For Wallace.*

In the barber's ear, the phone stopped ringing. Someone picked up.

Laurent didn't say anything. He didn't have to.

Without a word, he shut the phone. Message sent.

Fourth bookcase. Top shelf. Fast as can be.

Just like the client wanted.

*   *   *

46

He's gone," I say.

"Check his desk," Tot says.

I go cubicle to cubicle, passing my own in our office on the fourth floor, but I already know the answer.

When we first got here, I saw the metal wipe-off board and the little magnet heads with our pictures on them. There were two people in the IN column. Everyone else is OUT. Including the one archivist we came here to see: Dallas.

"No answer on his cell. Maybe he's downstairs," Tot says. "Or in the stacks."

"He's not," I say, heading back to the magnets in front. "You know how he is—he doesn't check out until the moment he's leaving. God forbid we shouldn't know that he's always working and—Hold on. Where's Clementine?"

Tot looks over his shoulder. The door that leads out to the hall-way is still open.

"Clemmi?" I call out, craning my neck outside.

She's sitting down, cross-legged on the tiles. "Sorry, I'm just— It's been a long day."

"Y'think? Usually, when I meet my long-lost father, and get nabbed by Security, and find secret writings that may lead me to a murder, I'm way peppier than that."

Forcing a smile, she reaches up and grips the doorframe to help her stand. But as she climbs to her feet, her face—it's not just white anymore. It's green.

"You're really not okay, are you?"

"Will you stop? I'm fine," she insists, forcing another smile. But

195

as she tucks a few stray strands of black hair behind her ear, I see the slight shake in her hand. I've had twenty years to romanticize Clementine's strength. It's the worst part of seeing old friends: when your rose-colored memories become undone by reality.

"We should get you home," I say, quickly realizing that, in all my excitement to see her, I have no idea where she lives. "Where in Virginia are you going? Is it far?"

"I can take the Metro."

"I'm sure you can. But where're you going?"

"By Winchester. Not far from Shenandoah University."

I look at Tot, who's already shaking his head. That's far. Real far. "You sure the Metro goes out there?" I ask.

"Metro, then commuter bus. Will you relax? I do it all the time."

I again look at Tot. He again shakes his head.

"Don't ask me to drive her," Tot says.

"I'm not asking you to drive her."

"And don't ask me for my car," he warns.

I don't say a word. Clementine's face is green; her hand still has the shakes. Tot may not like her. And he may not like how overprotective she's being. But even he can see it. She's not making it home by herself.

"I'm fine," she promises.

"Beecher..." Tot warns.

"It'll be good. You'll see."

"No. I won't see," Tot says. "I'm tired and I'm cranky, and thanks to your dictionary I got nothing done today. The last thing I need is a two-hour tour of Virginia. You take her home, you come back and pick me up."

"Right. Yes. You got it."

Within six minutes and nineteen seconds, Clementine and I are in the powder blue Mustang, pulling out of the Archives garage and plowing into the evening traffic.

I know Tot's worried. He's always worried. But when I think of what we've been through today...

How could it possibly get worse?

*   *   *

47

The archivist had to make one stop first.

With Beecher now gone, it wouldn't take long.

Just a quick moment to duck back into Finding Aids and head for the one...two...three...fourth bookshelf on the right. The archivist glanced back, but knew no one was here. That's why they picked this room in the first place.

The President was always so focused on the SCIF. And that made sense. The SCIF was secure. The SCIF was perfect.

Until yesterday, when it wasn't.

Reaching for the top shelf, the archivist shoved aside the black binders and went right for the book. *A Problem from Hell*.

From a pocket, the archivist took out a small plastic bottle about the size of a shot glass with a triangular nipple on top. The nipple was actually a sponge. The archivist flipped to the copyright page of the book, turned over the small bottle, and let the liquid mixture that was inside the plastic bottle soak into the triangular sponge. With a quick few brushes, the archivist painted the page.

Within seconds, small green handwriting revealed itself.

The archivist read it fast, already knowing most of it. But at the end...

The archivist nodded. When it came to Beecher...and this woman Clementine...That's exactly what had to happen.

The words faded back to nothingness as the archivist slapped the book shut and headed through the lobby, out into the cold of Pennsylvania Avenue.

"*Taxi!*"

A black-and-yellow cab bucked to a stop.

"Where you going tonight?" an older cabbie with a round nose and thick bifocals asked, handing the archivist a laminated card as he slid inside.

"What's this?" the archivist said.

"My mission statement."

Sure enough, the laminated card said: *To take you to your destination in an environment that is most pleasing to you.* Underneath was a listing of all the local radio stations.

Only in D.C. Everyone's a damn overachiever.

"Just turn the corner up here," the archivist said. "I'm waiting for some friends—they're in a light blue Mustang."

"Y'mean like that one?" the cabbie asked, pointing through the windshield as the classic car, with Beecher and Clementine inside, climbed up the security ramp and made a sharp right into traffic.

"That's the one. Beautiful automobile, huh?"

"Y'want me to follow it? Like the movies?" the cabbie asked.

"You can stay back a bit. Even if you lose them," the archivist said, holding *A Problem from Hell* on the seat, "I already know where they're going."

48

Y ou feeling any better?" I ask Clementine.

"Yeah."

"That doesn't sound better. That sounds like a yeah."

She sits with it a moment, staring into the mirror on her side of the car and eyeing the bright lights of the mob of cars behind us. Using the rearview, I do the same, making mental notes of who's behind us: a blue Acura, a few SUVs, a disproportionate number of hybrids, and the usual rush-hour taxis. Nothing out of the ordinary. It doesn't make me feel any better.

"Tot hates me," Clementine says.

"Why would you say that?"

"Y'mean besides the long glares and accusatory stares—or maybe when I answered my phone and he basically said, *Who're you talking to? I hate you?*"

"He's just worried about me."

"If he were worried, he'd be sitting in this car right now. He doesn't like me. He doesn't trust me."

"Well, *I* trust you."

As I tug the wheel into another right and follow the rush-hour traffic up Constitution Avenue, she doesn't respond.

"What, now I don't trust you?" I ask.

"Beecher, the fact you were there for me today—with Nico—I know how you feel. And I pray you know how I feel. In all these years . . . People aren't nice to me the way you're nice to me. But the only thing I don't understand: How come you never told me what you saw in those call numbers—y'know, in the book?"

She's talking about the invisible ink message:

Exitus

FEBRUARY 16

Acta

26 YEARS IS A LONG TIME TO KEEP A SECRET

Probat

WRITE BACK: NC 38.548.19 OR WU 773.427

"You know what those numbers mean, don't you?" she asks. "You know what books they are."

I shake my head.

"Beecher, you don't have to tell me. Honestly, you don't. But if I can help—"

"They're not books," I say.

Making a left and following the parade of cars as it edges toward I-395 and the signs for the 14th Street Bridge, I take another glance at the rearview. SUVs, hybrids, taxis—a few pushy drivers elbow their way in, but for the most part, everything's in the same place.

"Beecher, I was there. The guy in Preservation said—"

"The Diamond doesn't know what he—"

"Wait. What's the diamond?"

"Daniel. In Preservation. That's his nickname. *The Diamond*," I tell her. "And while he's clearly the expert on book construction and chemical reactions, he doesn't know squat about library science— because if he did, he'd know that neither of those is a call number."

She squints as if she's trying to reread the numbers from memory.

"NC 38.548.19 or WU 773.427," I repeat for her. "They *look* like library call numbers, right? But they're both missing their cutters." Reading her confusion, I explain, "In any call number, there're two sets of letters. The NC is the first set—the N tells us it's *Art*.

All N books have to do with art. The C will tell you what *kind* of art—Renaissance, modern, et cetera. But before the last set of numbers—the 19—there's always another letter—the *cutter*. It cuts down the subject, telling you the author or title or some other subdivision so you can find it. Without that second letter, it's not a real call number."

"Maybe they left out the second letters on purpose."

"I thought so too. Then I saw the other listing: WU 773.427."

"And the W stands for . . . ?"

"That's the problem. W doesn't stand for anything."

"What do you mean?"

"Years ago, every library had their own individual system. But to make things more uniform, when the world switched over to the Library of Congress system, every letter was assigned to a different subject. Q stood for *Science*. K stood for *Law*. But three letters—W, X, and Y—they never got assigned to anything."

"So if a book begins with an X—"

"Actually, Xs sometimes mean books that're held behind the main desk, maybe because they're racy or dirty—guess where *X-rated* comes from? But you get the picture. A book that starts WU . . . that's just not a book at all."

"Could it be something besides a book?"

"Ten bucks says that's what Tot's working on right now," I explain as I check in the rearview. The towering Archives building is long gone. "I know under the filing system for Government Publications, W is for the old War Department. But WU—it doesn't exist."

"So it can't be anything?"

"Anything can be anything. But whatever it is, it's not in the regular system, which means it could be in an older library that doesn't use the system, or a private one, or a—"

"What kind of private one? Like someone's personal library?" she asks.

I rub my thumbs in tiny circles on the steering wheel, digesting the thought. Huh. With all the running around for Dustin Gyrich, I hadn't thought about that.

"Y'think the President has his own private library at the White House?" she asks.

I stay silent.

"Beecher, y'hear what I said?"

I nod, but I'm quiet, my thumbs still making tiny circles.

"What's wrong? Why're you shutting down like that?" she asks. Before I can say anything, she knows the answer.

"You're worried you can't win this," she adds.

All I hear are Orlando's words from that first moment we found the book in the SCIF. *Name me one person ever who went up against a sitting President and walked away the same way they walked in.* "I *know* we can't win this. No one can win this. No one wins against a President."

"That's not true. As long as you have that book—and as long as he doesn't *know* you have that book—you have him, Beecher. You can use that to—"

I start breathing hard. My thumb-circles get faster.

"You okay?" she asks.

I stay silent.

"Beecher, what's wrong?"

Staring straight ahead, I motion outside. "Bridges. I don't like bridges."

She glances to her right as we're halfway up the incline. But it's not until the road peaks and we pass the glowing white columns along the back of the Jefferson Memorial that she spots the wide blackness of the Potomac River fanning out ahead of us. The 14th Street Bridge's wide road doesn't look like a bridge. But based on the shade of green that now matches my face with hers, she knows it feels like one.

"You're kidding, right?" she laughs.

I don't laugh back. "My father died on a bridge."

"And my father tried to kill the President. Top that."

"Please stop talking now. I'm trying not to throw up by visualizing that I'm back in colonial times writing letters with a dipped-ink pen."

"That's fine, but have you even seen what you're missing? This view," she adds, pointing out her window, "you can see the entire back of the Jefferson Memorial."

"I've seen the view. We have the finest shots in the world in our photographic records. We have the early files from when the commission was first discussing it. We even have the original blueprints that—"

"Stop the car."

"Pardon?"

"You heard. Stop the car. *Trust me.*"

"Clemmi, I'm not—"

She grips the handle and kicks the car door open. Blasts of cold air create a vacuum that sucks our hair, and a stray napkin on the floor, to the right. The tires of the car *choom-choom-choom* across the plates in the bridge's roadbed.

I slam the brakes and an opera of horns finds quick harmony behind us. As I jerk the wheel and pull us along the shoulder of the bridge, the open door of the Mustang nearly scrapes against the concrete barrier.

"Are you mental!?" I shout as we buck to a stop. "This isn't some eighth grade—!"

"Don't do that."

"Huh?"

"Don't go to eighth grade...don't talk about something old... don't bring up old memories that have nothing to do with who we are now. *This* is all that matters! *Today,*" she says as the horns keep honking behind us.

"The cops are gonna be here in two seconds," I say, keeping my head down and staring at my crotch to avoid looking over the bridge. "You can't stop at national monuments."

"Sure you can. We just did. Now look up and tell me what you see."

"I can't."

"You can. Just try. I know you can."

"Clemmi..."

203

"Try, Beecher. Just try."

In the distance, I hear the sirens.

"Please," she adds as if she's pleading for my soul.

In no mood to face another set of law enforcement officers, and still hearing Orlando calling me Professor Indiana Jones, I raise my head and quickly glance to the right. It lasts a second. Maybe two. The wind's made a wreck of Clementine's hair, but over her shoulder I have a clear view of the bright white dome of the Jefferson Memorial. I pause, surprised to feel my heart quicken.

"How's it look?" she asks.

"Truthfully? Kinda horrible," I say, eyeing the curves of the marble stonework. "It's just the back. You can't see the good part with the statue."

"But it's *real*," she says, looking over at the memorial. "And at least you saw it for yourself. Not in a book. Not in some old record. You saw it here—*now*—in the freezing cold, from the side of a bridge, in a way that no tourists ever experience it."

My fists still clutch the steering wheel. I keep my head down, again refusing to look outside. But I am listening.

"That was the part I liked," I say.

"You sound surprised."

"I kinda am," I admit as my heart begins to gallop. "I'd never seen it from this angle."

Turning away from the Jefferson Memorial, Clementine glances my way—just a bit as she peers over her shoulder—and looks back at me. Our eyes lock. She won't let herself smile—she's still making her point. But I see the appreciation for the trust.

"She did dump me," I blurt.

"Excuse me?"

"My fiancée. Iris. You asked before. She did dump me."

"I figured," she says. "It's pretty obvious."

"But it wasn't for another guy."

"For another *girl*?" Clementine asks.

"I wish. Then I would've at least had a good story."

This is the part where she's supposed to ask, *What happened?* But she doesn't.

My head's still down. My hands still clutch the wheel. As I relive the moment, she sees the pain I'm in.

"Beecher, if you don't want to, you don't have to say it. It really doesn't matter."

"She dumped me for the worst reason of all," I say as the sirens continue to get closer. "For absolutely no reason at all."

"Beecher..."

I clench my teeth to keep it all in. "I mean, if she fell in love with someone else, or I did something wrong, or I let her down in some unforgivable way...That, I'd understand, right? But instead, she said...it wasn't *anything*. Not a single thing. It was just *me*. I was nice. I was kind. We just...she didn't see the connection anymore." I look up at Clementine, whose mouth is slightly open. "I think she just thought I was boring. And the cruelest part is, when someone says something mean about you, you know when they're right."

Watching me from the passenger seat, Clementine barely moves.

"Can I tell you something?" she finally offers. "Iris sounds like a real shitwad."

I laugh, almost choking on the joy it brings.

"And can I tell you something else, Beecher? I don't think you're in love with the past. I think you're scared of the future."

I lift my head, turning toward her in the seat next to me. When we were leaving St. Elizabeths, Clementine said that the hardest part of seeing Nico was that so much of her life suddenly made sense. And I know I'm overstating it, and being melodramatic, and rebounding something fierce just because we raised the specter of Iris—but ever since Clementine returned to my life...life doesn't make complete sense. But it definitely makes more sense than it used to.

I turn toward the passenger seat and lean in toward Clementine. She freezes. But she doesn't pull away. I lean even closer, moving slowly, my fingers brushing her cheek and touching the wisps of her short black hair. As my lips part against hers, I'm overcome by her taste, a mix of caramel and a pinch of peach from her lip gloss.

There are great kissers in this world.

I'm not one of them.

I'm not sure Clementine is one of them. But she's damn near close.

"You got better since Battle of the Bands," she whispers as she takes a quick breath.

"You remember that?"

"C'mon, Beecher... how could I forget my first kiss?" she asks, the last few syllables vibrating off my lips.

Within seconds, I'm no longer leaning toward her. She's leaning toward me.

I'm overwhelmed by her scent... by the way her short black hair skates against my cheek... by the way her hand tumbles down my chest and slides so close to everything I'm feeling in my pants.

Behind us, a flood of red lights pummels the back window. I barely heard the siren from the police car, which is now two cars behind us, trying to get us moving.

Taking a breath, I slowly pull away.

"Feeling any better?" she asks.

"Definitely better. Though also pretty terrified that we're still on this bridge."

She offers a quick laugh. But as she settles back in her seat, she knots her eyebrows, offering a brand-new look—a sad silent confession that I've never seen before. Like yet another new door has opened—I'm starting to realize she's got dozens of them—and I finally get to see what's inside. "We're all terrified," she says as we race ahead and leave the bridge behind. "That's how you know you're alive, Beecher. Welcome to the present."

"Please make next... left turn," the female GPS voice announces through my cell phone over an hour later. *"Destination is... straight ahead... on the left."*

"Clemmi, we're here," I call out as I hit the brakes at the red light, waiting to turn onto her narrow block. As I've done at every stop since the moment we left the highway, I check the rearview. No one in sight.

When we first arrived in the small city of Winchester, Virginia, a huge brick residence hall and an overabundance of kids with back-packs told me we were in a college town. But as with any college town, there's the *good part* of the college town, and the *bad part* of the college town. The closer we weaved toward Clementine's block, those students gave way to boarded-up row houses, far too many abandoned factories, and even a pawn shop. Let's be clear: The good part of town never gets the pawn shop.

"Clemmi, we're ... I think we're here," I add as I turn onto the long dark block that's lined with a set of beat-up skinny row houses. Half the streetlights are busted. At the very last second, I also notice a taxi, its dim lights turning onto the block that we just left.

Two years ago, the Archives hosted a brown bag lunch for an author who was presenting a book about the effects of fear and its role in history. He said that when you go down a dark alley and you feel that tingling across the back of your neck, that's not just a bad feeling, that's a biological gift from God—the Gift of Fear, he called it. He said when you ignore that gift—when you go down the dark alley and say, *Y'know, I'm sure it'll be okay*—that's when you find real pain.

Next to me, while I'm still replaying our kiss, Clementine is fast asleep in the passenger seat, exhausted from the long ride as her chin rests on her clavicle. It's late enough and quiet enough that when I listen closely, I can hear the rise and fall of her breath-ing. But as I squint to read house numbers and pass one home with a door off its hinges, and another with a spray-painted sign across the front that reads PVC *pipes only, no copper inside*, all I hear right now is God's biological gift telling me this is not where I want to be.

Behind us, a car turns onto the block, then changes its mind and disappears.

"*Destination,*" the GPS voice announces. "*You have arrived.*"

BRAD MELTZER

Leaning forward, I double-check the house numbers: 355. This is it.

With a jerk of the wheel, I pull into the nearest open spot, right in front of a freestanding row house with a saggy old sofa on the front porch. I remember having a house like this. Back in college.

As I shift the car into park, my hand knocks into Clementine's purse, which sits between the bucket seats and opens its mouth at the impact. Inside, I spot the edge of a purple leather wallet, a ring of keys, and a single sheet of paper that makes me smile. Even with just the light from the lamppost, there's no missing what's on it—it's young me and Clementine, in a photocopied black-and-white version of the framed photo she gave me earlier today. She gave me the color one. But she kept a copy. For herself.

"Mary Mother of Christ! What you do to my girl?" a cigarette-stained voice calls from outside.

I jump at the noise, but as I scan the block, I don't see—

"*You!* You heard me!"

The sound takes me up the cracked brick steps, to the front door of Clementine's house. The screen door's shut, but thanks to the glow of the TV inside, I see the outline of an old woman with a bob of white hair.

"She said she'd call me back—she never called me back!" the woman shouts, shoving the screen door open and storming out into the cold wearing a faded pink sweatsuit. She hobbles down the stairs.

Right at us.

49

lemmi, this would be a good time to get up..." I call out, shaking her awake. As I kick the car door open, the woman—in her late sixties, maybe seventies—is already halfway down the stairs. She's a thin and surprisingly tall woman whose sharp features and natural elegance are offset by the slight hunch that comes with age.

"And I'm freezing!" she yells. "Where the hell you been?"

"Nan, you need to get inside," Clementine pleads, snapping awake and racing from the car.

Nan. Nana. Grandmother. Clemmi's grandmother.

"Don't you tell me where to go!" the grandmother explodes, narrowing her glassy blue eyes, which seem to glow in the night. As she reaches the curb, she shoves a plastic bottle of pills at Clementine's chest. "With dinner! You know I take my medicine with dinner!" Turning to me, she warns, "Don't you think I'm talkin' 'bout drugs either! Rectal cancer. I got cancer in my rectum," she says, patting the side of her leg. I didn't notice it at first. The lump that's hidden inside her sweatpants. A colostomy bag.

"What kinda person leaves ya with no way to open your medicine?"

"Nan, I'm sorry..."

At first, I assume it's Clementine's way to soften Nan's outrage, but the way Clementine won't look her in the eye...She's terrified of this woman.

On our far left, at the very end of the block, there's a loud *clink-clink*. Like a beer bottle spinning on concrete. Clementine and her grandmother don't even notice. I tell myself it's a cat.

"Of course you're sorry," Nan growls, snatching the now open prescription vial from Clementine's hands. Again turning to me, she adds, "Who're *you* anyway? You the one who did this to her?"

"Did what?" I ask.

"Nan!" Clemmi pleads.

"Y'know what this chemo costs? Two hundred dollars a bottle—and that's *with insurance!*"

"*Nan!*"

Nan stops right there, locking back on Clemmi. "Did you just raise your voice at me?"

"Don't talk to him like that."

Clearly smoldering, Nan slides her jaw off-center, opens her mouth, and pops her jawbone like she's cocking a gun. It freaks the hell outta me. From the look on Clementine's face, I'm not the only one.

"I know you want me dead," Nan says.

"I don't want you dead," Clementine pleads, cutting past her on the stairs. "If I wanted you dead, I would've never agreed to look after you."

"Look after me? *I'm not a cat!* This is *my* house! You live with *me!*"

At the end of the block, a car door slams. I squint, cursing how far it is. No way was that a cat.

"Um...Clemmi," I try to interrupt.

"I'm not fighting with you, Nan. Not tonight."

"Why? Because your boyfriend's here in his nice fresh suit? You're worried about him seeing the real you—the girl that lost her job at the radio station and is lucky to live with an old lady?"

Clementine freezes. Nan stands up straight, well aware of the damage.

"You didn't even tell him you lost your job, did you?" Nan asks almost as if she's enjoying herself. "Lemme guess—you're still try-ing to impress him."

"Will you stop?" Turning to me, Clementine adds, "I swear, I was gonna tell you—I just figured one lie at a time—"

"I absolutely understand," Nan interrupts. "A girl in your condition—"

"*Nan!*" Clemmi explodes, her voice echoing up the dark block. "Beecher, I'm sorry—I really am. She gets mean when it's late."

"Hold on, this is *Beecher*?" Nan asks. "This is the one you used to have the crush on? He's a nothing—look at him!"

"You know nothing about him!" Clementine threatens.

"I can see right now...!"

"No. You can't see anything. And y'know why?" Clementine growls, turning back and leaning in close on the staircase. "Because even on your very best day, you're not *half* the person he is. Not *even close*," she insists as Nan takes a small step backward, down to the lower step.

"Beecher, I'm sorry—I'll call you tomorrow," Clementine calls out as she tugs her grandmother by the arm. "Nan, let's go."

Anxious to disappear, Clementine races up the stairs. Her grandmother's about to follow, but at the last moment the old woman turns back to me, feeling my stare. "What? You being judgmental? Say it already."

"You're lucky you have her," I tell her.

Her jaw shifts off-center, and I again wait for the pop. The only thing that comes is her low whisper, each syllable puffing with a tiny blast of cold air. "Go lick yourself, Dudley Do-Right. If it wasn't for you knocking her up, she wouldn't even be in this mess."

A buzzing in my ears becomes deafening.

"Wh-What?"

"You think I'm blind *as well as* dumb? Would you really be coming back here if she didn't have you by the scrotum with this kid thing? I swear to Christ, they keep getting dumber."

"Nan! Come inside!" Clementine calls out.

With a final angry glare—a protective glare—the old woman makes her way back up the brick staircase, the colostomy bag swaying like a pendulum inside her pant leg.

For a moment, I just stand there.

Pregnant.

If it's true...it'd certainly explain why Clemmi was nauseous before—and more important, why now, of all moments, she suddenly started looking for her father.

Still, as it all sets in, as I realize where I am—alone...in the dark...with no one around—I need to get out of here.

Opening the door and sliding inside Tot's car, I notice a black leatherette glove in the passenger seat. The fingers are thin. Definitely Clementine's.

I look up the brick staircase. Both the screen door and the main door are shut. But I can still see the glow of the light inside.

I should leave her alone. She's had enough embarrassment for one night. But if I drop it off now...It'll only take a second. I can even make sure she's okay.

I elbow the car door open.

As I hop outside, a hard shove drills me from behind, knocking me face-forward to the pavement. I fight to stop the fall, but my arms—*zzzzppp, zzzzppp*—they're pinned...handcuffed...Whoever it is, he's strong. My arms are pinned behind my back.

Help! Someone help, I want to yell as my chin stabs the concrete and the wind's knocked out of me. A sharp knee digs into my back and long strong fingers stuff a smelly rag in my mouth. The smell... It's awful...Like burnt hair.

I try to spit out the rag, but the strong fingers grip my mouth and pinch my nose, making me take an even deeper breath.

Facedown on the pavement, I twist like a fish, trying to fight... to get free...to get a look at my attacker. A second knee stabs my back.

Dizziness sets in...

No, don't pass out!

I twist again and he shoves my face down, pinning my left cheek to the cold pavement, which now seems soft and warm. Like it's melting. The world seesaws and continues to tumble.

The very last thing I see, in the reflection of the Mustang's shiny hubcap, is an upside-down, funhouse-mirror view of my attacker.

*   *   *

50

I'm awake.

    I was unconscious, now I'm awake.

    It takes nothing to snap between the two. No time.

My eyes open, and I'm staring at bright yellow flowers. Sunflowers. My sister loves sunflowers.

I blink quickly, struggling to adjust to the light.

It's light. Is...is it daytime?

No, the curtains are closed. The light's in here.

There's the hum of central heating.

My brain's swirling. Is Clemmi...? Yeah...I remember... Clemmi's pregnant.

Nuhhh.

Clemmi's pregnant and my chin hurts. It hurts bad.

My shoulders are sore. A hard tug tells me why. My arms are still handcuffed behind my back.

But as I look down, what catches my eye is the chair I'm sitting in. It's got armrests. Upholstered fancy armrests. With nailheads.

I look back at the sunflowers. They sit in a fine Asian vase on a beautiful hand-carved coffee table.

In the Archives, I've read the top-secret reports of where the CIA brought all the terror suspects after 9/11. It wasn't a well-appointed room like this.

But even without the handcuffs, drugging, and kidnapping, I'm starting to think this is worse.

I glance around, trying to figure out how long I've been out. It looks dark through the closed curtains, but it could just as easily be early morning. I search the room for a clock. Nothing. In fact, the more I look around—at the little wastebasket, at the built-in library, where every leather-bound book is the exact same size—the whole room is so perfect, it makes me wonder if I'm in some kinda hotel, or...maybe this is someone's private SCIF...

On my left, I spot a framed black-and-white photograph of the White House covered with scaffolding and surrounded by dump trucks. It's from 1949, back when they were doing the construction that added the Truman Balcony.

Please tell me I'm not in the White House...

There's a flush of a toilet behind me.

I twist in my seat, frantically following the sound. Someone's in the bathroom. But what grabs my attention is the sliding mirrored door of the closet that sits next to it.

The closet's empty. No clothes...no shoes...not even a set of hangers.

It's the same all around.

No trash in the garbage. No photos on the walls...or the end tables...The chocolate brown leather sofa on my left has no give in any of the cushions. Like it's never been sat in.

What the hell is this place? Why aren't there any signs of life?

I try to fight free, but my head nearly caves in. Whatever they drugged me with...the dizziness...it's still taking its toll.

From the bathroom, there's a rush of water from the sink. Underneath the door, a shadow passes and...

Click.

I spin back as my weight jerks the chair into a half-spin. The bathroom door opens and my attacker reveals— That smell...Of cherry rum.

Cherry rum pipe smoke.

"Man, I really messed up your chin, didn't I?" Dallas asks, stepping forward, scratching at his little beard, and reminding me why he was always the most hated archivist in our office. "Sorry, Beech—we just needed to get you out of there. When I saw someone following—"

"What're you talking about? What the hell's going on?"

214

"I can explain."

"You damn well better explain!"

My brain flips back to yesterday. When they were taking Orlando's body out, I spotted Dallas with Rina, and they quickly ran for cover. Right now, though, he stands his ground, taking new pride in whatever it is he's up to.

"Remember when you first started at the Archives, Beecher?"

"Are you about to make a speech right now? Because if I get out of these handcuffs, I'm about to kill you."

"Listen to me," Dallas insists. "Remember that first night when you worked late, and visiting hours were over, and all the tourists were gone—and you made your way down to the Rotunda, just to stand in the darkness so you could have your own private viewing of the Declaration of Independence? Every employee in the building has that moment, Beecher. But as you stood there by yourself and you studied those fifty-six handwritten signatures that changed the entire world, remember that wondrous feeling where you dreamed what it would be like to be a part of history like that?" Dallas touches the gash on my chin. From the pain, I jerk my head up. He gets what he wants. I'm now looking him right in the eye. The smell of his pipe seeps off him. "This is your chance to add your signature, Beecher. History's calling you. All you have to do is help us."

"*Us?* Who's *us?*"

"The Culper Ring," Dallas says. "We're the Culper Ring. And with your help, we can catch the other one."

"The other *what?*"

"The ones who did this. The ones who killed Orlando. The other Culper Ring, of course."

51

It was cold and late—well past two in the morning—as Dr. Palmiotti stared at the drop phone that sat on his nightstand.

But as he lay there, wrapped in his down comforter, he knew he wasn't even close to sleep.

For a while, he tried his usual tricks: visualizing a walk in the wide green stretch of grass in the arboretum behind his college dorm. He didn't particularly like the outdoors. But he liked the idea of it. And he liked college. And usually, that was enough to do the trick.

Not tonight.

"Baby, you're gonna be exhausted tomorrow," Lydia said, rolling toward him as she faded back into her own slumber. "Stop worrying about him. If he needs you, he'll call."

He was still amazed to see her do things like that—to read him so clearly . . . to *feel* him being awake. He was lucky to have her. She understood him better in six months than his ex-wife did in nearly twenty years. And for a while, he thought about just that—in particular, about their night at the Four Seasons and the thing with the fishnet stockings she had done for his birthday—hoping it would be the key to his sleep.

But once again, the doctor's thoughts wandered back to his friend, and the message the President had written, and to this nightmare at the Archives—which of course took Palmiotti right back to his nightstand, to the phone with the gold presidential seal on the receiver.

If he needs you, he'll call.

It was good advice. But the one thing it failed to take into account was just how complex a President's needs were. In fact, it was those particular needs that caused the Ring to be created in the first place. Both Rings. And while it was bad enough that someone accidentally found the book, if the rest was true, if there was now a third party involved and the original Culper Ring was closing in . . . In med school, they used to call it CD. It had the same acronym in politics. Certain Death.

Palmiotti stuck his leg out from the comforter, trying to break his sweat. The drop phone would be ringing any minute.

But for the next hour and a half, nothing happened.

Palmiotti was tempted to call the medical unit. From there, the on-duty nurse could confirm that Wallace was upstairs. But Palmiotti knew he was upstairs. At this hour, where else would the President be?

By 4 a.m., the doctor was still tossing and twisting, eyeing the phone and waiting for it to ring. He knew his friend. He knew what had to be going through his head. He knew everything that was now at stake.

The phone *had* to ring.

But it never did. Not tonight.

And as Dr. Palmiotti stared up at his ceiling, both legs sticking out of his comforter, one hand holding Lydia, it was that merciless silence that worried him most of all.

52

"Why am I in handcuffs?"

"Beecher, did you hear a word I just said?" Dallas asks.

"Why am I in handcuffs!?"

"So you wouldn't do exactly what you're doing right now, namely throwing a fit rather than focusing on the big picture," Dallas shoots back. "Now. For the second time. Did you hear what I said?"

"There are two Culper Rings. I got it. But if you don't undo these cuffs..."

"Then what? You'll scream? Go. Scream. See what happens," he says, motioning at the barely lived-in room.

I take another glance around, still stuck in my seat. I'm not sure I believe there's really such a thing as a two-hundred-year-old secret spy unit. And even if I did, I'm not sure why they'd ever pick Dallas. But there's only one way to get answers. "Where are we anyway? What is this place?"

"I'm trying to tell you, Beecher. Now I know you don't like me. I know you've never liked me. But you need to understand two things: First, I want to get you out of here—the longer we keep you out of sight, the more suspicious it looks. Second, I'm on your side here. Okay? We're all on your side."

I'm about to unleash, but as my shoulders go numb, I stay locked on the priorities. "Undo the cuffs."

"And then you'll listen?"

"I can't feel my pinkies, Dallas. Undo the cuffs."

Squatting behind me, he pulls something from his pocket and

there're two loud snaps. As the blood flushes back to my wrists, he tosses the set of clear plasticuffs into the no-longer-empty trash can.

"Here...take this," he says, reaching for the bookcase and handing me a square cocktail napkin. I didn't even notice it before—an entire shelf in the bookcase is filled with a high-end selection of rum, vodka, scotch, and the rest. Whatever this room is used for, it clearly requires a good drink.

He pulls a few cubes from a silver ice bucket and drops them in my napkin. "For your chin," he explains, looking surprised when I don't say thanks.

"At Clementine's...to be there," I say as I put the ice to my chin. "How long were you following?"

"I wasn't *following.* I was trying to talk to you—to get you alone. I mean, yesterday in Orlando's office...this morning when Tot chased me away. Have you really not noticed how often I've been showing up?"

"So you gas and cuff me? That's your solution? Send an email next time! Or wait...just call! It's a lot less headache!"

Shaking his head, Dallas takes a seat on the leather sofa. "You really don't understand how this works, do you? Face-to-face—that's the only reason it's lasted. The problem is, every time I get near you, you're running off with your little group, and no offense, but...your high school first kiss? That's who you're trusting your life to?"

"I'm not trusting my life to her."

"You *are*, Beecher. You don't think you are, but you are. What you found in that SCIF—that was a miracle that happened—a true gift from God that you stumbled upon." I watch him carefully as he says the words. He's the only person besides Tot and Clemmi to even guess how this all started, which brings a strange reassurance that makes me think he's telling the truth. "But I promise you this," Dallas continues, "if you don't start being careful—when they confirm you have it—they'll put you in the ground even faster than Orlando. That's not just hyperbole, Beecher. That's math."

The ice on my chin sends a waterslide of cold down my Adam's apple and into the neck of my shirt. I barely feel it. "You keep saying *they*. Is that who you saw following me?"

"I couldn't see who they were. I think they spotted me first."

"Y'mean the car that almost turned down the block?"

"That wasn't just a car. It was a taxi. A D.C. taxi. Out that far in Virginia. Real hell of a commute, don't you think—unless that's your only choice because someone borrowed your car."

Omigod. The Mustang. "Is Tot's car...!?"

"His car is fine. We had it driven here, then sent a text from your phone saying you'd pick him up tomorrow. He didn't reply. You see what I'm getting at?"

I know exactly what he's getting at. "You think it was Tot in that taxi."

"I have no idea who it was, but I do know this: There's no way the President is pulling this off without help from someone inside our building."

The napkin filled with ice sends a second waterslide down the inside of my wrist, to my elbow. Orlando said it. Clemmi said it. Even I said it. But to hear those words—*the President*—not the president of some useless company—*the President of the United States*. This isn't just confirmation that the message in that dictionary was meant for Orson Wallace. It's confirmation that when it comes to my life— I can't even think about it.

"Tell me what the Culper Ring really is," I demand.

"The true Culper Ring?"

"The one that did this. The one the President's in."

"The President's in both."

"Dallas, I'm officially about to leap over that coffee table and stuff my foot through your teeth."

"I'm not trying to be coy, Beecher. I swear to you, I'm not. But this is two hundred years of history we're talking about. If you want to understand what the Culper Rings are up to now, you first need to know where they originally came from."

*　　*　　*

53

Clementine knew it wasn't good for her.

That's why she waited until the house was quiet.

And why she locked the door to her room.

And then waited some more.

There were enough surprises tonight—most notably the kiss from Beecher. Clementine knew he'd try—eventually he'd try—but that didn't mean it didn't catch her off guard. Plus, the old woman had already done enough. She didn't need to be there for this too.

For comfort, Clementine whistled a quick "psst psst—here, Parky" at her chubby ginger cat, and as he always did, Parker slowly circled his way up the arms of the forest green futon to Clementine's lap, rubbing his head into her palms.

The cat's kindness was one of the few things Clementine could count on these days, and it was exactly that thought that brought the sudden swell of tears to her eyes.

It reminded her of when she first moved to Virginia and ventured into the local Home Depot to buy a barbecue grill to celebrate the Fourth of July. Stopping one of the orange-overalled employees—a short man with chapped lips and greedy eyes—she asked, "Do I need to spend the few hundred bucks to buy a good grill, or would one of the fifty-dollar cheap grills do the job just as well?"

Licking his chapped lips, the employee said, "Let me explain it like this: I'm a car guy. I love cars. I love *all* cars. And I especially love my 1989 Camaro RS, which I recently spent over $3,000 on to put in a sunroof. Now. You ask yourself: Why would someone spend $3,000 to install a sunroof in some old car from 1989? You wanna know why? Because I'm a *car guy*. That's who I am. That's what I care about. So as you look at these grills, you need to ask yourself..." He took a deep breath and leaned in toward her. "Are you a grill gal?"

The man didn't need to say another word. Smiling to herself, Clementine grabbed a cheap fifty-dollar grill and marched toward the cash register. She wasn't a *grill gal*. Or a *car gal*, a *clothes gal*, or even a *shoe gal*.

She knew who she was. She was a *cat gal*.

No, it wasn't in that crazy-cat-lady way. And yes, there were plenty of people who love their cats and buy them cute plastic toys and high-end scratching posts. Pets can be the very best family members. But there were still only a few who annually throw their cat a real birthday party...or make appointments solely with *feline-only vets,* who only see cats as patients...or make sure that their cat's food and water bowls sit atop a wrought-iron base that keeps the bowls at cat-eye level so that their pet doesn't have to bend to drink.

Some people buy sunroofs. Some buy expensive grills. And some spend their money on a treasured pet. Clementine could even laugh at the insanity of it, but she was proud of being a cat gal—it was always her thing. Until she arrived at St. Elizabeths and saw her father so delicately and beautifully tending to all the cats there.

Just the sight of it made her feel like someone had hollowed out her body and stolen all her organs for themselves. Like her personal parts were no longer her own. It was the same feeling she had when she found out Nico was living so close to where she moved in Virginia. Or when he said that everything in life was already decided. Or when she read that he was almost her age when he had his first psychotic episode.

Of course she told herself none of that meant anything. Life was full of woo-woo coincidences.

But it was still her dad...her dad who lived near her...and looked so much like her...and somehow loved the exact same thing she loved so damn much. With everything else that she'd lost in life—the DJ jobs...the advertising jobs...even her mom—maybe in this moment, Clementine was due for a gain. Plus, it was still her dad. How could she not have some emotional connection?

And that was the one thing that Beecher—who lost his own father—understood better than anyone. Sure, seeing Nico was the hardest thing Clementine had ever done, but like any orphan, she wasn't tracking down her father to learn more about him. She was tracking him down to learn more about herself.

With the push of a button, Clementine's laptop hummed to life, and she sat back on the futon with Parker in her lap and the laptop by her side.

"I know, I know," she whispered to Parker.

It definitely wouldn't be good for her. And the worst part was, she knew the pain was only getting worse.

Of course, if she wanted, she could stop it. It'd be so easy to stop. All she had to do was shut the laptop. Slap it shut, go to sleep, and replay those moments of Beecher's reaffirming kiss.

Indeed, as her fingers flicked across the keyboard and she hit the enter key, all she had to do was close her eyes.

But the saddest truth of all? She didn't want to.

Onscreen, the video on YouTube slowly loaded and began to play. Clementine leaned toward the computer, wrapping her arms around Parker's body. She pulled the cat close—especially when the man with the big politician's grin stepped out onto the NASCAR track, his black windbreaker puffing up like a balloon.

On the far right of the screen, a man in a yellow jumpsuit entered the frame and raised his gun.

And as she had so many times before, Clementine felt her stomach fall as she watched her father try to murder the President.

54

I know about the Culper Ring," I tell Dallas. "They were George Washington's civilian spy group. They hid messages...they stayed secret...and from what I can tell, they stuck around long enough to have a hand in Gettysburg, World War I, and even somehow Hiroshima."

"How'd you know that last part?" Dallas challenges.

"You think you're the only history nut in the building? We all have access to the same records. Once we found the name Dustin Gyrich—"

"Gyrich. Okay. Okay, you're further than we thought," he says, almost to himself. "But you're wrong about one thing, Beecher: From Gettysburg to Hiroshima to anything else, the Culper Ring has never *had a hand* in these events. You're missing the mission completely."

"But we're right about the rest, aren't we? The Culper Ring that George Washington started, it still exists."

Leaning forward on the leather sofa, Dallas uses his top two teeth to comb the few beard hairs below his bottom lip. He does the same thing when our boss scolds him for falling behind on the quota we have for answering researchers' letters and emails. It's also my first clue that while he's happy to answer some of my questions, he's not answering all of them.

"Beecher, do you know what the President of the United States needs more than anything else? And I don't just mean Orson Wallace. Any President, any era. Obama, the Bushes, Thomas Jefferson. What's the one thing they need more than anything else?"

"You mean, besides smart advice?"

"No. Smart advice is easy. You're the President. Every genius in the world is banging down your door. Try again."

"This is already a stupid game."

"Just try again."

"Privacy?"

"That's top three. You're Reagan. You're Obama. You have more power than anyone. What's even more vital than privacy?"

"Trust."

"Getting warmer."

"Someone who cares about you."

"Getting colder. Think back to George Washington. Why'd he say the Culper Ring helped him win the Revolutionary War?"

"They brought him the best information."

"*Information!* There. *Bull's-eye.* You see it now, right? That is the most, and I mean *the most,* vital thing that a President needs to do his job: reliable information. You understand that?"

"I'm not an idiot."

"Then understand this: Our bureaucracy is so vast, by the time a piece of information makes its way to the President's desk, it's like a chewed-over dog bone. It goes from the guy on the ground, up to a supervisor, up to an analyst, up to a chief of staff, up to a deputy secretary, then up to the real secretary, then through the true honchos who pick through it...and then, if it's lucky, there it is... dumped on your desk, Mr. President. And now you have to take that drool-covered piece of info and use it to make a military, or environmental, or financial decision that'll affect millions or maybe billions of lives. You ready to rely on that?"

"It's not that simple."

"It *is* that simple. It's always been that simple. And it is—still— the greatest problem facing every President: You're the one man in charge, and every day you're making life-and-death decisions based on the work of total strangers with unknown agendas. And that's why, when you're sitting there with all those above-top-secret reports about every problem in the world, you can't help but wonder: *What* don't *I know? What'd they leave* out *of these reports? And what're the motives and biases built in to the info I'm getting?"*

"So the Culper Ring works for the President."

"No. The Culper Ring doesn't work for the President. It works for the *Presidency.* It serves the office, just as George Washington designed it—a built-in backstop to be used when it was needed most. Think about it, Beecher—before you drop the bomb on Hiroshima, wouldn't you want to be absolutely sure the Japanese weren't already about to surrender? Or before you went to slaughter your brother in Gettysburg, wouldn't you want to make sure you had the right general in place? Major General Meade was installed just four days before the fighting at Gettysburg began. Pretty good timing by Lincoln, eh?"

My mind swirls through the examples we found in the Archives—the Bay of Pigs...Sputnik...the *Lusitania*—each one its own critical moment in presidential history. It swirls even more when it reminds me that of all the theories we had, it's still Nico who was most correct. The President's definitely communicating through that dictionary. But it doesn't change the one thing I refuse to lose focus on:

"You said there were two," I tell Dallas. "Two Rings."

"And now you're seeing the problem," he says with a nod. "Every once in a while, there's kind of a...speed bump."

"Define speed bump."

"Beecher, I've already kept you here for too long. If they're watching—"

"Tell me about the second Ring, Dallas. Tell me, or I swear to you, I'll type up this crap and you'll be reading about it in the *Washington Post* tomorrow!"

"I know that's not true—that's not who you are. And if I didn't know that, we wouldn't even be having this conversation."

"Then have the damn conversation!"

Like before, he uses his teeth to comb at some stray beard hairs. But unlike before, his head is cocked to the side, his eyes staring off. Like he's listening to something.

"What're you doing?" I challenge.

He doesn't answer. But as he turns his head, I spot—in his ear—there's something in his ear.

"Is that an earpiece? Are you—? Is someone listening to us right now!?" I shout as I start to search the room. No mirrors. No cameras in the corners.

"They said to calm down, Beecher. You already passed the test."

"What test? Who's *they*? How the hell're they seeing us!?"

I rush to the little minibar, shoving the bottles of alcohol aside. I pull the top off the ice bucket. No wires anywhere.

It's on you, isn't it? You're wearing a camera!"

"Listen to me, Beecher—"

I hop over the coffee table, knocking the flowers to the floor. He leaps off the sofa and, like a lion tamer, grabs the armchair, trying to keep it between us.

"Will you listen to me!?" he says. "This isn't about you!"

"That's not true! This is *my life* you're screwing with!"

"You idiot! Your life's *already over!*"

I stop at the words.

His fingers dig into the back of the armchair.

"What'd you say?" I ask.

He doesn't answer.

"You said my life is over."

"We can protect you. We're protecting you right now." To prove the point, Dallas heads to the closed curtains and spreads them just a few feet apart, revealing a city block filled with parked cars, but empty of people and bathed in darkness. We're on the second floor of a brick townhouse, and though it takes me a moment, as I scan the restaurants across the street . . . that CVS.

"We're in Woodley Park," I say.

"We are. But we're also in the only residential house on a busy street where it's difficult to stop, making this building nearly impossible to observe without being observed. When it went up for sale, we were bidding against both the Israelis *and* the Palestinians."

"So this is . . . what? . . . some sorta safehouse?"

"You see that homeless guy across the street?" Dallas asks. "He'll be there until 4 a.m., at which point another 'homeless man' will clock in and take his place for a full eight-hour shift. Think about it, Beecher. There's a reason the FBI is the second biggest property renter in Washington, D.C. This is how you do it right."

I turn away as he lets the curtains shut. "You said my life is over."

"Beecher, you have to understand. When you found what you found..."

"I don't even know what I found. Tell me what I found."

"You found proof. That dictionary— That's proof that they exist."

"That what exists? A second Culper Ring?"

Dallas shakes his head, double-checking that the curtains are shut tight. "Don't call them that. They don't deserve to be called that."

"That's what they are, though, aren't they?"

Dallas sits with this a moment. I can't tell if he's thinking, or listening to whatever's being whispered in his ear, but eventually he says, "Every dozen or so administrations, it happens. It has to happen, right? Every person who's sworn in as President has his own agenda, and some of these guys—I heard the first was Millard Fillmore, though I think if you look at Ulysses Grant, or probably Harding—"

"I don't care about the 1920s or Teapot Dome."

"What about Watergate? You care about that one?"

"Time out. You're telling me that this other Culper Ring— whatever you want to call them—that they're the ones who pulled off Watergate?"

"No. Richard Nixon pulled off Watergate. But to make it happen, well..." Dallas heads over to the framed photo of the White House under construction. "Imagine the Culper Ring—our group, the *true* Culper Ring—as this giant *outer ring* that circles and has been protecting the Presidency for over two hundred years," he says, using his pointer-finger to draw a huge circle around the entire photograph. "And then imagine a guy like Nixon, who rides into power, and looks at that big wide outer ring and says to himself, 'Huh. I should have something like that around *me*.'"

"Like an *inner* ring."

"Like an inner ring," Dallas agrees, drawing a miniature little circle just around one of the White House windows. "Welcome to the speed bump. So he calls in a few friends that he knows he can trust—G. Gordon Liddy, Howard Hunt, and the rest of the crew— and voilà, Nixon has an inner ring that reports just to him. They call themselves the Plumbers. The rest, as they say, is you-know-what."

I stare at his imaginary circle around the White House window. At the Archives, we've got the original blueprints to the White House. Dallas didn't pick a random window. He picked the one on the second-floor Residence that I know President Wallace uses as his private office. "So you think—with the dictionary—you think that's what Wallace is doing right now? You think he's talking to his own personal Plumbers."

"You don't see the problem there?" Dallas asks.

"I guess I do, but . . . He's the President. Isn't he entitled to talk to whoever he wants, as secretively as he wants?"

"He absolutely is. But that doesn't mean he—or one of his group— is allowed to murder anyone they think is an accidental witness."

Orlando. Of course he's talking about Orlando. But for him to use that word. *Murder.*

"It wasn't a heart attack, was it?" I ask, though I already know the answer.

Once again, Dallas stays quiet. But unlike last time, he doesn't look away.

"Dallas, if you can confirm it, I need you to tell me," I demand. "I know the autopsy was today. If you have the results . . ."

"You don't need me to tell you anything," Dallas says with an emptiness in his voice that echoes like a battering ram against my chest. "They'll release the first round of tox reports in the next day or so, but you know what those results are. Just like you know nothing at this level is ever just an accident."

BRAD MELTZER

As the full weight of the battering ram hits, I nearly fall backward.

"Just remember, Beecher, when Nixon's Plumbers first started, they were on the side of the angels too, helping the White House protect classified documents." Like a woodpecker, Dallas taps his finger against the small window in the photo of the White House. "Absolute power doesn't corrupt absolutely—but it will make you do what you swore you'd never do, especially when you're trying to hold on to it."

I nod to myself, knowing he's right, but... "That still doesn't explain why you need me."

"You're joking, right? Haven't you seen the schedule?"

"What schedule?"

"Tomorrow. He's coming back for another reading visit." Eyeing the confusion on my face, Dallas explains, "The White House asked for you personally. You're his man, Beecher. When President Wallace comes back to the Archives tomorrow—when he's standing there inside that SCIF—they want you to be the one staffing him."

55

I t was only six seconds.

Six seconds of film.

Six seconds on YouTube.

But for Clementine, who was still curled on her futon, still clutching her cat for strength, and whose tired eyes still stared at the laptop screen, they were the most important six seconds of the entire video.

At this point, she knew just where to put her mouse on the progress bar so the little gray circle would hop back to 1:05 of the video. At 1:02, Nico first raised his gun, which you actually see before you see him. At 1:03, as he took a half-step out from the crowd of NASCAR drivers, you could make out just the arm of his jumpsuit— the bright sun ricocheting off a wide patch of yellow. At 1:04, the full yellow jumpsuit was visible. He was moving now. But it wasn't until 1:05 that you got the first clear view of Nico's full face.

The view lasted six seconds.

Six seconds where Nico's head was turned right at the camera.

Six seconds where Nico was calm; he was actually smiling.

Six quiet seconds—before the shooting and the screaming and the mayhem—where Clementine's father didn't look like a monster. He looked confident. At ease. He looked happy. And no question— even she could see it as his lips parted to reveal his grin—their expression was exactly the same. It was the only lie Beecher had told her. But she knew the truth. She looked just like her father.

Pop, pop, pop, the gunshots hiccupped at 1:12.

But by then, Clementine had already clicked her mouse, sending the little gray circle back to before the chaos began.

She'd been at it for a while now, over and over, the same six seconds. She knew it wasn't healthy.

Hoping to switch gears, she reached for her phone and dialed Beecher's number. Even with the long trek back, he should be home by now.

But as she held the receiver to her ear, she heard a few rings, then voicemail. She dialed again. Voicemail again.

She didn't think much of it. Instead, to her own surprise, she found herself thinking about their kiss.

She knew Beecher had it in him.

But as she was learning, Beecher was still full of surprises.

He's probably just asleep, she thought as she clicked back, and the video started again, and she watched again to see just how much she wasn't like her father.

"I know—I promise," she told her cat. "This'll be the last one."

56

Y ou should put the ice on your chin," Dallas says.

"I don't need ice," I say, even though I know I do. My chin's on fire. But it's nothing compared to what's coming. As I nudge the curtain open, I stare outside at a homeless man who's not a homeless man, from a residential townhouse that's not really a townhouse, and refuse to face my officemate, who I now understand is far more than just an officemate.

"Beecher, for Wallace to request you—it's a good thing."

"Yeah, that makes complete sense. In fact, it's absolutely obvious why locking me in an impenetrable bulletproof box with the most powerful man in the world—with no witnesses or anything to protect me—is just a perfect peach of an idea."

"We think he's going to make you an offer," he finally says.

"Who is? The President?"

"Why else would he ask for you, Beecher? You have something that was intended for him. So despite Orlando's death, and the FBI and Secret Service sniffing around the room, Wallace is coming right back to the scene of the crime, and he's asked for you to personally be there. Alone. In his SCIF. If we're lucky, when that door slams shut and those magnetic locks click, he'll start talking."

"Yeah, or he'll leave me just like Orlando."

Dallas shakes his head. "Be real. Presidents don't get dirt under their nails like that. They just give the orders. And sometimes, they don't even do that."

There's something in the way he says the words. "You don't think Wallace had a hand in this?" I ask.

"No, I think he *very much* had a hand in this, but what you keep forgetting is that what you found in that chair isn't just a book. It's a communication—and communications take two people."

"From the President to one of his Plumbers."

"But not just one of his Plumbers," Dallas corrects. "One of his Plumbers *who works in our building.* That's the key, Beecher. Whoever did this to Orlando...to be able to hide the book in that chair... to have access to the SCIF...it has to be someone on staff—or at the very least, someone with access to that room."

"To be honest, I thought it was *you.*"

"*Me?*" Dallas asks. "Why would it possibly be me?"

"I don't know. When I saw you in the hallway...when you were with Rina. Then when Gyrich came back to the building, you were the last person in Finding Aids."

"First, I wasn't *with Rina.* We got off the elevator at the same time. Second, I stopped in Finding Aids for two minutes—and only because I was trying to find you."

I see the way Dallas is looking at me. "You have someone else in mind."

"I do," he says. "But I need you to be honest with yourself, Beecher. Just how well do you really know Tot?"

57

ope. No. No way," I insist. "Tot would never do that."

"You say that, but you're still ignoring the hard questions," Dallas says.

"What hard questions? *Is Tot a killer?* He's not."

"Then why's he always around? Why's he helping you so much? Why's he suddenly giving you his car, and dropping everything he's working on, and treating this . . ."

". . . like it's a matter of life or death? Because *it is* a matter of life or death! My life! My death! Isn't that how a friend is supposed to react?"

"Be careful here. You sure he *is* your friend?"

"He *is* my friend!"

"Then how come—if he's the supposed master of all the Archives—he hasn't accepted a single promotion in nearly fifty years? You don't think that smells a little? Everyone else at his level goes up to bigger and better things, but Tot, for some unknown reason, stays tucked away in his little kingdom in the stacks."

"But isn't that why Tot *wouldn't* be in Wallace's Plumbers? You said Wallace's group is all new. Tot's been here forever."

"Which is why it's such a perfect cover to be there for Wallace— just another face in the crowd."

"And why's that any different than what *you're* doing with the Culper Ring?"

"What *I'm* doing, Beecher, is reacting to an emergency by coming directly to you and telling you what's really going on. What Tot—"

"You don't know it's Tot. And even if it was, it doesn't make sense. If he's really out for my blood, why's he helping me so much?"

"Maybe to gain your trust . . . maybe to bring you closer so he has a better fall guy. I have no idea. But what I do know is that he *is* gaining your trust, and he *is* bringing you closer, and he was also the very last person to call Orlando before he died. So when someone like that loans you his car, you have to admit: That's a pretty good explanation for why you're suddenly being followed by a taxi."

I'm tempted to argue, or even to ask him how he knew that Tot called Orlando, but my brain's too busy replaying "Islands in the Stream." Tot's cell phone—and, just like Clemmi said, the call that sent us racing up to Finding Aids at the exact same moment that Dustin Gyrich snuck out of the building.

"You need to start asking the hard questions, Beecher—of Tot or anyone else. If they work in our building, you shouldn't be whispering to them."

He's right. He's definitely right. There's only one problem.

"That doesn't mean Tot was the one in the taxi," I tell him. "It could've been anyone. It could've been Rina."

"I don't think it was Rina."

"How can you—?"

"It's just my thought, okay? You don't think it's Tot. I don't think it's Rina," he insists, barely raising his voice but definitely raising his voice.

As he scratches the side of his starter beard, I make a mental note of the sore spot. "What about Khazei?" I ask.

"From Security?"

"He's the one who buzzed Orlando into the SCIF. And right now, he's also the one spending far too much of his time lurking wherever I seem to be."

Dallas thinks on this a moment. "Maybe."

"*Maybe?*" I shoot back. "You've got a two-hundred-year-old spy network talking in your ear, and that's the best they come up with? *Maybe?*"

Before he can respond, there's a loud backfire. Through the curtain, a puff of black smoke shows me the source: a city bus that's now pulling away from the bus stop across the street. But what gnaws at me is Dallas's reaction to it. His face is white. He squints into the darkness. And I quickly remember that buses in D.C. don't run after midnight. It's well past 1 a.m.

"Beecher, I think we need to go."

"Wait. Am I . . . ? Who'd you see in that bus?"

He doesn't answer.

"Tell me what's with the bus, Dallas. You think someone's spying from that bus?"

He closes the shades, then checks again to make sure they stay closed. It's the first time I've seen him scared. "We'd also like to see the book."

"Wha?" I ask.

"The book. The dictionary," Dallas says. His tone is insistent. Like his life depends on it. "We need to know what was written in the dictionary."

He puts a hand on my shoulder, motioning me to the door.

I don't move. "Don't do that," I warn.

"Do what?"

"Rush me along, hoping I'll give it out of fear."

"You think I'd screw you like that?"

"No offense, but weren't you the one who just gave me that lecture about how every person in our building was already screwing me?"

He searches for calm, but I see him glance at the closed curtain. Time's running out. "What if I gave you a reason to trust us?"

"Depends how good the reason is."

"Is that okay?" he adds, though I realize he's no longer talking to me. He nods, reacting to what they're saying in his earpiece. Wasting no time, he heads for the closet and pulls something from his laptop bag, which was tucked just out of sight.

With a flick of his wrist, he whips it like a Frisbee straight at me.

I catch it as the plastic shell nicks my chest.

A videotape.

The orange sticker on the top reads: *12E1.*

That's the room...the SCIF...Is this...? This is the videotape that Orlando grabbed when we—

"How'd you get this?" I ask.

He shakes his head. "That's your get-out-of-jail-free card, Beecher. You know what would've happened if Wallace or one of his Plumbers had seen you on that tape?"

He doesn't have to say the words. I still hear Orlando: *If the President finds that videotape, he's going to declare war...on us.* The war's clearly started. Time to fight back.

From my back pocket, I pull out a folded sheet of paper and hand it to Dallas. He unfolds it, scanning the writing.

"This is a photocopy," he says. "Where's the original? Where's the book?"

This time, I'm the one shaking my head.

"You hid it in the Archives, didn't you?" he adds.

I still don't answer.

"Good. Well done. You're finally using your head," he says as he rereads the revealed note we found in the dictionary:

FEBRUARY 16

26 YEARS IS A LONG TIME TO KEEP A SECRET

WRITE BACK: NC 38.548.19 OR WU 773.427

"You know those aren't—"

"We know they're not call numbers," I agree. "But beyond that, we're stuck."

He stares at it for a few seconds more. "Unreal," he whispers to himself. "And the ink was green when you found it?"

"Bright green—new as can be," I tell him. "Whoever these Plumbers are, they like your formula."

He nods, definitely annoyed that there's someone else using their Culper Ring magic tricks. "How'd you know to look for the invisible ink?" Dallas asks. "Was that Tot?"

"It was someone else."

"Who?"

"Are you taking me to *your* leader?" I ask, pointing to his earpiece. "Then I'm not taking you to *mine*," I add, once again realizing just how valuable Nico's advice has been—and how I wouldn't even know about the invisible ink without him.

"So what do I do now?" I ask as he slides the photocopy into his briefcase. "How do I tell you what happens with the President? Do I just find you at work, or is there some secret number I should call?"

"Secret number?"

"Y'know, like if something goes wrong."

"This isn't Fight Club," Dallas says. From his back pocket, he pulls out his wallet, opens it up, and hands me a Band-Aid.

"What's this?"

"It's a Band-Aid."

"I can see it's a Band-Aid. But what is it? A transmitter? A microphone?"

"It's a Band-Aid," he repeats. "And if there's an emergency—if you need help—you take that Band-Aid and you tape it to the back of your chair at work. Don't come running or calling...don't send emails...nothing that people can intercept. You tape that Band-Aid up, and you head for the restroom at the end of our hallway. I swear to you, you'll have help."

"But what you said before...about my life already being over."

"Beecher, you know history isn't written until it's written, so—"

"Can you please stop insulting me, Dallas. I know what happens when people take on sitting Presidents. Even if I survive this, I'm not surviving this, am I?"

He studies me, once again combing his beard with his teeth. "Beecher, remember that mad scientist convention the government had last year?"

"You're insulting me again. I hate locker room speeches."

"It's not a locker room speech. It's a fact. Last year, the army had a 'mad scientist' conference, bringing together the wildest thinkers to predict what the most dangerous threats will be in the year 2030.

And y'know what they decided the number one threat was? *The destructive and disruptive capability of a small group.* That's what they're worried about most—not another country with a nuke— they're terrified of a small group with a committed goal. That's what we are, Beecher. That's what the Culper Ring has always been. Now I know you're worried about who you're going up against. But the Presidency will always be bigger than a single President. Do you hear that? Patriots founded this country, and patriots still protect it. So let me promise you one thing: I don't care if sixty-eight million people voted for him. Orson Wallace has never seen anything like us."

Dallas stands at the door, his hand on the top lock. He's not opening it until he's sure I get the point.

"That was actually a good locker room speech," I say.

"This is our business, Beecher. A fireman trains for the fire. This is our fire," he says, giving a sharp twist to the first of the three locks. "You help us find the Plumbers and we'll all find out who did this to Orlando."

"Can I ask one last question?"

"You already asked fifty questions—all you should be worrying about now is getting a good night's sleep and readying your best game face. You've got breakfast with the President of the United States."

As the door swings open, and we take a carpeted staircase down toward the back entrance of the building, I know he's only partly right. Before my breakfast date with the President, I've got one thing I need to do first.

58

Pulling into his parking lot, I give a double tap to the car horn and brace for the worst. It's nearly seven o'clock the next morning. Being late is the least of my problems.

As the door to his townhouse opens, even Tot's Merlin beard doesn't move. His herringbone overcoat is completely buttoned. He wants me to know he's been waiting. Uncomfortably.

"Get outta my car," he growls, limping angrily around the last few snow pucks on his front path.

"I'm sorry—I know I should've done that," I say as I scootch from the driver's to the passenger seat.

"No. *Out*," he says, pulling the driver's door open and thumbing me into the parking lot.

He won't even look at me as I climb past him.

"Tell me you didn't sleep with her," he says as he slides behind the wheel.

"I didn't." I take a breath. "Not that it's your business."

He looks up. His eyes are red. Like mine. He's been up late. "Beecher..."

"I'm sorry—I shouldn't've snapped—"

"Stop talking, Beecher."

I do.

"Now listen to what I'm saying," Tot adds, holding the steering wheel like he's strangling it. "Girls like Clementine...they look nice—but they can also be as manipulative as a James Taylor song. Sure, they're calming and bring you to a good place—but at their core, the whole goal of the damn thing is to undo you."

"That's a horrible analogy."

241

His glance tightens.

"What happened to your face—to your chin?" he asks.

"Brick steps. Clementine has brick steps. I slipped and fell. On my face."

He watches me silently. "That's a tough neighborhood you were in. Y'sure nothing else—?"

"How'd you know that?"

"Pardon?"

"The neighborhood. How'd you know it was tough?"

"I looked it up," he says without a moment's hesitation. "What else was I supposed to do when I was sitting in my office, waiting for you?"

A gust of cold air sends a whirlwind of remnant snow swirling in front of Tot's car. I ignore it, my gaze locked on Tot.

"Thank you for at least filling up the car with gas," he adds.

I nod even though it wasn't me. I forgot about the gas. The Culper Ring clearly didn't. I'm still not sure I trust them, but if I'm keeping score, including the videotape, that's at least two I owe them. And regardless of what they expect in return—regardless of what was really hidden in that dictionary—one thing is clear: Getting to the bottom of the Culper Ring and their enemies—these so-called Plumbers—is the only way I'm getting to the bottom of Orlando and saving my own behind.

"You getting in the car, Beecher, or what?" Tot asks.

As I circle around to the passenger side, I notice a redheaded woman walking a little brown dachshund. The thing is, it looks like the exact same dog that man with the plaid scarf was walking outside of my house yesterday. Still...that can't be the same dog.

"C'mon, we're late enough as it is."

As I plop into the passenger seat, Tot punches the pedal and blows past them without a second glance.

I watch them in my rearview until they fade from view.

With a flick of the dial, Tot turns the radio to his favorite country music station. If Dallas is right, and Tot's in with the Plumbers—though I'm absolutely unconvinced he's in with the Plumbers—this is the moment he'll try to gain trust by offering me another bit of *helpful* advice.

"So guess what else I found last night while I was waiting for you?" Tot asks as we join the morning traffic on Rockville Pike.

From his pocket, he takes out his own photocopy of the message that was in the dictionary:

FEBRUARY 16

26 YEARS IS A LONG TIME TO KEEP A SECRET

WRITE BACK: NC 38.548.19 OR WU 773.427

"Get ready to thank me, Beecher. I think I know what happened on February 16th."

59

You know who's the greeter this morning, right?" asked the President's young aide, a twenty-seven-year-old kid with a strict part in his brown hair.

In the backseat of the armored limousine, President Wallace didn't bother to answer.

Outside, there was a loud *crunk*, like a prison cell being unlocked. Through the Cadillac's green bulletproof glass, the President watched as one of the suit-and-tie Secret Service agents pressed a small security button underneath the door handle, allowing them to open the steel-reinforced door from the outside.

As Wallace knew, at any event, the first face he saw was always a super-VIP—someone with enough tug to wrangle the job of greeter. But in this case, as the door cracked open and revealed a heavyset woman in a navy blue dress, he knew this greeter was a familiar one.

"You're late," his sister Minnie barked.

"I'm always late. That's how I make an entrance," Wallace shot back, quickly remembering why he should've canceled this appearance.

Minnie flashed the largest half-smile that her stroke allowed, and then, like the nuns at their old school, rapped her flamingo-headed cane against her brother's polished shoes. "C'mon, I got people waiting."

With his big strides, it took no time for the President to make his way past the throngs of agents to the loading dock that led into the back entrance of the Capital Hilton. Barely a few steps down the sparse concrete hallway, Wallace heard the click-clack of Minnie's cane as she fought to speed-limp behind him. It'd been a while since they walked together. He slowed down—but he knew his sister too well. Even without the limp, she was forever trying to keep up.

"They tell you to thank Thomas Griffiths?" Minnie asked her brother.

"He knows about Thomas," the young aide called out, barely half a step behind them.

"What about Ross? You need to make a big deal. He's the one I answer to. Ross the Boss."

"He knows Ross too," the aide challenged as the smell of fresh croissants wafted through the air. Passing through a set of swinging doors, they followed the agents to their usual shortcut. Presidents don't arrive through front doors. They arrive through hotel kitchens.

"Just please...make him feel important," Minnie begged.

"Minnie, take my word on this one," the President said, nodding polite nods and waving polite waves to all the kitchen staff who stopped everything to turn and stare. "I know how to make people feel important."

"This way, sir," a short agent announced, pointing them to the left, through a final set of swinging doors. From the dark blue pipe-and-drape that created faux-curtains around the doorway, Wallace knew this was it. But instead of being in the main ballroom, he found himself in a smaller reception room filled with a rope line of at least two dozen people, all of them now clapping as he entered. Truth be told, he still loved the applause. What Wallace didn't love were the two private photographers at the front of the reception line.

"A photo line?" the aide hissed at Minnie.

"These are our top scientists—you have no idea how much they've done for brain injuries," Minnie pleaded.

"You said *one photo*...with just the executive director," the aide told her.

"I didn't agree to *any* photos," the President growled. Palmiotti was right. When it came to Minnie, he *was* a sucker.

245

"Sir, I apologize," the aide began.

With a cock of his head, the President flashed the aide a final look—the kind of angry, split-second daggers-in-the-eye that spouses share when they're entering a party but still want to say that this won't be forgotten later.

But as Wallace approached the crowd and waved the first guest into position, he couldn't help but notice how quickly Minnie stepped aside, leaving him alone in the spotlight. He'd seen it before—Minnie never liked cameras. All her life, she'd been self-conscious about her masculine looks that she got from the Turner syndrome. He knew that's why she didn't like the campaign trail, and why she never took a yearbook photo. But right now, as her colleagues gathered around her, there was a brand-new half-smile on her face. A real smile.

"Minnie, thank you so much for doing this," one of them said.

"—no idea what this means," another gushed.

A flashbulb popped in front of Wallace, but as the next person headed his way, he couldn't take his eyes off the . . . it was pride . . . real pride on his sister's face. And not just pride from being related to a President—or even from being an instant bigshot. This was pride in her work—for what she had done for this organization that had helped her so much all these years.

"Sir, you remember Ross Levin," the President's aide said as he introduced a bookish but handsome man with rectangular glasses.

"Of course, Ross," Wallace said, taking the cue and offering the full two-fisted handshake. "Can you give me one second, though, Ross? I want to get the real hero for these pictures. *Hey, Minnie!*" the President of the United States called out. "I'm feeling a little stage fright here without my sis near me."

There was a collective *awww* from Minnie's colleagues. But none of it meant as much as the bent half-smile that swelled across Minnie's face as her brother wrapped an arm around her shoulder and tugged her into the rest of the photos.

"On three, everyone say *Minnie!*" the President announced, hugging her even closer as the flashbulbs continued to explode.

Sure, Wallace knew he needed to get out of here. He knew he needed to deal with Beecher—just like they'd dealt with Eightball all those years ago. But after everything his sister had been through—from the teasing when she was younger, to the days right after the stroke, to the public hammering by Perez Hilton—would an extra ten minutes really matter?

No, they wouldn't.

Last night was a mess. But today... Beecher wasn't going anywhere.

60

Y'hear what I said?" Tot asks, his cloudy eye seeming to watch me in the passenger seat as he waves the photocopied sheet between us. "February 16th. Don't you wanna know?"

I nod, trying hard to stay focused on the traffic in front of us.

"Beecher, I'm talking to you."

"And I hear you. Yes. I'd love to know."

He turns his head even more. So he sees me with his good eye. I don't know why I bother. He's too good at this.

"You already know, don't you?" Tot asks. "You know what happened on February 16th."

I don't answer him.

"Good for you, Beecher. What'd you do—look it up when you got home?"

"How could I not?" I spend every day doing other people's historical research. All it took was a little extra footwork to do my own. "Khazei wants to pin the murder on me. This is my life on the line, Tot."

"So you saw the story? About Eightball?"

I nod. Even without his training, it wasn't hard to find. When it comes to figuring out what happened twenty-six years ago on February 16th, all you really need is a newspaper from the following day: February 17th.

Twenty-six years ago, President Orson Wallace was in his final year of college at the University of Michigan.

"You did the math, didn't you?" Tot asks.

"That what? That February 16th was a *Saturday*?"

This is when I'd usually see Tot's smile creeping through his beard. Right now, though, it's not there—even though I know Saturday was the breakthrough for him too. At this point, nearly every American has heard the story of how Wallace used to come home every weekend to check on his mom and his sick sister, who suffered from Turner syndrome. So if young Wallace was home in Ohio...

All I needed was the Cleveland News Index and their digital archives of the *Cleveland Plain Dealer*. I searched every keyword I could think of, including the names of family members. Not a single article on February 17th mentioned Wallace. But there was one—and only one—that did mention Wallace's hometown of Journey, Ohio:

Local Man Goes Missing

From my inside jacket pocket, I pull out the printed-out story, which was buried in the back of the newspaper. Just like Orlando. According to the piece, a twenty-year-old man named Griffin Anderson had gone missing the previous night and was last seen voluntarily getting into a black Dodge Diplomat with two other twenty-year-olds. All three men had tattoos of a black eight-ball on the inside of their forearms—a sign that police said made them a part of a Cleveland gang known as the Corona Kings.

"And that's all you found?" Tot challenges.

"Was there something else to find?"

"Tell me this first: Why were you testing me?"

"What're you talking about?"

"What you just did—you were testing me, Beecher. You came to pick me up, you knew you had done the same research, yet you stayed quiet to see what I offered up." If Tot were my age, this is the part where he'd say I didn't trust him and turn it into a fight. But he's got far more perspective than that. "So what's my grade?" he asks. "When I said the word *eight-ball*, does that mean I passed?"

"Tot, if you know something else..."

"Of course I know something else—and I also know I'm the one who told you not to trust anyone, including me. So I don't blame you. But if you're gonna insult me, try to be more subtle next time."

"Just tell me what you found!"

He ignores the outburst, making sure I get his real point: No matter how good I think I am, he's still the teacher. And still on my side.

"It's about the eight-ball tattoo, isn't it?" I ask. "I was going to look it up..."

"There's nothing else to look up—not unless you also happen to have an old colleague who still works in the Cleveland Police Department."

"I don't understand."

"You will," Tot says. "Especially when you hear who, twenty-six years ago, also happened to be in the original police report."

61

The barber knew the hotel well. But as he followed the curving staircase from the Capital Hilton lobby up to the second floor, it didn't stop the sense of dread that was now twisting into the small of his back.

"Sir, can I help you?" a passing hotel employee with close-cropped red hair asked just as Laurent hit the final step.

Laurent was nervous, but he wasn't a fool. He knew that when the President was in the building, the Secret Service disguised their agents in hotel uniforms.

"I'm fine, thanks," the barber said.

"And you know where you're going?" the hotel employee asked.

No question. Secret Service.

"I do," the barber said, trying hard to keep it together as he headed left and calmly turned the corner toward his destination: the far too appropriately named Presidential Ballroom.

"Good morning!" an older blonde with a homedone tint job sang out. "Welcome to the Caregivers' Conference. What can I do for you?"

"I should be on the list," Laurent said, abruptly pointing to the few unclaimed nametags—including the one he'd been using for so many months now. "Last name *Gyrich*."

"Mmm, let's find you," the woman said, scanning the names one by one, but also stealing a quick glance at his face.

Laurent felt the dread digging deeper into his back. It wasn't supposed to be this way. When Orson (he'd known the President since Wallace was little—he couldn't call him anything but Orson) first showed up all those years ago...in that rain...Laurent was just trying to do what was right. And when they first started in D.C....when he first agreed to help with the Plumbers, it wasn't much different: to do what's right...to serve his friend...to serve his country.

"Here we go! We have you right here, Mr. Gyrich," the woman said, handing the barber the nametag. "You're the one they called about...the guest of the White House. You should go in—he's just started. Oh, and if you like, we have a coat check."

"That's okay," he said, sliding the nametag into the pocket of his pea coat. "I'm not staying very long."

"This way, sir," a uniformed Secret Service agent said, motioning him through the metal detector that was set up just outside the main doors of the ballroom. From inside, he heard the familiar yet muffled baritone of President Orson Wallace booming through the ballroom's speakers. From what he could tell, Orson was keeping this one personal, telling the crowd about the night of Minnie's stroke and that moment in the ambulance when the paramedics asked her where she went to school, and the twelfth-grade Minnie could only name her elementary school.

In many ways, Laurent realized, it was the same problem at the Archives. The way they were rushing around—to even let it get this far—Orson was letting it get too personal.

"Enjoy the breakfast, sir," the Secret Service agent said as he pulled open the ballroom door. Underneath the brightly lit chandelier that was as long as a city bus, every neck was craned upward, all six hundred people watching the rosy-cheeked man who looked so comfortable up at the podium with the presidential seal on the front of it.

As always, the President glanced around the crowd, making eye contact with everyone. That is, until Laurent stepped into the room.

"...which is no different from the personal myths we tell ourselves every day," the President said, his pale gray eyes turning toward the barber in the back of the bright room. "The myths we create about ourselves are solely there so our brains can survive."

Across the red, gold, and blue carpet, the barber stood there a moment. He stood there waiting for the President. And when the two men finally locked eyes, when Laurent nodded just slightly and Orson nodded right back, the barber knew that the President had seen him.

That was it. Message sent.

Pivoting on his heel, the barber headed back out toward the welcome desk. The President cocked his head, flashing a smile and locking on yet another stranger in the crowd.

For the first time since this started, the Plumbers finally had something going their way.

62

So you've never heard of this guy Griffin?" Tot asks, stealing a glance at me as the Mustang zips through Rock Creek Park and we make our way to Constitution Avenue.

"Why would I've heard of him?"

"And there's no one you know who has an eight-ball tattoo?"

"Is this *you* testing *me* now?" I ask.

"Beecher, I'm seventy-one years old."

"You're actually seventy-two."

He thinks on this a moment. "I'm seventy-two years old. I have plenty of patience. I just don't like having my time wasted—and right now, since you're treating me like the enemy, you seem to be wasting it," he explains without any bitterness.

"I know you're not the enemy, Tot."

"Actually, you know nothing about me. For all you know, this is just another attempt to reel you in and grab you with the net. Do what you're doing, Beecher—keep asking the tough questions. And as for the toughest one so far: Every neighborhood in the country has a guy like Griffin."

"Meaning what?"

"Meaning according to the police report, Griffin's first arrest came when he was in high school—selling fake marijuana to a bunch of ninth graders. Then he got smart and started selling the real thing. His dad was a pharmacist, so he quickly graduated to selling pills. During one arrest—and remember, this is still in high school—Griffin spit in a cop's face, at which point he became the kid that even the tough high school kids knew you didn't mess with."

I see where he's going. "So when Griffin was kidnapped—"

"Not *kidnapped*," Tot corrects, approaching the end of Rock Creek Park. "They never use the word *kidnapped*. Or *abducted*. In the report, they don't even call it a *crime scene*. But you're painting the picture: When this guy Griffin finally disappeared, neighbors weren't exactly tripping over themselves to form a search party."

"It's still a missing kid."

"You sure? Griffin was twenty years old, no longer a minor. He got in a car—voluntarily—with two guys from his gang. And then he drives off into the sunset," Tot says as we make a left on Constitution Avenue and momentum presses me against the passenger door. "A crime? Where do you see a crime?"

"Okay," I say. "So where's the crime?"

"That's the point, Beecher. There isn't one. Griffin's dad goes to the newspaper. He begs the cops to find his son. But the cops see it as a young man exercising his independence. And they shut the case, I'm guessing secretly thrilled that Griffin and his eight-ball friends are someone else's problem."

"And now, all these years later, the case is back. So for the second time—where's the crime?"

Tot points his beard at the famous landmark all the way up on our left: the breathtaking home of President Orson Wallace. The White House.

"Don't tell me Wallace has an eight-ball tattoo," I say.

"Nope. Near as I can tell, Wallace was nowhere near this one."

"So what makes you think he's involved?"

As we pass the White House and weave down Pennsylvania Avenue and toward our building, Tot's smile finally pokes through his beard. "Now you're seeing the real value of an archive. History isn't written by the winners—it's written by everyone—it's a jigsaw of facts from contradictory sources. But every once in a while, you unearth that one original document that no one can argue with, like an old police report filed by two beat cops twenty-six years ago."

"Tot..."

"He was the one who gave them the info—the one eyewitness who told the cops everything he saw."

"The President was?"

"No. I told you, Wallace was nowhere near there." As we make a sharp right onto 7th Street and pull toward the garage, Tot picks up his photocopied sheet of paper and tosses it in my lap. It's the first time I notice the name he's handwritten across the bottom. *"Him! He was there!"*

I read the name and read it again. *"Stewart Palmiotti?"*

"Wallace's personal doctor," Tot says, hitting the brakes at the yellow antiram barrier outside the garage, just as the security guard looks up at us. "That's who we want: the President's oldest friend."

63

The cemetery reminded him of his mother.

Not of her death.

When she died, she was already in her eighties. Sure, she wanted a year or two more—but not much. She always said she never wanted to be one of those *old people*, so when it was her time to go, she went calmly, without much argument.

No, what the cemetery reminded Dr. Palmiotti of was his mother when she was younger...when *he* was younger...when his grandfather died and his mom was screaming—her face in a red rage, tears and snot running down her nose as two other family members fought to restrain her—about the fact that the funeral home had neglected to shave her father's face before putting him in his coffin.

Palmiotti had never seen such a brutal intensity in his mother. He'd never see it again. It was reserved solely for those who wronged her family.

It was a lesson Palmiotti never forgot.

Yet as he leaned into the morning cold and followed the well-paved, hilly trail into the heart of Oak Hill Cemetery, he quickly realized that this was far more than just a cemetery.

All cities have old money. Washington, D.C., has old money. But it also has *old power*. And Oak Hill, which was tucked into one of the toniest areas of Georgetown and extended its sprawling twenty-two acres of rolling green hills and obelisk-dotted graves deep into Rock Creek Park, was well known, especially by those who cared to know, as the resting place for that power.

Founded in 1849, when W. W. Corcoran donated the land he had bought from a great-nephew of George Washington, Oak Hill

257

held everyone from Abraham Lincoln's son Willie, to Secretary of War Edward Stanton, to Dean Acheson, to *Washington Post* publisher Philip Graham. For years, the cemetery management refused to take "new members," but demand grew so great, they recently built double-depth crypts below the main walking paths so that D.C.'s new power families could rest side by side with the old.

Welcome to Oak Hill Cemetery, the wooden sign read just inside the wrought-iron gate that was designed by James Renwick, who also designed the Smithsonian Castle and St. Patrick's Cathedral in New York. But what Palmiotti couldn't shake was the message at the bottom of the sign:

All Who Enter Do So At Their Own Risk

So needlessly melodramatic, Palmiotti thought to himself. But then again, as he glanced over his shoulder for the fourth time, that didn't mean it was any less unnerving. Using the Archives, or a SCIF, or even the barbershop was one thing. But to pick a place like this—a place so public and unprotected . . .

This was where they were going wrong. He had told the President just that. But right now, like that night in the rain with Eightball back when they were kids, Palmiotti also knew that sometimes, in some situations, you don't have a choice. You have to take matters into your own hands.

With a quick look down at his iPhone, Palmiotti followed the directions that took him past a headstone carved in the shape of an infant wrapped and sleeping in a blanket. He fought against the ice, trudging up a concrete path and a short hill that eventually revealed . . .

"Hoo . . ." Palmiotti whispered as he saw it.

Straight ahead, a wide-open field was sprinkled in every direction with snow-covered headstones, stately family crypts, and in the far distance, a circular Gothic family memorial surrounded by thick marble columns. Unlike a normal cemetery, there was no geometric grid. It was like a park, the graves peppered—somehow tastefully—everywhere.

Leaving the concrete path behind, Palmiotti spotted the faint footprints in the snow and knew all he had to do was follow them to his destination: the eight-foot-tall obelisk that sat next to a bare apple blossom tree.

As he approached, he saw two names at the base of the obelisk: Lt. Walter Gibson Peter, aged twenty, and Col. William Orton Williams, aged twenty-three. According to the cemetery visitor guide, these two cousins were relatives of Martha Washington. But, as Palmiotti continued to read, he saw that the reason they were buried together—both in Lot 578—was because during the Civil War they were both hanged as spies.

Crumpling the brochure, Palmiotti stuffed it in his coat pocket, trying to think about something else.

Behind him, there was a crunch. Like someone stepping through the snow.

Palmiotti spun, nearly slipping on the ice. The field was empty.

He was tempted to leave . . . to abort and walk away. But as he turned back to the grave, he already saw what he was looking for. Kneeling down, he brushed away the snow that had gathered at the base of the obelisk. A few wet leaves came loose. And some clumps of dirt. Then he heard the hollow *kkkkk*—there it was, the pale beige rock that was about the size of his palm.

The rock was round and smooth. It was also plastic. And hollow.

Perfect for hiding something inside.

Just like a spy would use, he thought to himself as he reread the inscriptions for Lt. Walter Gibson Peter and Col. William Orton Williams.

As a blast of wind galloped across the hill, Palmiotti reached into his jacket pocket and pulled out the folded-up note that said: *I Miss You.*

Simple. Easy. And if someone found it, they wouldn't think twice about it. Not unless they knew to read between the lines.

And so far, even if Beecher had figured out the ink, he still hadn't figured out how to read the true message inside.

259

With a flick of his thumb, Palmiotti opened the base of the rock, slid the note inside, and buried the rock back in the snow.

It took less than a minute in all. Even if someone was watching, he looked like just another mourner at another grave.

But as Palmiotti strode back to the concrete path and the snow seeped into his socks, he could tell—by the mere fact he was out here, and the fact that someone else had found out what they had done all those years ago—the end was coming.

This would all be over soon. It had to be.

To get this far, to climb this high, you had to be capable of a great many things. And on that night all those years ago—to protect their future...to protect his and Wallace's dreams—Palmiotti found out exactly what he was capable of.

It wasn't easy for him. And it wasn't easy for him now. But as he learned from his own father, big lives required big sacrifice. The thing is, growing up in Ohio, Palmiotti never thought he'd have a *big* life. He thought he'd have a *good* life. Not a big one. Not until that first day of fifth grade, when he met Orson Wallace. But if Wallace was proof of anything, it was that, for Palmiotti, the big life was finally possible.

Still, to look at all that Palmiotti had sacrificed over the years—his time, his marriage, his defunct medical practice—to look at his life and realize that all those sacrifices were about to become worthless...

No. Palmiotti was capable of far more than anyone expected. And that's exactly why the President kept him so close.

No matter what, this would be the end.

And there was nothing Beecher could do to stop it.

64

As Tot and I wait at the guardhouse, blocked by the yellow metal antiram barrier that sticks out from the concrete, we both reach for our IDs.

"Beautiful morning," the guard with the bright white teeth calls out, waving us through without even approaching the car.

The metal barrier churns and lowers with its usual shriek, biting into the ground. We both wave back, confused.

There's no ID check, no bomb sweep. Yesterday, we were enemies of the state; today we're BFFs.

The guard even adds a wink as we pass his booth and ride down to the garage. A wink.

"Something's wrong," Tot insists.

Of course something's wrong. But as I mentally replay Dallas's words from last night, my mind wanders back to a few years ago when the Archives released all the personnel records of the OSS, the early version of the CIA. Historians had estimated that there were about six thousand people who had spied for the agency back during World War II. When the records were unsealed, there were actually twenty-four thousand previously unknown spies, including Julia Child, Supreme Court Justice Arthur Goldberg, and a catcher for the Chicago White Sox.

The OSS lasted a total of three years. According to Dallas, the Culper Ring has been around for two hundred.

As Tot pulls into his parking spot, I look over my shoulder and up the ramp of the garage, where White Teeth is still watching us. And smiling.

Dallas never said it...never even hinted it...but only a fool wouldn't think that maybe this Culper Ring has a deeper reach than I originally thought.

"Look who else is visiting," Tot whispers, working hard to climb out of the Mustang. As I elbow open the car door and join him outside, I finally see who he's looking at: Over by the metal door that leads inside are two men in black body armor, both of them holding rifles. Secret Service.

From the look on Tot's face, he has no idea why they're here.

"Think Wallace is coming back?" he whispers.

"He's definitely coming back."

He shoots me a look. "How do you know?"

I take a breath, repracticing what I've been practicing all morning. It's one thing to play it safe—for now, while I gather info—by not mentioning Dallas and the Culper Ring. But to hide that I'll be with the President . . . to hide what I know Tot'll find out . . .

"I'm the one staffing him," I say as I slam the car door and head for the Secret Service.

Limping behind me, Tot's too smart to make a scene. But as we flash our IDs and give quick head-nods to the Service, I can tell he's pissed.

He doesn't say a word until we're in the elevator.

"When'd you find out?" Tot hisses just as the doors snap shut and we ride up to our offices.

"Last night. They emailed me last night."

His good eye picks me apart. I know what he's thinking.

"I was trying to tell you all morning," I add as the elevator bobs and stops at our destination. "But when you brought up this Dr. Palmiotti— Who knows, maybe being alone with the President is a good thing. Maybe he'll make me an offer or something."

"Make you an offer? Who gave you a stupid idea like that?"

"I-I just thought of it," I say, still thinking about what Dallas said last night. Whatever's been happening in that SCIF, it's between the President and someone on staff—or at least someone with access to the room.

Tot shakes his head, stepping out on the fourth floor. I'm right behind him, but as Tot throws open the door to our office and I follow him inside, there's a flash of movement on my right.

Like a jack-in-the-box, a head pops up from the far end of the grid of cubicles, then cuts into the main aisle. From the Mona Lisa hair, I recognize Rina immediately, but what catches me off guard... she was in my cube.

"What're you doing!?" I call out before I even realize I'm shouting.

Rina whips around, still standing in the aisle. "What? *Me?*"

"You heard me...!" I say, already whipping around the corner.

Like whack-a-moles, three more heads—all of them other officemates—pop up throughout the grid. One of them is Dallas. Everyone wants to see the fuss.

Still looking shocked, Rina stands there frozen.

My cube is next to Rina's. Yet as I race up the main aisle, Rina is standing outside *her* cube—not mine.

"W-What'd I do?" Rina asks. "What's wrong?"

I step back, confused. I double-check to make sure I have it right. I know what I saw.

"Beecher, you okay?" she asks.

I glance over my shoulder. Tot must've seen it too. But as I turn around, Tot's all the way by his desk, refusing to look my way. I get the picture. He's still pissed I didn't tell him about the President. This is my punishment: leaving me on my own.

That's fine. I know what I saw.

From his cubicle, Dallas shoots me his own glance. He saw it too. When Rina ducked into the aisle... she moved... she must've moved.

Relax, Dallas says with a slow nod. *Not in public.*

My cell phone rings. I pick up quickly.

"Is Mom okay?" I ask my sister Sharon.

"She's fine. Going to Jumbo's for lunch," my sister says. Hearing the strain in my voice, she adds, "What's wrong there?"

"Office politics. I'll call you later," I say, hanging up before she can pry.

"Beecher, you sure you're okay?" Rina asks.

"He's fine," Dallas tells her as he joins us in the main aisle. "He's just having one of those mornings."

"I can imagine," Rina says, cupping her palms and tapping her fingers together, more than happy to be rid of any confrontation. "I mean, it's not every day you get to staff the President, right, Beecher?"

I look back at Tot. His head's below the sightline of his cubicle, which means he's not even watching me anymore. The sad part is, I'm not sure if that's good or bad.

"Listen, if there's anything you need when you're in there," Rina offers, "I'm happy to help. I can even stand outside in case there're any new records the President might request."

"Thanks, but I'm okay, Rina," I say as I step into my cubicle and slide into my chair. On my desk, my eye immediately goes to my keyboard, which is slightly askew.

I hold my breath as I see it. My keyboard's never askew. I keep two neat piles on my desk. Both of them look messy. Like someone's thumbed through them.

Before I can react, my phone vibrates in my pocket. I assume it's my sister, but as I flip it open, caller ID says: *USSS*.

United States Secret Service.

"Beecher here," I say as I pick up.

"We've got Homerun ready to move," an agent with a stubborn Boston accent says. "You ready for us?"

"I'll be there in a minute," I tell him.

"You need to be there *now*," he challenges.

As he hangs up on my ear, I know the mess on my desk has to wait. I quickly dart for the stairs. I've got bigger problems to deal with.

65

During his early days at the White House, this was Orson Wallace's favorite part.

"Just an honor, Mr. President," an older man with a graying goatee offered.

"So nice to meet you, Mr. President," a woman wearing two diamond rings added.

"Thank you so much, Mr. President," a tall woman with wide black eyes said as she reached to shake his hand.

The speech was over, the applause was still going, and as President Wallace followed his aide to the swinging doors of the hotel's kitchen, he was riding such a swell of enjoyment, he tried to touch every outstretched hand of the insta-crowd that was now pressing so hard against the rope line.

It wasn't the adulation that got him going. What Wallace appreciated was just...the appreciation. The simple act of people saying *thank you*. These days, in this economy, that kind of crowd seemed to appear less and less often.

"Thank you so much, Mr. President."

"—just an inspiration, sir."

"—reinvigorated all of us, Mr. President."

"I hope you enjoyed the breakfast, Mr. President," the chef called out as Wallace weaved back through the kitchen.

"Just fantastic. We need to have you cook at the White House," Wallace called back, using the same compliment he saved for every chef in every hotel kitchen.

"—just want to thank you so much," Ross the Boss chimed in, leading the final row of handshakes—the VIP goodbyes—that

265

waited for Wallace at the far end of the service entrance and would take him to the waiting door of his armored limo.

"Hey—!" a female voice called out.

Wallace's arm was already extended in a handshake as he finally looked up at the last person in line: a heavyset woman in a royal blue dress.

"I love you," his sister Minnie said, leaning in and kissing him on the cheek.

"You're just saying that because I'm the President," Wallace teased.

With a whack, Minnie rapped her pink flamingo cane against his shin.

The President was still laughing as the Secret Service agent pushed the hidden button under the door handle, which unlocked the door so he could usher Wallace into the car. And for that moment, as he ducked inside and brother and sister shared their laughter, Wallace almost forgot about where he was headed next.

Almost.

"Homerun moving," one of the Secret Service agents whispered into his wrist, using the President's official Service code name. "Arrival at the Archives in approximately four minutes."

66

A s I tear full speed around the corner, my shoes slide across the twelfth floor's green terrazzo squares. If my timing's right, I've still got a few minutes on the President. I need them. Especially if I want to be ready.

"I need some ID," a calm voice announces just as I make the turn. His voice draws out each syllable so it sounds like *Eye. Dee.*

I know that voice.

But as I nearly plow into the man in the black body armor, I'm not focused on him or his black rifle. I don't even see the SCIF that sits at the end of the hall. All I see are ghosts. Ghosts of myself. And Clementine. And Orlando. Forty-eight hours ago, we were standing in this same pale blue hallway, with the same marble wainscoting, studying this same room with the matching pale blue metal door. I wish it were just déjà vu. Déjà vu is easy to dismiss. But this . . . this is like stepping on Orlando's grave.

A cold dread grips me, squeezing my Adam's apple until I barely remember how to breathe. It reminds me that the only reason to search for these Plumbers—and for what they put in that dictionary—is to prove that they're the ones who killed my friend.

"I said, *ID*," the agent insists.

"Y-Yeah . . . sure . . . sorry," I say, holding up my badge.

"Arms up," he barks, pulling out a black-and-yellow wand that looks like a flattened flashlight. Metal detector.

Of course. He saw my name. He knows I'm staffing him. No way they're letting me get close without making sure I'm clean.

As he waves the wand under my armpits, I blink once and see Orlando's dimpled chin and big-toothed smile as he clutched his little coffee cup and ushered me and Clementine inside. I blink again, and there's nothing but the empty pale blue hallway.

"Don't be so nervous," the Secret Service agent calls out, pinning a temporary metal clearance button on my lapel and motioning me toward the SCIF. "The President doesn't bite. Unless he's pissed."

I can't even pretend to laugh as I speedwalk up the hallway and stop at the call box that hangs on the wall. As I press the silver intercom button, a red indicator light blinks on.

"This is Beecher," I say into the intercom. "I'm opening SCIF 12E1." They're the same words Orlando said to Khazei two days ago.

I wait to hear Khazei growl something back. The way he's been watching, there's no way I'm seeing the President without him weighing in. But to my surprise . . .

"You're all set," a female voice replies. "Moses is four minutes away," she says, using our internal code name for him. "Enjoy."

The intercom goes silent, and I dart for the entrance to the SCIF. As I spin the combination lock, a sting of bile burns my throat.

I step inside the vault and catch a flash of shadow moving on my left. I'm not the only one in here.

"Oh, c'mon now," Khazei says as he slams the metal door shut and locks the two of us inside. "You really thought I'd miss this one?"

67

"Y ou shouldn't be here," I warn Khazei.

"Let me just say that's one of a variety of things you're wrong about," he counters.

As always, he's trying to keep me cornered. But just seeing Khazei here—just seeing his polished fingernails and his cocky grin—even I'm surprised how fast my fear gets swallowed by anger. "You're interfering with my work. And the work of the President," I shoot back.

"Oh, so now you and the President are a *team*?"

"I never said that. What I said was you were interfering."

"Beecher, do me a favor and take a seat," he says, pointing to the single table at the center of the room and the rolling research cart stocked with documents that sits next to it.

I stay where I am. He doesn't seem to care.

"Beecher, I've thought long and hard about this. I know I can keep putting the pressure on you. I can keep huffing and puffing and trying to blow your house down. Or I can be honest with you," he says, his voice softening to nearly a whisper.

"Before I started working here, y'know what my old job was?" Khazei asks as he leans a hand on the research cart. "I used to be a cop out in Virginia. The pay was good. The hours were bad. And the pension couldn't even touch what I get here, which is why I made the switch. But there's one thing I learned as a cop: Sometimes good people don't know how to be good to themselves. Y'understand what that means?"

"It means you've been reading too many self-help books."

"No, it means you have no idea how many guns are aimed at your

269

head. So let me do you one favor and tell you what I know: I know who your girlfriend Clementine is. I know who her dad is—which explains why you've been trying to hide her. Sure, I don't know why Orlando died—yet—but I do know that President Orson Wallace was scheduled to be in this room two days ago. I know that the Secret Service did everything in their power to clear out the CSI investigative folks from being here. And I know that despite the fact that there are over two dozen other SCIFs in this building that the President could've picked, he for some unexplainable reason asked for this room, *with you*, which puts him right back in the exact same place that, less than forty-eight hours ago, was the last known location that Orlando was seen before they found him lying downstairs on the carpet with his eyes permanently open. Now I know you're one of the smart ones, Beecher. Whatever deal you're working with the President—"

"I'm not working any deals!" I insist.

"Then you have even bigger problems than I thought. Look up and down at that totem pole you're stuck in. You're the lowest man. And when it comes to presidential scandals, when that totem pole finally tips and everyone starts yelling 'Timber,' you know what they call the lowest man? *The scapegoat*," he says, his dark eyes locked on mine.

"*We've got Moses outside the building*," Khazei's walkie-talkie squawks through the room.

"Beecher, I know you need a life preserver. This is me throwing you one. All you have to do is take hold."

"*Moses is in the elevator*," the walkie-talkie announces. "*One minute to arrival...*"

There's a hollow knock on the metal door. Secret Service want the SCIF opened and ready. Even Khazei knows he can't stop a request like that.

"Please, Beecher," he says as he reaches out and twists the metal latch on the door. My ears pop from the change in pressure as the door swings inward and the vacuum seal is broken. "I'm begging you to take hold."

It's the last thing I hear from Khazei. Without looking back, he steps out into the hallway, where three suit-and-tie Secret Service agents motion him out of the way.

An agent with blond hair and a tiny nose joins me in the SCIF, taking a spot in the back left corner. "Thirty seconds," he whispers to me as a courtesy. "Oh, and he's in a good mood."

I nod, appreciating the news.

Within a few seconds, everything goes silent.

The calm before the storm.

From outside, there's a quiet *clip-clop* as a set of finely polished dress shoes makes its way up the long hallway.

As Orson Wallace turns the corner and steps inside, I instinctively step back. I've never seen him face-to-face. But I know that face. Everyone knows that face. And those rosy cheeks. And those calming gray eyes. It's like the front page of a newspaper walking right at me.

"Sir, this is Beecher White. He'll be staffing you today," the blond agent announces as I realize that Wallace has come here without any staff.

There's another audible *pop* as the two-ton metal door slams shut and metal bolts *kunk* into place, sealing me in this windowless, soundproof, vacuum-packed box with the President of the United States.

"Nice to meet you, Beecher," Wallace says, heading straight for the desk, the research cart—and the single wooden chair—at the center of the room. "I appreciate your helping us out today."

68

That's the single dumbest idea I've ever heard," the barber snapped. "Why would you send him in like that!?"

Through the phone, Dr. Palmiotti didn't answer.

"I asked you a question!" the barber added.

"And I heard you. Now hear me: Be careful of your tone," Palmiotti warned through the receiver.

"There's no reason to put him at risk!"

"Be careful of your tone," Palmiotti warned again.

Taking a breath, the barber stared up at the brick walls of the narrow alleyway that was used as a breakroom behind the barbershop. An unkind wind shoved the rotting stench from the nearby garbage cans into his face.

"I'm just saying, he didn't have to go there," the barber said, far more calmly. He knew he was already out of bounds by making the phone call. But he never forgot the rules—especially after what they think happened. Not once did he refer to the President by name.

"I appreciate your concern," Palmiotti shot back, doing a poor job at hiding his sarcasm. "But we know what we're doing."

"I don't think you do. By bringing him in like that—"

"We know what we're doing, okay? He's not at risk. He's not in danger. And right now, he's in the best possible position to find out exactly who's holding the tin can on the other end of the string. So thank you for the concern, but this time, why don't you go back to doing what *you* do best, and we'll go back to doing what *we* do best?"

Before the barber could say a word, there was a click. Dr. Palmi-otti was gone.

Even when he was little, he was a prick, Laurent thought as he shoved his way through the back door of the barbershop, anxious to refocus his attention on his next haircut.

69

I'm waiting for it.

And watching.

And standing there, swaying in place as my hands fiddle in the pockets of my blue lab coat, pretending to fish for nothing at all.

The President's been here barely two minutes. He's sitting at the long research table, eyeing the various boxes and documents that are stacked in neat piles on the rolling cart.

"Do you need help, sir?" I ask.

He barely shakes his head, reaching for a file on the second shelf of the cart: a single-page document encased in a clear Mylar sleeve. I saw the request list. It's a handwritten letter by Abraham Lincoln— back when he was a regular citizen—requesting that better roads be built by the government. There's another on the cart from Andrew Jackson, petitioning for money well before he was elected. From what I'd heard, Wallace loves these records: all of them written by our greatest leaders long before they were our greatest leaders—and proof positive that life exists *before* and *after* the White House.

But today, as Wallace squints down at Lincoln's scratchy, wide script, I can't help but think that he's after something far bigger than life advice from his predecessors.

If Dallas and his contacts in the Culper Ring are to be believed— and that's a big *if*—they think Wallace is here to talk. With me.

I eye the blond Secret Service agent who's still standing in the opposite corner. He stares right back, unafraid of the eye contact. At the table, the President leans forward in his chair, both elbows on the desk as he hovers over the document. I watch him, picking apart his every movement like a mall cop studying a group of loud kids with skateboards.

The SCIF isn't very big. With three of us in here, the room temperature inches up just enough that I'm feeling it.

But that's not what's causing the heat that's swallowed my palms and is now plotting to take over the rest of my body.

At the table, Orson Wallace is calm as ever—ridiculously calm—like he's reading the Sunday paper.

For ten minutes, I stand there, my lab coat making me feel like a baked potato in tinfoil. The only movement I allow myself is licking the salty sweat mustache that's staked a claim on my upper lip.

Ten feet away, the President gives me nothing.

At twenty minutes, my back starts to ache from the lack of movement, and the sweat mustache doesn't even taste that salty anymore.

Still nothing from the President.

At the half-hour mark, he pulls a pencil—usually only archivists and researchers use pencils—from his jacket pocket and then flips to another set of presidential letters.

But otherwise, more nothing. And more nothing. Until…

Diagonally across the room, the blond agent puts a pointer-finger to his ear. Something's being said in his earpiece.

Without a word, the agent heads for the door and twists the metal latch. The President's used to people moving around him. He doesn't look up, even as our ears pop.

Sticking his head out the door, the blond agent listens to something being whispered by the agent outside. Something's definitely up. And the way the agent keeps looking back at me, then back to his boss, I can tell—clearance or no clearance, secure room or unsecure room—there's no way they're leaving me alone with the President.

"I need two minutes," the agent calls to me. He steps outside.

Before I can react, there's a sharp sucking sound as the door shuts and the vacuum again takes hold.

I look over at the rosy-cheeked President, who's still lost in his reading. But like before, all I see are the ghosts that float behind him: Orlando and Clementine...the spilled coffee...then the chair crashing to the floor. If it weren't for this room...and what we found...and what Orlando was fast enough to...

I almost forgot. What Orlando grabbed.

I glance up at the corner of the ceiling. The videocamera is right where it's always been. Watching us.

The sweat mustache puddles in the dimple of my lip.

That's why the President hasn't said a word. That's why he hasn't moved as he leans over the old documents. And that's why Dallas said Wallace created his so-called Plumbers in the first place.

He knows he's being watched. He's always being watched.

If he's sending a message, it has to be a subtle one.

That's fine.

I'm an archivist. I know how to wait.

Sticking to my corner and tightening the microscope, I study him sitting there—the way he favors his right arm, putting more weight on it as he leans on the desk.

I notice that he never touches the documents, always being respectful of their value.

I even observe the way he keeps both his feet flat on the floor. But beyond that...

Still nothing.

I wait some more.

More nothing.

He doesn't look up. Doesn't make eye contact. Doesn't ask any questions—just another five minutes of...

Nothing.

The door to the room unpuckers on my right as the blond Secret Service agent rejoins us. But he doesn't take his spot in the back corner.

"Sir, we really should get going," he says, staying by the door, which he holds open with his hand.

The President nods, tapping the eraser of the pencil against his chin. Still trying to get the last few seconds of reading done, he's quickly out of his seat, twisting himself so that it looks like his body is leaving the room even as his head is still reading.

"You have a good one now," the blond agent says to me.

As the President heads for the door—and toward me—it's the only other time the President's heavy gray eyes make contact with me.

"Thanks for helping us out," the leader of the free world offers as I crane my neck up to take in his six-foot-one frame. "Just amazing what you have here."

Then he's gone.

Poof.

He doesn't offer a handshake or a pat on my shoulder. No physical contact at all. All I get, as he cuts past me, is that he smells like talcum powder and Listerine.

As the silence sets in, I look over my shoulder, searching the room. The chair . . . the cart . . . everything's in place. Even the Mylar-encased document he was reading is still sitting there, untouched, on the desk. I rush over to it to make sure I didn't miss anything.

There's nothing.

Nothing.

Nothing.

And then I see it.

Something.

70

That's your great find? A *pencil*?" Dallas asks.

"Not just *a* pencil. *His* pencil," I say, pushing open the doors to all the bathroom stalls to make sure we're alone. "The President's pencil. That's what he left behind."

"Okay, so Wallace left a pencil. It's hardly the nuclear codes."

"You're really not seeing this? We were in the room..."

"I heard the story—you were in the SCIF, Wallace came in, and then, instead of reaching out to you, he spent the next forty minutes reading through old records. So fine, he held back. Maybe he got scared."

"He wasn't scared! Look at what he did: In the middle of everything, he reaches into his jacket and takes out a pencil—not a pen, like every other person outside the Archives uses. A pencil."

"Oh, of course—now I see it," he says sarcastically as he starts washing his hands in the bathroom sink. I'm not thrilled to be dealing with Dallas, but at this point—based on the info he gave me yesterday...based on his explanation of the inner and outer rings... and everything he anticipated about the President...and the safehouse and the videotape and the wireless ear thingie...plus with Tot now giving me the silent treatment—I can fight alone, or I can fight with his Culper Ring behind me. The answer's easy. Dallas may not have my complete trust, but for now, he's got some of it.

"I think Khrushchev and Mussolini were also pencil men," he adds with a laugh.

"I'm serious, Dallas. Think about it: Why does someone pull out a pencil? To follow our procedures for the research rooms—and to take notes, right? That's fine—that makes sense. But here's what

278

doesn't make sense. Wallace *wasn't* taking notes. The entire time, he didn't have paper...didn't have a notebook...didn't have or ask for a single thing to write on."

"Maybe he would've—but instead, he didn't find anything worth writing about. And even if that weren't the case, what's the big deal about having a pencil?"

"The big deal isn't *having* it. The big deal is that he *left it behind*! And truthfully, I wouldn't think it was such a big deal, except for the fact that—oh yeah—two days ago, we found a book in the same room that also wasn't a big deal...until we found it had a hidden message written in invisible ink."

At the sink, Dallas opens and closes his fists, shaking the excess water from his hands. He's listening. "So where's the hidden message in the pencil?"

"There are marks. Look at the pencil. Those indentations."

He picks up the pencil from the sink counter, holding it just a few inches from his nose.

He wants to tell me they're bite marks. But he knows they're not. In fact, as he looks close, he sees that the length of the pencil is dotted with perfect tiny pockmarks—like someone took the sharp point of a pin and made a few dozen indentations.

"Who does that to a pencil?" I ask.

"Beecher, I know you're all excited about the Culper Ring, but I think you're reading too many mystery novels. Not everything has to be a clue," he says, tossing me the pencil and rewashing his hands.

"You really don't see it?" I ask.

"I really don't—and even if I did, invisible ink is invisible ink. Since when are a few random dots a secret code?"

"Maybe now."

I toss him back the pencil. He tugs hard on the eraser.

"The eraser's attached. There's nothing hidden inside."

"You don't know that for sure," Dallas says.

"I do. I brought it downstairs and ran it through the X-ray. It's not hollowed out."

Dallas again brings the pencil close to his face—so close it almost touches his patchy beard.

"It still could be nothing," he says.

"It's *supposed* to look like nothing. And that dictionary was *supposed* to look like a dictionary. Until you find the exact right someone who knows how to read what's hidden underneath."

Standing at the sink, Dallas glances back at me. "You got someone in mind?"

For the first time today, I smile. "I very much do."

71

The archivist knew there was trouble when the cell phone started ringing.

The sound came from across the office, back by Beecher's desk.

Of course, he knew the ringtone—the theme song from the History Channel's *Last Days of the Civil War.* Everyone knew Dallas's phone.

But it wasn't until Dallas went darting out of the office that the archivist got concerned.

Being smart, the archivist didn't stand up...didn't panic... didn't even look up above the sightline of the cubicle.

Instead, all it took was the best tool in his arsenal—the one tool every historian must have.

Patience.

For sixteen minutes, the archivist sat there.

For sixteen minutes, the archivist waited.

He heard the door to the office again slam open. Dallas rushed in, bursting back into the office to grab something—sounded like winter coats sliding together—then darted back out again.

And then, giving Dallas time to make his way downstairs, the archivist turned to the one tool that served him, at this moment, even better than patience: the large plate glass window that doubled as an entire wall of his cubicle—and that gave him a perfect bird's-eye view of Pennsylvania Avenue.

Staring outside, the archivist watched as the two familiar figures bolted out of the building, racing across the street.

There they were.

Dallas. And Beecher.

Dallas and Beecher.

Definitely together.

The archivist's phone vibrated in his pocket. Just like he knew it would. No way would they let something like this slip by.

"Yeah, I see it," the archivist answered.

As they talked it through, an old silver Toyota—Dallas's Toyota—eventually stopped in front of the Archives. That's where Dallas and Beecher ran: to get Dallas's car. And from what it looked like, Beecher was the one driving. The car stopped and Dallas got out. From this height, four stories up, the archivist couldn't hear the screech. But he saw how fast Beecher drove off.

Like he was on a mission.

The archivist wasn't thrilled.

Now there was definitely no choice.

"I know . . . I see it too," Tot said into the phone, pressing his forehead against the cold plate glass window and watching as Beecher turned the corner and disappeared down 9th Street. "No, I don't know for sure, but I can guess. Yeah. No, of course we tagged the car. But it's time to tell the others," Tot added. "We've officially got ourselves a problem."

72

"ho you here to see?" the female guard with the bad Dutch-boy hair asks through the bulletproof glass window.

"We're on the list," I say, handing over my ID and stepping aside so she sees who I'm with.

From behind me, Clementine steps forward and slides her driver's license, along with her own temporary ID badge (the one that says she's a graduate student), into the open metal drawer just below the glass. With a tug, the St. Elizabeths guard snaps the drawer shut, dragging the contents to her side of the glass, but never taking her eyes off me. No question, she remembers me from yesterday.

"He's my assistant," Clementine explains.

"I don't care who he is. He still needs to be checked in," the guard pushes.

"I did. I called," Clementine pushes right back, tapping her thumb ring against the counter. Unlike last night with her grandmother, her voice is back to pure strength. "Check your computer."

The guard hits a few keys, and as her face falls, it's clear I was right to bring in Clementine. But as I take back my ID and the new sticker, and the guard motions us through the X-ray, it's also clear that Clementine's not exactly ready for the victory dance. "End of the hall," the guard says. "Escort'll meet you upstairs."

With a baritone *tunk*, the thick steel door on our left pops open, and we head inside to the heart of the building. Barely two steps in, we come to another steel door. This one's closed. It's the same system they have in prisons—a sally port—the next door won't open until the previous one is shut. That way, the patients can't escape.

Behind us, the first door clamps shut. I'm barely half a step behind Clementine. All I see is the back of her head, and a black beauty mark on the curve of her neck. But you don't have to be fluent in body language to see the way she's not moving. This is harder than yesterday. She knows what she's about to face.

"You don't have to do this," I whisper.

She doesn't look back.

"Clemmi, I'm serious," I add. "If you want, just wait here."

"How come you haven't asked me about last night?" she blurts.

"Wait. Are we fighting now? Is this about the kiss?"

"Forget the kiss. Last night. What you saw with Nan... why haven't you asked me about it?"

"I *did* ask you. You said you didn't want to talk about it."

"Well, now I do. Especially as I'm starting to hyperventilate in this tiny metal box."

Another metal *tunk* makes us both jump—the next door unlocks—and there's another long lime green hallway with an elevator at the far end. Clementine doesn't move, though it looks like she's trying to. In the past few days, I've seen her be both strong and weak, fearless and terrified, and also kind and protective. There are so many Clementines in that body. But when it comes to her family—especially her father—the girl who used to be prepared for anything reminds me that the number one thing she's not prepared for are her own insecurities.

"Y'know I don't judge you based on how you're treated by your grandmother," I tell her.

"I know you don't. But it's not just about how she treats me. It's about how I *let her* treat me. You saw it yesterday—I'm not... when she..." She presses her lips together. "I'm not my best with her."

I stand there, pretending I didn't see exactly that last night. "Sometimes you're so strong, I forget you can be hurt."

She shakes her head. "We can all be hurt."

I nod, thinking about the fact that Iris's bicycle is still sitting in my garage from where she accidentally left it. Iris loves that bicycle. But she still won't come pick it up.

As I study the single beauty mark on the back of Clementine's neck, it reminds me that there's nothing more intimate in life than simply being understood. And understanding someone else.

"How long've you been taking care of your grandma?" I finally ask.

"Four years. Ever since my mom died. And yes, I know it's good to take care of the elderly, but...living with a nasty old woman... having no job...which, also yes, I should've told you...and then finding out that Nico is my...*y'know*...I'm not saying I needed my life to be a symphony—I just never thought it'd turn out to be a country song."

"Yeah, well...it's better than realizing that your life is elevator music."

"Some people like elevator music," she counters.

I look over at her. She stands her ground, fearlessly locking eyes and reminding me exactly why her reappearance has slapped me out of the safe hibernation that's become my life. Even when she's afraid, this girl isn't afraid of anything. Or at least she's not afraid of me.

As she studies me, I want to kiss her again. I want to kiss her like last night—and I know this is my chance, a true second chance in every sense. A golden moment where the earth stops spinning, and the clouds roll away, and I get the opportunity to say the perfect words and prove that I can actually change my life.

"So...buh...your grandmother..." I stutter. "Her cancer's really bad, huh?"

"Yeah. It's bad," Clementine says, heading up the hallway. "Though mark my words, Nan's got eighteen lives. She'll bury us all and tap-dance on our graves."

I curse myself and contemplate cutting out my tongue. *How's the cancer?* That's the best I could come up with? Why didn't I just blurt out that I know she's pregnant and then make it a perfectly horrible social moment?

"Beecher, can I ask you a question?" Clementine adds as she jabs at the elevator call button. "Why'd you really come here?"

285

"What?"

"Here. Why here?" she says, pointing up. Three flights up to be precise. To her father. "You saw how crazy he is. Why come and see him?"

"I told you before—of all the people we've spoken to, he's still the one who first cracked the invisible ink. Without him, we'd still be thumbing through the dictionary."

"That's not true. He didn't crack anything. Your guy at the Archives...in Preservation..."

"The Diamond."

"Exactly. The Diamond," she says. "The Diamond's the one who cracked it."

"Only after Nico pointed out it was there. And yes, Nico's loopy, but he's also the only one who's handed us something that's panned out right."

"So now Tot's not right? C'mon, Beecher. You've got a dozen other people in the Archives who specialize in Revolutionary War stuff. You've got the Diamond and all his expertise about how the Founding Fathers used to secretly hide stuff. But instead of going to the trained professionals, you go to the paranoid schizo and the girl you first kissed in high school? Tell me what you're really after. Your office could've gotten you in here. Why'd you bring me with you?"

As I follow her into the elevator and press the button for the third floor, I look at her, feeling absolutely confused. "Why *wouldn't* I bring you? You were in that room when we found that dictionary. Your face is on that videotape just as much as mine is. And I'm telling you right now, Khazei knows who you are, Clementine. Do you really think all I care about is trying to protect myself? This is *our* problem. And if you think I haven't thought that from moment one, you really don't know me at all. Plus...can't you tell I like you?"

As the elevator doors roll shut, Clementine takes a half-step back, still silent. Between her missing dad, her dead mom, and the evil grandmother, she's spent a lifetime alone. She doesn't know what to do with *together*.

But I think she likes it.

"By the way," I add, standing next to her so we're nearly shoulder to shoulder. "Some of us like country music."

Clementine surprises me by blushing. As the elevator rises, she grips the railing behind her. "You were supposed to say that two minutes ago, genius—back when I said I liked elevator music."

"I know. I was panicking. Just give me credit for eventually getting there, okay?" Within seconds, as the elevator slows to a stop, I reach down and gently pry her fingers from the railing, taking her hand in my own.

It's a soaking, clammy mess. It's caked in cold sweat.

And it fits perfectly in mine.

For an instant, we stand there, both leaning on the back railing, both entombed in that frozen moment after the elevator bobs to a stop, but before the doors...

With a shudder, the doors part company. A short black woman dressed in a yellow blouse is bouncing a thick ring of keys in her open palm and clearly waiting to take us the rest of the way. Clementine prepared me for this: To help the patients feel more at ease, the staff doesn't wear uniforms. The silver nametag on her shirt says FPT, which is the mental hospital equivalent of an orderly. Behind the woman is another metal door, just like the ones downstairs.

"You're the ones seeing Nico Hadrian?" she asks, giving a quick glance to our IDs.

"That's us," I say as the woman twists a key in the lock and pushes the door open, revealing dull fluorescent lights, a scuffed, unpolished hall, and the man who's waiting for us, bouncing excitedly on his heels and standing just past the threshold with an awkward grin and a light in his chocolate brown eyes.

"I told everyone you'd be back," Nico says in the kind of monotone voice that comes from solid medication. "They never believe me."

73

That your pop or your granpop?" the muscular white kid with the laced-up army boots asked as the barber mowed the clippers up the back of the guy's head.

"My dad," Laurent replied, not even looking up at the crisp black-and-white photo of the soldier in full army uniform that was tucked next to the shiny blue bottle of Barbasol. In the photo—posed to look like an official army portrait in front of an American flag—his father was turned to the camera, a mischievous grin lighting his face.

"Those bars on his chest?" the client asked, trying to look up even though his chin was pressed down to his neck.

Laurent had heard the question plenty of times before—from people who wanted to know what medal his dad was wearing on his uniform.

The amazing part was, despite the photo, the barber rarely thought of his father as a soldier. As a strict Seventh-day Adventist, his dad was a pacifist, so committed to his faith that he refused to have anything to do with military service. But three days after Pearl Harbor, when the country was reeling and his prayers weren't bringing the answers he needed, his father walked into the recruitment office and enlisted.

He told his sergeants he wouldn't carry a weapon or dig ditches on Sabbath. They made him a cook, and of course let him cut hair too. Years later, after he returned home, Laurent's father remained just as committed to his faith. But the lesson was there—the one lesson he forever tried to drill into his children: Sometimes there's a greater good.

"He was actually a kitchen man," the barber said to his client, pointing the clippers back at the photo. "The medal's a joke from his first sergeant for being the first one to catch a lobster when they were stationed in San Juan."

The client laughed...and quickly rolled up his sleeve to reveal a crisp tattoo of a cartoony Marine Corps bulldog that was flexing his biceps like a bodybuilder and showing off his own tattoo, which read *Always Faithful* across his bulging dog arm.

The barber felt a lump in his throat, surprised by the swell of emotion that overtook him as he read the tattoo. No question about it, there was a real power that came with being faithful.

But.

He looked up and stole a quick glance at the photo of his father. At the miniature lobster that was pinned to his chest. And at the mischievous grin on his dad's young face.

There was also something to be said about the greater good.

74

Leading us past the nurses' station, past the TV alcove, past the section of small square tables covered by checkers sets, Nico keeps his chin up as he purposefully strides to what is clearly our destination: the only round table in the entire day room—and the only one with a green laminated card with the words *Don't Sit* on it.

"I made the card. So people don't sit here," Nico says.

"We appreciate that," I say, noticing that Clementine still hasn't said a word. It hasn't gotten any easier for her to be here. But the way Nico is staring more at me instead of her, I realize he still doesn't know she's his daughter. No question, that's better for all of us.

We all sit down. There are three of us at the table—and four seats. But as Nico's attention turns to the empty one, I have no doubt that, in his head, that empty seat is filled.

"It'll be quiet back here. That's why I like the round table," Nico says. Like every other table in the room, it's got a Plexiglas top. Makes it easier for the nurses to see what we're doing. Back by the nurses' station, the escort who walked us in is sitting at a computer, pretending not to stare at us. Pointing across the room to a set of swinging doors, Nico adds, "My room's back there."

There's a loud *kuh-kunk*. I follow the sound over my shoulder, where a soda machine—*kuh-kunk*—spits out a Diet Dr Pepper that's retrieved by a male patient with curly black hair.

"I can get us apple and orange juice for free. They make us pay for soda," Nico explains.

"I think we're okay," I say, hoping to move us along.

"You talk to me like the doctors," Nico says, placing both his hands flat on the see-through table. His feet are pressed perfectly together on the floor. "Like the newer doctors who are worried I might hurt them."

"Nico, I wasn't—"

"I know you're not her assistant. I know you said that just to get in here." There's a *kuh-kunk* behind us—another Diet Dr Pepper to another patient. "The Secret Service can arrest you for that, Benedict."

He's trying to take control, especially with the hokey move of calling me Benedict Arnold. But unlike last time, I've done my homework. Especially about him.

When Nico was first arrested for shooting the President, he was charged with a *federal* crime, which means he had *federal* records— including a psych profile—which means those records eventually came to the Archives, which also means it took nothing but a phone call to get them from our record center out in Suitland, Maryland.

To be honest, most of what I read was typical Psych 101 nonsense, but one thing did stand out: Yes, Nico's hyper-paranoid, and used to claim God talks to him . . . and yes, he's clearly well versed in all sorts of historical conspiracy theories, including delusional concerns about Thomas Jefferson and George Washington and a hidden pentagram in the street layout of Washington, D.C. But as a former decorated soldier in the army, the one thing Nico has always responded to best is a sure voice of authority.

"Nico, I'm here to talk about the Culper Ring," I announce. "Would you like an update or not?"

His hands stay flat on the table. His eyes flick back and forth, picking me apart. Then Clementine. Then the empty chair next to him. The profile said how methodical he was. But the way he starts biting the inside of his lip, he's also excited.

"I was right, wasn't I?" he blurts. "About the invisible ink . . ."

"You were. Messages were being sent."

"I knew! I—" He lowers his voice, glancing over at the nurses' station. The escort who brought us in is on the phone. Nico definitely hears what she's saying. And he's been here long enough to know what happens if he gets too excited. "I told you you were being tested," he insists, fighting to keep his composure. "I told you, didn't I?"

"We're all being tested," Clementine says, just like we practiced. "That's what life is."

"And here's your newest test," I jump in, already feeling guilty, but knowing that this is our only chance. "*This* is the message that came back."

From my front pants pocket, I pull out the pencil that was left behind by President Wallace and gently place it on the open table.

75

Nico's hand snaps out like a snake, snatching the President's pencil and cradling it in his open palm. His eyes again flick back and forth, soaking in every detail.

Eventually, he looks up. "I don't understand."

"The pencil...the indentations..." I say. "We think a message was hidden on that."

"On the pencil?" he asks.

"In the indentations," I say, pointing him back.

There's another *kuh-kunk* behind us. Diet Dr Pepper for another patient.

Clementine jumps and Nico blinks hard as the soda can hits. But Nico never loses sight of the pencil. Holding both ends, he twirls it slowly like the tips of a cartoon mustache. He devours every mark, every groove, every detail.

Eventually he looks up, his brown eyes peeking just above the pencil. "Tell me what it said in the invisible ink."

"Pardon?" I ask.

"The message. In the dictionary. I want to know what it said first. I want you to tell me."

"No. Absolutely no," I say, eyeing Clementine, who's staring through the see-through table at her own feet. She's not gonna last long. "That's not the game, Nico—I've got no time."

"Then I have no time for you," Nico challenges.

"That's fine. Then we'll leave. And you can sit here waiting another two years for your next visitor," I say, standing up from my seat.

"Sit."

"No. You're not driving this," I shoot back.

"Sit," Nico repeats, lowering his chin and trying hard to keep his voice down.

"Are you listening? You're not driving. So tell me what it says on the pencil, or have fun spending the rest of your afternoon with your free orange juice."

Next to me, Clementine rises from her seat, joining me to leave.

Nico looks over at the table's empty chair. He nods a few times. Whatever he's hearing, I pray it's good advice.

"It doesn't say anything," Nico blurts.

"Excuse me?"

"The pencil," Nico says. "There's no message."

"How do you know?"

"I can see. I can— I'm good with patterns. The doctors . . . they've told me . . . I can see what others can't. God gave me that gift," he says, again glancing at the empty chair. "The marks on the pencil . . . the indentations . . . there's nothing recurring. No repetition."

"So the Culper Ring . . . back in the day . . . they never used old carvings as codes?" I ask.

"These aren't carvings. These are . . . they're nothing. Nothing I can see. Now tell me what you haven't been saying. Tell me what was written in the invisible ink."

He says the words matter-of-factly, as if there should be no argument.

Clementine and I both stand there, silent.

"I know you came here for my help," Nico says. "You wouldn't be here if you weren't stuck. I can help with—"

He stops.

I know it's a trick. Nico isn't sly. He's not subtle. He's a whack job who acts like a giant child and thinks he's the reincarnation of George Washington. So I know he's just trying to get me to say . . .

"You can help me with *what*?" I ask, plenty annoyed, but curious enough to play along. I return to my seat.

He looks over toward the nurses' station, once again scanning the brightly lit room. Taped to a nearby square concrete column is a laser-printed sign that says:

Please keep voices low
And spirits up

"Nico, what can you help us with?" I repeat.

"I know about the Purple Hearts," Nico says.

"Okay, we're done—I've seen this scam already," I say as I again stand up.

"Where are you going?" Nico asks.

"This is the exact same thing you did last time—first you offer to help, then you start shoveling your whacky ghost stories."

To my surprise, Clementine grips my wrist, keeping me in place. "What about the Purple Hearts?" she asks.

"The medals. The military medals. Do you know who created the Purple Heart?"

"George Washington," I shoot back.

"I appreciate that. I appreciate you knowing your history," Nico says. "Yes, George Washington created it. It was one of the first medals introduced in the United States. But he didn't call it the Purple Heart—"

"He called it the Badge of Military Merit," I interrupt. "It got its name from the fact that the medal itself was a purple cloth in the shape of a heart. What else do you want to know?"

"Do you know how many Purple Hearts George Washington gave out?" Nico challenges.

This time, I'm silent. I'm good, but I'm not Tot.

"Three," Nico says. "That's it. Three. Three men—all of them from Connecticut. As part of the honor, Washington wrote their names into a special book he called the Book of Merit. And do you know where this Book of Merit is today?"

"In that warehouse with the Ark of the Covenant?" I ask.

"No one knows where it is," Nico says, oblivious to my joke as he flashes us a grin of excitement. Clementine looks even worse than she did yesterday. She's not lasting much longer. "Washington's book disappeared. Forever. In 1932, they revived the honor of the Purple Heart—it's been given in our military ever since. But to this day, no one—not anyone—has any idea where Washington's original Book of Merit—with the original names—actually is."

"And this matters to us because . . . ?"

"It matters because today, the Purple Heart goes to those who are wounded in battle. But originally, back then, Washington's badge had nothing to do with injuries. In his own words, Washington said it was for *extraordinary fidelity*. Do you know what *extraordinary fidelity* means?"

"It means someone who's loyal," I say.

"It means someone who can keep a secret," Nico counters. "I didn't know this. I looked it up. I found it after your visit. I have a lot of time here."

"Just get to the point."

"I have been. You're not listening to it. Like your predecessor—"

"Don't compare me to a predecessor. Don't call me Benedict Arnold. Don't start with all that reincarnation hoo-hoo," I warn him, still standing across from him. "If you want us to listen, stay in reality."

His eyes flicker back and forth. His chest rises and falls just as fast. But to his credit, Nico bites the inside of his lip and stays on track. "The very first recipient of the Purple Heart was a twenty-six-year-old named Elijah Churchill," Nico explains. "Elijah served under someone I think you've heard of—Benjamin Tallmadge."

Clementine looks my way.

"Tallmadge was the organizer of the original Culper Ring," I say.

"Then when you look at the third name on that list—Daniel Bissell from Windsor, Connecticut—guess why his name was put in the Book of Merit? He was one of our best spies, who helped infiltrate Benedict Arnold's own corps," Nico says, his eyes flicking faster than ever. "And according to some, that's the *real* reason the Book of Merit disappeared. It wasn't stolen. It was hidden—by

Washington himself, who collected our best men and used them to build the greatest secret corps that history never knew..."

"The Culper Ring," Clementine says.

"I'm not asking you to believe it," Nico says. "But even America's secret history has its experts. Let me help you with this. You know I can help you. This is the world I know best."

I'm tempted to argue, but we both know he's right. When it comes to conspiracies, Nico's got a PhD.

"Tell me what you found in the invisible ink," Nico says. "Tell me and I'll share what I know. If I fail, you can leave and we're done."

I look over at Clementine, who replies with an awkward shrug. I can't help but agree. At this point—especially with the President's pencil apparently being a bust, and still not knowing why Wallace brought me to that room—what do we have to lose?

From my back pocket, I unfold the photocopy of the dictionary page and slide it across the round table.

Unlike before, Nico doesn't snatch it. He stays calm, hands again flat on the table. But as he leans forward and reads the words, I see the thick vein starting to swell on his neck.

FEBRUARY 16

26 YEARS IS A LONG TIME TO KEEP A SECRET

WRITE BACK: NC 38.548.19 OR WU 773.427

There's a loud *kuh-kunk* behind us. Another Diet Dr Pepper for another patient, this one a young Asian man with a dyed blond stripe running down the middle of his head like a skunk streak.

"Get away from us, Simon—this isn't your business!" Nico growls without turning around as he covers the photocopy by pressing it against his own chest. The Asian man flips Nico the finger, then heads for the swinging doors that lead back to patients' rooms.

Barely noticing, Nico focuses back on the photocopy. His lips move as he reads.

His lips move as he reads it again.

Over and over, he rereads the document. The vein on his neck swells larger than ever.

He finally looks up—not excited, not energized . . . not anything.

"I know where you need to go," he says.

76

The barber had gloves in his pocket. But he didn't put them on.

It wasn't that he wasn't cold. Out here—especially out here in the snow-covered graveyard—the weather was freezing. He was most definitely cold.

But for now, he wanted to feel it.

In fact, as he walked up the twisting concrete path of Oak Hill Cemetery, he knew that was his real problem. For too long now, especially the past few years, he hadn't felt the cold, or fear—or most anything at all. Instead, he'd been lulled. And worst of all, he hadn't been lulled by anyone. He'd been lulled by himself.

It was the same reason he came here today.

He knew he shouldn't. Palmiotti would tear him apart if he found out he'd trekked all the way out here in the snow. But as he spotted the headstone that was carved in the shape of a baby swaddled in a blanket, the barber couldn't help but think what else he'd lulled himself into.

He'd only lived in Washington a few years now. But he'd been here long enough to know where the real strings were pulled. Right now, Palmiotti was the one with the office in the White House. And the private parking spot in the White House. And the best friend who sat in the Oval Office. All the barber had was high rent on his barber chair and a set of presidential cuff links. So if this really was the moment where the tornado was about to uproot the house, Laurent knew who'd be the first one that house was landing on.

Damn right he needed to come out here and start feeling this stuff for himself.

But as he took his first step off the concrete path and into the snow, he heard the faint rumbling of voices behind him.

Hobbling and hiding behind a section of trees that surrounded the edges of the wide-open graveyard, Laurent didn't have any trouble staying out of sight. Out here, no one was looking for anything except the dead—which is why it made such a perfect drop point.

In the distance, two voices were fighting, arguing, and far too busy to see what was really going on in the cemetery.

Still, it wasn't until they reached the top of the path that Laurent peered out from behind the apple blossom tree and spied who was making all the noise.

That's him, the barber thought as the bitter cold settled between the thin bones of his fingers.

"Stop!" the girl called to the guy with the sandy blond hair.

The guy wasn't listening. But there he was. The one who could take away everything they had worked for.

Beecher.

77

Beecher, *stop* ...!" Clementine calls out, chasing behind me. I keep running, my lungs starting to burn from the cold, my shoes soaked from the snow as I climb the concrete path and pass a double-wide headstone with an intricate carved stone owl taking flight from the top.

No doubt, Oak Hill Cemetery is for people with money. But if Nico's right, it's also for people with something far more than that.

"Beecher, you need to be smart!" Clementine adds. "Don't jump in without knowing where you're going!"

I know she's right. But thanks to the GPS in my cell phone, I know exactly where I'm going.

"*542 feet northwest,*" it says in glowing green letters. There's even a red digital arrow that points me in the right direction. Yet as I look down to check it, my phone vibrates in my hand.

Caller ID says it's the one archivist who I know is a member of the actual Culper Ring. Dallas.

"Beecher, that's it! You cracked it!" Dallas blurts before I even say hello.

I know what he's talking about. The note. The invisible ink. *Twenty-six years is a long time to keep a secret. Write back: NC 38.548.19 or WU 773.427.* Since the moment we found it, we knew those numbers weren't call numbers on books. So then we kept thinking, *What's NC? What's WU?*

Until Nico said it was another old George Washington trick.

"Nico's the one who cracked it," I remind him.

"The point is, he was right. One of our guys—he works at the

301

Supreme Court of all things—he said Nico's story checked out: Washington apparently used to write these long rambling letters that seemed to go nowhere...until you read just the first letter, or third letter, or whatever letter of every word. When we tried that here, it's like he said: NC and WU became..."

"N and W. North and West," I say, repeating what Nico told me, and I told Dallas a half hour ago when I said to meet us here.

As I head up the main path, I understand why no one wants to take Nico at his word, but even I have to admit, it was amazing to watch. Once Nico had the N and W, he played with the decimals and the message became a bit more familiar: *Write back: N 38° 54.819 W 77° 3.427*—a GPS address that converts to the same latitude and longitude system that's been in place since Ptolemy put them in the first world atlas nearly two thousand years ago. That's why we were stuck for so long. We were looking for *book* coordinates. These were *map* coordinates. "Where are you anyway?" I ask.

"Just getting to Oak Hill now," Dallas explains. "I just passed the front gate. Where're you?"

"I don't know—where all the headstones and dead people are. Up the hill on the left. There's..." I glance around, searching for landmarks. "There's a wide-open field and a huge stone statue of a...she looks like a farm girl, but her face is all flat because the weather's worn away her nose."

"Hold on—I think I...I see you," Dallas says. "I see you and—" He cuts himself off. "Please tell me that's not Clementine with you."

"Don't even start. Y'know I needed her to get into St. Elizabeths."

"And what about here? Why bring her here? We talked about this, Beecher. No matter what you think, we don't know this girl."

I hang up the phone, tired of the argument. It's no different than what Tot said. But what neither of them understands is, without Clementine, I never would've made it all the way here. And like I told her earlier, she was in that SCIF too. I can't leave her behind.

"Beecher, hold up!" a faint voice calls out behind us.

I turn, spotting Dallas just as he comes around the corner, half-way down the crooked path. He's less than fifty yards away. He's running fast to catch up.

But not as fast as me.

"Who's that?" Clementine calls out, clearly freaked out.

"Don't worry. Just Dallas," I say.

"Why'd you tell him we were coming here?" Clementine asks, remembering Tot's advice to not trust anyone.

I don't answer.

On my cell phone, GPS says we've got another 319 feet to go. But I don't need a snazzy cell phone to see my true destination.

An expansive pie crust of snow covers the ground, and a narrow minefield of footprints burrows straight at a single grave: an eight-foot-tall obelisk that looks like a miniature Washington Monument.

"That's it, isn't it?" Clementine whispers behind me.

As I sprint from the paved path, my feet are swallowed by the ice. I stick to my left, careful to steer clear of the evidence. The footprints look new—like they were made this morning. There's also another set of prints that leads back, back, back to the ring of trees that surround the field.

"You think someone's out there?" Clementine asks, spotting the same prints I do.

I don't answer. But what catches my eye is what's sitting at the base of the obelisk: wet leaves...clumps of soil...and a neat little hole in dirty brown snow...

Like something's buried underneath.

Scrambling forward, I dive for the little rabbit hole, stuff my hand down it, and pat around until...

There.

The beige rock is smooth and flat, perfect for skimming in a lake. Dallas and Clementine both rush to my side. But as I pull the rock out, I know something's wrong. The weight's not right.

"It's plastic," I say. "I think...I think it's hollow."

"Of course it's hollow. That's how they hide stuff in it," Dallas says as if he sees this all the time. "Open it up. See what it is."

I flip the rock over. Sure enough, the bottom swivels open.

All three of us hunch over it like mother birds over an egg.

And we finally get to see what's inside.

78

Tot purposely chose one of the SCIFs on the opposite side of the building.

He picked one that was assigned to the Legislative folks. The head of the Legislative SCIFs was a middle-aged guy who spent his nights playing Adams Morgan clubs with a happy but untalented rocksteady and reggae band. He'd never know the room was being used.

Still, Tot was careful as he came over. He did his usual weaving through the stacks, kept his face off the cameras, and even knew to avoid the elderly volunteers who they'd packed into one of the suites on the eighteenth floor to sort through the recently unearthed Revolutionary War widow pension files.

In fact, to actually get in the room, he was smart enough to avoid using the regular door code.

And smart enough to instead use the security staff's override code.

And smart enough to pick one of the few SCIFs in the building that didn't have a single surveillance camera (which is how most Senators and Members preferred it).

But the one thing Tot did that was smartest of all?

He made sure he wasn't working this alone.

On his right, the quarter-inch vault door clicked and thunked, then opened with a pneumatic pop.

"You're late," Tot said.

"You're wrong," Khazei said as the door slammed behind him. "I'm right on time."

*   *   *

79

othing."

"No. Can't be," Dallas says.

"It can. And it *is*," I say, tipping the hollow rock so he and Clementine can get a good view.

Dallas squints and leans in, examining the small rectangular compartment inside the rock. No question, there's nothing there, which means . . .

"Someone already picked up the message," Clementine says, looking back at the footprints that lead out to the treeline, which curves like a horseshoe around us.

"Or no one's put one in yet," I say, trying to stay positive, but unable to shake the feeling that Clementine may be right. I follow her gaze to the treeline in the distance. Nothing moves. Nothing makes a sound. But we all recognize that out-of-body gnawing that comes when you think you're being watched. "I think we need a place to hide. Someone could still be coming."

Dallas shakes his head, pointing down at the grave. "If that were the case, where'd these footprints come from?"

"Actually, I was thinking they came from you," Clementine challenges, motioning at Dallas even as she eyes the ones back to the treeline. "I mean, even with Beecher calling you, that's a pretty amazing coincidence that you show up at the exact moment we do."

"Funny, I was thinking the same about *you*," Dallas shoots back. "But I was going to be cordial enough to wait until you left and tell Beecher behind your back."

"Can you both please stop?" I plead. I'm tempted to tell Clementine what Dallas did last night—how he spotted that person in the taxi...and gave me the video of us in the SCIF, keeping it away from Khazei...and told me the true story about the Culper Ring and the President's private group of Plumbers. But it doesn't change the fact that with this rock being empty..."We're more lost than ever."

"Not true," Dallas says, licking flicks of snow from his beard.

"What're you talking about? This was the one moment where we had the upper hand—we knew the location where the President and his Plumbers were dropping their message, but instead of catching them in the act, we're standing here freezing our rear ends off."

"You sure this message is between the President and his Plumbers?" Dallas asks, his voice taking on that timbre of cockiness that it gets when he thinks he's in control.

"What's a Plumber?" Clementine asks.

"His friends. Like Nixon's Plumbers," I explain. "The people Wallace is working with."

"But you see my point, right?" Dallas adds. "If this note really was between the President and his Plumbers—and they knew you found out about it—"

"Why didn't they simply change the meeting spot?" I ask, completing the thought and looking again at the mess of footprints.

"And on top of that, if the big fear was the fact that you'd rat him out, why didn't the President make you an offer when he had you in the SCIF? He's supposedly who the message in the dictionary was for, right?"

It's a fair question. And the one assumption we've been relying on since the moment this started: that when we found the dictionary in the SCIF, it held a message between the President and someone from his inner circle. But if that's not the case...

"You think the President may've been trying to communicate with someone *outside* his circle?" I ask.

"Either that or someone outside his circle may've been trying to communicate with the President," Dallas replies.

As I turn away from the treeline, my brain flips back to the original message: *February 16. Twenty-six years is a long time to keep a secret.*

"Maybe that's why the President asked for you to staff him this morning, Beecher. Maybe he wasn't trying to *give* you a message— maybe he was waiting to *get* one. From *you*."

I see where he's going. It's the only thing that makes sense. All this time, we thought the dictionary held a letter that was written to Wallace by one of his friends. But if this is really from someone who's *not* on his side . . . and they somehow found out about his Plumbers, and were hoping to reveal something from twenty-six years ago . . .

"You think someone's threatening Wallace?" Clementine asks.

"I think they're way beyond threats," I say as a cloud of frosty air puffs out with each syllable. "If this is what I think it is, I think someone's blackmailing the President of the United States."

80

Entering the SCIF, Khazei did his own quick scan of the windowless room.

"You think I'm stupid?" Tot asked as he fiddled with the TV that sat atop the rolling cart. "There're no cameras."

Khazei checked anyway. For himself. Sure enough, no cameras. But that didn't mean there was no VCR.

"Where'd you even find it?" Khazei asked, motioning to the videotape as Tot slid it in and turned on the TV.

"In his house. He had it hid in a box of tampons."

"Why'd he have tampons? I thought he lived alone."

"He's got a sister. And had a fiancée. He's not throwing their stuff away," Tot scolded.

Khazei didn't respond. Instead, he looked down at his recently polished nails, tempted to start biting the cuticle of his thumb.

On TV, the video began to play, showing Orlando, Clementine...and of course Beecher—and what they found in the SCIF that day.

"Eff me," Khazei muttered.

Tot nodded. "I think they already did."

81

E ightball?" Dallas asks.

"Has to be Eightball," I agree with a nod.

"What's Eightball?" Clementine asks.

I look over at Dallas, who shakes his head. He doesn't want me telling her. He also didn't want me bringing her to see Nico. But that's the only reason we got in. And got here.

"Beecher, if you don't want to tell me, you don't have to," Clementine says. "It's okay. I understand."

"Listen to the girl," Dallas whispers.

But what Dallas will never understand is what Khazei said this morning—once everything finally gets out and they verify that Orlando's been murdered, Clementine's just as high on the suspect list as I am, and therefore has just as much of a right to know what the hell is really going on.

"Eightball's a person," I say as Clementine stands frozen in the cold. "He's a kid, really—or *was* a kid—named Griffin Anderson. He was twenty years old when he disappeared."

"Disappeared? As in abducted?"

"No one knows. This guy Eightball was the town bully, complete with an eight-ball tattoo on his forearm. The point is, *he's* what happened twenty-six years ago. February 16th. That's the night he disappeared from the President's hometown in Ohio."

"Which means what?" Clementine asks as a twig snaps back by the treeline. We all turn to look. It's too hard to see anything. "You think that when the President was younger, he had some hand in this?"

"I have no idea, but . . . well . . . yeah," I say, still scanning tree by

310

tree. "Think about it. Something happens that night, Wallace loses his cool, and—I don't know—the future President goes all *Mystic River* and he and his boys somehow make Eightball disappear..."

"Until somehow, someone from the past suddenly shows up out of nowhere and starts resurrecting the story," Dallas says, his eyes tightening on Clementine.

"Dallas, leave her alone," I say.

"No, Dallas, say what you're thinking," Clementine says.

"I just did," he shoots back.

"And that's your grand scenario? You think I got my hands on some old info, and then what? I've been using Beecher in hopes of terrorizing the President?"

"There are more ridiculous ideas out there."

"And just to complete your delusion, tell me what my motive is again?"

"I've seen where you live, Clementine. I was out there last night," Dallas says. "No offense, but that house...that neighborhood... you could clearly use an upgrade."

"Dallas, that's enough!" I say.

"You do *not* know me," Clementine growls, making sure he hears each syllable, "so be very careful what you say next."

"Ooh, nice threatening ending. I didn't even have to bring up how far the apple tumbles from the tree. Like father, like dau—"

Springing forward, Clementine leaps for Dallas's throat. *"You smug piece of—!"*

I dart in front of Dallas, catching Clementine in midair, inches before she clobbers him. She's a whirlwind of wild punches, her weight hitting my chest at full speed and knocking me backward.

"Clemmi, relax!" I insist as I dig my feet into the snow. She still fights to get past me, our chests pressing against each other.

"Don't you dare compare him to me! You take those words back!" she continues, still raging at Dallas.

"He didn't mean it," I plead as I try to hold her in place.

"You take it back!" she howls, her hot breath pounding against my face. It's even worse than when she lost it with Khazei.

"Clementine! Stop!" I order, gripping her shoulders hard enough that I know she feels it.

Her eyes turn my way, her anger still at full boil. The scariest part is, for that half a second, she looks *exactly* like her father. She again grits her teeth, and the big vein swells. I wait for her to attack.

"You can let go now," she says in a low voice. Her arms are still tensed.

"You sure?" I ask.

"Let go, Beecher. I want you to let me go. Now."

As she tugs free of my grip, I shoot Dallas a look, hoping he'll apologize. He doesn't.

"Dallas didn't mean it," I tell her.

"I know who I am!" she shoots back, struggling to find control. "I know I'm impulsive. And passionate. I know I have a temper—but I'm *not him*, Beecher! I'm not *that*," she insists, refusing to say her father's name.

I reach out to calm her.

She again pulls away. By now, I know she's good at hiding her wounded side. And her scared side. But this anger...this venom that erupts and stings so brutally...Some things can't be hidden—especially when it's who we really are.

"The least you can do is pretend to stick up for me," she adds, catching her breath.

"C'mon, you know I don't think you're like Nico."

"I know you can *say* it, Beecher. The point is to *mean* it."

The words bite as she lets them freeze in the air.

Before I can say a word, she turns around, walking back to the path alone.

"Apologize later," Dallas says, gripping my arm as I go to chase her. "Right now, let's get back to the group so we can figure out what's going on."

"The group? Your super-bad-ass Culper Ring?" I ask, my eyes still on Clementine, who needs some time to calm down. "In case you haven't noticed, Dallas, for all the bragging you've done, they didn't get anywhere until I gave them Nico's answer. And in case you hadn't noticed that, everything else has failed: The rock was empty, all the messages are gone, and we've got no leads to follow."

"That's not true. You said Tot found that police report—the one that had the President's doctor..."

"Stewart Palmiotti."

"...that when Palmiotti was home from college, he was the last one who saw Eightball alive...that he told the police he saw Eightball voluntarily get into that car. While you were running around with Clementine, I had our guys confirm it. They found the report. Palmiotti knows what really happened that night, which means we can—"

"We can *what*? We can send some Culper Ring guys to go confront Palmiotti? Is that the new master plan—that they march into the White House, stick a finger in his face, and accuse the President's oldest and most trusted friend of harboring an old secret?"

"You'd be surprised what people will say when they think you have the upper hand."

"But we don't have the upper hand! All we have is a sheet of paper with someone saying, *I know what you did last summer*, which is proof of *nothing*! And I'm telling you right now—I don't care how many brainiacs you've got in that Ring—if you go in there with nothing and start yanking on the tail of the lion, that lion is going to take out his claws and show us firsthand why they crowned him king of the jungle. And the first claw's coming at me."

As Clementine heads back down the curving concrete path, Dallas for once doesn't argue. He knows I'm right. He knows that the moment those tox reports come back and Khazei can prove that Orlando was murdered, every single eye is going to be aimed at the last person Orlando was seen with: me. And when that black hole opens, there's no slowing it down. Not until it swallows every one of us in its path.

"That still doesn't mean we shouldn't focus on Palmiotti," he says, again motioning to the footprints. "Our people are looking. They can find anything. So whatever happened all those years ago, we'll find out what they saw, or who was there...or even where they were—"

"Wait," I blurt. "Say that part again."

"We'll find what they saw?"

"No. *Where they were.* If we find where they were..." I pull out my phone, quickly dialing a number.

"What're you doing?" Dallas asks.

"If we want to take down the lion," I tell him, "we need to get a bigger gun."

82

"W hat're you doing?" Dallas asked.

"If we want to take down the lion," Beecher replied, "we need to get a bigger gun."

Still watching from the treeline, the barber had to hold his breath to hear what they were saying. He tried to tell himself it was still okay. But as Beecher dialed whatever number he was dialing in the distance, Laurent knew the truth—and he knew just how far he was from *okay*.

From what he could hear, Beecher and his group weren't just guessing anymore. They had details. They had names—and not just the President's. They had Palmiotti...plus, he heard them say *Eightball*...

If they—for them to know about that...for them to know what happened that night...

On the side of the apple blossom tree that hid Laurent from sight, a small patch of snow, clinging like a white island to the bark, was slowly whittled down by the intensity of the blowing wind. As he watched the island shrink, flake by flake, Laurent knew it was no different here.

Erosion over time.

For a while now, Palmiotti said he could stop it. That somehow, he could make it all go away. But confidence is no different than friendships or secrets. They're all susceptible to the same fate...

Erosion over time.

It was so clear to Laurent now. This wasn't the beginning of the tornado.

This was the beginning of the end of it.

A few inches in front of the barber, the island of snow was the size of a quarter, worn down by another slash of wind. Across the snowy field, Beecher was having much the same effect. Indeed, as the last bits of snow were tugged from the bark, Laurent once again felt a thick lump in his throat and the matching swell of emotion that overcame him earlier when he read his client's tattoo.

If Laurent wanted to stop the tornado, there was only one way to make it go away. Until this exact moment, though, he didn't think he had the courage to do it.

But he did.

Reaching into his jacket pocket, Laurent gripped tight to the item he'd instinctively grabbed from the shop, one of only a few mementos his father brought back from the war: the Master Barbers straight-edge razor with the abalone handle.

As he slid it out and flipped the blade open, the lasts bits of snow were blown from the tree bark.

Across the field, both Beecher and Dallas had their backs to him.

The tornado was about to start swirling a whole lot faster.

83

National Archives," a familiar voice says through my phone. "How may I direct your call?"

"Katya, it's Beecher. Can you transfer me over to Mr. Harmon in Presidential Records?" Standing in the snow and reading the confusion on Dallas's face, I explain, "The goal is to find what really happened on February 16th, right? The problem is, the only record from the sixteenth is that police report, which is a record that Palmiotti created himself. But what if we could find out where Palmiotti and Wallace were on the seventeenth . . . or even the eighteenth?"

Dallas's eyes tighten as he tries to put it together. He knows the problem. Twenty-six years ago, Wallace wasn't President. But that doesn't mean there aren't any presidential records.

"Okay, so when this happened . . . Twenty-six years ago, the President was . . . back in college," Dallas adds, quickly doing the math.

Dallas knows how the Archives work. He knows what we keep. And knows that when Wallace or any other President gets elected, the very first thing we do is start a file for them. But most of all, we start *filling that file*—by preserving that person's history. We start collecting photos and family pictures, mementos and birth records and elementary school reports.

It's how we have those baby photos of Clinton—and how we know what was written in Bush's and Obama's fifth-grade report cards. We know those documents are eventually headed for a presidential library, so the moment a new President is elected, the government starts grabbing everything it can. And best of all, guess who's in charge of storing it?

"You think there're records from where Palmiotti was on February 16th?" Dallas asks.

"We know he was in Ohio. The police report says so. He and Wallace were both home from college, which means—"

"This is Mr. Harmon," a curt voice snaps through the phone. As one of our top people in Presidential Records, Steve Harmon doesn't apologize for being impatient, or for referring to himself as Mr. Harmon. A former navy man, all he cares about are facts.

"Mr. Harmon, this is Beecher calling—from Old Military."

"Katya told me."

"Yes, well, er—I have a request here for some records from when President Wallace was in college, and—"

"Most of those records haven't been processed yet."

"I know, sir, but we're trying to track down a particular date— the week of February 16th—back during the President's final year of college." As I say the words, even though she's way down the path and nearly a football field away, Clementine glances over her shoulder. I don't care whose daughter she is. No way can she hear me. She turns away and continues walking. "It's for a friend of the foundation," I tell Harmon.

In Archives terms, *friend of the foundation* means one of the big-shot donors who help sponsor so many of our exhibits.

From the silence on the phone, I know Mr. Harmon's annoyed. But he's also well aware that the only reason we're still allowed to display one of the original Magna Cartas is because a friend of the foundation—the head of the Carlyle Group—loans it to us.

"Put the request in writing. I'll take a look," Mr. Harmon says.

The click in my ear tells me he's gone.

"Wallace's college records?" Dallas asks as I put away my phone and we both stand there, our feet eaten by the snow. "You really think the smoking gun's in some old English paper? 'What I Did During Spring Break—And How We Hid Eightball's Body,' by Orson Wallace?"

"There's no smoking gun, Dallas. What I'm looking for is a time-line. And if we're lucky, this'll tell us whether, during that week,

Wallace came back to class or was so traumatized by what happened, he spent some time away."

"So you're looking for attendance records? Hate to remind you, but they don't take attendance in college."

"And I hate to remind you, but you have no idea what they take. Maybe when Wallace got back to school he spoke to a guidance counselor, and there's an incident report still floating in his old student file," I say as I look over Dallas's shoulder, where Clementine is just a tiny speck of coal in the white distance.

Another twig snaps back by the treeline. "We should get out of here," I say.

Watching me watching Clementine, Dallas follows me to the graveyard's concrete path, which still holds the trail of her impacted-snow footprints. "Beecher, do you have any idea how the Culper Ring has managed to successfully stay secret for over two hundred years?"

"Trust."

"Exactly. Trust," Dallas says. "Two hundred years of trusting the right people. Now let me ask you a question: Did you tell Clementine everything I said about the Culper Ring?"

"You told me not to."

"I did. But the point is, you listened. And y'know why you listened? Because even though, when it comes to Clementine, there's a little voice in your pants that's been telling you what to do—when you thought about telling her about the Culper Ring, there was a second voice—the voice in your head—that told you *not* to. For whatever reason, something in your brain told you that Clementine shouldn't know this one. And that's the voice you need to listen to, Beecher. It'll lead you far better than the voice in your pants," he says as he steps out onto the concrete path and plants his own snow footprint right over Clementine's.

"I appreciate the talking-penis analogy, but let's be honest, Dallas—if I didn't have Clementine with me this morning, I never would've even gotten in to see Nico."

"And that's so bad?"

"If Nico didn't see that sheet, we wouldn't've gotten here," I point out, catching up to him and holding out the empty rock.

"What're you talking about?"

"The coordinates. North 38 degrees, west 77 degrees—"

"Go back," Dallas says, stopping on the path. "You showed him the actual invisible ink sheet?"

"No, I—" I pat my jacket pockets, then my jeans. Don't tell me I—

"*What*, Beecher? You *gave* Nico the sheet?"

"Of course not. In the rush...we were so excited...I think I left it."

"You didn't *leave* it, Beecher. He *took* it. Didn't you see *Silence of the Lambs*? He absolutely *took* it—which means in your quest to figure out who's messing with the President, you gave the full story to the mental patient who once tried to assassinate one!"

I try to tell myself that Nico doesn't know that the note was for Wallace, but it's drowned out by the fact that there are only two types of people who ever come to see Nico: fellow crazies and desperate reporters.

"You better pray he doesn't have access to copiers or scanners," Dallas says, reminding me exactly what'll happen if Nico puts that sheet of paper in the hands of either of those two groups.

I look downhill, checking for Clementine. She's gone. In her place, all I see is Nico and the calm, measured way he said *thank you* when I left. He definitely took it.

"Don't tell me you're going back to St. Elizabeths," Dallas calls out, though he already knows the answer.

"I have to," I tell him as I pick up speed. "I need to get back what Nico took from us."

84

It was something that the one with the ungroomed beard—
Dallas—it was something Dallas had said.

Squinting through the front windshield as the morning sun
pinged off the piles of soot-capped snow, the barber couldn't help
but notice the sudden increase in the number of the neighborhood's
liquor stores and laundromats. Of course, there was a barbershop.
There was always a barbershop, he knew, spying the hand-painted
sign with the words *Fades To Braids* in big red letters.

Kicking the brakes as he approached a red light, he didn't regret
holding back at the cemetery. He was ready. He'd made his peace.
But when he heard those words leave Dallas's lips, he knew there
was still one box that needed to be checked.

Twenty-six years ago, he'd acted in haste. Looking back at it,
though, he didn't regret that either. He did the best he could in the
moment.

Just as he was doing now.

As the light winked green, he twisted the wheel into a sharp left
turn, fishtailing for a split second in a mass of gray slush. As the car
found traction, Laurent knew he was close.

This was it.

He knew it from the moment he saw the building in the distance.

He knew it as he felt the straight-edge razor that still called to
him from his pocket.

He knew it as he saw—parked at the top of the hill—the silver
car that Beecher had been driving.

And he knew it when he spotted, just next to the main gate, the thin black letters that spelled out those same two words that had left Dallas's lips back in the cemetery.

St. Elizabeths.

The greater good would finally be served.

85

It takes me nineteen minutes to drop Dallas at the Archives, eleven minutes to drive his silver Toyota back to St. Elizabeths, and a full forty seconds for me to stand outside, working on my story, before I push open the front door of Nico's building.

"I . . . hi . . . sorry . . . I think I left my notebook upstairs," I say to the guard, feigning idiocy and holding up the temporary ID sticker that she gave me a little over an hour ago.

The guard with the bad Dutch-boy hair rolls her eyes.

"Just make it quick," she says as a loud *tunk* opens the steel door, and I take my second trip of the day through the metal detector.

"Don't worry," I tell her. "I'll be lightning."

Trying hard to stand still, I fight my body as it follows the rhythmic sway of the rising elevator.

An hour ago, when I was standing here, I was holding Clementine's hand. Right now, I lean hard on that thought, though it does nothing to calm me.

As the doors rumble open and I step out, the same black woman with the same big key ring is waiting for me.

"Forgot your notebook, huh?" she asks with a laugh. "Hope there's no phone numbers in there. You don't want Nico calling your relatives."

I pretend to laugh along as she again opens the metal door and leads me down the hallway, back to the day room.

"Christopher, can you help him out?" the woman asks, passing me to a heavy male nurse in a freshly starched white shirt. "We got some more visitors coming up right now."

323

As she leaves me behind, I take a quick scan of the fluorescent-lit day room: patients watching various TVs, nurses flipping through various clipboards, there's even someone feeding coins into the soda machine. But as I check the Plexiglas round table in the corner...

No Nico.

"Who you here for again?" the heavy male nurse asks as he fluffs pillows and straightens one of the many saggy sofas.

"Nico," I say, holding up my ID sticker like it's a badge. "I was here seeing Nico, but I think I left my notebook."

He does his own scan of the area, starting with the round table. He knows Nico's routine.

"I bet he's in his room—711," he says, pointing me to the swinging doors on the far left. "Don't worry, you can go yourself. Nico's got room visitor privileges."

"Yeah...no...I'll be quick," I say, taking off for the swinging doors and reminding myself what they first told me: This is a hospital, not a prison. But as I push the doors open and the bright day room narrows into the far smaller, far darker, far quieter hospital hallway, the sudden silence makes me all too aware of how alone I am back here.

At the end of the hall is an internal metal staircase that's blocked off by a thick glass door so no one on this floor can access it. I still hear the soft thud of footsteps as someone descends a few floors above.

Counting room numbers, I walk past at least three patient rooms that have padlocks on the outside. One of them is locked, bolted tight. I don't even want to know who's in there.

By the time I reach Room 711, I'm twisting out of my winter coat to stop the sweat. Nico's door also has a padlock and is slightly ajar. The lights are on. But from what I can tell, no one's inside.

I look back over my shoulder. Through the cutaway in the swinging doors, the male nurse is still watching me.

"Nico...?" I call out, tapping a knuckle softly on the door.

No one answers.

"Nico, you there?" I ask, knocking again.

Still nothing.

I know this moment. It's just like the moment in the original SCIF: a scary door, an off-limits room, and a spectacularly clear opportunity. Back then, I told Orlando we shouldn't be that guy in the horror movie who checks out the noise coming from the woods. The thing is, right now, I need what's in those woods.

Clenching my jaw, I give the door a slight push, and the whiff of rosewater perfume takes me back a dozen years. It's the same smell as Clementine's old house. As I lean forward, the nylon on my winter coat rubs the door like sandpaper. I crane my neck just enough to see—

"What the hell you doing?" an angry voice snaps behind me.

I spin around to find a tall brown-haired man—nurse...another nurse—standing there wearing plastic gloves and carrying a stack of Dixie cups in a long plastic sheath.

"You got no business being back here!" the nurse scolds, plenty pissed.

"The other nurse...the guy up front...in the white," I stutter, pointing back the way I came. "He said Nico had visitor privileges."

"Christopher? Christopher ain't no nurse! He runs the juice cart! And don't think I don't know what you're doing..."

"Doing? I-I'm not doing anything."

"You say that. But then every year or so, we still get one of you showing up, hoping to get an autograph or grab some personal item—last year, some guy put a Bible that he said belonged to Nico up on eBay. I know you think it's cool, but you've got no idea how hard Nico's working. It's not easy for him, okay? Let the man live his damn life."

"I am. I want to. I'm...I'm just trying to get my notebook," I tell him.

"The what?"

"My notebook. I was visiting with him earlier. Doing research. I think I left my notebook."

The nurse cocks his head, studying me for a full two seconds. He believes me. Pointing me back to the swinging doors of the day

325

room, he explains, "Nico's doing his janitor work in the RMB Building. You wanna ask him something, go find him there. You're not going in his room without his okay. Now you know where RMB is?"

"The redbrick building, right?" I say, rushing for the door, remembering where Nico feeds the cats. "I know exactly where it is."

86

ippy out today, huh?" a young guard with a big gold class ring asks as I shove my way out of the wind and into the toasty lobby of the redbrick RMB Building.

"I'm from Wisconsin. This is summer for us," I say, working extra hard to keep it light as I approach the desk and yet again scribble my name in a sign-in book. "So who'd you play for?" I add, motioning to the gold football that's engraved into his ring.

"Floyd County High School. Out in Virginia," he says. "It's class A, not AAA, but still... state champs."

"State champs," I say with a nod, well aware that there's only one thing I really care about from high school.

"So you're the Nico guy?" the guard asks.

"Pardon?"

"They called me from the other side—said you'd be coming. You're the one looking for Nico, right?" Before I can answer, a lanky black woman with bright red statement glasses shoves open the locked metal door that leads to the rest of the building. After finding me outside Nico's room, they're not letting me get in this building unattended.

"Vivian can take you back," the guard says, motioning me through what looks like a brand-new metal detector. But as the red-glasses nurse swipes her ID against a snazzy new scanner to open the metal door, I'm all too aware that this building has a far more high-tech security system than the ancient giant key ring that the nurses rely on in the other one.

"So you a reporter?" Red Glasses asks as she tugs the door open and invites me inside.

"No...no...just...I'm doing some research," I say, following behind her.

"Like I said—a reporter," she teases as I notice a sign on the wall that says:

Gero-Psych Unit

In the hallway, there's an empty gurney, an empty wheelchair and a state-of-the-art rolling cart. Everything's scrubbed neat as can be. Outrageously neat. Even without the industrial hand sanitizer dispensers along the walls, I know a hospital when I see one.

"I didn't realize you had a full medical unit back here," I say as we pass an open room and I spot an elderly man in a hospital bed, hooked to various monitors and staring blankly at a TV.

"Our population's aging. We need someplace to take care of them. You should put that in one of your articles, rather than all the usual stuff you write about us." She's about to say something else, but as we reach our destination—the nurses' desk that sits like an island at the center of the long suite—she stops and arches an eyebrow, looking confused.

"Everything okay?" I ask.

"Yeah, I just...Nico was just mopping back here."

I follow her gaze down to the floor. Sure enough, the tiles are still shiny and wet.

"Gimme half a sec," the nurse says, picking up the desk phone and quickly dialing a number. As she waits for it to ring, I trace the wet streaks on the floor to...

There.

Just a few feet ahead, along the tile, there're two parallel streaks—from the wheels of a mop bucket rolling along the wet floor—that run like train tracks, then make a sharp right into one of the patient rooms.

"Pam, you see Nico up there?" the nurse says into the phone.

As she waits for an answer, I follow the streaks a few steps toward the open room. Inside, the lights are off, but there's sunlight coming in from the window. Stretching my neck, I peek around the corner, into the room, and...

Nothing. No mop bucket...no Nico...nothing but another patient hooked up to another set of machines.

"Great—he's up there?" the nurse says behind me, still talking on the phone. "Perfect. Great. Sure, please send him down."

As she hangs up the phone, I take one last glance at the patient in the bed. He's maybe sixty or so, and propped on his side, facing me. It's not by his choice. There are pillows stuffed behind his back. His body's frozen, and his hands rest like a corpse's at the center of his chest. They did the same thing when my mom had her heart surgery: turning him to prevent bedsores.

The oddest part are the man's eyes, which are small and red like a bat's. As I step in the room, he's staring right at me. I raise my hand to apologize for interrupting, but I quickly realize...he's barely blinking.

I tighten my own gaze. There's nothing behind his eyes. He's not seeing anything at all. He just lies there, his whole body as stiff as his arms on his—

Wait.

His arm. There's something on his arm.

My face goes hot, flushing with blood. Every bone in my body feels paper-thin and brittle, like a fishbone that's easily snapped.

I didn't see it when I first walked in—I was too busy looking at his empty eyes—but there it is, faded and withered on the lower part of his forearm:

A tattoo.

A sagging, faded black tattoo.

Of an eight-ball.

87

Twenty-six years ago
Journey, Ohio

That'll be seventeen dollars and fifty-four—"

"No...hold on...I got coupons," the heavy customer with the thick neck interrupted, fishing out wads of crumpled coupons and handing them to the supermarket cashier.

The cashier shook her head. "Son, you should've—" But as the cashier finally looked up and made eye contact, she realized the customer with the ripped black concert tee and the matching punk black Converse wasn't a *he*. It was a *she*. "I...hurrr...lemme just... ring these up," the cashier stuttered, quickly looking away.

By now, after sixteen years of living with Turner syndrome, Minnie Wallace knew how people saw her. She was used to awkward stares. Just like she was used to the fact that as she stepped past the cashier and into the bagging area, every single bagboy in the store had somehow subtly made his way to one of the other cashier lanes.

No way around it—people always disappoint, Minnie thought as she sorted cans of cheap tuna fish away from the cheap generic aspirin, and bagged the rest of her groceries herself.

"New grand total...fifteen dollars and four cents," the cashier announced, stealing another quick glance at Minnie's broad chest and low, mannish hairline. Minnie caught that too, even as she brushed her black bowl-cut hair down against her forehead in the hopes of covering her face.

With a final hug around the two brown bags of groceries, Minnie gripped them tightly to her chest, added a sharp lift, and headed for the automatic doors.

Outside, the drab Ohio sky was still laced with a few slivers of pink as the sun gave way to dark.

"Y'need some help?" a voice called out.

"Huh?" Minnie asked, turning off balance and nearly dropping both bags.

"Here, lemme...*Here*," a boy with far too much gel in his spiky brown hair said, taking control of both bags before they tumbled.

"Man, these *are* heavy," he teased with a warm smile as he walked next to her. "You're strong."

Minnie stared, finally getting her first good look at his face. She knew him from school. He was a few years older from being left back. Twelfth grade. His name was Griffin.

"Whattya want?" she asked, already suspicious.

"Nothing. I was— You just looked like you needed—"

"If you want my brother to buy you beer, go ask him yourself," she said, knowing full well what Orson had been doing since he'd been back on spring break.

"No...that's not— Can you just listen?" he pleaded, readjusting the bags and revealing the tattoo on his forearm. A black eight-ball. "I just was hoping—I don't know...maybe..." Griffin stopped at the corner, working hard on the words. "Maybe we could...maybe go out sometime?"

"You're serious?"

"Sure...yeah. It's just...I've seen you around school—always wearing that concert shirt—the Smiths," he said as Minnie's big cheeks burned red. "The Smiths are cool."

"Yeah, they're...they're kinda cool," she replied, unable to do anything but look straight down, study her black Converse, and try extra hard to slide open her leather jacket so he could see her current English Beat concert tee, which was stretched tight by her round belly.

"Yeah, English Beat's cool too," Griffin added, nodding his

approval as he readjusted the brown paper bags and stole another glance at her.

As they crossed the street, Griffin pointed to a parked black Dodge Aspen that had been repainted with a cheap paint job. "If you want, I can drive you home," he offered.

"You don't have to do that."

"I know," he said, again peering over at her, this time for longer. "I'd like to. I'd really like to."

It wasn't the offer that caught Minnie off guard. Or even his smile. It was the way he looked at her. Right at her. For sixteen years, unless someone was staring, no one looked at her.

But Griffin did. He looked. And smiled.

He was still smiling, even as Minnie shyly looked away.

Feeling like a cork about to leave a bottle, Minnie couldn't look away for long. Standing up straight—completely unafraid—she looked back at him. "Okay," she said, standing by the passenger side of the car and waiting for him to open the door.

Still holding both bags, he leaned in and reached past her, his forearm about to brush against her own. He was so close, she could smell the Wonder Bread in the grocery bag—and the black cherry soda on his breath.

She looked right at him, waiting for him to say something.

The only sound was a muffled *rat-a-tat-tat* . . .

. . . of laughter.

It was coming from her left. She followed the sound over her shoulder, just around the corner, where two guys—one black with a high-top fade, one white wearing an Oakland Raiders jersey—were snickering to themselves.

"No, ya Guido—the deal was you gotta do the kiss!" the white one shouted.

"You lose, brother! Game over!" the black one added.

"That's not what we said!" Griffin laughed back.

Minnie stood there, still struggling to process.

"C'mon, you should be thanking me," Griffin said, turning back to Minnie. "I gave you a full two minutes of what it's like to be normal."

Minnie wanted to scream. She wanted to hit him. But her body locked up and her legs began to tremble. Still, there was no way she'd cry for him. No way. She tried steeling herself, but all she saw was how hard all three of them were laughing. From her nose, twin waterfalls of snot slowly ran down.

"Bye, freak," Griffin said, dropping both bags of groceries. The eggs shattered in one bag. From the other, a single can of tuna fish cartwheeled down the sidewalk.

"You even realize how much you look like a boy? Whatchu got down there, boy parts or girl parts?" Griffin asked, flicking his fingers against her crotch. The trembling in her legs only got worse. "It's boy parts, innit?"

Minnie shook her head, fighting the tears. "I'm a girl," she whispered.

"And you're telling me all those girl parts work? No chance," Griffin challenged, getting right in her face. "No chance those parts work."

Minnie watched the can of tuna fish roll into the street and tip on its side, making a small repeating circle like a spun nickel approaching its stop.

"I'm right, ain't I?" Griffin added as the can of tuna continued to spin in front of the car. Minnie shut her eyes, her legs trembling worse than ever. "You got nothing working down there, do ya?" he shouted. "Take the hint, animal. God did it for a reason—He don't want no more mongrels like you!"

Minnie's legs finally stopped trembling. She could feel the result running down her legs.

"Did you just wet your—!?" Griffin took a step back, making a face. That smell..."Is that—? Ohh, *nasty*!"

"She just took a dump in her pants?" the white kid asked.

"She crapped her pants!" Griffin laughed.

Scrambling backward, Minnie tripped over the rest of her

groceries, landing on her rear with an awful squish that set Griffin and his friends howling.

In the street, the can of tuna sat there.

Climbing to her feet, Minnie looked up at Griffin and his eight-ball tattoo as the world melted in a flush of tears.

"Check it out—a face made for an abortion—and the stench of one too!" one of them said, laughing.

"Where you going, Elephant Man!? You forgot your groceries!" Griffin called out as she fought to her feet and started running up the block. "Whatcha gonna do—go tell your mom!?"

She didn't respond, but as she ran as hard as she could and tried to avoid thinking of what was running down her legs, Minnie Wallace knew the answer. She knew exactly what she was going to do.

She was going to get her brother.

88

I stumble backward, bumping into the spine of the open hospital room door.

"Good news!" the red-glasses nurse calls out behind me. "Nico's upstairs. He's on his way down."

I barely hear the words. I'm too focused on the patient with... eight-ball. He's got an eight-ball...

"I-Is he...? Is that...?"

"Relax. He's fine," the nurse says. "He's PVS. Persistent vegetative state. Been like that since he got here—though actually, you should talk to Nico. We ask our patients to go in and do therapy for him: play music, rub his face. But Nico swears that he's heard him speak—just mumblings, of course."

I spin back to face her. It's the first time she sees the panic on my face. "You okay?" she asks.

"Is that his name? *R. Rubin?*" I blurt, reading the name from the medical chart clipped to the foot of his bed. "How long has he been here?"

"Actually, that information is—"

"How long's he been here!" I explode.

The nurse steps back at the outburst. Eightball doesn't move, his bat eyes barely blinking.

"Ten years," the nurse says coldly. "Now I need to ask you to leave. If you want to speak to Nico—"

Nico. I almost forgot. Nico's headed here right now.

"I changed my mind. I don't need to see him," I say, cutting past the nurse and rushing back to the lobby. "And don't tell him I came. You'll only upset him," I warn, meaning every word.

As I shove the metal door open and dart back into the cool air of the lobby, my brain is still swirling, trying to do the math. If Eightball's here, then— No. Don't even think it. Not until I know for sure.

"Well that was fast," the guard with the big football ring calls out from behind the security desk.

"Can I—? Your sign-in book," I blurt, pointing to the black binder on the edge of his desk. "You need me to sign out?"

"Nah. I can do it for you."

"It's fine, I'm right here," I say, flipping open the book and grabbing the pen. My name's on the last page. I purposely flip to the first, scanning names as quickly as I can.

For Eightball to be here... If Nico knew—or even if he didn't know—there's no way this was pulled off without help.

The first page in the overstuffed book dates back to June, over six months ago. There're only two or three visitors per day, which, as I continue to flip through the pages, makes it easy to see who's been in this building five months ago... four months ago... three months ago...

Oh. Shit.

No... it can't be.

But it is.

My ribs contract, gripping my lungs like thin skeleton fingers. But before I can react, my phone vibrates in my pocket.

Caller ID tells me it's Dallas.

"You ready to pass out?" I ask as I pick up.

"Don't talk. Just listen," he insists. "We've got an emergency."

"Trust me, the emergency's here."

"No, Beecher. The emergency's *here*. Are you listening? I had some folks—some of our folks here—I had them run Clementine's info to see if they could find something new. But when they looked up her address—"

"The address isn't in her name. I know. It's her grandmother's place. Her grandmother owns the house."

"You said that last night. But that's the problem, Beecher. When they ran her name—according to everything we found..." He takes a breath, making sure I'm listening. "Clementine's grandmother died eight years ago."

Inside my ribcage, the skeleton fingers tighten their grip. I'm still flipping through the sign-in book. But I can't say I'm surprised.

"I know," I tell him.

"What're you talking about?"

I look down at the sign-in book and reread the one name that is in here over and over and over again. Three months ago, two months ago, even last month—the signature is unmistakable. An effortless swirl from the one person who I now realize has been coming to see Nico not just since yesterday, but for over three months now.

Clementine.

89

Twenty-six years ago
Journey, Ohio

It was Thursday, and the barbershop was open late.

The young barber wasn't thrilled—in fact, if it were any other client, he would've already locked up and left. Especially tonight. Tonight was card night, and with Vincent hosting, that meant they'd be playing bid whist and eating those good pierogies Vincent always ordered from around the corner. They were probably already eating them now, Laurent thought as he glanced down at his digital watch and then out the plate glass window where the rain had just started to springboard from the black sky.

Ten more minutes. I'm not waiting a minute more than that, he promised himself, even though he made the same promise ten minutes ago.

And ten minutes before that.

Again, if it were anyone else, Laurent would've already left. But he wasn't waiting on just any client. This was one of Laurent's *first* clients—back from when Laurent was still in high school and his dad first gave him the scissors and a chair of his own.

In a town like Journey, where the same man has been cutting the same hair for nearly four decades, it takes more than just bravery to try out the untested new barber.

It takes trust.

And like his father with his own first clients, Laurent would

338

never—not ever—forget that fact, not even years later when he was asked to stay late on a cold, rainy card night, when every store on the block was closed and every second waiting here decreased the chances of him seeing a pierogi or—

Diiiing, the bell rang at the front of the barbershop.

Laurent turned as the door slammed hard into the wall, nearly shattering the plate glass. It wasn't his client. It was a crush of young men in their twenties rushing in from the rain, stumbling at the threshold. They were soaked...slipping...dripping puddles across the black-and-white tile floor.

For those first seconds, Laurent was pissed. He hated dealing with drunks, especially drunk college kids who suddenly see a barbershop and think they want a Mr. T mohawk. But it wasn't until they tumbled inside that Laurent finally saw the true cause of their lack of balance: The young man in the middle sagged facedown to the ground. His friends weren't walking with him. They were carrying him.

As he lay there, not moving, his right arm was bent awkwardly in a way that arms don't bend. Sliding down from his soaked hair, drips of blood tumbled into the new puddle of rainwater, seeping outward as they turned the floor a strangely beautiful light pink. But even in the midst of the chaos, even with the blood still coming, the young barber, who would forever regret staying late that night, immediately recognized the tattoo on the bleeding man's forearm.

An eight-ball.

He'd cut the hair of one other person with the same mark. He knew what it meant—and what gang it came from.

"Get inside! Shut the door!" one of the boys said, screaming at the overweight boy—no, that was a girl—who was still standing out in the rain, looking like a chubby phantom and not saying a word.

"They're gonna kill us!" the other boy called out, his haunting gray eyes locking on the barber with an almost spiritual clarity. Laurent knew him too—he'd known him for years—back from when the boy was little and his father would bring all sorts of trouble to the shop. Even back then, even when it got bad, Laurent never saw the boy get riled. Until now.

"I mean it, Laurent. *Please...*" the young twenty-year-old who would one day be the President of the United States pleaded as his gray eyes went wet with tears. "Please can you help us?"

90

Beecher..." Dallas warns through the phone.

"I'm already gone," I say, shoving open the lobby's glass door and darting out into the cold. My body bakes in the weird sensation from the heat in my winter coat mixing with the brutal wind from outside. But as I weave past the concrete benches in front of the brick building...

"Make sure Nico's not following," Dallas says, reading my mind.

I check. And check. And recheck again.

The glass door is shut. From what I can tell, there's no movement inside.

"Get out of there!" Dallas adds as I run for the narrow black path that snakes through the snow and leads back up to the parking lot. I recheck one more time, but as I turn around, my legs feel like toothpicks, ready to snap and unable to hold my weight. But this time—all the times—I'm not looking for Nico. I'm looking for *her*.

For Clementine.

My mind swirls into rewind, replaying every moment, every interaction, every conversation we've had since she "magically" returned to my life. I thought I was lucky. I thought I was blessed. How many guys get to reconnect with the girl they used to dream of? The answer's easy. None.

I replay our night on the bridge... and the homemade photo she made of us... and how she understood me in a way that Iris never did. I try to tell myself how stupid and cliché and dumb every precious moment was—but the toughest truth, as the bitter pain in my belly tells me, is how bad I still want every damn second of it to be real.

Still running on toothpicks, I tear as hard as I can, putting as much space between myself and the building as possible. My stomach nearly bursts, feeling like a rolled-over carcass. *How could she do this to me?*

"Beecher, are you—?"

"I-I saw him," I tell Dallas.

"Nico?"

"No. I saw him. He's here. I saw *Eightball!*"

"What're you talking about?"

"He's alive. We assumed he was dead—that Wallace killed him all those years ago—but he's—" At the top of the hill, the path dumps me back in the parking lot that sits right across from Nico's home building. Within seconds, I beeline for Dallas's old Toyota and fish the keys from my pocket. "Don't you see, Dallas? We were right—about Eightball...and the blackmail...That's what they were doing. That's how they found out what happened all those years ago," I add as I whip open the car door and slide into the front seat. "Maybe they found Eightball...or Eightball whispered it—either way, they used that to blackmail—"

"I think it'd be best if you put down the phone now," a soft gentlemanly voice suggests from the backseat.

"Whatthef—!" I jump so high, my head slams into the roof.

"I also highly recommend not turning around," the man warns. "I see what you're doing," he adds as we lock eyes in the mirror. He's an older black man with silver hair and a matching silver mustache. "I'm begging you, Beecher—this is the time when you want to use that big brain of yours. Now please...put the phone down, and put your hands on the steering wheel."

His voice is kind, almost soothing. But there's no mistaking the threat, especially as I spot his shiny silver weapon just above the back of my headrest.

At first, I assume it's a gun. It's not.

It's a straight-edge razor.

* * *

91

Twenty-six years ago
Journey, Ohio

U p here...left up here!" the kid with the tight curly hair—
the one called Palmiotti—insisted, sitting in the passenger seat and pointing out the front windshield of the
young barber's white van.

"The hospital's to the right!" Laurent shouted, refusing to turn
the wheel.

"No...go to the other hospital—Memorial. Stay left!" Palmiotti
yelled.

"Memorial's twenty minutes from here!" Laurent shot back.
"You see how he's bleeding?"

Behind them, in the back of the van, Orson Wallace was down
on his knees, cradling the head of the unconscious kid with the
eight-ball tattoo, trying to stop the bleeding by tightly holding towels from the barbershop against his head.

An hour ago, Wallace threw the first punch. And the second. He
would've thrown the third too, but Eightball got lucky, knocking the
wind out of Wallace's stomach. That's when Palmiotti jumped in,
gripping Eightball in a tight headlock and holding him still as Wallace showed him the real damage you can do when, in a moment of
vengeful anger, you stuff your car keys between your knuckles and
stab someone in the face.

Years later, Wallace would tell himself he used the keys because
of what Eightball did to Minnie.

343

It wasn't true.

Wallace was just pissed that Eightball hit him back.

"He's not moving anymore," Wallace's sister whispered from the back corner of the van. She was down on her knees too, but just like in the barbershop, she wouldn't get close to the body. "He was moving before and now he's not."

"He's breathing! I see him breathing!" Wallace shouted. "Stewie, get us to Memorial!"

Palmiotti turned to the barber. His voice was slow and measured, giving each syllable its own punch. "My father. Works. At Memorial," he growled. "Go. Left. Now."

With a screech, the van hooked left, all five of them swayed to the right, and they followed Spinnaker Road, the longest and most poorly lit stretch of asphalt that ran out of town.

Passing field after field of pitch-black farmland, the barber used the silence to take a good look at Palmiotti in the passenger seat. New jeans. Nice Michigan Lacrosse sweatshirt. Frat boy hair.

"Can I ask one thing?" the barber said, finally breaking the silence. "What was wrong with your car?"

"What's that?" Palmiotti asked.

"You got those nice clothes—the new Reeboks. Don't tell me you don't have a car. So what's wrong with yours that we gotta be driving in mine?"

"What'd you want me to do? Run home and get it? My brother dropped us off downtown—then everything else exploded with the fight."

It was a fast answer. And a good one, Laurent thought to himself. But as he looked over his shoulder and saw the pool of blood that was now in his van—in his carpet—and could be linked just to *him*, he couldn't help but notice the look that Palmiotti shot to Wallace in the passenger-side mirror.

Or the look that Wallace shot back.

As a barber who spent every day watching clients in a mirror, Laurent was fluent in talking with just your eyes. He knew a *thank-you* when he saw one. And right there, in that moment, he also knew the hierarchy of loyalties that would drive their relationship for the next twenty-six years.

"There... *pull in there!*" Palmiotti said, eventually motioning to the putty-colored building in the distance with the backlit sign that read *Emergency Room.* "There's parking spots in front."

Even before the van bucked to a stop, Palmiotti was outside in the rain. With a tug, he whipped open the side door of the van, and in one quick motion, he and Wallace scooped up Eightball and—shouting the words "Wait here!"—carried him off like tandem lifeguards toward the sliding doors of the emergency room.

There was a hushed *whoosh* as they disappeared, leaving the barber breathing heavy in the driver's seat, still buzzing with adrenaline. But as fast as reality settled in, all the mental avoidance of the past half hour faded with equal speed. To drive out here... to even take them at all... Laurent had said they should call an ambulance—but in the rush of chaos... the way Eightball was bleeding... and all that screaming... Wallace seemed so sure. And when Wallace was sure, it was hard to argue. They had to take him themselves. Otherwise, he would've died.

"You okay?" a soft female voice coughed from the back of the van.

Laurent nodded.

"I-I'm sorry for this—I really am," she added.

"You have nothing to apologize for," Laurent insisted, staring out at the raindrops that slalomed down the front windshield. "This has nothing to do with you."

"You're wrong."

"I'm not. They told me what happened when you came back—Eightball grabbing a baseball bat... It shouldn't've escalated like that, but lemme tell you—"

"You weren't there."

"—if someone did that to my sister... and *I* was your brother—"

"You weren't there," Minnie insisted, her voice cracking. "You didn't see what happened. Orson wasn't the only one who made him bleed."

345

The words hung in the van, which was battered by the metal pinging of raindrops from above. Laurent slowly twisted in his seat, turning to the chubby girl with the wet hair and the now dried train tracks of black mascara that ran down her face. She sat Indian-style, looking every bit her young age as she picked at nothing in the bloodstained carpet.

The barber hadn't noticed it before. Hadn't even registered it. But as he thought about it now, Orson's clothes—just like Palmiotti's—were mostly clean. But here, in the back of the van . . .

The front of Minnie's leather jacket . . . her neck . . . even her English Beat T-shirt . . . were covered in a fine spray of blood.

Just like you'd get if you hit something soft. With a baseball bat.

Still picking at nothing in the blood-soaked carpet, Minnie didn't say a word.

In fact, it took another ten minutes before her tears finally came—pained, soft whimpers that sounded like a wounded dog—set off when her brother exited from the sliding doors of the emergency room, stepped back into the rain, and told them the news: Eightball was dead.

92

Y ou have no idea how hard this is," the man with the razor says as he sits directly behind me in the backseat of the car.

"Listen," I plead. "There's no reason to—"

"Beecher, I've asked you two times now. Please put your phone down."

"It's down...I put it down," I say, though I don't tell him that I haven't hung up. If I'm lucky, Dallas can hear every word we're saying. "Just please...can you lower the razor?"

In the rearview, the man barely reacts, though the razor does disappear behind my headrest. Still, the way he manically keeps shifting in his seat—sitting up so close I hear him breathing through his nose—he's panicking, still making his decision.

"I'm sorry you found him," the man says, sounding genuine as he stares down at his lap. "That's why you were running just now—all out of breath. You saw him, didn't you?"

"I don't know what you're talking about. I was here picking up a notebook—"

"Please don't do that to me. I was being honest with you," he says, sounding wounded, his head still down. I feel a slight nudge in my lower back. From his knees. His feet tap furiously against the floor, making the whole car shake. Whatever he's about to do, it's weighing on him. "I know it's over, Beecher. I know you saw Griffin."

"If you think I'm the one doing this...with the blackmail...It's not me," I tell him. "I swear to you—Clementine's—"

"They know the roles. They know who's done this. And when it comes to the fight you've picked...the poor girl's as dead as you are."

It's the second time in two days someone's mentioned my death as if it's inevitable. It's starting to piss me off.

Behind me, the man with the razor continues to lean forward, elbows resting on his still bouncing knees. He again takes a heavy breath through his nose. It's not getting any easier for him. "You're a history guy, right, Beecher?" Before I can answer, he asks, "Y'ever hear of a guy named Tsutomu Yamaguchi?"

I shake my head, searching the parking lot and scanning the grounds for a guard...for an orderly...for anyone to help. There's no one in sight.

"You never heard of him? Tsutomu Yamaguchi?" he repeats as I finally place his accent. Flat and midwestern. Just like the President's. "In 1945, this man Yamaguchi was in the shipbuilding business. In Japan. Y'know what happened in 1945 in Japan?"

"Please...this—whatever this is about. You can let me go. No one'll ever know. You can say I—"

"Hiroshima. Can you imagine? Of all the towns that this guy's shipbuilding business sends him to, on August 6, 1945, Yamaguchi was visiting Hiroshima at the exact moment one of our B-29s dropped the atomic bomb," he continues as if I'm not even there. "But ready for the twist? Yamaguchi actually *survives*. He suffers bad burns, spends the night in the city, and then quickly races to his hometown, which is guess where?"

I don't answer.

"Nagasaki—which gets hit with the second bomb three days later. And God bless him, Yamaguchi *survives that too*! Blessed by God, right? A hundred and forty thousand are killed in Hiroshima. Seventy thousand die in Nagasaki. But to this day, this one man is the only person certified by the Japanese government to have survived *both* blasts. Two atomic bombs," he says, shaking his head as he continues to stare down at the blade in his lap. "It may be on a smaller scale, but I can tell you, Beecher. In this life, there are days like that. For all of us."

I nod politely, hoping it'll keep him talking. On my phone, it says my call has been connected for four minutes and twenty-seven seconds. If Dallas and his Culper Ring are as good as I think they are, it won't be long until the cavalry comes running.

In the small of my back, the man's knees stop shaking.

"Mine was that night in the rain," he adds as his voice picks up speed. "I knew it the instant they brought him in. Forget the blood and the bits of bone that they said she drove into his brain..."

She? Did he just say she?

"...I knew it from the split second I saw the looks on those boys' faces. It was more than terror, more than remorse. The pain in their eyes was like...it was like they knew they'd never be able to face God Himself again." He looks up from the blade. His eyes are red and bloodshot. "Y'ever been around a victim of crime—someone who's been raped or beaten or even mugged? The depth of their horror—you feel that pain through the pores of your skin. I didn't want to admit it, but that night...that was my own Hiroshima sitting right there in front of me."

As he says the words, my own pores—my whole body—I feel the despair rising off him. He doesn't have a choice. From here on in, there's only one way to keep me from talking. Outside, I eye the service road that leads up from the front gate. Still no cavalry. If I run, the knife's close enough that he can still do damage. My hands stay gripped to the steering wheel. I search between the seats... across the floor...looking anywhere for a weapon.

"The worst part was how easy it was to pretend otherwise and keep it all silent. Not just with Griffin. With her too. With the stroke..."

The stroke? I think for a second. He said *her. Does he mean...?*

"They blamed it on the Turner syndrome, but when someone takes the long accordion hose from her vacuum cleaner, hooks one end to the tailpipe of her family's Honda Civic, and then loops the other end into the window of the driver's seat? That's not Turner syndrome. That's *penance*," he says. "Palmiotti didn't find her for four hours. To this day, him pulling her out...it's a miracle she even survived."

My chest cavity feels hollow—all my organs gone—as I try

to take a breath. All this time, we thought Wallace was protect-ing himself. But he was actually trying to protect...*her*. His sister. "You're saying Minnie...that Minnie Wallace was the one who... and she tried to commit—?"

"You're not listening! *I need you to listen to me!*" he explodes, his face contorting with pain. "I was just the driver! I didn't do anything—I was just trying to help some...they were *kids!*"

"Then you need to listen to me now," I interrupt, trying to make eye contact in the rearview. "If that's the case, you need to tell your story. You have nothing to worry about. You didn't do anything wrong."

"I didn't," he agrees as the pain on his face only gets worse. "I just took them to the hospital. They told me Griffin was dead."

"Then there you go. That's what matters," I say, knowing the benefits of agreeing. The sooner I win him over, the more I can buy myself more time. "All these years...you had no idea."

"It's true...I-I was just the driver. How am I supposed to know they gave him a fake name—or—or—or transferred him here once Wallace got his Senate seat? They told me he was dead."

"Exactly—they told you he was dead. That's all you knew, right?"

I wait for his answer, but this time there's only silence from the backseat.

I glance again in the rearview. Our eyes lock.

"That's all you knew, right?" I ask for the second time.

But as a watery glaze fills his bloodshot eyes, I quickly under-stand. The worst lies in life are the ones we tell ourselves.

"You knew..." I say. "You *knew* Eightball was here."

"Only recently."

"How recently? A week? A month?"

His face goes pale like an onionskin. "I lied to my own soul."

"How long?" I ask.

"Two years. Two and a half years," he whispers, his head slop-ing down as if his neck no longer works. The car still sits in the parking lot. I search the service road. Still no one there. "You have to understand, when I found out...when I confronted Palmiotti... They said they moved him here to keep an eye on him—to take care of him—but I was the only one who came to visit him. He needed to know...I needed to tell him what Wallace had done. For me. I didn't do it for the greater good. It was only good for me. But I had no idea Nico heard me," he adds, his voice at full sprint. "That's why, at the cemetery...when you said you were coming here...I knew. I knew it! This was my chance to end it. I'm sorry for being so weak, Beecher—but this is what I should've done the moment this started..."

Over my shoulder, he raises his blade to cut me.

But in the mirror, I see it.

It's already covered in blood.

I look down, patting my neck. I didn't feel anything...

Without warning, the blade drops from his hand, bouncing and falling into the front seat.

His onionskin face goes practically transparent. He sags backward, sinking in his seat.

Oh God. Has he been shot?

I check the front window...the sides. All the glass is intact. But as I spin back to face him...in the seat...There's blood. So much blood. It's not splattered. It's contained. A small pool. On the seat... on his arms...No. Not his arms...

It's coming from his wrists.

"What'd *you do*?" I yell.

"She paid her penance," he whispers through a hard cough. "I need to pay mine."

"*What the hell'd you do!?*" I repeat as a slow red puddle blooms in the backseat, raining down to— On the floor. I couldn't see it before.

At his feet, a larger pool of blood seeps into the carpet. From the size of the puddle...all that red...He did this. When we were talking. He wasn't just staring down at the razor. He'd used it.

"You tell them—you tell them there's a cost," he sputters, about to pass out. "Every decision we make in life, there's always a cost."

"Gimme your wrists! I can stop it!" I tell him.

"You're missing the point," he stutters, no longing cringing. Whatever pain he was feeling is finally gone. "For thirty years, I wondered why they stumbled into my store that night. They could've picked any store. Or no store. But it's no different than that guy . . . from Hiroshima. It's no different than Yamaguchi. We spend our lives thinking history's some arbitrary collection of good and bad moments stirred together in complete randomness. But look at Yamaguchi. When history has your number, there's . . . there's nowhere on this planet you can run."

He sags sideways, his breathing sputtering as he collapses against the back door.

I kick open my own door, rushing outside. Whatever I think of him, he still needs my help. But as my feet hit the concrete and I reach for his door, my face nearly collides with the chest of the man who's just arrived outside the car and is now blocking my way.

I know he's got ground privileges. He followed the path right back the way he came. To the parking lot across from his building.

"Don't look so scared, Benjamin," Nico says, barely noticing that he's standing in my personal space. "I'm here now. Everything's going to be all right."

93

ou need to move," I say to Nico as I try to cut around him to get to the back door of the car.

Nico doesn't budge. Doesn't move. But he does see what I'm looking at. In the backseat. The black man covered in blood.

"I know him," Nico blurts. "He's the barber."

"What?"

"He comes to give haircuts. To Griffin. But sometimes when he leaves—I check. Griffin's hair isn't cut at all. I told them, but they never—"

"Nico, get out of the way!"

"The barber...for you to do this to him...he was watching me, wasn't he? I know their eyes are everywhere."

"Nico..."

"That's why you came back, isn't it? To do this. To protect me..."

"Protect you?"

"I see your razor. In the driver's seat," he says, his eyes flicking back and forth as he dissects the contents of the car. "I see how you killed him."

"That's not—"

"It makes perfect sense," he adds, nodding feverishly. "It's what I said. This was your mission...your trial. The test of Benedict Arnold. And you—you—don't you see?—you finally passed, Benjamin! Instead of betraying George Washington, you were given a chance...a chance to protect him. *And you did!* You risked your life to protect me!"

Annoyed by the nuttiness, I shove him aside, tear open the back door of the car, and feel for a pulse. Nothing. No heartbeat.

Across the long field that leads back to the medical building, a security guard turns the corner, heading our way.

"You need to go," Nico says to me, eyeing the guard. "They can't know you did this."

"I didn't do anything!" I say, still staring at the barber.

"There's no need to mourn him. He's moved on to his next mission."

"Will you stop? *There is no mission!*" I explode, slapping his hand from my shoulder. "There's no test! There's no trials! There's no George Washington—and stop calling me Benedict Arnold! All that matters is *this*! This, *right here*," I hiss, pointing back at the body of the barber. "I know you and she . . . you *caused* this! I saw the sign-in sheet! I saw Clementine's name! And if it'd help you get out of here, I know you'd do anything, including making your daughter blackmail the Pr—!"

"What'd you call her?"

"Don't tell me you don't know she's your daughter," I challenge.

He takes a half-step back and stands perfectly still. "She told me she was a graduate student. But students . . . students don't come to see me. That's how I knew," Nico admits, blinking over and over and suddenly looking . . . he actually looks *concerned*. He opens his mouth to say something, then closes it just as fast. He's fitting his own pieces together. But as his eyes stop blinking and the concern on his face slowly turns to pain, I can't help but think that I have it wrong. Maybe this isn't the father-daughter operation I just thought it was.

"When I fed the cats, Clementine used to— I saw her one Wednesday. When the barber was cutting hair," Nico blurts. "She helped him. She told the barber Griffin's hair looks better when it's long in front. He listened. It made her smile more."

On my right, across the field, the security guard is less than fifty yards away. On my left, down by the front gate, the guardhouse's white-and-orange-striped gate arm rises in the air. A black car pulls up the service road. Someone's just arrived.

"It made me smile more too," Nico adds, barely noticing. "But she heard the barber, didn't she? She heard his confession."

"Nico, you need to get away from here," I tell him as the guard picks up his pace, coming right at us.

"She did this...she caused this, didn't she?" Nico says, motioning to the barber.

On the service road, the black car picks up speed.

"The doctors here...they say I have a sickness," Nico says. "That's what put the evil in my body—the sickness did. And so I prayed—I begged God—I begged God since the first day she came to visit...I worried she had it too."

"Nico, get out of here," I insist, tempted to jump in the car and take off. But I don't. The barber's dead—I can't take him with me. But if I stay and try to explain, there's only one place I'm going if they find me with Nico and a bloodied corpse.

"All these years, I knew my fate. I always knew what God chose me for," Nico adds. "But when Clementine came...when she reached out to me like that...I thought I finally got— I was lucky. Do you know what that means, Benjamin? To be a lucky man?" he asks, his voice cracking.

"Nico, please get out of here," I beg, grabbing my phone from the front seat.

The black car knifes to the left, heading straight for our parking lot.

The security guard is now running.

"But there is no luck, is there, God?" he asks, talking to the sky. "I knew that! I knew it all along! But when I met her...when I saw her...how could I not hope? How could I not think that I'd finally been blessed—the truest blessing—that despite the sickness inside myself, that You made her different than me." He stares up at the sky, his eyes swollen with tears. "I begged You, God! I begged You to make her different than me!"

"Nico, back to your building! *Now!*" the security guard shouts in the distance.

Behind me, the black car speeds up the service road, its engine roaring.

"*You!* Away from Nico!" the guard yells at me.

There's a loud screech. The black car skids into the parking lot, punting bits of frozen gravel at us. But it's not until the passenger door bursts open that I finally see who's driving.

"Get in! Hurry!" Dallas shouts from behind the steering wheel.

"*Nico, don't you move!*" the guard yells as he reaches the parking lot. That's still his priority.

"Nico, I'll see you next week!" I call out, trying to make it all sound normal as I dart to the black car, which is already pulling away.

As I hop inside and tug the door shut, Dallas kicks the gas and we're off. Behind us, the guard grabs Nico by the arm. The guard looks relieved. Problem solved. That's still the top St. Elizabeths priority. No escapes.

The road isn't long. Within ten seconds, we're rolling past the main gate. Dallas offers a casual wave to the man in the guard-house. The fact that he waves back tells us the guard in the parking lot still hasn't found the barber's body. Word's not out yet.

"That guy with the knife...the barber—" I say.

"I know. I could hear," Dallas says, holding up his phone as we pull out of the gate and reach the main street. "I think I was able to get most of it on tape."

"Then we should—"

"No," Dallas says, twisting the wheel as we speed toward the highway. "Right now, there's only one place we need to go."

94

From the front seat of the white van that was parked down the block, it wasn't hard to spot Beecher.

Or Dallas.

There are two of them now, the driver of the van thought, watching their black car bounce and rumble as it left St. Elizabeths. Two of them to deal with.

From the look on Beecher's face, he was terrified, still processing. Dallas wasn't doing much better.

It was no different for the driver of the white van.

It had all gone so bad, so quickly.

But there was no choice. That's what Beecher would never understand.

For a moment, the driver reached for the ignition, but then waited, watching as Dallas's car coughed up a small choke of smoke and disappeared up the block.

This wasn't the time to get spotted. More important, the driver wanted to see if anyone else was following.

For a full minute, the driver sat there, watching the street and every other parked car on it. No one moved.

Beyond the front gate, up the main service road that ran inside St. Elizabeths, there was a swirl of orange sirens. On-campus security. No doubt, Nico was already being medicated for whatever mess the barber's panicking had caused.

The driver was tempted to go up there, but again, there was no choice.

There was never any choice.

Not until the one problem that had caused so many others was dealt with. The problem that she could only blame on herself.

Beecher.

By now, the black car was long gone, zipping toward its destination.

With a deep breath, Clementine pulled out onto the road and did her best to stay calm.

Beecher's head start didn't matter.

Not when she knew exactly where they were going.

95

Four months ago
St. Elizabeths Hospital

The man with the black leather zipper case was never late.

He always came on Thursdays. At 4 p.m. Always right on time.

But as Clementine glanced down at her watch and saw that it was already a few minutes past four...

"Heya, Pam," the older black man with the silver hair and silver mustache called out as he shoved his way through the swinging doors, approached the nurses' station, and eyed one of the many open rooms. Like an ICU, the rooms of the Gero-Psych Unit didn't have any doors. "How's your Thursday?"

"Same as my Wednesday," the nurse replied, adding a flirty laugh and crumpling up the foil wrapper of her California Tortilla burrito.

Over by the sinks, Clementine pretended to fill one of the cats' water dishes as she watched the same exchange she'd witnessed the week before—and so many weeks before that. By now, she knew his patterns. That's how she knew when to send her dad upstairs for more cat food. She knew the old black man wouldn't be late. Like all barbers, he knew the value of keeping an appointment.

"They ready for me?" the barber asked.

"Not like they got much choice," the nurse added along with another flirty laugh.

Dumping and refilling the same water bowl and strategically using the room's pillars to stay out of sight, Clementine watched as the barber unzipped the leather case that held his sharpened scissors. It had been nearly two months since she first saw him enter the unit, saying he was there to give haircuts to patients. No reason to look twice at that—until Clementine noticed that although he rotated through a few of the rooms, he always finished with the exact same patient:

The guy with the tattoo of the eight-ball.

Clementine tried not to think about it. She didn't want to be a suspicious person, or assume the worst about people. But as she learned when her mom was lying there in hospice and finally told Clemmi her father's real name, there are certain traits that God puts in each of us. There's no escaping them.

It's who we are.

Indeed, when Clementine first peered across the unit and into the room, she couldn't help but notice how the barber, with his back to her, was standing next to Eightball's bed, clutching the bed's guardrail as if he needed it to stand. He wasn't cutting Eightball's hair. His hands didn't move...his shoulders were slumped. He was crying. And more than anything else, that's what drew Clementine to take that first step toward them.

She told herself she wasn't trying to pry—she was just hoping to console him—but as she neared the room, she heard those two words that made her stop midstep. The two words that forced her to cock her head and look twice at the barber, and that had her coming back week after week to fill in the rest of the story. Two simple words: *Orson Wallace*.

From that moment, Clementine knew she'd never mention it to Nico. She still hadn't told him she was his daughter—and there were plenty of reasons for hiding that. So she certainly wasn't going to tell him this. Indeed, over the next few months, as she eventually put together the full picture, Clementine knew that what she'd been witnessing was far more than just a simple visit from a barber. What she'd been given was a chance. A real chance to answer the original questions she'd come searching for—to find out the things even her father didn't know.

With the changes in her body and everything she was going through—was it really such a sin to want to know the truth?

"Laurent here," the barber said today, flipping open his cell phone and pacing back and forth in Eightball's small room. "Yeah. I can do it tonight or first thing tomorrow. Just tell me when."

Dumping and refilling the cat's water bowl for the fifth or sixth time, Clementine listened carefully to every detail she could hear. She knew she was getting close. She knew about Wallace and his group of Plumbers, who were running errands for him. Of course, there was only so much one could get from eavesdropping. She had no idea what Minnie did with the baseball bat—or about how Palmiotti held Eightball down while Wallace worked on his face with his car keys. But she did know the Plumbers were helping him hide Eightball. No way could Wallace afford to let that get out. And best of all, after all this time, she knew where the barber was talking about.

"Same place?" the barber asked. "At the Archives?"

Ducking back toward the sink, Clementine had heard him mention the Archives before.

"I found a salmon flavor," Nico interrupted, reentering the room with a big bag of Meow Mix cat food under his arm. "They like salmon flavor."

Across the unit, the barber shut his phone, knowing better than to make eye contact with Nico. Clementine stayed by the sink, so as to not look out of place.

"Anything we're forgetting?" Nico called out to Clementine.

"I don't think so," she replied, shutting off the water and stealing one last glance at Eightball's room. She was definitely getting close. And as she thought about it, if she needed to, she even had a way to get into the Archives. That guy whose name she saw on the high school page. On Facebook.

Beecher.

For a moment, she felt that familiar pang of guilt. It didn't last long. If she'd learned anything during this time with her father... There was no avoiding it. Or escaping it.

This was who she was—or at least who she had to be...if she wanted to find the truth.

"I think we're set," Clementine said, balancing the full bowl of water as she followed her dad back outside. "I've got everything we need."

96

D on't say those words to me," Tot warned, gripping the receiver at his desk.

"Will you just listen?" Khazei asked through the phone.

"Do you know where Beecher is or not?"

"Don't blame this on me. You said Dallas's car was tagged last night—that all I had to do was track them on GPS."

"That *is* all you had to do. In fact, isn't that why you went racing to St. Elizabeths? To find them?" Tot asked. "So are they there or not?"

"The car's here, sure. But you should see what else is here—sirens swirling...there's no going in or out—total lockdown. As I pulled up, they had half their security force gathered around Dallas's car that Beecher drove here. So yes, that gray car is still in the same GPS spot as it was a half hour ago. But I'm telling you, Tot—there's no Beecher...no Clementine...no one's here."

Glancing out the plate glass window of his office, Tot stared down at Pennsylvania Avenue, then tightened his focus so that all he saw was his own gray beard in his reflection. "Something's wrong."

"Do not panic on this."

"You're not listening. Something's wrong, and Beecher's gone," Tot insisted. "And the only way we're salvaging this is if we somehow find him."

"That's fine. You're the one who knows him so well. Tell me what's next?"

Tot thought about it for a moment. He thought about it again. And for the first time in a long time, he had no idea.

*   *   *

97

She hasn't said *yes* yet?" the President challenged.

"It's not that simple," the young aide replied as they rode up in the White House elevator.

"It *is* that simple, son—you ask a girl out, she says yes or she says no," Wallace teased, tossing a wink at the usher who ran the elevator. "You want me to issue an executive order for you? I'll handwrite it on the good stationery: *Go out with my aide Patrick, or face formal charges. Signed—Me.*"

The young aide forced a laugh, pretending he hadn't heard the joke fifty times before. He didn't mind, though. Like any job, everyone's happy when the boss is in a good mood.

The elevator door unclenched on the second floor of the White House Residence, and as the President made a sharp right up the hallway, the aide knew that mood was about to get even better.

"You tell him who he's eating with?" the usher in the elevator whispered to the aide.

"Why you think he's walking so fast?"

At the far end of the hallway, the President spotted the small antique Georgian serving table that every day would hold a silver tray filled with small place-cards, each one in the shape of a thin, pointed collar-stay that was made of fine thick paper. On each one would be a calligraphed name, and the way the place-cards were organized in two neat columns—that same order would be the seating assignment for the day's presidential lunch.

Today, however, there were no place-cards.

No seating chart.

No calligraphed names.

"Okay, who's ready for mac and cheese?" Wallace called out playfully, clapping his hands together as he made a final sharp right and entered the narrow Family Dining Room, with its pale yellow walls and long mahogany table.

On most days, there'd be two dozen people gathered here.

Today, the table was set for two. Him and Andrew.

"No mac and cheese," announced a disappointed eight-year-old boy with a mess of brown hair and glowing gray eyes. Just like his father's. "They said we can't."

"*Who* says we can't?" the President challenged.

Just outside the dining room—and knowing better than to come inside—the nanny who was in charge of Wallace's son shook her head. Wallace knew that look. Andrew had mac and cheese last night. And probably the night before that.

"He'll live," Wallace said. "Two mac and cheeses."

As young Andrew's gray eyes lit up, Wallace couldn't even pretend to contain his own smile.

"Chocolate milk too?" the boy asked.

"Don't push it," Wallace teased.

It was tough being President. But it was even tougher being a father in the White House. So at least once a week—or at the very least every other week—there was an uninterrupted meal with no staff, no scheduling, no briefings, no press, no VIPs, and no Members of Congress who will vote your way if you invite them to have lunch with you at the White House.

Some days, the Family Dining Room had to be for just that. Family.

With a playful shoo of his hand, the President got rid of the nanny and the other staffers, closed the door to the dining room, and flicked off the lights.

"Dad, I got two new ones—and found the one where they're plumbers." Andrew beamed, flipping open his laptop and angling it so they could both see. With the push of a button, a black-and-white episode of *The Three Stooges* started playing onscreen.

As President, Wallace knew he could use the White House

movie theater downstairs. But as a father, just as he'd done long before he won the election, there was nothing better than being hunched over some mac and cheese, watching the classics with his son.

Kuuk-kuuk-kuuk.

Someone knocked on the door.

Wallace turned, all set to unleash on his staff—until the door opened and he saw who was knocking.

"It'll take only a second," Dr. Palmiotti said.

The President shot him a look that would need ice later. Sliding inside, Palmiotti didn't care.

"Sorry, Andrew—I'll be fast," the doctor added, trying to sound upbeat. "It's about your haircut," he told the President.

As Palmiotti leaned to whisper in his ear, Wallace knew lunch was over.

"I'm on this. I'm taking care of it. And I'm sorry," Palmiotti whispered. "He's gone. They found him dead. Slit wrists."

Nodding as if he were hearing a baseball score, the President stared across the table at his eight-year-old son.

"Y'have to go now, don't you?" the boy asked his father as Palmiotti left the room.

"You kidding?" the President asked, reaching for the laptop and hitting the play button himself. "What kinda dad misses mac and cheese with his boy?"

As the theme music began and Moe, Larry, and Curly jumped around onscreen, Wallace sat there in the semidark room, listening to his son laugh hysterically, while trying hard not to think about the dead friend he'd known since he was nearly the same age as his boy.

98

"You don't have to come if you don't want to," Dallas says.

"I'm coming," I tell him. "It's just— The caves?" I ask from the passenger seat. "They're far."

"They're in Pennsylvania," Dallas says, gripping the steering wheel with both hands. "We just cut through Maryland and the facility's right there."

I know where he's talking about. In our downtown building, we house nearly one billion documents. There're another 3.2 billion out in College Park, Maryland. And there's overflow storage in places like Suitland, Maryland, whose building is the size of more than twenty football fields and houses over 6.4 billion documents. But since the most important issue—and biggest cost—surrounding document storage is room temperature, the Archives saves millions of dollars each year by using the natural cold of underground caves all across the country, from Lee's Summit, Missouri, to Lenexa, Kansas, to, in the case of documents coming in from Ohio, the caves in Boyers, Pennsylvania.

"Can I ask you one last question?" I say, my eyes catching my own reflection in the windshield. "When you were back at the office . . . why'd you pick up my phone?"

"What?"

"Before. After we left the cemetery. You went back to the office; I was going back to see Nico. You said they called. You said you spoke to Mr. Harmon yourself," I add, referring to the guy from Presidential Records who I called from the cemetery. "You said that while they didn't find anything in Wallace's old college records—"

"Which I said they wouldn't."

"—I was still right about one thing: Our Archives staff collects every document from every place Wallace ever visited, including elementary school, junior high, and...even the records from the hospital he was born at."

"But do you understand what happened, Beecher? That hospital—sure, it's great that they have the President's birth records. But when Mr. Harmon started digging, he also found another file with Wallace's name on it: for a broken finger that Wallace had treated in the emergency room *twenty-six years ago*. That means that emergency room—"

"—is the same emergency room they took Eightball to that night. I know. The barber told me they were there. I know what happened."

"I'm sure you do. But every word that barber said to you—from Minnie being the one to swing that bat, to Wallace covering it up to protect his sister, to transferring Eightball and keeping him hidden all these years, to however Clementine found out about it and started blackmailing them—y'know what that amounts to? *Nothing*. Not a single thing, Beecher. Every word that barber said is hearsay from a dead man. If you go and shout it in public, you'll get about as far as any other Kennedy conspiracy nut who swears that Jack Ruby whispered all his secrets from his jail cell. But. If we get these hospital records, you have the one thing—*the only thing*—that works when you're going up against a sitting President. Proof. That file is *proof*, Beecher. Proof that Wallace was there that night. That file in Pennsylvania will save your life."

I know Dallas is right. And I know when it comes to the massive piles of incoming records, our office won't fax them or scan them until they're officially processed, which starts with the vital documents and takes years to work its way down to something as small as a childhood broken finger. Yet..."You're not answering my question," I say, still locked on our reflection in the windshield. "You said Mr. Harmon *called*. That you spoke to him yourself. But when we were at the cemetery, I didn't give Mr. Harmon *your* number. I gave him mine."

Dallas turns, cocky as ever.

"And that's what you're all sulky about? That I picked up your phone? You were already at St. Elizabeths—I was back in the office and heard it ringing—so yeah, of course I picked it up. Considering what happened, you're lucky I did."

I nod. It's a perfect explanation. But it doesn't lift my mood.

"How're you not thrilled?" Dallas asks. "This is gonna be the nail for the coffin."

"I've already seen the coffins! Two men are dead! Orlando... and now this barber— He came to me! The barber came to me and died in front of me! All because of— Because she—" I stay with the reflection, trying hard not to see myself.

Outside, the sun argues with the snow that lines both sides of I-270. A brown-and-white highway sign tells me we're nearing Hagerstown and the Pennsylvania border. But I'm still staring at my own reflection.

"You didn't cause those deaths, Beecher. And just so you actually hear it: She wasn't exploiting your weakness. She was counting on your strength."

"What're you talking about?"

"What Clementine did—the only reason she was able to pull it off—was because you're someone who helps people. And that's a good thing."

"It doesn't feel so good right now," I say as I again replay every single moment over the past two days. The only thing that's worse is how easily she pulled it off. For Clementine to have everything that the barber confessed to Eightball... for her to somehow figure out all the Plumber details... and when we first were in the SCIF... I don't think she *found* that old dictionary. I think she was actually sneaking it in, but then when the coffee got spilled, she had to improvise...

"Listen, I know she and Nico stabbed you plenty deep—"

"No. Don't blame Nico for this. You didn't see him—the way he reacted... Nico's not in this. And I know it's hard to believe because he's such a nutface, but when you listen to him—there was

369

one thing Nico was always right about." Up above, the sun blinds me. But not for long. "Nico said we're all here for a reason. He's not wrong. So when this is done—when Clementine's captured, and Orlando's family has their answers, and we tell the world the real story about the President—"

"You don't have to say it, Beecher. They're watching," Dallas says, leaning hard on the word *they*, which is how he always refers to the Culper Ring. "They'll make sure you're taken care of."

I nod, pretending that's what I'm really after.

"So I assume they're the ones who gave you this car?" I ask.

"And the gray one too," Dallas says.

"Yeah, I was thinking about that. So I shouldn't be worried that the barber's body is still sitting in it?"

"If Jesus himself came down and searched that car, he'd still never be able to trace it."

"I drove it on the grounds. They're not going to link it to me?"

"They said not to worry about that either."

"So that's it? The Culper Ring just waves their hands and magically takes care of it all?"

"It's not magic, Beecher. It's loyalty. Loyalty and efficiency. They'll get there well before the cops, and then...well...think of what you're seeing with Wallace and Palmiotti. Especially in this town, never underestimate the power of loyalty."

"I'm not. That's why, when everything settles..." I take a breath and think again about that guy from Hiroshima. "I want to be introduced."

"What're you talking about?"

"To them. To the Culper Ring. When this is all done, I want in."

"Beecher, I know you've got a lot of adrenaline flowing..."

"This isn't adrenaline. And don't think it's some silly revenge fantasy either. I know what Clementine did to me. I know I let her do it. But when I was in that car at St. Elizabeths—when I thought the barber was about to take that knife and slit my throat—I kept waiting for my life to flash in front of my eyes...or for some hypersensitivity, or slow motion, or whatever the other clichés are, to kick in. But instead, all I could think was that it felt...*right*. Does that make sense?"

"It doesn't make any sense at all."

"I don't mean *right* that I was about to be murdered. I mean *right* that, when I was in that spot...when I was in that danger...I felt like I was shaken awake. After Iris...after everything she made me feel...I made a decision and went to sleep. Do you know what that's like—trying to go to sleep, and lose yourself in the hopes of burying the worst fears in your life? It was the one thing Clementine didn't lie about: I wasn't in love with the past. I was terrified of my own future—and then when Clementine came along, I thought she was my second chance. But she's not. *This* is. I want my second chance. It's like my life finally makes sense."

"That's still the adrenaline speaking."

"It's not adrenaline. It's what we're here for, Dallas. It's what I thought I was here for, but instead...Do you know how many years I've spent staring into old books and thinking I was touching history? But that's not where history is." I look at the rearview and lean to the side until I again see myself. All this time, I thought Clementine was the one reviving me. But when your world feels dead, there's only one person who can bring you back to life.

"I can do this, Dallas."

"I'm sure you can. You can do lots of things. But this isn't what you're meant for."

"You're not listening to me," I say, giving him a good long stare. "Look at my life. I'm tired of doing what I'm meant for."

From the driver's seat, Dallas peers my way, using his top teeth to chew the few beard hairs below his bottom lip.

"I can do it," I insist. "I'm ready."

He doesn't say a word.

And then, as we race for the caves...and for the proof...and for the records that will end this mess, he finally does.

"Y'know what, Beecher? I think you're right."

*　　*　　*

99

Carla Lee knew it was going to be a bad day. She knew it when her two-year-old son woke up at 5:40 in the morning all excited to play. She knew it when the little yellow tub of margarine for her morning English muffin was completely empty, even though her husband had put it back in the fridge. And she knew it when she was racing back from her 3 p.m. meetings and saw the dead animal on Franklin Road.

She'd seen dead animals before on the highway. In these parts of western Pennsylvania, there were always deer and foxes and loads of unlucky possums. Carla had even stopped for a few (she was a dog owner—she couldn't just ride past if it was a dog). But here, on Franklin Road, which was hilly and rarely traveled, if you did see a dead animal, it never looked like this.

Carla couldn't see the fur anymore—couldn't even tell what kind of creature it was. The animal was— Carla squinted as she veered around the tight curve in her banged-up maroon Camry. There was no other way to say it. The animal was run-through. Run-through over and over again. People probably couldn't even see it if they were coming fast around the turn. But Carla was a mother. With three kids. And a sweet Maltese that peed on the floor every time someone came in the door. It'd been years since she went fast around the turns.

For that reason, she had a perfect view of the poor creature that was a mess of twisted red and black organs covered in flies.

For Carla, the mother and Maltese owner, that was the worst part of her bad day—being stuck with that image in her head.

She couldn't shake the image as she turned onto Brachton Road.

She couldn't shake it as she pulled into the enormous employee parking lot that sat across the road from the underground storage facility known as Copper Mountain.

And as she left her car, stepped into the cold wind that was whipping off the nearby Pennsylvania hills, and rushed for the arriving white school bus that served as the employee shuttle, she still saw that mess of red and black.

It was that image, still floating in her mind, that took all of her attention as she and her fellow employees packed together to get on board the arriving bus.

It was because she was thinking of that image that Carla didn't even notice, in the usual crush to get on the bus, the young black-haired woman standing so close behind her.

"Please—go ahead—you were first," Clementine said, flashing a warm smile and motioning politely.

"Thanks," Carla replied, climbing aboard without even noticing how much Clementine's hair and overall coloring matched her own.

Within minutes, the white school bus rolled through security and pulled up to the main entrance at the mouth of the cave. After all these years, Carla was used to working underground. But as they entered the cave, and a long slow shadow crept across the roof of the bus and swallowed the remaining daylight, Carla felt that familiar wiggle in her belly. Spotting the armed guards that always greeted them as they stepped off the shuttle, she then reached into her purse, fished for her ID, and—

"Craparoo," she whispered to herself. "I need to go back," Carla called out to the bus driver.

"Everything okay?" Clementine asked.

"Yeah. I think I just left my ID in my car."

"I do that all the time," Clementine said, heading for the front of the bus, where she took out the ID she'd lifted from Carla's purse, flashed it at the guard, and followed the other employees along the concrete path into Copper Mountain.

Carla Lee was definitely having a bad day.

But Clementine, so far, was having a great one.

Especially if they'd found the file she was looking for.

100

I t's under us," Dallas says.

"Whattya mean?" I ask.

"The place. The caves," Dallas explains as the narrow two-lane road sends us rising and falling and rising again over yet another set of low twisting hills, which are getting harder to see as the 4 p.m. sky grows dark. "That's why the road's like this. I think the caves are right under us."

I nod, staring down at my phone, which casts a pale blue glow in the car and is still getting enough signal for me to search the websites of all the D.C. TV stations to see if anyone's covering the story.

I search for Nico's name...for my name...even for the word *homicide* or *murder*. Nothing. No mention of St. Elizabeths, no mention of a dead barber, and most important, no mention of me being wanted as a fugitive.

"Now do you understand why no one's heard of us in two hundred years?" Dallas asks, once again trying to put me at ease. It almost works—until I gaze out at the snow-covered trees and we blow past the red, white, and blue road sign with the picture of George Washington.

Welcome to the Washington Trail—1753

It's silly and a meaningless coincidence, but I can't help but imagine Nico's joy if he knew that we were driving the same path that George Washington marched on back in 1753.

"Beecher, stop thinking what you're thinking," Dallas warns.

"You have no idea what I'm thinking."

"I saw the sign. It's not an omen."

"I never said it was an omen."

Dallas hears my tone. He believes me. "Though it is kinda haunted house," he admits.

"It's definitely haunted house," I say with a nod.

With a few quick turns, Dallas weaves us deeper into the hills, where at every curve in the road the nearest tree has a red reflector sunk into its trunk. Out here, the roads don't have lights, which we need even more as the winter sky grows black.

"You sure this is right?" I ask.

Before he can answer, my phone vibrates in my hand. Caller ID tells me who it is.

"Tot?" Dallas asks.

I nod. It's the fourth time he's called in the last few hours. I haven't picked up once. The last thing I need is for him to fish and potentially figure out where we are.

As we round the final curve, the hills level out and a brand-new glow blinds us in the distance, forcing us to squint. Straight ahead, giant metal floodlights dot the long field that stretches out in front of us. A familiar churn in my stomach tells me what my eyes can't see.

"This is it, isn't it?"

Dallas doesn't answer. He's staring at a white bus that slowly rumbles through the brightly lit parking lot on our left.

The only other sign of life is a fluorescent red triangle that looks like a corporate logo and is set into a haystack-sized man-made hill and serves as the sole welcome mat. You don't come this way unless you know what you're looking for.

Just past the red triangle, at the only intersection for miles, a narrow paved road slopes down to the left, toward a high-tech check-in building, then keeps going until it dead-ends at the base of the nearby stone cliffside that surrounds the little canyon that we're now driving in.

But as we make the left toward the check-in building, it's clear that the road doesn't dead-end. It keeps going, into a black arch-way that looks like a train tunnel, inside the cliff and down under-ground.

"Stay in your car! I'm coming to you," a guard calls out in a flat western Pennsylvania accent, appearing from nowhere and pointing us away from the check-in building and toward a small freestanding guardhouse that looks more like a construction shed.

I look again to my right. There are two more sheds and a bunch of workers wearing hard hats. The check-in building is still under construction.

"Here...right here," the guard says, motioning us into place out-side the security shed—and into view of its two different security cameras. "Welcome to Copper Mountain," he adds as Dallas rolls down his window. "I assume you got an appointment?"

101

Racing in the golf cart, our hair blows in a swirl as Dallas and I whip down one of the cave's long cavities.

"...just so glad to have you both here," gushes Gina Paul, our driver, a short, overfriendly woman with a pointy-beak nose, smoker's breath, and straight blonde hair that's pulled back so tight, it acts as a facelift.

"I'm sorry it's such short notice," I tell her.

"Short notice...it's fine. Short notice is fine," she says as I realize she's just like my aunt who repeats everything you say. Her nametag says she's an account manager, but I don't need that to know she's in sales. "So, so great to finally meet you, Beecher," she adds even though she doesn't mean it.

She doesn't care who I am.

But she does care where I work.

Fifty years ago, this cave was one of Pennsylvania's largest limestone mines. But when the limestone ran dry, Copper Mountain, Inc., bought its 1,100 acres of tunnels and turned it into one of the most secure off-site storage areas on the eastern seaboard.

And one of the most profitable.

That's a fact not lost on Gina, who, by how fast this golf cart is now moving, realizes just how much money the National Archives spends here every year.

We're not the only ones.

The narrow thin cavern is about as wide as a truck, and on our right a painted red steel door is set deep into the rock, like a hanging red tooth on a jack-o'-lantern. Above the door, a military flag hangs down from the ceiling. I know the logo. *U.S. Army.* As the golf cart picks up speed, there's another door fifty yards down from that—and another flag hanging from the ceiling. *Marines.*

It's the same the entire stretch of the cavern: red steel door after red steel door after red steel door. *Air Force. Navy. Department of Defense.*

"I'm surprised they put their names on them," Dallas says as we pass one for the FBI.

"Those are the rooms they want you to see," Gina says with a laugh. "We've got over twenty-two miles of tunnels back here. You don't want to know how much more space they've got."

I pretend to laugh along, but as we go deeper into the cave I can't take my eyes off the ceiling, which seems to be getting lower.

"You're not imagining things," Gina says. "It *is* getting lower."

Dallas shoots me a look to see if I'm okay.

Throughout the cavern, the jagged rock walls are painted white, and there are fluorescent lights hung everywhere, presumably to make it feel more like a workplace instead of an anthill.

To my surprise, it works.

On our right, two employees wait at an ATM that's built into the rock. Next to that, there's a red awning over a fully functioning store called the "Roadway Café."

I thought being this far underground would feel like I was being buried. Instead...

"You've got a full-blown city down here," Dallas says as we pass a new group of construction workers—this one putting the finishing touches on an area that holds vending machines.

"Almost three thousand employees. Think of us as the Empire State Building lying on its side and buried three hundred feet underground. We got a full-service post office...our own water treatment plant to make the toilets work...even good food in the cafeteria—though of course, it's all brought in. There's no cooking permitted on site. We get a fire and—forget burning the files that're stored down here—y'know what kinda death trap we'd be standing in?" she asks with a laugh.

Neither Dallas nor I laugh back—especially as we both look up

BRAD MELTZER

and notice the cargo netting that's now running along the length of the ceiling and keeping stray rocks, cracked stalactites, and what feels like the entire cavern from collapsing on our heads. Back by the café and the ATM, we were in the cave's version of Times Square. But as the employees thin out and we head deeper into the catacombs, this is clearly one of its darker alleys.

"Home sweet home," Gina says, flicking on the golf cart's lights.

Straight ahead, it looks like the cave dead-ends. But as the golf cart's lights blink awake, there's no missing the yellow police tape that keeps people from turning the corner, or the enormous red, white, and blue eagle—part of the National Archives logo—that's painted directly on the cave wall. Above the eagle's head is a par- tially unrolled scroll with the words: *Littera Scripta Manet*, the Archives motto that translates as "The Written Word Endures."

Damn right it does, I think to myself, hopping out of the golf cart and darting for the bright red door that serves as the entrance to the Archives' underground storage facility.

102

Anything else I can help with?" Gina calls out, standing in the cave, outside the threshold of the open red door.

"I think we're fine," I tell her.

Dallas is already inside the storage unit.

I'm anxious to follow.

Gina never leaves her spot. As a sales rep, she's in charge of clearing our visit with Mr. Harmon and the Presidential Records Office, checking our IDs, and even putting in the six-digit code that opens the steel door (and the secondary door that sits just behind that). But without the necessary security clearance, she can't join us in here.

"Both doors open from the inside," she assures us as the cold air pours out from the room. Just inside the door, I take a quick glance at the hygrothermograph on the wall. The temperature is at a brisk fifty-eight degrees, which is colder than we usually keep it.

"If you think of anything else, just gimme a call," she adds, tapping the leather phone holster on her hip. Reading my expression, she says, "Reception's great. We've got cell towers throughout."

Her point hits home as my own phone starts to vibrate.

As I glance down, caller ID tells me it's Tot. Again.

"I should grab this," I say to Gina, who nods a quick goodbye, keenly aware of when a client needs privacy.

As the red steel door slams shut and my phone continues to vibrate, I spin toward our destination and step through the second door, where the damp darkness of the cave has been replaced by an enormous bright white room that's as big as an airplane hangar and as sterile as our preservation staff can possibly manage. In truth, it's just a taller, brighter version of our stacks in D.C., filled with row after row of metal shelves. But instead of just books and archive boxes, the specially designed shelves are also packed with plastic boxes and metal canisters that hold old computer tape, vintage film, and thousands upon thousands of negatives of old photographs.

There's a reason this stuff is here instead of in Washington. Part of it's the cold temperature (which is better for film). Part of it's cost (which is better for our budget). But part of it—especially the archive boxes that are locked in the security cage on my left—is what we call "geographical separation." It's one of the National Archives' most vital—and least known—tasks. If there's ever a terrorist attack that turns Washington into a fireball, we're fully ready with the documents and paperwork to make sure our most vital institutions survive.

But as I step into the room, the only survival I'm really worried about is my own.

"You find it yet?" I call to Dallas, who's racing up the center aisle, checking record group numbers on each row of shelves that he passes.

His only answer is a sharp right turn as he disappears down one of the far rows in back. We're definitely close.

My phone vibrates for the fourth time, about to kick to voicemail. I have no idea if Tot knows where we are. But now that he can't get in the way, it'd probably be smart to find out.

"Beecher here," I answer, waiting to see how long it takes him to fish.

"Where the hell are you?" Tot asks. "I left you half a dozen messages!"

"I didn't get them. I'm just . . . it's been a crazy day."

"Don't. I know when you're lying, Beecher. Where are you? Who're you with?"

I take a moment to think about a response. Even through the phone, I swear I feel Tot's good eye picking me apart. "Tot, you need to—"

"Are you still with Clementine? I thought she left after the cemetery."

I pause. "How'd you know I was at a cemetery?"

"Because I'm not an idiot like the rest of the idiots you seem to be in love with!"

"Wait . . . time out. Did you have someone following me!?"

Before he can answer, my phone beeps. I look down and recognize the number. It's the only person who could possibly take me away from this one.

"Tot, hold on a sec."

"Don't you hang up on me!"

With a click, I put him on hold.

"Mr. Harmon?" I ask the man in Presidential Records who not only helped us get into the cave but also knows exactly what document we're looking for. "I-Is everything okay?"

"That's my question for *you,*" he says, though his tone surprisingly seems softer and more helpful than usual. That's all I need to be suspicious. "Everything going okay down there?"

"It's . . . we're fine." I pause a moment, confused. "Is there a reason we *shouldn't* be fine?"

"Not at all," he says, back to his military matter-of-factness. "Just making sure you got there. I'd asked the Copper Mountain folks to stay a little later when I heard you lost the directions."

"When I lost the *what?*"

"The directions I sent. Your secretary said—"

"My secretary?"

"The woman who called. She said you lost the directions."

Up on my left, back in the stacks, there's a metal *thunk.* The problem is, Dallas is all the way down on my right.

According to the hygrothermograph, it's still a cool fifty-eight degrees. But suddenly the long white room feels like an oven. Clearly we're not alone in here.

"Mr. Harmon, let me call you right back," I say, hanging up the phone.

"Dallas, we got problems!" I shout, racing up the aisle and clicking back to Tot.

"Wait—you're with *Dallas!?*" Tot asks, hearing the last bits through the phone.

"Tot, this isn't—!"

"Beecher, you don't know what you're doing!"

"You're wrong! For once, I know exactly what I'm doing!"

"*Pay attention!*" Tot explodes. "I know what Clementine did...
I know her grandmother's long dead...I even know how she did it!
We got the tox report—they found a dose of oral chemo in Orlando's
blood, even though he never had cancer. That's how she poisoned
him—she put it in his coffee! Now where in God's name are you so
I can get you someplace safe?"

My brain kicks hard, fighting to find the right places for each
new puzzle piece. What's amazing is how quickly each one fits.

"Where are you, Beecher?" Tot asks again.

There's a part of me that knows to stay quiet. It's the same part
that has kept Tot at arm's length since the night I went out to Clementine's house. But no matter how easy it is to paint him as the
enemy, the one picture I can't shake is the one from three years
ago, at lunch in our dungeony cafeteria, when Tot finally trusted me
enough to tell me about the first night, after fifty years, that he slept
alone in his house after his wife died. He said he couldn't bring
himself to sleep under those covers as long as she wasn't there.

I don't care what anyone says. There are some things that can't
be lied about.

"Tot, listen to me: I think Clementine is here. With us."

"What're you talking about? Where's *here*? Who're you with
besides Dallas?"

"Them. The Culper Ring."

I hear him take a deep breath.

"You need to get out of there, Beecher."

"We are...we're about to," I say as I reach the back of the room
and spot Dallas down one of the rows. He's on his knees, rummaging through a cardboard file box—a new box—that's marked *Wal-
lace/Hometown* in thick magic marker. "We're just getting—"

"Forget the Culper Ring. *Get out of there!*"

"But don't you see? You were right about them. Dallas brought
me in and—"

"Dallas *isn't in* the Culper Ring!"

Turning the corner, I hit the brakes, knocking a square file box from the shelf. As it tumbles and hits the concrete floor, it vomits sheets of paper in a wide fan.

"What'd you say?" I ask.

"Dallas isn't in the Culper Ring. He never *was*."

"How do you know?"

Tot takes another breath, his voice more of a grumble than a whisper. "Because *I'm* in the Culper Ring, Beecher. And I swear to you—the moment he finds what he's looking for, Dallas is going to end your life."

At the end of the row, down on his knees and flipping through one particular file, Dallas looks my way and peers over his scratched black reading glasses. "Y'okay, Beecher?" he calls out. "You don't look so good."

103

I-I'm great," I tell Dallas, who quickly turns back to the file he's flipping through.

"Turn around and walk away from him!" Tot barks through the phone. "Dallas has been in the Plumbers from the start—his uncle is Ronald Cobb, the President's law school pal, who used to work at the Archives and got Dallas the job here! That's why they picked him!"

It makes no sense. If that's the case, why'd Dallas bring me here? But before I can ask it—

"If you think I'm lying, at least get out of there," Tot adds. "At the very worst, I keep you alive!"

I take a few steps back, my body still in shock. It's like staring at your reflection in the back of a spoon. In front of me, the spoon flattens—the distortion fades—and life slowly becomes crystal clear. Since the start of this, I've learned how good the Culper Ring was at keeping secrets...how they protect us like a big *outer ring* without ever revealing their existence...and how hard they've worked to shut down corrupt Presidents like Nixon or Wallace when they start their own private, self-serving *inner rings* like the Plumbers. But last night, within the first three minutes of being in that safehouse, Dallas spilled every secret, revealed his own membership, and took control of my entire search for the Plumbers, including making sure that I stopped sharing with Tot.

I thought it was for my own good.

But if what Tot says is true...if Tot's the one in the Culper Ring and Dallas has been lying...the only ones who really benefited were Wallace...Palmiotti...and...

"This is it ... !" Dallas shouts, excitedly pulling out a few sheets of paper and slapping the file folder shut. "We got it, Beech. *Here it is!*" Closing the file box, he shoves it back on the shelf and rushes right at me.

"*Get away from him, Beecher!*" Tot yells in my ear.

Dallas stops right in front of me, the hospital file clutched at his side.

"Who're you talking to?" Dallas asks, pointing to my phone and sliding his reading glasses back into his jacket pocket.

"*He found the file? Do not let him have that!*" Tot adds as another noise—this one louder, a metal thud—erupts from this side of the stacks. Whoever's in here, they're getting closer.

"That noise ... you think that's Clementine?" Dallas asks, side-stepping past me and racing into the main aisle, back toward the door. What Tot said first is still my best move. I can deal with Dallas later. Right now, though, I need to get out of here.

"*Watch him, Beecher!*" Tot says in my ear as we pick up speed.

With each row we pass, I glance down each one. Empty. Empty. Empty again.

The air feels frozen as we run. It doesn't stop the even colder sweat that's crawling up my back.

The red doors are just a few feet away.

We pass another empty row. And another.

"Do we need a code to get out!?" Dallas asks.

"She said it opens from—"

Kuh-kunk.

The metal door flies wide as Dallas rams it with his hip. It's the same for the next door, the outer red door, which whips open, dumping us both back into the dusty air and poor lighting of the cave. We're still moving, skidding, slowing down. It takes a moment for my eyes to adjust to the dark.

That's the reason we don't see who's standing there, waiting for us.

There's a soft click. Like the hammer on a gun.

"Put the phone down, Beecher," she says, and I drop it to the ground. To make sure Tot's gone, she picks it up and hangs up the phone herself.

I was wrong. She wasn't inside. She was out here the whole time.

"I'm sorry. I really am," Clementine adds as she points her gun at Dallas's face, then over to mine. "But I need to know what they did to my dad."

104

You really think I believe a word you're saying?" I ask, my eyes narrowing on Clementine's gun.

"She's a liar," Dallas agrees. "Whatever she's about to tell you, she's a liar."

"Don't let Dallas confuse you," Clementine says. "You know what's true...you met Nico yourself. They ruined him, Beecher. They ruined my dad's life."

"You think that excuses everything you did? You killed Orlando! And then that lying...exploiting our friendship...!" I shout, hoping it's loud enough for someone to hear.

There's a small group of employees all the way down by the cave's cafeteria. They don't even turn. They're too far.

She points with her gun, motioning us around the corner as we duck under the yellow police tape with the word *Caution* written across it. Back here, the lights are dimmer than those in the main cavity. From the piles of metal shelving on our right, and the rolls of cable wire piled up on our left, it looks like this section of the cave is mostly used for maintenance and storage. No one's hearing us back here.

My brain whips back to our old schoolyard and when she tied that jump rope around Vincent Paglinni's neck. Two days ago, when Clementine saw her father, I thought the girl who was always prepared was finally undone. But I was wrong. As always, she was prepared for everything.

"Beecher, before you judge," she says. "I swear to you...I tried telling you the truth."

"When was that? Before or after you hired someone to play your dead grandmother?"

"I didn't hire anyone! Nan's the woman I live with—the land-lord's mother-in-law. Instead of paying rent, I take care of her!"

"Then why'd you say she's your grandmother?"

"I didn't, Beecher! That's what *you* said! And then— You cared so much about it, and I just wanted— You have no idea what's at stake."

"That's your response!? You're not even pregnant, are you? That was just to suck my sympathy and lead me along!"

"I didn't tell her to blurt that! She saw me throwing up and that's what she thought! The woman hates me!"

"You still let me believe some old woman was your dead grand-mother! You understand how sick that is?"

"Don't say that."

"You're sick just like Nico!"

"Don't say that!" she erupts.

"You killed my friend!" I erupt right back. "You murdered Orlando! You're a murderer just like your crazy-ass father!"

She shakes her head over and over, but it's not in anger. The way her chin is tucked down to her chest, she can't look up at me. "I-I didn't mean to," she pleads. "I didn't think he would die."

"Then why'd you bring that chemo with you!? I know how you did it—don't say it's an accident, Clementine! You came in the building with that chemo in your pocket—or was the real plan to use that on me?"

"It wasn't meant for anyone," she says, her voice lower than ever.

"Then why'd you bring it!?"

Her nostrils flare.

"Clementine..."

"Why do you think I brought it? Why does anyone carry around oral chemo? It's mine, Beecher. The medicine is for me!"

My eyebrows knot. Dallas shakes his head.

"What're you talking about?" I ask.

"Orlando...He wasn't supposed to be there," Clementine stut-ters. "When Orlando opened that SCIF and handed me his cof-fee...I thought the chemo would just...I thought he was in the

Plumbers—that he was watching me for the President . . . that they'd found out about me. I thought it would knock him out . . . but I never thought it'd . . ."

"What do you mean, *the medicine's for you*?" I ask.

"Ask yourself the real question, Beecher: After all these years, why now? Why'd I pick *now* to track down my father?" Her chin is still down, but she finally looks up at me. "They diagnosed me eight months ago," she says, her hands—and the gun—now shaking. "I'm dying, Beecher. I'm dying from . . . back when Nico was in the army . . . I'm dying from whatever they did to my father."

105

S he's a liar," Dallas insists.

"They changed him!" Clementine shouts. "Whatever the army put in Nico...that's what made him insane!"

"You see that, Beecher? It's pure delusion," Dallas says.

"It's not delusion," Clementine says. "Ask him, Beecher. He's in the Plumbers, isn't he?"

"I'm not in the Plumbers," Dallas insists.

"Don't let him confuse you," Clementine says. "I knew it when I saw him at the cemetery. But when I first found out about Eightball...ask him what I was blackmailing Wallace for. It wasn't money. Even when they nibbled and replied to my message in that rock at the graveyard—I never once asked for money."

"Is that true?" I say to Dallas.

He doesn't answer.

"*Tell him!*" Clementine growls, her hand suddenly steady as her finger tightens around the trigger. "He knows you're working with the President and the barber and all the rest of his ass-kissers who've been hiding the truth for years!"

Dallas turns my way, but never takes his eyes off Clementine's gun.

"She asked for a file," Dallas finally says. "She wanted Nico's army file."

"His *real* file," Clementine clarifies. "Not the fake one they dismissed him with." Reading my confusion, Clementine explains, "My mother told me the stories. She told me how Nico...she told me how he was *before* he entered the army. How when they were younger...how she used to keep the phone on her pillow and he'd sing her to sleep. But when he finally came home...when he left the army—"

"He didn't *leave* the army. They *kicked him out*—for trying to use a staple remover to take out one of his superiors' eyes," Dallas says.

"No—they kicked him out because of what they put inside him...what they turned him into," Clementine shoots back. "Have you even bothered to read his fake file? It says he got transferred from army sniper school in Fort Benning, Georgia, to the one in Tennessee. But I checked. The address in Tennessee was for an old army medical center. Nico wasn't just a sniper! He was a patient— and he wasn't the only one!" she adds, looking right at me. "You know another one! You know him personally!"

"What're you talking about?" I stutter.

"My mother—before she died—she told me, okay. You think they came to our tiny town and just took one person? They took a group of them—a bunch of them. So you can think I'm as crazy as you want, but I'm not the only one with the results of their experiments in me, Beecher. You have it in you too! You have it from what they did to *your* father!"

I shake my head, knowing she's nuts. "My dad died. He died on the way to the recruitment office. He never even got a chance to sign up."

"And you believed that. You believed that because that's what they told you, okay. But he was there. He and Nico and the others...they were enlisted long before anybody knew it. Your father was alive, Beecher. And if I'm right, he still may be!"

My lips go dry. My stomach crumples, folding in on itself. She's a liar. I know she's a liar...

"You can look for yourself," she adds. "Ask them for the records, okay!" It's the third time she's ended a sentence with the word *okay*, and every time she uses it, every time her voice cracks, it's like a fracture, a faultline that's splintering through her, threatening to

393

undo everything she always keeps so neatly packed in place. "My mom told me—the experiments were all going right—until everything went wrong—!"

"Do *not* listen to her!" Dallas says. "She spent months planning this—months to manipulate you and blackmail us. She's an even bigger psychopath than Nico!"

"Beecher, do you know what kind of cancer they found in me?" Clementine asks as I replay the last words Nico said to me back at the hospital: Nico begged God to make Clementine different from him. He wanted her to be different. "The kind of cancer no one's ever heard of. *Ever*," she adds. "Every doctor... every specialist... they said there're over one hundred and fifty types of cancer in the world, but when they look at mine, they can't even classify it. The mutation's so big, one doctor described it as a DNA spelling mistake. That's what my body is. That's what yours may be! A spelling mistake!"

"Beecher, I know you want to believe her," Dallas interrupts. "But listen to me—no matter what she's saying—we can still help you walk away from this."

"You think he's stupid!? Your Plumbers caused this!" Clementine yells.

"Will you stop?" Dallas insists. "I'm not in the Plumbers—I'm in the Culper Ring! I'm one of the good guys!"

"No," a brand-new voice—a man's deep voice—announces behind us. "You're *not*."

There's a hushed click.

And a muffled boom.

A small burst of blood pops from Dallas's chest. Lurching backward, Dallas looks down, though he still doesn't register the fresh gunshot wound and the blood puddle that's flowering at his chest.

Even before we spin to face his attacker, I know who pulled the trigger: the one man who benefits most from having all of us out here, in one place—the man who will do anything to get this file—

and who's spent nearly three decades proving his loyalty while protecting his dearest friend.

"Don't look so surprised," Dr. Palmiotti says, his eyes burning as he turns the corner and points his gun at us. "You had to know this was coming."

106

That's not…No…" Dallas stutters, barely able to stand and still not registering his wound. "You told me…you said I was in the Culper Ring—"

Ignoring him, Palmiotti steps in close and snatches the file from Dallas's hands. "You need to know you were serving your country, son."

Dallas shakes his head, his body still in shock.

I try to take a breath as the stale air fills my lungs. Tot had it only part right. Yes, Dallas was in the Plumbers. But he didn't *know* he was in the Plumbers.

"Beecher, you see what these people are capable of?" Clementine snaps as all the doubt, all the sadness, all the weepiness she just showed us is suddenly gone. For the past few days, every time Clementine had a mood shift or revealed a new side of herself, I kept saying it was another door opening inside her. She had dozens of rooms. But as I look at her now, I finally understand that it doesn't matter how many rooms she has. It doesn't matter how striking the rooms are. Or how well they're decorated. Or how mesmerizing they are to walk through. What matters is that every one of her rooms—even the very best one—has a hell of a light switch. And it flips. Instantly. Without any damn warning. Just like her father.

On my left, Dallas looks down at his chest, where the blood puddle has blossomed, soaking his shirt. His legs sway, beginning to buckle.

Wasting no time, Palmiotti turns his gun toward me. I see the blackness of the barrel. I wait for him to make some final threat, but it doesn't come. "My apologies, Beecher," he says as he pulls the trigger and—

Ftttt.

The air twists with a brutal hiss.

Palmiotti doesn't notice. Not until he looks down and spots the singed black hole, like a cigarette burn, that smolders in his forearm. A thin drip of blood begins to run down.

It's not like the movies. There's no wisp of smoke twirling from the barrel. There's just Clementine. And her gun.

She saved me.

Palmiotti stands there, stunned. His gun drops from his hand, bounces along the floor, and makes a dull thud near Dallas's feet.

Dallas can barely stand, but he knows this is his chance. His last chance. He spots Palmiotti's gun.

But before Dallas can even bend for it, he grabs his own chest. He's bleeding bad. His legs buckle and he crumples, empty-handed, to the dusty floor.

"I'm leaving now," Clementine says, keeping her gun on Palmiotti and once again tightening her finger around the trigger. "You can hand me that file now, please."

107

*D*allas...!" I yell, sliding on my knees and trying to catch him as he falls forward.

I'm not nearly fast enough. I grab his waist, but his face knocks with a scary thud against the concrete.

Out of the corner of my eye, I see Clementine holding her gun inches from Palmiotti's face. Without a word, she plucks the file from his grip.

"Dallas, can you hear me!?" I call out, rolling him on his back.

"I-I didn't know, Beecher..." Dallas stutters, holding his chest, his eyes hopping back and forth, unable to focus. "I swear I didn't know..."

"Dallas, listen—"

"You shoot him back!" Dallas interrupts, reaching out and pointing to Palmiotti's gun. He wriggles—and reaches all the way out, finally grabbing it.

Next to us, Palmiotti's bent over, dealing with his own pain and putting maximum pressure on the bullet wound in his arm.

Dallas fights hard to shove the gun in my hand, but his movement's too jerky. The gun bounces off my wrist, crashing to the ground.

I pick it up just as Clementine races at us.

Clementine stops. Her ginger brown eyes lock with my own. She has no idea what I'm thinking. No idea if I'm capable of picking this gun up and shooting her with it. But whatever she sees in my eyes, she knows she has no chance of making it all the way to the front entrance of the cave—all the way down the long well-populated main cavern—without us screaming murder. Switching directions, and not seeming the least bit worried, she tucks the file in the back of her pants and takes off deeper into the cave.

In my lap, Dallas is barely moving. Barely fighting. *"Beecher, why can't I see in my left eye?"* he cries, his voice crashing.

As the blood seeps out beneath him, I know there's only one thing he needs.

A doctor.

"You need to help him," I say, raising my gun and pointing it toward Palmiotti.

But Palmiotti's gone. He's already racing to the back of the cave, chasing after Clementine.

"Palmiotti, do *not* leave him!" I yell.

"She has the file, Beecher! Even you don't want her having that on the President!"

"Get back here . . . !" I insist.

There's a quick drumroll of footsteps.

Palmiotti—and Clementine—are long gone.

108

allas's head is in my lap. He struggles to sit up. He can't.

"D-Don't you dare sit here and nurse me," he hisses, his breathing quick, but not out of control. "What Palmiotti did to us... you take that, Beecher!" He motions to Palmiotti's gun. "You take that and do what's right!"

Behind me, I still hear the echo of Palmiotti chasing after Clementine. I watch Dallas's chest rise and fall, making sure he's taking full breaths.

"*Beecher, y-you need to do what's right,*" Dallas begs.

But as he fights to get the words out, the only thing I hear is Tot's voice in my head. Two days ago, he said that history is a selection process—that it chooses moments and events, and even people—that it hands them a situation that they shouldn't be able to overcome, and that it's in those moments, in that fight, that people find out who they are. It was a good speech. And for two days now, I've assumed history had chosen me.

I couldn't have been more wrong.

History doesn't choose *individual* people.

History chooses everyone. Every day.

The only question is: How long will you ignore the call?

I've been waiting for Tot... for Dallas... for the Culper Ring... for just about anyone to save me. But there's only one person who can do that.

"I got it," I tell him.

Holding Palmiotti's gun, and still thinking about what Clementine said about my dad, I glance to my right. On the wall, there's a small red fire alarm built into the rock. I hop to my feet and jab my elbow into the glass. The alarm screams, sending a high-pitched howl swirling through the cave.

That should bring Dallas the help he needs far faster than anything I can do. But as I check to make sure he's still conscious...

"*I'm fine...*" Dallas whispers, drowned out by the alarm. "*I'm fine. Go...*"

Far behind us, there's a low rumble as hundreds of employees follow their protocol and pour into the cave's main artery, ready to evacuate. I barely hear it—especially as my own heartbeat pulses in my ears.

This isn't history.

But it is my life. And my father's. What she said...

I need to know.

Running full speed with a gun in my hand, I turn the corner and head deeper into the cave.

Clementine's out there. So is Palmiotti.

I know they're waiting for me.

But they have no idea what's coming.

109

et back here...!" Beecher's voice bounced off the jagged walls as Palmiotti picked up speed and barreled deeper into the cave.

Using his tie as a makeshift tourniquet, Palmiotti knotted it twice around his forearm. Luckily, it was a through-and-through. The bleeding wasn't bad. Still, he had no intention of waiting. Not when he was this close to Clementine...this close to catching her...and this close to grabbing the hospital file and finally ending this threat to him and the President.

No, this was the benefit of having everyone in one place, Palmiotti thought, ignoring the pulsing in his forearm and being extra careful as he reached another turn in the cave. Unsure of what was waiting around the corner, he stopped and waited. He'd seen what happened earlier. It wasn't just that Clementine had a gun. It was how effortlessly she'd pulled the trigger.

Without a doubt, Wallace was right about her. She was an animal, just like her father. But as Palmiotti now knew, that didn't mean that Wallace was right about everything. Palmiotti tried to tell him—based on what Dallas was reporting—that even though Beecher let Clementine into the Archives, it didn't mean Beecher was also helping her blackmail Wallace and the Plumbers. That's why the President came back and requested Beecher in the SCIF— he had to test Beecher. He had to know. But even so, once Beecher had the book...once he started sniffing down the right path...and the hospital file—and then to bring in Tot and the attention of the *real* Culper Ring...No, at the level that things were happening, there was only one way to protect what he and the President had worked so hard for. Palmiotti knew the risk of coming here himself. But with everyone in one spot, he could put out every last fire. And not leave anything to chance.

Those were the same lessons now, Palmiotti thought as he craned his neck out and found nothing but another empty cavity, slightly longer than a grocery aisle, with another sharp turn to the right. It was the fourth one so far, as if the entire back of the cave ran in an endless step pattern. But as Palmiotti turned the corner, down at the far end of the next aisle, there was a puddle of water along the floor and a red spray-painted sign that leaned against the wall with the words *Car Wash* on it.

Racing down the length of the dark brown cavern—back here, the walls were no longer painted white—Palmiotti felt the cave getting warmer. He also noticed two yellow sponges, still soapy with suds, tucked behind the *Car Wash* sign. Whoever else had been back here, they haven't been gone long, making Palmiotti wonder for the first time: Clementine was prepared for so much. Maybe there was another cave exit she knew about.

Reaching yet another turn, Palmiotti stopped and slowly leaned forward, peeking around the corner. But this time, instead of another long narrow tunnel, there was a cavern—wide as a suburban cul-de-sac—and a dead end. Straight ahead, the tunnel was blocked and boarded off by tall sheets of plywood. It looked like one of those protective walls that surround a construction site. On the wall was a rusty metal sign that read *Area 6.*

But the only sign that Palmiotti cared about was the glowing one above the red steel door on the far right of the cul-de-sac. *Emergency Exit.*

Sonuvabitch.

Leaping for the door and grabbing the handle, Palmiotti gave it a sharp tug. It didn't open. He tried again.

Locked. It was definitely locked. In fact, as he looked closer at the industrial keyhole, there was an old key broken off and stuck inside. It didn't make sense. Clementine couldn't've got out here. But if she didn't get out here, then she should still be—

Behind him, Palmiotti heard a small chirp. A squeak.

Spinning back, he rechecked the cavern. A mess of muddy wheelbarrows were piled up on his left. Next to that were two enormous wooden spools of thick cable wire and another mound of discarded metal shelving, all of it rusty from the heat and dampness at this end of the cave. Diagonally across was another red metal door. Stenciled letters on the front read: *Treatment Plant*. But before Palmiotti could even run for the door, there was another squeak...

There. On his right.

He didn't see it at first: Cut into the plywood wall, like a human-sized doggie door, was a hinged piece of wood that didn't sway much.

But no question, it was moving. Back and forth.

Like someone had just passed through it.

Rushing to it, but working hard to stay quiet, Palmiotti studied the door. Back and forth...back and forth. It was barely swaying now, letting out a few final squeaks as it settled to a stop. A crush of rocks crackled below his feet. A bead of sweat ran down his cheek, into the tie that wrapped his forearm.

Either Clementine was standing on the other side of this door, waiting to put a bullet in his face, or she was still running, following wherever the tunnel led.

Only one way to find out.

Pressing his open palm against the plywood, Palmiotti gave it a push. Inside, unlike the rest of the cave, there were no lights. Total black. Nothing but silence.

Out of nowhere, the shrill scream of a fire alarm echoed from every direction. Palmiotti jumped at the noise, nearly bashing his head into the top threshold of the doggie door. No doubt, the alarm was pulled by Beecher, who was probably still panicking back where Palmiotti left him.

But a distraction was a distraction. Seizing the moment, Palmiotti shoved the plywood forward, lifted his left leg, and took a full step through the giant swinging door. His foot landed with a squish. His socks...his dress shoes...his entire foot was submerged in water.

Ducking inside, he hopped wildly to his right foot, trying to get to dry ground. Again, he landed with a wet squish as he—

Fttt.

He slapped his neck like he was swatting a mosquito bite. On impact, a wet splash sprayed through the spaces between his fingers. It was too dark for him to see the blood. Like before, he didn't even feel it. As he stood there in the knee-high water, it was the smell that hit him first: the charred smell of burnt skin. His skin.

She shot me. Again. The nutty bitch shot me again!

But before the words traveled the synaptic pathway from his brain to his mouth, Palmiotti was hit again—tackled actually—his attacker ramming him from the right, purposely grabbing at the hole in his forearm as momentum and the electric jolt of pain knocked him sideways, into the shallow water that fed the water treatment area.

Before Palmiotti could get a single word out, two hands gripped his throat, sharp thumbnails digging into his voicebox.

Tumbling backward, he fell like a cleaved tree. The shallow water parted at the impact, then knitted back together over his face. Under the water, Palmiotti tried to scream as his lungs filled with the inky brown lake water. She clawed her way on top, sitting on his chest.

Palmiotti never got to see her.

But he knew Clementine wasn't letting go.

110

*A*nybody there...?" I call out, holding tight to the gun as I turn yet another corner in yet another poorly lit stretch of cave. "*Clementine...?*"

The only answer comes from the fire alarm, whose howl rings hard at the base of my skull.

A minute ago, I thought I heard the muffled thuds of Palmiotti running, but now...

Nothing but alarm.

Racing forward and holding the gun out in front of me, I lick the salty bits of sweat from my lips. At first, I told myself it was nerves. It's not. The deeper I go, the hotter it gets.

This isn't just the maintenance area of the cave. By the hum that rumbles just below the fire alarm, this is where all the HVAC and mechanical equipment is.

Picking up speed, I rush past a dusty spray-painted *Car Wash* sign and some still-soapy sponges, yet as I turn the next corner, there's a sudden dead end.

On my right, there's a door for an *Emergency Exit*. But straight ahead, built into the construction wall, there's a swinging panel that...*huh*...is still swinging.

My fingers tighten around the trigger. There's no question where they are. I can wait here for help. I can play it absolutely safe. But if either of them gets away...

I take my first step toward the wooden wall, and the fire alarm stops, leaving me in a sudden vacuum of silence that's so severe, the only sound that exists is that phantom hum that follows you home when you leave a loud rock concert.

Straight ahead, the doggie door continues to swing, squeaking off-key.

Below my feet, with every step, bits of rock pop like glass.

In the distance, there's a chirp I can't place.

But what hits me like an axe in the stomach—as I approach the swinging panel and use the barrel of the gun to shove it open—is that there's not a single noise coming from inside.

111

Palmiotti knew what to do.

Even now... with his head underwater... with her hands around his throat... Palmiotti knew what to do if he wanted to breathe again.

Thrashing wildly, he clapped his arms together so his fists collided with Clementine's ears.

He couldn't hear her scream. But he did feel her let go. His head broke the surface of the water. Gasping for fresh air, he heard the fire alarm still ringing. Water dripped from his nose, from his ears, from his chin. His neck—where he'd been shot—was burning now. From the amount of blood that soaked his right shoulder, he knew his internal jugular vein was lacerated. It was bad. Much worse than his forearm. But at least he could breathe.

Still coughing uncontrollably, he rolled sideways in the shallow water. He couldn't see much, but there were small cracks of light in the plywood wall. His eyes adjusted fast.

Clementine rushed at him, raising her gun to—

Krkkk.

Palmiotti kicked hard—it was nothing but instinct—as his heel rammed Clementine's unbent knee.

The crack was audible. Clementine's leg nearly hyperextended as muscles and tendons were pulled like piano wire. Tumbling forward, she nosedived into the water.

She fought hard to get up, quickly climbing to her good knee. She knew what was coming.

She wasn't nearly fast enough.

The first kick slammed into her stomach, lifting her off the ground and taking all the wind out of her.

"D'you even realize how stupid you are!?" Palmiotti growled, spit flying with every syllable. "Even before the hospital file—just on the threat of you knowing what we did to Eightball—we were willing to give you everything! *You had us!* You'd actually *won!*"

Clementine's head was still down. Palmiotti gripped the back of her hair, twisting her head until she faced him and...

Pmmmp.

He rammed his knee in her face, sending her tumbling backward, splashing into the water. As fast as she could, she crabwalked back, trying to get away. She had no chance.

"Instead, when you heard about the file, you had to come here and be greedy...!" Palmiotti added, standing over her and grabbing her by the shirt. With a sharp tug, he lifted her up until the water reached her waist, then he punched her square in the face.

This time, though, it was Palmiotti who wasn't letting go. He felt the throbbing at the wound in his neck. He could feel himself getting light-headed. He didn't care. Cocking his arm back, he hit her again. And...

There was a loud *click* behind him.

"That's enough," a familiar voice announced.

Palmiotti turned, glancing over his shoulder. "Go away. This isn't your problem anymore."

"You are so incredibly wrong about that," Beecher warned, aiming his gun straight at Palmiotti. "Let go of her now, and put your hands in the air."

112

Y ou're done—you're both done," I warn Palmiotti.

"She still has her gun!" he insists, pointing back at Clementine.

I look down to check for myself. The brown water is almost to my knees, though it looks like it gets deeper as it snakes down the length of the cavern and winds into the darkness like the River Styx. This isn't some small puddle. It's a man-made lake.

In the darkness, it's near impossible to see anything but a glassy reflection off the surface. But there's no missing Clementine. Or the way, as she wipes her mouth and backs away from us on her knees, she keeps her other hand conspicuously below the water.

"He hit me, Beecher," she pleads, still slowly moving backward. "I swallowed my tooth—he knocked it down my—"

I point my gun at her and pull the trigger.

The barrel booms with a thunderclap that reverberates through the cavern. From the back of the cave, a speedy red bird—the chirping I heard before—zips out, flies in a few wild circles, and disappears again.

"Gah!" Clementine screams as the bullet slices her thigh, sending bits of skin and flesh flicking across the water. Palmiotti's already injured. Whatever else happens, I'm not letting either of them—and especially her—get away.

At first she looks mad, but as she falls back on her ass and tucks her knee toward her chin, her eyebrows quickly unknot and her eyes go round and weepy. "H-How could you...? You shot me..." she moans.

"What you said about my father—is it true?" I ask.

"Beecher...the documents they're hiding—there's even more in that file. And if we have that, it's not just our word against theirs—"

"*IS IT TRUE!?*" I explode.

The cave is silent, except for the red bird cheeping in the distance. "Th-That's what my mother told me. I swear to you—on her dead body. But if I don't get out of here—"

"No. Do *not* do that," I warn her. "Do *not* manipulate me. Do not try to get away. I've seen that show already—I know how it ends."

"Make her raise her hands!" Palmiotti shouts, stumbling back a few steps and leaning against the cave wall. I didn't notice it until now—all that red on his shoulder...the way he's holding his neck. He's been shot again.

"Don't let Palmiotti twist you," Clementine warns, ignoring her own pain and fighting to stay calm. I can see the wet file folder sticking up from behind her back, where she tucked it in her pants. "Even with everything I did—you know I'd never hurt you. And before...I-I saved you."

"You need to shoot her!" Palmiotti insists. "She's got her gun under the water!"

"Clementine, raise your hands," I insist.

She shifts her weight, raising both hands, then lowering them back in the water, which, from the way she's sitting, comes just above her waist.

"She kept the gun *in her lap!*" Palmiotti adds. "She still has it!"

"I don't have anything!" she shouts.

I don't believe either of them. And even if her gun is still in her lap, I don't know if a gun can work once it's underwater. But the one thing I do know is I need to see for myself.

"Clementine, *get up!* Stand up," I tell her.

"I can't."

"Whattya mean *you can't?*"

"You shot me, Beecher. In the *leg.* I can't *stand,*" she explains, pointing to her leg that's bent.

"The bullshit is just never-ending!" Palmiotti says. "If you don't shoot her, she's going to—!"

"Dr. Palmiotti, *stop talking!*" I yell.

"Then use your brain for once instead of thinking with your scrotum!" Palmiotti begs, reaching my way. "If you want, give me the gun and I'll—"

"Do *not* come near this gun," I say, aiming the barrel at his chest. "I know who you are, Doctor. I know you tricked Dallas into thinking he was fighting for the good of the Culper Ring. And since I know you're the top plumber in the Plumbers, I know where your loyalty lies."

Palmiotti doesn't move.

Across from us, Clementine doesn't either.

"Beecher, listen to me," Palmiotti says. "Whatever you think our mission is, we can fight about this later. But if you don't shoot her— if you don't protect us—she's gonna kill both of us."

"I know you don't believe that," Clementine jumps in, her eyes flicking back and forth between me and Palmiotti. "Of course he wants you to shoot me, Beecher. Think of why he put that bullet in Dallas's chest! He's cleaning up one by one...and once I'm gone, you're the only witness that's left. And then...and then..." She slows herself down as the pain takes hold. "Guess how quickly you'll be dead after that?"

"So now *we're* the bad guys?" Palmiotti asks, forcing a laugh. "For what? For trying to protect the leader of the free world from a blackmailer and her crazy father?"

"No—for helping your boss bury a baseball bat in the side of someone's head! I saw Eightball's medical chart. Puncture wounds in the face! Shattered eye socket; broken cheekbones! And brain damage from an in-driven fragment of his skull! Lemme guess: You held Eightball down while Wallace wound up with a hammer. Did it feel good when you heard that boy's eye socket shatter? What about all these years when you helped the President of the United States keep him in storage like a piece of old furniture—and then used all the real Culper Ring's methods to hide it!? How'd that one feel?" Turning to me, she adds, "Pay attention, Beecher. Palmiotti wants you to think *I'm* the bad guy. But remember, he didn't need you and Dallas to get the file. Once you found it, he could've had Dallas take you home, and he could've grabbed it himself. So what's the benefit to Palmiotti of having all of us in an underground cave in the middle of nowhere...?"

"Jesus, Beecher—even if you think she's telling the truth—make her stand up!" Palmiotti pleads.

"...because even if they smoke that hospital file, the last thing Palmiotti and the President need is you running around, bearing witness to the world," Clementine says, as serious as I've ever seen her. "That's the only reason you're here, Beecher—that's the big ending. Whether you shoot me now or not, you're gonna die here. *I'm* gonna die here. Both of us...with what's in our blood...don't you see...we're history."

Behind her, the bird isn't chirping. There's only silence.

"That's not true," I say, still pointing my gun at her.

"You lie. And worst of all, you lie to yourself," she tells me. "Think of everything you've seen: You saw him shoot Dallas. You've already seen what they'll do to protect what they have in that White House. You pull that trigger on me, and I guarantee you you'll be dead in ten minutes—and you wanna know why? Because that's your role, Beecher. You get to play Lee Harvey Oswald...or John Hinckley... or even Nico. That's your big part in the opera. Think of any presidential attack in history—you can't have one without a patsy."

"Beecher, make her stand the hell up!" Palmiotti begs, his voice cracking. His face should be a red rage. Instead, it's bone white. The way he's gripping his neck and using his free hand to steady himself against the wall, he's losing blood fast.

I look back at Clementine sitting in the water. Both of her legs are straight out, like she's coming down a waterslide. The water's above her waist. I still can't see if she has her gun.

"You know I'm right," she says as she starts to breathe heavily. The pain in her leg is definitely getting worse. But as she sits there, she starts using her good leg to slowly push herself backward in the water. "This is your chance, Beecher. If we leave together...with this file...Forget making them pay—we can finally get the truth."

"Beecher, whatever you're thinking right now," Palmiotti pleads, "she has the file tucked in her pants and her gun in one of her hands. Do not assume—*for one second*—that the moment you lower your gun, she's not going to raise hers and kill the both of us."

"Help me up, Beecher. Help me up and we can get out of here," Clementine says, reaching out with her left hand. Her right is still underwater as she stops maneuvering back.

"S-She's the one who killed Orlando!" Palmiotti says, coughing wildly.

"Clementine, what you told me before ... about being sick," I say. "Are you really dying?"

She doesn't say a word. But she also doesn't look away. "I can't be lying about everything."

"*She can ... she admitted it, Beecher ... She killed your friend!*"

From the back of the cave, the trapped red bird again swoops through the darkness, and just as quickly disappears with a high-pitched chirp.

I look over at Palmiotti, who's got no fight left in him, then back to Clementine, who's still holding one hand out to me—and hiding her other beneath the water.

The answer is easy.

There's only one real threat left.

I aim my gun at Clementine and cock the hammer. "Clementine, pick your hands up and stand up now, or I swear to God I'll shoot you again," I tell her.

Two minutes ago, Clementine said we were history. She knows nothing about history. History is simply what's behind us.

"*Thank you!*" Palmiotti calls out, still coughing behind me. "Now we can—"

Palmiotti doesn't finish the thought.

As Clementine is about to get up, there's a loud splash behind me.

I turn to my right just as Palmiotti hits the water. He lands face-first, arms at his side, like he's frozen solid. For half a second, I stand there, waiting for him to get up. But the way he lies there, facedown ...

His body jerks. Then jerks again, wildly. Within seconds, his upper body is twitching, making him buck like a fish on land. I have no idea what that gunshot to the neck did. But I know a seizure when I see one.

"*Palmiotti...!*" I call out even though he can't hear me.

I'm about to run at him, when I remember...

Clementine.

"He's gonna die," she says matter-of-factly, fighting to climb to her good leg. Her one hand is still hidden below the water. "You may hate him, but he needs your help."

"If you run, I'll shoot you again," I warn her.

"No. You won't. Not after that," she says, pointing me back to Palmiotti, whose convulsions are starting to slow down. He doesn't have long.

If the situation were reversed, Palmiotti would leave me. Gladly. Clementine might too. But to turn your back and just leave someone to die...

Right there, I see the choice. I can grab Clementine. Or I can race to help Palmiotti.

Life. Or death. There's no time for both.

I think of everything Palmiotti did. How he shot Dallas. And how, if I save him, President Wallace will pull every string in existence to make sure Palmiotti walks away without a scar, mark, or paper cut.

I think of what Clementine knows about my father.

But when it comes to making the final choice...

...there's really no choice at all.

Sprinting toward the facedown Palmiotti and tucking my gun into my pants, I grab him by the shoulders and lift him, bending him backward, out from the water. He's deadweight, his arms sagging forward as his fingertips skate along the top of the water. A waterfall of fluid and vomit drains from his mouth.

I know what to do. I spent two summers lifeguarding at the local pool. But as I drop to my knees and twist Palmiotti onto his back, I can't help but look over my shoulder.

With her back to me, Clementine climbs to her feet. She tries to steady herself, her right hand still down in the water.

As Palmiotti's head hits my lap, his face isn't pale anymore. It's ashen and gray. His half-open eyes are waxy as he gazes through me. He's not in there.

I open his mouth. I clear his airway. I look over my shoulder...

My eyes seize on Clementine as she finally pulls her hand from the water...

...and reveals the soaking-wet gun that she's been gripping the entire time.

Oh, jeez.

Palmiotti was right.

She lifts the gun. All she has to do is turn and fire. It's an easy shot.

But she never takes it.

Scrambling and limping, Clementine heads deeper into the cave, leaving a wake in the water that fans out behind her. The gun is dangling by her side. I wait for her to look back at me.

She doesn't.

Not once.

I tilt Palmiotti's head back. I pinch his nose. He hasn't taken a breath in a full minute. His gray skin is starting to turn blue.

"Help...!" I call out even though no one's there.

Palmiotti's only movement comes from a rare gasp that sends his chest heaving. *Huuuh.* It's not a breath. He's not breathing at all.

He's dying.

"We need help...!" I call out.

I look over my shoulder.

Clementine's gone.

In my lap, Palmiotti doesn't move. No gasping. No heaving. His eyes stare through me. His skin is bluer than ever. I feel for a pulse, but there's nothing there.

"Please, someone... I need help...!"

*   *   *

113

Clementine is gone.

I know they won't find her.

Dallas is dead. So is Palmiotti.

I know both are my fault.

And on top of all that, when it comes to my father, I've got nothing but questions.

In the back part of the cave, the first ones to reach us are Copper Mountain's internal volunteer firefighters, which are made up of a group of beefy-looking managers and maintenance guys who check me for cuts and scrapes. I don't have a scratch on me. No punches thrown, no black eyes to heal, no lame sling to make it look like I learned a lesson as I went through the wringer.

I did everything Clementine and Tot and even Dallas had been pushing me to do. For those few minutes, as I held that gun, and squeezed that trigger, I was no longer the spectator who was avoiding the future and watching the action from the safety of a well-worn history book. For those few minutes, I was absolutely, supremely *in the present*.

But as the paramedics buzz back and forth and I stand there alone in the cave, staring down at my cell phone, the very worst part of my new reality is simply . . . I have no idea who to call.

"*There. I see 'em . . .*" a female voice announces.

I look up just as a woman paramedic with short brown hair climbs out of a golf cart that's painted red and white like an ambulance. She starts talking to the other paramedic—the guy who told me that the water treatment area has a waste exit on the far side of the cave. Clementine was prepared for that one too.

But as the woman paramedic gets closer, I realize she's not here for me. She heads to the corner of the cave, where Dallas's and Palmiotti's stiff bodies are covered by red-and-white-checkered plastic tablecloths from the cafeteria.

I could've shot Clementine. Maybe I should've. But as I stare at Dallas's and Palmiotti's covered bodies, the thought that's doing far more damage is a simple one: After everything that happened, I helped *nobody*.

The thought continues to carve into my brain as a third paramedic motions my way.

"So you're the lucky one, huh?" a paramedic with a twinge of Texas in his voice asks, putting a hand on my shoulder and pulling me back. "If you need a lift, you can ride with us," he adds, pointing me to the white car that sits just behind the golf cart.

I nod him a thanks as he opens the back door of the car and I slide inside. But it's not until the door slams shut and I see the metal police car–type partition that divides the front seat from the back, that I realize he's dressed in a suit.

Paramedics don't wear suits.

The locks thunk. The driver—a man with thin blond hair that's combed straight back and curls into a duck's butt at his neck—is also in a suit.

Never facing me, the man with the Texas twang drops into the passenger seat and whispers into his wrist:

"We're in route Crown. Notify B-4."

I have no idea what B-4 is. But during all those reading visits, I've been around enough Secret Service agents to know what *Crown* is the code word for.

They're taking me to the White House.

Good.

That's exactly where I want to go.

*　　*　　*

114

I try to sleep on the ride.

I don't have a chance.

For the first few hours, my body won't shut off. I'm too wired and rattled and awake. I keep checking my phone, annoyed I can't get a signal. But as we pass into Maryland, I realize it's not my phone.

"You're blocking it, aren't you?" I call out to the driver. "You've got one of those devices—for blocking my cell signal."

He doesn't answer. Too bad for him, I've seen the CIA files on interrogation. I know the game.

The longer they let the silence sink in and make this car seem like a cage, the more likely I am to calm down.

It usually works.

But after everything that's happened—to Orlando...to Dallas...and even to Palmiotti—I don't care how many hours I sit back here, there's no damn way I'm just calming down...

Until.

The car makes a sharp right, bouncing and bumping its way to the security shed at the southeast gate. Of the White House.

"Emily..." the driver of our car says, miming a tip of the hat to the female uniformed guard.

"Jim..." the guard replies, nodding back.

It's nearly ten at night. They know we're coming.

With a click, the black metal gate swings open, and we ride up the slight incline toward the familiar giant white columns and the perfectly lit Truman Balcony. Just the sight of it unties the knots of my rage and, to my surprise, makes the world float in time, like I'm hovering in my own body.

It's not the President that does it to me. It's this place.

Last year, I took my sisters here to see the enormous Christmas tree they always have on the South Lawn. Like every other tourist, we took photos from the street, squeezing the camera through the bars of the metal gate and snapping shots of the world's most famous white mansion.

Regardless of who lives inside, the White House—and the Presidency—still deserve respect.

Even if Wallace doesn't.

The car jolts to a stop just under the awning of the South Portico.

I know this entrance. This isn't the public entrance. Or the staff entrance.

The is the entrance that Nixon walked out when he boarded the helicopter for the last time and popped the double fingers. The entrance where Obama and his daughters played with their dog.

The private entrance.

Wallace's entrance.

Before I can even reach for the door, two men in suits appear on my right from inside the mansion. As they approach the car, I see their earpieces. More Secret Service.

The car locks thunk. The taller one opens the door.

"He's ready for you," he says, motioning for me to walk ahead of them. They both fall in right behind me, making it clear that they're the ones steering.

We don't go far.

As we step through an oval room that I recognize as the room where FDR used to give his fireside chats, they motion me to the left, down a long pale-red-carpeted hallway.

There's another agent on my left, who whispers into his wrist as we pass.

In the White House, every stranger is a threat.

They don't know the half of it.

"Here you go..." one of them says as we reach the end of the hall, and he points me to the only open door on the hallway.

The sign out front tells me where we are. But even without that, as I step inside—past the unusually small reception area and unusually clean bathroom—there's an exam table that's covered by a sterile roll of white paper.

Even in the White House, there's no mistaking a doctor's office.

"Please. Have a seat," he announces, dressed in a sharp pin-striped suit despite the late hour. As he waves me into the private office, his gray eyes look different than the last time I saw him, with the kind of dark puffiness under them that only comes from stress. "I was worried about you, Beecher," the President of the United States adds, extending a hand. "I wasn't sure you were going to make it."

115

You look like you have something on your mind, Beecher," the President offers, sounding almost concerned.

"Excuse me?" I ask.

"On your face. I can see it. Say what you're thinking, son."

"You don't wanna hear what I'm thinking," I shoot back.

"Watch yourself," one of the Secret Service agents blurts behind me. I didn't even realize they were still there.

"Victor," the President says. It's just one word. He's not even annoyed as he says it. But in those two syllables, it's clear what the President wants. *Leave us alone. Get out.*

"Sir, this isn't—"

"*Victor.*" That's the end. Argument over.

Without another word, the two agents leave the doctor's office, shutting the door behind them. But it's Wallace who rounds the desk, crosses behind me, and locks the office door with a hushed *clunk.*

At first, I thought he brought me here because of what happened to Palmiotti. But I'm now realizing it's one of the only places in the White House where he can guarantee complete privacy.

With him behind me, I keep my eyes on Palmiotti's desk, where there's a small box that looks like a toaster. A little screen lists the following names in green digital letters:

POTUS: Ground Floor Doctor's Office
FLOTUS: Second Floor Residence
VPOTUS: West Wing
MINNIE: Traveling

Doesn't take a medical degree to know those're the current locations of the President, First Lady, Vice President, and Minnie. I'd read that Wallace made the Secret Service take his kids' names off the search grid. There was no reason for staff to know where they were at any minute. But he clearly left Minnie on. It's been twenty-six years since the President's sister tried to kill herself. He's not taking his eyes off her.

Otherwise, the office is sparse, and the walls—to my surprise—aren't filled with photos of Palmiotti and the President. Palmiotti had just one, on the desk, in a tasteful silver frame. It's not from the Oval or Inauguration Day. No, this is a grainy shot from when Palmiotti and Wallace were back in ... from the early-eighties hair and the white caps and gowns, it has to be high school graduation.

They can't be more than eighteen: young Palmiotti on the left; young Wallace on the right. In between, they've both got their arms around the real star of the photo: Wallace's mother, who has her head tilted just slightly toward her son, and is beaming the kind of toothy smile that only a mom at graduation can possibly beam. But as Mom stretches her own arms around their waists, pulling them in close, one thing's clear: This isn't a presidential photo. It's a family one.

With the door now locked, the President moves slowly behind me, heading back toward the desk. He's silent and unreadable. I know he's trying to intimidate me. And I know it's working.

But as he brushes past me, I spot ... in his hand ... He's holding one of those black oval bulbs from the end of a blood pressure kit.

As he slides back into his chair, I don't care how cool he's trying to play it. This man still lost his oldest—and perhaps *only*—real friend today. He lowers his hands behind the desk and I know he's squeezing that bulb.

"If it makes you feel better, we'll find her," he finally offers.

"Pardon?"

"The girl. The one who took the file ..."

"Clementine. But whattya mean we'll find—?" I stop myself, looking carefully at Wallace. Until just this moment, he had no idea that Clementine was the one who had the file.

His gray eyes lock on me, and I realize, in this depth of the ocean, just how sharp the shark's teeth can be.

"Is that why you brought me here? To see if I was the one who still had the file?"

"Beecher, you keep thinking I'm trying to fight you. But you need to know—all this time—we thought *you* were the one who was blackmailing *us*."

"I wasn't."

"I know that. And that's the only reason I brought you here, Beecher: to thank you. I appreciate what you did. The way you came through and worked so hard to protect Dallas and Dr. Palmiotti. And even when you found the rest . . . you could've taken advantage and asked for something for yourself. But you never did."

I stare at the President, who knits his fingers together and gently lowers them in prayer style on the desk. He's not holding the blood pressure bulb anymore.

"Can I ask you a question, sir?"

"Of course."

"Is that the same speech you gave to Dallas?"

"What're you talking about?" the President asks.

"The polite flattery . . . the moral back-pat . . . even the subtle hint you dropped about the advantages you can offer and how much you can do for me, without ever directly saying it. Is that the way you made Dallas feel special when you invited him into the Plumbers, and he thought he was joining the Culper Ring?"

The President shifts his weight, his eyes still locked on me. "Be very careful of what you're accusing me of."

"I'm not accusing you of anything, sir. But it is a fair calculation, isn't it? Why risk a head-on collision when you can bring me inside? I mean, now that I think about it—is that the real reason you brought me here? To keep me quiet by inviting me to be the newest member of your Plumbers?"

The President's hands stay frozen in prayer style on the desk. If his voice was any colder, I'd be able to see it in the air. "No. That *isn't* why I brought you here. At all."

424

He takes another breath, all set to hide his emotions just like he does on every other day of his life. But I see his tongue as it rolls inside his mouth. As good as Wallace is, his friend is still dead. You don't just bury that away.

"I brought you to say thank you," he insists for the second time. "Without you, we wouldn't know who killed that security guard."

"His name's Orlando," I interrupt.

Wallace nods with a nearly invisible grin, letting me know he's well aware of Orlando's name. He's anxious to be back in control—and I just gave it back to him. "Though you'll be happy to hear, Beecher—from what I understand, the D.C. police already have Clementine's picture up on their website. They were able to link her chemotherapy prescription to the drugs they found in Orlando's bloodwork."

"What're you talking about?"

"I'm just telling you what's online. And when you think about it, that young archivist—Beecher whatshisname—who tracked her down, and looped in the President's doctor, and even followed her all the way out to those caves—that guy's a hero," he adds, his eyes growing darker as they tighten on me. "Of course, some say Beecher had a hand in it—that he violated every security protocol and was the one who let Clementine inside that SCIF—and that together they planned all this, and were after the President, and they even went to visit her father, who—can you believe it?—is Nico Hadrian, who may be trying to kill again."

He pauses a moment, looking over at the office's only window. It has a perfect view of the South Lawn—except for the iron bars that cover it. I get the point. All he has to do is say the words and that's my permanent view. His voice is back to the exact strength he started with. "But I don't want to believe that about him. Beecher's a good guy. I don't want to see him lose everything like that."

It's an overdramatic speech—especially with the glance at the iron bars—and exactly the one I thought he'd give. "I still know about the two Culper Rings," I say. "I know about your Plumbers. And for you especially . . . I know your personal stake in this."

He knows I mean Minnie.

"Beecher, I think we all have a personal stake in this. Right, son?" he asks, putting all the emphasis on the word *son*.

I know he means my father.

It's an empty threat. If he wanted to trade, he would've already offered it. But he's done debating.

"Go tell the world, Beecher. And you find me one person who wouldn't protect their sister in the *exact same way* if they saw her in trouble. If you think my poll numbers are good now, just wait until you turn me into a hero."

"Maybe," I say.

"Not *maybe*," he says as if he's already seen the future. He leans into the desk, his fingers still crossed in prayer. This man takes on entire countries. And wins. "The press'll dig for a little while into what the doctor was up to, but they'll move on to the next well—especially when they don't strike oil. *The President's doctor* is very different than the *President*."

"But we all know this isn't about *the President*. Even for *you*, it's never been about you. It's about *her*, isn't it, sir? Forget the press... the public...forget everyone. We wouldn't still be talking if you weren't worried about something. And to me, that only thing you're worried about is—if I start doing the cable show rounds and say your sister's accident was actually an attempted suicide out of guilt for what she did to Eightball—"

"Beecher, I will only say this once. Don't threaten me. You have no idea what happened that night."

"The barber told me. He told me about the vacuum hose—and the tailpipe of the Honda Civic."

"You have no idea what happened that night."

"I know it took you four hours before you found her. I know how it still haunts you that you couldn't stop it."

"You're not hearing me, Beecher," he says, lowering his voice so that I listen to every syllable. "I was there—I'm the one who found her. You. Have. No. Idea. What. Happened. That. Night."

His burning intensity knocks me back in my seat. I look at the President.

He doesn't look away. His baggy eyes narrow.

I replay the events...The barber...Laurent said it took four hours before they found Minnie that night. That Palmiotti was the one who pulled her from the car. But now...if Wallace says he's the one who found her first...

You have no idea what happened that night.

My skin goes cold. I replay it again. Wallace was there first...he was the first one to see her unconscious in the car...But if Palmiotti is the one who eventually pulled her out...Both things can be true. Unless...

Unless Wallace got there first, saw Minnie unconscious, and decided that the best action...

...was not to take any action at all.

You have no idea what happened that night.

"When you saw her lying there...you didn't pull her out of the car, did you...?" I blurt.

The President doesn't answer.

The bitter taste of bile bursts in my throat as I glance back at the silver picture frame. The family photo.

The one with two kids in the family.

Not three.

"You tried to leave her in that smoke-filled car. You tried to let your own sister die," I say.

"Everyone knows I love my sister."

"But in that moment, after all the heartache she caused...If Palmiotti hadn't come in, you would've stood there and watched her suffocate."

Wallace juts out his lower lip and huffs a puff of air up his own nose. But he doesn't answer. He'll never answer. Not for what they did to Eightball. Not for hiding him all these years. Not for any of this.

I was wrong before.

All this time, I thought I was fighting men.

I'm fighting monsters.

"That's how you knew you could trust Palmiotti with anything,

including the Plumbers. He was there for your lowest moment—
and the truly sick part is, he decided to stay even though he knew
you would've let your sister die," I say. "You belong together. You
ditched your souls for each other."

There's a flash on the digital screen that lists the First Family's
location. In a blink, Minnie's status goes from:

MINNIE: Traveling

to

MINNIE: Second Floor Residence

Now she's upstairs.

"No place like home," Wallace says, never once raising his voice.
He turns directly at me, finally undoing the prayer grip of his hands.
"So. We're done now, yes?"

"We're not."

"We are. We very much are."

"I can still find proof."

"You can *try*. But we're done, Beecher. And y'know why we're
done? Because when it comes to conspiracy theories—think of
the best ones out there—think of the ones that even have some
semblance of proof...like JFK. For over fifty years now, after all
the Jack Ruby and Lee Harvey Oswald stories...after all the witnesses who came forward, and the books, and the speculation, and
the Oliver Stones, and the annual conventions that still happen to
this very day, you know what the number one theory most people
believe? *The Warren Commission*," he says dryly. "*That's* who the
public believes—the commission authored by the U.S. government.
We make a great bad guy, and they all say they hate us. But at the
end of every day, people *want* to trust us. Because we're their *government*. And people trust their government."

"I bet you practiced that monologue."

"Just remember where you are: This is a prizefight, Beecher.
And when you're in a prizefight for a long time—take my word on

this—you keep swinging that hard and you're only gonna knock yourself out."

"Actually, the knockout already happened."

"Pardon?"

"Just remember where *you* are, Mr. President. Look around. By the end of the week, this office will be empty. The photo in the silver frame will be, I'm guessing, slipped inside Palmiotti's coffin. Your doctor's gone, sir. So's your barber. Your Plumbers are finished. Goodbye. All your work did was get two loyal men killed. So you can try to pretend you've got everything exactly where you want it, but I'm the one who gets to go home for the rest of my week—while you're the one at the funerals, delivering the eulogies."

"You have nothing. You have less than nothing."

"You may be right. But then I keep thinking...the whole purpose of the Plumbers was to take people you trust and use them to build a wall around you. That wall protected you and insulated you. And now that wall is gone," I say. "So what're you gonna do now, sir?" Standing from my seat and heading for the door, I add, "You have a good night, Mr. President."

116

St. Elizabeths Hospital
Third floor

Nico didn't like card games.

It didn't matter.

Every few months, the doctors would still have a new pack of playing cards delivered to his room. Usually, they were cards from defunct airlines—both TWA and Piedmont Air apparently gave out a lot of free playing cards back in the day. But Nico didn't know what the doctors' therapeutic goal was. He didn't much care.

To Nico, a card game—especially one like solitaire—could never be enjoyable. Not when it left so much to chance. No, in Nico's world, the universe was far more organized. Gravity...temperature...even the repetition of history...Those were part of God's rules. The universe definitely had rules. It *had* to have rules. And purpose.

So, every few months, when Nico would receive his playing cards, he'd wait a day or two and then hand them back to the orderlies, or leave them in the day room, or, if they found their way back to him, tuck them into the cushions of the couch that smelled like urine and soup.

But tonight, at nearly 10 p.m. in the now quiet main room, Nico sat at one of the Plexiglas tables near the nurses' station and quietly played a game of solitaire.

"Thanks for being so patient, baby," the heavy nurse with the big hoop earrings said. "You know how Mr. Jasper gets if we let him sit in his diaper too long."

"Oooh, and you're playing cards so nice," the nurse crooned, making a mental note and clearly excited for what she'd inevitably be telling the doctors tomorrow.

It wasn't much. But Nico knew it mattered. The hospital was no different than the universe. Everything had rules. And the number one rule here was: If you don't please the nurses, you're not getting your privileges.

It was why he didn't complain when they let someone else feed the cats tonight. Or when Rupert brought him apple juice instead of orange.

Nico had been lucky earlier today. When he approached that car—the one with the barber and the blasphemous wrists—he was worried the blame would be put on him.

It wasn't. And he knew why.

Whoever had burned Beecher—whoever had caused all that pain—the last thing they wanted was Nico's name all over this. If that had happened, a real investigation would've been started.

The ones who did this . . . They didn't want that.

In the end, it didn't surprise Nico. But it did surprise him that, when it came to that investigation, they had the power to stop it.

Right there, Nico knew what was coming next.

"I see you put Randall's Sprite cans in the recycling—cleaned up his crackers too," the nurse added. "I know you're sucking up, Nico—but I appreciate it. Now remind me what you're waiting for again? Your mail?"

"Not mail," Nico said. "My phone. Any new phone messages?"

The nurse with the hoop earrings gripped a blue three-ring binder from the shelf above her desk and quickly flipped to the last pages.

Nico could've snuck a look at the book when she wasn't there.

But there were rules.

There were always rules.

And consequences.

"Lemme see . . . according to this . . ." she said as her chubby finger skated down the page. "Nope. Sorry, baby. No calls." Snapping the book shut, she added, "Maybe tomorrow."

Nico nodded. It was a good thought. Maybe it'd be tomorrow. Or the day after that. Or even the day after.

But it was going to happen. Soon.

Nico knew the rules.

He knew his purpose.

Beecher would be coming back. He definitely would.

It might take him a month. Or even longer. But eventually, Beecher would want help. He'd want help, and he'd want answers. And most of all, he'd want to know how to track down Clementine— which, if Nico was right about what was in her, was the only thing Nico wanted too.

Shoving his way back through the swinging doors and still thinking of how his daughter had misled him, Nico headed back to his room.

Soon, he and Beecher—George Washington and Benedict Arnold—would again be working together.

Just like the universe had always planned.

117

The White House
Second-Floor Residence

Where's he, upstairs?" Minnie asked a passing aide who was carrying the newest stack of autographed items, from personal letters to a red, white, and blue golf ball, that the President had just finished signing.

"Solarium," the aide said, pointing up as Minnie headed for the back staircase that would take her the rest of the way.

Minnie always loved the Solarium, which sat above the Truman Balcony on the top floor of the White House and had the best view of the Mall and the Washington Monument.

But Minnie didn't love it for the view. Or because it was the one casual room in the entire Residence. She loved it because it reminded her of home. Literally.

Lined with old family photos from when she and the President were kids, the narrow hallway that led up and out to the Solarium rose at a surprisingly steep incline. Even with her pink flamingo cane, it was tough for Minnie to navigate. But she still stared as she passed each old photograph—the one when she and ten-year-old Orson are smiling with all the chocolate in their teeth... the one with Orson proudly holding his first cross-country running trophy... and of course, the one right after she was born, with her mother placing baby Minnie for the first time in her brother's arms. Back then, the side of her face was covered with skin lesions. But little Orson is smiling down, so proud to be the new big brother. Wallace had personally made sure that picture made the list.

"Don't you dare do that," Minnie called out to her brother, rapping her cane against the floor. As she entered the room, which was decorated with casual sofas, she saw the problem.

With his back to her, the President stood there, hands in his pockets as he stared out the tall glass windows at the bright glow of the Washington Monument.

"Don't do that," she warned again, knowing him all too well.

"You know this was the room Nancy Reagan was in when they told her the President had been shot?" her brother announced.

"Yeah, and I know from the last time you were all upset and moody, it's also the room where Nixon told his family he was going to step down. We get it. Whenever you start staring out at the monuments or talking about other Presidents, you're in a piss mood. So just tell me: What's it this time? What's in your craw?"

He thought about telling her that Palmiotti was dead. It'd be on the news soon enough—complete with the story of how the doctor was blackmailed and lured down to the caves by the criminal Clementine. But Wallace knew that his sister was still riding the high of the morning's charity event.

"Actually, I was just thinking about you," Wallace replied, still keeping his back to her as Minnie hobbled with her cane toward him. "Today was really nice."

"It was, wasn't it?" Minnie said, smiling the half-smile that the stroke allowed. "Thanks again for coming and doing the speech. It made the event..." She paused a moment, trying to think of the right word. Her brother had heard all of them.

"It felt good to have you there," she finally said.

The President nodded, still standing there, staring out at the snow-covered Mall. From behind, Minnie playfully tapped his leg with the head of the flamingo cane. "Make room," she added, forcing him aside. With a sisterly shove, Minnie stepped close to him so they were standing shoulder to shoulder, two siblings staring out at the stunning view.

"It was fun being there. I mean, for me too," the President admitted.

"You should do it more often then. We have a fund-raiser next month out in Virginia," Minnie said.

Wallace didn't reply.

"Orson, I'm *kidding*," Minnie added. "But I did mean what I said before: Having you there... I probably don't say this enough, but—"

"Minnie, you don't have to say anything."

"I do. And you need to hear it. I just want you to know...my whole life...I appreciate everything you've given me," she said, motioning out at the monuments and the Mall. "You're a good brother."

The President nodded. "You're right. I am."

Minnie rapped him with her pink cane, laughing. But as she followed her brother's gaze, she realized Wallace wasn't staring out at the Washington Monument. He was staring *down*, at the paved path of the South Lawn, where two Secret Service agents were walking a blond staffer—he looked like all the other young aides—down toward the southeast security gate.

"Who's that?" Minnie asked.

The President of the United States stared and lied again. "Nobody important."

118

I know they want to throw me out.

They want to grab me by the nape of my neck and heave me into the trash, like they do in old comic strips.

But as the two Secret Service agents walk me down the paved path that borders the South Lawn, I stay two steps ahead of them. Still, I feel how close they are behind me.

"Taxis won't stop here," the agent with the round nose says as we reach the black metal pedestrian gate and wait for it to open. "Go down a block. You'll be better off."

"Thanks," I say without looking back at them.

From the security shed on my right, the female uniformed agent never takes her eyes off me. She pushes a button and a magnetic lock pops.

"Have a safe night," the agent with the round nose adds, patting me on the back and nearly knocking me through the metal gate as it swings open. Even for the Secret Service, he's far too physical. "Hope you enjoyed your visit to the White House."

As I rush outside, the gate bites shut, and I fight the cold by stuffing my hands in my pockets. To my surprise, my right pocket's not empty. There's a sheet of paper—feels like a business card—waiting for me.

I pull it out. It's not a business card. It's blank. Except for the handwritten note that says:

15th and F.
Taxi will be waiting.

I glance over my shoulder at the agent with the round nose. His

436

back is already turned to me as he follows his partner back to the mansion. He doesn't turn around.

But I know he wrote that note.

I look down, rereading it again: 15th and F Street. Just around the corner.

Confused, but also curious, I start with a walk, which quickly becomes a speedwalk, which—the closer I get to 15th Street— quickly becomes a full-out run.

As I turn the corner, I'm shoved hard by the wind tunnel that runs along the long side of the Treasury building. At this hour, the street is empty. Except for the one car that's parked illegally, waiting for me.

It doesn't look like a cab.

In fact, as I count the four bright headlights instead of the usual two, I know who it is—even without noticing the car's front grille, where the chrome horse is in mid-gallop.

It's definitely not a cab.

It's a Mustang.

I take a few steps toward the pale blue car. The passenger window is already rolled down, giving me a clear view of Tot, who has to be freezing as he sits so calmly inside. He ducks down to see me better. Even his bad eye is filled with fatherly concern.

Just the sight of him makes it hard for me to stand. I shake my head, shooting him a silent plea and begging him not to say *I told you so.*

Of course, he listens. From the start, he's been the only one.

"It'll be okay," he finally offers.

"You sure?" I ask him.

He doesn't answer. He just leans across the passenger seat and opens the door. "C'mon, let's get you home."

*   *   *

119

Fourteen years ago
Sagamore, Wisconsin

*B*eecher...*customer at buyback!*" Mr. Farris shouted from the back office of the secondhand bookshop.

At sixteen years old, Beecher had no problem darting up the aisles, past the overstuffed shelves that were packed with old paperbacks. The only thing that slowed him down was when he saw who was waiting for him at the register.

He knew her from behind—from just the sight of her long black hair.

He'd know her anywhere.

Clementine.

Ducking underneath the drawbridge counter and sliding to a stop behind the register, Beecher worked hard to keep it cool. "Clementine...Hey."

"I didn't know you worked here," she offered.

"Yeah. I'm Beecher," he said, pointing to himself.

"I know your name, Beecher."

"Yeah...no...that's great," he replied, praying better words would come. "So you got stuff for us?" he added, motioning to the blue milk crate that she had lugged inside and that now sat by her feet.

"I heard you guys pay fifty cents for old records and CDs."

"Fifty cents for records. Fifty cents for paperbacks. And a full dollar if it's a new hardcover—though he'll pay a lot if you've got the '69 Bee Gees *Odessa* album with the original foldout artwork."

"I don't have the Bee Gees," she said. "I just have these..."

From the milk crate, she pulled out half a dozen copies of the CD with her mom's photo on it: *Penny Maxwell's Greatest Hits*.

Beecher knew the rules. He could buy back anything he wanted—as long as the store didn't already have too many copies.

Two hours ago, Clementine's mom came in and told Mr. Farris that her family was moving to Detroit for her singing career and could they please buy back a few dozen of her CDs to raise some much-needed cash. Of course, Mr. Farris obliged. Farris always obliged, which was why the store's front window still had a crack in it and the air conditioning would never be fixed. So as Beecher looked across the counter at Clementine's exact same offerings...

"We can definitely use a few extra copies," he finally said.

"Really? You sure?"

"Absolutely. I've listened to them. Your mom's got a real voice. Like early Dinah Washington, but softer and with better range— and of course without the horrendous drug overdose."

Clementine couldn't help but grin. "I know you already bought my mom's copies—and you're stuck with those."

"And we have thirty copies of *To Kill a Mockingbird*. But each new school year, we sell every damn one."

Cocking her head, Clementine took a long silent look across the counter. It was the kind of look that came with its own internal cal-culation. "You're not a jackass like everyone else."

"Not true," Beecher said, motioning to the milk crate. "I'm just buttering you up so I can lowball you on that *Frankenstein* paper-back you've got there. That's a British edition. I can get big bucks for it. Now what else you got?"

Lifting the crate, Clementine dumped and filled the counter with at least twenty other paperbacks, a few hardbacks, and a pile of used CDs including Boyz II Men, Wilson Phillips, and Color Me Badd.

"I also got this..." Clementine said, pulling out a frayed blue leather book with a heavily worn spine, torn soiled pages, and a shredded silk ribbon bookmark. "It's not in good shape, but...it's for sure old—1970."

Tilting his head, Beecher read the gold lettering on the spine. *One Hundred Years of Solitude* by Gabriel García Márquez. "Good book. This your mom's?"

"My mom hates to read. I think it's my grandmother's. Oh, and there's one other problem...the cover is..." She flipped the leather book over, revealing that it was missing its front cover.

"Y'know the pages still stay together," Beecher pointed out.

"Huh?"

"The pages...*look*..." he said, lifting the book by its remaining cover and dangling it in the air so all the pages spread out like a fan. "If the binding's good, all the pages stay in place."

"That some sorta used bookstore trick?"

"Actually, it's from my mom. When my dad...when he passed... Reverend Lurie told her that even when one cover gets torn away from a book, as long as the other cover's there, it'll still hold the pages together. For me and my sisters...he said my mom was the other cover. And we were the pages."

Clementine stood there silently, staring down at the old blue leather book.

"He was trying to make an analogy about life," Beecher pointed out.

"I get it," Clementine said, still studying the old volume. She was quiet for nearly a minute, resting her left elbow on the counter. Within a decade, that elbow would be covered with deep white scars from an incident she'd never tell the truth about.

"You think this copy could've belonged to my dad?" she finally asked.

Beecher shrugged. "Or it can just be a book."

Clementine looked up and offered another grin at Beecher. Her widest one yet. "Y'know, my mom and I are moving to Detroit."

"I heard."

"Still...we should really stay in touch."

"Yeah. Great. I'd like that," Beecher said, feeling the excitement tighten his chest—especially as he saw Clementine reach out and slide the leather copy of Márquez's masterpiece back into her milk crate. "Let me give you my email address," he said.

"Email?"

"It's this thing...it's new and— Actually, it's stupid. No one'll use it." Grabbing one of the small squares of paper that Mr. Farris would make by cutting up used, discarded sheets, Beecher quickly scribbled his mailing address and phone number. Clementine did the same.

As they exchanged sheets, Beecher did a quick tallying of her buybacks and paid out a grand total of thirty-two dollars (rounding up the last fifty cents).

"Make sure you look me up if you ever get to Michigan," Clementine called out as she headed for the door.

"You do the same when you come back here and visit," he called back.

And with twin genuine smiles on their faces, Beecher and Clementine waved goodbye, knowing full well they'd never see each other again.

120

One week from now
Chatham, Ontario

W ould you like to order, ma'am—or are you waiting for one more?" the waiter asked, leaning in to avoid embarrassment.

"I'm by myself," the woman in the stylish chocolate brown overcoat replied as she again scanned the entrance to the outdoor café, which was overdecorated to look like an old Tudor-style shop from an English village square. Just outside the metal railing, as it'd been for the past twenty minutes, the only people around were the lunchtime pedestrians passing along King Street. Next to her table, the heating lamp was on full blast. It was January. In Canada. Far too cold for anyone to be sitting outside.

But for the woman in the chocolate brown overcoat, that was the point.

She could've come somewhere private.

A nearby hotel.

St. Andrew's Church.

Instead, she came to the café.

Outside. In public. Where everyone could see her.

"How're the fish cakes?" she asked, making prolonged eye contact with the waiter just to see if he'd recognize her.

He didn't.

Of course he didn't.

Her hair was long now. And blonde. But to anyone who knew her, there was no mistaking that grin.

Just like her father's.

"Unless you have something even better than that," Clementine Kaye said, pulling a breadstick from the basket and turning her head just enough so the pedestrians could see her.

"I think you'll like the fish cakes," the waiter replied, scribbling down the order.

As another wave of locals strolled past the café, Clementine threw a quick smile to a five-year-old girl who was walking with her mom.

Even in a week, it had gotten easier. Sure, her leg still hurt from the shooting, and her wanted-for-questioning photo was still posted across the Internet, but it was still the Internet. The world was already moving on.

Which meant she could get back to what really mattered.

Lifting her menu off the table and handing it back to the waiter, Clementine looked down at the thick manila envelope. As the waiter left, she pulled out a water-stained file folder with a familiar name typed in the upper corner. *Wallace, Orson.*

This was it: the unprocessed file that Beecher had tracked to the cave's underground storage area—the original records from the night twenty-six years ago when they brought Eightball into the hospital, and the future President of the United States was treated for his broken finger. As best as Clementine could figure, this was the only proof that the future President was there that night.

But it paled next to the one priceless detail that Clementine never anticipated finding. Indeed, even with what she now knew about the Plumbers, none of it compared to the two-hundred-year-old spy network that'd been operating since the birth of the United States:

The Culper Ring.

Clementine knew all about the Culper Ring.

Including at least one person who was in it.

Above her, the heat lamp sizzled with a fresh burst of warmth. Clementine barely noticed as she looked out at the Chatham police car that pulled up along King Street.

At the traffic light, the car slowed down. The officer in the passenger seat didn't look at her. Didn't even see her.

But as the light blinked green and the car took off, Clementine reminded herself that there were hazards in rushing blindly.

Sure, she could go public now. She could put Tot and the Culper Ring on the front page of every newspaper and website, and then sit back and watch the world take President Wallace and Tot and toss them all in the shredder.

But that wouldn't get Clementine what she was really after.

For so long now, she had told herself this was about her father. And it was. It always was.

But it was also about her.

And so, after nearly three decades of wondering, years of searching, six months of planning, and the next few months of healing, Clementine Kaye sat back in her seat and—in a small town in Canada, under a baking heat lamp—started thinking exactly how she'd finally get the answers she wanted.

Beecher had taught her the benefits of patience.

The Culper Ring had taught her the benefits of secrecy.

But from here on in, it was no different than when she grabbed that jump rope and leapt onto Vincent Paglinni's back in the schoolyard all those years ago.

Even the hardest fights in life become easy when you have the element of surprise.

121

Washington, D.C.

There's a double tap of a car horn, honking from outside.

Every morning for the past week, I've ignored it. Just like I ignored the calls and the texts and the knocks on the door. Instead, I stared at my computer, searching through the lack of press and trying to lose myself in a few cutthroat eBay battles over photo postcards of a 1902 pub in Dublin as well as a rare collection of World War I battleships.

It doesn't help like it used to.

Grabbing my dad's soft leather briefcase and threading my arms into my winter coat, I head through the living room and pull open the front door.

Of course, he's still waiting. He knew I'd eventually wear down.

To his credit, as I tug open the door of the powder blue Mustang and crawl inside, he doesn't ask me how I am. Tot already knows.

He's seen the President's rising poll numbers. In fact, as the car takes off up the block, Tot doesn't try to cheer me up, or put on the radio, or try to distract me. It's not until we get all the way to Rock Creek Park that he says the only thing he needs to . . .

"I was worried about you, Beecher."

When I don't reply, he adds, "I heard they finally released Dallas's and Palmiotti's bodies."

I nod from the passenger seat, staring straight ahead.

"And the barber's," he says, turning the steering wheel with just

445

his wrists. The car rumbles its usual rumble as we veer onto Constitution Avenue. "Though there's still no sign of Clementine."

I nod again.

"Which I guess means you still have no proof," Tot says.

"I'm well aware."

"And with no proof, you got nothin'."

"Tot, who taught you how to give a welcome-back talk? The Great Santini?"

"If it makes you feel better, while you've been playing hermit and answering all the FBI and Secret Service questions, I spoke to Orlando's wife. I know it doesn't help much...or bring him back... but—" His voice goes quiet. "They did get some closure from knowing who did this to him."

I try to tell myself that's true. But it's not.

"The only thing I don't understand is: On that night you came back from the caves, why'd he bring you to the White House, Beecher? I know you said it was to ask you to join the Plumbers, but think about it: What was the real point of that meeting with the President that night?"

"You mean besides reminding me what'll happen to my life if I open my mouth? I gave this great macho-y speech, but the truth is, he knew how it'd play out. He was just rubbing it in."

"Not a chance," Tot says, asking it again. "Why'd he bring you to the White House?"

"You do realize we lost, right? So if this is you being rhetorical—"

"Ask yourself, Beecher. Why'd he bring you to the White House?"

"I have no idea! To scare me?"

"Damn right to scare you! That's why he wanted to invite you in—that's all it was about: to scare you," Tot confirms, his beard swaying as he cocks his head. "And y'know the only reason why someone tries to scare you? Because he's *worried* about you. *He's* the one scared of *you*!"

"Then he's a bigger moron than we thought. Because for the past week, I've been racking my brain, trying to think of other places we can find proof, or a witness, or anything else about what happened that night. And believe me, I'll keep trying. I'll dig as long as it takes. But when it comes to being the Ghost of Christmas Past, it's not as easy as you think."

"That's not the ghost he's worried about."

"Come again?"

"Think of what you just said. When that first ghost comes to visit Ebenezer Scrooge...the Ghost of Christmas Past is the one that *fails*. The Ghost of Christmas Present—he fails too. But the ghost that actually gets the job done—the one that does the most damage—that's the Ghost from what's Yet to Come."

"Are you trying to make a really nice metaphor about history or the future? Because if you are—"

"Life isn't metaphor, Beecher. History isn't metaphor. It's just life."

I stare out the front of the car, looking down Constitution Avenue. The Washington Monument is all the way down, but from the angle we're at, thanks to the trees and the lightposts on our right, it's a completely obscured view. A horrible view. Just like that night at the Jefferson Memorial.

It's not metaphor. It's just a fact.

"Beecher, you've spent all this time fighting alone. You don't have to. If you want, we can help you find Clementine."

"It's not just her, Tot. What she said...about my father... She said he didn't die, and that maybe I have cancer. But if he's alive..."

"What she said was complete manure designed to manipulate and take advantage of an emotionally vulnerable moment. But we can find the truth. If he's alive, we'll find him. Same with the cancer. We can help you find all of it. And if we do it together—and we do it right—I promise you, you'll have the chance to make sure that every loathsome bastard—including the one in that big White House—pays for every ounce of pain they caused," Tot says, his voice finding speed. "You thought finding that old dictionary was when history chose you. That wasn't the moment. *This* is. The only question is—and it's a simple question: They think they won the war with you. Are you ready to declare war back?"

"I thought your Culper Ring worked *for* the President?"

"We work for the *Presidency*. And that Presidency has now been corrupted. So. Are you ready to declare war back?"

He called it a simple question. It's not simple. But it is easy. I look right at him. "Tot, are you asking me to join the Culper Ring?"

I wait for him to turn away and stare out the front window. He looks me right in the eye. "It's not for everyone."

"You're serious? This is real?"

"Some days you get peanuts; some days you get shells. This is a peanut day."

"And that Secret Service guy who walked me out of the White House and slipped me that note that you were waiting for me... He's a peanut too?"

"Some people are with us. Some people owe us a favor. We're a small group. Smaller than you think. And we've survived for only one reason: We pick our own replacements. I'm seventy-two years old, and... what you went through these past weeks... They know you're ready. Though if it makes any difference, I thought you've been ready for years."

With a twist of a knob, the radio hiccups to life and the car is filled with the sounds of Kenny Rogers singing "The Gambler."

"'The Gambler'?" I ask. "That's what you had cued up? You were trying to make this a little moment, weren't you?"

"Beecher, it's a moment even without the music."

I let the country twang of Kenny Rogers flow over me as a small grin lifts my cheeks. He may be right.

With a hard punch of the gas, the engine clears its throat and we cruise past the White House on our left.

"I won't let you down, Tot."

"I know, Beecher," he says without looking at me. "I'm just glad you finally know too."

Straight ahead, the morning sun is so bright I can't see a thing in front of me. It feels fantastic.

"So where we going?" I ask as we reach 9th Street and Tot blows through the turn. He keeps heading straight on Constitution. On most mornings, he makes a left.

"Where do you think I'm going?" Tot asks as the car picks up speed and we leave the White House behind. "Now that we finally got you in the Culper Ring, well...don't you want to meet the others?"